The Viewport Technician

The Viewport Technician:
A Guide to Portable Software Design

Michael Brian Bentley

Scott, Foresman and Company
Glenview, Illinois   London

Library of Congress Cataloging-in-Publication Data

Bentley, Michael Brian.
The viewport technician.

Bibliography: p.
Includes index.
1. Software compatibility.   I. Title.
QA76.754.B46   1988   005   87-15912
ISBN 0-673-18383-1

1   2   3   4   5   6   RRC   92   91   90   89   88   87

ISBN 0-673-18383-1

Notice of Liability

The information in this book is distributed on an "As Is" basis, without warranty. Neither the author nor Scott, Foresman and Company shall have any liability to customer or any other person or entity with respect to any liability, loss, or damage caused or alleged to be caused directly or indirectly by the programs contained herein. This includes, but is not limited to, interruption of service, loss of data, loss of business or anticipatory profits, or consequential damages from the use of the programs.

Scott, Foresman Professional Publishing Group books are available for bulk sales at quantity discounts. For information, please contact the Marketing Manager, Professional Books, Professional Publishing Group, Scott, Foresman and Company, 1900 East Lake Avenue, Glenview, IL 60025.

Trademark Lines

Introduction

I wrote this book to answer my own questions about software portability, questions that first arose when I wanted to move a small project from one computer to another. In my spare time I was developing a project on my second computer, a Heath/Zenith H/Z100. The project, a diagram builder, needed graphics, so I wrote a small graphics system. It also really needed a parser generator, so I wrote one based on a public-domain version for a different machine and language.

My wife and I really like to use Macintosh software, so we decided to buy a Macintosh, although we didn't have enough spare cash to set it up for developing code and the hard disks I already owned wouldn't work on the Macintosh. I wanted to move the project to the Mac, but it wasn't feasible for me to do that yet.

For an entirely different reason I built a PC clone from random parts that I bought at the 1985 Dayton Hamvention.

Somewhere along this spare-time timeline I discovered Digital Research's Gem, and decided that it could be used for my project; the Gem screen looked like the Macintosh, except that at the time it was slower and rougher. Gem graphics worked better than my simple graphics, and I wanted to get on to working with the business end of my project.

Ah, a problem. Which to use: the Macintosh, with its excellent support but no hard disk, or Gem, since it ran on the IBM PC (which had the hard disk) and was more than adequate for my uses? The intellectual voice hidden in me piped up and said, "You are a software engineer! Write the code so that it is portable!"

After looking at the problem, which involved scanning the volumes of loose documents for the Mac and someone else's Gem documentation, I decided that I had no idea how to do that.

I asked around town (Chicago) to find out if other people were trying to do ports from the Mac to the IBM or vice-versa, and if so, how they were doing it. I found out that, yes, many companies were fascinated by the market they hadn't tapped yet, and yes, they were in the process of porting, or had attempted to port their existing software from machine A to machine B.

In the early attempts nobody succeeded. Games that appeared on both machines at once were developed in parallel by two different programmers working on two different machines, sometimes never bothering to call each other and sometimes simply not knowing that other versions were being written. Programs that were originally written for the Mac didn't make it to the IBM. Code that was written for the IBM and moved to the Mac had to be drastically modified to conform to the higher user-interface standards.

Currently there are some programs that were developed completely on one machine and then moved to another. In these cases the source code for the different versions is maintained separately.

There were (and are) some programs on the Mac that use a subset of the Mac user-interface guidelines. Code that was written on the IBM, worked in the IBM mode, and was moved to the Mac without modification didn't sell well (or at all). Mac users feel contempt for software companies that try to sell them line-oriented software; they bought the Mac to get away from that kind of code! Although the Macintosh is merely an embodiment of local progress, and not the end-all or be-all of user-interface design, Mac users knew what they wanted (they had seen enough to know) and the stuff that came from text-oriented machines was not it.

Writing portable code is not very difficult if you don't use most of the features of a machine; this is a decision (marketing loves it) that doesn't work when using machines like the Macintosh. Reviewers for the major computer magazines annihilate or (more likely) never review products that aren't as good as they could be for the given system. Users gravitate toward simpler and friendlier software, and following the user-interface guidelines has been a path toward that goal.

I decided that I was going to be in for a difficult time, and had to choose between the Mac and the IBM. As I write this I still have not made that decision, because I decided to write this book instead.

OBJECTIVES

This book compares, feature by feature, the abilities of existing window systems. It also gives ideas that may help you write a program that can be moved to another system (and its windowing software) without rewriting everything. One goal is to have the same code compile, link and perform magnificently on two different machines without modification. The ultimate goal (which used to be possible) is to have the same executable file run just as fast on both machines without changes. I believe that the first goal is a reasonable one to expect. The differences between window systems make the ultimate goal very hard.

The following machines and windowing environments are the primary subjects:

☐ Amiga with Intuition by Commodore-Amiga
☐ Atari ST by Atari, with Gem by Digital Research (at least initially)
☐ IBM PC family clones, with Gem by Digital Research and with Windows by Microsoft, Inc.
☐ Macintosh and the IIGS by Apple Computer, Inc.

There are many things to discuss. This book contains material on the following topics:

☐ program organization
☐ source code organization
☐ coding hints
☐ data structures
☐ environment services
☐ support programs
☐ program orchestration

This text is *not* intended to be a critical review of the machines or the window and graphic environments. I want it to be a useful "get up to speed" tool for a programmer who must write code and take advantage of as many features of each machine as time will allow.

ACKNOWLEDGMENTS

Many, many people helped me get this book done. Those most important were:

Jeff Duntemann, for daily advice, for mental exercise, and for getting me into this by example (he wrote *The Complete Turbo Pascal* and *Turbo Pascal Solutions*);

Richard Swadley, an editor with patience;

Bill Leininger, for the many bits of wisdom and words of advice;

Marty Franz, for grinding through the manuscript before it was ready, telling me what was wrong with it, and for providing most of the C coding hints section;

Hugh Daniel, who bends ears in unique and wondrous ways;

Al McNeil, a cauldron of Mac know-how;

Bob Meyers, for his Atari ST knowledge;

Lisa Golladay, for without her adept technical writing the proposal for the book wouldn't have had that "certain something";

The folks at Digital Research, Apple Computer, and Microsoft;

And Alice, one very wonderful partner and patron, for being near even when it wasn't necessary.

The text, graphics and some of the listings in this book were produced entirely on a 512K Macintosh with a Levco MonsterMac 2 megabyte add-on card, the old 64K ROMs, and *one* (count it) 400K disk drive. Some listings were generated on Unix System III, Unix System V, and MS-DOS machines and then cross-loaded to the Macintosh. A considerable amount of background information came from Usenet, BBSes, and a couple of dial-up services. It took 30 hours to print the manuscript on an Imagewriter I. The principal production facilities were MacWrite, MacPaint, MacDraw, Switcher, TML Pascal, Dungeons of Doom, and GridWars.

For comments or corrections, the author can be reached through a number of methods. Mike's MCI electronic mail address is Michael Brian Bentley, ID number 258-5112. His Genie account is BENTLEY, his Compuserve account is 75026,315, and his amateur radio call sign is N9FJD (his packet radio BBS should be up by now). Mike's Usenet mail address is not constant, but he lives in the Chicago suburbs and is rarely far away from node ihnp4. Otherwise, try contacting him through the publisher.

Brief Contents Listing

Contents

PART 3   Environment Services

PART **4**   Program Orchestration

Appendixes

Index

1 Overview

1.1   The New Assignment

You are a programmer working for a medium-sized corporation whose products have nothing at all to do with the computer industry. Your work involves a couple of small computers, a mainframe, and a minicomputer, and you own one computer that you keep at home.

You walk into your office at the beginning of your work day. Taking your jacket off, you see an unfamiliar stapled document on top of your desk. It has one of those yellow self-stick notes on the cover. "Oh, oh . . ." you think, hanging your jacket on the hook behind the door. Sitting down in the squeaky chair, you read the note without touching the document.

It says that you have just been given the job of writing a program for the folks at corporate HQ (which is, incidentally, at the other end of the continent). You skim through the specifications. The program is no big deal, but it needs graphics and a "friendly countenance." It needs only careful high-level language coding and little-to-no assembly language, to run fast, but HQ wants it to run on as many of the following machines as possible:

IBM AT

Apple Macintosh

Apple IIGS

Atari ST

Commodore Amiga

There are a wide variety of machines, mostly Macintoshes, IBM PCs, and IBM ATs, at work (the note refers you to Appendix B for the numbers). Many of the people who work at HQ have those machines as well as Ataris and Amigas (and IIGSs) at home, and would like to (pleeeeeeeeeeeeeze?) use the software on their machines after normal hours. The folks at HQ wouldn't normally have stuck an Apple II on the list, but they got wind that the IIGS is pretty close to the Macintosh in terms of software support. Corporate has left it up to you to decide which computers will get the software.

1.2 Analyzing What's Needed

Here are the contents of Appendix B, showing the number of small computers owned by the company, and employees of the company, as of May 1987.

IBMs and clones:

lapheld	300	(plus 12 at home)
PC:	2429	(plus 83 at home)
AT:	252	(plus 6 at home)
386 based	23	(plus 3 at home)

Apples:

Mac Plus	1500	(plus 120 at home)
Mac II and SE	37	(plus 3 at home – new!)
IIGS	10	(plus 40 at home)

Ataris:

1024   25   (plus 57 at home)

Commodores:

Amiga   4   (plus 80 at home)

Appendix B also says that any IBM PC equipped with a Color Graphics Adapter (CGA) (minimal graphics resolution) or a Monochrome Adapter (no graphics capability) may have to be upgraded to run the software. The company will spring for more hardware such as memory, a better display card, or an accelerator card, but only for the office machines; folks with home systems are on their own.

The bulk of the computers are IBM PCs and clones and Mac Plus systems, so deciding which two machines get the software first should be easy. That is, until you recall that you are one of the folks with an Amiga at home, and you also remember that the CEO really likes her Atari 1024 ST. The members of your programming group own a variety of computers, most of which are not on the list; the one member who owns a DEC PDP-8 will probably *insist* that the software be ported to his machine.

So, for statistical, political, strategic, tactical, and obvious reasons, your program will have to be portable. But what exactly does that mean? How do you write easy-to-use, portable code for these machines? And, once a portable program is written, how much effort will it take to port the program to a new machine?

1.3 The Services of a Window System

A window system provides many additional **services** to both application developers and end-users. A software service is a job that is handled by an already-written component of a system. The new services handled by the window systems are not provided solely by linking new function library routines to an application's executable file. Rather, the window systems are implemented as part of the operating environment, sometimes standing on top of the old disk operating system, and sometimes mingling with it. Services are done by the environment outside the body of the application.

This book discusses the differences between various **user-interface** services, and deals with related topics that have to do with graphics on the display screen and user input from several devices. It provides only a cursory investigation of the differences between the supported file systems, although it does describe the contents of some types of files (and a little more than that for memory management concerns). Multitasking is discussed because this capability has a profound influence on the organization of a program when supported by the user-interface package.

All the small computers mentioned in this book have at least a minimal file system. All the other services that are essential for running a single program are accounted for. Some of the routines and data structures are different, particularly for the Macintosh. These differences have been treated with some success by the support libraries supplied with language compilers, and are treated in depth elsewhere in the literature.

Here is a list of the **higher-level** services, like the user-interface, that you will be getting from machines with windowing software:

Alerts   Boxes that appear on the display to announce, warn, or merely prompt. They contain very few **controls**.

Controls   Graphic icons that emulate real-world control devices like on-off buttons, sliding volume controls, and light switches.

Dialogs   Boxes that appear on the display and contain a number of controls and text fields.

Events   Records from the OS or a program that tell of something that has happened, such as a key being pressed, a disk being pushed into the drive, or the arrival of a character via a serial port.

Fonts   Collections of characters in a unique typeface designed to be used at screen or higher resolutions (laserprinters, Linotype machines).

Graphics   Display points, lines, ellipses, rectangles, polygons, bitmaps, text, fill patterns, and animation.

Data Memory Management   Allocating, deallocating, and moving data areas in RAM.

Menus   A bar across the top of the screen (or a window in some systems) with text or iconic entries; when the user points to one of the menu bar entries (and, in some systems, presses a mouse button), a hidden list of commands appears in a box just below the entry. These individual commands are selected by positioning the mouse cursor over them and pressing (or in some systems, releasing) a mouse button.

Multitasking   The ability to interleave the running times of programs so that they appear to all be running at the same time. This comes in handy for long program runs where the interactions may be preordained and would tie up the machine and display for minutes to hours (compiles, links, and murderous spreadsheet and database calculations). Electronic mail programs also need to use a few system resources but must be active 24 hours a day and free from interference by other software packages to be effective.

Resources   Environment support for giving a group of bytes a name and a type in RAM, on disk, and in executable files. If resources are supported, then the contents of executable files are divided into resources. When a program is running, resources are yanked in from disk when needed. Blocks of code and data are resources, as are menus, dialog and alert boxes (complete with controls), and fonts; the Macintosh has quite a few different predefined resources, and you can define your own. Resources are an example of object-oriented constructs in the windowing environments.

Scrap Buffer Operations

An area of RAM or disk used as a common temporary store for cut and paste operations. The contents of the buffer are identified by type so that applications know how to treat the contents. Any kind of data is a candidate for the scrap buffer. This is one way programs transfer data to each other.

Code Segment Management

Historically RAM was a limited resource, addressability was limited, and the early micros didn't have hardware memory management. The OS, CPU, and windowing packages permit (or require) blocks of code to be segmented. The code segments can be loaded into memory and flushed at will during execution; the entire program need not be present in RAM at once.

Text Editing

A good set of text manipulation routines provided by the environment makes development much, much easier: you don't have to worry about the consequences of displaying different fonts or supporting text edit interactions; your program can be supplied with sections of text built and extracted using a different program; and a user will already know exactly how to edit text in your program.

Windows

Rectangular areas of the display that act like malleable blackboards: programs write on the blackboard from the back side, and you see what it does from the front (see Fig. 1–1). A display can have a bunch of windows, either next to each other or in front of one another; bringing a window in front of a pack of windows is a quick way to see what is in it. Having a flock of windows on one display is a way to have more than one display's worth of graphics and text information available at a touch; the window frames act as visual references and as controls to access the information they contain.

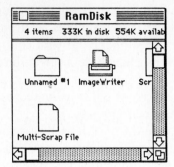

Figure 1–1 An active window, with controls

Every windowing package does not support all the items in the list. The 68000-based Macintosh does not have multitasking, nor does Gem. The Apple IIGS and the Amiga do not support resources. The rest are present in all the targeted machines as part of the user-interface support, but (despite one manufacturer's claims) each instance is unique in the same way that one passage of writing changes between each language of the Rosetta Stone. It takes forethought to work with these partly-diverging systems to make chunks of your program machine-independent and corral the system-dependent chunks.

If you had to write software for each of the computers, your development plan might include the following points:

☐ Careful selection of a language.

☐ Analysis, design, and selective prototyping of the program before implementation. Modifications of the program structure during implementation may affect more than one version of a section of system-dependent code, and thus are costly and annoying.

☐ Good source file organization so that confusion is kept in check, files are not lost, and duplication of code is minimized.

☐ Authoring resilient code. There is no substitute for knowing what good and bad code look like and writing only the good stuff.

☐ Determining what changes the future may bring to the program environments, and making preparations for minimizing the effects. This is the "keep an ear to the rail" guideline.

☐ Keeping abreast of developments by third-party vendors. This is the "keep the other ear to the other rail" guideline. Bear in mind that the "not invented here" point of view has valid things to say about licensing, reliability, and maintenance problems associated with using third-party libraries.

☐ Knowing the extent of, and the differences between, the operating system and user-interface services on the target machines. Knowing this ahead of time may keep you from using unique features of one machine that can't easily be duplicated in the application code on another system.

☐ Keeping the system-dependent code out of the system-independent code areas.

The last two points must be significant, since not following them was the cause of a number of failed software porting efforts early in the life span of the Macintosh, Gem, and Microsoft Windows.

This book is an attempt to put some of the necessary portability research into words and in one place. Otherwise you would need to plow through some of the following large tomes for the same information:

Apple Computer, Inc.: *Inside Macintosh*, Vols. I–IV

Microsoft, Inc.: *Windows Development Toolkit Manuals*

Commodore, Inc.: *Amiga Manuals*

Digital Research, Inc.: *Gem Programmer's Toolkit Manual*

The basic stuff is in this book. Once you start cooking on the design and coding, you will use the real manuals more because they contain much more about what the manufacturers say is in their products.

1.4 A Short Description of the Machines

In this section I take the liberty of providing a short description and history of each of the machines that is considered to be a current major player in personal business computers. These descriptions are, of course, opinionated.

APPLE MACINTOSH

The Macintosh was Apple Computer's third attempt to create a popular successor to the Apple II line of personal computers.

The first attempt, the Apple III, had essentially the same microprocessor technology as the Apple II, but used an unwieldy main memory mapping system to fit "10 pounds of program into a 5-pound bag." To handle the complicated paging mechanism, Apple engineers crafted SOS, one of the most powerful and flexible operating system environments for a computer the size of the Apple III.

In the second attempt, the Apple Lisa was armed with a much more competitive processor (the 68000), the best (at the time) chip-based memory management hardware (to run large programs without a large amount of RAM), a battalion of operating system routines, a small number of system utilities, and a medium resolution black-and-white display. Every manufacturer calls its display resolution "super" for emotional reasons; a *high* resolution display really means 1024 by 1024 color pixels or more.

The Lisa's operating environment shared none of the drawbacks of the Apple II or III environments, except the need for low cost. It was designed under the assumption that at least a half-megabyte of memory would be available, enabling Apple's engineers to take advantage of years of research in user-interface design in-house, at Xerox PARC, and elsewhere in the industry. The Lisa, however, suffered from reliability problems, and its market penetration was very slow in comparison with the exploding market based on the Intel 8088 and the IBM PC design. This was primarily due to the steep initial cost, which was around $10,000. The Lisa's user-interface was excellent, but it never had the voracious third-party software developer support that the IBM PC family enjoys.

The Macintosh is another story. It is equipped with a faster version of the Motorola 68000 than the Lisa has. The Mac has a cheaper hardware design and a smaller physical form—it is portable. The Mac is not equipped with a full memory management facility, but few programs working on micros these days approach the need for more than a megabyte of working RAM, and paging memory management, unless used heavily, serves only to slow down the operation of a system. In addition, the Mac is equipped with reworked, heavily optimized, and debugged versions of the system software that first saw action in the Lisa a year before. Sales figures for the first Macintoshes, each equipped with only 128K of

RAM, were astonishing. Third-party support of the Macintosh is strong and sophisticated.

The 68000-based Macintosh supports one application running at a time. It has a big ROM with a generous number of user-interface support routines, including basic graphics (the Quickdraw package), fonts, windows, menus, dialogs, and text management, to name a few. The machine supports resources, which means that it can grab from the disk (and treat as objects) entire menus, dialog boxes, code, pictures, and more. Controls, such as check boxes and push buttons, are emulated by the software graphically, and can be used easily by application code. The Macintosh has a segment loader for loading and moving code segments between disk and RAM. There is a software memory manager for shuffling data objects during an application's runtime without interfering with the application. An event manager posts all the standard I/O transactions to a queue polled by applications to see if anything has happened recently.

The most recent models of the Macintosh have been embellished with card slots, completely unlocking the once jealously guarded architecture; however, the Mac II and the Mac SE use entirely different bus architectures and incompatible "DIN" bus connectors.

IBM PC FAMILY

IBM came out with a machine that seemed to follow most of the rules in the Hacker's Ethic, befuddling a tremendous number of people. It didn't use the standard Apple, S100, or Intel busses, for IBM is IBM, after all — they invented their own. The guts were wide open, not closed, and the operating system was open.

The reaction to this nifty new machine was: *gimme!* IBM, perplexed, "ramped up" production — up and up and up. The IBM PC, and its successful copies, are sold in such numbers today that they are treated as commodities!

The original IBM PCs use an Intel 8088, which is about 3 to 4 times slower than the 68000, as the central processor unit. The Intel 8086 processor is faster than an 8088; the Intel 80286 processor, the cpu of the IBM AT, is about as fast as a 68000; and the Intel 80386 processor, not currently used in a commercially-available IBM machine, is *much* faster than the 68000. The other complication to this formula is the Intel 8087 math coprocessor, which speeds up basic math operations over software emulation by a considerable margin. The 68000 machines do not win over from 8088 machines many people who are interested in crunching numbers with a small computer, since the 68000 technically doesn't have a math coprocessor (although the 68020 does).

The standard operating system is called PC-DOS (or MS-DOS); it provides essential operating system services like file I/O, console I/O, and interrupt handling. There is a small section of the operating system, called the BIOS or Basic I/O System, that is normally kept in a small ROM. It contains some of the lowest-level I/O software in the system. At the time of writing, the BIOS (and a small Microsoft BASIC interpreter, only on the IBM PC) is the only thing kept in ROM for this family of systems, but rumors floating around the industry suggest that this may change.

Because the IBM PC and MS-DOS/PC-DOS were not released with an extensive library of graphics support, and because the speed of the 8088 processor is not very good, most of the software developed for the IBM PC that does graphics writes directly to the RAM areas used by the displays, bypassing the operating system and the BIOS.

Other operating systems for this family of machines exist; Unix by AT&T and Concurrent PC-DOS (or CPC-DOS) by Digital Research are two of them. Some Unix ports for the IBM machines contain support to run MS-DOS programs, and CPC-DOS is a multitasking OS currently compatible with versions of MS-DOS up to 3.2. Neither Unix nor CPC-DOS provides anything beyond essential graphic services without additional software.

There are quite a few commercially-available libraries and software packages that can be layered on top of MS-DOS or linked into an application to add many services that aren't provided by MS-DOS. The two packages I know to be most successful at providing a Macintosh-like program environment are the Digital Research Gem and the Microsoft Windows. The other packages are missing one thing or another, which separates them from any hope of accommodating application ports to or from the Macintosh. Some have graphics but are missing support for dialogs, fonts, menus, scrap buffers, windows, controls, resources, or desktop software.

Gem is a lean package that adequately provides graphics services with punctuality. Microsoft Windows is a larger package that not only realizes the essential services found in the Macintosh, but also has efficient multitasking as well. Gem contains a limited multitasking kernel, and relies on the native operating system for more complete tasking services. Windows allows concurrent programs to use different windows on the display at the same time.

About the only thing wrong with these two packages is that programs that are written using them tend not to perform very well on 8088-based machines. This is to say that they seem to run like molasses. Since most business machines today use an 8088, conservative factions in the industry write off the impact that Windows and Gem will have because, for one thing, Windows and Gem applications run so "slowly." There is more to a product than just *selling* it; it has to be written, and the use of Gem or Windows may be the only difference between a program that fails and a program that works reliably.

My personal opinion is that their market penetration may be slow, but noticeable improvements in current applications on the IBM PC aren't going to go anywhere without the software that does what Gem and Windows provide. Software with a good horse underneath it, and a window system to handle the user interface, will easily out-demo older IBM software. Some applications, like desktop publishing programs, are *very hard* to use on 8088-based systems, and are very hard to write (economically) without the help of Gem- or Windows-like library. However, there is always plenty of room for someone who will finance the development of a huge 80 to 100% assembly-code written package, using a small group of completely dedicated programmers to capture a market. I expect that, rather than writing applications in assembly language, most new major packages will eventually support 80286 and 80386 systems only, despite the current large number of 8088 systems, for two reasons: the cost to upgrade to an 80286/80386 from an 8088 will be very low, and major packages written in assembly language are expensive to produce and maintain and take longer to write. It will be much easier and cheaper to induce customers to upgrade.

ATARI ST

The Atari ST is another 68000-based system. Its long suit is that it is a very lean, inexpensive color system. The ST is known in the United States but is more popular in Europe. It is designed to be cheaper than the Macintosh, with color graphics and higher resolution.

The low-level operating system is called TOS; above that are the Gem Virtual Device Interface (VDI) and the higher-level Application Environment Services (AES) modules. The VDI and AES are present on both the ST and IBM. Disk I/O is supported by a number of routines supplied in library form by compiler developers.

Software development support for the Atari ST is not as vast as that for the established Macintosh or IBM. This book is dedicated to helping people develop code on any one of the machines mentioned here and move it to another, so that a sophisticated program will not be limited to a one-user base. At this writing, despite Gem's presence, the window system guidelines for the Atari ST are fragmented. Many programmers have found Gem to be incompatible with their needs, and have developed their own library of user-interface routines.

COMMODORE AMIGA

The color display hardware of this 68000-based machine is the most sophisticated on the list. Most of these capabilities are used to fluidly move predefined color bitmaps around on the display.

The contents of the Amiga display are not implemented as a single, contiguous block of RAM at a set location. Very simply put, the Amiga display hardware follows a list of instructions telling it the addresses and dimensions of the blocks of RAM to be displayed and where on the display they should appear. This display list is like a program to the Amiga display processor; the entire display list is executed once every time the electron beam passes over the entire display. The instrument that executes the display list is the **copper**, the display (co)processor.

The size of the blocks of RAM (bitmaps) has nothing at all to do with the size of the display; if the bitmap is too large, then only part is visible. The Amiga display hardware includes a blitter which is at the beck and call of the display processor to handle bitmap-bitmap interactions. Blit means **block image transfer**, so a **blitter** is a piece of hardware or software that copies blocks of memory from one place to another. Blit operations involve logical operations on and between blocks of memory before the result is placed elsewhere in RAM. For example, one block of memory can be inverted, where all the bit values are flipped ($1\rightarrow0$, and $0\rightarrow1$). The result of this operation is **XORed** with another block of memory, and the final result is shown on the display as a rectangle with a pattern in it. Blit operations (see Fig. 1–2) make the most sense when applied for use with raster graphics, and are discussed in full in the chapter on graphics in Part 3 of this book.

The Amiga doesn't provide much hardware acceleration for drawing line-based graphic primitives in real time. The operating system provides

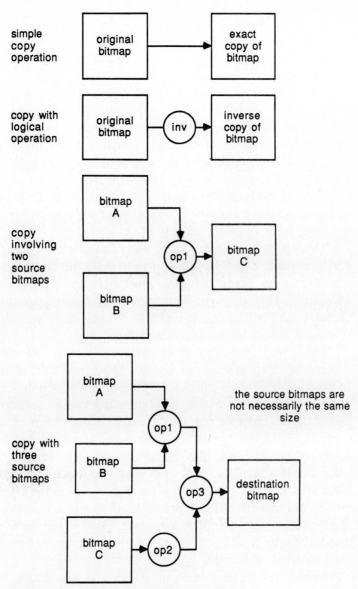

Figure 1–2 Examples of blitter operations

multitasking. The advanced graphics functions (screens, windows, menus, etc.) are provided by the software package called Intuition. Intuition fully supports multitasking; it allows concurrent programs to have different windows on the screen at the same time.

APPLE IIGS

The Apple IIGS is an upgrade for the Apple II line of computers. Apple Computer has sold an awful lot of Apple IIs, and as a consequence has many satisfied Apple II owners. Apple wanted to create an option so that these satisfied customers could inexpensively upgrade to a faster machine without having to abandon their software base. Much of the Apple II software is very sensitive to the speed of the processor, the properties of the disk drive, and other quirks of the Apple II, so if there is anything different about a new machine, it can't be made to work. Therefore, an upgrade machine must be compatible at least to the 95-percent level to have any hope of being successful.

This upgrade must be significantly cheaper than going out and getting a Macintosh or else it has no reason to exist, but that likely means that the upgrade as an entire machine must be considerably cheaper than the Macintosh. How does Apple design a significant upgrade to the II that is cheaper than a Macintosh and has a color display, without eroding the pricing structure of the Macintosh family?

The central processor in the IIGS, a Western Design Center 65816, has two instruction sets: the first is 100 percent 6502-compatible, and the second implements a unique 16-bit processor. Apple Computer has re-written much of the Macintosh operating system software for the IIGS; this includes most of the ROM calls, in one form or another, for the support of the user-interface. There are a number of basic differences between the IIGS and the Macintosh software support: the IIGS has a color display, the Mac Plus does not; the Macintosh has resources, the IIGS does not; the Macintosh is much faster than the IIGS (even in 16-bit mode); and the IIGS development team seems to be more protective than the Macintosh group of data structures used in the user-interface and the operating system, so there are more routines provided in the IIGS that are used solely to hide data.

Apple gets to keep both the IIGS and Macintosh, even though the IIGS is much cheaper than a Macintosh but potentially can run the same applications with some modifications. The most significant difference is the speed of the 65816 in 16-bit mode; it runs code significantly faster than a 6502, but significantly slower than a 68000. It is unclear, despite the savvy marketing and engineering decisions backing this machine, whether a sufficient market exists for Macintosh and IIGS ports for the effort to be worthwhile to developers.

1.5 | Conclusion

Part 1 describes my motives, and the machines that were in mind at this writing. It glosses over the entire span of material, parts of which the rest of the book treats in some depth. The 1987 machines are not entirely part of the literature (except in speculation), so their contribution to the rest of the book is minimal, but the services that they (will) provide are (going to be) similar to those in machines on the market now. The constraints on the design of applications will not change much. This is much easier to predict than Chicago weather.

Part 2 discusses what an application must do to talk to the window systems, and the constraints and additional responsibilities that are placed upon application code. Windowing applications, in order to handle a myriad of real-time user interactions as well as the standard operating system responsibilities, are now designed to centralize and emphasize the user I/O processing code. This has a sweeping impact on how business programs are organized, both in source and in binary form; they suddenly look like real-time process control programs.

Also, some of the window systems provide support for *editing executable files* without recompilation or relinking, to enable in-the-field adjustments to initialization, adding and subtracting capabilities, and text language translation. Support for **resources** has a wholesale impact on how components of programs are thought of and how binary files are partitioned.

2 Program Organization

2.1 | Introduction

Programs that are written to use one or more of the windowing packages are not much different from programs that aren't. There are no magic incantations to be intoned, no sacrifices to be made for the goodwill of obscure computer science deities. The present design philosophies impose constraints that might be annoying, but we programmers have put up with an awful lot in the past, and we always, always make it better in the long run. This implies that what *is* different cannot be disregarded.

Showing the differences between each of the five highlighted systems mentioned on the cover is intended to achieve two lofty goals. The first is to make knowing any one of the five systems easier. The second is to help produce a portable program that will run on the target systems with few changes. To help write portable programs, or at least programs maintainable on just one machine, this book presents material on three fronts:

Program Composition — how executable files are arranged; programs are *not* simply code and data. There are discussions of real-time user interaction, response time, display objects, and responsibilities; events, event messages, event loops, and event routines; and the differences in existing code design between single-tasking and multitasking systems.

Source File Organization — big programs in general, and portable programs in particular, are more pliant when the code is divided into parts and kept in a myriad of small files. The files contain different kinds of code. Projects involving more than one machine and having at least radiation-proof (that is, obvious) partitions between the portable code and the system-dependent code are simpler to port and maintain. Manpower, language, and compiler-system constraints are big factors that are discussed in this section.

Coding Hints — this book uses the two big high-level implementation languages of the 1980s' small machines, C and Pascal, because only those two are well-supported by the manufacturers of the windowing packages. Just writing a program in C or Pascal is not enough to guarantee slick execution and easy ports. The available language compilers implement variations that can get in the way of portability (particularly in Pascal, but C developers can also get stung). This section discusses some of the major and minor gotchas by comparing selected existing compilers.

2.2 Program Composition

RESPONSE TIME AND RESPONSIBILITY

Programs that work under windowing environments not only have more responsibilities than programs that don't, they can get away with a good deal less. The weight of added responsibility, and the intolerance of improper and inconsistent function, is why I/O has become *the* prominent voice in windowing programs. The changes in the way programs are implemented is a reaction to the threat of bulky, clumsy, slow, and misbehaving code; fancy I/O is an area where problems grow on trees.

Microcomputers are cheap enough to be single-user *and* popular machines. When it comes to basic character I/O and applications that don't tax the system, microcomputers are more responsive than larger machines (multiuser minicomputers and mainframes). On micros, screen-based editors react immediately to keypresses and leave multi-user system screen editors in the dust. Any program that does simple I/O operations, and is written in a normal, linear fashion without much attention given to real-time considerations, is still going to be responsive on a micro. Since users aren't added to a single-user micro, response time never gets bad for that reason.

Micros are like small two-seat sports cars. A sports car is a fiesty machine that can carry one or two people and a little bit of luggage somewhere. The engine barks and growls enthusiastically, and the passing acceleration is great. Larger computers are like larger cars (limos, vans). They are not designed to be as responsive, but can carry more weight.

The trouble starts when microcomputer applications start to do windowing and interactive graphics and handle input from sources other than the keyboard. The processor time required to do the graphics is enormous, and handling I/O from several different devices is a costly guessing game. The overhead skyrockets and the responsiveness drops like a stone.

The interactive feel of micros is something that until now has been taken for granted. It was something that could be aided by clever engineering in the operating system: keeping the OS lean. There is now little alternative, since just making the processor faster will not solve many of the problems. Both the application code and the operating system environment have to pay more attention to real-time I/O transactions, the asset that is most hurt by the added responsibility.

Simple Non-Real-Time User I/O

When user I/O is simple, users send commands and data with a console keyboard, or something emulating the keyboard like an indirect command file. The program does not operate in **real time**—it accepts input only when *it* is ready, and doesn't have to respond in jig time. The program is not required to accept user I/O without showing a prompt first, much less whenever input does or can appear. A non-real-time program will prompt for input only when it can accept input. Normally prompts appear only after a chunk of program code has executed to the next input statement, and the program then sits there until the input statement has been satisfied.

An unsophisticated program, or a program running in a lean environment, expects to be "forewarned" with a typed-in user command before a change is made to the machine configuration it is running on, for instance, changing a disk; a program is likely (expected) to ignore input it doesn't expect, or to greet the request with a minimum of feedback. There are other nuances.

A Non-Real-Time Example

Figure 2–1 is an example of an interactive session with a program that does not require the software to work in real time.

Real-Time User I/O

Windowing programs must expect user input to appear from several sources. The mouse, the keyboard, and inserting a disk into a drive are all possibilities.

The meaning of a mouse button press depends on where on the screen the mouse cursor is at that moment, the number of consecutive presses, and which mouse button is being operated (if there is more than one). Both the windowing program and the windowing system have to do some of the decoding, with **real-time constraints**: the decoding may have to be done, and the program react, before something else happens. It is clear that the processor time that is sometimes needed will make real-time interaction impractical, but at other times windowing programs do not have the luxury of making the user wait. The burden has shifted toward the application, windowing system, and machine, and away from the patience of the user.

```
Login: bentley
Password: xxxxxxxxxx
Last Login: 5 January 1987
Bentley 1> timelog
Just a moment...
*** TimeLogger v 1.25 ***
Identify the account to bill: RustScupper
Please specify start time: 8:00
And now the end time: 16:30
And finally the idle time: 1:20

That entry is for RustScupper, from 8:00 to 16:30 with
  1:20 worth of holes during the session.

Make another log entry? (y/n) > n

Thank you! These times will be added to your log.
Have a pleasant day, and thank you for observing
all safety precautions!

*** TimeLogger v1.25 ***

Bentley 2> logout
Logged out in the nick of time!
Login:
```

Figure 2–1 Example of an interactive session requiring no real-time responses

Poor real-time behavior is the reason that windowing systems do not succeed on slow personal computers. Windowing applications rely on real-time feedback, but slow computers find real-time interactions difficult to keep up with while trying to handle graphics too.

A Real-Time Example

Here is a simple example of a sequence of operations that must be allowed to happen in real-time. The mouse cursor is positioned over an object on the screen. The mouse button is pressed, signifying (in this case) that the object should be "picked up." The cursor is then moved by moving the mouse; the selected object is dragged with the cursor because the mouse button is being held down. In the hands of a skilled user, the time between selecting the object with the mouse and mouse cursor and dragging it to a new location is negligible. The application must quickly identify what the pressing of the mouse button means in that case. The dragging operation also occurs in real-time. The cursor is supposed to match the movement of the mouse nuance for nuance. If the movements of the object image and mouse cursor do not exactly match the movements of the mouse, or appear erratic or jumpy and not smooth, then using that software is uncomfortable (see Fig. 2–2).

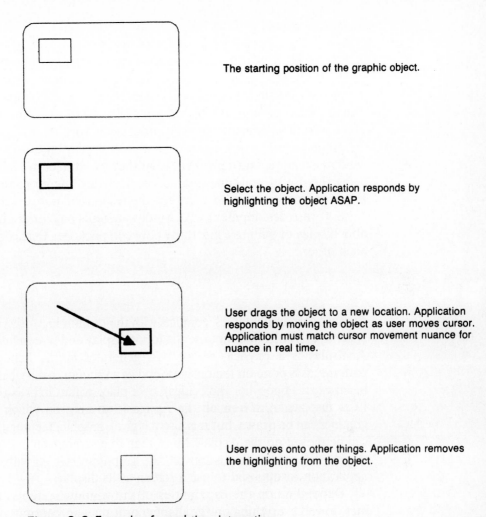

The starting position of the graphic object.

Select the object. Application responds by highlighting the object ASAP.

User drags the object to a new location. Application responds by moving the object as user moves cursor. Application must match cursor movement nuance for nuance in real time.

User moves onto other things. Application removes the highlighting from the object.

Figure 2–2 Example of a real-time interaction

DISPLAYS AND DISPLAY OBJECTS

Window system application code is arranged around **display objects** (and the mouse), so here is a brief introduction to them. These display objects, with other services, are discussed at length in Part 3.

Display objects are predefined graphics that are supported (as services) by the window system. They are used to divide the display fairly between the warring factions of functions, tasks, and coordinate systems;

to accept orders from the user with the mouse and keyboard; and to show current status. Since display objects are defined and supported by the window packages, they are established as standards and are used in program after program. Learning a new program that uses known services is much easier than learning one that doesn't. For example, people who already know how to use Macintosh's MacWrite word processor already know how most Macintosh word processors work!

An interesting thing about the common display objects (screens, menus, windows, dialogs, and controls) is that they *all* interact in real-time, encouraging the use of real-time interaction. They are therefore provided to enhance the machine, and not to keep the responsibilities of a machine down.

Software development with window systems has turned into a remarkable display of willing conformity between packages that compete against each other.

The Display

Because of manufacturers' conflicts with the terminology used in the window systems, this book does not use the terms display and screen interchangeably. A **display** is a physical device that generates visible light in controlled patterns, as is done on the business end of a vacuum tube (where an electron beam excites phosphor molecules), or a place where light is reflected, as in LCD displays. A **screen** on the Amiga is an area on which windows and graphics can be drawn, but it is also a logical, graphic, rectangular object that can be moved on the display. More than one screen can exist on an Amiga display. When a screen is moved, the graphics on it go with it. An Amiga application is supposed to use a screen as its display.

Depending on the capabilities of the window system, an application may "own" everything on the **display** or it may be "permitted" to use just a part of the display. In the first case the window system will receive user interactions with the display and send them all to the currently executing application. In the second case the window system has to first determine which application program should get notice of each interaction.

When an application owns the display (or an entire logical **screen**, as may be the case on the Amiga), it doesn't have to use any of the predefined objects like windows to contain things that belong to it. The application knows that any mouse picks will involve it. There are reasons why you might not want to do that, but there is no real reason why you couldn't.

When an application doesn't own the display, it might be sharing the display with other programs. The window system then requires that the application define windows and keep its data within them. Amiga screens can also be shared between programs, but the Amiga system doesn't require the use of windows; it leaves conformity up to the developers. Figures 2–3, 2–4, and 2–5 show some examples of different displays.

The Use for a Window

The window is the first example of a display object. It contains zero or more related data items that are properly displayed together. The data items could comprise anything, from the image of a map to a list of those who are naughty and those who are nice, with pictures. Windows are often used as "windows" into a large **world coordinate system** in which data or graphic objects are drawn.

Windows have properties that help show meaningful information: they keep one kind of data from involuntarily occupying the entire display; they can be used to show part of a region of data that is bigger than the display; and they can be moved around on the display, sized to taste, or removed completely. Windows also indicate where data should and shouldn't appear on the display.

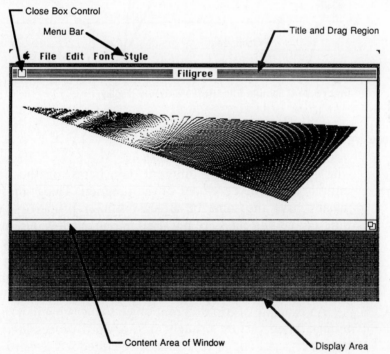

Figure 2–3 Macintosh display with one window and menu bar

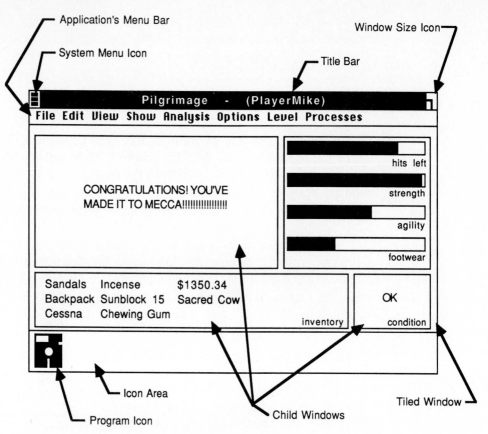

Figure 2–4 Sample Microsoft Windows display

Appearance versus Editing Rules

The criteria for placing different data items together in a window are entirely up to the developer of the program. Things that go in a window usually have the same or at least similar properties, so that entirely different editing rules are not used in one window. However, the appearance of completely unrelated objects in the same window happens all the time in windowing applications like desktop publishing programs. It is common that some things that can *appear* in a window have to be *created and edited* in another window (or program) and pasted in.

An example of two different objects coexisting in a single window is a bitmap-based picture brought into a word processing program from a paint program. The picture cannot be edited in the word processor, but it can be pasted into the file so that text can be written around it. The edit

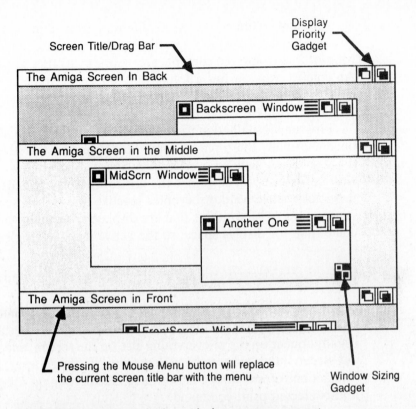

Figure 2–5 An Amiga display with three screens present

window can be used to fully edit text, but is limited to cut and paste operations with any other kind of data.

Editing completely unrelated objects in the same window is not recommended, but don't let me stop an unusual but appropriate approach for unusual data.

Active Display Objects

An **active** window is one in which a user can directly select or edit the contents. An **inactive** window is one that is on the display, like an active window, but that has to be made active first before any other interaction. The inactive window is selected as a whole, usually with a mouse pick over any part of the window. If the select succeeds, the window becomes active and the user can then interact with the contents of the window. Usually activating one window will deactivate another window.

An active window display is different from that of an inactive one. Usually the active window is displayed with color and texture in the window frame, and the contents are displayed as they normally should be. An inactive window has a frame that is missing some color and texture, and the contents are diffused, with diminished contrast and brightness (see Fig. 2–6).

Programs usually don't have all their windows available or active at once. Normally the topmost overlapping window is active, with the rest inactive. To activate an overlapping window, the window itself is selected with the mouse, which brings the entire window to the foreground. The previously active window becomes inactive and is sent somewhere in the background. With windows that are displayed without overlap, there is no contention for display space, so the active/inactive toggle is optional.

Dialog Windows

There are a number of different types of windows, some of which are significant enough to get their own name. Dialogs are special windows that usually appear on top of everything else on the screen, and usually require any screen interactions to be with *them* until they go away. Dialogs are for interactions of immediate importance, like setting up the parameters for a just-selected print command.

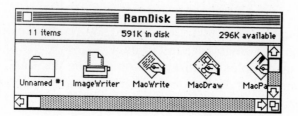

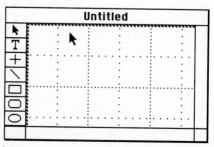

Figure 2–6 Active and inactive window

Dialogs usually contain controls, which are small, user-controlled devices that represent with graphics the current state of an adjustable program option. The graphics of the controls help identify the nature of the option. Is it a boolean (yes/no, on/off, true/false)? Is it the name of a file? Will the selection of the control invoke an immediate response? Figure 2–7 shows an example of a dialog box.

Menus

Menus are other display objects that are used to make the most of the display. A menu contains a list of menu items, short text phrases, or graphics with an optional check mark. A menu item can be selected with a pointing device, and usually represents a command or a simple program option. Menus are not displayed until selected because they take up too much display space. Instead, a menu is represented by a menu title in a menu bar which takes up a single line at the top of the display, screen, or a window (depending on the window system) (see Fig. 2–8).

User Behavior

Anything that can be placed on the screen at one time has to be placed there by software. A window system display contains selectable objects and nonselectable objects. As a rule, users try to interact with *anything* on the display, even nonselectable objects.

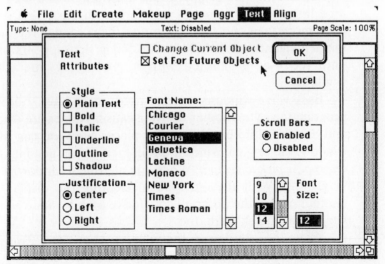

Figure 2–7 Macintosh modal dialog box (from DESIGN by Meta Software)

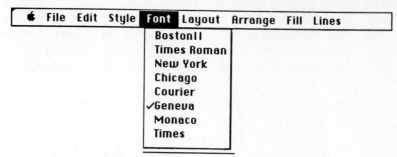

Figure 2–8 Menu bar and menu

If there is a selectable object on the display, there must be code that handles the interaction. If a user tries to select something with the mouse, it is appropriate to have the application react even if the interaction is senseless—especially if the user does it over and over.

Under the Hood

If an application can have several windows on the display at one time, the code to handle the contents of the display is initially accessed from the same part of the program. The implementation varies depending on the window system, but most programs use one standard "screen" on which all of their windows and graphics may appear (see Fig. 2–9).

Window system applications emphasize opening and closing a window when different data or operations are wanted. If a program has to go off on a tangent, it does not "create a new display," but it might close and open more than one window, and perhaps change the menu bar. Usually minor tangents are handled by a dialog that appears in the foreground until the user is finished with it, preventing interactions with other windows.

Back when windows weren't used, you'd have to leave one part of a program to get to another drawing causing the entire display to be erased and drawing different data in its place. Now you can just open another window; the original window is still there if you need it, and *you only need one mouse pick to get to it.* When you activate a window, it usually activates in a blink. With the old system, clearing the display and starting up another part of the program could take a while, and you could need a few keypresses to get there, too.

When the user presses the mouse button, the software only has to find out if the cursor is over an active window or the menu bar. Using the menu bar leads to several predefined operations. Finding out which one was picked is simple: the window system usually tells you. If the mouse pick occurred in an inactive window, the program activates it and deactivates another. The rules for interacting with the data in all but one of the open windows can be discounted, since those windows are probably inactive. Even though the application must be ready for anything that can happen in one small section of its code, narrowing it down to the window (and soon an operation) is simple. When an active window is involved, the hard part happens: the mouse pick has to be correlated with the coordinate system displayed by that window. If the interaction involves a predefined control, the window system may absorb most of the effort; anything else will require more application code.

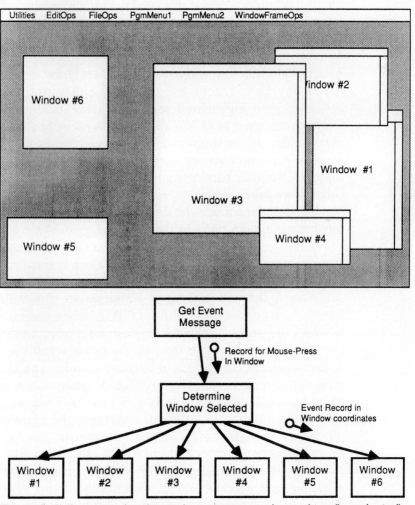

Figure 2–9 Example of multi-window program with matching (hypothetical) structure chart of mouse-button event handling routines

MODES

A **mode** exists in software when an action, such as a screen pick, attempted more than once on the same data produces different reactions. If you have used Wordstar and toggled its Insert and Overwrite Modes, then you have experience with a mode. A mode also exists when the program you are using siphons you off to a dark corner and keeps you there for a while. There is nothing unique about the interactions with the software, but the effects are unique.

Software modes are clearly identified to reduce the possibility of confusion and accidental misuse. Historically modal software didn't have adequate feedback and reinforcement from the program for a user's actions, and was the most difficult kind to learn. The visual aids of the Macintosh, Gem, Windows, and Amiga are used to make avoiding modes easier. Palettes, like those found in MacDraw and MacPaint, are for identifying the commonly used modes in either program. The active mode is shown by a highlighted selection in the palette. Both palettes and windows are used in ODS/Consultant to identify all the program's available modes and to show which mode is active (see Fig. 2–10). A dialog window that won't get out of the way until it is satisfied is called a **modal dialog**; if another window can be activated over the dialog window, it is called a **modeless dialog**.

In MacPaint a mode starts when a choice in the palette has been made; any further screen picks in the graphics window are for that mode, until the next palette pick. Picking the spray can starts the spray can mode. The spray can mode ends when the eraser block is selected. Menu selections don't change the graphics window mode.

When used with tight-fisted moderation, consistency, and a bit of feedback, modes aren't confusing. A window system program is likely to make the ground rules for lesser-used modes unarguably obvious by: 1) plastering a dialog box over all the active windows in the foreground; 2) presenting all the options in large type; and 3) chaining you up until it's done with you. It is difficult with large programs or a suite of smaller ones to avoid modes, though it is usually possible to simplify the design and reduce the number. In addition, sometimes the customer wants modes.

Figure 2–11 shows the change window in MacWrite. The mode is represented by the appearance of a foreground window. When a screen pick outside of the change window is made, the change window becomes a background window and is hidden behind the large editing window. The change window can be made to vanish altogether by picking its

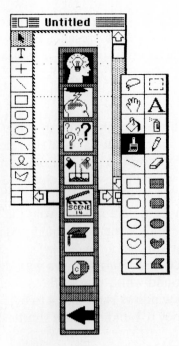

Figure 2–10 Palettes from MacDraw, MacPaint, ODS/Consultant

Change
Find what	
Change to	
(Find Next) (Change, Then Find) (Change) (Change All)
● **Whole Word**   ○ **Partial Word**

Figure 2–11 The change window from MacWrite

Macintosh "go away" box at the top left-hand of the window. Since this is exactly how most windows behave on the Macintosh, much of how the change command works is already understood by someone who knows how windows work. This experience is easily garnered by doing other, more common things with the machine. The use of the window forces the programming of the operations in that window to follow the standards for windows specified in the user-interface rulebook, not because it's "The Law," but because the program will otherwise bomb or behave unpredictably. Placing a mode in unique surroundings to make it obvious where you stand helps remove the modality.

If a window supports accesses to data that are different from what the other windows in a program display, its presence is less an indication of modality and more a demonstration of problem complexity.

Boundary Conditions

Windows are used to encapsulate entirely different sets of rules and data, but multiple windows can be used on the same set of rules and data. It is conceivable that someone might want to dedicate one window per palette option into a single graphics workspace; when a change is made in one of the windows, the change could be reflected in what all the other windows display. This appears to be a legitimate way to avoid the use of a palette and modes, but it makes sense only if there is enough space on the display to hold all the windows at one time (if a big display is at one's disposal or the palette has very few selections). For machines with display resolution of around 640 by 480 black-and-white pixels, the general limit on the number of useful foreground windows is around 4 to 6. If there are more, users will probably feel like they're building space shuttles in linen closets.

EVENTS AND THE EVENT LOOP

Operating systems are on the prowl for things that need their attention. How it notices them is paramount for a successful personal computer. Nobody likes a personal machine that drops disk blocks or ignores keypresses and mouse clicks. Each click is a demand for the machine to do something. When the task is complete, the machine must return quickly to the matters at hand.

Windowing application software has to be written properly to use the capabilities of the machine to handle the inevitable flurry of interactions, or **events**. The operating system software can and does handle these events, to a limit, but it is up to the application software to do something with them. Otherwise, the operating system may gag on the backlog of unanswered events, be forced to lose the oldest one, or have to refuse new ones.

The window systems discussed in this book *demand* that the application software have an answer for all the events that can occur. This is why it is harder to write windowing software. Older programs simply don't worry about fielding a variety of voluntary inputs. They wait for the carriage return, process a line of text, and then wait for another carriage return.

Mouse clicks (pressing and releasing the mouse buttons) are interesting events because the meaning of a click is dependent on the location of the display cursor; the event needs more sleuthing. A simple mouse click is disarmingly complicated, but worth the extra effort; it is a good way to interact with a variety of commands without needing typing skills.

Other event sources are serial and parallel ports, networking ports, disk drives, and any other peripheral devices. Software may also be the source of events, especially in multitasking environments. This happens in AT&T's Unix System V, Commodore's Amiga operating system, and Digital Research's Concurrent PC-DOS. Application software for the windowing packages covered in this book is entirely capable of creating and posting event messages.

The operating system handles the interrupts from the standard peripheral devices, such as disk drives and serial ports, and when appropriate turns them into events for the application to see. However, the events that originate from the user can be properly interpreted only by an application program.

Busy Wait versus Ready Blocked: A Little Operating System Theory and Some Historical Observation

One key difference among window systems is their support of multitasking. The effects are felt squarely by the event-handling code in the application.

The Macintosh has not supported a true multitasking environment, which has affected the recommended programming styles for application software. As time passes the number of Macintosh programs written in the recommended style will increase, making it harder for the world in general to adjust to a Macintosh environment that does efficiently support multitasking, if one becomes available. This idea has to be looked at if you are trying to write portable software, since some of the target machines do support multitasking, and their "event loops" are crafted differently. The portable software must be implemented efficiently on these machines and must not be hampered by the original philosophies of any one design group.

I assume that, while this book is in print, multitasking will manage some popularity on personal computers. Multitasking is a step beyond foreground/background jobs, in which any number of programs can be running on the machine, competing for machine resources. Simple background tasks, like printer spoolers and alarm clock routines, are then joined by electronic mail programs that can accept and send messages by radio or telephone without having to usurp the machine from the person at the terminal. The multitasking ability will become popular for the following reasons:

- [ ] RAM has become inexpensive in quantities that can accommodate large programs.
- [ ] The CPUs used in the newer machines are fast enough to be idle most of the time, even when someone is using the machine interactively. The Motorola 68020 and Intel 80386 are the eligible candidates.
- [ ] Designers and programmers are starving for multitasking, and users would use it if they knew about it and could use it. There has always been a need for multitasking but not enough horsepower, and the ability has been shrouded under inelegant implementation.

The hacking community was ready for a multitasking micro-based computer back in late 1980, but then IBM came out with a machine that was an evolutionary improvement over the majority of personal computers, 64K-bounded 8080-, 6502-, 6800-, and z80-based systems. It was clear that the machine was not fast enough to easily permit fluid multitasking or drive interactive graphics. As Spock says, "The needs of the many outweigh the needs of the few . . . or the one," and the entire community was bowled over by the sudden ferocious demand for what many considered to be an uninteresting machine.

It was Apple's 1983 contention that a 68000-based machine didn't have enough horsepower to provide multitasking and great graphics without cranking up the expense, based on their experience with the Lisa. The Macintosh, released in 1984, was designed to support graphics and not multitasking.

The 1985 Commodore Amiga removed some of the CPU-intensive graphics operations from the responsibility of the main processor, making room for multitasking. It became economically possible, in their view, to provide the custom coprocessors in a competitive, mass-produced machine.

The 1985 Atari ST machines do not have hardware accelerators as the Amiga does, and consequently Atari did not initially provide a multitasking environment, but bought **Gem** from Digital Research, Inc. The standard disk operating system support software is not a full multitasking operating system. Neither is TOS, which provides the lower-level OS functions. Gem, however, is designed to permit operation in a multitasking environment.

Some programs on the ST will predictably run smoother and faster than the same programs on the Amiga because of the difference between multitasking and single-task environments.

The success of multitasking operating systems on the IBM PC and clones has not been good; 8088s simply aren't fast enough, their memory address space is too small. Certainly RAM is cheap enough.

Being Busy While Waiting

Why should we be concerned about the issue of multitasking machines versus single foreground task machines? We should be concerned because the program code can be sloppier in single foreground task machines, and certain kinds of sloppy code in a multitasking environment will "murder" performance. A **busy-wait** is one example: busy-waits are the recommended Macintosh programming technique for designing event loops.

Here is an example of a busy-wait, in the form of a standard Macintosh program segment:

```
PROCEDURE YeMainEventLoop;
VAR Event: EventRecord;
BEGIN
   REPEAT
      SystemTask;                              {Desk Accessory Support}
      IF (GetNextEvent(EveryEvent,Event)) THEN
      CASE Event.what OF                       {We have an event: what kind?}
         mouseDown:      MouseDowns(Event);
         KeyDown:        KeyDowns(Event);
         ActivateEvt:    Activates(Event);
         UpDateEvt:      Updates(Event);
      END;                                     {of Case}
      do_other_stuff
   UNTIL Finished;                             {We're outa here}
END;
```

The code in the REPEAT–UNTIL block is a polling loop in which execution of the code between REPEAT and UNTIL is continuous. The loop executes, sampling GetNextEvent until an event occurs. When an event is present, the loop calls another section of code. The code executed depends on the type of event.

In the example a routine called **do_other_stuff** is called every time the loop iterates. There is usually a good reason for this routine, but it is entirely up to the application. It is not required in all event loops for the Macintosh. The routine can be used to spur timing loops.

Even if **do_other_stuff** didn't have to be there, the above loop could be called a busy-wait. It has the attention of the CPU whether or not something useful is being done. If an event occurs once each second, this busy-wait loop is still using nearly 100% of the machine waiting for something to happen. Busy-waits are acceptable if there is only one foreground task.

The tasks of the printer spooler and the other menial I/O tasks get plenty of CPU time by having the operating system or the application poll them. This polling can happen whenever simple I/O requests are made by the event loop, or whenever timer- or buffer-ready interrupts are fired.

On the Macintosh the main application intercepts the events for desk accessories. It is up to the application to forward the event to the desk accessory. It is also the responsibility of the main application to allow some compute time to the desk accessories. The responsibility of the event loop is much larger on the Mac than on the other machines.

Waiting for Events

In a multitasking environment you don't want software that isn't doing anything to be soaking up CPU time. Other software, such as sophisticated electronic mail systems or number-crunching jobs, could use those moments. There are many tasks without the need for space on the system display that nevertheless need the CPU!

When a program in a multitasking environment wants an event, the program tells the operating system that it is waiting for some input to occur and that the CPU should wake up the program when the input becomes available. The program then stops executing. Nothing on the display changes, so it looks like the program is still running. The program goes into a state called **ready-blocked**, which translates into "I can't do anything until someone gives me a command!" This state isn't unusual. For the first program to do anything on a single processor machine, the second program has to be temporarily put aside.

Compared to normal business or utility software, the unusual aspect of multitasking code on a personal computer is the application program **stepping aside voluntarily**. Try these examples:

Gem

The Gem **evnt_multi** routine returns when a qualifying event becomes available. You get to specify what kinds of events are qualified. You also get to provide the storage required for each different kind of event expected. These are two of three reasons why the call is parameter-heavy.

```
MainEventLoop()                     /* in C language */
{
    BOOLEAN       done;

    key_input = FALSE;
    done = FALSE;

        /* This executes continuously after initialization has been done.
           It is the event loop from which all commands are interactively
           begun. The only way to escape this loop is to exit the program.
           The other environments have similar architectural designs. */

    FOREVER
    {
                /* Wait for next event of appropriate type. */

        ev_which = evnt_multi(MU_BUTTON | MU_MESAG | MU_M1 | MU_KEYBD,
                    0x02, 0x01, 0x01,
                    m_out,
                    (UWORD) work_area.g_x, (UWORD) work_area.g_y,
                    (UWORD) work_area.g_w, (UWORD) work_area.g_h,
                    0, 0, 0, 0, 0,
                    ad_rmsg, 0, 0,
                    &mousex, &mousey, &bstate, &kstate,
                    &kreturn, &bclicks);

        wind_update(BEG_UPDATE);        /* Begin window update region.
                                           We may change the window
                                           contents in the following
                                           code, so window is reserved.*/

        if (!(ev_which & MU_KEYBD))     /* Process a nonkeyboard event.*/
        {
```

```
            if (key_input)
            {
                    curs_off();
                    key_input = FALSE;
                    save_work();
            }
    }


    if (ev_which & MU_MESAG)         /* Process a message event. */
            if (hndl_msg())
                    break;


    if (ev_which & MU_BUTTON)        /* Process a mouse button event.*/
            if (hndl_button())       /* Arbitrary mouse button proc. */
                    break;


    if (ev_which & MU_M1)
            if (hndl_mouse())
                    break;


    if (ev_which & MU_KEYBD)         /* Process a keyboard event. */
            if (hndl_keyboard())     /* Arbitrary keyboard event proc.*/
                    break;


    wind_update(END_UPDATE);         /* End window update zone. */

  }

}
```

MS Windows

The code at the end of this paragraph is a main message (event) loop for a Windows program. The loop waits for messages to appear. The Windows program wakes up the task when a message becomes available. The code is in MS Pascal, which is in keeping with this book's use of Pascal rather than C; however, Windows seems to be more friendly to C programmers because a number of type casts are required when using the standard include files from Microsoft. Type casts are contrary to the ideology of

Pascal. The special intrinsic command **RETYPE**, used a few times below, makes the code four times bulkier than it needs to be.

```
(* Wait for the next event message. *)
WHILE (GetMessage(RETYPE(LPMSG,ADS msg_),RETYPE(HWND,NULL_),0,0)<>0) DO BEGIN
     EVAL(TranslateMessage(RETYPE(LPMSG, ADS msg_)));
     EVAL(DispatchMessage(RETYPE(LPMSG, ADS msg_)));
END;
```

The loop above takes the message handed to it, filters it with TranslateMessage, and hands it to DispatchMessage. The filter routine converts Windows' virtual key messages into character messages before they are dispatched. DispatchMessage is used to send the message to the appropriate **window procedure**, a routine that accepts messages only for a particular window. It is common for an application to have only one tiled window on the display; one window procedure would be used to drive it.

Below is a Windows application window procedure. **AnyOleWndProc** directly handles create, destroy, size, and paint messages, and watches the mouse button messages, too. Since Windows provides standard message handling, the other messages are returned to the Windows runtime environment for handling. Default responses are made with a call to **DefWindowProc**, the Default Window Procedure.

```
FUNCTION AnyOleWndProc(  hWindow: HWND;
                         message: UNSIGNED;
                         wParam: WORD;
                         lParam: long): long [ PUBLIC, WINDOWS ];
VAR ps: PAINTSTRUCT;
BEGIN
    CASE message OF
      WM_CREATE: DoCreate( RETYPE(HWND, NULL_ ));
      WM_DESTROY:PostQuitMessage( 0 );
      WM_SIZE:   DoSize( hWindow );
      WM_PAINT:  BEGIN
                  EVAL(BeginPaint( hWindow, RETYPE( LPPAINTSTRUCT, ADS ps)));
                      DoPaint( hWindow, ps.hdc_ );
                  EndPaint( hWindow,  RETYPE( LPPAINTSTRUCT, ADS ps));
                 END;
```

```
        WM_RBUTTONDOWN,
        WM_LBUTTONDOWN: DoMouse( hWindow, lParam );
        OTHERWISE BEGIN   { If it isn't one of the above message types,... }
            MuzzleWndProc := DefWindowProc(hWindow, message, wParam, lParam);
            RETURN;
          END { OTHERWISE }
      END;   { CASE }
      AnyOleWndProc := 0;
      RETURN;
END;
```

Note the unique features of MS Pascal used above, such as the RETYPE function, the OTHERWISE clause in the case statement, the special attributes after the function type declaration, and the use of a RETURN statement. If your application is in Pascal, these system-dependent features have to be carefully sprinkled on top of your portable code. This subject is further discussed in the chapter on coding hints.

Amiga

Amiga is a multitasking machine, so it is appropriate to use the Wait routine. Calling **Wait** with an argument causes the task to wait without running until the condition of the argument becomes true. After your message queue gets something, your program has to make a copy of it, tell the environment that it has received this message, and then use the message. The reply must be made quickly after a copy is made, lest the program's universe get out of sync.

```
FOREVER {                                          /* In C language */

    /* Don't do anything until a message resource becomes available. */

    Wait( 1 << Mywindow->UserPort->mp_SigBit );

    MouseMoved = FALSE;                 /* assume the mouse hasn't moved */
    while (message = GetMsg(MyWindow->UserPort)) { /* got a message? */
      CopyMsg( MyCopy, message );       /* Make a copy of the message, */
      ReplyMsg( message );              /* reply ASAP, then process message */
```

```
      if ( MyCopy.class == MOUSEMOVE )
        MouseMoved = TRUE;
      else ProcessMessage( MyCopy );
    }
  if ( MouseMoved )
    ProcessMove( MyCopy.x, MyCopy.y );
}
```

EVENT LOOP PORTABILITY

Because the event loop is the highest-order code in a window system application, it is a great place to begin talking about writing portable code. The event loop invariably assumes that the work environment has already been initialized for it to operate, so the loop is not the first chunk of code to execute in a program. However, it is where most interactive commands are launched, modes are begun, and I/O is routed.

The structure of an event loop is not complicated. Processing I/O transactions is a function of the user-interface code. The code that properly belongs in an event loop merely receives events. The rest of the processing should be done in other routines, as is shown in Figure 2–12. The lined routine appears to be a feature of Microsoft Windows, and the dotted routines seem to be characteristic of the Macintosh and IIGS event loops.

Architecturally Gem, Amiga, and Windows are similar enough to each other so that designing programs that can be moved between them is far from hopeless. The function calls and handling of the system-dependent record types make the event loop code, as it is presented here,

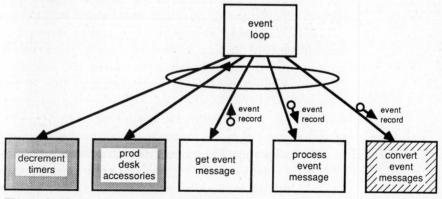

Figure 2–12 A generic event message loop

system-dependent. Part of the event loop code can be made to be system-independent by using a control routine that calls other routines to handle the system-dependent details. Here is a list of some of the requirements for such a routine:

- ☐ Check loop escape condition.
- ☐ Support desk accessories.
- ☐ Handle event loop iterations in two ways:
  busy-wait and ready-wait.
- ☐ Use an independent set of data structures and constants to define the event message contents.
- ☐ Support timing call requirements in case the event loop is busy-wait based.

On the other hand, the event loop code is short; little will be gained by making it system-independent, but there are reasons to make some of the code just underneath it independent.

The two culprits that undermine a portable approach are:

- ☐ Using system-dependent data structures in what could be system-independent code.
- ☐ Making system-dependent function calls in similarly inappropriate places, especially when those functions need system-dependent arguments.

One approach is to expand system-dependent records, such as event records, so that they become system-independent. Little time can be spent on the conversion, because window systems have real-time constraints. Conversion of dependent data structures everywhere will cost execution time.

Just by looking at a variety of coding examples provided by the windowing environment authors, one can see that the example application code is "polluted" with system dependencies. Judging from their style it may seem inappropriate to write anything that is independent of the system function calls and datatypes used in the parameters. It is important to note that the examples are not intended to demonstrate how to write portable code; they demonstrate only how the window software works.

It is not impossible but not easy to write portable code. It is also very confusing if you are writing for all of the environments covered in this book. Although this book discusses six different hardware/software combinations, you don't have to implement your application code with *all six* in mind. This may help you reduce the number of special cases, retain some coding efficiency, and sacrifice some of the portability.

A detailed breakdown on the composition of event and event message records, types of events and messages, and related function calls, is discussed in the chapter on event managers.

INITIALIZATION AND CLEANUP

This section describes what typically has to be done during initialization regardless of the function of the program. The coding examples that follow do some things that aren't absolutely essential but are common; nevertheless, the nonessential code is kept to a minimum.

Macintosh

A main Macintosh application has to initialize its environment. Any Mac program, whether a desk accessory or an application, is expected to claim what it needs from memory and to explicitly return its allocations when it is done.

Here is an example of a simple global initialization routine for the Macintosh:

```
PROCEDURE InitEnviron;                           {In Pascal}
Begin
    InitGraf(@thePort);                          {Make a grafport for the screen.}
    ClockCursor := GetCursor(watchCursor);       {Reserve the cursors to be used.}
    HLock(Handle(ClockCursor));                  {Lock cursors.}
    SetCursor(ClockCursor^^);                     {Display watch during setup.}
    InitFonts;                                   {Fonts manager init.}
    InitWindows;                                 {Window manager init.}
    InitMenus;                                   {Menu manager init.}
    TEInit;                                      {Text edit manager init.}
    InitDialogs(Nil);                            {Dialog manager init.}
    Finished := False;                           {Init ugly program escape flag.}
    FlushEvents(everyEvent,0);                   {Zotz ancient, cobwebbed events.}
End;
```

Other initialization code will be needed to establish menus, windows, etc. Some of these things are defined as resources, and have to be brought in and handed to the system to become visible.

Cleanup code is minimal on the Macintosh, since each main program that runs reinitializes everything when it begins to run. Files must be closed, and modified system resources should be put back the way they were.

Macintosh and IIGS Desk Accessory Initialization

Desk accessories on the Apple IIGS are not handled as they are on the Macintosh. Desk accessories, which are technically small applications, are supposed to *avoid* initializing the program environment, even when invoked from the desktop. There is no way to start a desk accessory unless a main program is executing; the Finder qualifies as a main program.

Mac DAs are not used as individual executable files; they are intended to be added to the system file before they can be used. There are shareware and public domain desk accessories that yank DAs from disk and allow them to be used. With either the Macintosh or the IIGS, it isn't a good idea for a DA to initialize any of the managers, because that will upset the operation of the currently running main application.

There are actually two kinds of IIGS desk accessories, Classic desk accessories and New desk accessories. **Classic desk accessories** (CDAs) are designed to operate in a nonwindowing/event environment where they get the entire screen and the whole machine. Classic DAs are activated by a keypress and are responsible for saving and restoring the execution environment to avoid destroying the progress of main applications. Classic DAs are also responsible for handling their own I/O requirements.

New desk accessories (NDAs) are those similar to Macintosh desk accessories. New desk accessories are normally loaded by the operating system at boot time. To use them, Quickdraw, LineEdit, and the Event, Window, Menu, Scrap, and Dialog manager toolsets must be loaded and initialized first. NDAs must save and restore globals.

Using the IIGS's TaskMaster greatly simplifies what has to be done at initialization time and during application execution, as TaskMaster handles some of the system calls for you (like OpenNDA, SystemTask and SystemClick).

The IIGS InitRoutine is called for each installed NDA at desk startup or shutdown time.

Gem

Gem programs are not required to initialize the environment. They are not in absolute control of the environment as Macintosh applications are. Applications do have to open I/O devices, including the screen device.

Gem protects itself somewhat from application mishandling, but doesn't do this very well in the case of blatant mishandling. For example, if Gem is passed a misformed parameter block, the system will detonate. It is assumed that the Gem binding routines provide some protection, but all the windowing systems have a difficult time withstanding parameter mismatches and values that are out-of-range.

```
GlobalInit()                               /* In verbose C code. */
{
    WORD    work_in[11];
    WORD    i;

    gl_apid = appl_init();                 /* Initialize the libraries. */
    if (gl_apid == -1)                     /* If not good, return to sender. */
            return(4);
    return(0);
}
```

Other code is inserted as needed to set up the virtual workstation, define windows, load resources, build menus, establish undo buffers, etc.

Gem does require some cleanup. The following segment of code should provide a pretty good example.

```
Cleanup() {
    wind_close(TheWindow);        /* Close the window. */
    wind_delete(TheWindow);       /* Remove the window. */
    menu_bar(0x0L, FALSE);        /* Zotz the menu bar. */
    dos_free(AllocatedSpace);     /* Return allocated space. */
    v_clsvwk( VdiHandle );        /* Close the virtual workstation. */
    wind_update(END_UPDATE);      /* Not updating the window any more. */
    appl_exit();                  /* Exit, stage left. */
}
```

MS Windows

MS Windows is like Gem in that the environment is already initialized and running by the time an application starts to run. Programs run under the watchful eye of the environment; they make calls to obtain system resources.

Windows is a true multitasking environment. One application talks to another using Windows-supported messages, but one application does not have direct control of another, as is the case on the Macintosh with the relationship between desk accessories and applications. Windows does not have desk accessories; they are considered to be small Windows programs, and do not need special treatment as desk accessories do on the Macintosh.

The system supplies some objects, like predefined brushes, whenever the application wants them. Below, some are requested right at startup time for the program.

Any application, if it needs a window (most need a tiled or overlapping window at least), has to create one using a window template that has been registered with the environment.

```
{    Every MS Windows WinMain procedure is called by Windows runtime each
     time a new instance of the application is created. This example
     is in Pascal. }


FUNCTION WinMain( hInstance,
                  hPrevInstance:         HANDLE;
                  lpszCmdLine:           LPSTR;
                  cmdShow:               INT ): BOOL [PUBLIC];
VAR  msg_ : MSG;
     hWnd_: HWND;                               { handle to a Window }
BEGIN
     { TemplateInit is called for the first instance, to establish the
       template for the class of window required by this program. }

     if (RETYPE(BOOL, hPrevInstance) = FALSE_) THEN      { 1st instance? }
       IF (TemplateInit( hInstance ) = FALSE_) THEN BEGIN {then do this }
         WinMain := FALSE_;                              { whoops... }
         RETURN ;
       END;


     hbrWhite := GetStockObject( WHITE_BRUSH );    { define a few brushes }
```

```
hbrBlack := GetStockObject( BLACK_BRUSH );
hbrGray  := GetStockObject( GRAY_BRUSH );

    { Create a window instance with the Template defined via TemplateInit.}

hWnd_ := CreateWindow(
            RETYPE(LPSTR, ADS 'Example' * CHR(0)),
            RETYPE(LPSTR, ADS 'Example' * CHR(0)),
            WS_TILEDWINDOW,
            0,                                { x is the preferred col #  }
            0,                                { y is ignored  }
            0,                                { cx is ignored  }
            100,                              { cy is the preferred height }
            RETYPE(HWND, NULL_),              { there is no parent }
            RETYPE(HMENU, NULL_),             { use class menu }
            RETYPE(HANDLE, hInstance),        { the window instance handle }
            RETYPE(LPSTR, BYLONG(0, NULL_))   { no arguments here... }
        );

EVAL(ShowWindow(hWnd_, cmdShow));            { Make the window appear }
UpdateWindow(hWnd_);

{ additional global setup is arranged anywhere above the message loop }

{ the message (events) loop is called from here }
}
```

At cleanup time the tiled window has to be closed, but little else has to be done.

Amiga

On this machine much of the standard initializations involve grabbing onto libraries and establishing ownership of devices. The usual window creation occurs, as does screen creation. A screen is a backdrop for group of related windows.

Below is some sample init code that establishes some of the devices. Much of the context has been removed to make the key comparisons between environments clearer, although the exact meaning of the Amiga code may be obscured. More initialization work is done in Amiga code because the Amiga does not support resources. Programmers can set up structures for system calls with C variable declaration initializers, in data files, or in inline code.

```
{                                              /* Part of an Amiga init function in C.*/
  .
  .

  .
  if ((IntuitionBase =
    (struct IntuitionBase *)OpenLibrary("intuition.library", INTUITION_REV))
              == NULL) error("There is an Intuition problem.");
  if ((GfxBase =
     (struct GfxBase *)OpenLibrary("graphics.library",GRAPHICS_REV))
              == NULL ) error("There is a graphics library problem.");
  if (p_screen == 1) {
     if ((myscreen = (struct Screen *)OpenScreen(&NewScreen)) == NULL)
       error("The screen doesn't want to open.");
     NewWindow.Screen = myscreen;
  }
  if(( mywindow = (struct Window *)OpenWindow(&NewWindow) ) == NULL)
    error("The window is stuck.");
  myviewport    = (struct ViewPort *)ViewPortAddress(mywindow);
          /* ---- Open read port. ---- */
  Read_Request = (struct IOExtSer *)
    AllocMem((long)sizeof(*Read_Request),MEMF_PUBLIC|MEMF_CLEAR);
  Read_Request->io_SerFlags = 0L;
  Read_Request->IOSer.io_Message.mn_ReplyPort = CreatePort(0,0);
  if(OpenDevice(SERIALNAME,NULL,Read_Request,NULL))
    error("Can't open Read device.");
          /* ---- Open a timer port. ---- */
  Timer_Port = CreatePort("Timer Port",0);
  Script_Timer_Port = CreatePort("Timer Port",0);
  if (OpenDevice(TIMERNAME, UNIT_VBLANK, (char *) &Timer, 0) ||
      OpenDevice(TIMERNAME, UNIT_VBLANK, (char *) &Script_Timer, 0))
    error("Can't open timer device.");
    .
    .

    .
}
```

Here is some sample Amiga end execution code. The menu strip is cleared, devices that have been opened are closed and deleted, and buffers are deallocated. If a screen is left with no windows, it is automatically removed by Intuition.

```
EndProgram() {                              /* The end of program execution. */
    ClearMenuStrip( mywindow );
    CloseDevice(&Timer);
    DeletePort(Timer_Port);
    CloseDevice(Read_Request);
    DeletePort(Read_Request->IOSer.io_Message.mn_ReplyPort);
    FreeMem(Read_Request,(long)sizeof(*Read_Request));
    CloseWindow( mywindow );
}
```

IIGS

Although this machine's initialization routines differ from those of the Macintosh, the ideology is untouched. However, there is a difference in the way the desk accessories are handled. The IIGS keeps DAs where they belong (in my opinion), in a specified folder on the disk; they do not have to be added to the system file.

EXECUTABLE FILE ORGANIZATION

Executable files come in all sizes, from a few bytes to megabytes. When executable files are used, their internal composition is not clear to most people because most people avert their eyes. Those who look by using the equivalent of a Type command get a snootful of random bytes. Those who look at executable files with more appropriate tools can usually determine (after a while) what the file contains, even to the point of understanding what the assembly code is doing. Beyond that, unless something has gone wrong or a copy protection scheme has to be dealt with, most folks keep away. In fact, to dissuade copy protection busting and reverse engineering, there have been attempts in some states to pass legislation making it unlawful to disassemble and read binary files!

This book has to cover executable files from the inside a little bit because, on the Macintosh and under Gem and Windows, executable files are more complicated and interesting. The design constraints that are forced upon application code are discussed here. Neither of these subjects requires you to buy a debugger, since resources, events, and multitasking will require only high-level thinking and not low-level scrutiny. Because of the three, however, software organization is much different now than it was in the average business program of time past.

Files and Resources

A **resource** is the name for a block of bytes in an executable file that can be referenced with an ID string or number. Any program can ask the environment software for a specific resource from a file (usually its own). On the Macintosh, doggone nearly everything is kept in an individual resource: code, arbitrary data, menus, and dialog boxes. Using resources makes it possible to define and change many things about a program without having to compile the code and link the modules together. Not all the windowing packages support using resources, and the support that is there varies from package to package, but when present resources are very useful. To understand resources, see Figure 2–13, which shows how the contents of executable files are arranged.

Macintosh

A Macintosh file has two major components. The first is the **resource fork**, which may contain resources. The second is the **data fork**, which is used by an application for storing data. Either fork can be empty. Since resource and data forks are present in any file on the Macintosh, even small or ungainly programs can do some wild things.

For example, a game or editor can store text data in the data fork and unique font resources in the resource fork; the font is then used to display the text. This system requires no extra coding effort to arrange, and no special effort to use.

The Mac supports its file organization with several file and resource manager routines, down to the lowest levels of the OS.

There is a significant difference in the ways environments interact with applications. The Mac environment is mundane in that the operating

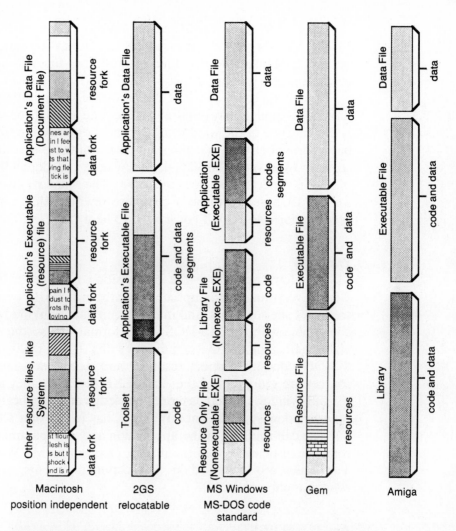

Figure 2–13 Comparing common executable and nonexecutable files

system is polled by the application for information. This is considerably different from the MS Windows environment, described shortly.

Gem
Gem runs on top of an operating system, which is responsible for the file system. The executable code for a Gem application is kept in one file, and its resources are stored in another. Under MS-DOS and on the Atari ST the names for executable files normally have **.APP** for a suffix; the files containing resources have a **.RSC** suffix.

Gem code files aren't divided into resources as files are on the Macintosh. One reason for this is that the display technology varies widely on the IBM machines; a different resource file may be required for machines with different displays, but the code file doesn't have to change.

The architectural limits of the hardware, or limitations caused by the linker or compiler, may require that the code and data be segmented. Gem is the only one of the windowing packages discussed in this book that has been ported between machines, and some of these machines force you to segment your code. The 8088 definitely does and, depending on what kind of code is generated, so does the 68000. The Mac/Lisa-like window system for the IIGS seems to be a complete rewrite using many of the same specifications, so I don't consider it to be a "port" of the original code.

Windows

MS Windows executable file composition is closer to Macintosh than Gem. Everything winds up conveniently in a single executable file: resources, code segments, and initialization data. A Windows application is compatible with the MS-DOS .EXE format file, so the name has up to eight characters and the mandatory suffix .EXE. Unlike the Macintosh, MS-DOS doesn't support resource and data forks. Like the Mac, resources are grouped together in a .EXE file, since they are added last.

MS Windows demands more knowledge of its applications than do the other window systems, since Windows has to not only start applications, but also call routines in the application and pass parameters. This needs some sophistication from the linking phase of an MS Windows program. The issues are discussed in the section on events, multitasking, and event-handling code.

Amiga and IIGS

The Commodore Amiga and the Apple IIGS do not currently support resources (I am surprised by their omission on the Apple machine), but it is something that can be provided by third-party developers; do it if you think it will make some money.

Resources

Grouping executable files into resources produces several benefits. The first is that you can edit an executable file, as far as the author of the module is willing to let you. You are not editing the source code used to create the binary file; this is the binary file itself. Since code resources aren't easily modified, it is common practice to keep things that should not be modifiable by users in code resources.

For example, it is common for companies to release demonstration packages that have been lobotomized to disable the save and print options on one of the pull-down menus. That is, you can do anything you want except save or print your results. If the menu is in a menu resource, then it can be edited by a user in the executable file. If you didn't remove the save and print code from the module, and just set the menu items to be disabled, then users of medium sophistication could use a resource editor and quickly turn the options back on! By not using a resource for that menu, and by eliminating the save and print code altogether, you can prevent this.

Resources are used by programs as black boxes. For example, your program knows that there is a resource in its executable file on disk that defines a complete dialog box; the program has the ID number for the resource. Your code only has to go get it from the disk to use it, which is usually done with one function call. A function doesn't have to be written to build the dialog box at runtime.

The resources in any Macintosh file are accessible by any application, as long as the application knows what to look for. Macintosh applications can use system resources, resources within their own executable module, other executable modules, or from any other files, regardless of to whom they belong. Normal use of someone else's resources is read-only, unless the program is a system utility like ResEdit. The important thing is that the ability is there.

With code resources (or fancy code segments) comes the freedom of not having to load an entire executable image into RAM before running the program. Components are brought into RAM only when it is a good idea. Both Macintosh and Windows provide code segment management. The capability is very important when working with large programs. Otherwise they can take forever to load and occupy most of RAM, though most of the code will not be used.

For the Macintosh (and eventually for the other packages) any program can grab a resource from a file. Since resources have a defined format, special **resource editors** have been written using this property to create and modify a number of different resource types.

This means that even though the application has been compiled and linked, it is still possible to:

- [ ] Add, subtract, or exchange code segments in a file, extending its capability without needing recompilation, relinking, and replacing of the entire module.
- [ ] Change the text portions of the program to a different language without changing a line of code.
- [ ] Adjust the default initialization values for a program, again without changing the original source.
- [ ] Swap predefined bitmaps (icons, fonts, and pictures) to adjust for different pixel ratios and densities.

Gem

The resources under Gem are not as well-supported as Macintosh resources, but the approach Gem has for supporting graphics is general and flexible. Gem graphics are defined with **object trees**, which are linked lists each of which defines a graphic object in terms of graphic primitives. An object tree is constructed and the resource is built from that. There is little difference between object trees. When a Gem function is given one, the function assumes that the construct is in the form that it will understand and interprets it that way. For example, the **objc_draw** routine draws all the object trees, no matter the purpose; the **form_do** routine expects the object tree it is given to define a Gem form, and interprets user interactions with it accordingly.

Amiga and IIGS

Again, neither the Amiga nor the IIGS supports resources.

SYSTEM DEPENDENT (PRE-COMPILE) FILES

Macintosh, IIGS, Windows, Gem, and Amiga have some different ideas on what files have to be present for the successful creation of an executable module, independent of the source code. Of the bunch, it seems to me that Windows wins the prize for "most complicated."

Amiga

Amiga code development is heavily influenced by Unix. There are source and include files that are used to build an Amiga executable file. Since there aren't any special or unusual constructs (like resources), extra files used to contain that information aren't present.

The Amiga was originally a C language machine, and it continues in that vein despite the existence of other compilers and interpreters.

Gem

There are source and include files that are used to build Gem executable files (those with a .APP suffix). Another program has to be written to create the resources for the application and build the .RSC file, using the Gem Resource Construction Set, since at the time of this writing a resource compiler is not available for Gem. A full-fledged resource editor is also not available, though smaller utility editors exist for two or three types of resources.

Gem is primarily a C language environment, though there are other languages available: FORTH, Modula-2, and Pascal.

Macintosh

The normal source and include files are present. A file with the suffix **.r** (for example) is an input file to a resource compiler. A .r file is a readable text file that is fed to a program that creates resources. Here is a piece of a resource compiler input file:

```
/*-------------------------------------------------------------------------

        Sample.r    -  Resources for the Sample Application

        Copyright Apple Computer, Inc. 1985, 1986  All rights reserved.

-------------------------------------------------------------------------*/


resource 'WIND' (128, "Sample Window") {
    {64, 60, 314, 460},
    documentproc, visible, nogoaway, 0x0, "Sample Window"
};


resource 'DLOG' (128, "About Sample…") {
    {66, 102, 224, 400},
    dboxproc, visible, nogoaway, 0x0, 128, ""
};


resource 'DITL' (128) {
```

```
        {
/* 1 */ {130, 205, 150, 284},
            button {
                enabled,
                "CONTINUE"
            };
/* 2 */ {104, 144, 120, 296},                    /* SourceLanguage Item */
            statictext {
                disabled,
                ""
            };
/* 3 */ {88, 144, 105, 218},                     /* Author Item */
            statictext {
                disabled,
                ""
            };
/* 4 */ {8, 32, 26, 273},
            statictext {
                disabled,
                "Macintosh Programmer's Workshop"
            };
/* 5 */ {32, 80, 50, 212},
            statictext {
                disabled,
                "Sample Application"
            };
/* 6 */ {56, 16, 74, 281},
            statictext {
                enabled, "Copyright © 1985,1986 Apple Computer"
            };
/* 7 */ {88, 16, 104, 144},
            statictext {
                enabled, "Source Language:"
            };
/* 8 */ {104, 16, 120, 144},
            statictext {
                enabled, "Brought to you by:"
            }
        }
};
```

```
resource 'MENU' (128, "Apple", preload) {
    128, 0x7FFFFFFD, enabled, apple,
    {
        "About Sample…",
                noicon, nokey, nomark, plain;
        "-",
                noicon, nokey, nomark, plain
    }
};
```

At writing time, the Macintosh with its resource editing software, is much better off than the other window packages though the Mac's support is still far from perfect. Resource-support development is a tall order. The resource file above is not the same as the Microsoft Windows **.RC** file, mentioned later in this section, and not the same as Gem's solution. From the point of view of this book, a resource compiler input language strikes me as something that could easily be standardized.

The Macintosh started out as a Pascal cross-development environment on the Lisa. Then third party C compilers became available. Now (finally), decent C and Pascal compilers can be bought, and most package development seems to take place in those two languages. There are significant Mac products written in FORTH, and the Mac toolbox is supported by most of the languages for the machine, so the variety and support of Macintosh languages are excellent.

Windows
Windows usually requires a minimum of three files for small applications. One file is the one with the source in it, like EXAMP.ASM, APPLIC.PAS, or MAGIC.C, as they would appear in an MS-DOS directory. As usual, more complex programs have more than one source file and many include files.

The second kind of file contains the module definition information. It carries the same base name as the primary source file, but the file name suffix must be **.DEF**. Examples are: EXAMP.DEF, APPLIC.DEF, and MAGIC.DEF. The module definition file is used for describing the global parameters of the program being created for the Windows environment. Here is an example .DEF file:

```
NAME NameOfProgram

DESCRIPTION 'Description string for program.'
LIBRARY     Libname
STUB  'WINSTUB.EXE'
CODE MOVEABLE
DATA MOVEABLE MULTIPLE
HEAPSIZE    10000
STACKSIZE   10000
EXPORTS
     ProgWinProc @1
```

There is a description of the module definition file elsewhere in this book.

The third kind of file contains the **resource script** for the program to be built. As in the module definition file, the base name is usually the same as the primary source file. The file suffix is .RC. Examples are EXAMP.RC, APPLIC.RC, and MAGIC.RC. The purpose of a Windows resource script is the same as that of a resource compiler input file on the Macintosh, but the syntax is somewhat different. Gem doesn't currently have a resource compiler.

Here is what part of a resource script looks like (this script defines a dialog box and two menus):

```
DTFIND DIALOG 25, 25, 104, 44
STYLE  WS_POPUP | WS_DLGFRAME | WS_VISIBLE
BEGIN
     RTEXT  "Find:"        3,     4,    8,     20,    8
     EDITTEXT              4,    28,    6,     72,    12,   WS_GROUP | WS_TABSTOP
     DEFPUSHBUTTON "Ok",          IDOK,      7,24,40,14,   WS_GROUP | WS_TABSTOP
     PUSHBUTTON    "Cancel",      IDCANCEL, 57,24,40,14,   WS_GROUP | WS_TABSTOP
END
StdMenu MENU
BEGIN
    POPUP    "File"
    BEGIN
       MENUITEM    "New",            NEW
```

```
    MENUITEM     "Open...",        OPEN
    MENUITEM     "Save",           SAVE
    MENUITEM     "Save As...",     SAVEAS
    MENUITEM     "Print",          PRINT
    MENUITEM     "Print All",      PRINTALL
    MENUITEM     "Merge...",       MERGE
END
    POPUP    "Edit"
    BEGIN
        MENUITEM     "Index...",      HEADER
        MENUITEM     "Cut",           CUT
        MENUITEM     "Copy",          COPY
        MENUITEM     "Paste",         PASTE
        MENUITEM     "Restore",       UNDO
        MENUITEM     SEPARATOR
        MENUITEM     "Words"          I_TEXT,   CHECKED
        MENUITEM     "Graphic"        I_BITMAP
        MENUITEM     "Sound"          I_ROBOT
    END
END
```

A file with a **.ICO** extension contains an **icon definition** for an MS Windows program. Each Windows application has a unique icon that is shown on the bottom of the console when the application's tiled window is not open and the application is in RAM and running. A double-select of the icon will cause the icon to disappear from the console and make the window reappear. The icon definition file is binary and maintained with an icon graphics editor.

Other Files

An MS Windows **link command file** has the extension **.LNK**, and contains all the required linker commands. The **make command files**, at least the ones from Microsoft, have no extension; most make programs accept as an execution time parameter the name of the file to get the commands from. There are equivalent files (and utility programs) available under all of the window systems.

2.3 | Source File Organization

This section discusses how to organize the source files of a project, and all the different kinds of files that are involved. It discusses the limitations of ISO Pascal source file organization, and compares it with how Modula-2, C, and extended Pascal files can be arranged. Also mentioned in this section are:

- ☐ Large versus small projects.
- ☐ Include files.
- ☐ Make files and code vaults.
- ☐ Linker files.
- ☐ Resource definition files.
- ☐ Source file preprocessors and macro processors.
- ☐ Separate versus independent compilation.

Individually, these topics are standard fare. Here they are presented together in the context of window system application development since they affect ease of development, maintenance, and porting. Many of the problems with portability are completely language-dependent, so a meaty portion of this section talks about it.

THE LANGUAGE SHOW

When Wirth designed Pascal in the early 1970s, his objective was to create a language that could be used to clearly demonstrate elementary and advanced coding techniques. With Pascal the important thing was the easy understanding of a coded algorithm. One doesn't want to spend the entire class teaching students how to write in a language when the purpose of the course is to learn data structures!

The folks at Bell Laboratories, meanwhile, were designing the C programming language to be a small-systems language, with the language itself being small. The compiler had to generate fast, efficient code so that programmers could avoid having to write code in assembler. The source code in this implementation language would be fast without the benefit of automatic optimization by the compiler, because the language permits statements to be "folded" together in the source, allowing the hip programmer to write fast code. The compiler could be *lean*.

These two languages are the hit of the 1980s, with souped-up implementations of Pascal available for around $60, and free C compilers available through user groups. Neither language is free of problems, but much work can be economically completed using them.

Wirth, with his Modula-2 definition, has a viable language that addresses some of the major problems with Pascal that the ISO standard for Pascal has not fixed. In ISO Pascal, large program development with a small team of programmers is not easy, and neither is doing anything fancy with standard Pascal I/O. Implementing operating system code in standard Pascal is a questionable practice. Scientific and engineering programming is still done in FORTRAN and this will probably continue for some time, although little of the new integrated circuit and circuit board computer-aided engineering software is being written in FORTRAN. The popularity of C has absorbed some of the work that had been done in assembler (wonder of wonders) and FORTRAN. Even some business applications, once implemented in woefully inefficient form, are being rewritten for micros in C.

Small programs can fit entirely in one source file, but problems aplenty arise when organizing a bigger program the same way. For example, the editor may be adequate for working with small files, but it may bog down with larger ones. The system may not have enough resources or the compiler may not be written for large enough files for the compiler to process the entire source of a large program at once. The source of one program may not fit on a single backup disk, and may not fit on the work disk either. There may be several people working on this program, so placing all of the source of a large program in one file makes for some interesting problems that people prefer to avoid. Finally, when all else is taken into account, it may take considerably longer to debug large single file programs because it takes a long time to recompile the entire program, no matter how fast the compiler system is.

The alternative is to divide the source of a large program into several files. With an ISO standard Pascal compiler, the only way to do this is with an **include file** compiler directive. Each of the compilers that implement an extended Pascal has its own way of dealing with the problem, requiring special considerations for code portability between Pascal systems. C, Modula-2, and FORTRAN compiler systems have been standardized to allow either independent or separate compilation. The big question is then whether a compiler that may be involved in a port of a program *at least* follows the de facto or specified standards for the language.

HANDLING CODE DIFFERENCES

For each program, each different environment, and each language system, there will be differences in the implementation. This section describes the good and bad aspects of ways to handle these differences.

Each of the new software environments, Macintosh, Gem, Intuition, and Windows, is different enough to guarantee a large amount of system-dependent code for any good program that uses them. A bad program is presumably one that turns its back on the majority of the services provided by these environments by having the screen emulate a glass teletype — an attempt to shrink the user interface system-dependent code. This will happen if a program was originally written for an older environment (and was designed to use a glass tty) and ported to one or more of the new environments, but probably will not occur much with new software that doesn't have to be ported outside the realm of the new environments. Interactive programs that are written only for portability don't get favorable magazine reviews; they run slowly and take a long time to get to know.

Here are ways to organize system-dependent sections so that reading and changing the code isn't made more difficult than it has to be:

☐ Inline runtime conditionals.
☐ Runtime initialization and prompting.
☐ Preprocessor (compile time) conditionals.
☐ Link time decisions.
☐ Overlays.
☐ Directory and file grouping.

Runtime Conditionals

Runtime conditionals are used (in this sense) when the outside world of a program is uncertain. The code for all the possible different options is present in the executable module. A query is made at some time during execution by the program, and a decision on which section of code has to be run is based on the answer. For example:

Runtime conditionals are to be avoided when they are not necessary, because they charge when it costs the most, which is while the user is interacting with the software. One of the positive effects of having an unexpandable architecture for the Macintosh is the reduction of runtime conditionals like this, which results in a reduction of code bulk and duplicate effort for one machine.

```
Procedure SetResRatio;                    { a Pascal example }
begin
    if (printer=mx80) then begin
        ...
    end
    else if (printer=fx80) then begin
        ...
    end
end;
```

Runtime Initialization and Prompting

Runtime initialization usually goes hand-in-hand with runtime conditionals. One instance where it doesn't is the case where the exact hardware
environment is specified in a file, which is read at the beginning of
execution. Based on the information from the file, some pointers to
sections of code are set. These pointers are set only at initialization, yet
they have an effect on the way the program executes later. The C language
allows one function to reference another via a **pointer to a function**. Pascal
pointers are used to point only to data elements in the heap. Two Pascal
functions are required to provide this capability: an **AddressOf** function,
which will provide the runtime address of anything with a static address
during the expected lifetime of the returned value, and a **Call** procedure
that accepts the address of a procedure or function and a variable number
of parameters, and feeds the code at the address with the parameters.
Though this method avoids runtime ifs, the domain of Pascal does not
presently include self-modifying code at runtime.

Use of the AddressOf and Call functions in Pascal is not common.
What is common in all the systems studied in this book is the use of
software interrupts, or traps, to get to the operating system and user-
interface software. The AddressOf operation is replaced by a simple
integer number that, by prearrangement, means a particular routine.
When the software interrupt is generated, the requested software is run
and control is then returned.

Preprocessor Conditionals

One use of source preprocessors that is used constantly in C programs,
and rarely in Pascal, is to adjust the source of a program to local customs
before the compiler works on the code. For example, here is part of a C
program that contains code written for two machines:

```
#if IBMPC

          set_bar_counter(0);

          swing_density(ZAXIS);

#endif
#if IBMAT

          set_bar_counter(1);

          limit_tasks(1);

          swing_density(YAXIS);

#endif
```

The code could not be run as is through a C compiler because of the preprocessor commands embedded in the source. After the preprocessor has done its work, the source looks like:

```
set_bar_counter(1);

limit_tasks(1);

swing_density(YAXIS);
```

Presumably, if this program were compiled and run on an IBM PC instead of an IBM AT, something would go wrong. The decisions regarding which lines of code would be executed weren't made at runtime. Note that in the above case, all the ways the code could be arranged are listed in the same place in the same file. This makes inspection simple.

Preprocessors work, but it is not good to use them exclusive of the other methods. If there are many preprocessor commands in one source file and some commands are nested within other commands, the source becomes hard to read, the code loses continuity, and the file expands in size. When this could happen, using other methods is more appropriate. This method should not be used simply to keep a routine or file "system-independent," although this happens all the time during the maintenance phases of large software projects.

Link Time Decisions

With standard C language systems, it is possible to independently compile files, creating files of object code. The object code files are then processed by a linker to create an executable file. It is also normal to process a group of object code files with a librarian program to create a single library file, parts of which can then be extracted by the linker for use in creating an executable file.

It is possible to create different versions of a group of functions or files, keep them all handy, but use one set rather than another in creating an executable file. Just tell the linker to use the IBM PC I/O library rather than the IBM AT I/O library. To make these different libraries or object code files, there may be several copies of the same source file with grossly different contents. Or, one copy of the source file may be kept around, but have some preprocessor commands that can be set differently when the preprocessor creates the output file to be then fed to the compiler. When there are several files to chose from, they are normally stored in different directories (or file folders) but have the same name as other versions of object files that evolved from the same source file. This is the normal way to handle system-dependent code.

System-dependent code can suffer from a proliferation of special versions of routines. This makes the maintenance of programs harder, and even makes the original development team take longer to write the *first* version. Try to reduce or eliminate code that would otherwise be system-dependent. When a routine has to be system-dependent, it should be treated as such, especially if there are many lines of code. Putting in a road may be a good idea initially, but the consequence may be having to maintain 4 million miles of built road.

Overlays

One other method of organization is through overlays, which are sections of executable code that are dragged into memory from disk when needed. Sometimes an overlay is brought into memory, overwriting another overlay since they share the same main memory space. The program may decide at runtime that it needs the IBM AT version of several routines, rather than the IBM PC version, and yanks in the AT overlay. Depending on how the overlay manager is written and how the code in the overlay works, the program need not ever bother with any other overlay for the rest of the run. Different overlays, each made with the same list of routine names but with the routines written differently, can peacefully coexist.

INCLUDE FILES

Include files are implemented in one form or another in most compiler systems. For most C programs using them is mandatory. In large FOR-TRAN programs it is a good idea. For ISO Pascal programs, and for one of the ways of dealing with Turbo Pascal on IBM PCs, extensive use of the include file compiler directive is the way to evade monolithic source files.

Include files are used for things that are used in a number of programs and source files: defining constants, types, macros, short functions and procedures, and FORTRAN common declarations. Putting them in included files keeps them from cluttering up files with "the good stuff" in them, and changing the one instance of a declaration in an include file means you have changed all the places where the item is declared. A source file may have only 40 lines of code and comments in it, but with the addition of the contents of the files brought in during compilation with the include directives, it may balloon to 1000 lines or more. It usually isn't necessary to have these definitions around the original code that uses them, except at compile time. Properly used, code readability improves.

Somewhere, anywhere in the source file of a program, an include file directive can be stored. In C the include directive is implemented as a standard preprocessor command:

```
#include <stdio.h>
```

— or —

```
#include "/usr/harvey/include/wallbanger.h"
```

— or —

```
#include "../include/wallbanger.h"
```

The pound sign "#" has to be in column one of the source file. The first instance of the C #include preprocessor directive uses a file name, in this case stdio.h, and surrounds it with a less-than "<" and a greater-than ">" pair. This says that the file resides in the special systemwide directory where standard include files live.

The second example uses double-quote marks and the full pathname of the file. This works if the file system being used works like the hierarchical one in AT&T's UNIX operating system. MS-DOS and Macintosh compilers can deal with this. It is an example of an absolute pathname.

The third example uses a ". ." in the pathname, which means "climb up a directory." If the present working directory is "/usr/harvey/work," then the above path describes the include file wallbanger.h as being in the directory up one level and down into another directory (called include). This is a relative pathname.

In Pascal files are included with a compiler directive. For example:

```
{ $I Filename }
```

— or —

```
(* $I Filename *)
```

or, in some systems, even

```
{ $I /usr/harvey/wallbanger }
```

It is possible to use the C preprocessor on Pascal source files with embedded preprocessor commands like "#include." Some Pascal compiler systems don't provide the $I compiler directive, and rely on the use of the C standard preprocessor. If you are using one of the windowing packages, you probably aren't using a compiler like that.

Nested Includes

One interesting difference between the Pascal standard compiler directive and the C preprocessor command is that the Pascal compiler include doesn't allow nested references, but the C preprocessor include command does. That is, if a Pascal source file has a $I directive and the file brought in also has a $I directive, the included file's $I will *not* be processed. Turbo Pascal, in fact, will detect the nested $I and stop processing, reporting the attempted nested include as an error.

The standard C preprocessor's allowance of nested includes is used in C programs used with the UNIX operating system. On one hand, they are a nuisance during debugging and unit testing; you have to specifically watch out for #include statements in included files, even if you know they are permitted. Missing one could lead to a confused search for days! On the other hand, once in a blue moon, the added capability comes in handy. The compromise between legibility and function is to allow nested includes, but (I think) only near the top of any source text and with their use clearly highlighted. The following is an example of using include statements. Note the extra comment highlighting to make them stand out.

```
/* ******************************************************** */
/*                  INCLUDED FILES                          */
/* ******************************************************** */


#include "TheSun"
#include "TheMoon"
#include "And_TheStars"


/* ******************************************************** */
```

A Full-fledged Pascal Example

The following is a listing of a simple program written in Pascal. All it does is demonstrate how include files can be used:

```
program ShowIncludes;
    const
            {$I Show.consts }
    type
            {$I Base.types }
            {$I Show.types }
    var
            sex: all_sexes;
            ssno: all_ssnos;
begin
    writeln(' Doesn''t do much. ')
end.
```

Here are the contents of the file Show.consts:

```
lowssno = 100000000;
highssno = 999999999;
```

The following is contained in Show.types:

```
all_sexes = ( female, male );
```

The following is in Base.types:

```
all_ssnos = integer;        { some Pascal compilers have integer types
                              that can't handle numbers this big }
```

All the constant and type declarations can be used in several source files and programs without having to retype the text or copy the text into the program source files. If the included files are very long, they will keep out of the way while you edit the file containing ShowIncludes.

Caveats

If you are *not* working with a strictly ISO standard Pascal or 3.0 or earlier version of Turbo Pascal (i.e., you have a Pascal that allows independent compilation), then I suggest that include files are a bad place for defining variables and nontrivial functions and procedures. This is if you are also using the extensions that allow independent compilation. It is easier for me to track the goings-on in a program by having present the local variables used in the file. It is more difficult for me to make sense of some code if the sources of the routines can be in several different kinds of files or directories. It is, to me, better discipline if the variables that are used in a file are the only variables declared in that file. I have seen projects where there was only one include file for a number of source files; the include file contained every constant and variable used in the suite. When debugging the contents of one file, it is detrimental to have to work around the unnecessary noise generated by the contents of every other file in that system.

With Turbo Pascal versions 1.x, 2.x, and 3.x (the versions currently available before this is printed) and ISO Standard Pascal, the lack of an accessible linking phase of the compiler makes it harder to keep the source code in a number of small files rather than have everything in one big file. It becomes necessary to use the include file ability in a slightly different fashion. This other way entails creating one "master" source file, in itself not very long. It has include directives for the constants and the types, but it also has a separate include directive for each "slave" source file. Each of these included source files contains one or more related procedures and functions used by the program.

This method isn't bad, for it *should* be more portable across Pascals than any use of independent compilation. Some Pascal systems are designed to process many small files into object code, one at a time, and then link them together, rather than compile and link one large file. The first few passes of such a Pascal compiler may not be able to handle a monolithic file built from a master source file that includes a number of other source files (making a 50,000 + line program). This is despite careful crafting of the component functions and procedures. There may be need, for example, of a large temporary file on disk. The question is not important to users of Turbo Pascal on an IBM PC because, without resorting to chaining and overlays, PC Turbo Pascal code is limited to fit in a single code segment.

Here is a Pascal program that uses include files to keep constant and type declarations and other include files for major parts of the program.

```
program IncludeSource;                    { Written in Pascal. }
const
     {$I ConstDefs }
type
     {$I TypeDefs }
```

```
var
    FirstWizard,
    LastWizard,
    WizIndex:     all_wizards;          { note that globals are still declared
                                          in the file in which they are used. }


    { -------------------------------------------------- }
    {    Inclusion of files containing utility routines   }
    { -------------------------------------------------- }
    {$I OrderFil }
    {$I OpenFil }
    {$I SetPtr }
    {$I ReadRec }
    {$I NameWr }
    {$I AddrWr }
    {$I TelWr }
    {$I ClosFil }
    { -------------------------------------------------- }
    {                     Main program text               }
    { -------------------------------------------------- }
begin
    writeln(' WizCon IV Convention Attendees ');
    OpenWizardFile;
    GetLastWizardNumber;
    for WizIndex := FirstWizard to LastWizard do
            ListWizards;
    writeln(' ---------- End Of List ------------ ');
    CloseWizardFile
end.
```

Portable Pascal Code

Someone wants to write a system in Pascal and have it run on a number of different systems, aiming to have only one set of source files. No matter how big the program, it is annoying to deal with copies of the same file that differ only because they are arranged differently. It is bad enough hassling with legitimately dependent code (code that is written differently for each environment).

It isn't possible to deal with all the popular versions of Pascal for microprocessor-based systems with just the standard Pascal Include directive ($I). If you want to implement a Pascal program using small, independently-compiled source files while avoiding having to have n copies of the system-independent code (one for each implementation), then you will have to be careful which Pascal compilers you use. In the context of this book, only implementations like Borland International's Turbo Pascal will be difficult. Using a preprocessor can deal with the problem, but the quick edit/compile/debug cycling that is the hallmark of the Turbo package will be lost, as only the preprocessor and the editor, not the compiler, get to work with the original source files. The compiler sees source files that are generated from the original with a preprocessor.

Preprocessors are discussed in another section of this book. One very brief suggestion: following a PC Turbo Pascal source file organization standard, avoiding independent compilation, should produce a relatively movable program. It is especially important to identify the target machines and map the differences between compilers.

The Turbo Pascal compiler for the Macintosh doesn't share the insane limitations of the IBM PC's most popular Pascal compiler, for it supports UNITs and resources. The 68000 version of the Mac Turbo compiler may not allow resources to be longer than 32K bytes each, but at least you can have more than one!

INDEPENDENT COMPILATION

One step beyond "the single file contains all the code" is the idea of compiling the contents of two (or more) files—one perhaps on Monday, the other on Tuesday—and on Wednesday incorporating both compiled modules into an executable program. Each small compilation creates an **object file** from the source file. These object files are in themselves nonexecutable; they exist to be linked together by a linker program, in a predetermined way, to build the executable file.

Each object file is generated from its source file. The act is independent from other source or object files, unless a source file is yanked in using an include directive or a preprocessor command.

PC Turbo Pascal does not presently have an identifiable linking phase that can be used separately from the rest of the compiler system, but Macintosh Turbo does. The closest that PC Turbo gets is when the compiler is used to build PC Turbo overlays. There have been indications that PC Turbo Pascal will someday be provided with a linker, or that the compiler will be able to generate individual object files so that someone else's linker can be used to create executable files. There are third-party products that permit Turbo executables to be constructed with more than a single code segment. Borland's Modula-2 compiler has to have all that and more to follow the Modula-2 standards described by Wirth.

SEPARATE COMPILATION

Separate compilation is a more complicated mechanism than independent compilation. The example below illustrates the difference with two source files. The first file contains the Pascal program, and the second file contains a Pascal routine called by the main Pascal routine in the first file.

```
program test;
      procedure example(a: integer; var b: char ); external;
begin
      example(2,'c')
end.
```

```
procedure example( a: integer; var b: integer );
begin
      writeln(a,b)
end;
```

The parameter list for the procedure called Example is intentionally misspecified in the file with the main routine for the program.

If this program's files were independently-compiled, the discrepancy would not be detected at compile time. What happens when this program is linked together and then run depends on the quality of the compiler and dumb luck. The source error may not cause anything to be wrong. An error may be detected during execution, causing the program to come to a premature but orderly halt. The system may crash. It is this problem with independent compilation that makes working with some extended Pascals interesting.

If the compiler system supported separate compilation, then the discrepancy would definitely be detected at compile time, and an error message generated. This is done by maintaining a database of procedure interface information in a handy file. The compiler checks this database every time a file wants to use a routine in a different file, ensuring that there is perfect agreement regarding that routine's parameter list. A compile time detection of this error is much better than finding the error during testing or afterward, when there may be a good chance that it will go undetected for some time.

A Common Solution to the Pascal Separate Compilation Problem

The Macintosh standard for separate compilation is to adopt a form of the UCSD extensions to Pascal, where the keywords units, uses, initialization, interface, and implementation are used.

A normal Pascal program used to fit in one (big) file, with the keyword **program** at the top and **"end."** at the end. For separate compilation, the main file begins with the program keyword, but other files begin with the keyword **unit**. In a suite of source files that form one program only one file starts with the keyword program; the rest start with unit.

The **uses** clause identifies from where procedures and variables that are declared in another file are coming. The uses clause mentions the name of the units that the borrowed constant, type, variable, and procedure/function names are from.

The **interface** part of a unit is used to list the constants, types, variables, and procedures/functions of the contents of that unit that are public. This implies that most of the things in each file can be hidden away, and only the items that are intended to be accessible are public. The interface part shows how those public items are declared, including constants and types.

The **implementation** part of a unit contains private declarations of constants, types, variables, and procedures and functions, and also the procedure and function blocks — the code.

The **initialization** part is used to contain code that is to be executed at the beginning of runtime.

When a file is being compiled and the compiler encounters a uses clause, it tracks down the unit mentioned in the statement and includes the items mentioned in the unit's interface part in its symbol table. This is how datatype declaration problems between source files are detected at compile time.

The Apple Pascal compilers have established a very strong standard that the other compiler developers (at least for the Macintosh) are following. I know that Borland's Mac Turbo Pascal has one major difference (no get/put) and a number of minor ones. It does not follow the de facto UCSD standard to the letter.

MS Pascal also uses UCSD extensions, also without following the UCSD module exactly, and differing as well from the Macintosh compilers.

More details on the unique extensions and shortcomings (features) of the various Pascal compilers are in the coding hints section.

PREPROCESSORS AND MACROS

This section describes preprocessor programs and how they differ from Macro preprocessor programs. Uses for these preparatory programs are also discussed.

Introduction

Compilers accept input files and generate a variety of output files. Some of these files are text and are readable, others are not; a priori knowledge of what's in the latter kind of file (or different programs to aid their understanding, like debuggers and disassemblers) is needed if someone wants to look at their contents. Compilers are nothing unusual, as programs go.

All that the compiler cares about, really, is if the source input files follow the rules that it knows so that it can generate kosher output files. It is therefore OK to create other programs that come both before and after a language compiler. Programs that are run before the compiler can generate legitimate input files for the program. Programs that work on the output files of the compiler, like linkers and optimizers, can create executable modules (in some cases) and faster executable programs, respectively.

FORTRAN

The FORTRAN language, originally designed to work on some of the earliest machines powerful enough to support a defined language higher than assembler, has been redefined a few times over the years. The present ANSI 1977 FORTRAN standard for FORTRAN code is a conservative couple of steps behind the more recent languages, like C, Pascal, and Modula 2, which are overwhelmingly more popular on the micro-based systems. A different popularity story is told for the larger machines, where less work is done for the "fun of it" and the variety and support of language experimentation is anemic enough to stifle liberal approaches to development. Despite the inelegance and inefficiencies of FORTRAN, it is *still* the language of choice for scientific endeavors, such as particle physics. To avoid working directly with FORTRAN, standard operating procedure is to use a preprocessor. There are a number of preprocessors that accept a well-defined input language (Ratfor is one) and generate ANSI standard FORTRAN files as output.

cpp

Some preprocessor languages are designed along the lines of full-fledged programming languages. Others, like the standard C preprocessor, scan but do not process the entire input file, turning every line of input source code into a line of output source code. The C preprocessor searches for a special flag character, normally "#", in column 1 of a source file. If the preprocessor sees this flag character, it knows that the next few characters on that line are a message for the preprocessor. If no pound sign is in column 1, then the preprocessor knows not to touch that line of code, and (unless a previous command says otherwise) copies the line of code verbatim to the output file.

Here is a list of the important standard C preprocessor commands:

#define Identifier TokenString
means that any instance of Identifier should be replaced by Token-String.

#define Identifier(Identifier,Identifier, . . . ,Identifier) TokenString
defines a macro. The first identifier is the name of the macro; the identifiers within the parentheses are arguments. For example, the macro definition and the following text:

```
#define this(that,the,other) that = the + other;
    this(a,b,c)
```

would produce:

```
a = b + c;
```

#undef Identifier

is used to remove any previous definitions of Identifier.

#include < filename >

is used to include the source content of filename into the preprocessor output file. The "<" and ">" indicate that the directory the file comes from is a Unix specially arranged include file directory. Just as common is the form:

#include "filename"

where the files come from the directory whose path is explicitly described as filename.

#if ConstantExpression

If ConstantExpression is nonzero, then it is TRUE, and the code that follows will be included in the output file up until the matching #endif starting in column 1. If the expression evaluates to zero, then the code between the #if and #endif will be skipped.

#ifdef Identifier

If the identifier has been defined already during that session with the preprocessor, this statement evaluates to TRUE and the code contained by the #ifdef #endif will be included in the preprocessor's output file.

#ifndef Identifier

If the identifier has not been defined, the statement evaluates to TRUE, and the code within the block will be included in the output file.

#else

Used between an #if, #ifdef, or #ifndef, and an #endif. The #else marks the beginning of the block to be written to the output file if the test fails.

An Example

Here is an example C program source file with C preprocessor commands. It is followed by the pure C version of the same file after the preprocessor is done with it. Unless a user wants it that way, it is unusual for any program, let alone a preprocessor, to overwrite the input file with the output file (I am unfortunately very good at this). The example contains a multiline macro definition, which is described in the following section on macros.

```
        /* C with preprocessor commands in the source: */
#define TRUE 1
#define APPLE TRUE
#if APPLE
#define LineDraw(a,b,c,d,e)      Absolute(a,b);\
    SetFGPattern(e);\
    LineTo(c,d);\
#else
#define LineDraw(a,b,c,d,e)      Style(e); /* Use alternative method. */\
    Points[0] = 2;\
    Points[1] = a;\
    Points[1] = b;\
    Points[1] = c;\
    Points[1] = d;\
    PolyLine(Points);
#end


extern int CurPattern;    /* Contains the value of the current line pattern. */


Line(x1,y1,x2,y2)
    int x1, y1, x2, y2;
{
    LineDraw(x1, y1, x2, y2, CurPattern);
}


    /* C source after preprocessing: */
Line(x1,y1,x2,y2)
    int x1, y1, x2, y2;
{
    Absolute(x1,y1);
    SetFGPattern(CurPattern);
    LineTo(x2,y2);
}
```

Modula 2

Modula 2 is a language designed to avoid having to use any form of
preprocessing. It is based on the successes and failures of language design

and implementations of the 1970s, including C and Pascal. If a preprocessor is run before a Modula 2 compiler, chances are the compiler program will detect it, become indignant, *slag* the preprocessor, and leave the premises.

Macros

Some preprocessors implement macros to some degree. The previous example has a multiline macro definition in it, about as extensive as the standard C preprocessor can handle. Others that process code slower than cpp do much more.

There are systems in use today that use two preprocessor languages. One implements more powerful control structures for an undernourished language; most I've seen are for FORTRAN-66. The second provides a high-powered macro capability. A macro is a block of code that fully takes the place of its identifying name in every place the name is used in a source file. A macro is different from a subroutine, procedure, or function, in that the latter three occur publicly in a program once (the number of private copies is limitless), but can be called or referenced by name any number of times. A routine name is not physically replaced in a source file by its entire block of code (like a macro) , but is replaced in the executable file by the address of the routine in RAM.

Other preprocessors rarely do better than cpp in speed; cpp is designed to run and then get out of the way. It does "just enough" to get its job done. The tradeoff is that cpp doesn't handle macro defines close to the theoretical ideal.

A good macro processor handles nested macros properly; you can define macros in terms of other macros. Entire programs can be written completely in nested macros, instead of using procedures that call each other. Even recursion can be properly handled with macros. Macros aren't popular because of the nasty side effects: unless the processor builds a database of macro definitions that it keeps current, it is *not* going to be a speed demon, and any such database will be a big one.

Preprocessor Difficulties

There are problems with using a preprocessor or macro preprocessor with Pascal compiler systems, among others. The following is a synopsis:

☐ The preprocessor has to be ported to all the machines and environments in which the target program is going to be used. It's my experience that it is otherwise harder to deal with the porting process.

☐ The preprocessor requires time to execute. This may be a *long* time. The time it takes a preprocessor to handle a file is added to each compile time. Macro processors are hogs.

☐ The preprocessor input source file may be very difficult to read. Some of those macro languages have deceptively simple rules that either mask the logic of a section of code or force you into scanning a program line-by-line for global details.

☐ Some Pascal systems do not expect the use of a preprocessor. Borland's PC Turbo Pascal comes to mind.

☐ Some people take to using preprocessors too much, especially macro processors. Indications of overuse include developing subdialects of macro definitions and the need for creating cross-reference indices of macro libraries. It is *simple* to define too many macros!

☐ Source level debugging gets a little more interesting. Instead of just throwing out the files that are the output of the preprocessor and the input of the compiler (you normally won't need them), sometimes you have to keep them for use with a debugger.

☐ Preprocessors can do unexpected things to the source. On the input side the code looks fine, but on the output side the code may look like hash browns.

On the other hand, we are far from perfecting machines and preprocessors. This stuff may not suit your purposes today, but this may not be true tomorrow. Macro processing is a potentially powerful way to overcome portability problems.

CHAINING AND OVERLAYS

It used to be (pre–IBM PC) that the personal computer software market catered to the hot-rod or specially configured personal computer by accommodating some very rare hardware configurations. This was because *all* configurations were rare! Software developers clung to whatever commonality that did exist, like the CP/M operating system, but this would only get your foot in the door! Accommodative CP/M developers spent half their development time building an army of software drivers for a myriad of different peripherals and main displays.

Also both RAM and disk space were expensive back then, with most machines capable of directly addressing only 64K of RAM. Many software packages even then couldn't fit in 64K. To get all the software to fit, common minicomputer and mainframe tricks were adopted, among which were overlays and chaining. Neither of these two tricks are lost in time, for overlays and chaining are supported in strange and wonderful forms by the new environments, and not simply by compilers or interpreters.

Chaining

Chaining is simpler than overlaying. An example: Program A gives the user five options. Selecting option two causes the program to close all its open files and "chain" to another program that has the code to accommodate the user's request. When one program **chains** to another, the chained-to program (on micros, anyway) is pulled off the disk and dropped right on top of the place in RAM that the chained-from program was running, obliterating the copy of the first program. The chained-to program then starts to execute in place of the first program.

Some language systems allow communication between two chaining programs by way of unmodified regions of data space in RAM. Some, on the other hand, allow no such communication except through file I/O. The file I/O trick is no trick at all; for example, program A drops a message in file COMM.TXT which program B then reads.

Chaining from one program to another without the two covertly communicating with each other except via files, is common practice. The code that does the chaining is most certainly not portable, but this code should not amount to much, especially in the context of this book.

Below are descriptions of the chaining facilities for each window system.

Macintosh

The Macintosh ROM includes a Chain call. It is an advanced segment loader routine that starts an application without changing the application heap. The Launch routine restores the heap to its original size; it is otherwise the same as the Chain call. Both Chain and Launch must be called from an assembler routine, since they don't follow Pascal or C parameter stack rules. To get to the calls from a higher-level language requires writing (or using) an assembly routine that accepts the required parameters in C or Pascal standard form, rearranges them, and invokes the call.

Gem
Most of the MS-DOS compilers and interpreters have a chain command, in one form or another. Gem itself provides the shell library function **shel_write** for informing Gem which application to run next.

Windows
The version of Windows I have doesn't appear to have either a spawn task message or a routine that starts a task in place of the current one.

Windows does provide several module-manager functions that are used in combination to bring in code modules and data areas. These routines are listed in the following section on overlays.

Amiga
The Amiga's multitasking kernel provides a few routines for manipulating concurrent tasks and handling intertask communication. The Intuition package doesn't get involved in process scheduling, but it does control access to the display for cooperating tasks. Programs may spawn processes using AddTask and control task execution with the other Exec calls.

Overlays

Overlays are a bit more flexible than simple chaining. Overlays are used when only a part of a program, not the entire program, is read into empty RAM or over another expendable part. Part of the program is normally in RAM. These days, the overlays can be relocatable.

There are various methods for supporting overlays. It is easy to write a program that will not fit on most of the target machines without chaining or overlays, especially if the target machine performs multitasking, and the running program should not assume that all the available memory belongs to it. It is possible that two language compilers, compatible in every other way, differ in how they handle overlays, and that difference can be a killer.

The environments covered in this text tend to have their own overlay systems. Overlay management, which was once the responsibility of a compiler's support library (on micros), now falls to the operating system, where it belongs.

Macintosh

The Macintosh overlays are called **code segment resources**. On 68000-based Macintoshes, code segments are limited to 32K bytes. This is so that most jump instructions within the same segment can be offsets from the beginning of the segment when located in memory. It permits both relocatable code and shorter instructions to achieve the jumps. The bad side effect of this is felt most by people who have to move mammoth programs from older environments onto the Mac. *Unless* their code is well structured, they will be in for a battle on steep hillside with the wind against them should they try to move their software to this machine.

A Mac application can track down and use resources from several files, including the system. There are two groups of routines for dealing with resources: the **segment loader** is used to manipulate code segments, whereas the resource manager works with resources in general. Oddly, there's only one high-level routine in the segment loader that directly manipulates segments.

UnloadSeg	Unload a segment (it can then be purged/moved)
CountAppFiles	Report on number of files selected with application (via Finder, Juggler, or Servant, etc.)
GetAppFiles	Identify one of the files selected with application
ClrAppFiles	Tell Finder (or other) you've processed a file
GetAppParms	Obtain information about the current application
ExitToShell	Release application heap and run Finder in place of current application

Underneath, two assembly-accessible routines (**_LoadSeg** and **_Unload-Seg**) are stack-based.

IIGS

The memory system of the IIGS is segmented (pages are 64K in size) and the system is slower, both of which limit freedom of action on the part of the system and application developers. There is, however, a generalized OS mechanism called the *Tool Locator* that will track down components that are needed by an application. Custom toolsets can be developed and used with the Tool Locator. Using the Tool Locator is not the same as using Macintosh code resources.

Amiga

The Amiga doesn't currently provide an overlay manager in the ROM, though it does have a multitasking kernel.

Gem

Gem does not directly support overlay, code segment, or code resource management.

Windows

The Module Manager routines are used to access procedures and data in executable modules. The Macintosh lumps code resources with every other kind of resource, but Windows treats code and data blocks to their own set of access routines. In Windows code and data aren't resources. A list of the routines follows:

GetModuleHandle	Return a handle to a module specified by name
GetModuleUsage	Return the reference count for a module
GetModuleFile-Name	Return executable file name containing the indicated module
GetInstanceData	Copy data from an older instance to the current instance of a program
GetProcAddress	Return the RAM address of indicated routine
MakeProcIn-stance	Assign a data segment of an instance to a procedure
FreeProcInstance	Detach a procedure instance from a data segment assigned using MakeProcInstance
GetCodeHandle	Returns the handle to a code segment that contains the indicated function.
Throw	Copies the current execution environment into the provided buffer.
Catch	Restores the execution environment stored in the buffer indicated.

Future Overlay Systems

I foresee a growing interest in the faster machines that, almost incidentally, sport virtual memory systems (where the disk and the available RAM get together with the processor to fake having more RAM). Virtual memory is an economic virtue that does for large programs what windows do for graphics on displays. For example, a computer may have only 2 megabytes of RAM physically in the box. A virtual memory system may simulate, with much disk space, a memory address space that is billions of bytes wide!

For a 5 megabyte program to fit in 2 megabytes of physical memory, it is necessary to keep a copy of the program on disk and have the system copy blocks of the program to memory as it needs them. Large data arrays are handled the same way, except that a new or changed block is written to the disk before it is overwritten or after the program has finished running.

A personal machine with a virtual memory system is going to be a hot-rod for a while. Virtual memory systems run "more slowly" than nonvirtual systems for small numbers of small programs. RAM chip design has been improving rapidly enough to make it cheap to own "enough" memory without resorting to a fully virtual system. Although virtual systems can get along on a slow 40-megabyte hard disk or smaller, there will be another reason to motivate faster, bigger drives for micros. Segmenting code and data will not go away, because intelligent program partitions go farther to accelerate performance than does a global virtual memory system. In some cases it is too unproductive to partition a program, and the work has to be handled by the virtual system.

MODULES AND UNITS IN PASCAL

This section describes the primary differences between a number of Pascal compilers that are considered by this book, with an occasional special mention of UCSD Pascal. The UCSD Pascal extensions are popular among Pascal compilers, particularly by Lisa Pascal compatible compilers (such as LightSpeed Pascal, TML Pascal, MPW Pascal, and Turbo Pascal for the Macintosh). The keynote compilers are:

PC Turbo Pascal	Keystone of the popularity of Pascal on micros
Pascal/MT+	Digital Research's Pascal compiler; currently obsolete, but mentioned because DRI produces Gem
MS Pascal	Microsoft supports Windows applications with both their C and Pascal compilers
UCSD Pascal	Originated several extensions to Pascal that are commonly employed in successful Pascal compilers today
Lisa Pascal	The model used by *all* the present generation of Macintosh Pascal compilers

Languages that support development on the Amiga and the Atari ST are perhaps unfairly not represented here; however, I hope that the syntactical variety of the Pascals mentioned above is sufficient to carry the points across.

As a bonus, this section also includes a description of how Modula 2 handles separate compilation and modules. I thought it would be proper to discuss major differences between Pascals with respect to large program development, and contrast them all with the Modula 2 standard.

Finally, a word or two on C language considerations ends this section.

In General

As originally designed, Pascal is a language that is supposed to provide expressive power without requiring the compiler to be written by a large team of high-paid software developers.

One of the features that didn't make it into the Pascal language definition is anything to do with independent or separate compilation. A Pascal program nominally consists of a single source file, with the word *program* at the top and the word *end* at the bottom.

Because a Pascal compiler can be a single-pass compiler, things like variables, types, constants, and procedures have to be defined before they are used. This results in the familiar but odd characteristic of Pascal programs being organized "backward," where the body of the main procedure and the most significant procedures and functions are listed at the bottom. The least significant procedures and functions are declared at the top of the file.

Monolithic file organization is murder on team development. It is agonizing to have more than one person work on the same file at one time, and the smallish personal computer doesn't take to expediently processing 100,000-byte source files. Most Pascal compiler writers have fortunately added a few things to their Pascal compilers that permit spreading the code across several source files. These source files can then be compiled one at a time. Unfortunately, although some are close, none of these compilers extends Pascal exactly the same way. Most are different enough to require special attention if portability is an issue.

Turbo Pascal for the IBM PC

Turbo Pascal (up to and including v3.0) for the IBM PC, et al., does not have a unit declaration or a MODULE declaration. No form of independent compilation is supported. A Turbo Pascal program may access software that is coresident, using software interrupts or externals with absolute addresses. No linker is available for Turbo Pascal programs.

The Turbo Pascal program header is optional. With it you can list the devices or files the program will use to do I/O. For example:

```
        program phillipe( input, output );
```

To develop large programs using PC Turbo Pascal, the common trick is to use the compiler's Include directive in the main program's source file.

```
program phillipe(input,output); { Turbo Pascal Main Program }
const
      {$I consts.lib }              { All the constants in file consts.lib }
type
      {$I types.lib }               { All the type declarations there }
var
      this,
      that,
      theother: integer;


          { The following include commands yank in all the
              routines described in separate source files. }


      {$I neatIO.src }              { This file contains three routines }
      {$I utils.src }              { This file contains 12 routines }
      {$I proc1.src }              { This file contains one large routine }
      {$I proc2.src }              { ditto }
      {$I proc3.src }              { again, ditto }

begin                              { the program code }
      proc3( this, that );
      proc2( that, theother );
end.                               { program phillipe }
```

Pascal/MT+ for the IBM PC

The declaration for a Pascal/MT+ program may have the optional program parameters, but the compiler ignores them.

Pascal/MT+ supports modules. The beginning of a module has the word *module*, followed by the name of the module. The end of a module is represented by the word *modend*. The **external** attribute is used before each variable or routine declaration whose body exists outside that module.

Pascal/MT+ modules are *independently compiled* if they are in different files. Assume for the following example that module a and module b are each in their own source files. Assume that the parameter list of a routine in module a does not match the parameter list that module b incorrectly understands routine a to have. Grief may be met in the form of runtime errors. These errors are likely to be difficult to track down. No error messages will be generated either at compile time or during the link phase. A cure for this is to use include files, or a cpp or m4-like preprocessor, to handle the procedure declarations for all the modules in a program. Using cpp or m4 for this is demonstrated later in this chapter. The idea is to have all the files cooperate and use one physical declaration of each routine's parameter list declaration.

Use include files or a preprocessor for type declarations, for the same reasons that include files or preprocessors are used for Pascal/MT+ external procedure declarations.

Pascal/MT+ code is organized in much the same way as Microsoft Pascal code can be if modules, and not units, are used in the Microsoft Pascal version. Pascal/MT+ modules do not have an initialization section, as do Microsoft Pascal modules. Microsoft external declarations have the keyword extern *after* the procedure name and parameter list, and Microsoft Pascal has reasons to require initialization different from Pascal/MT+.

An MT+ module must contain at least one procedure or function.

The following is a two-file example of a Pascal/MT+ program. One file contains the program declaration MT example, and the second contains a module called WhyNot. The program accesses a procedure called InModule that is defined outside of the block where it is used.

```
program MTexample( input, output );
    const   a = 1;
    var     c: char;
            pass_down_value: integer;
    external procedure InModule( var i: integer; var xyz: char );
begin
    pass_down_value := a;
    InModule( a, c );
    writeln( c )
end.

module WhyNot;
    const   LeConstant = 'z';
    procedure DisplayValue( ShowValue: char ); forward;
```

```
procedure InModule( var x: integer; var y: char );
begin
        DisplayValue( y );
        y := LeConstant;
end;


procedure DisplayValue;
begin
        writeln( 'the value from the main program = ', x:3 );
end;


modend.
```

Microsoft Pascal for the IBM PC

Program declarations work the way they are described in standard Pascal, with the parameter list describing I/O devices or files.

Microsoft Pascal modules are started with the word **module** and ended with the word **end**. Optional attributes may be specified within square brackets after the module declaration (e.g., **module this [public]**;). These attributes apply globally to the module.

Microsoft modules have an optional initialization block. If a module declares any file variables, then the module has to be declared as a parameterless extern procedure somewhere else in the program and called before anything in the module is accessed.

Microsoft units are much more complicated (but safer) than modules. A unit is composed of an **interface** division, where the name of the unit is declared, and an **implementation** division, where the code for the unit is described. The Microsoft version of this extension is much different from the original UCSD version and the versions adopted by Apple.

The root of the difference is the sophistication of the compile-time database. UCSD and Apple compilers extract and compare interface information from already compiled object files. With the Microsoft compiler the text of the interface block must be in the source file that is using the public features of that unit; this is commonly done with include directives.

Any use of a unit in a module, program, or another unit requires the declaration **uses** in the source where the unit is being used. The keyword *uses* is followed by the name of the unit being used.

An optional list can be specified after the uses declaration, for example:

```
uses unitname(penup,pendown);
```

This is a list of entry points into the unit (such as all the public procedure and function names). A similar list of entry points must be made in the original unit declaration if this list is to be used. This list contains the real names of the routines. Together these lists translate local names of routines to the actual names as they are implemented in the unit.

This feature allows one unit to be linked to "one or the other" of a version of a given unit, without text changes. For example, one version of unit devdraw may have the **pen_up** routine actually called **hp_pen_up**, and the **pen_down** routine really called **hp_pen_down**. To the code using that or another version of the **unit devdraw**, the first routine is **pen_up** and the second is **pen_down**. For example:

```
unit devdraw(hppendown,hppenup);
```

Changing the physical names of the routines in one part of a software system has no effect on the need to recompile other parts of the system.

If the optional routine list after the unit declaration is omitted, the absolute names of the routines must be used in the code using those routines.

The presence of a begin before the last end of either an interface or implementation section in MS Pascal means that initialization code for the unit is to follow.

An initialization block for a unit is mandatory if any file variables are declared in that unit. Executing the initialization code is handled automatically at the beginning of runtime. MS Pascal does a runtime check of all the internal version numbers of the interfaces used to compile all the units, warning of mismatches.

Interface divisions are required for describing the interfaces of used units. With Microsoft Pascal, the unit and uses declarations occur within interface and implementation divisions. The interface of a unit has to be present in a source file with code that uses that unit. Usually the text of the interface is inserted in the text at compile time using the include compiler directive (an MS-Pascal "metacommand").

The following is a sample Microsoft Pascal program using modules:

```
program MSexample( input, output );
    const   a = 1;
    var     c: char;
            pass_down_value: integer
    procedure InModule( var i: integer; var xyz: char ); extern;
```

```
    begin
        pass_down_value := a;
        InModule( a, c );
        writeln( c )
    end.


module WhyNot;
    const   LeConstant = 'z';
    procedure DisplayValue( ShowValue: char ); forward;

    procedure InModule( var x: integer; var y: char );
    begin
            DisplayValue( y );
            y := LeConstant;
    end;


    procedure DisplayValue;
    begin
            writeln( 'the value from the main program = ', x:3 );
    end;
modend.
```

UCSD Pascal (a Portable Language Environment)

In UCSD Pascal the unit declaration comes before the interface declaration and the implementation declaration of that unit, unlike in MS-Pascal. The interface and implementation declarations of a unit occur only within the unit. It isn't necessary to include the text of the interface declaration in any separately compiled source files.

The uses declaration, if used, must be placed immediately after the program, interface, or implementation declaration. If a procedure described in a uses declaration comes from a library file, the compiler directive $U libname must be used to name the library file.

As in MS-Pascal, anything declared in an interface section is global to code outside of that unit. Other sections of code using the routines must credit the originating unit with a uses statement. Anything belonging to a unit that is left out of the interface section is private and not directly accessible to code outside of that unit.

The initialization section of a unit exists if there is a begin before the last end of the unit. The section is normally exclusively initialization, but if a

***;

appears anywhere in this last part of a unit, then the code above that line is used for initialization, while the code below the line is used for termination. Both sections are automatically executed at the appropriate moments during runtime.

```
UNIT GreenBack;             { An example UCSD Pascal unit. }
    INTERFACE
        USES                { In case items mentioned in the interface section
                              are based on knowledge from other units. }
            {$U Diam.CODE} DiamInfo;    { A name of another unit. }
        CONST       indigo,
                    murkcount: integer;
        TYPE Fresnel = record
               FocLen:      integer;
               Diam:        DiamRec;
               Density:     real;
             end;
        VAR LensDescriptor: Fresnel;
        FUNCTION QueryLens( A: LensDescriptor ): BOOLEAN;


    IMPLEMENTATION
            { The following USES statement is used to borrow public
              constants, types, variables, procedures and functions from
              other units. These items must be listed in the INTERFACE
              section of the other units. }
        USES {$U Grind.CODE }    GrindVals,
             {$U Gravity.CODE }  SpecGravity;
        TYPE { Private type declarations here, global to the unit. }
        VAR GrooveCount: integer;
            { Other private var declarations here. }
        FUNCTION QueryLens;      { Must not have parameter information. }
        BEGIN
            { The QueryLens code goes here. }
        END;
```

```
                    { The following init/termination code is optional.  }
          BEGIN           { If this begin is present, then an init/term block exists.}
          { The unit initialization code goes here. }
          ***;            { <- An optional statement used to separate init/term code. }
          { The unit termination code goes here. }
      END   { This END must be present. }
```

Lisa Pascal (for the Macintosh XL)

The unit mechanism for Lisa Pascal is the same as that found in UCSD Pascal (see above), except that units do not have an initialization section and global labels may not be declared in a unit. Initialization has to take place explicitly with the standard entry points mentioned in the interface section of the unit to be initialized.

```
UNIT MPWBack;               { An example Lisa/MPW Pascal unit. }
    INTERFACE
        USES                { In case items mentioned in the interface section
                                are based on knowledge from other units. }
            {$U DI}      DiamInfo,    { The name of another unit. }
            {$U Grind}   GrindVals,
            {$U Gravity} SpecGravity;
        CONST indigo, murkcount: integer;
        TYPE Fresnel = record
                FocLen:    integer;
                Diam:      DiamRec;
                Density:   real;
            end;
        VAR LensDescriptor: Fresnel;
        FUNCTION QueryLens( A: LensDescriptor ): BOOLEAN;


    IMPLEMENTATION
            { There is no USES statement in the implementation block. }
        TYPE { Private type declarations go here that are global to the unit. }
        VAR  GrooveCount: integer;
            { Other private var declarations go here. }
        FUNCTION QueryLens;      { May have the same parameter info as above. }
        BEGIN
```

```
      { The QueryLens code goes here. }
  END;
END. { This end is not optional; it must be present. }
```

Separate Compilation in Modula 2

This section describes how the language Modula 2 provides independent or separate compilation.

The formal specification for Modula 2 includes a more than adequate method for supporting separately compilable modules, so there is little danger of incompatible Modula 2 standards springing up. It becomes blessedly unnecessary to use preprocessors to make up for the nonportability of code using independent or separate compilation in the source. It is possible to entirely avoid preprocessing; the code for one routine isn't scattered to the four edges of a floppy disk, and there doesn't have to be non–Modula 2 code in the source. The option to use a preprocessor, except in closed systems such as Borland's Turbo Pascal, is still available.

Modula 2 is syntactically less forgiving than ISO Pascal. The reserved keywords ALL HAVE TO BE IN UPPERCASE. Modula 2 is a case-sensitive language, like C and unlike Pascal. Pascal is a case-insensitive language, where the variables goshwow, GoshWow and GOSHWOW are considered to be the same. They are three different variables in Modula 2 and C. I prefer to have goshwow be the same as GOSHWOW. Some implementations of Modula 2 have extensions that allow case-insensitive code.

Modula 2 modules are organized in either one or two parts. A one-part module is declared simply with the word MODULE and the name of the module, followed by the contents:

```
MODULE doodah;

  .
  . (* contents of MODULE doodah here *)
  .
END doodah.
```

A two-part MODULE has a DEFINITION MODULE part and an IMPLEMENTATION MODULE part. If

```
DEFINITION MODULE fitzgig;
```

exists, then there has to be

```
IMPLEMENTATION MODULE fitzgig;
```

The definition module contains the list of types, procedures, and variables that may be imported by other modules. The variables declared in the definition module exist for the life of the executing program. The types, if declared likewise, are accessible by the world outside that module. If something in the corresponding implementation module is not mentioned in the definition module, it is private and not directly accessible by other modules.

A Modula 2 module may contain **EXPORT** statements, which are used to come right out and say which variables and procedures are accessible by code outside the module. There are also **IMPORT** statements, which describe what variables and procedures are being used by that module. Here are examples:

```
DEFINITION MODULE farout;
    EXPORT QUALIFIED this, that, TheOtherThing, GetGovtData,
                    PutGovtData, GetSecretData, PutSecretData;
    TYPE    GovernmentData = RECORD (* this definition is public *)
                    ssno:  INTEGER;
                    sex:   AllSexes;
                    name:  NameRecord;
            END;
            SecretData;         (* Note that the definition of this type is
                                    not made accessible to the public. *)
    VAR    this, that:       INTEGER;
           TheOtherThing:    GovernmentData;

    PROCEDURE GetGovtData(   VAR x: GovernmentData): BOOLEAN;
    PROCEDURE PutGovtData(   VAR x: GovernmentData): BOOLEAN;
    PROCEDURE GetSecretData( VAR x: SecretData):     BOOLEAN;
    PROCEDURE PutSecretData( VAR x: SecretData):     BOOLEAN;
END farout.
```

The keyword QUALIFIED comes in handy with separately compilable modules. When the word QUALIFIED is present in an export declaration, not only do other modules have to say the name of the variable or procedure they are using, they also have to say from which module it comes. For example, the module InOut has the following statement in its definition module part:

```
EXPORT QUALIFIED EOL, Read, Write, WriteIn, WriteCard;
```

This forces the module farout to have the import list shown in the following example of an implementation module part. Module farout gets several routines and variables from a module called InOut:

```
IMPLEMENTATION MODULE farout;
     FROM InOut IMPORT EOL, Read, Write, WriteLn, WriteCard;


     PROCEDURE GetGovtData( VAR x: GovernmentData): BOOLEAN;
     BEGIN

          ...

     END;


     PROCEDURE PutGovtData( VAR x: GovernmentData): BOOLEAN;
     BEGIN

          ...

     END;


     PROCEDURE GetSecretData( VAR x: SecretData): BOOLEAN;
     BEGIN

          ...

     END;


     PROCEDURE PutSecretData( VAR x: SecretData): BOOLEAN;
     BEGIN

          ...

     END;
END farout.
```

Modula 2 modules can either be separately compilable or be local. Local modules are modules that are nested inside other modules. An interesting property of local modules is that they behave like reverse procedures! Specifically, a variable declared inside a nested module can be made accessible by code outside of that module, which isn't possible using just a procedure. A variable declared outside the nested module is assumed to be ignored, rather than assumed to be accessible. There are times when defensive programming is smart; local modules make it *easy*.

In the following example of local modules, the keyword QUALIFIED is not used because it would be overkill. Local modules in one file are usually written by one developer, so that he or she can pick the names of things so that they don't clash. Separately compilable modules, on the other hand, require the use of QUALIFIED because of the unpredictability of the use of names across separate module boundaries.

```
VAR x, z: INTEGER;


MODULE WowTheReader;
    IMPORT z;                    (* We let z in. *)
    VAR   x, y: INTEGER;         (* We want our own copies of x and y. *)
                                 (* This x is different than the one outside. *)

        MODULE Fortress;
            IMPORT x;            (* Obtain the x from WowTheReader. *)
            EXPORT w;            (* Provide WowTheReader with w. *)
            VAR   w: INTEGER;    (*    Fortress declares it,
                                         NOT WowTheReader! *)


        (* right here, x and w are accessible, but not y or z.
           Fortress can inherit y if it wants, but it doesn't. *)


        END Fortress;


    (* From here, y, w, z, and the global x are all accessible. The
          x from Fortress is not available to WowTheReader. *)


END WowTheReader;
```

Independent Compilation in C

Most C language compilers support independent compilation. Portable C programs are routinely developed using many individual source files, with routines that reference other routines in other files. No parameter list checking for routines is done at compile-time, either between routines in the same file or between routines in different files.

De facto standard C does not have the equivalent of Units/Interface/Uses statements that extended Pascal and Modula 2 have, but ANSI C does have function prototypes.

A program called lint is commonly available for making the routine type and parameter list checks. Implementations of lint sometimes check references made across file boundaries. It is up to a developer to run lint on a suite of source files; lint is not automatically run as a consequence of running the compiler.

There are two standards used for the declaration of variables in C in a program with many source files. The first standard, the one most commonly supported, allows the following two-file program to compile and link together without problem:

```
/* file number 1 */

int a;
main() {}

/* file number 2 */

int a;
grok() {}
```

The second standard says that only one file may declare a global variable; the others have to specify that the variable is externally declared. The above example would not link properly if the compiler followed the second standard, because the integer a is declared twice. The correct syntax would be:

```
/* file number 2 */

extern int a;
grok() {}
```

The ANSI C standards committee has been deliberating about this and other related topics for eons, in an effort to establish a significant standard for the C language (rather than an incomplete standard like ISO Pascal). In the above case, I believe the correct approach, though not necessarily the most portable, is to use the extern keyword.

AUTOMATING FILE AND PROGRAM CONSTRUCTION

Since I advocate developing a large program as a metropolis of small files, I would be remiss if I didn't indicate solutions for the problems that will appear.

Big projects can have an overwhelming number of small files, far too many to keep track of by hand. The same projects generate different variations of the same software: production versions, special-function versions, one development version for each programmer, versions for testing, small memory model versions, versions for the 80386, versions for Gem/ST, etc.

Once in a while, someone with a version of the program in hand will ask the inevitable questions: "OK, will someone tell me how this program was built? What exactly is in this module?" Without the proper tools and techniques, you may never get an answer. This is an uncomfortable moment, for that module might be the one that works in a couple of days.

There are two programs that go hand-in-hand to protect your investment (not including the backup program) and enable the concurrent existence of all these special versions of programs and files. Following a list of directions, the first program orders other programs to execute and report back. The second program acts as a bank vault for source and other files, protecting them from unconsidered access and keeping track of changes. To use these programs, you don't need a hierarchical file system, though I don't recommend large program development without one. Even if there is only one programmer working on a project, a tree of directories can come in handy.

Program 1: The Make Utility

The Make program accepts a text input file (a **makefile**), which is the recipe for a program. The makefile mentions the names of files and contains command lines. The filenames are used to form **dependency rules**, which simply identify all the files that are dependent on other files. For example, if file A is used to build file B, then file B depends on file A.

The first key to the Make program is the last modification date for each file mentioned by name in the makefile. For example:

File Name	Last Modification Date
ExecutableFile	6 Jun 87 13:40:30
SourceA.c	6 Jun 87 13:29:30
SourceB.c	6 Jun 87 12:42:30
SourceC.c	6 Jun 87 11:33:30
SourceD.c	6 Jun 87 15:10:30

In the above directory listing, The file ExecutableFile is built by compiling and linking four C language source files, SourceA.c through SourceD.c. When Make checks to see if any of the source files have been changed since the last time ExecutableFile was built, Make will discover that SourceD.c has indeed been modified. Depending on what the makefile says, Make will have the file recompiled and will also have ExecutableFile relinked.

The second key to Make is that it can start other programs, like C and Pascal compilers, and tell them what to do. Based on the description in the makefile, Make effectively creates a command file, but it creates and fires off the commands one at a time. Also, depending on the makefile contents (and the operating environment), Make will wait until the current operation has finished before applying the next command. Make is interactively working with the rest of the system to build whatever is described in the makefile.

Make is general enough to not have to know what the nature of the dependencies are or what kinds of files it is dealing with, so Make is good for more than compiles and links. You can build an up-to-date hard copy of a manual for a custom version of a software package.

Makefiles can be huge and convoluted. The instructions on how to build hundreds of files can be kept in a single makefile. A single program can be composed of hundreds of source, object, resource, and other data files, and one makefile will describe it all. When you type:

```
make WorldBeaterProgram
```

Make will track down all the files that it has to find, check when they were last modified, and re-create only the files that are out-of-date, or are not present and should be. You don't have to be sitting by the computer invoking each command by hand. Since the work is selective, it needs much less time than it would take to re-create everything. The process is also much less error-prone than keeping track of dependencies by hand.

At AT&T, Make is used to automate building *suites* of enormous modules. To recompile everything would take weeks. Losing a makefile under this circumstance can be catastrophic.

Make not only follows dependencies, it will go anywhere in the file system that it is told to go to find a file, provided that it has the required security permissions (if applicable). The makefile can also say in which directory to place a newly created file, or where to move an old one.

Special copies of makefiles can describe how to construct custom or development versions of packages. These makefiles can be convenient, permanent records of how modules were created.

The syntax of a makefile varies among implementations of Make. They tend to be pretty cryptic, in the tradition of computer science in the 1970s. An example of a makefile is shown in Figure 2–14.

A Special Trick: Source File ID strings In Binary Files

Two things can be done to answer the questions, "How was this module created? What is in this module?" The first is to create a makefile to exactly describe what modules from what directories go into the result file;

```
#
#   Standard command line definitions
#

cp=cl -d -c -AS -Gsw -Os -Zpe

#
#   Standard inference rules
#
.c.obj:
    $(cp) $*.c

#
#   The C File List
#

fonttest.obj: fonttest.c fonttest.h

fonttest.res: fonttest.rc fonttest.h fonttest.ico
    rc -r fonttest.rc

fonttest.exe: fonttest.obj fonttest.def fonttest.res
    link4 fonttest,fonttest/ALIGN:16,fonttest/MAP,slibw,fonttest.def
    mapsym fonttest
    rc fonttest.res
```

Figure 2–14 An Example Makefile (From Microsoft Windows Developers Toolkit)

if you know which makefile was used, then you know which files were used and where they are.

The second thing is a neat trick that can prevent ulcers. At the top of each source file, define a private array of characters in whatever language you are using, a string that will never be used anywhere in the executable part of the code. For example, in C:

```
static char FileID[80] = "$%ID baseio.c %%D %%T %%P\0";
```

The %%D, %%T, and %%P character groups are macros that are translated into the date, time, and file directory pathname substrings when appropriate. The file is compiled with this string in it. Eventually, the executable file will be built; each of the object files in the executable file contributed its own version of the FileID character array.

When the fateful questions are asked, one only need run the binary file through a simple program that searches for and prints all the occurrences of a string that starts with a unique-enough flag pattern, such as "$%ID", and is NULL terminated (ends with an ASCII 00). Part of the list might look like:

```
baseio.c 9sep87 12:23
grec.c 9sep87 9:12
gspline.c 4sep87 3:23
ggrok.c 5sep86 12:12
heaven.c 29feb87 23:59
any.68k 23apr87 22:12
ArthurModsV12.c 30feb86 15:23
```

The good side effect is accountability; the bad side effect is the space occupied by hundreds of FileID strings. If the product version goes out with those FileID strings inside, any customers can find them (if they bother to look). Who knows if the information will be significant to customers or not? Encrypting part of the strings will help.

Program 2: The Code Vault

The second package is what I call a **code vault** (more commonly called a **code control system**). This is software that is responsible for keeping track of the whereabouts of files, permitting controlled access to files, and recording file changes.

When a code vault is set up in a directory system, normal read/write access to any file inside the vault is restricted. For write access you have to **check out** the file to be changed. To return the file to the code vault, you have to check it back in. New files are registered. Obsolete files are removed with a code vault delete command that does more house cleaning than the system's delete command.

The benefits of protecting an investment with a code control system are listed below:

- [ ] Prevent files from being checked out (and modified) by two people at once.
- [ ] Track file modifications, noting when a file is changed and what was modified.
- [ ] Enforce a no-write policy on certain files, such as those used to build a product that is in the field.
- [ ] Control several versions of a package.
- [ ] Control large projects or several small ones.
- [ ] Report on current valid information, such as who currently owns a specified file for modification.

The exact benefits vary, depending on the code control system.

When a new file is added to the vault, a copy of the file is placed in a directory structure reserved for the vault. The contents of the file may be checked (depending on the code control software) for FileID strings, which are modified to reflect when the file was inserted into the vault.

When a file in the vault is checked out, a copy of the file is made and handed to the borrower. A lock is placed on the original copy in the vault so that nobody else can check it out. Clearly, there have been times when several (nay, hundreds!) of people wanted to change a file at the same time; this automatic mechanism heads off many problems. At the very least, developers will know that the file is in demand, rather than discovering it after the fact and much too late.

A file access control system doesn't work unless it can enforce some of the paths into and out of the vault. The file system has to have a security system that can prevent direct modifications of the original copies without checking the file out. Perhaps the control system can modify the directory files in the vault to control access should the applicable file security not be provided by the operating system.

Code control systems don't take up a great deal of space; if you have to keep revisions around, they are quite efficient. However, there is a bad side; some consume excessive amounts of processor time to check in changed files.

PORTABLE PASCAL USING PREPROCESSORS

Defining the Problem

FORTRAN, C, and Modula 2 have well-defined rules for independent/separate compilation and other design considerations. Pascal compilers employ different solutions to deal with the same questions, nurtured by limited, ill-defined standards for the language.

Early Pascal didn't flexibly accommodate part-by-part compiling, for the design goal of the language was to keep it simple for use in teaching elementary computer science. The explosion in Pascal's popularity for everyday development was certainly not anticipated. An excellent computer science teaching language became a workhorse that was woefully underdefined for its new role. The standards were changed, in slow reaction to the demand, but the changes did not go far enough.

Current standards haven't stopped implementors from extending their Pascal compilers, because the market has been egging them on. Standards don't reward developers, but the market does; standards can only help or hinder. What we have now are many good Pascals that are somewhat incompatible with each other, and not just for independent compilation. So, how do you write an application in Pascal on an IBM PC and on a Macintosh, and still have to maintain the product code with one set of source files? That question is dealt with here.

This book uses Pascal more than C for the examples, despite clear evidence in the literature that Pascal is not ideal for writing portable code, especially between extended environments. The reason is that Pascal has been the language of choice for many, particularly on the IBM PC and Apple machines. It is understood that the current language of choice for product development on micros is C; it seems that C programmers have no trouble understanding Pascal examples, but people who know Pascal do not necessarily know C. C programmers already know how to use preprocessors to adjust for differences in implementation and compiler system differences.

Since preprocessors are rarely used with Pascal, some Pascal programmers may not have much experience with them. This section shows how a single set of source code for a large program can be processed by different Pascal compilers with the help of preprocessors. The example uses cpp for the preprocessor, and for languages involves Borland's Turbo Pascal for the IBM PC, Digital Research's Pascal/MT+, Apple's Lisa Pascal, and Microsoft's MS-Pascal.

The scope of the experiment described in this section includes the declaration of programs, units, modules, procedures, and functions. It does *not* include code within procedures, functions, or programs. The example attempts to show two significant things: the impact of not having good standards, and a way to get around the problem for Pascal.

The example is long, and it is complicated by its handling of four different compilers where two probably would have been sufficient. However, current trends seem to imply a proliferation of window systems, so I decided to illuminate a hypothetical (but certainly not easy or unlikely) situation.

Compiler Idols
UCSD Pascal has well-defined rules that have been adopted by Microsoft and Apple for their versions of Pascal. These extensions are discussed at length in the coding hints chapter, which appears in Part 2 of the book. If you are unfamiliar with the UCSD extensions to standard Pascal and the Apple/Microsoft variations of those extensions, you may want to skip ahead and read about them first.

Preprocessor Tools
Normally supplied with the AT&T Unix system are two preprocessors, cpp and **m4**. **cpp** is the C language preprocessor, and **m4** is a macro preprocessor. Both of these programs take standard, human-readable ASCII text as input, generate readable text output files, and report errors. The commands for cpp are formulated differently from the way m4 commands are formulated, making it harder for the m4 program to accidentally expand a cpp command (if both are used to successively process the contents of a single file).

One viable way to make Pascal code portable is to use a preprocessor such as cpp or m4. Unix manuals mention that cpp is for use on C source files only, and that the C preprocessor is likely to change over the years as the C language changes. They also say that m4 should be used instead.

Problems with Macros

While experimenting with both m4 and cpp for this experiment, I discovered that m4 is decisively better at processing files. After several iterations with the C preprocessor, a program source file "template" was developed. One of the recurring problems with cpp is its noncooperation when doing fancy things. For example (similar to others in this chapter), the #define command has a form where it can accept a parameter:

```
#define A(B) B+C
```

If the above #define were used in a source file with the following text:

```
KingArthur = A(CosmicDust) + excalibur;
```

then the preprocessor would produce the following code:

```
KingArthur = CosmicDust + C + excalibur;
```

Well, here is a simplified version of "something fancy." Using this #define in a Pascal source file:

```
#define HDRFILENAME(F) "F.hdr"
```

the following cpp command was attempted:

```
#include HDRFILENAME(test)
```

The idea was to be have cpp expand the macro HDRFILENAME before it processed the #include command, in order to find a method to pass a name to an include file preprocessor command that is embedded in another included file. In the case of this example, the included file has to have a .hdr extension at the end of its name.

This did not work; it confused cpp to the point that the rest of its work beyond the use of the above #include command made no sense.

It was necessary to use the cpp commands simply; if fancier versions of cpp existed, their extra features could not be used—that would limit the portability of the source code. It was assumed that the existing form of the AT&T Unix cpp would be the base version followed by C compilers from other software houses for other operating systems.

The m4 processor handles this case properly. The processing of the following lines of m4 commands results in the text of file test.hdr inserted into the output stream:

```
define(HDRFILENAME,$1.hdr)
include(HDRFILENAME(test))
```

How does the presence of preprocessor commands affect the readability of Pascal code? When used sparingly, preprocessor commands can help readability. Usually, though, using a preprocessor for portability reasons does not help, since the code is more verbose. It becomes difficult to find the native code underneath. A large suite of production source files that are hard to read is also uncomfortable to maintain. The results described here were not entirely successful, but to be fair this experiment describes circumstances that are pretty bad. There are wide differences between the selected compilers; therefore, I consider this a worst-case demonstration. Any application of this technique for a smaller set of target Pascal compilers isn't going to need so many different files and so much cryptic code for handling differences in the compiled language syntax. Certainly C source code with embedded preprocessor commands does get complicated, but rarely this complicated.

The discussion on the pitfalls of processing macros now leads into a discussion of the mechanics of preprocessing Pascal code, and how preprocessors can be used to create different versions of source code from one set of source files.

The Portable Pascal Example

This example of Pascal code with embedded cpp commands has three primary source files. One file contains the program block and the other two contain functions and procedures.

There are many other files. For any one of the four versions of the generatable program source, some of the files are unnecessary, but they are needed for cpp to be able to make the other versions. Using m4 would simplify some of this work.

File Naming Conventions

Each type of file involved in this example has been assigned a suffix (or extension), as with common MS-DOS/PC-DOS file names. For example, test.src is a source file, and test.use contains the USES information that some Pascal compilers need in the source code. Files with the same base name are closely associated with each other, so test.hdr is a closer relation of test.src than either nonse.src or nonse.hdr.

This file naming convention is complicated. It is designed to fight against a different problem: *too many* kinds of files. A list of all the file types is given below, with a short description of each type of file:

File	Comment
name.src	A Pascal source file with preprocessor commands. It contains variable declarations and the text of executable procedures and functions, and also contains include commands to grab other files listed below.
name.hdr	A human-readable file containing many preprocessor commands and Pascal code for each supported compiler system. This file type contains the code for the top of the name.src file.
name.int	A human-readable file containing preprocessor commands and Pascal code. It contains the INTERFACE block for the name.src file. The content may be used by other .src files if the public contents of name.src are used by them.
name.use	A human-readable file containing preprocessor commands that has the USES section of an extended Pascal program for the name.src file.
name.sfl	A human-readable file with preprocessor commands. This type contains a list of source files (other than name.src) that is to be "included" in any preprocessing and compiling of the file name.src.
name.dcl	A human-readable file with preprocessor commands. A file of this type contains the many forms of declarations that a Pascal procedure may have, depending on the Pascal compiler used. For example, the Turbo Pascal compiler uses:

```
Procedure A(B,C: integer); forward;
```

near the top of the file, and:

```
Procedure A;
begin ... end;
```

where the procedure is fully described. Lisa Pascal, on the other hand, uses the same form for the forward reference, but can use the full form of the declaration where the procedure is fully described:

```
Procedure A (B,C: integer);
begin ... end;
```

All the forms of the declaration of a Procedure are in the same file because it is easier to track down errors in the parameter lists of a procedure or function when they're all in the same place, at least for this example.

name.ext   Used to contain the list of external declarations (a Pascal file may require a number of variables, procedures, and functions that are declared externally). The .ext file may contain the actual external declarations, or it may reference the .dcl files of other .src files to get that information. Doing the latter may be reasonable if the number of external references is low, but could get very hard to deal with for a large number of externals.

name.fwd   Similar in use to .ext files, but for forward references.

name.pub   Contains public type, variable, and routine declarations for a given extended Pascal source file (as used in Lisa Pascal, for example).

name.mid   Contains the preprocessor code to yank in forward reference lists and external references.

The following are .def files used to contain global preprocessor defines and other commands. There is only one of each for a given project.

global.def   Contains important preprocessor commands and Pascal code shared by all the files involved in a compile. There is no file called global.src; files with a .def extension are unique and do not have associated files with the same base name and suffixes like .src and .dcl.

header.def   Used to contain compiler directives and similar details that are present in each preprocessed source file.

lingo.def   Contains the compiler system-dependent defines (an intentionally short file). There are enough commands in this file to define TRUE and FALSE and which compiler is being used. Also, the define for the macro name LANGUAGE has a test before it: if the name LANGUAGE has been defined, then none of the following defines will be processed. This test is provided to evade attempts to redefine macros without using the #undef preprocessor command. This file contains the command to include global.def, which is where any additional global defines should be stated.

This structure has been devised to accommodate the unextended Pascal compiler. Most of what such a compiler system would consider "noise" has been relegated to separate files. These files are not included in the compilable text file by the preprocessor. This is controlled with an appropriate combination of defines made in the lingo.def file. (The big picture is portrayed in Figure 2–15.)

Handling differences between code to talk to the window packages is a different matter that is not addressed by this example, since the solution requires more than conditional compilation.

The Example

The following three short files are the original source files that are fed through the cpp preprocessor. They are disarmingly simple.

The first file is called test.src, which is the main source file for this example; it contains the body of the main procedure and sets up the declaration block. The first thing test.src does is include four other files:

lingo.def   Identifies for cpp which Pascal dialect to generate.

prcset.def   Creates temporary definitions that are used for defining procedure headers.

test.hdr   Contains the information needed to define the declaration part or preamble of a Pascal source file. Some of the contents are subject to the defines created in prcset.def.

prcrst.def   Tears down the temporary cpp defines set up with prcset.def.

The next include statement is used to define forward references and externs. Since some standard Pascal compilers don't permit multiple instances of the keywords VAR, CONST, and TYPE to occur in the same

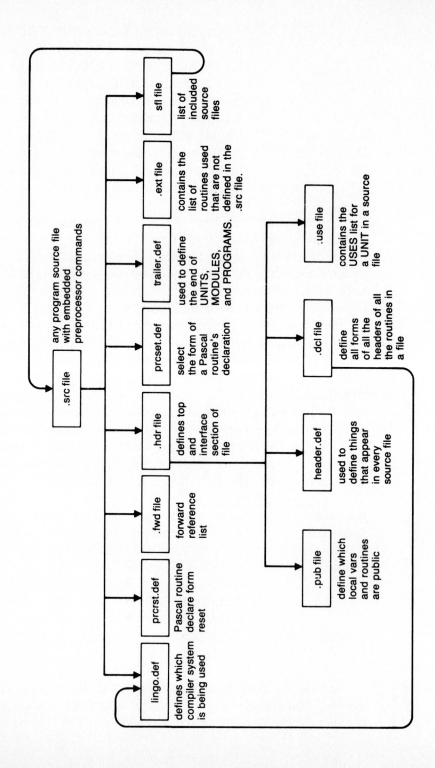

Figure 2–15 File Types Used in Preprocessed Pascal Example

part of a declaration part, the include command for test.mid is brought in within a variable declaration part.

Here are the contents of test.src:

```
(* A very simple, three procedure Pascal test case. *)

#include "lingo.def"
#include "prcset.def"
#include "test.hdr"
#include "prcrst.def"

{**** The Main Program for Test ****}

const
    { The global constant declarations are brought in here. }
type
    { The global type declarations are yanked in here. }
var
    nits,
    picks: integer; { Global variables are declared here. }


#include "test.mid"

begin
    { The program test code follows. }
    whatthis(1,2,3,4,5);
    nonsense(6,7,8,9,10);
    writeln('Thats all she wrote.');
end.
```

The other two files, nonse.src and what.src, contain the body of the procedures that are used in the example program. In this case they are used by the main procedure, but this isn't necessary. They are in separate source files because we want them to be separately compilable when it is possible to do so. Here is a listing of nonse.src:

```
{nonse.src}
#include "lingo.def"
#include "prcset.def"
#include "nonse.hdr"
#include "prcrst.def"
```

```
begin
        { The procedure nonsense code goes here. }
end;


#include "trailer.def"
```

And this is what.src:

```
    (* what.src: This contains the body of procedure whatthis. *)


#include "lingo.def"
#include "prcset.def"
#include "what.hdr"
#include "prcrst.def"


begin
        { The procedure whatthis code goes here. }
end;


#include "trailer.def"
```

The file trailer.def is used to properly end the contents. When these files are compiled with the contents of the main source file (as they would be when working with Turbo Pascal for the IBM PC), no module end is needed. When the files are compiled individually, some form of module end is used. MT+ Pascal uses MODEND., whereas Microsoft and Lisa Pascal use END.

Here are the contents of trailer.def:

```
(* The trailer.def file; provides the appropriate termination for each
   section. *)



#if TURBO
{ Turbo Pascal has no Module ends except at the end. }
#endif
#if MTPLUS
modend. { Pascal MTPLUS Module }
#endif
#if MCRSFT
end. { Microsoft Pascal Module }
#endif
```

```
#if LISA
end. { Lisa Pascal Module }
#endif
```

The contents of lingo.def for this example follow. This version is set up for generating Pascal/MT+ code:

```
#ifndef LANGUAGE
#define FALSE 0
#define TRUE 1
    (* This is lingo.def, where the compiler dialect is selected
       and the global definitions are pulled in. The constants should
       be defined only once per constructed source file. Consequently,
       If this message appears more than once, something is w0rng...   *)
#define LANGUAGE TRUE
#define TURBO FALSE
#define MTPLUS TRUE
#define MCRSFT FALSE
#define LISA FALSE
#include "global.def"
#endif
```

The prcset.def file determines the form of procedure header declarations based on the language being used and where in the current source file the prcset.def file is included. For this example the procedure headers can take three forms: the normal form, a forward reference form, and the forwarded reference form. The *normal form* is where arguments are listed in the normal fashion.

```
function strange( a: integer; b: real ): integer;
```

The *forward reference form* is the normal form followed by the key word FORWARD:

```
function strange( var a: integer; b: real ): integer; forward;
```

The *forwarded* (or *short*) *reference form* is used in the declaration of a procedure that has a prior forward reference declaration in the file. The heading is kept, but the parameter list and typing are dropped:

```
function strange;
```

Some compilers don't enforce this requirement.

Here is a listing of the prcset.def file used in this example:

```
(* prcset.def is used to conditionally define which header format is used. *)
#if TURBO
#   if FORWARD
#     define FORWARD_HDR TRUE
#   else
#     if FORWARDED
#        define SHORT_HDR TRUE
#     else
#        define STANDARD_HDR TRUE
#     endif
#   endif
#endif
#if MTPLUS
#   if FORWARD
#     define FORWARD_HDR TRUE
#   else
#     define STANDARD_HDR TRUE
#   endif
#endif
#if MCRSFT
#   if FORWARD
#     define FORWARD_HDR TRUE
#   else
#     define STANDARD_HDR TRUE
#   endif
#endif
#if LISA
#   if FORWARD
#     define FORWARD_HDR TRUE
#   else
#     define STANDARD_HDR TRUE
#   endif
#endif
```

To counter the defines made in prcset.def, here is what's in prcrst.def:

```
(* This file, prcrst.def, resets the header type constants. *)
#if STANDARD_HDR
```

```
#    undef STANDARD_HDR
#endif
#if FORWARD_HDR
#    undef FORWARD_HDR
#endif
#if SHORT_HDR
#    undef SHORT_HDR
#endif
```

The next file type, the .hdr files, can be more complicated than the ones mentioned previously. The header file has to establish or bring in whatever goes before the variables, constants, and type declarations. This involves any INTERFACE, USES, and UNIT details. In the .hdr file for test.src, the includes within are used for the following file types where appropriate:

.dcl	Contains the different forms of headings or procedures used in a source file. The results of .dcl files being included depend on prcset.def.
.int	Contains the INTERFACE part of a module, if any.
.use	Contains the USES statement for a module. Alternatively, the .use files are included by .int files when a USES statement is within an INTERFACE.
.pub	Normally used for public declarations. The .pub files used in this example contain comments only and aren't listed.

Here is a listing of test.hdr:

```
(* test.hdr: the program's header file. The .hdr files contain any
   of the compiler-dependent header information prior to the
   implementation block. It is intended to include public declarations
   within the interface block. *)
#if TURBO
PROGRAM Test;
#    include "test.dcl"
#endif
#if MTPLUS
#    include "test.dcl"
```

```
#endif
#if MCRSFT
#include "test.int"
#include "nonse.int"
#include "what.int"
MODULE test[];                      (* MODULE rather than PROGRAM for Windows. *)
#    include "test.use"
#    include "test.pub"
#    include "test.dcl"
#endif
#if LISA
     { The regular or special preamble is stuck in here for the
       main program source file. }


PROGRAM test;

       { The header.def file is not included here; this is the main file. }


#    include "test.use"
#    include "test.pub"


       { No implementation statement for the main program source file is
           needed for Lisa/Macintosh. }
#endif
```

The .hdr files for the satellite source files (what.src and nonse.src) use the key word MODULE instead of PROGRAM, but their content is similar to that of test.hdr. Here is a listing of what.hdr:

```
       (* what.hdr: This is used for yanking in the appropriate top part of a
           source file (for declarations and uses). *)

#if TURBO
#    include "what.dcl"
#endif

#if MTPLUS
Module WhatIsThis;
```

```
#    include "what.dcl"
#endif


#if MCRSFT
#    include "what.int"
     IMPLEMENTATION OF what;
          USES
#    include "what.use"
#endif


#if LISA
#    include "header.def"
     UNIT WhatIsThis;
     INTERFACE
       USES
#    include "what.use"
#    include "what.pub"
     IMPLEMENTATION
#endif
```

Here is nonse.hdr:

```
(* This is nonse.hdr, used by nonse.src to decide which include files
   contain the right public or global interface and declarations
   section for a source file. *)


#if TURBO
#    include "nonse.dcl"
#endif


#if MTPLUS
Module Nonsense;              (* MT PLUS Pascal requires "MODULE" etc. *)
#    include "nonse.dcl"
#endif


#if MCRSFT
#    include "nonse.int"
#endif
```

```
#if LISA
#    include "nonse.int"
#endif
```

The next file type, .dcl, is used to establish in the preprocessor output file an appropriate copy of the procedure headings that are declared in .src files. For example, nonse.dcl contains the various forms of the procedures and functions kept in nonse.src.

The file test.dcl doesn't contain anything more than a comment, so the file isn't listed individually. The nonse.dcl file contains:

```
(* nonse.dcl: This is used for extracting an appropriate procedure header. *)

#include "lingo.def"
#if STANDARD_HDR
procedure nonsense(a,b,c,d,e,f: integer); { Inline, normal. }
#endif
#if FORWARD_HDR
procedure nonsense(a,b,c,d,e,f: integer); forward; {Near the top of the file.}
#endif
#if SHORT_HDR
#if PROC==nonsense
procedure nonsense;    { At the top of each appropriate procedure declaration.}
#endif
#endif
#if INTERFACE_HDR
        { The list of routines in the module go here. }
#endif
```

Here is what.dcl:

```
#include "lingo.def"
#if STANDARD_HDR
procedure whatthis(a,b,c,d,e,f: integer);
#endif

#if FORWARD_HDR
procedure whatthis(a,b,c,d,e,f: integer); forward;
```

```
#endif

#if SHORT_HDR
procedure whatthis;
#endif
```

The repetitive includes to lingo.def are harmless, except for the time required. However, under certain circumstances these might cause lingo.def to be included by cpp into the input stream for the first time, and it is very important that cpp knows which compiler it is supposed to deal with.

Here are the listings for the .int files, which contain the source code held in the INTERFACE parts of a file. First, the simplistic test.int:

```
    (* test.int contains the interfaces that are required for test.int to be
        properly compiled and linked and arent part of the application
        source code.    *)
#if MCRSFT
INTERFACE;                          (* Microsoftese UnitSpeak. *)
  Unit paslibw (
    {$include:'stdincl.inc'}
  );
  {$include:'windows.inc'}
END;
#endif
#if LISA
#endif
#if TURBO
#endif
#if MTPLUS
#endif
```

Second, the contents of the **nonse.int** file:

```
(* nonse.int contains the INTERFACE declarations for nonse.src. *)
#if MCRSFT
INTERFACE;
    UNIT Nonse(
```

```
                    Nonsense
        );
                procedure Nonsense(a,b,c,d: integer);
END;
#endif
#if LISA
#    include "header.def"
     UNIT Nonsense;              (* LISA uses UCSD Units. *)
     INTERFACE
       USES
#    include "nonse.use"
#    include "nonse.pub"
     IMPLEMENTATION
#endif
```

Finally the what.int file:

```
#if MCRSFT
INTERFACE;
     UNIT What(
          whatthis
     );
     procedure whatthis(a,b,c,d: integer);
END;
#endif
#if LISA
#endif
```

The three USES definition files are next. First, test.use:

```
(* test.use: The list of used routines for test.src is inserted here. *)
(* This file isnt referenced if the compiler doesnt have USES. *)

#if LISA
     {$L-}  { Turn off listing option for used files. }
     USES                        {$U-}
          {$U nonse } nonsense,
```

```
                    {$U what   } whatthis;
        {$L+}  { Kick the listing option back on. }
#endif


#if MCRSFT
    { Insert Microsofts standard USES syntax here. }
    USES paslibw (
      {$include:'stdincl.inc'}
    ),
     Nonse(Nonsense),
     what(whatthis);
#endif


#if TURBO
     { PC Turbo Pascal doesn't do linking, so no USES statement. }
#endif


#if MTPLUS
     { MT+ Pascal doesn't have INTERFACE/IMPLEMENTATION/USES statements. }
#endif
```

The nonse.use and what.use files don't contain anything more than comments, and so are not listed here. When files are empty like this, they don't have to be around at all.

The .pub files are used for containing things that are declared public. This example does not use them but you might want to know where to place such declarations when necessary, so they are mentioned here.

The one .mid file used in this example, test.mid, is used by Turbo Pascal for the IBM PC merely to yank the appropriate .fwd (forward reference) and .sfl (source file list) files. Here are all those files for test:

```
      (* test.mid contains the forward and external file includes. *)
      (* Extern declarations are used when using modules instead of units. *)
#if TURBO
#    include "test.fwd"
#    include "test.sfl"
#endif
#if MTPLUS
```

```
#     include "test.ext"
#endif
#if LISA
    (* LISA doesnt do forward references or externs in this example. *)
#endif
#if MCRSFT
        (* Microsoft isnt doing forward refs or externs in this example. *)
#endif
```

Here is test.fwd. It isn't much:

```
    (* test.fwd: All forward declares are made via this file *)


#define FORWARD TRUE
#include "what.dcl"
#include "nonse.dcl"
#undef FORWARD
```

Here is test.sfl, which is a list of all the satellite source files that have to be included in the monolithic form of the compilable source file for the IBM PC Turbo Pascal compiler:

```
    (* test.sfl: This is used for including all the bodies of procedures and
        functions when they have to be compiled in the same file as the
        main program, Test. *)


#include "nonse.src"
#include "what.src"
```

The penultimate file is test.ext, which describes the external routines used by the code in test.src. This file is used in this example only for the Pascal/MT+ dialect, since the UCSD-like extensions for separate compilation aren't supported by Pascal/MT+, and IBM PC Turbo Pascal doesn't currently use a linker:

```
    (* test.ext: External routines are listed here, if any. Do not
        include this file unless you WANT procedure declarations
```

```
                    with externs on them. *)


#if MTPLUS
external procedure whatthis(a,b,c,d,e: integer);
external procedure nonsense(a,b,c,d,e: integer);
#endif


#if LISA
procedure whatthis(a,b,c,d,e: integer); external;
procedure nonsense(a,b,c,d,e: integer); external;
#endif


#if TURBO
(* PC Turbo Pascal doesn't presently do linking as we know it. *)
#endif


#if MCRSFT
procedure whatthis(a,b,c,d,e: integer); external;
procedure nonsense(a,b,c,d,e: integer); external;
#endif
```

The last file before the output files are listed is header.def. It is a handy file that contains the compiler option commands needed in any of the source files processed by the compilers. Here is a listing of header.def that is not used by the example, but should give you the idea.

```
    (* header.def: This contains global compiler directive text for the
        different compiler systems. *)


#if TURBO
#endif


#if MTPLUS
#endif


#if MCRSFT
    { The repetitive, invariant file preamble is defined here, along with
      several other things. (header.def) }
```

```
    {$windows+}
    {$stackseg+ $debug- $symtab-}
#endif


#if LISA
    { The repetitive, invariant file preamble is defined here, along with
        several other things. (header.def) }
#endif
```

The Example's cpp Output Files

These are sample outputs. The first is generated with TURBO in lingo.def is set to TRUE and the other language system identifier flags are set to FALSE. The second is generated when LISA is set to TRUE.

To generate the Turbo Pascal version, only the file test.src has to be explicitly processed using cpp, as the preprocessor commands include the other .src files. With the Lisa version each of the .src files has to be individually run through cpp. The C preprocessor also has a habit of generating spurious blank lines that fill the output file; these have been edited out of the following listings for clarity. Also, cpp generates many status lines for the C compiler such as:

```
    # line 23 test.src
```

These have been removed for clarity. Any good version of cpp provides an option that turns off the line statement generation. Some versions of cpp are built into the C compiler and do not exist as separate executable modules.

Turbo Pascal, IBM PC Version

```
(* A very simple, three procedure Pascal test case. *)

    (* This is lingo.def, where the compiler dialect is selected
       and the global definitions are pulled in. The constants should
       be defined only once per constructed source file. Consequently,
       If this message appears more than once, something is w0rng...   *)


    (* This is the global.def file, where the partition strategy for the
```

```
           dielect of Pascal is stated. If the compiler is to use an
           INTERFACE section, the PINTERFACE define will be true. *)

(* prcset.def is used to conditionally define which header format is used. *)

           (* test.hdr: This is the program's header file. The .hdr files contain
              the compiler-dependent header information prior to the
              implementation block. It is intended to include public declarations
              within the interface block. *)

PROGRAM Test;

           (* test.dcl: There could be some procedures in the main source file,
              other than the program declaration, that have to be forward
              referenced. This file, test.dcl, takes care of that for the
              matching .src file. *)

(* prcrst.def resets the header type constants. *)

{**** The Main Program for Test ****}

const
     { The global constant declarations are brought in here. }
type
     { The global type declarations are yanked in here. }
var

     nits,
     picks: integer; { The global variables are declared here. }

     (* test.mid contains the forward and external file includes. *)
     (* Extern declarations are used when using modules instead of units. *)

     (* test.fwd: all test's forward declares are made via this file. *)

     (* nonse.dcl: This is for extracting an appropriate procedure header. *)

     (* test.sfl: used for including all the bodies of procedures and
        functions when they have to be compiled in the same file as the
        main program, Test. *)
```

```
        (* prcset.def is used to conditionally define which header format is used. *)


            (* this is nonse.hdr, used by nonse.src to decide which include files
                that contain the public or global interface and declarations
                section of a file. *)


            (* nonse.dcl: This is for extracting an appropriate procedure header. *)

procedure nonsense(a,b,c,d,e,f: integer); { inline, normal }

(* prcrst.def resets the header type constants. *)


begin
        { The procedure nonsense code goes here. }
end;


(* The trailer.def file provides the appropriate termination for each
    section. *)

{ Turbo Pascal has no Module ends except at the end. }

        (* what.src: This contains the body of procedure whatthis. *)

(* prcset.def is used to conditionally define which header format is used. *)

        (* what.hdr: This is for yanking in the appropriate top part of a file.*)

procedure whatthis(a,b,c,d,e,f: integer);

(* prcrst.def resets the header type constants. *)


begin
        { The procedure whatthis code goes here. }
end;


(* The trailer.def file provides the appropriate termination for each
    section. *)
```

```
{ Turbo Pascal has no Module ends except at the end. }

begin
     { The program test code follows. }
     whatthis(1,2,3,4,5);
     nonsense(6,7,8,9,10);
     writeln('That''s all she wrote.');
end.
```

MS Pascal Version

```
(* A very simple, three-procedure Pascal test case. *)

     (* This is lingo.def, where the compiler dialect is selected
        and the global definitions are pulled in. The constants should
        be defined only once per constructed source file. Consequently,
        if this message appears more than once, something is w0rng...   *)

     (* This is the global.def file, where the partition strategy for the
        dielect of Pascal is stated. If the compiler is to use an
        INTERFACE section, the PINTERFACE define will be true. *)


(* prcset.def is used to conditionally define which header format is used. *)


     (* test.hdr: the program's header file. The .hdr files contain any
        of the compiler-dependent header information prior to the
        implementation block. It is intended to include public declarations
        within the interface block. *)

     (* test.int contains the interfaces that are required for test.int to be
        properly compiled and linked, and that aren't part of the application
        source code.      *)
```

```
        INTERFACE;                          (* Microsoftese UnitSpeak *)

           Unit paslibw (
              {$include:'stdincl.inc'}
           );
           {$include:'windows.inc'}
        END;


        (* nonse.int contains the INTERFACE declarations for nonse.src. *)


        INTERFACE;
              UNIT Nonse(
                    Nonsense
              );
                    procedure Nonsense(a,b,c,d: integer);
        END;


        INTERFACE;
              UNIT What(
                    whatthis
              );
              procedure whatthis(a,b,c,d: integer);
        END;


        MODULE test[];                      (* MODULE rather than PROGRAM for Windows *)

        (* test.use: The list of used routines for test.src is inserted here. *)
        (* This file isnt referenced if the compiler doesnt have USES. *)


           { Insert Microsoft's standard USES syntax here. }
           USES paslibw (
              {$include:'stdincl.inc'}
           ),
            Nonse(Nonsense),
            what(whatthis);
```

```
(* test.pub: Public types and routine declarations for test.src. *)
(* -- there arent any. *)
(* test.dcl: There could be some procedures in the main source file,
    other than the program declaration, that have to be forward
    referenced. This file, test.dcl, takes care of that for the
    matching .src file. *)


(* prcrst.def resets the header type constants. *)

{**** The Main Program for Test ****}

const
    { The global constant declarations are brought in here. }
type
    { The global type declarations are yanked in here. }
var
    nits,
    picks: integer; { The global variables are declared here. }

    (* test.mid contains the forward and external file includes. *)
    (* Extern declarations are used when using modules instead of units. *)


      (* Microsoft isnt doing forward refs or externs in this example. *)


begin
    { The program test code follows }
    whatthis(1,2,3,4,5);
    nonsense(6,7,8,9,10);
    writeln('That''s all she wrote.');
end.
```

Lisa Pascal Version

```
(* A very simple, three-procedure Pascal test case. *)

    (* This is lingo.def, where the compiler dialect is selected
       and the global definitions are pulled in. The constants should
       be defined only once per constructed source file. Consequently,
       if this message appears more than once, something is w0rng...   *)

    (* This is the global.def file, where the partition strategy for the
       dielect of Pascal is stated. If the compiler is to use an
       INTERFACE section, the PINTERFACE define will be true.  *)

(* prcset.def is used to conditionally define which header format is used. *)



    (* test.hdr: This is the program's header file. The .hdr files contain
       the compiler-dependent header information prior to the
       implementation block. It is intended to include public declarations
       within the interface block. *)



      { The regular or special preamble is stuck in here for the
        main program source file. }

PROGRAM test;

      { The header.def file is not included here, this is the main file. }

(* test.use: The list of used routines for test.src is inserted here. *)
(* This file isnt referenced if the compiler doesnt have USES. *)

      {$L-}  { Turn off listing option for used files. }
      USES                      {$U-}
            {$U nonse } nonsense,
            {$U what  } whatthis;

      {$L+}  { Kick the listing option back on. }
```

```
(* test.pub: Public types and routine declarations for test.src.*)
(* -- there arent any. *)


    { No implementation statement for the main program source file
        needed for Lisa/Macintosh. }


(* prcrst.def resets the header type constants *)


{**** The Main Program for Test ****}


const
    { The global constant declarations are brought in here. }
type
    { The global type declarations are yanked in here. }
var
    nits,
    picks: integer; { The global variables are declared here. }


    (* test.mid contains the forward and external file includes. *)
    (* Extern declarations are used when using modules instead of units. *)


    (* Lisa doesnt do forward references or externs in this example. *)


begin
    { The program test code follows. }
    whatthis(1,2,3,4,5);
    nonsense(6,7,8,9,10);
    writeln('Thats all she wrote.');
end.
```

Pascal/MT+ Version

```
(* A very simple, three-procedure Pascal test case. *)

    (* This is lingo.def, where the compiler dialect is selected
        and the global definitions are pulled in. The constants should
```

```
                          be defined only once per constructed source file. Consequently,
                          If this message appears more than once, something is w0rng...   *)


              (* This is the global.def file, where the partition strategy for the
                 dielect of Pascal is stated. If the compiler is to use an
                 INTERFACE section, the PINTERFACE define will be true. *)



(* prcset.def is used to conditionally define which header format is used. *)



              (* test.hdr: This is the program's header file. The .hdr files contain
                 the compiler-dependent header information prior to the
                 implementation block. It is intended to include public declarations
                 within the interface block. *)


              (* test.dcl: There could be some procedures in the main source file,
                    other than the program declaration, that have to be forward
                       referenced. This file, test.dcl, takes care of that for the
                       matching .src file. *)


(* prcrst.def resets the header type constants. *)

{**** The Main Program for Test ****}

const
      { The global constant declarations are brought in here. }
type
      { The global type declarations are yanked in here. }
var
      nits,
      picks: integer; { The global variables are declared here. }


              (* test.mid contains the forward and external file includes. *)
              (* Extern declarations are used when using modules instead of units. *)


              (* test.ext: External routines are listed here, if any. Do not
                 include this file unless you WANT procedure declarations
```

```
     with externs on them. *)


external procedure whatthis(a,b,c,d,e: integer);
external procedure nonsense(a,b,c,d,e: integer);


begin
    { The program test code follows. }
    whatthis(1,2,3,4,5);
    nonsense(6,7,8,9,10);
    writeln('Thats all she wrote.');
end.
```

2.4 Coding Hints

This section contains coding suggestions for the focus languages, Pascal and C. Basic, C++, Forth, fourth-generation database languages, Cobol, and Modula 2 are not really covered, despite their utility and present or future popularity.

The coding hints described here are concerned with the "minor arcana" of language, such as naming conventions, use of datatypes, and construction of routines. The "major arcana," such as modules, programs, units, construction of files, and data/memory management, are covered elsewhere.

Although only a few compiler systems were examined for the C and Pascal minor arcana, I feel that the material presented here will give you a good idea of what to watch out for. Compiler systems are well-maintained products, so the old irritating limits are continually being replaced by new and different ones. The best micro-based compilers that are available today make the best ones available 2 years ago look just terrible!

I prefer to use a language that doesn't require different syntax for different compilers, if I know ahead of time that I will have to port the product; a program that needs no changes when it is moved from one system to another makes a programmer happier. Such a language system has to be able to handle large project development, allow ways to access the operating environment in a consistent fashion, and gracefully acknowledge differences between working environments.

The number of FORTRAN compilers in use today that support a single language standard make it a trustworthy, if not comfortable, language with which to develop portable code. The language is notoriously hostile toward people trying to flex the standard I/O facilities, and structure manipulation is terrible — two reasons why FORTRAN isn't popular on micros for new product development.

The standardization of C compilers is good, considering the expressive power of the language. Since C is used to write operating systems and system-level programs, applications written in C often involve intimate operations with data components that are normally the domain of the operating system software. The Unix operating system, written almost entirely in C, has been ported to many machines of similar hardware architecture (and to some odd ones). Even though it may be impossible under some conditions to write portable code, it is usually possible to get around the problem with another resource. The standard workaround tool for the C language is the standard C preprocessor, cpp.

The language C++ is better than C for portable applications because of its modern construction and its reduced need for a preprocessor (having a preprocessor phase is slower than not having one). The poor availability of C++ compilers at the time of this writing makes whatever advantages C++ has moot. At this writing some C++ preprocessors for normal C compilers have become available; they may be a short-term solution, but I don't consider them adequate for the long-term.

The existing implementations of the Pascal language provide as rich a working environment as that provided by C. *Standard* Pascal is inappropriate in my opinion for professional portable application development. The urge to rely on language extensions is strong. Of C, Pascal, and FORTRAN, I consider Pascal to be the most ornery in which to write portable code. The Pascal compilers are different from others, and the lack of a standard preprocessor to act as go-between has made it an ordeal to solve the problem with conditional compilation. Pascal, however, seems to be the most popular compiled language.

If you are about to develop a new product, remember the rapidly changing world when making decisions, but weigh your decisions in favor of existing products. Remember, although the C standard is stronger than the current Pascal standard, if only two machines are planned you only need two compilers. More languages qualify.

THE PASCAL MINOR ARCANA

Naming Conventions

Pascal is a case-insensitive language. The lowercase form of a letter is interchangeable with the uppercase form in any identifier (i.e., FRED = fred). It is possible to use both lowercase and uppercase letters in Pascal source. Some Pascal systems have built-in editors that force reserved keywords to be uppercase, but this shouldn't affect the interpretation of the keyword. Variable, function, procedure, constant, and type names allow numbers, characters, and some nonalphanumeric characters to be part of the name, such as the underscore.

The trend for naming conventions appears to be heading toward using capitals for clarity, such as

```
ThisOldMan
IDnumber
```

rather than using the underscore for the same purpose, as in

```
this_old_man
id_number
```

The present form of the Modula 2 definition excludes the use of the underscore in identifiers, though some Modula 2 compilers provide a switch to allow it. Digital Research's Pascal/MT+ compiler eliminates the underscore from significance, so that the name

```
ID_number
```

is the same as

```
IDnumber
```

Lengths of Names

The length of the significant portion of a name is unpredictable, though most compilers permit names in the source to be arbitrarily long, using the first n characters for practical use. The PC Turbo Pascal compiler has no apparent limit for the number of significant digits in a single identifier, although the Turbo Pascal editor has a limit of 127 characters per line of source. Names in Turbo Pascal for the Macintosh are significant to the first 63 characters; characters beyond the first 63 are allowed but not significant. MPW Pascal also allows 63 characters in a name.

An identifier must fit on a single line. Pascal/MT+ allows long identifiers, up to the length of a single line, but truncates them internally to eight characters. Externally declared identifiers are truncated to seven characters. Microsoft Pascal identifiers are significant to a minimum of 19 characters (in some implementations, 31) but must fit on one line; Microsoft Pascal generates a warning message when an identifier is longer than the number of significant characters. Early Lisa Pascal supports long identifiers, the first eight characters being significant. The first 16 characters of TML MacLanguage Series Pascal (v1.0) identifiers are significant; v2.0 of TML allows much longer identifiers.

Normally the real constraint on the length of significant characters in an identifier is not caused by the Pascal compiler, but by the utilities that are used during development, such as linkers and debuggers. A linker phase exists in most compiler systems. Although people seem to avoid using a large number of characters in identifiers, most people prefer to occasionally use more than what is considered a "safe" number of significant characters (six for external identifiers and seven otherwise). Turbo Pascal for the Macintosh doesn't appear to have this problem.

Except for Microsoft Pascal's minor warnings, no compilers complain about long identifiers. Therefore, do not use anything other than letters and numbers in identifiers; underscores appear to be the only portable exception.

Labels

Standard Pascal labels may contain one to four numeric characters, but many compilers have extended the definition for labels to allow alphabetic characters. It is suggested that the use of labels (and gotos) should be so limited that following the standard Pascal convention shouldn't be a problem. TML MacLanguage Series Pascal (v1.0) considers the labels 1 and 0001 to be equivalent, as leading zeros are insignificant. Turbo Pascal for the Macintosh allows a digit sequence or an identifier to be a label, but portable solutions shouldn't use identifiers as labels. Turbo Pascal/ Macintosh also limits the range of gotos to the current block (that is, you can't leap out of procedures).

Modula 2 Considerations

Modula 2 is a case-sensitive language. If you forsee an eventual need to convert Pascal applications into Modula 2, make an effort to have the identifiers defined and used consistently with regard to case-sensitivity. This will reduce the number of undeclared identifier errors encountered during a Modula 2 compilation (unless there is a switch available to allow case-insensitivity, as provided by the Turbo Modula 2 compiler). This author prefers case-insensitivity to case-sensitivity, but when in Rome . . . .

Reserved Words

Never use an identifier that could be used as a reserved word in any compiler. The error messages that arise will usually mislead you. The significant length of identifiers in some compilers may work in conjunction with the reserved word list to drive you up a wall. For example, the variable name

```
IOresultFromDiskAccess
```

is perfectly legal in Turbo Pascal, but Pascal/MT+ will generate an error since all it sees is **IOresult**, which is a predefined identifier.

Archaic Syntactic Differences

Some compilers allow the symbol (. to represent a left square bracket, [, and the symbol .) to represent the right square bracket,], because in the bad old days some keyboards were missing some standard ASCII symbols, such as the square and curly brackets. Curly brackets aren't necessary to Pascal code, but square brackets are used all over the place, so a software workaround was provided. Few machines in use today have this problem with the bracket symbols, so don't use the workaround.

Pascal Constants

Pascal constants are designed to be straightforward, but are inflexible. You may have float, character, string, and other constant identifiers (with optional signs), as well as integer values, but arithmetic operations are no-no's. The following are legal:

```
const  irving  =    12;          (* Years of age. *)

       pi      =    3.14;        (* An imprecise example. *)

       name    =    'Irving';    (* String constant. *)

       Let1    =    'I';         (* Character constant. *)

       BigNo   =    9E12;        (* Obese. *)

       SmNo    =    -8E-12;      (* Slim. *)

       groan   =    -irving;     (* Whatever. *)
```

These are not legal:

```
const Zip  =       irving + 2;
      Fname  =     name + '.DAT';
```

The annoying thing about this is that there are times when several constants are related to one another but aren't going to have the same value. Instead of

```
const key = 35;
      maxindex = key − 1;
      minindex = key − 20;
```

you have to say:

```
const key = 35;
      maxindex = 34;
      minindex = 15;
```

The above example is not sensitive to this constraint, but working with several constants gets very annoying. One of the ways around the standard is to use a preprocessor in which you can define identifiers in terms of arithmetic statements and have the preprocessor replace all occurrences of the identifier in the source file with the final result of the constant value. This approach assumes that your preprocessor is also portable or at least available on every target machine, that you are patient enough to preprocess source files on one machine and compile them on another, *or* that you are cross-compiling your source on a single machine.

MS-Pascal Constants

Microsoft's MS-Pascal supports a number of extensions to constant declarations, including structured datatypes like constant arrays, records, and typed sets. It also supports constant expressions. MS-Pascal allows you to redeclare predeclared constants, like true and false. One thing to watch out for in MS-Pascal (or any other compiler) is the difference between the ranges of real constants and real values; for example, real constants in

MS-Pascal are single-precision only when using the Microsoft standard floating point system.

MS-Pascal also allows constants to be specified in different numbering bases, like base 16 (for example, 16#10AF) for integer, word, or integer4 constants. Use of nondecimal constants is not portable.

Turbo Pascal Typed Constants and Constant Expressions

Turbo Pascal for the IBM PC has an extension called **typed constants**, which consists of variables given initial values. Though typed constants are declared in the constant declaration area, their values can be changed. Use of typed constants is not portable between implementations of Turbo Pascal, since Turbo Pascal for the Macintosh (v1.0) does not have this extension.

TML and Lisa Pascal

The Apple compilers permit constant expressions in place of constants. Early versions of TML Pascal did not, but v2.0 does. Turbo Pascal for the Macintosh, incidentally, does not permit constant expressions.

Recommendations

Only the standard methods for defining Pascal constants should be used for portable code. Do not redeclare predeclared constants. Do not tempt the gods when playing with the limits of the real number systems! Portability problems will surface when working with constants that are based on datatypes unavailable on one of the target machines. If some changes to the code are allowed during porting, make sure that all the target machines implement something close to what is needed before you use the extension.

Constant expressions are *very* useful. If the compilers you are using don't permit constant expressions in place of constants, perhaps you can rely on a preprocessor to evaluate the expressions before running the compiler.

Pascal Types

Base Types

Standard Pascal provides integer, real, boolean, and char (character). Embellished implementations add string (in Microsoft Pascal, called lstring), byte, word, integers with different ranges (8088-based compilers normally provide 2-byte integers, with long integers using 4 bytes), and different reals (4, 6, or 8 bytes each). Also common are BCD numbers for business applications. Pascal/MT+ provides both a BCD routine library and a real number routine library, but you can't use both at the same time. Borland has a version of Turbo Pascal that provides BCD reals.

To get around naming differences between compiler systems of similar base datatypes, you may want to use an include file that defines neutral types in terms of the system-dependent versions of the names. Using these type names rather than the base names will centralize the unique names in a single file, but that file then has to be included in every compilable source.

Sets

The maximum size of a set varies between Pascal compilers. MS-DOS Turbo Pascal, Pascal/MT+, and MS-Pascal allow 256 elements in a set. Lisa Pascal permits 4088 elements in a set, with set operations being very fast when the number of elements is less than 32, which fits nicely in a register. The code speed degrades as the set size increases. There is a special Lisa Pascal note: If the base type is a subrange, the elements must fit in the range 0. .4087. TML Pascal (v1.0) is constraining, as it allows only 32 elements in a set and integer subrange base types have to fit in the range 0. .31. TML Pascal (v2.0) allows a range of 0. .4087. However, Turbo Pascal for the Mac (v1.0) permits only 256 byte-sized elements in a set.

Tangling With Strings

The portability of Pascal programs using the fancy string datatype is not guaranteed. Most of the Pascals use the same kind of string datatype extension. The first (zeroth or [0]) element of a character string array contains the length of the valid character data in the array. Some Pascals permit access of the length value by accessing the index zero element of the array, but some don't; the length value is always available via the length function. Declaration of variables with the string datatype varies. For example, note the following string declaration:

```
var snookems: string[255];
```

With Turbo and Lisa Pascal the static size attribute (for example, "[255]") must be present. With Pascal/MT+, the space allocated for the string is 80 if the size attribute is left off. With TML Pascal, leaving the size attribute off is the same as specifying a static size of 255.

Variable-length strings are declared differently in Microsoft Pascal. The normal Microsoft string type is defined as a super array, specifically a packed array of character. The super array class permits the fancy use of size attributes in both variable declaration and dynamic heap allocation.

However, the result of this powerful extension is that strings are declared and used in a manner different from that in any other Pascal compiler. Variables of the type string are declared as follows:

```
var MicrosoftString: string(10); (* Note the use of parentheses. *)
```

The above declaration makes a string of ten characters. In Microsoft Pascal, variables of type string don't contain data of varying length; the length of the string at declaration time is the length of the contents during execution. This means that assignments and comparisons between string variables of different length *cannot* be made. Microsoft provides the lstring type for more automatic string features, and this is described below.

Note the use of parentheses for the size attribute of a variable's type that is derived from a super array type. If you leave off the size attribute, you avoid defining the length of the array. Leaving off the static size attribute of a declaration ("derived" from a super type) in the var section of a Microsoft Pascal program is illegal, because the var section is used to create new variables, whose length must be known. Leaving off the size attribute of a parameter in a parameter declaration list is another matter; that's how conformant arrays are implemented in Microsoft Pascal, so it is legal. Using super types in parameter lists allows a routine to not know the exact length of a Pascal array. For example:

```
program TheTest;
    type AnyLength: string;
    var victim: string(12);
    .

    .

    .

    procedure test( var a: AnyLength ); { Works on any lstring long enough.}
    begin
        a := 'this works';           {Original must have length>=10 chars.}
    end;


begin
    test(victim);
end.
```

The Microsoft Pascal super array type lstring provides both the static size allocation of the type string and the dynamic content length of the string data found in the string types of other extended Pascal compilers. The lstring type contains a length value at the zeroth element. If the following declaration is made:

```
var google: lstring(20);
```

then the maximum string size that can fit in google is 20 characters, and the actual data length in google is accessible either by google[0], which is of type char, or by google.len, which is of type byte.

String Operators

Turbo Pascal (IBM PC and Macintosh) allows the plus sign operator to be used to concatenate strings. In the following example, a, b, and c are variables declared to be of type string[80]:

```
a := b + c + '.doc'; { This is legal in PC Turbo but not in other
compilers.}
```

'.doc' is considered to be a string constant. The Turbo relational operators all work with strings in comparisons.

Pascal/MT +, Microsoft Pascal, and Lisa Pascal do not permit the plus sign operator to work with strings. The relational operators of these compilers, however, do work.

TML Pascal operators generally work like Lisa Pascal operators. TML Pascal, LightSpeed, and Macintosh-resident Pascal compilers all use the Lisa Pascal and the later MPW Pascal systems as the de facto standards for Pascal on the Macintosh family. Turbo Pascal for the Macintosh (v1.0) does not support constant expressions, an exponent operator, or short-circuit boolean expressions.

String Maximum Lengths

Pascal/MT +, Turbo Pascal, Lisa, Microsoft (**lstring**), and TML Pascal permit a maximum static size of 255 characters for the automatic string datatype. Longer character arrays are possible in all the implementations, with varying limits. Microsoft has a limit of 65,534 bytes per structured type variable. The 68000-based languages tend to have a data structure size limit of 32K bytes; this limit doesn't exist in compilers capable of generating code specifically for the 68020 processor, but using the capability isn't recommended—the code wouldn't work on 68000s.

I suggest that any operation involving automatic strings, like an assignment or relational operation, be embedded in its own system-dependent function or procedure. For example, to add two strings together, invent a procedure called AddString that accepts two strings and returns a third. AddString should be a procedure and not a function because some implementations of Pascal don't permit returning a structured datatype or a string as the value of a function. The ISO standard permits the return of pointers and simple types, but returning fancier types is an extension. Microsoft Pascal has this extension, Lisa Pascal didn't have it but does now (v3.1), MPW Pascal has it, TML Pascal (v1.0) does not have it, and PC/Macintosh Turbo Pascal and Pascal/MT+ permit returning string type variables but nothing else.

Predefined String Functions

The Macintosh compilers covered in this book all have access to the rich routine libraries and ROM calls of the Macintosh. The routines listed here are the kinds usually provided with a Pascal compiler and not with the environment support libraries or ROM routines.

The Pascal/MT+, Turbo, Lisa, and TML Pascal compilers provide the following basic string functions:

length	Returns the length of a given string.
pos	Finds an instance of a substring in a given string.
concat	Returns the concatenation of two or more strings.
copy	Returns a substring of a given number of characters from a given string.
delete	Removes a few characters from a given string.
insert	Inserts a few characters into a given string.

PC Turbo Pascal provides two additional routines:

Str	Converts a real or integer value into a string.
Val	Converts the given string contents into a real or integer number (as specified).

Turbo Pascal for the Mac doesn't have Str and Val. The entire Mac Toolbox and ROM are available, though, and the language does have C-style casting (type coercion).

Microsoft Pascal provides a stranger assortment of routines; they do almost the same things, but some of the names are different (Microsoft development products are usually well-stocked with a large library):

concat	A procedure that concatenates a string to the end of an lstring.
copylst	Copies a string's content to an lstring.
copystr	Copies one string to another string.

delete	Deletes a specified number of characters from a string.
insert	Inserts a string into an lstring at any location.
positn	Starting the search at a given character position, finds the given substring in the specified string.
scaneq	Scans until the given character is found or until the specified number of characters is skipped; this routine can be told to scan backward.
scanne	Scans until the first character that isn't the specified character is encountered; this routine can also be told to scan backward.

There are other Microsoft Pascal routines that operate on strings (at the system level use with caution):

fillc	Fills a region of memory with a specified number of copies of a given character; relative address type version.
fillsc	Fills a region of memory with a specified number of copies of a given character; segment address type version.
movel	Relative address block move.
movesl	Segment address block move.
mover	Relative address block move; like movel but moves characters in reverse order.
movesr	Segment address block move; like movesl but moves characters in reverse order.

Predefined Constants
There are a number of predefined constant values, such as Maxint, that define the highest integer value attainable in a given Pascal implementation, and true and false. Other predefined constants are not portable. This is no big deal; if the constant isn't defined by one compiler system, define it yourself in a system-dependent include file.

Declaration Order in a Program Block
The rules for the order of declarations have been relaxed in some compilers to permit more readable code and additional flexibility when using include files. It isn't just constants, types, variables, and then procedures and functions any more. Items that are related to one another

can reside in the same location in a file now, and there can be more than one declaration block of the same kind:

```
.

.

.

type    a = 4;

var     c: integer;

const   j = 4.3;

type    all_things_considered = (equal, not equal);

var     widget: all_things_considered;

function doit( thing: all_things_considered): all_things_considered;

begin ... end;

const kk = 99;

{$I Ops.Src}

.

.

.
```

Pretty Printing and Inline Documentation

Rarely do inline documentation, indentation guidelines, or other presentation concerns effect portability, except insofar as modifications are done faster when the code presentation is consistent and helpful. The curly brackets as comment delimiters are not present in Modula 2, so if you have any interest in an eventual Pascal to Modula 2 conversion, use (* and *) instead of curly brackets. This is not a big deal, since a global search and replace would take care of the problem too. Using a } to end a comment started with (*, or *) to end a comment started with {, are never recommended, though some compilers work that way.

Datatype Conversion

Pascal was designed to hamper ad hoc use of datatypes and unplanned data conversion, which is one reason any kind of Pascal is painful to use for operating system applications. When you are using datatypes that are not exactly right for the task (i.e., declaring a variable as an integer where a subrange or an enumerated type is appropriate), portability problems may occur.

For example, the case statement in the ISO Pascal standard does not have an else or otherwise clause (the equivalent of the C language switch statement's default clause), and therefore technically all the possible values of the case index expression have to be itemized. Using an integer variable as the case index provides your software an excuse for runtime errors that abruptly halt execution, because most compilers can't handle more than 255 separate case values. If PC Turbo Pascal encounters a case index value not mentioned in the list of case values, it looks the other way and proceeds without a runtime error, acting as though a blank else clause were present in the case statement.

```
(* If x = 4 when this procedure runs, the program may stop with
   a runtime error. *)


procedure EnormousCaseIndex( x: integer);
begin

     case x of    (* =x= is the case index. *)
           1:;
           2:;
           3:;
     end;
end;
```

The consequence of the IBM/Macintosh Turbo Pascal feature is that, to fully debug software, there should always be an else clause for a case statement. This else clause needs to be provided with a runtime error/debug message stating where it is and what happened. Otherwise you'll never know that weird values are coursing through your case statements.

Appropriately typing a variable as a subrange or enumerated type makes a louder statement, but restricts the freedom of that variable's use. Data conversion from an enumerated type variable to an integer variable is easy; going the other way is usually not as straightforward, requiring a conversion routine. Since a popular conversion is to make a text representation of a value and convert text to an ordinal or real value, most implementors don't bother with enumerated types when conversion is expected. They have been using the vanilla, inexplicit integer type, and the provided text conversion routines (write, read, writeln, and readln).

This is especially true when the compiler system does not generate very fast code for case statements; case statements with a long list of cases are potential performance bottlenecks. Case statements are an obvious method of converting integer values to enumerated values. A way to avoid the slowness of legal data conversion is discussed in the next section on allocation.

Pascal/MT+, like Turbo Pascal, does not stop with a runtime error when a case label fails to match the value of the case index when an else clause is not specified. Pascal/MT + also uses the keyword else to indicate the default part of the case statement.

Microsoft Pascal uses the keyword otherwise for its else clause. Microsoft Pascal provides code that generates a runtime error if the case index value is not mentioned in the list, and no otherwise clause is specified, if range checking is turned on. Microsoft Pascal attempts to generate very fast code for case statements with a long list of cases (it generates a jump table). If the range checking is turned off there is no otherwise clause, and the case statement is confronted with an unaccommodated-for index value, then the code may try to index to a nonexistent entry in the jump table and execute arbitrary bytes anywhere in RAM.

Microsoft Pascal and Turbo Pascal for the Mac "cheat" by providing an extension for C-like casting. TML Pascal case statements work like Turbo and MT +, except that they use the keyword otherwise for the else clause, according to the Apple Macintosh family standard presented by Lisa Pascal (v3.1,3.9).

For portable code avoid using variables that use primitive datatypes, like integer or char, as case indices. This should keep the number of case values to something that can be handled without resorting to the else/otherwise clause. Since most people (including me) will use the else clause in a case statement despite this strong recommendation, a change utility program should be handy when moving the source suite from machine to machine. Change searches for all occurrences of a specified string in an entire directory of files and converts them to a different string, so all occurrences of "otherwise" could be switched with one command to the string "else." It should be mentioned that going the other way and changing all "else" strings to "otherwise" is not a good idea; it is left as an exercise for the reader to figure out why.

Storage, Stack Allocation, and Pointers
It is unsafe to assume that in the example:

```
var a, b, c: integer;
```

when the variables a, b, and c are allocated space in memory (either on the program stack or elsewhere) they are assigned contiguous memory locations. It is also not safe, though finding out is easy enough, to assume that any two Pascal compilers allocate storage in exactly the same way. Pascal programmers are by definition not allowed to know the order in which space is allocated for structured types like records. Members of a structured type may be stored pretty close together; so much for idealism.

There are times when knowledge of storage allocation may be imperative. Two different compilers on the same machine with interchangeable linkable object files must allocate storage at least in agreement, if not exactly the same way.

The common example of using the intimate knowledge of storage allocation is the use of a variant record for datatype conversion. For example, on the IBM PC a Pascal pointer into a heap usually requires 32 bits, 16 for the Intel 8086 offset register and 16 for the segment register. Normally Pascal pointers are used to follow linked lists, and not to traverse arrays or reference absolute memory locations (this is a standard diet for the less-controlled C pointer). The mechanisms provided by ISO standard Pascal do not allow easy access to the pointer datatype for arbitrary assignment, so there is no legal way to set the value of a pointer except by using the intrinsic function new, a pointer component of a record in a linked list, or another pointer. A pointer can be assigned an arbitrary value by using the following variant record:

```
var cheat = record
        case integer of         (* ISO std. says integer here is no-no. *)
                1: ( segval, offsetval: integer);
                2: ( mempointer: ^char);
        end
end;
```

Using this beast as a means to poke into memory as follows:

```
cheat.segval := 20;
cheat.offsetval := 30;
cheat.mempointer^ := 'a';
```

The first two lines set the address in memory pointed to by the pointer. The third line treats the two integer variables as a full-powered pointer, assigning a character value to the RAM location indicated by the character pointer.

There can be no runtime or compile-time error checking for this end-around the tight type checking of Pascal compilers, so the above syntax is "portable," but some machines may disagree with it. The code above assumes that a pointer for a given machine is 32 bits wide. Pointers on smaller machines (i.e., 8080-based systems) are 16 bits wide. Since the 68000 only uses 24 bits for physical addresses, the compiler system may not provide a 32-bit pointer. Both the byte storage order and the word storage order may vary between processors. Fortunately, even if the storage order is different, each machine has consistency; though processors will use the code differently, the results may be consistent.

Pointer Expressions

The safest Pascal code uses pointers in the following ways. In assignment statements, pointers are used without unique compiler-dependent operators, like Lisa Pascal's @ operator. Pointers may also be passed as parameters, by value or by reference. The address to which they point may be passed as a parameter (when dereferenced with the ^ character) or can be used in a regular assignment statement. In conditional tests the only portable operation is equality, = (or inequality, < >). What passes for a NIL or UNDEFINED value should be assumed to vary from machine to machine; NIL is usually 0, whereas UNDEFINED is usually what happened to be at a given memory location when it became a pointer variable. Some operating systems, like Unix, take steps to fill the entire data region with zeros before the program begins execution, which means that early on an UNDEFINED pointer is going to have the value 0 — but don't bet on it, check for it first.

PC Turbo Pascal Pointers

PC Turbo Pascal pointers are made of a 16-bit segment address, stored as the 2 most significant bytes, and a 16-bit offset address, stored as the 2 least significant bytes. Each 16-bit component is stored with the least significant byte first and the most significant byte following. A cross-section of memory would look like Figure 2–16.

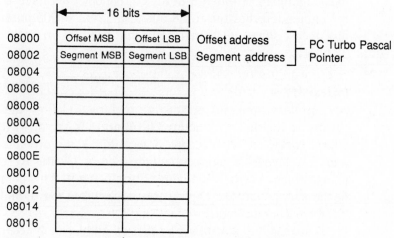

Figure 2–16 Full PC Turbo Pascal pointer in memory

Most compilers provide alternate methods of obtaining the address of a data component or setting the address value of a pointer. MS-DOS Turbo provides the following functions that work with variables and routines as x:

ofs(x)	Returns the 16-bit offset component of the address of x.
seg(x)	Returns the 16-bit segment component of the address of x.
addr(x)	Returns a 32-bit address of x.
cseg	Returns the code segment address.
dseg	Returns the data segment address.
sseg	Returns the stack segment address.

Turbo Pascal/Macintosh Address of Operator

Turbo Pascal for the Macintosh also uses the @ symbol as the "address of" operator. Though the language system doesn't itself provide anything that uses this information, the Mac ROM environment does.

TML Pascal Pointers

TML Systems MacLanguage Series Pascal, like all of the Macintosh Pascal compilers (Lisa, LightSpeed, MPW), uses a 32-bit pointer. The Lisa compiler uses the @ operator, which provides the same service as the C language "&" operator; it gets the absolute address of the following variable or routine in memory. On 68000s the address is 32 bits, but the most significant 8 bits are not used; 68000s only have a 24-bit address. I recommended that the top 8 bits of a 32-bit 68000 pointer be left alone, just in case someone wants to run that product on a 68020, which uses all 32 bits.

Pascal/MT+

A compiler command option is provided to allow the @ character to substitute for the ˆ character. This feature is at odds with the Macintosh Pascal compilers; at this time, Pascal/MT+ maintenance and marketing may not have been aggressively pursued by Digital Research, Inc., and I know of very few development efforts using it. This compiler is included in the survey because Digital Research wrote Gem, and it is possible to write small Gem applications using Pascal/MT+.

Pascal/MT+ provides the function **addr**, which accepts the name of a variable or function and returns a pointer value to it.

Microsoft MS-Pascal Pointers

MS-Pascal provides 16- and 32-bit address types used for arbitrary operations directly with machine addresses; the MS-Pascal manual states that "the pointer type is only applicable to variables in the heap." Using the 16-bit variety leads to faster processing and fewer memory needs, but restricts operations to the singular default 8086 data segment. Making a 16-bit relative address variable requires the use of the phrase **adr of** before the type; a 32-bit segment address variable needs the phrase **ads of**.

```
var    ANumber:      integer;
       PtrToNumber:  adr of integer;
       AnotherPtr:   ads of integer;


begin
       PtrToNumber   := adr ANumber;
       AnotherPtr    := ads ANumber;
       AnotherPtr^   := 5;
       PtrToNumber^  := PtrToNumber^ + 1;
       ShowValue(AnotherPtr^);
end;
```

The value 6 would be displayed by the routine ShowValue.

The difference between adr and ads is that adr (on an 8086) assumes use of the default data segment, whereas using ads means "go far" for the address of the segment as well as the offset into the segment.

MS-Pascal Pointer Types

MS-Pascal allows the use of the character ? to act as a substitute for the character ^.

MS-Pascal provides both **new** and **dispose**, and **mark** and **release**. Except that the MS-Pascal names are **markas** and **releas**.

MS-Pascal Data Allocation (Extended new and dispose)

Normally MS-Pascal puts every kind of data element within the default data segment, providing a puny maximum of 64K bytes. Regardless of what extended tricks are employed to escape the 64K limit, file variables must be placed in the default data segment. To create and use long linked lists (for example, those that may extend beyond 64K bytes), it is necessary to use the MS-Pascal segmented address type and not use the standard functions new and dispose. The following functions are provided for that purpose:

allmqq	Allocates segmented memory blocks (of bytes).
fremqq	Frees a block (does not have error handling).
getmqq	Calls allmqq and checks for error returns.
dismqq	Calls and checks for error returns.

A check after the call is needed to see if enough memory is being provided.

MS-Pascal provides a number of additional routines for mundane system and application level chores. The following were selected because they provide services similar to the routines listed above for MS-DOS Turbo Pascal:

hibyte

hiword

lobyte

loword

Conclusions

The MS-Pascal solution to extending Pascal to accommodate system program development is very thorough, but is inconsistent with respect to other Pascal compiler systems. If Pascal is the language of choice for a development effort and the MS-DOS version of Microsoft Windows is to be used as the windowing/graphics environment for the IBM PC/AT version of the program, then all operations that allocate and deallocate space in segmented data regions must be placed in system-dependent source files, or a preprocessor must provide syntactic changes. Declarations of pointers for use with areas outside the default data segment require the use of either adr of or ads of, which make parts of the variable and type declaration blocks system-dependent. This can be handled with system-dependent include files or preprocessors, but I am loathe to recommend system-dependent files for isolating this dependency; the use of pointers can be so extensive that program source code could become *entirely* system-dependent! However this concern is treated, it will be a very influential factor, and ought not be left until after the port of a working program is started.

Pointer Validity

Because the support environments are becoming dominant, algorithms involving pointers have additional things to watch out for. Since programs can be subdivided into resources which can be brought in from disk independent of other parts of a program, it is now possible for a resource to be overwritten during program execution. A pointer aimed at something in a resource that has been swapped for another resource is no longer valid. A common mistake among Macintosh programmers is to assume that a pointer, or a pointer to a table of pointers, is still valid over a period of computing time involving system calls. In the new environments quite a bit of system data is kept in a heap region. You have to keep "asking the bank" what your balance is, because keeping your receipts isn't good enough.

ABSOLUTE Addresses (for Variable Instantiation)

This is an extension that is not at all portable between any of the compiler systems. When associating an absolute address with a declared variable or function, we want to have that block of code or data item bound to a specified beginning address in memory. Pascal/MT+ requires the attribute keyword ABSOLUTE followed by a full address within square brackets in a declaration:

```
var x: absolute[$4000:$1000] char;
```

The character $ indicates a hexidecimal value and the colon separates the segment address from the offset address for the MS-DOS and CP/M-86 versions of Pascal/MT+. Variable x is thus placed at the address 4000:1000 (base 16).

Microsoft MS-Pascal provides the ORIGIN attribute, which does the same thing as Pascal/MT+'s ABSOLUTE. The use is slightly different:

```
var x [origin 16#0001: 16#4000]: char;
```

Note that the keyword is within the square brackets. Also note the different notation for hexidecimal values.

In Lisa Pascal assigning an absolute address is done at runtime using pointers. It is possible to do so in Pascal/MT+, although the portability is then subject to the extensions provided for assigning arbitrary addresses to Pascal pointers (listed in this chapter). It is understood that absolute address requirements change between hardware bases, yet there may be a need to know or work with absolute addresses on two entirely different machines.

Control Flow

Some Pascal compilers have extensions that emulate the C language flow control statements break and continue. Microsoft Pascal has break, cycle (the same as C's continue), and return; both keywords break and cycle may be followed by a label. Modula 2 has a return statement much like the C return, but the capabilities provided by the other keywords aren't a common extension. Lisa Pascal has similar extensions (cycle and leave), but Mac Turbo Pascal does not.

Redeclaration of Identifiers in One Scope
Some compilers allow you to declare something as a type and then declare it as a variable in the same scope, but this is not a portable practice.

Interrupt Routines and Events
Events and interrupts are discussed elsewhere in this text; this section provides insight on some extensions to Pascal for interrupt and event handling. Programs written using the libraries provided by systems like Gem, Macintosh, and Windows must recognize a number of different events, but usually the support library has prior knowledge of most or all of them. The standard has been to write programs to voluntarily poll or check whether an event has occurred at appropriate times. For example, a program may say:

```
if HasEventHappened then          { returns TRUE if event occurred}
    ServiceEvent( GetEventRecord ); { process the event }
```

The only way for an application program to know that something happened (aside from a power failure or someone slapping the reset button) is to ask.

Underneath the layer of support routines that volunteer event information are procedures that start executing when something else causes an interrupt. Normally there's a single procedure that handles the processing to be done for an interrupt. Such procedures do things like take a single character and stick it in a circular buffer, set a flag to true, and then return. Interrupt procedures are rarely called by application software routines or even other system-level routines.

Pascal does not need extensions to deal with events, but the language has been stretched to embrace interrupt handlers and (for quick development but slow performance) device drivers.

An interrupt routine is never called by another routine in the application code. When the interrupt routine executes, it saves the current program status (which is not its own) on the stack, and then processes the interrupt. When finished, the program status and control are restored to what they were before the interrupt procedure was run.

An early compiler, Pascal/MT+, provides the attribute keyword IN-TERRUPT to associate with the declaration of a procedure when that procedure is to execute when a specified interrupt occurs. For an example, see Figure 2–17.

```
Program QuickInterruptDemo;                { Demo Pascal/MT+ Interrupt Proc Syntax}

CONST
      Device1 = $23;                       { The device uses interrupt #23 }
TYPE
      Ptr = ^Integer;                      { We are using MTPLUS Addr Function }
VAR
      DeviceProd:  Boolean;                { Convert event to polled variable }
      DevVector:   ABSOLUTE[0:$8C] PTR;{ Locate the Interrupt Vector in RAM }

      PROCEDURE INTERRUPT [Device1] Watch1;   { When int #23 occurs, do this }
      BEGIN
            DeviceProd := TRUE             { May be set once per thousand hours }
      END;

      PROCEDURE Grind; External;           { Do whatever is required in here }

BEGIN
      DevVector := Addr(Watch1);           { Have Int. Vector point to proc Watch1}
      DeviceProd := FALSE;                 { Initialize our polled var }
      repeat
            Grind;                         { Grind until interrupt occurs }
      until DeviceProd                     { Then exit gracefully }
END.
```

Figure 2–17 Example DRI Pascal/MT+ Interrupt Procedure for an 8086-based System

MS-Pascal provides the same attribute for its interrupt procedures, but the association made between an interrupt procedure and its interrupt is achieved by using an MS-Pascal library procedure, vectin, in the application program, rather than when the program is loaded at the beginning of runtime. For an MS-Pascal example, see Figure 2–18.

Pascal/MT+ provides nothing equivalent to the function vectin, so the associations must be made explicitly. The addresses of the interrupt procedures are assigned to pointer variables (for example) that have been declared using the absolute attribute to be at the interrupt vector address-es. MS-Pascal provides enabin and disbin to enable and disable interrupts; the Pascal/MT+ manual suggests the use of inline code to insert 8086 CLI and STI instructions to enable and disable interrupts.

Two Flavors Of The Keyword inline

Lisa Pascal, TML Pascal, et al., allow the definition of an inline procedure:

```
procedure LeATrap; inline 2;
```

```
Program OtherInterruptDemo;              { Demo MS Pascal Interrupt Procedure}
CONST
    Device1 = $23;                       { The device uses interrupt #23 }
VAR
    DeviceProd:  Boolean;                { Convert event to polled variable }

    PROCEDURE Watch1 [INTERRUPT];        { When int #23 occurs, do this }
    BEGIN
         DeviceProd := TRUE              { May be set once per thousand hours }
    END;

    PROCEDURE Grind; External;           { Do whatever is required in here }

          { Vectin associates an interrupt vector with a procedure }

    PROCEDURE Vectin( vector: WORD; intProc: PROCEDURE); EXTERN;

BEGIN
    DeviceProd := FALSE;                 { Initialize our polled var }
    Vectin( Device1, Watch1 );           { Set up the appropriate int. vector }
    repeat
         Grind;                          { Grind until interrupt occurs }
    until DeviceProd                     { Then exit gracefully }
END.
```

Figure 2–18 Example Microsoft Pascal Interrupt Procedure for an 8086-based System

The inline keyword indicates that an A trap, one of the 68000's 1010 (hexidecimal) traps, is to be executed directly. The unsigned integer following the keyword inline is the trap that is to be executed. This is a no-fooling-around method to make direct Macintosh ROM calls.

There are differences between the TML Pascal inline procedure and the MS-Pascal and Pascal/MT + interrupt procedure. On the Macintosh the interrupt (trap) procedure is assumed to be present and needed; with MS-Pascal or Pascal/MT+ the interrupt procedure *is* a trap routine that you can write.

The keyword inline is used in other compilers, like Pascal/MT+, to indicate that the code following is not Pascal code, but rather assembler or raw decimal or hexidecimal values that are to be placed in the executable program file exactly as they are stated. For example, in MT+:

```
writeln('hi there');    { display the string "hi there"}
inline('hi there');     {stick characters in the execution stream??}
writeln('hi there');    { display the string "hi there"}
```

The inline command creates a group of characters that are placed, not on the stack or in a data segment, but directly in the code segment before the second writeln. In this case the program and machine will probably execute the machine instruction formed by the hex values of the first two to four characters in "hi there." Most programmers use the inline (in this context) to define known assembly code or machine instructions if it is intended that the program try to execute the sequence. The above example may result in the program crashing. Inline can be used to define readable copyright messages in the midst of a human-unreadable executable file; just stick the inline statement in a procedure that is never called.

Use of inline in any case is highly system-dependent, which means that it should not be used in system-independent modules. The syntax and use of inline are likely to be different in each implementation of extended Pascal.

Conformant Arrays and Functions as Parameters

Two features that have historically been left out of early versions of so-called ISO-compatible Pascal compilers are conformant arrays and the passing of procedures and functions as parameters. A conformant array declaration is used when you want to avoid specifying the range of elements in a given dimension of an array parameter of a routine. This permits separate calls to the same routine to have arrays of different sizes as parameters. It can also be useful to pass a procedure or function as a formal parameter so that a routine may execute the passed procedure or function at its leisure, though I know few Pascal programmers who would avoid buying a compiler because it was missing the latter feature. Conformant arrays have proven to be very useful when building libraries of Pascal routines, so it is recommended that conformant arrays be present in any legitimate implementation.

Turbo Pascal for the Mac (v1.0) and IBM PC (v3.0) do not permit procedure and function arguments.

MS-Pascal supports conformant arrays by way of its unstandard but internally consistent industrial-strength supertypes. Any use of conformant arrays will have to be changed slightly to conform to the MS-Pascal compiler. For the record, conformant arrays are not part of the level 0 definition of the ISO standard (they're part of level 1).

Get And Put

Borland leaves get and put out of their Pascal compilers, including the extensive Macintosh version, even though the other Mac compilers have them. Using get and put, however, is not recommended on the Macintosh when doing anything "fancy" for speed and efficiency.

THE C MINOR ARCANA

C is the preferred language for work in hostile or cranky environments, and is used with Gem, Amiga, Windows, and of course Unix. An awful lot of personal computer software products are written in C. We will now look at some of the dos and don'ts of writing C programs that are portable across many different systems and compilers.

Overview

C is, by experience, a portable programming language, but portability between different systems and compilers requires a more disciplined coding style than most C programmers are used to. Since most programmers are not in the habit of testing their code on several machines at once, the code is designed, debugged, and tested without the added perspective of the results from the other machines.

Well-written C code is as readable and maintainable as excellent Pascal code. It is considerably easier to write bad C code than it is to write bad Pascal code, yet bad C code can still be moved from machine to machine whereas some good Pascal code may not be. Historically much more C software than Pascal software has been written and ported. Much of that C code was badly written, but the systems were still movable, sometimes needing only some tweaks to the preprocessor commands. Though it doesn't help that the definition of the C language left some features up for interpretation until the recent efforts by ANSI, IEEE, and of course AT&T, this hasn't stopped many people.

C Compiler Documentation

The documentation for C compilers has been poor, making it difficult to provide a feature-by-feature comparison of each available system. Figuring out the differences due to bugs is like asking that a full validation suite be run on all the candidate compiler systems. Since the list of existing bugs changes from version to version, the timeliness of a catalog of them is not going to be very good. An excellent (but brief and expensive) summary of C language gotchas, using some older compilers as references, is *C Programming Guidelines* by Thomas Plum.

The Macintosh Programmer's Workbench (MPW) C compiler comes with a good manual, as do the Microsoft compilers, although Microsoft manuals are a little cryptic and the languages are peppered with extra "features."

You'll Poke Your Eye Out

Once again here is a most important point: the way to insure that the C programs you write are portable is to design them that way. This means you should write your application using functions that isolate system dependencies (be they the windowing package you are using, the operating system, or the hardware) from the rest of the application. It is much harder to add portability as an afterthought than it is to build it into your programs from the beginning.

C Portability Don'ts

Naked Type Usage

A standard C compiler has a rich set of base datatypes, most of which are variations on a theme: integer, very short integer, short integer, long integer, or unsigned integer. Unsigned long integer is also common. These integer types differ as to how many bits are used to represent them.

Even between compilers on the same hardware, the length of types such as int and unsigned will vary. Some large model 8088 C compilers define the int datatype as a 16-bit entity, while others define it as a 32–bit entity. Assuming an int will always be a specific width is really asking for trouble when you move to a C compiler on a different system. Kernighan and Ritchie's landmark *The C Programming Language* (known as K & R) states that " ... int will normally reflect the most "natural" size for a particular machine." This of course means that it could be *anything*. K & R also states that " ... short and long should provide different lengths of integers where practical." Consequently, using the base datatypes for operating system parameters may require changes throughout the code to change the sizes of the variables containing the data. Although the lengths of short and long integers are more stable than the unmodified int type, none have guaranteed lengths.

For data that require a specified large range of values, document in the code how big the range actually has to be. Also, don't use a base datatype directly; use a preprocessor define constant as follows:

```
/* INT4B has to be a 4-byte integer for the range to be wide enough. */
#define INT4B long
INT4B ford_car_count;   /* This tallies yearly production of Ford Cars. */
```

✹ **Don't use "naked" types (char, int, unsigned) to hold operating system objects like handles and ports.**

Sign Extension

While type char usually refers to an 8-bit quantity, some C compilers sign-extend the 8 bits when lengthening is done, while others will fill the high byte of the int with zeros. The lengthening happens, for example, during an assignment to a variable of type int. If you intend to do arithmetic operations with 8-bit variables, be aware that K & R says that sign-extension is machine-dependent.

Hard-Coding Memory Locations and Interrupts

Another practice that makes conversion difficult is "hard-coding" system interrupts or memory locations. Even on the same hardware, these can change between releases of the operating system or windowing environment. It's far better to wrap these dependencies in functions or macros and use those throughout the rest of your application.

✶ **Don't directly call system interrupts or memory locations.**

Using Unproven Compiler Systems

The C compiler you use should at least support the Unix Version 7 standard for the language and library. Anything less *is a toy compiler that will cause big problems*. You must have access to a full working preprocessor and typedefs so you can create your own semantic types and macros.

Many C compilers, while otherwise obeying "the standard," add nonstandard extensions. For example, Microsoft's C compiler offers a * width specifier for formatted I/O functions. While the specifier is convenient to use, it is supported on practically no other compiler. This means you should avoid using this feature if you plan to transport your code; pretend you are writing in Pascal.

The Pascal language is designed to be a quick test, but C is designed to be a small, expressive language; it is tougher to exhaustively examine all the combinations that you just can't do in Pascal. Therefore, many of the C language portability problems are attributable to interpretations of the standard and to bugs.

In the olden days of microcomputing it was very tedious to check out a large product before releasing it. The machines are faster now, at least the ones that have windowing packages running on them. This means that it is now possible to *test* the compiler.

For C compilers two different backbreaking suites are used: one to explicitly exercise operators, syntax, and boundary conditions with respect to the hardware and the other to make sure the new compiler can compile and execute the old production software that has worked in the past. These test suites can be enormous and require a long time to run once, much less the several iterations it takes to get the bugs out. An example of the first suite is the C compiler test suite from Human Computing Resources of Toronto; when shown to me it required 70 megabytes of disk space. The best example of the second suite that I know of is a selection of standard Unix utilities, such as grep, yacc, lex, awk, etc. If your compiler successfully compiles that code, "it's Miller time."

When you buy your compilers for portable applications, you get to grill the technical folk who are responsible for the compiler to find out about their testing procedures. Never trust the advertising in a magazine, and only partially trust good results from other development projects.

One test for the preprocessor of a compiler system, strangely enough, is to determine whether the preprocessor can handle multiline macro definitions. Here is an example of a multiple-line definition:

```
#define A(B,C,D,E) AssignFileType(B,E);    \
CreateFileBlockEntry(B,C,D);    \
OpenFileAttribute(B);
```

✱ **Don't use a nonstandard or minimal C compiler to write production-quality software. Make sure the compiler has been tested.**

K & R Standards versus ANSI Extensions
The ANSI extensions to the C language are not currently supported by all C compilers. While they do bring an extra measure of portability and error checking to your programs, the standard is still in flux and some conversion may be needed later if it changes. A "better" language standard is the Unix Version 7 standard. An exception is the void function type, which can be easily simulated with a typedef and makes your functions more readable. If you can count on the ANSI standard being supported by all the compilers you plan to use, then go ahead.

✱ **Don't use ANSI extensions unless they will be available on all the compilers and systems you plan to use.**

Function Libraries
Your portable programs will certainly use:

□ your own functions
□ the standard libraries
□ services provided by the windowing environment

Many compiler vendors provide additional nonstandard libraries. Although convenient, these can cause big problems when you switch to a new system or compiler. If you must use one of these functions, be prepared to write a C version of the function for inclusion when the program is converted.

Like nonstandard libraries, add-on aftermarket libraries are potential trouble spots. A large number have been released on the IBM PC especially, supporting everything from keyed file retrieval to asynchronous communications, but *none* of these libraries were written to support code *off* the IBM PC! If you must use one of these libraries, it must be available in source code for conversion to another system (somewhat likely) or available on all target systems (highly unlikely).

✴ **Avoid nonstandard or machine-specific library functions, even when source code is available.**

✴ **Don't use aftermarket libraries unless they are available on all target machines.**

Using Pointers as Integers and Vice Versa

One of the C coding glitches I continually run into is accidentally using a pointer as an integer or an integer as a pointer. The symptoms are everything that can go wrong: the entire system bombs, the printf function displays ridiculous values, or entire sections of code apparently don't run at all. It is an easy error to make because pointers are used heavily in any C program, and the difference between a pointer and a value is either the ampersand & or asterisk *. Leaving these two symbols off or using them by accident will often not be detected at compile time.

Sometimes it is convenient to intentionally use a pointer as an integer value (for example, adding two addresses together to obtain a third). Doing this assumes that there is a constant relationship between pointers to data items and the integer datatype. This *may* be true on one machine, but it is an extremely common C language usage error, and certainly isn't portable. Even using longs instead of ints won't always work, because on the IBM PC small-memory model compilers do not lengthen pointers correctly to long. The proper form is to use casts whenever you are performing this type of conversion. Better yet, avoid them where possible with a union.

Unfortunately this problem often shows up after a program has been running successfully in scaled-down form on a small-memory model. Some IBM PC compilers, such as Mark Williams', can be instructed to check for such "puns." Another way to catch these errors is to use the lint program.

✳ **Don't freely interchange pointer and integer references.**

Byte Storage Order

If you use pointers to ints (or int *), you can't always freely use a pointer to a char (or char *) to access the same data. Some machines, like the 8086 family, store integers low-order byte first. Other machines, like the 68000 family, store integers high-order byte first.

✳ **Don't assume byte order.**

Most of the problems discussed above can be avoided by not accessing system objects (buffers, handles, etc.) directly. If it has to be done, try confining the dependency to a single function with a well-defined interface.

Compiler Error Detection

Here's something that varies all over the place: Pascal compilers have very stringent error detection that is executed whenever the compiler is used to generate code. The error detection provided by C compilers is intentionally more relaxed, so that some errors detected by Pascal compilers are not normally flagged by C compilers. However, the Unix utility lint is provided to focus on expressions that have been singled out to be sources of common mistakes and bad practice. Since some compiler systems are not provided with anything like lint, their error detection facilities are sometimes designed to take up some of the slack and generate more warnings or error messages.

The recommendation here is to avoid using features in one compiler that generate error messages in another, even if the code that is generated works. Other developers may be concerned if they have to fix something else only to discover that a flock of modules upsets one of the compilers. Programmers judge the status of someone else's module partly by whether it compiles cleanly; error messages, even warnings, will generate bad vibes.

✳ **Production code should compile cleanly; don't pass the code if it generates error messages when compiled.**

Tame Commentary

The C preprocessor can do strange and unexpected things to code before handing the code to a compiler. For example, C comments are normally removed by the preprocessor before the compiler sees the code; using comment fields for clever compiler commands, a la Pascal, won't work. Also, comments that are on the same line as a #define sometimes become part of the definition. If the inline documentation is particularly verbose, as it can be in files with many #define commands, some preprocessors may not be able to handle all the preprocessor definitions, and the compiler may not either. The comments are not removed because some preprocessors do not back up after an expansion to scan a line for macros; consequently, the comments are left in.

Both the preprocessor and the C compiler have to be able to deal with nested comments. Nested comments are very nice for iterative debugging, but I don't consider it good practice to leave them in production source files.

Some Dos of Software Portability

Length and Composition of External Names

The safe length for externals in portable code is six significant characters. That isn't good, just safe. Most language systems support at least seven characters, but six- or seven-character significance is unsatisfactory for programming in the 1980s.

The MS-DOS linker allows eight characters in an external name, but at present the linker is apparently designed more for use with Pascal than with C; external identifiers are case-insensitive. It is common for linkers to consider the underscore, dollar, and at signs to be valid characters.

Nonexternal name lengths also vary, but the problem is always more acute with external names. I recommend using names that are unique in the first six characters, even though this is surprisingly difficult to do when you have worked with longer descriptive names. If you are certain of the properties of all the target compiler systems, such as eight-character significance, go ahead and expect that number of characters to be significant.

Another way of dealing with the problem is for the master source files to contain longer names which are boiled down to shorter versions by the preprocessor.

✳ **Know the significant length of internal and external names for all the compilers before defining names.**

Identification of System and Functional Dependencies

Across different systems, *anything* can change. Even the lowly system printer may have to be accessed in a variety of ways. This is in contrast to programs that run on only a single operating system, where only functional dependencies exist.

Some candidates for isolation from the rest of your application include:

Screen handling

Printer handling

Memory management

File access

Keyboard access

Communications devices (modems, serial ports)

Any interface to the outside world can change when your program is moved to another system. Clearly identify what this interface must be before writing your application; this can help you isolate the parts that must change from the "functional" part that does the work.

✳ **Identify system dependencies as well as functional ones.**

Semantic Typing

Define and use your own types for variables and functions. Use no basic or primitive types directly. This will allow you to easily convert programs to machines with differing fundamental type sizes by simply changing one include file. The de facto standard is to use the file called **stdtype.h** to contain these semantic type definitions. Here is a sample stdtype.h:

```
/* ------------------------------------------------------- */
/* A collection of standard types for portable C programs.*/
/* From Whitesmiths Inc. Portable C Compiler System       */
/* and T. Plum's Book C Programming Guidelines.           */
/* ------------------------------------------------------- */
#ifndef STDTYP_H
#define STDTYP_H
typedef char tbits, tbool;
typedef int bool;
typedef unsigned sizetype;
```

```
typedef long lbits;
typedef short bits, metachar;
#ifdef USHORT
typedef unsigned short ushort;
#undef USHORT
#else
typedef unsigned ushort; /* This assumes a 16-bit machine. */
#endif
#ifdef TINY
typedef char tiny;
#undef TINY
#define TINY(n) (char)(((n) & (0x80) ? (~0x7f | (n)) : (n))
#endif
#ifdef UTINY
typedef unsigned char utiny;
#undef UTINY
#define UTINY(n) (unsigned char)(n)
#else
typedef char utiny;
#define UTINY(n) (unsigned)((n) & 0xff)
#endif
#ifdef VOID
typedef int void;
#endif
#endif
```

In this header file the symbols VOID, UTINY, TINY, and USHORT are set from the compilation command line if the compiler can handle these types. If not, alternate declarations using other fundamental types are used.

Reasons for Using the Preprocessor

Use the C preprocessor to select code for compilation based on machine type, memory model, and compiler. The idea behind this book is to encourage the development and support of one set of source code files that supports all the machines on which your product must run, rather than separate source files. Separate files encourage variations in the interface as well as content of a module, and therefore should be minimized.

What To Do About Assembler Language

Assembler language is a necessary evil of system-level programming. You should treat assembler language code at a functional level and avoid placing it directly inline. Better yet, maintain separate assembler object modules and link them together with your C code if your systems support a robust macro assembler.

Some compiler systems use glue routines to interface with the environment and special routines, and some compilers effectively provide the glue themselves. For example, special keywords are provided in Microsoft C to indicate that the called routine uses the parameter stack the Pascal way. Some compilers don't have this special keyword and require a small routine to make the necessary adjustments.

✳ **Wrap inline assembler in a function call.**

Which Compiler to Use

Portability is easier to ensure if you can use a single vendor's compilers over a range of target machines. Usually a vendor will supply custom routine libraries for each family as an enticement. Historically, the Whitesmith compilers have gone to great lengths to ensure portability between their various target systems, though they haven't generally been the easiest of compilers to use (I'm writing from experience). Aztec C is another compiler available on a wide range of machines.

Oddly, the compiler developers have not reacted to the needs of the windowing environment market by beefing up their routine libraries with graphics routines that look the same on different machines. I suspect that this will change when windowing environments have a strong presence on the IBM family machines.

✳ **Take a good look at a single vendor's family of compilers.**

The Syntax Police

Lint, while often verbose and difficult to use, can spot many portability problems overlooked or "optimized" away by the compiler. Lint has been reimplemented for the environments of particular interest here (MS-DOS, Macintosh, Amiga, and ST), since it doesn't have to be very interactive. If you plan to do a lot of porting between different systems, definitely consider purchasing an implementation of lint or an equivalent and using it regularly. Lint can dredge up some eye-opening things.

Limits

C compilers are subject to local custom, like any other piece of software. On 68000-based machines there is normally a size limit of 32K bytes for any structure. The C source code looks no different, yet the program with 50K-byte structures will not successfully compile.

On the 8088 and 8086 there are a flock of different ways to link modules together. Usually the compilers can't handle structures larger than a single data segment, which is 64K bytes, and single functions can't be larger than a code segment, which is also 64K bytes.

The 68020 does not have the 32K-byte limit of the 68000, and the 80386 doesn't have to have the 8088 segment size. I expect that people will develop code on the new machines using the older limits to stay compatible. For how long? Programmers will use the older limits for as long as the customers can stand using the old equipment. Look at how many people are still using Apple IIs.

3.1 Introduction to Part 3

Part 3 is the nitty gritty, where we discover what code has already been written for you *four times over*, each time slightly differently. Much of this stuff has actually been done many more than four times; on the IBM PC there are a zillion different libraries that "do windows." Some libraries handle windows and multitasking, some handle menus, and some others handle graphics. Out of this variety the IBM packages Gem and MS Windows were selected. Here are some of the reasons:

- They *provide* (not merely *support*) a graphics environment.
- They provide a set of interactive tools primarily controlled with a mouse.
- They provide a medium where applications can communicate with one another and exchange data.
- They advocate the establishment of a consistent user-interface that is considerably friendlier and more predictable than just a DOS prompt.
- With Resources they provide ways to make special versions of packages (i.e., a Japanese or a German version) in the field without recompilation by editing the compiled executable program.
- They provide a flexible way to accept program stimuli (via events and messages) and to generate graphics.
- They provide working device drivers for a wide variety of popular I/O devices.

The services discussed here are primarily those unique to windowing environments: graphics, events, menus, dialogs, controls, advanced text editing, resources, and scrap buffer management. Many facets of the user-interfaces provided by the Amiga, Gem, Macintosh, and MS Windows are compared to one another. Because of the amount of the material to be covered, less attention is paid to the lower-level services, like memory managers and file I/O.

3.2 | Foundations

These few lower-level nuggets are common to each of the windowing packages, and are discussed first:

Runtime Interfaces	How applications talk to the windowing packages.
Primitive Datatypes	The essential base datatypes that are used as environment function arguments.
Handles and Pointers	A special section focusing on the use of pointers and the differences between handles for each environment.
Miscellaneous	Some comments on the differences between stack-based and register-based function calls, Pascal and C function calls, and extended Pascal and normal C-style strings.

THE RUNTIME INTERFACE

Each windowing package has a set of rules that must be used by application software to communicate with the runtime system. These interfaces are unique, though techniques may be similar. On the 68000, A-line traps (explained below) are a popular way to call ROM-based routines from application code, and the 8088's software interrupts are not wasted by any application support package.

The developers of these environments have been standing on the shoulders of the folks who have made horrible mistakes before them. Though the access methods and the data structures are different, the design philosophies do not fly in many different directions.

A Gem Roadmap

Gem runs on small computers that are based on the Intel 8086 family and Motorola 68000 family of processors. The Atari ST line supports Gem, as can the generic computer with an 8088 and MS-DOS. Figure 3–1 describes the major blocks of code and the normal chain of command on an MS-DOS/PC-DOS machine. Figure 3–2 shows the calling tree on an Atari ST with Gem.

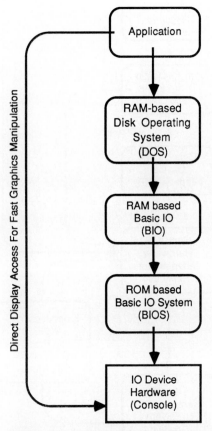

Figure 3–1 MS-DOS Calling Hierarchy

Bare Bones Gem

The interface between Gem and applications is austere. The Gem runtime system talks to application software with a small number of one-dimensional arrays that are provided by the application. Most of the arrays illustrated below contain 16-bit integers; one array contains 32-bit values. The application carefully inserts numbers into prespecified locations in these arrays for each of the Gem-supported functions. The application also has to carefully extract numbers that are returned by Gem.

The following is a Pascal/MT + definition of the arrays used to talk to the two major components of the Gem runtime software, the Gem Virtual

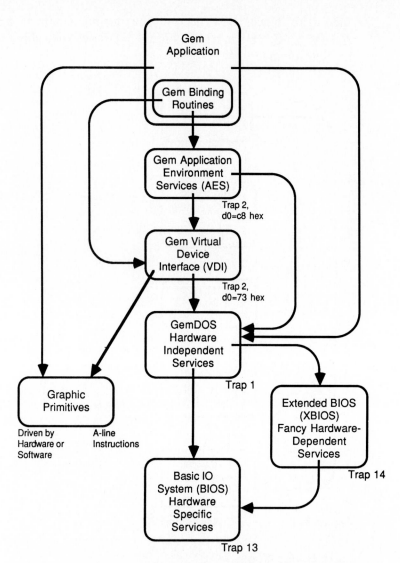

Figure 3–2 Atari ST (Gem) Calling Hierarchy

Device Interface (VDI) and the Gem Advanced Environment Services (AES). An application does not use the same set of arrays to talk to the GEM VDI and the Gem AES.

```
{ The declarations for the Gem VDI communications arrays. }


const       cntl_max =          11;
```

```
            intin_max =           131;
            intout_max =          139;
            pts_max =             144;


      { Note that these arrays begin at 0, not 1. }


type        contrl_array =        array[0..cntl_max] of integer;
            intin_array =         array[0..intin_max] of integer;
            intout_array =        array[0..intout_max] of integer;
            ptsin_array =         array[0..pts_max] of integer;
            ptsout_array =        array[0..pts_max] of integer;


      { These are the VDI communications arrays. }


var         contrl:       contrl_array;
            intin:        intin_array;
            intout:       intout_array;
            ptsin:        ptsin_array;
            ptsout:       ptsout_array;


      { These are declarations for the Gem AES communications arrays. }


const       ac_max =      4;
            ai_max =      15;
            ao_max =      6;
            ag_max =      14;
            aad_max =     3;


type        ac_array =    array[0..ac_max] of integer; { Note: zero based. }
            ai_array =    array[0..ai_max] of integer;
            ao_array =    array[0..ao_max] of integer;
            ag_array =    array[0..ag_max] of integer;
            aad_array =   array[0..aad_max] of longint; { 32 bit integers. }


var         gcontrol =    ac_array;
            global =      ag_array;
            gintin =      ai_array;
            gintout =     ao_array;
            addr_in =     aad_array;
            addr_out =    aad_array;
```

The Gem VDI and Gem AES both use one entry point that is accessed with a single software interrupt. When the Gem VDI or AES is called, the address sent is pointing to a list of addresses that point to either the VDI or the AES parameter arrays. When Gem returns control, some data are placed in the arrays for return to and use by the application code.

An Example

One of the functions in Gem VDI is the Close Virtual Screen Workstation, which turns off the virtual display. Using the variable declarations described above, the contents of the arrays sent to Gem VDI must be set to:

```
contrl[0] := 101;        { Only the contrl array is set on input. }
contrl[1] := 0;
contrl[3] := 0;
contrl[6] := DeviceHandle;
```

The 16-bit quantity contrl[0] contains the decimal opcode 101, which to Gem means (oddly enough) Close the Virtual Screen Workstation. Array element contrl[6] contains a Gem handle that indicates which device is involved. When the operation is complete, Gem VDI returns (in this case) zeros in contrl[2] and contrl[4].

Gem Binding Routines

Filling the Gem parameter arrays with seemingly arbitrary numbers gets old immediately. To help improve the code, write some binding routines that have understandable names and accept more meaningful values from the application code. The binding routines stuff the arrays, call Gem, and return any significant results. Digital Research's *Gem Toolkit* comes with a separate binding routine for each identifiable Gem VDI and AES operation, and compilers that are intended to be used with Gem are provided with binding routine libraries.

GVDI and GAES, the Lowest-Level Binding Routines

In the entire set of bindings the routines closest to VDI and AES are the routines that execute the software interrupt. These two routines, GVDI and GAES, fill in the registers of the CPU with the appropriate information before invoking their respective GEM runtime packages.

For the MS-DOS version GVDI builds an array of pointers to the VDI arrays and places the address of the beginning of this array in registers ds and dx of the 8086. Gem VDI also sticks a hexidecimal 473 in register cx and then executes the software interrupt 0ef hexidecimal. It is very important that the order of the pointers to the VDI communications arrays in the array of pointers be correct, with the array of type contrl _array first, the ptsout_array last, and the middle ones likewise in the order indicated above.

GAES for the MS-DOS version of Gem builds an array of pointers to the AES communications arrays and sticks a hexidecimal 200 in register cx. GAES then calls software interrupt 0ef hex. The AES is likewise sensitive to the order of the array pointers in the pointer array.

Watch For Software Interrupt Conflicts

The commercially available MS-DOS package called Btrieve currently uses the same software interrupt, 0EF hex, that Gem uses. This could cause problems if you attempt to use both Btrieve and Gem on one application. Make certain that none of the packages you intend to use conflicts with another's use of software interrupts and traps. There won't be conflicts with Gem on the Atari ST, but Gem is "just another package" on the IBM PC.

An Example Binding Routine

One case of a higher-level binding routine provided by the Gem Toolkit, v_clsvwk, is used to effect the Close Virtual Screen Workstation function mentioned above. It accepts only one parameter, the handle to the device to be closed, also mentioned above. A Pascal version of the function declaration might look like:

```
{ Close Virtual Screen Workstation }
function v_clsvwk( handle: integer ): integer;
```

The above function call is cordial and meaningful in contrast to the nondescript verbose code within that sets the communications arrays and invokes the software interrupt to Gem.

Binding Routine Flexibility

Because the Gem binding routines and include files are custom-made for each compiler system by the language implementors, they can vary from machine to machine and from compiler to compiler. The type and constant declarations can vary. The routine names and their parameter lists may differ from (or be a subset of) the bindings in the Gem Toolkit.

A Microsoft Windows Roadmap

The data structures used in applications to interface to Microsoft Windows are more involved than those needed to talk to Gem by way of the binding routines. Figure 3–3 shows a simplified calling map of an MS-DOS machine running Windows and an application program.

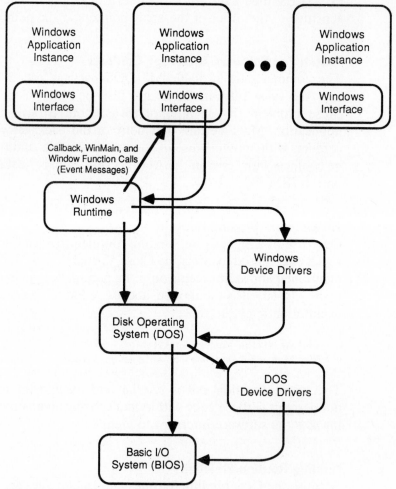

Figure 3–3 MS Windows Calling Tree

How Windows Talks to Applications

While there is a kind of visible, logical barrier between the application code and the Gem runtime system, with the binding routines acting as a bridge, there is none in evidence with Windows. Developers using the Gem Toolkit for MS-DOS deal with both the binding routines and the communications arrays underneath them, because both are displayed prominently in the manuals. The Microsoft Windows development package does not include the source for any access routines, except include files for both Microsoft C and Pascal. The manuals provide information for the high-level access routines that are kept in library files. In this sense, communicating with Windows is a matter of calling well-defined routines and linking the executable ones with the appropriate libraries.

Intel Program Models and Optimization

Microsoft has a "thing" about allowing developers to *optimize* their Windows application code; my early copy of the Windows development package comes with multiple sets of object libraries for supporting a variety of programming models. This is a common practice among the more popular products of the MS-DOS compiler systems shops.

There is a performance difference between code using 32-bit jumps and that using 16-bit jumps. Support for the different program models allows you to minimize the number of long jumps needed for the size of the program. Supporting different Intel program models also permits using 16-bit offsets into default data segments, rather than employing 32-bit addresses, if the amount of static, stack, and heap storage can be predicted. On a slow or segmented machine these tuning tricks can make a big difference.

Encapsulation

The Microsoft manuals don't give information on the composition of most of the Windows internal data structures. This can be considered an act of self-defense. To get to the data Microsoft provides many specialized data structure setup and access routines. Providing these controlled access paths eliminates a number of easily committed, annoying, and difficult-to-trace mistakes that can happen when playing directly with data structures. Microsoft has given itself more freedom to change things underneath the protective function call layer and to improve the package without inadvertently breaking application code. On the other hand, Microsoft Windows confronts you with a different kind of complexity, and it may also be hard to get around Windows' control management for whatever important reason you may have. This is a policy that Apple is adapting with the Macintosh and the IIGS.

A Macintosh Roadmap

Figure 3–4 describes a rough profile of the Macintosh address space.

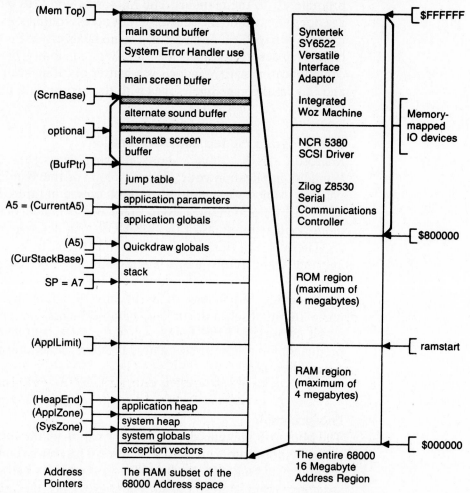

Figure 3–4 A Macintosh roadmap

Figure 3–5 shows a typical Macintosh calling arrangement.

Locations of Macintosh Utility Routines

There are three places from which a Macintosh developer can get utility routines. A number of support routines for the Macintosh are available in object library files that can be linked into an application. Also, many of the

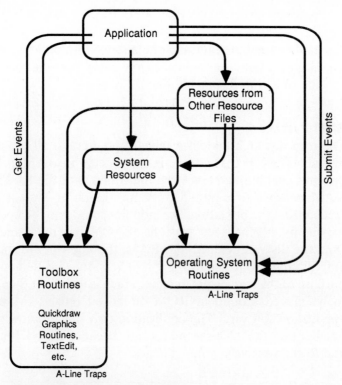

Figure 3–5 Macintosh Hierarchy

available routines are stuffed into 128K ROM. Finally, application programs may communicate with or use other application programs, such as Apple's Switcher.

The Macintosh ROM used to be 64K, but the smaller ROM has been replaced by 128K ROM. The old ROM is still used in machines that haven't been upgraded. There is at least one mandatory line of code that Mac applications must check to see which version of ROM is present; the differences between the two versions are considerable. The Mac SE and the Mac II also have more new code in ROM.

Routines in a Mac application program can directly call routines that are linked into the application. The exact ramifications of this are discussed later. Routines in ROM are accessed indirectly.

There are two general classes of ROM routines: operating system routines and toolbox routines. To get to them, an application program loads include files at preprocessor or compile time that contain the external declarations of the ROM routines in the form:

```
PROCEDURE InitGraf(globalPtr: Ptr); INLINE $A86E;
```

The tailing attribute indicates the address of a pointer to the routine in a trap dispatch table somewhere in low RAM, and that the routine is on the far side of a trap dispatch table.

ROM Patches

The **trap dispatch table** is a table of pointers to all the routines that are available in ROM. The table is constructed in RAM at boot-time, using information obtained first from the contents of the ROM. The table is in RAM because it is modified by the operating system software that is loaded from the boot disk. The modifications from the boot disk are mostly for bug fixes. When new versions of ROM-based routines are brought in from the disk and placed into RAM, the appropriate trap dispatch table entry is changed to point to the new version. This demonstrates the main purpose of the trap dispatch table, which is to permit the routines in ROM to be moved around in ROM or moved into RAM without affecting application software. The application only has to know the proper index number into the table for the routine, because the pointer out of the table and to the routine is what changes.

Macintosh ROM Calls in Excruciating Detail

Apple uses a unique 68000 opcode (not used by Motorola for any machine instructions) to indicate the execution of an OS or toolbox ROM call. Since the 68000 doesn't use machine instructions beginning with the binary pattern 1010 (or A in hexidecimal), the 68000 generates an exception trap when it finds such an instruction. On seeing an instruction like $A86E, the normal act of loading, storing, or performing an arithmetic operation is suspended. The 68000 does four things instead: (1) it places three 16-bit words (the current processor context, including the 32-bit program counter, and the 16-bit status register) on the supervisor stack; (2) it uses the value 28 hex to add to the contents of the 68000 vector base register; (3) it finds the vector in the vector table pointing out where to go; and (4) it goes there. All the 68000 instructions starting with the value $A cause what is called an **A-line trap**. On the Macintosh a trap dispatcher routine written by Apple waits for the processor beyond the A-line trap vector. That routine looks at bit 11 of the instruction. If the bit is 0, it's an OS call, and if the bit is 1, it's a toolbox call. Bits 0 through 7 indicate one of 256 possible OS calls, and bits 0 through 8 indicate one of 512 possible toolbox calls. These values are used to index into the two trap dispatch tables (one for OS, the other for the toolbox) and grab the vector that really does point to the routine to execute.

From an application program's point of view, all that really must be understood is that each ROM routine has its own 32-bit hexidecimal number; these numbers, and the use of the attribute INLINE in the above TML Pascal example, are unique to the Macintosh. The presence of the INLINE $A86E, rather than the reserved word external, is one of the significant differences when comparing the use of ROM routines and routines in linkable libraries on the Macintosh.

The data structures used for communicating with Macintosh library and ROM routines are very sophisticated. The complexity is spurred by the sheer bulk and breadth of the support software, but there is also more stuff visible in the Macintosh environment than in the other environments. Each comparable data structure for each environment is examined later in this chapter.

A IIGS RoadMap

The IIGS memory map is banked and not contiguous, so everything is "more interesting" on the IIGS compared with the Macintosh.

The IIGS low-level code was designed to be accessed quickly, because the 65816 processor is not as swift as a 68000, and every cycle counts.

Each IIGS tool function is uniquely addressed by two 8-bit values: a tool set number and a function number. To give you some idea what a tool set looks like, here are the numbers that have been assigned at the time of writing:

1   Tool Locator
2   Memory Manager
3   Misc.
4   QuickDraw II
5   Desk Manager
6   Event Manager
7   Scheduler
8   Sound Manager
9   FDB Tools
10   SANE (arithmetic package)

All tool functions are executed by going through the tool locator. The locator uses the function's tool set number to track down the tool set entry in a Tool Pointer Table. This entry points to another table called the **Function Pointer Table**. The Function Pointer Table entry corresponding to the function number contains the address of the function. Each of the pointer entries in the tool pointer and function pointer tables takes up 4 bytes, so there is no skimping in the addressing scheme here.

The delay in getting to some tool set functions using the tool locator may be too long, so Apple allows some custom tools to bypass the tool locator system and be called directly.

An Amiga Roadmap

The Amiga is organized with much of the low-level system software kept in "ROM," much like the Atari ST and the Macintosh. Early in the Amiga's history the bootstrap program transferred much of what is supposed to be in ROM from the boot disk into a write-once RAM bank; subsequent (spurious) attempts to write to that area were disallowed, making it act as ROM. It looks as though Amiga did this because they considered their system software to be more volatile than that found on the Atari or Macintosh machines, and it was more economical for Amiga to provide updates on disk rather than burn a batch of new ROMs.

Like the Mac and Atari machines, Commodore-Amiga has gone to great lengths to avoid allowing the use of absolute RAM addresses for their system software. They have set up a mechanism that requires programs to register requests to access system libraries; otherwise, accessing system software is pretty much like calling any C function.

Libraries

System routines are kept in Amiga libraries. To use routines, a program must open the library with the routine OpenLibrary. The OpenLibrary call tells the system that the program would like to use the routines; the system returns the base address of the routine library.

Some libraries are kept on disk and some aren't. The OpenLibrary call serves to yank in the necessary code from disk before the program really needs it.

The Amiga system is permitted to keep routines wherever it thinks is convenient. The system does not have to tell anyone where routines are until they're needed during runtime. Once the base address of the library node is specified, the library node can't be moved. The jump vector addresses of the library (for the routines) are also stationary, so you can play some optimization games by caching or keeping those pointers in registers.

When an application is finished, it must make a call to CloseLibrary with the base address of the library as the argument.

Determining how long it takes to access routines in runtime libraries may be a good exercise; the time will probably change as the Amiga kernel improves, and will probably impact how you write temporally sensitive applications. Figure 3–6 shows an example of an Amiga calling tree.

Calling Standards

Stack versus Register Calls

There are system-level routines that expect parameters to be in registers or in static locations in system or global data regions. These routines are normally incompatible with routines written in high-level languages, because HLL routines expect that parameters will be placed on a stack and that the valid stack pointer will be provided. There is a good reason for using registers: Accessing parameters on the stack is slower than having the data already in registers (for the compilers I have studied). Everyone avoids using the stack for arguments in time-critical code. Even if the routine is very short, it might be called a million times.

Most of the routines in Macintosh ROM that are usually called from applications are written to get and place parameters on the supervisor stack, but there are a few ROM routines that use registers.

What the Gem bindings expect depends on the language system they support. For C or Pascal code the bindings probably expect arguments to be provided on the stack as with any normal routine. Since the bindings are implemented by whoever writes the language system, other Gem bindings are *not guaranteed to follow these rules*. Below the binding routines, Gem itself expects a list of pointers to arrays, the addresses of which are passed in a register.

The Amiga is a C programming machine that expects system call arguments to be provided in C standard order. Not unlike the other environments, there are a number of low-level routines that accept and provide arguments in registers and ignore the stack.

MS Windows functions are all stack-oriented.

Pascal versus C Calls

The order of Pascal parameters on the stack is normally the reverse of the order that arguments take when programmed in C. The solutions used in

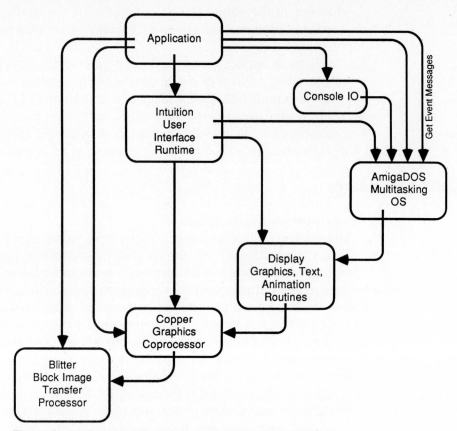

Figure 3–6 Who normally calls or uses whom on the Amiga

different language systems are similar enough. Megamax C provides the attribute Pascal for C routines calling Pascal routines; the code generated should insert parameters onto the stack in reverse order. Another approach is to simply leave it up to the developer to reverse the parameter list order in the source with respect to the routine being called. A third method is to have the Pascal or C compiler habitually use the calling standard of the other language. Ideally this sort of thing should be handled automatically, with nary a thought given to it.

Windows is a little strange in that most of the examples are written in C, yet the application entry points for the Windows environment (such as WinMain, About, and WndProc) are to be defined with the Microsoft attribute PASCAL. Routines that are used within an application follow the calling standards of the implementation language.

PRIMITIVE DATATYPES

To begin to understand each system's novelty, here is a comparison of some of the simple datatypes that are used as arguments or as parts of structure arguments in calls to each environment. These are made of the essential datatypes given by each of the languages provided by Apple, Atari, Commodore, Digital Research, and Microsoft, as well as of some of the declared datatypes in the many include files that are provided with each language system.

Macintosh General-Purpose Pascal Datatypes

```
type SignedByte    =      -128..127;    { Any signed byte. }
     Byte =               0..255;       { Any unsigned byte. }
     Ptr =               ^SignedByte;  { A Generic data pointer. }
     Handle =            ^Ptr;          { A Pointer to a pointer. }
     ProcPtr =           Ptr;           { A Pointer to a procedure. }
     Fixed =             LongInt;       { A Mac fixed point data type. }


     { Data types based on automatic strings of up to 255 characters. }


     Str255 =            String[255]; { The biggest autostring. }
     StringPtr =         ^Str255;
     StringHandle =      ^StringPtr;
```

Note that the Byte defined in the list above is not the Pascal datatype char found in Jensen and Wirth's *Pascal User Manual and Report.*

Windows General-Purpose Pascal Datatypes

```
     { Standard compiler-provided types. }


type  integer =    -32767..32767;
      integer2 =   integer;
      word =       0..65535;
      char =       0..255;
      boolean =    (false,true);
```

```
real =        real4 | real8       {This depends on a compile option.}
real4 =       1.0E-38..1.0E38;
real8 =       1.0E-306..1.0E306;


{ Include file definitions. }


type int         =        INTEGER;
     short       =        INTEGER;
     long        =        INTEGER4;
     unsigned    =        WORD;
     unsignedlong =       INTEGER4;
     LPshort     =        ADS OF short; {Note the use of nonstandard ptr here.}


const FALSE_  =           0;
      TRUE_   =           1;
      NULL_   =           0;


type DWORD =              INTEGER4;
     BOOL  =              int;
     PSTR  =              ADR OF INTEGER1;
     LPSTR =              ADS OF INTEGER1;
     LPINT =              ADS OF BOOL;
```

The include files are clearly used to make Pascal emulate C by defining C-like datatypes and using them in application code. The ADS and ADR features of Microsoft Pascal are used respectively to make 32-bit address pointers (with half being the offset and the other half the segment) and to make 16-bit address pointers. The standard Pascal pointers in Microsoft Pascal are 16-bit pointers limited to the default data segment. Portable Pascal code that avoids ADS and ADR is limited to a 64K heap in Microsoft Pascal. Again, the difference between the standard pointer and the ADR/ADS features is that Microsoft expects you to write system-level (aka "filthy") code, whereas the standard Pascal pointers are clean, low-danger datatypes. The trouble is that standard pointers are limited to the single default data segment in this implementation of Pascal. Handles are other datatypes that can be used to avoid difficulties with the range of Pascal pointers; they are described later.

Gem General-Purpose Pascal Datatypes

```
{ Regular Pascal compiler datatypes }

type char =        0..255;              { 8 bits }
     boolean =     true, false;         { 8 bits }
     integer =     -32768..32767;       { 16 bits }
     longint =     2**32-1..-2**32      { 32 bits }
     byte =        0..255;              { 8 bits }
     word =        0..65535;            { 16 bits }
     real =        10**-307..10**307    { 8 bytes }
```

The types described above aren't anything special, despite including byte, word, and longint. Further along are the definitions used for interfacing with the actual Gem runtime package at the lowest level, and for interfacing with a set of Gem binding routines at a higher level.

To employ GemVDI and GemAES directly and on a minimum budget requires attention to numerous details, and the effort can be error-prone. There is but one call to exchange data and commands with the Gem runtime system. The generality of this call does not influence the production of natural, self-documenting code. Fortunately, a layer of binding routines is normally provided to hide the low-level, verbose details of accessing Gem. It is unfortunate that some people have to know the low-level details, but given a good set of binding routines, most do not. The source of the binding routines may be furnished, as they are for the C language in Digital Research's Gem Toolkit for MS-DOS, or they may be provided in a library file, ready to be linked in.

Amiga General-Purpose Datatypes

Judging from both the style of the programming manuals and the coding style, Amiga system software may have been inspired by Unix ideology, although the function of the kernel and utilities do not reflect a Unix-based design. The Amiga is *definitely* a C language machine. The following listing is offered in C because: (1) Amiga is a C machine, and (2) I don't have sample Pascal material for the Amiga at this writing.

Incidentally, although the following code is at least readable, I recommend that *portable* code be written without comments on the same line as a preprocessor define command, since some preprocessors get upset.

```
#define GLOBAL extern          /* An external declaration. */
#define IMPORT extern          /* An external reference. */
#define STATIC static          /* A static var declaration. */
#define REGISTER register      /* If in upper case, it must be true.*/
typedef long LONG;             /* A signed 32 bit integer. */
typedef unsigned long ULONG;   /* An unsigned 32 bit quantity. */
typedef unsigned long LONGBITS; /* A 32-bit bitfield or set. */
typedef short WORD;            /* A signed 16 bit integer. */
typedef unsigned short WORD;   /* An unsigned 16 bit quantity. */
typedef unsigned short WORDBITS; /* A 16-bit bitfield or set. */
typedef char BYTE;             /* For system use, really. */
typedef unsigned char UBYTE;   /* For system use. */
typedef unsigned char BYTEBITS; /* For system eyes only. */
typedef unsigned char *STRPTR; /* An Ascii text pointer definition. */
typedef STRPTR APTR;           /* An ASCII text pointer definition. */
typedef float FLOAT;           /* The real numbers. */
typedef double DOUBLE;         /* Double precision real numbers. */
typedef short COUNT;           /* The system counting variable type. */
typedef unsigned short UCOUNT; /* Another system counting type. */
typedef short BOOL;            /* Expected to be TRUE or FALSE only. */
typedef unsigned char TEXT;    /* Really for arrays of characters. */
#define TRUE 1                 /* The standard ubiquitous TRUTH. */
#define FALSE 0                /* The standard ubiquitous FALSE. */
```

Extended Pascal versus C Strings

C strings are the same as in every C compiler, with most of the support library routines written to assume that a NULL (ASCII 0) character is used to terminate a string of characters. Pascal automatic strings, on the other hand, are usually implemented, but the exact details sometimes clash. Normally there is a length byte at the beginning of the string record, and the actual data follow.

The Macintosh system was written using assembler and Pascal, and for a while the only support language was Pascal. The Macintosh low-level support software uses the extended Pascal version of automatic strings. C compilers for the Mac have been provided with simple C-to-Pascal and Pascal-to-C string convert routines, and now there are ROM versions of these routines in the 128K ROM.

Microsoft Windows is currently supported by two compilers, MS Pascal and Microsoft C. Microsoft Pascal supports the extended string type in a unique way, but the C-style string is implemented in the portable way.

Amiga is a C-based environment, and therefore the system and Intuition functions are supported by C-style strings.

A Caveat Regarding String Conversion

There have been C programs written for the Macintosh that regularly convert C-style strings to Pascal for ROM and Toolbox use and convert Pascal-style strings (sent from the ROM/Toolbox) to a NULL-terminated character array before the application code really does anything with it. Before you know it, your program is running several times slower than it has to. These conversions are probably frequent enough to make a remarkable dent in performance. Where possible, avoid the conversions entirely. Try NULL-filling the string memory first and then overlaying the string data on top; or allocate an extra byte at the end (for those 255-character strings), drop a NULL at the end of the string when appropriate, and use a string pointer that jumps over the length indicator. "Correct" conversion routines might copy the Pascal string data to a character array starting at an address (this is a slow solution).

HANDLES AND POINTERS

Gem does not have a predefined record type for window definition information. The application code is responsible for keeping track using appropriate measures, which I assume partially means defining its own window record.

All but one of Gem's window library binding routines do not accept or provide pointers to data structures in the manner of the Macintosh or Microsoft Windows libraries.

Macintosh's GetNewWindow and NewWindow functions provide pointers to the created record of type WindowRecord for a window. Similar functions exist for the IIGS, but the system authors prefer that you not manipulate the fields of the window record directly.

Microsoft Windows' CreateWindow routine provides an hWND typed handle to a "mysterious" window entity. Microsoft Windows has a number of access routines for editing data fields associated with a given window via an hWND.

Gem normally provides a simple window reference number of type integer. This number is a Gem handle, dissimilar to the Macintosh handle. Gem will know what you mean when the number is used in the right places.

The Amiga doesn't work with handles directly. Most data structures can be directly manipulated by the application code. All the defines, typedefs, and structures are listed in a description of all the system header (.h) and assembler interface (.i) files in the back of volume II of the *Amiga ROM Kernel Manual*.

Macintosh

In the Macintosh a pointer can be used by code when that code controls the whereabouts of the data pointed to it. If the Macintosh Memory Manager can move the data "out from under the pointer," rendering the pointer invalid, then a mere pointer is no good. A handle is used by code when the block can be moved without prior knowledge by that code.

The operating systems in which Gem and Microsoft Windows reside don't necessarily provide memory allocation with equal sophistication. In their cases a pointer is the same as a Macintosh pointer (although with possibly different sizes depending on the Intel Program Model being used) and a handle is an indirect pointer. A Gem or Windows handle could be interpreted as a 16-bit pointer to another pointer in memory, an index into an array of pointers, or an index into a linked list of pointers.

Gem

Gem accepts pointers (full 32-bit pointers, even on the PC-DOS version) to objects in object trees, buffers filled for and by Gem message pipes, filename strings, recorded user event buffers (these are associated with a Gem feature that is like Macintosh journaling), the Gem mouse form definition block, scrap buffers, buffers containing directory specifications that are displayed by file selector dialog boxes, a buffer that contains the item selected from the file selector dialog box, resource filename strings, and resource data structures.

Gem *provides* a pointer only via the Gem AES call rsrc_gaddr, which gives the address of any known data structure in memory, such as those of Gem type object, tedinfo, iconblk, or bitblk.

Type Casts and Generic Pointers

Much use of type casting is evident in some of the coding examples provided by the authors of the windowing environments. Lisa Pascal examples tend to avoid constructs like type casting. Though there is less evidence of type casting in the examples of Gem code, Gem handles and pointers are declared and used "generically" to point to any kind of data structure supported by the Gem system.

Here is a fragment of a switch statement from a Microsoft Windows example application. This example was selected because of the variety of casts used within eight lines of code, not because it uses five casts (which isn't unusual):

```
case WM_ERASEBKGND:                           /* Erase Background msg code */
    GetClientRect( hWnd, (LPRECT)&rect );
    hbr = CreateSolidBrush( GetSysColor(COLOR_WINDOW) );
    hbrOld = SelectObject( (HDC)wParam, hbr );
    FillRect( (HDC)wParam, (LPRECT)&rect, hbr);
    SelectObject( (HDC)wParam, hbrOld );
    DeleteObject( hbr );
    break;
```

Casting leads to small, efficient C code, but it is also the hallmark of harder-to-understand code. When learning how a program works, one thing to do is to trace the hierarchy of variable and type declarations and see how they are used in routines. When values are cast or pointers are used generically, the datatype hierarchy is leaning against a nearby wall to support itself; you cannot be certain if a particular pointer or handle is associated with a specific data structure by way of its type declaration. In practice you could give the variable a very specific name, diminishing the impact of my complaint. The responsibility of resolving misdirected pointers and handles then falls entirely to the programmer, since the type-checking of the compiler system has been bypassed. Regardless of variable naming conventions, type casts and generic pointers or handles make it harder to understand what data structures are being brought into play when. It is unnecessary for the *code* to distinguish between a pointer to a window and a pointer to a picture record, since pointers to different kinds of data structures are (internally) normally of the same datatype. Using different types for pointer variables is helpful to programmers and authors of books like this one who appreciate every bit of help they get.

Pointing out this problem with type casting, generic pointers, and handles should help you understand why some sections of Gem, Windows, and the Macintosh system are a little hard to understand. In the Gem toolkit documentation, when the header to a Gem binding function contains the datatype handle, you have to ask yourself, "A handle to what?" and understand that the question must be clearly answered by the code you write.

Hiding Details

Looking at the way Microsoft Windows declares the type hWnd will demonstrate a minor moment of confusion that can materialize when one is confronted with the loose threads of generic pointers.

In the C include file windows.h, hWnd is declared

```
typedef HANDLE HWND;
```

while HANDLE and related types are declared

```
typedef WORD          HANDLE;
typedef HANDLE        *PHANDLE;
typedef HANDLE NEAR   *SPHANDLE;
typedef HANDLE FAR    *LPHANDLE;
```

Similarly, in the Pascal include file windows.inc, hWnd is declared

```
TYPE
    HWND = HANDLE;
```

Here are some of the other Pascal-type declarations:

```
TYPE
    HANDLE =          ADR OF INTEGER1;
    SPHANDLE =        ADR OF WORD;
    LPHANDLE =        ADS OF WORD;
    FARPROC =         ADSMEM;
    NEARPROC =        ADRMEM;
    GLOBALHANDLE_ =   HANDLE;
    LOCALHANDLE_ =    HANDLE;
```

These type declarations are repeated here exactly as they appear in their respective include files, including the case of the letters. With the Pascal form of the declarations the case is not relevant, so it doesn't matter if they appear in uppercase or lowercase. The C code is case-sensitive.

The type hWnd appears to be a handle to a specific data structure or object in memory somewhere. Upon inspection the include files reveal other handles:

```
typedef HANDLE HSTR;
typedef HANDLE HICON;
typedef HANDLE HDC;
```

```
typedef HANDLE HMENU;
typedef HANDLE HPEN;
typedef HANDLE HFONT;
typedef HANDLE HBRUSH;
typedef HANDLE HBITMAP;
typedef HANDLE HCURSOR;
typedef HANDLE HRGN;
```

We have a bunch of datatypes that are used to define handles to a variety of data structures. So far, so good. However, look at the following:

```
typedef struct {
    HDC hdc;
    BOOL fErase;
    RECT rcPaint;
    BOOL fRestore;
    BOOL fIncUpdate;
    BYTE rgbReserved[16];
} PAINTSTRUCT;
typedef PAINTSTRUCT *PPAINTSTRUCT;
typedef PAINTSTRUCT NEAR *NPPAINTSTRUCT;
typedef PAINTSTRUCT FAR *LPPAINTSTRUCT;
```

Note that with the C language pointers defined immediately above, the data-structure type to which they point is defined with them. With the handle type declarations, it isn't. What is occurring above, is that the handle is being defined generically because the exact composition of the data structure is intentionally not explicitly defined.

Typography

Be aware of a small detail involving the Microsoft Windows documentation used to prepare this text. In the chapters that describe how each Windows routine works, the parameters for each routine are loosely described in two ways: with a pseudocode type and with a sentence or paragraph describing the significance and operation of the parameter. The typesetting of the documentation had nothing to do with the presentation of the actual datatype declaration in either the Pascal or C include files provided with the Windows toolkit. For example, in the manual the type of a function parameter may be presented as "hWindow," whereas the actual definition in either language's include file is HWND.

In contrast, the presentation and description of datatypes in the include files on the Macintosh (and Lisa, aka Mac XL) environment is very close to what is in *Inside Macintosh*. The *Gem Toolkit* manual is very good about defining the parameters to Gem calls in terms of both the contents of the low-level parameter arrays and the associated higher-level binding routine. *Gem Toolkit* defines the datatype of each parameter and the return value of the function (if any) as they are defined in the include files and in the source of the provided binding routines. There are some differences between source files and documentation on the Atari ST version of GEM; the use of underscores in some names isn't documented in the manuals.

3.3 | Event Managers

Event handling is the major organizational influence in Amiga, Gem, Windows, and Macintosh applications. Less interactive software is rarely arranged the way software is arranged when using a windowing package.

An **event** is a small record handed to an application from the operating environment. The record describes something that the user has done or something that the system routinely sends to an application in case the application needs to know it. Common events are sent in reaction to the following things:

pressing or releasing the mouse button

pressing or releasing a keyboard key

holding a keyboard key down

activating a window

updating a window

having a timer expire

inserting a disk

Included in the event record are data pertinent to the type of event being reported. If a mouse button is pressed, the mouse button–down event tells where the cursor was on the screen, which button on the mouse was pressed, and which keyboard keys were being held down.

When an event is generated, it is directed to the application's event queue where the application can pick it up (in an order that varies from system to system) at its leisure.

OVERVIEW

Macintosh Events

There are two Mac event managers, the operating system event manager and the toolbox event manager. The OS event manager handles lower-level events.

An application controls the Mac event queue with OS event routines, as there are functions for removing and inserting events and masking event types from getting into the queue. In normal usage toolbox event routines are used for extracting events from the queue, and the OS event routines are used to insert event records into the queue.

The design of the Mac event manager revolves around the assumption that when an application is present on the screen it has control of all the resources of the machine. The design ideology is clearly reflected by the fact that the highest-level block in a Mac application, the event processing code, is written as a busy-wait loop. The application asks the event manager if certain events are present in the queue. The event manager returns yes if they are and no if they aren't. The event loop repeats the question until an event does appear. Some of the application may execute whether or not the machine has the events to give it. These are the fingerprints of a singletasking system.

I consider getting the Mac or the Mac + to handle multitasking a great challenge. The results that I have seen thus far have been less than ideal, but all it takes is one *good* multitasking manager.

Gem

The Gem event manager is designed to work in a multitasking environment. Event handling is done on the basis of the operating system waking up the application when something has happened. If an application has to periodically maintain data structures, file contents, or screen contents (such as updating the time being displayed in a window) even if the user hasn't done anything, there are timer events that can be set to go off at prearranged times and wake up the application.

The Gem event manager does not provide a wide variety of functions, but these routines can handle a reasonable selection of event types, although the number of predefined events and event messages is relatively small.

Windows

The Windows message handling system is also based on a multitasking model. All the events are generalized into message records. There are many predefined application, system, and clipboard messages; the reason for so many predefined messages is that they are simpler than Gem messages, and have to cover more ground. The scope of the Macintosh event manager is smaller than that found under Gem or Windows.

MOUSE BUTTONS

Windows directly supports two mouse buttons by providing separate messages for each up or down action of each button.

Gem can handle at least three buttons and, depending on the implementation, should be able to juggle more. *The Gem Programmer's Toolkit AES* manual for the IBM PC says 16 buttons, as the status of each button is identified in an event message as 1 bit in a 16-bit value. Before you ask why, remember that there are quite a number of "no fooling around/Major Domo" CAD/CAM packages that use as many buttons on a puck as they can get away with; a reasonable minimum seems to be four buttons. The package developers for the IBM PC and others seem to be happy with whatever they can get, though, and are using the keyboard for additional cursor-context sensitive picks.

The Mac mouse has one mouse button and the Macintosh event manager support is for a single-button mouse, but the status of some keyboard keys is routinely provided with certain types of events.

RECOMMENDATIONS

Restricting a package to a single mouse button, relying on menu-selectable modes, and possibly holding some of the keyboard keys down for additional mouse-pick operations appear to be the constraints that are required to achieve the simplest portability.

Requiring that portable software on the Macintosh use two mouse buttons forces the user to find a different mouse and additional hardware and system software to interface the two-button mouse to the Macintosh.

Extra-button mouse-picks may have to be solved by using keyboard keys. When an environment doesn't provide some keyboard key status data when a mouse button is pressed, some gymnastics must be performed. For example, when an appropriate keyboard key event hits, the application code must ask the system where the mouse cursor is *immediately* after the keyboard event occurs, since a separate function call is required to get the mouse location—the mouse cursor could be moved before the location is reported.

The Amiga, Gem, and MS Windows environments support at least two-button mice, but the IIGS and Macintosh support only one-button mice.

EVENT DATA STRUCTURES

Macintosh

The following is an event record:

```
TYPE EventRecord = RECORD
        what:         INTEGER;    {The event code.}
        message:      LONGINT;    {The event message.}
        when:         LONGINT;    {The number of ticks since startup.}
        where:        Point;      {The mouse location.}
        modifiers:    INTEGER;    {Some modifier bit flags.}
    END;
```

The what field identifies the type of event that took place. The message field contains the followup data important to the context of the event type.

Inside the event queue the record takes a slightly different form:

```
TYPE EvQE1 = RECORD
        qLink:          QElemPtr;   {The next queue entry.}
        qType:          INTEGER;    {The queue type.}
        evtQWhat:       INTEGER;    {The event code.}
        evtQMessage:    LONGINT;    {The event message.}
        evtQWhen:       LONGINT;    {Number of ticks since startup.}
        evtQWhere:      Point;      {The mouse location.}
        evtQModifiers:  INTEGER;    {Some modifier flags.}
    END;
```

Gem

The event data structures, like everything else directly into or out of Gem, are simple entries in a bunch of arrays. Records may be defined depending on the sophistication of the binding routines provided by the language implementor (and also if the binding routines were written to follow the standard defined by Digital Research in the example bindings provided with the Gem Toolkit).

The Toolkit binding routines pass on the stack to Gem individual integer values, and pass the addresses of integer variables to Gem for return values.

Common Gem input parameters are:

Mouse button data:

ev_bclicks	Number of mouse button presses
ev_bmask	Active mouse buttons
ev_bstate	The button state that will activate the event

Mouse movement data:

ev_moflags	Return on entry or exit to specified rectangle
ev_mox	X-coordinate of mouse rectangle
ev_moy	Y-coordinate of mouse rectangle
ev_mowidth	Mouse rectangle width
ev_moheight	Mouse rectangle height
ev_moresvd	Always equals the value 1 (RESERVED)

Event message present data:

ev_mgpbuff	Where to put the 16-byte message when it shows up

Timer data:

ev_tlocount	Low word on a long value (in milliseconds)
ev_thicount	High word of a long value (in milliseconds)

Double-click speed setting data:

ev_dnew	New double-click speed (1 through 5)
ev_dgetset	1 if setting speed, 0 if getting speed

Common Gem output parameters are:

Mouse button data:

ev_bmx	X-coordinate of mouse pointer
ev_bmy	Y-coordinate of mouse pointer
ev_bbutton	Mouse button state
ev_bkstate	State of modifier keys on the keyboard

Message event data:
The 16-byte message is returned in the buffer pointed to by ev_mgp-buff. The predefined message types are defined elsewhere in this section.

Timer event data:

ev_tresvd	Equals the value 1

Common Gem function return parameters are:

keyboard data:

ev_kreturn	The standard keyboard code

mouse button data:

ev_breturn	The number of presses in the specified time

mouse data:

ev_moresvd	The value 1

message data:

ev_mgresvd	The value 1

timer data:

ev_tresvd   The value 1

event_multi:

ev_mwhich   The event(s) that actually occurred

double-click data:

ev_dspeed   The double-click speed

Windows

Here is the message structure:

```
MSG = RECORD
        hwnd_:      HWND;       {A handle to window receiving msg.}
        message:    WORD;       {The message type.}
        wParam:     WORD;       {Additional info depending on type.}
        lParam:     LONG;       {Additional info depending on type.}
        time:       DWORD;      {The time that the message was posted.}
        pt:         POINT;      {The position of mouse when msg posted.}
END;
```

The Windows message record may be the tip of an iceberg when it appears, since lParam may be a pointer to one of a number of different data structures, depending on the message type. For example, the WM_CREATE message tells the application that a window is being created; lParam in this case is a long pointer to a CREATESTRUCT record, with fields that match the parameters sent to the CreateWindow function. lParam may be used, depending on the message type, to contain the following:

A long pointer to a CREATESTRUCT data structure

The width and height of a window

High word = TRUE, low word = handle to a window

X and Y coordinates of window location (top left corner of window)

X and Y coordinates of the mouse cursor in a window

A keyboard key transition record (repeat count, down or up, key code)

A window handle and a control notification code

The scrollbar "thumb position" value

A long pointer to a PAINTSTRUCT record

A long pointer to a text buffer

A long pointer to a null-terminated string

The other all-purpose (but shorter) field wParam may contain, depending on the message type, the following kinds of data:

TRUE or FALSE

A window handle

A resizing value (SIZEICONIC, SIZEFULLSCREEN, SIZENORMAL)

A display context handle

Virtual key status bit values

Virtual key codes

ASCII key codes

Dead key codes (that is, no forward carriage movement when printed)

A timer ID

A menu item or control ID

A scroll-bar code

A control item handle

The maximum number of characters to copy during a copy text operation

Amiga

The MsgPort record is defined as follows:

```
struct MsgPort {                /* An Amiga message port. */
    struct Node    mp_Node;     /* A standard Amiga Node record. */
    UBYTE  mp_Flags;            /* The event arrival actions. */
    UBYTE  mp_SigBit;           /* The signal bit number. */
    struct Task    *mp_SigTask; /* A ptr. to signalled task or structure. */
    struct List    mp_msgList;  /* A list header for queued messages. */
}
```

The Message record is defined as follows:

```
struct Message {
    struct Node     mn_Node;           /* An Amiga node record. */
    struct MsgPort *mn_ReplyPort;      /* The port to reply to. */
    UWORD           mn_length;         /* The message body length in bytes. */
}
```

The Intuimessage record is defined this way:

```
struct IntuiMessage {
    struct Message ExecMessage;        /* A Standard message record. */
    ULONG  Class;                      /* Bits correspond with IDCMP bits. */
    USHORT Code;                       /* Arbitrary value or raw data code. */
    USHORT Qualifier;                  /* Some key modifier codes. */
    APTR   IAddress;                   /* Intuition object assoc. with msg. */
    SHORT  MouseX, MouseY;             /* The mouse coords at time of event. */
    ULONG  Seconds, Micros;            /* The system clock time at event. */
    struct Window *IDCMPWindow;        /* Ptr to originating Intuit. window */
    struct IntuiMessage *SpecialLink;  /* The manuals do not say what it is. */
}
```

EVENT QUEUES

Macintosh

Whenever a new event is created, it is inserted at the end of the singular event queue. An application sampling the event queue using the function GetNextEvent usually gets the oldest event in the queue that matches the preference list. The preferences are specified through a 16-bit mask passed to GetNextEvent.

An application may skip through the normally first-in/first-out queue to get selected types of event records. Another routine, EventAvail, can be used to get an event record without having it yanked from the queue. If the event queue fills, the oldest event records are removed to make room for new event records.

The Mac has a small number of queue manipulation routines, such as FlushEvents and GetNextEvent.

Gem

The Gem event queue is called a **message pipe**; there is a message pipe for each executing application. The keyboard, mouse button, mouse, and timer events do not use the message pipes, and require less information than the predefined message events that do use the pipes. There are two Event Library routines that are used to obtain message events from a message pipe: evnt_mesag and evnt_multi.

When applications are *creating* messages to be inserted into message pipes and consumed by themselves (not common, but done) or other processes, the Gem AES Application Library routine appl_write is used.

The Application Library routine appl_find is used to find another application program running under Gem; it returns the application ID number if found. Once the ID is known, communications can be established.

The appl_read function is used to read a message from a message pipe buffer belonging to an arbitrary process.

Extraction of messages from the message pipe is strictly first-in/first-out through the normal channels. There are no routines provided to select message event types of interest over other types in the pipe.

Windows

There are two types of Windows message queues, the **hardware queue** and the **application queues**. The hardware queue is public to all applications, but read access to an application queue is reserved for the owner of the queue.

When an application makes a request for a message, Windows first provides messages (if any) from the top of its application queue. If no messages are available, then a message is obtained from the hardware queue.

GetMessage is used to wait for a message to become available (it will not return empty-handed). PeekMessage is used to poll the application queue for a message, returning even if none are present.

SendMessage sends a message to a window without returning until the message has been processed. PostMessage sends a message to a window (via its application queue), returning without delay.

Amiga

Intuition provides two ways to obtain input. The first way is used to transact simple event messages to and from Intuition, and is called an **Intuition Direct Communications Message Port** or, cryptically, an **IDCMP**. The second way is via the **console device**, which provides standard

Input transactions like ASCII characters rather than key presses, and escape sequences rather than screen events.

The console device is a throwback to the lazy text-only I/O days, and is adequate for testing purposes. Since this chapter is about event management, discussion of the console device I/O is not discussed further here.

The IDCMP

The IDCMP consists of a pair of standard Exec message ports, one for Intuition and one for an application. Once the IDCMP is open, it should be monitored for incoming messages. The types of event messages that come through an IDCMP can be controlled, as the Mac event queue can, but the mechanics are different. Message transactions are made via PutMsg, GetMsg, and ReplyMsg. GetMsg doesn't wait for a valid message to be present in the queue; if nothing is there, it returns the value 0. To have a program wait for a port message to become available without using a busy-wait loop, the Msg routines must be used with the exec's signal routines: AllocSignal, FreeSignal, SetSignal, Signal, and especially Wait. After Wait is called, it will not return until the indicated signals have occurred, which could indicate that messages are available from a port.

If the IDCMP is closed without acknowledging all the queued messages (via the ReplyMsg routine), those messages are lost.

Messages that originate from Intuition can be a special form of exec message, called an **Intuimessage**, which contains additional information that makes sense coming only from Intuition: qualifier key status when the event was generated, the mouse coordinates, the clock time, an optional address of an Intuition object associated with the event, the address of the Intuition window originating the event, and a special code field for menu item numbers or raw key values.

IDCMP Message Port Creation

An IDCMP is created automatically when the IDCMP flags are set appropriately when defining window structures. The ModifyIDCMP function is available to build and take down ports and change the types of events that can get through.

IIGS

The IIGS event manager may look familiar to Macintosh programmers, with the usual number of exceptions that are common to all the managers of the Macintosh and IIGS. The IIGS has the same sort of event queue that is used on the Mac. The IIGS has GetNextEvent, PostEvent, FlushEvents, GetOSEvent, and OSEventAvail for manipulating queued events.

RECEIVING EVENTS AND MESSAGES

Macintosh

An application has one event loop routine defined close to (if not inside) the main procedure of the program. The event loop checks for events by polling the Macintosh environment; the polling has to be done when events are expected, including when programs go "solo" for extended periods. Users expect to be able to cancel long commands in progress without detrimental effect to the files and the memory image.

When an application is accepting events, it doesn't have to accept every kind of event and throw out or throw back into the queue the ones it doesn't want. A mask is passed to GetNextEvent to select timely events and exclude meaningless ones. A common error during code development is to exclude too many event types, sometimes by selecting the wrong bit pattern in the mask.

A Macintosh application gets to intercept events to desk accessories, since the desk accessory is using the resources of the machine with the grace of the main application.

When GetNextEvent returns, the event loop of the application decides if an event was returned (via the return value, a boolean). If so, it determines the kind of event (described by the what field of the EventRecord) and then decides what the application has to do. This is simple, but not quite the same as what is done under Gem or Windows.

The OS event manager is used primarily to insert event records into the event queue; the toolbox event manager is used by the application to extract them.

```
procedure MacMainEventLoop;      (* An example Event Loop, in Pascal. *)
var  Event:        EventRecord;
     AnEventHere: Boolean;
begin
   LemmeGo := false;             (* The ever-popular boolean escape valve. *)
   Repeat
      SystemTask;                (* This is used to support desk accessories. *)
      AnEventHere := GetNextEvent(AllEvents,Event); (* Return false if none. *)
```

```
    if AnEventHere then
      case Event.what of
        mouseDown:      MDownHandler( Event );      (* Mouse button *)
        KeyDown:        KDownHandler( Event );      (* Keyboard key *)
        ActivateEvt:    ActHandler( Event );        (* Window selection *)
        UpDateEvt:      UpHandler( Event );         (* Redraw request *)
      end;
    until LemmeGo;
end;
```

Gem

Since Gem is designed to be used in a multitasking environment on smallish computers, there is a big difference in the design of a Gem application. The busy-wait event loop is replaced with the relatively recent (vintage 1966) concept of blocking a task from execution until the request for a resource is satisfied. In this case the resource is most immediately in the form of an event or an event message. The Gem application informs the Gem AES what it wants, and then does not run until "something happens."

The Gem function normally called is event_multi. Unlike Apple's GetNextEvent and Microsoft's austere GetMessage, the call to the event-_multi binding routine is accompanied by a gaggle of parameters: 16 integer input parameters, 7 integer output parameters, and 1 address input parameter. The call will always result in something interesting being returned.

Please refer to Part 1 for an example of the event loop code for Gem.

Windows

Windows is a multitasking environment that cannot handle the idea of application programs executing busy-waits until something interesting happens. The Windows' "Main Procedure," in the vernacular of C programs, is both the routine in an application that executes first and the routine that accepts (event) messages from Windows. It is the main procedure by virtue of its name; it *must* be called WinMain.

Only messages that belong to an application will be made available to that application. Some messages are broadcast to all applications sharing space on the display (like User Requested That Windows Terminate, which causes applications to scramble to clean up and close files).

When a message appears, WinMain calls WndProc indirectly, using another routine called DispatchMessage. WinMain obtains messages by calling GetMessage. Some processing of the message information can be done (by TranslateMessage) prior to a call to DispatchMessage.

WndProc decides which messages can be handled by the application code. The rest are handed back to Windows via DefWindowProc, which effectively carries out the default processing of messages. Having the application receive all the messages first and allowing it to hand the ones that it doesn't want to process back to Microsoft Windows gives an application control over messages that concern it.

IIGS

Event receiving and handling with the IIGS is about the same as with the Macintosh.

Amiga

If a program is being written along the lines set up for Windows, Gem, and Macintosh, then an Amiga event loop looks much like those found on those machines. An IDCMP is created either when a window that owns one is created or when application code establishes one. Intuition and the Amiga exec will funnel event messages to the application via IDCMPs. The application sets up which event messages are acceptable, and then calls Wait; when the appropriate signal appears, the task is reawakened and the incoming messages are read out of the port queue one at a time. Each message must be answered via the ReplyMsg routine.

The kind of IDCMP event messages that come over the transom are delegated with the IDCMP flags, settable when the associated window is created or via the ModifyIDCMP routine. Here are some of the options:

MOUSE-	
BUTTONS	Send mouse button up/down events
MOUSEMOVE	Mouse movements events (expect *tons* of messages)
DELTAMOVE	Mouse movements events (in terms of deltas)
GADGETDOWN	Send gadget selection event
GADGETUP	Send gadget release event
CLOSEWINDOW	Send close window gadget selected message
MENUPICK	Menu mouse button event, menu item number returned
MENUVERIFY	Determine if window drawing is complete event

REQSET	Generate message when first requester opens
REQCLEAR	Generate message when last requester closes
REQVERIFY	Application wants window draw finished before requesters appear over window
NEWSIZE	Intuition should send message when window is resized
REFRESH-WINDOW	Send message to application when window should be refreshed
SIZEVERIFY	Must finish drawing to window before resize request
ACTIVEWINDOW	Message sent if window activated
INACTIVE-WINDOW	Message sent if window deactivated
RAWKEY	Send raw key codes in Code field of message
NEWPREFS	Send message when preferences have been changed
DISKINSERTED	Send message when disk is inserted
DISKREMOVED	Send event message when disk is removed

KEYBOARD EVENTS

Macintosh

Some of the Macintosh keys do not generate key-down and key-up events. These modifier keys are Shift, Caps Lock, Option, and Command (aka Splat). The status of the modifier keys is reported by a Macintosh keyboard key event, which is generated when a regular keyboard key is pressed or released.

The Mac keyboard is missing some keys that are common on other keyboards, like ESCAPE and BREAK. The Mac keyboard is also missing a number of the IBM PC keyboard keys, including function keys, ALT, and PRINT SCREEN. Existing software occasionally uses the Command key as the control key; the odd finger stretch to type CONTROL-Q while connected to a bulletin board or other remote system is slightly annoying, but only because it is different. The idea of the Mac keyboard is that application software is supposed to rely less on special key combinations and more on the mouse. The Mac + keyboard is not much different. The Mac II and SE keyboards are redesigns with the missing keys put back.

The old Mac has an optional keypad that has an ESCAPE key and four arrow keys. On the new Macs a numeric keypad is standard equipment.

In addition to the normal key-down and key-up events there is the **autokey** event, which reports when a key has been held down for a specified period. Autokey is used to implement a repeat key operation.

Gem

Gem has to rely on the machine's operating system for providing basic keyboard services. The Gem keyboard event returns a 16-bit value, with a normal ASCII code in the low byte (if one is available for the pressed key) and a binary code in the high byte. On the IBM PC, for example, all the ALT-modified keys and all the function keys have low bytes of 00; the normal uppercase and lowercase letters and the numbers have regular ASCII values in the low byte and various machine-dependent values in the high byte.

The Gem keyboard event (evnt_keybd) returns only the 16-bit key ID and not the status of the mouse button or the keyboard modifier keys. For that information the IBM PC version of the Gem VDI routine vq_key_s provides the current state of the keyboard modifier keys. Also, the Gem AES function graf_mkstate provides the vq_key_s modifier key data, the current state of the mouse button, and the screen coordinates of the mouse. There is no equivalent to the Macintosh autokey event. The IBM PC modifier keys are Control, Right Shift, Left Shift, and ALT.

Windows

There is a small complement of messages to handle keyboard key events. The lParam field of the keyboard key message contains an 8-bit scan code and a repeat count, the latter serving the same function as the Mac's autokey event. The wParam field contains a 16-bit virtual key code.

The messages WM_KEYDOWN and WM_KEYUP are obtained through the GetMessage function. They provide "raw" character information that can be used as is or converted into something more obvious with the routine TranslateMessage. TranslateMessage simply accepts messages like WM_KEYDOWN and returns messages like WM_CHAR and WM_DEADCHAR. WM_CHAR is for normal ASCII characters; the wParam field contains the ASCII value and lParam carries both a repeat count and an auto-repeat count. WM_DEADCHAR is for a character with no forward motion (in other words, a character that is combined with another character to form a third character). An example of a dead character is an accent mark, normally intended to coexist with another character.

There are messages similar to WM_CHAR and WM_DEADCHAR generated when a user is accessing a window's system menu, size box, or scroll bars. They are WM_SYSKEYDOWN, WM_SYSKEYUP, WM_SYSCHAR, and WM_SYSDEADCHAR. They are distinct messages because the origin of the messages is significant.

Since the keyboard is a limited resource that can't be used by more than one window or application at a time, the routine SetFocus assigns the ownership of the keyboard to the window specified by the function parameter. GetFocus obtains the Microsoft Windows handle to the current owner of the keyboard. GetKeyState, a routine that returns the current state of the specified virtual key, yields information that will usually make sense only to the owner of the focus (Microsoft lingo for "system keyboard").

Through GetKeyState the status of a toggle key can be obtained. A toggle key is more modal than other kinds of keys, since its physical position doesn't always imply the same state; press and release the CAPS LOCK key once and the CAPS LOCK is activated, but a second press and release will reset the control and allow lowercase characters again.

Amiga

Amiga keypresses can work either through the IDCMP ports or through a console device. Since we are more interested in portable solutions, we are excluding the console device, which is only a source of data and not of event information.

When a keypress event Intuimessage comes in, the raw data can be in the Code field of the message, and the positions of qualifier keys (SHIFT, CTRL, etc.) are described in the Qualifier field of an Intuimessage.

Recommendations

Simple programs won't have to deal with unusual key combinations when using a windowing package—that's what the mouse is for. Keypress shortcuts can be supplied for menu entry selections, but on large programs it will be difficult to supply all the possible menu options with keypress equivalents. Although the names and numbers of the modifier keys and the availability of function keys vary among machines, creating system-dependent routines to provide character input with a consistent interface for your specific requirements will be straightforward. Remember that function keys and control keys are to be used strictly for shortcuts, and should *never* be considered the principal or first-choice method for activating application operations.

MOUSE EVENTS

Macintosh

Since the Mac has but a single button, there is less to worry about when creating code that uses it. The first thing to do when a mouse-down event arrives (via GetNextEvent) is find out where the mouse cursor is and what the keyboard-modifier keys are doing. The message field of the mouse event doesn't contain anything useful, but the where field reports where the cursor is on the screen. That XY coordinate should be handed to the function FindWindow (of the window manager) to determine if the cursor was in a window, a system window, the menu bar, a content region, a drag region, a grow region, or a goaway region. The application's reaction to the mouse pick will depend on whether the window (if any) should be considered active or not.

The toolbox TextEdit routines are clever in that they can process mouse events intelligently. They know what to do when a double-click occurs, for example. Otherwise a double-click will have to be determined by the application code by measuring the time difference between the occurrence of two mouse-down events.

There are a few support routines bundled within the toolbox event manager that are mouse event-related. The procedure GetMouse provides the current mouse cursor location. The function Button returns TRUE if the mouse button is down and FALSE if it is up. StillDown returns TRUE if the button has been held down since the last mouse-down event. WaitMouseUp is strange; if there is a mouse-up event in the event queue (meaning the mouse button is now up), the mouse-up event in the queue is removed and WaitMouseUp returns FALSE. If Wait-MouseUp has to "wait" for the button to be released, it returns a TRUE. It does not wait for the button to be released.

Gem

The mouse events in Gem are simple, and are different from Mac mouse events because of the singletask/multitask ideology differences. As far as an application can tell, the differences fade outside of the event loops.

A mouse event can occur when the mouse cursor is moved into a rectangular region so that the mouse cursor can be switched by the application (Gem is watching the mouse). Both the evnt_button and evnt_mouse events provide the coordinates of the mouse cursor, the state of the keyboard modifier keys, and the state of each mouse button. The evnt_button event can be told how many button presses are necessary in a preset time period for the event to go off; the evnt_mouse event is told from which mouse rectangle the mouse cursor has to escape for that event to sound.

Mouse events, as mentioned previously, can be numerous. Gem informs the application when the state of a mouse button has changed, but only if the application has told Gem that it is interested (using a mask).

Windows

The WM_MOUSEMOVE message is generated when the mouse is moved. The states of the two Windows-supported mouse buttons and the shift and control modifier keys are included in the message (in the wParam field). The lParam field contains the coordinates of the mouse cursor relative to the top left corner of the window/application receiving the message.

WM_LBUTTONDOWN is the message generated by pressing the left mouse button. WM_RBUTTONDOWN is generated by pressing the right mouse button. WM_LBUTTONUP and WM_RBUTTONUP are generated when the appropriate mouse buttons are released. The WM_LBUTTONDBLCLK and WM_RBUTTONDBLCLK messages appear when the respective mouse buttons are pressed twice within a preset time. All the mouse button messages contain the same information as WM_MOUSEMOVE. The quirk here is that only windows created with a class that includes the CS_DBLCLKS style can receive double-click messages, and a double-click action will generate a down, an up, and a double-click message (three messages).

AMIGA

Button Dynamics

The left button is the **selection button**, and is used to select graphic and text items in a window. The right one is the **information transfer button**, also known as the **menu button**. Holding the menu button down displays the menu bar associated with the currently active window across the top of the current Intuition screen. Double-clicking the menu button activates a special "double-menu" requester to be used to transfer information.

Holding the right mouse button down permits selection of multiple menu items with the left mouse button.

Mouse Button Message Types

The event type MOUSEBUTTONS can be generated with the following associated codes:

SELECTDOWN	Left button down
SELECTUP	Left button up
MENUDOWN	Right button down
MENUUP	Right button up

If mouse events occur over gadgets and menu items, different event message types are generated.

DEVICE DRIVER EVENTS

Macintosh

The meanings of device driver events are sensitive to the contexts of the different drivers that generate them. It is a discretionary event type that ought to be used by low-level hardware-interface software. Adding custom device drivers hasn't been common because the original Mac, the 512K Mac, and the Mac+ are not equipped with high-speed hardware buses for adding devices excluding memory to the system. It is common but not obligatory for parts of a device driver to be provoked by a hardware interrupt.

Gem and Windows

Gem and Windows are both designed to handle a large variety of devices, especially graphic devices. Both windowing packages use drivers to translate device-independent commands to hardware-dependent ones. When, for example, a Gem device driver has to tell Gem or a Gem application that something is occurring, two things are likely to happen. The first is that a hardware interrupt will fire, awakening a small interrupt-based I/O routine that will take care of the basic needs of the interrupt service and no more. The second is that a larger component of the device driver will, at Gem's behest, find out what the interrupt routine had to do and finish the job by formulating the appropriate event structure and placing it in the correct queue or stack location. Gem starts the ready but blocked receiver of the event structure, and the application reads its mail. Windows is no different. The exact nature or composition of device drivers for both Gem and Windows is not public knowledge, because Microsoft and Digital Research consider that information to be more proprietary.

Amiga

For device drivers and other system sources, regular exec messages are generated and accepted by an application via an IDCMP port.

EVENT PRIORITIES

Macintosh

Mac event types vary in priority. Activate events are the highest priority; they are never really inserted into the event queue, though the GetNext-Event routine will produce an activate event (if one is available) as though the event were sitting at the top of the queue. Lower in priority are the mouse button and key events, the disk-inserted event, network events, Mac device driver events, and application-defined events; they are inserted into the queue in first-in/first-out order. The autokey event is next, reporting that a keyboard key is being held down. The lowest priority event is update; update events are also not inserted into the event queue, but are generated by the event manager when two conditions are met: first, when a call to GetNextEvent occurs and the queue is empty, and second, when the contents of a window have been changed.

Gem

The message pipes are strictly first-in/first-out queues. Other than getting the oldest message event in the queue, there is no standard mechanism provided for extracting selected messages out of FIFO order from the queue (unlike the Mac and Windows event managers). Since the keyboard, mouse, mouse button, and timer events don't use message pipes, their importance is completely separate from the message events, leaving their priority up to the application. The Gem keystone event manager function, evnt_multi, will return with the first event message of any type specified by the application, but one kind of message event can't be favored over another.

Windows

The application queues are normally first-in/first-out queues, but Windows manipulates the order of queued messages for overall improvement in the behavior of the entire system. For example, Windows keeps paint messages at the back end of the application queue. Nonpaint messages are inserted into the queue before any already-queued paint messages. If two paint messages are present in an application queue, they are merged to form a single paint message. Sizing requests are not controlled like paint messages; they are always extracted from the queue before paint messages. Since sizing messages may correspond with paint messages, special attention has to be given to processing size messages quickly.

Amiga

I don't believe there is (currently) a way to manipulate the order in which messages are stored in an IDCMP port queue. Messages can be selectively extracted from the queue by modifying the allowed message types with calls to the ModifyIDCMP routine.

3.4 Graphics

USING THE GRAPHICS LIBRARY

Aside from much of the application code being system-dependent, many adjustments to a portable application are for differences in the operation of the back ends of the compiler systems, meaning the linkers and (lately) resource builders/editors. It seems that all systems use different roads for the last leg of the journey to get to the same town. The back end differences are a factor, but not as voluminous a tide as the stuff discussed in this section—how each of the graphics subsystems and many of the routines work, and how they compare with one another.

Macintosh

QuickDraw in ROM
The software base for Macintosh graphics manipulation, **Quickdraw**, is embedded in ROM in every Mac. The contents of the major versions of ROM don't vary from machine to machine. At this time the Mac+ and older, upgraded Macs contain 128K of ROM. The 512K and 128K Macs that haven't been upgraded contain 64K of ROM. The differences between the 64K and 128K ROM cannot be treated lightly. Since the upgrade from 64K to 128K of ROM involves some money, it is not advisable to assume that a software package only has to run on machines with the new ROM. The new Mac II and SE have more ROM code that is in addition to the 128K ROM. The differences are handled where possible with disk-based update system software.

Pascal Calling Standards
Calls to the Quickdraw routines (the Mac embedded graphics routines) are made using the standard Macintosh Pascal calling rules. That is, parameters must be placed on the stack in the order that they appear in the Pascal source, implying that the first parameter in the list is pushed onto the stack first. Applications implemented using good high-level language systems don't have extra "baggage code" to do anything special to get to the ROM functions, since the compilers/linkers try to absorb the details. Some systems may need a special PASCAL attribute in C source code to warn the compiler system to store the parameter list backward on the stack (with respect to C code).

Assembly Concerns
The Quickdraw routines have a short list of caveats when accessed using assembly language. This isn't a normal concern for portability, but someone may be trying to port assembly code from machine to machine. Here are some warnings:

> The contents of registers a0, a1, d0, d1, and d2 are destroyed by Quickdraw routines.
>
> Booleans require a single byte on the stack.
>
> Characters and integers require a word (16 bits) on the stack.
>
> Pointers, reals, long integers, and handles need 32 bits.
>
> All VARs require a pointer pushed on the stack.

Records that are smaller than 4 bytes may be placed directly on the stack, but anything bigger can't be; a pointer to the record should be used instead.

Other routines that are not included in ROM are available in library files that can be linked into the executable module. There are third parties that sell utility libraries intended for making application writing much simpler; these libraries provide immense help in producing portable software with commercial/industrial quality. To find out about these libraries join APDA, the Apple Programmer's and Developer's Association, read *Mac Tutor Magazine*, join one or more of the major dialups (like CompuServe or Genie), or get into a developer's group.

External Declarations

From the Pascal language point of view accessing routines from another module requires declaring the external routines; these declarations are commonly found in readable files that are included at compile time using the standard Pascal $I metacommand (or something like it). The external declarations describe the many hiding places in which the routines are lurking, like ROM (accessed via A-TRAP) or a nearby code resource.

The following example Macintosh C declaration involves a ROM routine called TESetText. It uses Pascal calling conventions, so the declaration begins with the pascal keyword.

```
pascal void TESetText(text,length,hTE) /* example external declaration in C */
    Ptr         text;               /* =test= is a Pointer type */
    long        length;             /* parameter =length= is a long int */
    TEHandle    hTE;                /* hTE is a handle to an edit record */
                extern 0xA9CF;      /* ah! a friendly A-TRAP entry */
```

Here is the same external declaration from one of the TML Pascal include files:

```
PROCEDURE TESetText(    inText: Ptr;
                        textLength:  LONGINT;
                        h; TEHandle );        INLINE $A9CF;
```

Here is a TML Pascal declaration involving a routine that isn't in ROM, but in a library file that has to be linked with the rest of the application code for the routines to be accessible. Note that the keyword EXTERNAL is used instead of INLINE.

```
FUNCTION SpeechOn( ExcpsFile:    Str255;
                  VAR theSpeech: SpeechHandle): SpeechErr; EXTERNAL;
```

Gem

No members of the IBM PC "horde" currently contain more than a minimum of firmware; the entire Gem runtime environment resides on disk. The Atari ST line was initially released with all the operating system and runtime environment on disk, but much of the common code has since been migrated to ROM. The time reduction to load the remainder of the operating environment on disk when using ROM is significant. The reconfiguration doesn't require changes in existing executable modules.

The standard Digital Research Gem binding routines are written in C and are used without special arrangement. Direct communication with Gem AES is done using a list of pointers to arrays of integers and longs (containing a variety of datatypes); the Gem VDI requires its own list of pointers to a different set of arrays. A different set of binding routines is provided with each compiler system working under Gem. The extents of these routines vary widely. The unwritten guidelines on providing the binding routines for a compiler include striving to make a superset of the de facto standard library (the DRI IBM PC version of the Gem binding routines) and using the same names as those used by the DRI binding routines. There are a small number of developer aids provided for the Atari ST version of Gem that are intended to be library add-ons for existing compilers.

Windows

In the present form Windows seems amenable only to those languages that use the Microsoft linker. The version of Windows made available for the development of this book includes a special Windows linker, presumably to handle newer object file formats that aren't included in older, standard release versions of Microsoft's linker for MS-DOS.

In the application some routines are required to be declared with special attributes, like PASCAL and FAR, depending on the implementation language. For example, WndProc and WinMain are two routines that must exist in every application that is intimate with the Windows environment. They must be declared with the PASCAL keyword. The WndProc declaration must also be declared with the FAR keyword.

Assembly Conventions

The Windows Toolkit includes a file, cmacros.inc, containing assembly language macros used to emulate the high-level language interface conventions needed for an assembler application program to talk to Windows. There are a few things that have to be defined for the macros to work properly: the Intel memory model to use (small, middle, large, compact, or huge), the calling convention (C, Pascal), and the presence of Windows epilog and prolog code used to define the current procedure's data segment.

What do the macros look like? Here is a list of those available at the time of writing:

createSeg	Create new segment with given name and attributes
sBegin	Open a segment (similar to MASM's SEGMENT)
sEnd	Close a segment (similar to MASM's ENDS)
assumes	Ref's relative to seg reg (MASM's ASSUME)
dataOFFSET	Generate relative offset into named group's data segment
codeOFFSET	Generate relative offset into named group's code segment
*segName***OFFSET**	Generate offset relative to beginning of group that segName segment is a member of
staticX	Allocate private static memory for storage
globalX	Allocate public static memory for storage
externX	Used to define external variables or procedures
labelX	Used to define one label for external variables or procedures
cProc	Used to define the name and attributes of a procedure
parmX	Used to define procedure parameters
LocalX	Used to define frame variables for a procedure
cBegin	Define the entry point for a procedure specified
cCall	Push specified arguments onto the stack, save some registers, and call the specified procedure
Save	Used to specify the registers to be saved by the next use of the cCall macro
Arg	Used to define the arguments to be passed by the next use of the cCall macro.
DefX	Define a specified name so that it can be referenced elsewhere

Smashes	Used to mention which registers are rubbed out by the procedure indicated
RegPtr	Make a 32-bit pointer indicated by a segment and index register pair
errnz	Display an error if expression specified doesn't evaluate to zero
errn$	Display an error if the address of the present location, subtracted from the first parameter of this macro and added to the second parameter, is not zero

Here is another tidbit garnered from the Microsoft Windows manuals regarding procedure calls: For the C calling convention registers S and DI must be saved if they are used, and the BP register must always be saved.

IIGS

By design the higher-level software differences between Mac's Quickdraw and Cortland's Quickdraw II are small. That is not to say that the changes that have been made for the IIGS are trivial! The basics of the IIGS and Mac are not the same, and the piper must be paid somewhere.

The standard Macintosh display is a bitmap of 512 by 342 square black-and-white pixels. The "super-hires" IIGS display is 640 by 200 pixels (the same size as the standard IBM PC color graphics display), with 4 colors at a time and rectangular pixels. The IIGS display also supports 16 colors at a time, but the number of displayed pixels is then cut way down.

The IIGS uses a 65816 processor, which is much different from the 68000 in a Macintosh. The 65816, for example, is much slower. It appears from the preliminary documentation that Apple engineers expect developers to write more IIGS code in assembler than was expected on the Macintosh, perhaps because of the difference in speed. That is not to say that much of the application code for the Macintosh isn't written in assembler; much of it is.

Amiga

The Amiga ROM kernel is undergoing changes that may dramatically affect application code. Data structures that most would consider to be within the domain (and under the protection) of the system have fields that are directly accessible by application code. This would not be so bad if the structures aren't changed, but they are. The best way to react to a system like this is to create or use a custom set of data structure access routines that act to consolidate the adjustments. For example rather than saying:

```
a := b^.c;
```

it is safer to use:

```
a := CField(b);
```

since changes to the record type will force a change in the contents of the procedure (CField), but the use of the procedure will probably not change. The second form of the statement is also slower, since it involves the additional overhead of a function call and return.

Assembler Concerns

The 68000 registers d0, d1, a0, and a1 are scratch, and do not have to be saved prior to function calls. Consequently, don't expect them to retain values placed in them during function calls. *All* other data and address registers have to be saved. The values of functions (results) are returned in register d0. Register a6 is off limits within the system kernel, as it is used as the base address for a function vector table.

COORDINATE SYSTEMS

Macintosh

The Macintosh global coordinate plane ranges from -32768 to $+32767$ in both axes. The origin coordinate (0,0) is at the center of the grid. Grid coordinates are integer values. Negative values are either to the left of or above the origin (note the orientation in Fig. 3–7).

The existing Macintosh standard display is a 512-by-342 pixel monochrome bitmap. The Mac II supports color and has a larger bitmap. A few add-on display devices have been created to enlarge the existing Mac display bitmap, in one case to 1024 by 1024 pixels. From this experience we have learned that it is important for software to be written so that the display size is not *assumed* to be 512 by 342 pixels. Doing so prevents the immediate use of the larger bitmap real estate. This is a common problem, and the solution is normally in the application code.

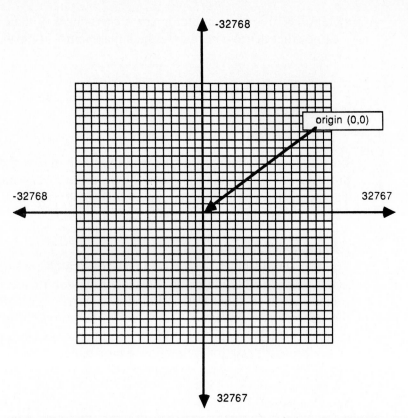

Figure 3–7 The Macintosh Quickdraw coordinate plane. The 2GS Quickdraw II coordinate plane isn't as large: − 16K to 16K on both axes.

The Macintosh coordinate grid is not the same as the display bitmap. This distinction is not insignificant, for there are two common ways to address bits on the coordinate plane although the difference may seem capricious.

The grid lines have length but no width, so the lines have no trouble fitting between the screen pixels. Within the bounds of the Mac display the pixel that corresponds to a grid coordinate is below and to the right of the coordinate point (see Fig. 3–8).

Lines are drawn (see Fig. 3–9) with a pen nib that may have a width or height larger than a single bit; the drawing location that corresponds to a grid coordinate is still below and to the right of the coordinate point, extending farther to the right and downward as required (see Fig. 3–9).

When a rectangle is drawn (see Fig. 3–10), the coordinates of the rectangle contain all the bits that visually represent the rectangle; the right

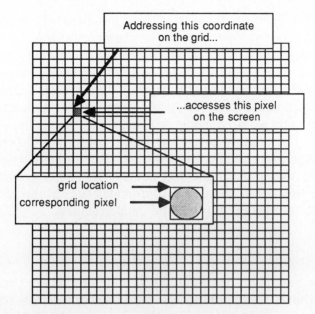

Figure 3–8 How pixels correspond with grid locations

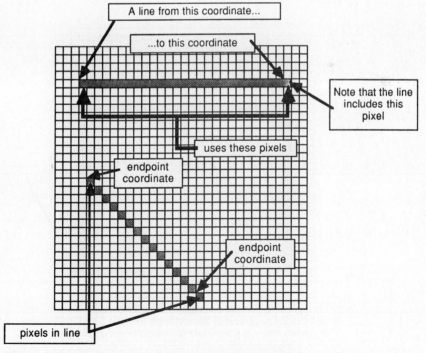

Figure 3–9 Lines drawn in the Mac coordinate system

side border is to the right of the drawn right side line, and the lower border is below the lower side of the drawn lower line.

Other graphic primitives are based on having a defining rectangle that is used to draw ovals, round-edged rectangles, polygons, regions, and arcs. All the routines used for drawing these objects follow the described rules except one: FramePoly, which permits lines to be drawn just below or to the right of the defining rectangle.

The origin (0,0) of the Macintosh display bitmap is at the top left corner. In agreement with the global coordinate system, local coordinates increase to the right and downward. There is more on the difference between local and global coordinates later in this chapter, particularly in the sections on bitmaps and data structures.

Gem

Because Gem machines are all different, as are their displays, the Gem Virtual Device Interface is more concerned with accommodating differences in physical displays; Gem has a mechanism that makes the coordinate systems for each different display match: **Normalized Device Coordinates (NDC)** (see Fig. 3–11).

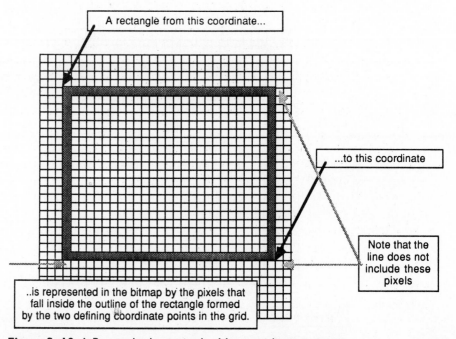

Figure content labels:
A rectangle from this coordinate...

...to this coordinate

Note that the line does not include these pixels

..is represented in the bitmap by the pixels that fall inside the outline of the rectangle formed by the two defining coordinate points in the grid.

Figure 3–10 A Rectangle drawn in the Mac coordinate system

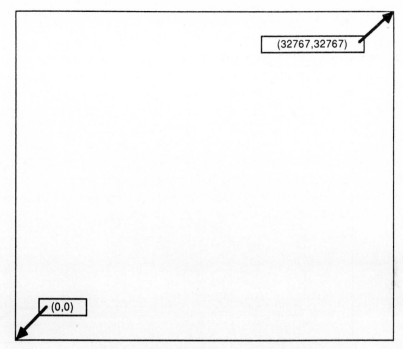

coordinates are expressed in terms of logical units

Figure 3–11 Gem Normalized Device Coordinate plane for a graphics device

The NDC space is 1-quarter as large as a Macintosh coordinate space, with the coordinates (0,0) mapped to the lower left corner, and (32767,32767) assigned to the top right of the display. The trick behind the NDC is that a Gem application pretends that the physical display is the entire NDC space, which has 32768^2 pixels. Gem VDI is then responsible for knowing the true resolution and dimensions of the display and the pixel proportions. When a Gem VDI graphics routine is called and given NDC coordinates, Gem VDI converts the NDC coordinates into pixel coordinates to change the display.

The raster coordinate space (see Fig. 3–12) is the coordinate system that has the closest relation to the bit image on the display; if the display is 640 by 200 pixels, then the raster coordinate space is 640 by 200. If NDC is used, all the individual NDC values must be mapped into raster coordinates before becoming visible.

When mapping Normalized Device Coordinates to raster coordinates, different scale factors are used on each axis to adjust the final image for variations in the shapes of the pixels and the dimensions of the display; this conversion can be time-consuming.

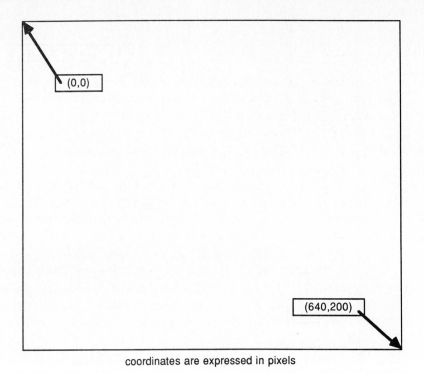

coordinates are expressed in pixels

Figure 3–12 Gem Device Coordinate plane for an IBM PC CGA display

The use of NDC for an open device is optional; an application can address the display using either the Normalized Device Coordinates or the raster coordinates. The system used depends on how the device was opened by the application (via the Gem VDI v_opnwk or v_opnvwk routines). Many applications are certainly better off directly using raster coordinates.

Simple but important differences between environment coordinate systems include the orientation of coordinate space axes and the relative positions of a coordinate and its corresponding screen pixel. A Gem raster coordinate is to the lower left of its corresponding pixel. The origin of a raster coordinate space is at the upper left corner, and (MaxX,MaxY) is at the bottom right corner. Yup, the Gem RC map orientation is different from that of Gem NDC space, but the RC axes have the same orientation as Mac local coordinate axes.

A significant observation is that Gem VDI routines only understand screen coordinates, either normalized or raster. This means that, while the Macintosh has some automatic coordinate-space to screen-space mapping supported in the lower graphic routines, Gem VDI does not.

For example, if a graphics command is made on the Macintosh, say via a FrameRect call (which draws the outline of a rectangle), the routine is given coordinates that are not screen coordinates; there is always some logical to physical coordinate mapping going on. Prior to the FrameRect call there must have been some arrangements made with whatever data structures control the current status of this mapping. Consequently, no matter what happens, more work is being done on the Macintosh to figure out where points are to be drawn on the display. The VDI routines are lower and closer to the display.

The Gem AES routines use VDI routines for all drawing; AES routines (like objc_draw) usually work with screen coordinates, leaving any fancy coordinate space translation to the application code.

Gem AES supports creating data records that contain a variety of predefined graphic objects that can then be manipulated with other Gem AES routines. The data records are members of linked lists; parent-child relationships can be defined between objects. The coordinates of a child object are then relative to the parent-object domain, but they are *still essentially the same as screen coordinates*. The parent object covers equal or more screen real estate than the child object; when a child object is drawn, the Gem clip rectangle is defined to be the part of the screen occupied by the parent object.

Windows

The Microsoft Windows version of a Macintosh GrafPort or a Gem virtual workstation is the **display context**. The display context contains the current location, draw attributes, and other device information. There tends to be a display context for each window, with each window having its own coordinate mapping systems. Display contexts are covered at some length in the data structures section of this chapter, and are also covered a little in the chapter on windowing.

One of the values kept by the display context is the **coordinate mapping mode**, which describes the principle rules for the coordinate space. There are seven supported mapping modes. The default coordinate mapping mode for a display context is MM_TEXT, which means:

☐ The coordinate origin is at the upper left corner
☐ The Y axis is upside-down (the numbers increase going down)
☐ The coordinate scale is screen or device pixels

Other coordinate mapping modes are MM_LOMETRIC, MM_HI-METRIC, MM_LOENGLISH, MM_HIENGLISH, MM_TWIPS, MM_ISOTROPIC, and MM_ANISOTROPIC. Each of these mapping modes differs in scale and orientation of each axis (the directions in which the values are increasing and decreasing).

Each of the following modes have positive X to the right and positive Y upward:

MM_LOMETRIC	0.1-millimeter scale
MM_HIMETRIC	0.01-millimeter scale
MM_LOENGLISH	0.01-inch scale
MM_HIENGLISH	0.001-inch scale
MM_TWIPS	1/20th-point scale (for typographers)

These modes have definable axis scales and axis orientation:

MM_ISOTROPIC

MM_ANISOTROPIC

MM_ISOTROPIC differs from MM_ANISOTROPIC in that the former requires that both axes have the same scale, while the latter has no such restriction (that is, Y could be in inches and X could be in millimeters). In fact, all the mapping modes except MM_ANISOTROPIC have both axes of the same scale.

To set the definable axis units, orientation, and scale, the routines SetWindowExt, SetViewportExt, SetWindowOrg, and SetViewportOrg are provided. Microsoft Windows assumes that with all this variety your application deals in something other than pixels. MS Windows is more than happy to oblige the whims of the application, but this means that there is a little more to the coordinate system support vehicle for programmers to pick up.

The first trick in knowing MS Windows graphics is understanding the differences between windows and viewports.

The **window** on the display is a nifty mechanism used to give a program some of the display. How much of the screen is given to the window depends on what the user wants, and is influenced by what is needed to show the data intelligently. Sometimes, though, the real estate requirements are not constant over time, so the size of the window will shrink and expand.

On the other side of the window are the data being displayed. Normally, not all the data are displayable on the screen at once, much less in a window on the screen. To show more, make the window bigger; to see different information, move the window around with respect to the data. It is like moving the scroll bar in a text editor to "push the text up and down."

Graphics editing programs such as AutoCAD and MacDraft enable you to slap graphic entities like boxes and widgets onto a mythical worksheet that could be as large as the floor of a bullring if the worksheet physically existed. The graphic entities on the worksheet are assigned coordinates relative to that worksheet, so if a part of the worksheet were displayed you'd see all the graphics on that part. If the designer were working in inches everything would be placed on that worksheet in terms of inches; for example, at the location 4 inches from the top and 3 inches from the left side of the sheet there is a circle ½ inch in diameter.

In most drafting applications it is impractical to draw everything on a one-to-one scale. The ability to draw objects that are 1 foot wide as 1-inch objects on paper is very important, yet sometimes it would be nice to see the object as though it were drawn as a 10-inch object (a close up).

In this zoom operation, obviously the physical size of the window on the screen doesn't change, and nothing changes on the drawing or in the database, but the drawing apparently "gets closer" to the screen. In Microsoft Windows all that changes are a couple values in the display context.

In addition to the screen, the window on the screen, and the worksheet (aka the application's coordinate space, or **world coordinate space**), there is also a viewport. The **viewport** is not visually represented by anything on the display or in the world coordinate system; it is a construct that is used to help determine what to show from the world coordinate space. A viewport is not useful alone.

The description would be straightforward were it not true that somewhere along the progression of computer science the term "window" picked up two meanings; this is where those two meanings clash.

When used with a viewport a window is the visible area of the world coordinate space (see Fig. 3–13). For example, if a worksheet is a 10-foot by 10-foot plane, the window may be set to look at the area at the bottom right corner of the worksheet. The window settings might be (9.3, 8.0, .6, .4), meaning that the top left corner of the window is over the location $X = 9.3$, $Y = 8.0$, and the window includes the visible information extending 0.6 feet to the right and 0.4 feet downward; that would put the bottom right corner of the window over the location $X = 9.9$, $Y = 8.4$.

A viewport (Fig. 3–14) is used to turn world coordinates into screen coordinates. The viewport area is mapped on top of the window into the

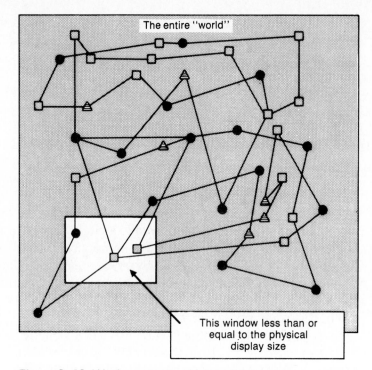

The entire "world"

This window less than or
equal to the physical
display size

Figure 3–13 Window over world coordinate space

world coordinate space, so only things that are within the window are also
within the viewport. To keep the coordinate transform calculations fast,
the world coordinates space window and the viewport are rectangles
rather than fancy shapes like arbitrary polygons.

The viewport does not provide the final piece of the puzzle, the
location of the image on the screen. The location is kept in the display
context and represented visually (in this case by the location of the window
frame on the screen and the Client Rectangle within it).

The size or **extent** of a viewport is described in terms of device
coordinates, like pixels. The window extent is described in terms of the
world coordinates used to reference the graphic data, for example, measurements. The **window origin** is where the upper left corner of the
window hovers over the world coordinate system.

The viewport enters the example with its definition:

```
(0,0, screenloc.right-screenloc.left, screenloc.top-screenloc.bottom)
```

The first two numbers are the X and Y coordinate values for the top left
corner of the viewport. The (0,0) means that the top left corner of the

viewport is where the origin of the world coordinate space window should be mapped. This does *not* mean that the viewport is positioned at pixel (0,0) on the screen—the viewport is not on the screen—but it does mean that the viewport is so many pixels high and so many wide.

The physical width and height of a viewport are defined using screen coordinates (pixels). The width is the third number in the viewport definition, and the fourth number is the height. Again, the screenloc structure is used only to determine size.

We have a window into the world coordinate space, a viewport somewhere on the screen, and a relationship between the viewport and the coordinate space window (see Fig. 3–15). We can now display the contents of the world coordinate space on the screen (Fig. 3–16).

In Figs. 3–17 and 3–18, we change the sizes of both the viewport and the window, one at a time, to see what happens.

In Fig. 3–19, we change the relationship between viewport and window origins.

That should be enough background material to understand what the Windows environment and its routines provide. Now, for those routines.

SetWindowExt is used to assign the X and Y extents of the window into a logical (or world) coordinate space. The window belongs to the specified display context. The function returns the previous extent settings in a long integer; the high-order word is the old Y extent and the low-order word is the old X extent. GetWindowExt returns the current extent settings.

SetViewportExt assigns the extents of the viewport associated with the specified display context. The function returns the previous extent settings in one long integer, like SetWindowExt. GetViewportExt returns the current extent settings.

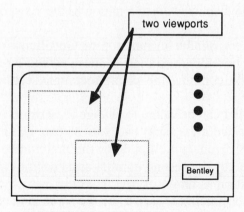

Figure 3–14 Two viewports on a display

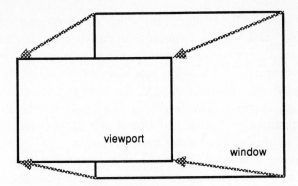

Figure 3–15 Relationship between window and corresponding viewport

SetWindowOrg sets the origin of the specified display context's window into the world coordinate space. The function returns the old origin in a long integer, with Y being the high-order word and X the low-order word. GetWindowOrg returns the current window origin location.

SetViewportOrg sets the origin of the specified display context's viewport. The function returns the old origin in a long integer, like SetWindowOrg. GetViewportOrg returns the current window origin location.

SetMapMode sets the map mode of the display context mentioned in the parameter list. The returned value is the previous mode. The GetMapMode function returns the current map mode.

Another useful routine, GetClientRect, provides the coordinates of the onscreen rectangle that is accessible by an application—the drawing area for that application. The device coordinates are returned in a record that specifies the upper left and lower right corners of the client rectangle. This information is used for determining the extents of the viewport associated with the display context common to the viewport and the client rectangle.

GetWindowRect, similar in function to GetClientRect, provides the dimensions of the bounding rectangle of the specified screen window. The bounding rectangle contains the client rectangle, caption, border, and scroll bars (if any).

ScaleWindowExt can be called to change the extents of a window. The new extents are calculated using two sets of two numbers and the old extents. The old X extent is multiplied by the first number in one set, and the result is divided by the second number and becomes the new X extent. The same calculation is made on the Y extent with the second pair of numbers. ScaleViewportExt is used to do the same kind of modification to the viewport extents.

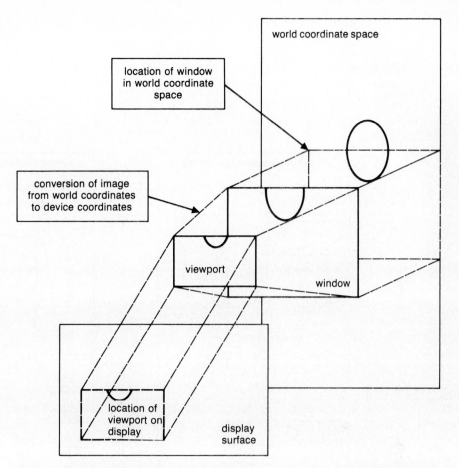

world coordinate space

location of window
in world coordinate
space

conversion of image
from world coordinates
to device coordinates

viewport

window

location of
viewport on
display

display
surface

Figure 3–16 Image mapped onto display using viewport and window over world coordinate space

OffsetWindowOrg and OffsetViewportOrg are used to move the origin of a window or a viewport, respectively, relative to the current value. This is done by adding a change in X value to the current origin's X-coordinate value, and by adding a change in Y value to the origin's Y-coordinate value.

IIGS

The IIGS global coordinate plane ranges from -16384 to $+16383$ in both axes, with the origin $(0,0)$ in the center of the grid. Like the other machines, the IIGS grid coordinates are INTEGER values. IIGS Quickdraw II supports a world coordinate space that is one quarter the size of

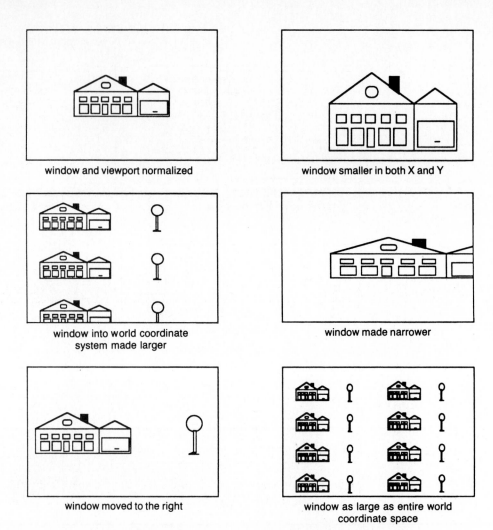

window and viewport normalized

window smaller in both X and Y

window into world coordinate
system made larger

window made narrower

window moved to the right

window as large as entire world
coordinate space

The window origin is not changed, except in the bottom-right example.

Figure 3–17 Window and viewport in normalized proportion, and then changing
the window size

the Macintosh logical coordinate space. To avoid slowing the code down, there are no range checks made on the coordinate values, so it is possible to specify a number far outside the supported range of the coordinate system with possibly wild results.

The coordinate system works exactly the same for Quickdraw II as for Quickdraw, with a point corresponding to a pixel above and to the left of the pixel.

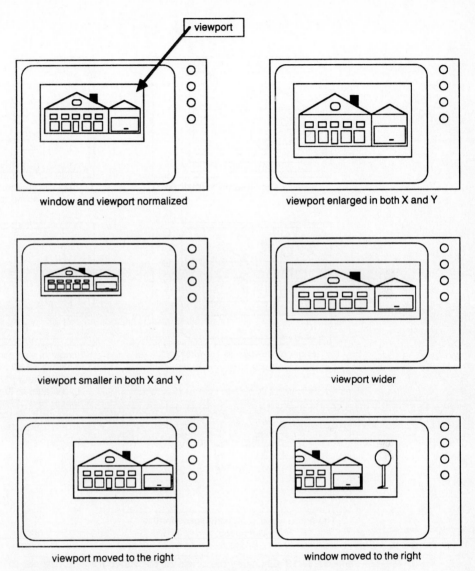

Figure 3–18 Exercising the viewport, and a window change for contrast

The IIGS has some hidden bells and whistles: Each scan line on the display has an attribute byte called a **Scanline Control Byte** (or **SCB**). No such thing exists in the Mac or Mac+ systems, since the SCB contains scan line resolution and color attributes, neither of which is variable on the monochromatic Mac display. The Mac II displays also support color in a different way.

Quickdraw II permits using any section of system RAM for drawing, including the display RAM, but the entire destination pixel map must be

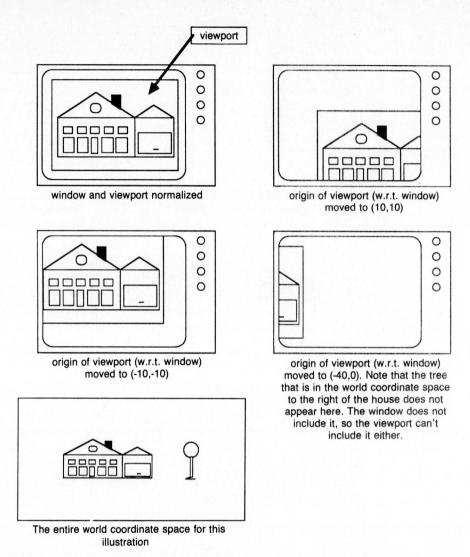

viewport

window and viewport normalized

origin of viewport (w.r.t. window) moved to (10,10)

origin of viewport (w.r.t. window) moved to (-10,-10)

origin of viewport (w.r.t. window) moved to (-40,0). Note that the tree that is in the world coordinate space to the right of the house does not appear here. The window does not include it, so the viewport can't include it either.

The entire world coordinate space for this illustration

Figure 3–19 Changing the origin of the viewport with respect to the corresponding window to the world coordinate space

in a single bank. Overwriting parts of the operating system with graphics isn't recommended.

The BoundsRect is the Quickdraw II rectangle that describes the size and shape of the pixel map. It imposes a local coordinate system on the map. The PortRect encompasses the active data space area. The Mac equivalents are portbits.bounds and portRect, respectively.

Some Quickdraw II routines are being placed in the ROM areas of the machine, and some are being relegated to RAM and, consequently, disk. It is assumed that these routines will be improved over time, as were the Mac Quickdraw routines, so the system ROM profile will change dramatically over time.

Amiga

Amiga's RastPort record is similar in purpose to Mac's GrafPort, Windows' display context, and Gem's virtual workstation. A more complete definition for RastPort is given in the section on data structures later in this chapter. The RastPort record contains everything known about a bitmap, including pen position, current drawing modes, pen colors, patterns, text information, layer information via a pointer to the appropriate layer record (soon to be discussed), virtual sprite, and blitter object animation data via a pointer to a GelsInfo record. The RastPort is not described in full yet because to do so properly would require pretty good descriptions of the other related record types (RasInfo, BitMap, ViewPort, View, Region, Layer, ColorMap, CopList, CprList, AreaInfo, TmpRas, ClipRect, UCopList, and LayerInfo). It's too soon for all of that, but it is time to talk a little about bitmaps and layers.

The function and macro libraries provided for use by application software do not support a coordinate system that is independent of or of a larger scale than the physical, pixel-based coordinate system used for addressing in Amiga bitmaps. Though there are many, many graphics, layer, and animation routines, they are all in support of the low-level capabilities provided by the Amiga display hardware. There are no virtual-to-physical coordinate system conversion routines. There should be many ways to fill this gap, perhaps by using new libraries provided by either Commodore-Amiga or third parties. There is a hardware-supported mechanism for converting physical coordinates to other physical coordinates.

The **layer** mechanism (supported by the Amiga's graphics hardware) allows a larger physical coordinate system to exist than what would be permissible within the boundaries of the display. A layer "owns" a bitmap; the Amiga system understands that a layer bitmap has some additional, commonly used properties that ordinary bitmaps don't have. A **Layer record** contains the extra data used for a layer bitmap.

An application program draws on one or more layer bitmaps. Then part or all of the layer bitmaps are displayed on the screen, controlled by what the Layer records say. The Layer record contains pointers to clipping rectangles and the RastPort in control of the layer; it also contains a boundary rectangle structure, a clipping region structure, some layer access control variables (a task can lock the layer to prevent it from being modified), two variables used to keep track of the scroll position of a superbitmap layer bitmap, pointers to layers to be displayed in front of and behind it, and so on.

The screen, which is itself a bitmap, is not accessed directly by the application tasks. The private layers, whose bitmaps have been drawn on by owner tasks, are displayed by the system according to the information in *all* the Layer records without total chaos appearing on the screen. Layers are used, not just raw bitmaps, for the system to display a multitude of windows.

There are three kinds of layers. The difference between them, as far as coordinate systems are involved, is the size of the addressable bitmap. The layer with the largest raster bitmap, a **superbitmap layer**, can have coordinates that range from 0 to 1024 along both axes. Enough memory has to belong to the bitmap to handle addresses that high; bitmaps can be tremendous memory hogs, especially when many colors are involved. The coordinates for a smaller, common raster bitmap range from 0 to 320; exact sizes are up to the programmer. The top left corner of any bitmap is the origin (0,0), so the Y-axis pixel coordinates increase downward and the X-axis pixel coordinates increase to the right.

There is much more on layers and bitmaps later in the section on bitmaps.

THE POINT

Macintosh

The point data type in Pascal is defined as:

```
TYPE  VHSelect = (V,H);

      Point = RECORD CASE INTEGER OF
          0: (   v: INTEGER;
                 h: INTEGER);
          1: (   vh: ARRAY[ VHSelect ] OF INTEGER)
          END; { Point }
```

The Mac's definition allows access to both X and Y coordinate values as fields of the record or as elements of an array, although the distinction here is moot. This use of the integer type for the variant is considered by some to be poor style. Using a variant record like this is also considered poor style, since it assumes that the storage allocation order is consistent. Some Pascal compilers may place h before v in memory, for example. It was the language originator's intention to teach how to code while still avoiding these questionable tactics. Obviously, it didn't turn out that way.

One routine that operates with the Point type is SetOrigin, which moves the origin to a new coordinate; this affects later drawing (not what is on the display already), such as screen updates. There are also a number of calculation routines: AddPt, SubPt, SetPt, EqualPt, GlobalToLocal, and LocalToGlobal. AddPt adds two coordinate locations together, returning the result in place of the second coordinate. SubPt subtracts the first coordinate from the second, returning the result in place of the second coordinate. SetPt does the absurdly simple task of assigning two integer values to be the coordinates of a point. EqualPt returns TRUE if two specified points are the same.

The last two routines, LocalToGlobal and GlobalToLocal, map the point coordinates between the private coordinate system of a Macintosh GrafPort and the global coordinate plane (see Fig. 3–20).

Gem

All the reference materials viewed before and during the development of this text were devoid of references to anything like a point structure or record. Normally Gem application and binding code passes the X and Y components of coordinates to routines separately as word or integer parameters. The definition of a Gem point is understood to be nothing unusual or different.

The Gem AES objc_offset function returns the screen coordinates of the specified graphic object. The object could be the child of a child of an object: The coordinates of a child object are stored relative to the parent object.

Angles are specified in tenths of a degree. For absolute angles the 3 o'clock position is 0 degrees, and thereafter the values increase counterclockwise.

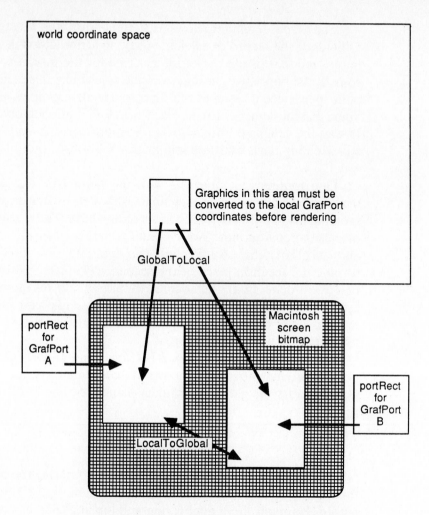

To draw in the GrafPort portRect from the world coordinate space,
the world coordinates must be converted to GrafPort local coordinates via
GlobalToLocal. To do operations between two GrafPorts, the coordinates must be
converted to a mutual coordinate system via LocalToGlobal.

Figure 3–20 Local and global coordinate planes

Windows

The point record for Windows in Pascal is:

```
TYPE POINT = RECORD
      x:    int;
      y:    int;
```

```
END;
PPOINT = ADR OF POINT;          { Just down the block. }
LPPOINT = ADS OF POINT;         { Way in the next county. }
```

For single coordinate pairs Windows doesn't use function parameters with type POINT; instead it uses separate integer values for X and Y. In fact, it is very common for Windows routines to return 32-bit values, with the X value in the low 16-bit word and the Y value in the high 16-bit word; otherwise a return address would be involved, or the return values wouldn't be ignorable (C compilers permit ignoring the existence of the return value of a C function). The Windows routines that handle a variable (and possibly large) number of coordinate points, like Polyline and Polygon, accept as a parameter a pointer to an array of type POINT.

The routine GetPixel retrieves the RGB color value of the pixel at the specified point. If the pixel corresponding to the specified point is within the current clipping region, SetPixel will assign the pixel the specified RGB color.

IIGS

The IIGS Point datatype is the same as on the Macintosh. The Quickdraw II routines AddPt, SubPt, SetPt, and EqualPt work the same as the originals. The global coordinate plane is smaller on the IIGS than the Mac, so the Quickdraw II versions of LocalToGlobal and GlobalToLocal abide by the limit, but otherwise they behave the same as their Quickdraw counterparts. All of these routines are ROM-based.

Amiga

Amiga-supported coordinates are physical, with respect to a Raster bitmap that may belong to a layer. The Amiga is primarily a C language machine, and the low-level support layer at this time can't be considered as airtight as those of the other machines discussed here. Amiga data structures aren't fleshed out as much as those of the other systems. There is no point datatype (but there are a number of other structures, as described later in this chapter). To describe a coordinate, the low routines accept separate parameter values for X and Y. Application software, in the absence of libraries with virtual (world, global) coordinate system support, must provide their own.

To obtain the color value of a pixel in a Raster bitplane, ReadPixel is given a pointer to the RastPort and the Raster Coordinate space X and Y coordinates. ReadPixel returns a value from 0 to 255. ReadPixel builds the pixel color value by checking the corresponding bits in each bitplane of a Raster bitmap.

To understand how bits are mapped back to a color value, read the Amiga description in the color section in this part.

WritePixel is used for setting a pixel belonging to a RastPort Raster bitmap to the RastPort's current foreground color. WritePixel needs a pointer to the RastPort record, an X coordinate, and a Y coordinate value; the coordinates are in terms of the Raster bitmap coordinate space, not screen coordinates.

FUNDAMENTAL, MODAL, AND TEMPORAL CONCERNS

Macintosh

There are a few things that ought to be known by any graphics system when it is asked to draw something on the screen: What (the object it should render), How (what attributes should be involved when the object is drawn), and Where (which includes where the object should and where it should not be drawn).

The Quickdraw package deals with the attributes of drawn lines (like the line width) and the rendering of graphics separately. This means that, before an object is drawn, it is necessary to tell Quickdraw how to set up the pen with separate Quickdraw routine calls. The line draw information is not included in the Quickdraw datatype records used to describe the primitive graphics elements. The obligatory exceptions to this rule are discussed in this part.

The present grafPort record contains all the current truths about the accessible portion of the Mac display; these truths include how lines are to be drawn. The fields describing line width, draw mode, etc., must be set properly before the contents of the screen are changed.

A full description of grafPorts is provided in the data structures section of this part.

Gem

There are VDI routines that, like their Macintosh equivalents, set attributes or modes for drawing. There is no defined structure in Gem equivalent to the grafPort, yet the following functions exist:

vswr_mode	Select the writing mode.
vs_color	Map a color index to three RGB relative color intensities.
vsl_type	Choose a predefined line draw pattern.
vsl_udsty	Define the user-definable line draw pattern.
vsl_width	Specify the line width.
vsl_color	Pick the line draw color index.
vsl_ends	Choose a line endpoint symbol.
vsm_type	Choose the polymarker type.
vsm_height	Choose the polymarker height.
vsm_color	Choose the polymarker color index.
vst_height	Set the character height in absolute mode.
vst_point	Set the character height in points mode.
vst_rotation	Set the character baseline vector.
vst_vont	Set the character face (the same as a Mac font).
vst_color	Pick the color index of text.
vst_effects	Choose the text drawing style.
vst_alignment	Set the text alignment.
vsf_interior	Choose the fill interior style.
vsf_style	Choose the fill style index.
vsf_color	Set the fill color index.
vsf_perimeter	Turn on/off the fill perimeter visibility.
vsf_udpat	Define the user-defined fill pattern.

There are also a number of Gem VDI inquiry functions that return the current modes and options. All these attributes are associated with a (virtual) workstation.

Windows

Under Windows, as mentioned before, the display context is the equivalent of the Mac's GrafPort, also referred to as the DC in the *Microsoft Windows Programmer's Guide* and *Reference Manual*. The unique fields of the DC are the field for indicating either relative or absolute line draws (both may not be active at once), the aforementioned window and viewport origin and extents, and a polygon fill mode field.

IIGS

The Quickdraw II version of the GrafPort record is not the same as the Macintosh grafPort. There have been field name changes, changes in the field order, additions of new fields, and removal of fields. Apple recommends that developers religiously avoid direct contact with GrafPort fields and use the existing Quickdraw set and access functions. Exact details are available in the data structures section of this part.

Amiga

The Amiga was designed around coprocessors to help with the graphics chores. The Amiga is more graphics display/list-oriented than the other machines. Using the extra hardware and the display lists produce strange consequences. For example, the order of graphic object records in the lists is significant. The display hardware can't react intelligently when list items are out of video-beam scanning order, so it is necessary to call a low-level routine to sort the list order before displaying the list. There are also a number of coprocessor control routines that must be used if anything is going to work properly.

The Amiga has a hardware Blitter (RasterOp). To control the blitter, the routines provided are BltClear, BltPattern, BltBitMap, BltTemplate, ClpBlit, DisownBlitter, OwnBlitter, QBlit, QBSBlit, and WaitBlit. Blt-Clear is discussed in the miscellaneous section near the end of this part; BltPattern is described in the section on Pattern Fills; and BltBitMap, BltTemplate, and ClipBlit definitions are in the section on bitmaps; and the rest are mentioned in the section on specialized processor control near the end of the graphics chapter.

The Amiga also has a higher-level coprocessor called the Copper, whose job is to execute Copper instruction streams that are built from the Amiga display lists. The Copper does the actual rendering of the image, using the blitter to operate on bitmaps and then displaying the result, all in real-time. A Copper instruction stream describing the entire screen contents is executed once per video frame (see Fig. 3–21).

THE LINE

Macintosh

Quickdraw does not require an explicit line record type definition, since all its line drawing routines involve moving from the present pen coordinates to either an **absolute** coordinate address (you'll wind up there no matter where you start) or a **relative** location (where you'll wind up depends on

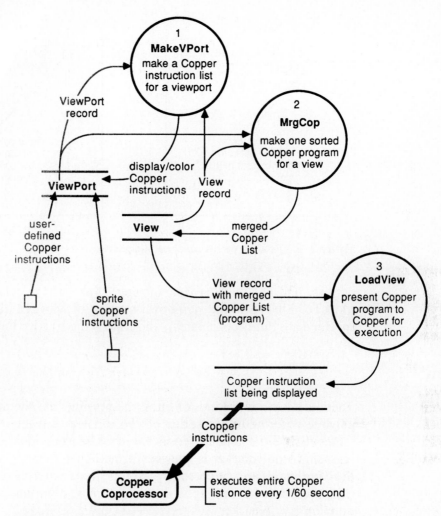

Figure 3–21 Displaying Amiga Copper instruction lists

where you start). Figure 3–22 illustrates relative versus absolute addresses. Relative coordinates are described in terms of changes in the X and the Y coordinates, and always start from the present spot. The present pen coordinates, incidentally, are kept in the pnLoc field in the current grafPort record.

There are a small number of line draw routines. MoveTo accepts a single set of absolute coordinates to which to move the pen. The coordinates are local to the current Macintosh grafPort, and the pen nib is up (no drawing is done). On these fancy display-based windowing systems, there is a big distinction between drawing, drawing with the background color/

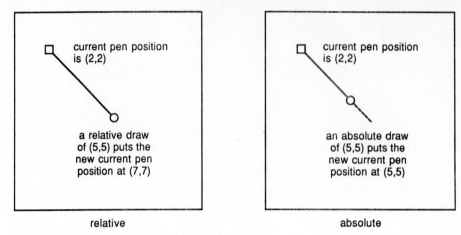

Figure 3–22 Relative versus absolute addressing

pattern, and not drawing (but moving). Move is the relative version of MoveTo. LineTo is the pen-down version of MoveTo (it draws to the specified absolute coordinates), and Line is the relative line draw routine.

Gem

There are two major kinds of lines, the polyline and the polymarker. The **polyline** is formed by a series of coordinates connected by drawn line segments; there can be as few as two coordinates and a single drawn line segment. A **polymarker** is likewise formed by a series of coordinates, but the coordinates are connected by the repeated rendering of a small symbol (like the asterisk). The polyline function is v_pline and the polymarker function is v_pmarker.

A dynamic structure like a polyline is not built using Gem VDI or AES calls. The application code does the work of filling values into arrays or structures. A Gem dynamic structure is usually drawn with one routine call.

The Gem structure that contains the dynamic data points is usually accessible using a direct memory address (like a static array) or a pointer

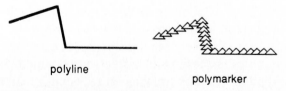

Figure 3–23 Polyline and Polymarker

(when space is created using the standard alloc routine). A Mac dynamic structure is usually referenced only with a handle (a pointer to a pointer).

One interesting difference between the Macintosh and Gem environments is the way that the Macintosh Quickdraw code helps to build dynamic data structures. They are built with the application code making repeated calls to Quickdraw routines after telling Quickdraw to "start building a dynamic data structure." The created structure can then usually be drawn with one Quickdraw call.

Repeated calls to Gem functions are not done in the same way as with Mac routines, since Gem does not have a built-in data structure building mode. Gem AES instead provides support for the modeless construction of heap-based linked lists of graphic objects. The goals of these two methods are not exactly the same, as is discussed later in this part.

The Quickdraw system is designed to permit access to variable-length data structures only by using Quickdraw calls and handles. Gem applications tend to use direct pointers. A Gem application has direct control over dynamic data structures, which is more than Mac applications normally exercise. When going through Quickdraw the length of dynamic data structures can be changed at any time. A Gem application handles its own memory allocation for a dynamic structure; a Mac application can optionally do its own dynamic allocation management, but could leave that work up to Quickdraw and the Macintosh memory manager.

Windows

Routines used on some of the current drawing attributes are pertinent to line drawing. The display context (DC) relabs flag indicates whether the coordinates passed to Windows Graphics Device Interface (GDI) routines are relative or absolute. The function SetRelAbs accepts RELATIVE, where each move is relative to the last pen position, or ABSOLUTE, where each move is relative to the current DC origin. SetRelAbs returns the old relabs setting. The function GetRelAbs returns the current relabs flag. The relabs flag default value is ABSOLUTE.

The MoveTo routine moves the current pen position to the specified coordinates (without drawing). The return value is the previous pen position.

LineTo is similar to MoveTo except that a draw takes place. The current pen is used for the line rendering. If a line is actually drawn, LineTo returns TRUE, FALSE otherwise.

The Polyline routine is equivalent to Gem's Polyline. The Windows Polyline is given a pointer to an array of POINT, and ignores the current pen position value in the display context record.

MS Windows also provides LineDDA, which accepts two coordinate pairs, a pointer to a function that is to be called by LineDDA and a pointer to data that the supplied function may need. LineDDA calculates all the points on a line between the first and second coordinate pairs, and feeds each point to the supplied function along with the pointer to the supplied data. The LineDDA call to the supplied function is in the form Function(X,Y,supplied_data_pointer).

IIGS

Move, MoveTo, Line, and LineTo are used in exactly the same way as their Macintosh equivalents are used.

Amiga

The Draw routine is used to draw a line from the current pen position of the specified RastPort to the indicated location, given in terms of the RastPort's raster coordinates. PolyDraw is used to draw a number of connected lines, starting with the location specified by the first coordinate pair in the provided coordinate pair array, and continuing to the last coordinate pair. PolyDraw is also given a RastPort pointer and the number of coordinate pairs in the array.

THE PEN

Macintosh

The Mac pen control routines do not directly produce graphics; they set the drawing modes for routines that affect the display. The adjustable pen characteristics are the pen location, nib size, drawing mode, and draw pattern. Each characteristic has a field in the grafPort record.

HidePen is used to override attempts by other Quickdraw routines to draw to the current grafPort. HidePen decrements a value in pnVis field of the current grafPort record; while that value is negative, no drawing can appear. ShowPen increments pnVis, and so leans toward making draws visible again (though it won't become true until pnVis is positive, so immediate results aren't guaranteed).

The routine GetPen returns the current pen location in local coordinates. GetPenState and SetPenState can be used to manipulate the small variety of drawing modes all at once. These two routines use as a parameter a record that contains only the grafPort fields containing the pen location, size, mode, and pattern.

PenSize is used to specify the height and width of the pen nib. The height and width are separate parameters.

The PenPat routine sets the draw pattern for a pen in the current grafPort. The windowing environments don't believe in just black ink; on the Mac you have choices of white, black, three shades of grey, and any other new pattern you care to define (you have an 8-by-8 bit square of two colors in which to fit the custom pattern).

PenMode controls how to draw the pattern. It is used to tell Quickdraw to copy the pattern verbatim to the GrafPort's part of the screen, to or the pattern with the contents of the GrafPort's bitmap, to xor the pattern, to bic the pattern, or to invert the color (not). The other pen modes are not or, not xor, and not bic. PenMode sets the pnMode field of the current grafPort; more detail on drawing modes is provided below.

PenNormal resets all the pen-affiliated fields of the current grafPort to a predefined state; the nib size is 1-bit by 1-bit, the mode is copy, and the pattern is solid black.

Gem

The pen analogy is emphasized less under Gem. There is no mechanism for emulating a pen lift from the drawing surface by routines that render lines draws invisible, nor are there equivalents of the relative pen move and the relative pen draw routines. Gem does not keep the current pen location. Also, there are two ways to draw lines: with a polyline and with a polymarker.

There are two inquiry routines: vql_attributes and vqm_attributes. vql_attributes returns the values for all the current polyline settings, including line type, line color, line width, end styles, and draw mode. vqm_attributes likewise returns the current polymarker settings, including the marker type, color, height, and drawing mode. The routines that follow are used to set the current attributes.

vsl_type is used to select the current polyline line style from a minimum of six styles. The first six styles are predefined, and a seventh is for one user-definable pattern. More device-specific styles may be implemented. vsl_udsty is provided to give the user-definable style. The styles are 16-bit patterns that are used repetitively.

vsl_width is used to set the current polyline line width. All the selectable line widths involve an odd number of pixels, starting with one, three, five, etc. One will be subtracted from any even number of make it odd.

vsl_color selects the current polyline color index. A color index is a preset handle to a specific RGB color value triad; rather than specifying each red, green, and blue gun intensity for each time a color specifier is needed, one can assign a color index to an RGB triad once and use the color index. The routine that maps a color index to an RGB color triad is vs_color.

vsl_ends selects one of three available endpoint styles for a polyline. The three are rounded, arrowed, and squared. The squared end is the default.

vsm_type is used to select the current polymarker symbol. There are six definite symbols (and perhaps more device-dependent symbols) to select from. The first six symbols are point, plus, star, square, diagonal cross, and diamond.

vsm_height assigns the current polymarker symbol height; and

vsm_color is provided to set the current polymarker color index.

Windows

There are a small number of pen attribute routines. GetStockObject sets a number of attributes at once by the name — actually a C preprocessor definition that translates into a predefined index value — of a group of attribute settings. GetStockObject also sets brush and font attributes.

CreatePen returns a handle to a newly created Pen definition. There are three parameters: the pen style, the width of the pen nib, and the RGB color of the "ink." The pen styles are Solid, Dash, Dot, Dash and Dot, and Dash and two dots. The width is given in logical units. Another routine, CreatePenIndirect, does the same thing except that it is given a pointer to a LOGPEN data structure containing the same appropriate values. If either routine should fail for any reason, the value of the returned handle will be NULL. Here is the LOGPEN definition in Pascal:

```
TYPE LOGPEN = RECORD
        lopnStyle:    WORD;
        lopnWidth:    POINT;        {Passed as part of a record.}
        lopnColor:    INTEGER4;
END;
PLOGPEN = ADR OF LOGPEN;           {A short pointer.}
LPLOGPEN = ADS OF LOGPEN;          {A long pointer.}
```

IIGS

The routines HidePen, ShowPen, GetPen, GetPenState, SetPenState, PenSize, PenMode, PenPat, and PenNormal all work the same way their Macintosh equivalents do.

Amiga

The Amiga RastPort record contains the current pen location for the RastPort's bitmap.

The Move routine is used to nudge the pen of the specified RastPort to a new position in the raster coordinate space without drawing.

SetAPen sets the foreground pen color. This color is used for lines, area fills, and text. SetAPen requires a pointer to the affected RastPort and a pen color that can range from 0 to 255 bytes. The RastPort field containing the foreground pen color is FgPen.

SetBPen sets the background pen color, which is contained in the RastPort field BgPen. The SetBPen parameters are a pointer to the affected RastPort record and a pen color ranging from 0 to 255 bytes.

SetOPen changes the color of the third current pen color (the outline color) which is stored in the AOlPen field of a RastPort record. The AolPen color is used for (1) outlines of polygons that are filled with the foreground pen color and (2) as the boundary color for area foreground color floodfills.

DRAWING MODES

Macintosh

The PenMode procedure sets the way in which the pnPat field of the current GrafPort is to be used when shapes and lines are drawn. SetPenState sets the current mode as well as the pen location, size, and pattern. GetPenState, along with all the other current pen characteristics, returns the current drawing mode.

All the available drawing modes are:

patCopy	Source pattern overwrites destination.
patOr	Source OR'd with destination.
patXor	Source XOR'd with destination.

patBic	Destination cleared (0) if source set (1).
notPatCopy	Source pattern inverted.
notPatOr	Source pattern inverted and then OR'd with destination.
notPatXor	Source pattern inverted and then XOR'd with destination.
notPatBic	Destination cleared if source cleared.

The Macintosh II, in addition to the old Mac's eight basic drawing/transfer modes, provides modes that work with bitmaps with depth greater than one plane (for more colors). The additional modes work properly with the new record definitions provided on the Mac II to handle multi-plane pixel images, pixMap (rather than bitMap) and pixPat. If you are using the old black-and-white standard Macintosh data structures, the color draw modes revert to the old transfer modes. There are more Mac II details in the sections on color, bitmaps, and data structures.

The new drawing modes are:

AddOver	The destination pixel is assigned the color closest to the sum of the source and destination RGB values MOD 65535. For single-bit pixels, AddOver reverts to Xor.
AddPin	The destination pixel is assigned the color closest to the sum of the destination RGB values, pinned to a maximum-allowable RGB value assigned using the routine OpColor. For single-bit pixels, AddPin reverts to Bic. If AddOver doesn't provide the expected results, then try AddPin.
SubOver	The destination pixel is assigned the color closest to the difference between the source and destination RGB values. If the result is a negative value, that value is subtracted from 65535 to get the RGB value.
SubPin	The destination pixel is assigned the color closest to the difference of the source and destination pixels, pinned by a maximum RGB value set with the routine OpColor.
Max	The destination pixel is assigned the highest red, the highest green, and the highest blue component values taken from the source and the destination RGB

values. The RGB color that results may differ from the originals. For 1-bit pixels, Max turns into Bic.

Min   Min works like Max, except that the lesser component values are used. Min reverts to Or for single-bit pixels.

Blend   A weighted average of the source and destination colors becomes the new destination color. The weight value is set with the OpColor routine, and the algorithm used is:

```
dest=(source*weight/65536)+(dest*(1-weight/65536))
```

For single-bit pixels, Blend turns into Copy.

Gem

There are four drawing modes: replace, transparent, XOR, and reverse transparent. In **replace** mode the line style overwrites the screen. In **transparent** mode the bits set in the line style overwrite the screen; the 0 bits in the line style don't effect the display. In **XOR** mode the line style bit and the screen bit are XOR'ed together to produce a new value. In **reverse transparent** mode the 0 bits in the line style overwrite the screen.

Windows

There isn't a great deal of variety to be found with the predefined line patterns; there are five, including solid. Using the routine **LineDDA** is the prescribed way to circumvent the limit; you must write your own patterned line draw routines.

The Windows drawing mode is defined as the way the color of the pen interacts with the color of the display. There are two routines for manipulating the mode: SetROP2 and GetRop2 [sic]. GetRop2 returns the current drawing mode. SetROP2 is used to set the current drawing mode, and returns the old one. Here are the predefined drawing modes:

Mode	New Pixel Color
R2_NOP	Display color (no color change whatsoever)
R2_NOT	Inverse of display color

R2_BLACK	Always black
R2_WHITE	Always white
R2_COPYPEN	Pen color
R2_NOTCOPYPEN	Inverse of pen color
R2_MERGEPEN	Combination of pen and display colors
R2_NOTMERGEPEN	Inverse of combination of pen and display colors
R2_MERGEPENNOT	Combination of pen and inverse of display colors
R2_MERGENOTPEN	Combination of display and inverse of pen colors
R2_MASKNOTPEN	Combination of display and inverse of pen colors.
R2_MASKPENNOT	Combination of pen and inverse of display colors
R2_XORPEN	Combination of colors in pen and display, excluding the colors in both
R2_NOTXORPEN	Inverse of R2_XORPEN color
R2_MASKPEN	Combination of colors common to both pen and display
R2_NOTMASKPEN	Inverse of R2_MASKPEN color

IIGS

The integer values for the transfer modes are not the same as those on the Macintosh and the mnemonics are slightly different, but the transfer modes are the same. The IIGS has COPY, notCOPY, OR, notOR, XOR, notXOR, BIC, and notBIC. This is the same whether working with text, pen, or pixel transfers.

There are also special text modes, applicable when rendering a monochrome bitmap on a 2- or 4-bit (color) world. There are foreCOPY, notforeCOPY, foreOR, notforeOR, foreXOR, notforeXOR, foreBIC, and notforeBIC. The background pixels are never altered.

Amiga

The function SetDrMd is used to assign the current drawing mode of the RastPort record indicated by the first parameter. The second parameter is the drawmode, of which there are presently four: JAM1, COMPLE-MENT, JAM2, and INVERSVID.

> The **JAM1** drawing mode is used to force addressed pixels to the current foreground pen color.

> The **COMPLEMENT** mode is used to take the value of an addressed pixel and complement it.

> The **JAM2** mode is used with patterns only. If the addressed pixel coincides with a bit set to 0 in the pattern the pixel becomes the background pen color; coinciding with a 1 bit forces the pixel to adopt the foreground color.

> The **INVERSVID** mode inverts the video effect of the foreground and background pen colors.

These modes can be mixed and matched for delightful effects, though some of the combinations don't make sense.

THE RECTANGLE (AND FRIENDS)

Macintosh

Rectangles are very simple constructs that on the Macintosh are handled the same way as ovals and round-corner rectangles. They are defined by two corner points, and shapes appear inside (or are the same as) the rectangle defined by the two points. The two defining corners are the top left and bottom right corners. Here is the Mac data structure:

```
TYPE Rect = RECORD CASE INTEGER OF
       0:    (top:         INTEGER;
              left:        INTEGER;
              bottom:      INTEGER;
              right:       INTEGER);
       1:    (topLeft:     Point;
              botRight:    Point)
END;
```

As with the Point datatype, the variant record trick used here is intended to call the same data by different names, not to store different data in the same location of memory at different times.

Note that when drawing a rectangle or any object defined using a rectangle, if the rectangle is v by h in size (where v is the number of vertical coordinates and h is the number of horizontal coordinates), then the drawing of the rectangle will actually be v − 1 pixels high and h − 1 pixels wide. The coordinates of the rectangle define the outside dimensions of the rectangle; the bits used to draw the rectangle fit inside.

The routines for graphic operations with rectangles are

FrameRect draws a hollow outline just inside the specified rectangle using the pattern specified within the present grafPort

PaintRect paints the inside of the specified rectangle using the current draw mode and pen pattern

EraseRect paints the inside of the specified rectangle using the current background pattern without using the current draw mode

InvertRect swaps black pixels with white ones and vice versa (remember the monochromatic nature of standard Mac 128K, 512K, and Mac+ displays)

FillRect paints the inside of the specified rectangle using the specified pattern and ignoring the foreground and background patterns and the draw modes specified in the current grafPort record.

There are equivalent routines for drawing ovals; FrameOval, PaintOval, EraseOval, InvertOval, and FillOval do the same thing for ovals as their counterparts do for rectangles, except that an oval is drawn inside the specified rectangle.

There are similarly named routines for rendering round-corner rectangles: FrameRoundRect, PaintRoundRect, EraseRoundRect, InvertRoundRect, and FillRoundRect.

Another small cluster of routines is provided to draw arcs and wedges (Fig. 3–24); like those previously mentioned, these routines use a rectangle to define a shape (an oval in this case if it were completely drawn). The arc routines use two other INTEGER values that define the location extent of the arc or wedge to be drawn within the rectangle. The first value, startAngle, specifies in degrees where the arc begins relative to the 12 o'clock position, with positive angles going clockwise. The second value, arcAngle, is the extent of the arc in degrees. The routines are PaintArc, EraseArc, InvertArc, and Fillarc.

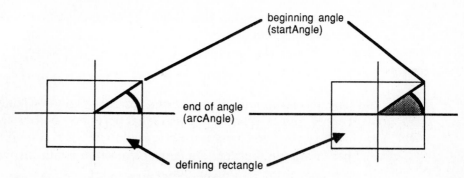

Figure 3–24 Macintosh arcs and wedges

Gem

The VDI routine vr_recfl fills a rectangular screen area with the current area fill pattern. The current fill outline is not used.

The Gem VDI GDP (Generalized Drawing Primitive) function handles all of the graphic primitive drawing. Fortunately, most of the Gem Binding routine libraries provide a separate routine for each primitive.

v_rbox is the routine that draws a round-corner rectangle. Again, Gem rectangles, unlike those on the Macintosh, are specified by using the lower left and upper right corner coordinates. v_rfbox defines a filled round-corner rectangle using the current fill interior style and color index.

v_cellarray is an interesting routine that draws a rectangle at the specified location on the screen with the current color. Also provided as parameters are the numbers of rows and columns into which the area of the rectangle is to be subdivided. The color of each subdivision is specified by another parameter, a color index array.

The Gem AES Object Library manipulates a few rectangular objects. Gem AES rectangular objects are called **boxes** and normally contain additional graphics stored in memory as child object records. The rectangular object types are:

G_BOX	A box that contains graphics.
G_BOXTEXT	A box that contains graphic text information.
G_PROGDEF	A programmer-defined object (could be anything).
G_IBOX	A box without fill pattern or color; the border may not be visible.
G_BOXCHAR	A box that contains one text character.
G_FBOXTEXT	A box containing formatted graphic text.

The Object Library routines and data structures are described in detail later in this part.

Windows

The Rectangle function is given an MS Windows handle to a display context and two coordinate pairs that describe a pair of defining points for a rectangle. The current brush is used to fill the rectangle, and the current pen draws the border. The current position is not involved. A TRUE is returned if the rectangle is drawn.

FillRect fills a specified rectangle with the specified brush.

FrameRect draws a border for the specified rectangle. The brush indicated in the parameter list is used to draw the border.

The RoundRect function draws a rectangle with rounded corners. A third coordinate pair is provided to specify the width and height of the ellipse form used to draw each of the four corners.

Bounding rectangles are also used by the Ellipse, Arc, and Pie functions.

InvertRect operates on a selected rectangular area of the display, inverting the color of each pixel within the rectangle.

IIGS

The rectangle structure in the IIGS is the same as that in the Macintosh. Rectangles, ovals, and round-corner rectangles are defined the same way in both machines, as are the arc routines.

Amiga

RectFill is used to draw a filled rectangle for the indicated RastPort. The current pen (outline and secondary colors) and pattern are used. Two coordinate pairs are provided to define the rectangle in the raster coordinate space.

COMPLICATED RECTANGLE OPERATIONS

The rectangle, being the useful shape that it is, can do much more than the simple graphics-rendering operations mentioned in the previous section. The different windowing packages provide varying numbers of advanced rectangle routines.

Macintosh

The routine SetRect is a simple thing used to assign values to the two defining coordinate points of a given rectangle. Also easy is the OffsetRect routine, which is used to globally move the defining coordinates of a rectangle; an INTEGER value is added to the Y coordinates and a separate value is added to the X coordinates.

InsetRect provides a way to shrink or enlarge a rectangle; one provided value is added to the left-side and subtracted from the right-side X coordinate, and the other value is added to the bottom and subtracted from the top Y coordinate. The function SectRect provides the coordinates for a rectangle defined by the intersection of two specified rectangles, returning FALSE if the rectangles don't intersect. UnionRect calculates the smallest rectangle that encompasses two other rectangles, whether they intersect or not.

PtInRect returns TRUE if the pixel corresponding to a specified coordinate is contained within a specified rectangle. Pt2Rect returns the smallest rectangle that contains two specified points.

PtToAngle calculates the INTEGER angle between a vertical line from the center of a rectangle and a line from the center of the rectangle to a specified point. PtToAngle uses amusing geometric math; if the line to the point goes through the top right corner, that angle will be 45 degrees, even though the rectangle may not be square.

EqualRect compares two rectangles and returns TRUE if they have identical boundary coordinates. EmptyRect returns TRUE if the specified rectangle isn't much of a rectangle (i.e., has length and width of zero).

Gem

The standard Gem environment does not come with advanced rectangle operations.

Windows

There are a couple of advanced rectangle routines that work with clipping rectangles. IntersectClipRect makes a new clipping rectangle with the intersection of the old clipping rectangle and an arbitrary rectangle defined with device coordinates. OffsetClipRgn moves the clipping rectangle on the device according to a pair of offsets (one value for X, another value for Y). For more information on clipping rectangles and regions for MS Windows, read the section on clipping.

MS Windows also has SetRect, SetRectEmpty, CopyRect, Inflate-Rect, IntersectRect, UnionRect, OffsetRect, IsRectEmpty, PtInRect, and RectVisible.

SetRect assigns the coordinates of a rectangle.

SectRectEmpty sets a rectangle to have all zeros for coordinates.

CopyRect copies the contents of one Rect type record to another one.

InflateRect expands the size of a rectangle by X units above and below and Y units to the left and right.

IntersectRect determines the intersection of two rectangles and stuffs that rectangular definition into a third Rect type record.

UnionRect creates a rectangle that encompasses two other rectangles.

OffsetRect is used to merely move a rectangle by X and Y units.

IsRectEmpty returns TRUE if a specified rectangle is empty and FALSE if it isn't.

PtInRect accepts a pointer to a rectangle and a point record; it returns TRUE if the point is within the rectangle, and FALSE if it isn't.

RectVisible returns TRUE if the specified rectangle lies within the clipping region of the specified display context, and FALSE if it does not.

IIGS

The Mac Quickdraw routines SetRect, OffsetRect, InsetRect, SectRect, UnionRect, PtInRect, Pt2Rect, EqualRect, EmptyRect, and Pt2Angle are all present in Quickdraw II.

Amiga

The Amiga doesn't have advanced rectangle routines. Most of the bitmap and layer manipulations involve rectangular objects, as discussed previously.

THE REGION

A number of arbitrarily selected points can be brought together as a group, and a wide variety of operations can be performed on that group. Such a group, called a **region**, can form a "splotch" on a screen, with a number of points within the body of the splotch excluded. Regions are commonly used for clipping graphics; some environments support a region defined as a completely arbitrary set of bits, with the bits in the region corresponding to writeable pixels in a bitmap (e.g., the Macintosh). Other environments permit less anarchistic region definitions (the Amiga).

The operations on regions are similar to those applicable to other graphic primitives, involving to some degree the three major transformations: **translation** (which simply amounts to moving an entire object to a different part of the screen), **scaling** (shrinking or expanding an object's dimension along the X and/or Y axis), and **rotation** (effectively rotating an object around the origin (0,0) of the coordinate system).

A rectangle record contains two endpoints and when drawn usually involves many more points than the two in the record. In contrast, the points expressly included in a region must be specified in the region data structure. A region has more brute force than other primitives; it is designed to be a memory hog. Bigger, more complicated regions need more memory space, since they must contain more data points.

Part of the state of the art in the software business is the design of compact methods for keeping regions in memory that do not need to sacrifice much execution time for manipulating the contents of a region.

The difference between a region and bitmap (described later in the chapter) is that a bitmap is most definitely rectangular, whereas a region is not, though a region does have a defining rectangle for determining what the region's coordinates are. Also, bitmap data are displayed, whereas region data are used to manipulate displayed data and are not normally visually exciting in themselves.

Macintosh

The Mac region record has two fixed fields and a variable-length field that contains the member point information:

```
TYPE Region = RECORD
     rgnSize:      INTEGER;      { The number of bytes in the region. }
     rgnBBox:      Rect;         { The region-enclosing rectangle. }
     { *** An optional region definition data section goes here ***}
END;
```

Macintosh regions can change in size with time, and therefore tend to move around in memory at the whim of the Macintosh memory manager.

For this reason Mac regions ought to be referenced with handles (not pointers) when used by application software.

A handle on the Macintosh is a pointer that points to another pointer. The second pointer points to the actual data record in memory. The second pointer normally resides in a block of pointers, and this block is manipulated by the operating system. This indirect route permits both the application code and the operating system to manipulate regions without getting in each other's way. The application may manipulate the handle (the indirect pointer), but the job of changing the direct pointer belongs to the operating system. In a Macintosh Pascal system the notation for a handle declaration is:

```
var    ThingHandle: ^ThingPointer;    {handle declaration}
       ThingPointer: ^Thing;          {pointer declaration}
```

Some sample code might be:

```
ThingHandle^^.whatever := 10; {Application code uses handle only.}
```

The simple difference between handles and pointers is shown graphically in Figure 3–25. Handles allow the Macintosh memory manager to move things around in memory without explicit permission from or knowledge by the application software. Because of the dynamic sizing of regions, this ability is mandatory.

Here are the declarations of the common region handle and pointer types:

```
TYPE RgnPtr = ^Region;
     RgnHandle = ^RgnPtr;
```

There are a number of region manipulation and display routines in Quickdraw. The function NewRgn is used to create a virgin region in memory. The region's extent rectangle is defined to be (0,0,0,0), which is not very large in any coordinate system. Because regions are complicated, use of the normal heap allocation routines (the new routine in Pascal, or any of the alloc routines associated with the C language or Unix) isn't sufficient.

The principal method for building a region is to use Quickdraw commands that are sandwiched between calls to OpenRgn and CloseRgn (see Fig. 3–26). The OpenRgn call signals to Quickdraw that all the Line, LineTo, and framed-shape drawing routines (SetRect, FrameOval, etc.) are to be used to build up the outline of the region rather than to modify

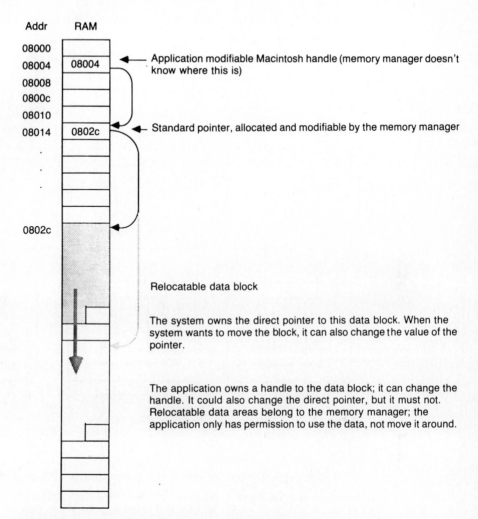

Addr   RAM

08000

08004   08004 ◄— Application modifiable Macintosh handle (memory manager doesn't know where this is)

08008

0800c

08010

08014   0802c ◄— Standard pointer, allocated and modifiable by the memory manager

0802c

Relocatable data block

The system owns the direct pointer to this data block. When the system wants to move the block, it can also change the value of the pointer.

The application owns a handle to the data block; it can change the handle. It could also change the direct pointer, but it must not. Relocatable data areas belong to the memory manager; the application only has permission to use the data, not move it around.

Figure 3–25 Comparing Macintosh handles with pointers

the contents of the display. The CloseRgn call is to end the collection of region graphics and save the image into the region data structure. The data structure is indicated by the RgnHandle parameter of CloseRgn.

DisposeRgn can be used to return the space once used by a region to the free memory pool. DisposeRgn is given the handle to the region to be removed. Use of the unchanged region handle afterward serves no purpose, since it won't point to anything significant.

CopyRgn copies the contents of one region to another. NewRgn must be used to create both regions before the copy operation, but CopyRgn handles the space allocation required by the duplication.

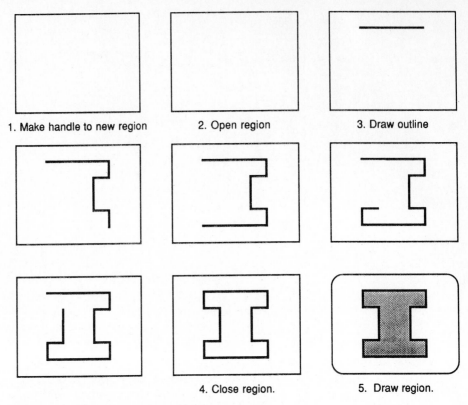

1. Make handle to new region   2. Open region   3. Draw outline

4. Close region.   5. Draw region.

Figure 3–26 Region building example (Macintosh)

OffsetRgn is used to move the coordinates of a region, but does not cause a screen update to take place. InsetRgn independently shrinks or expands a region in the X and Y directions. SectRgn fills an existing region with the intersection of two other regions. UnionRgn fills an existing region with the union of two other regions. DiffRgn fills an existing region with the difference between two other regions. XorRgn fills an existing region with the "difference between the union and the intersection" of two other regions. PtInRgn returns TRUE if a specified pixel is within a specified region. RectInRgn returns TRUE if a given rectangle intersects a specified region.

Two regions can be compared using EqualRgn, which returns TRUE if they are equivalent. EmptyRgn returns TRUE if a specified region is empty.

FrameRgn draws an outline around a region and PaintRgn fills the specified region, both commands using the current pen pattern, size, and mode. EraseRgn fills the specified region with the current background pattern. InvertRgn inverts the color of all a region's pixels. FillRgn is used to fill a region with a *specified* 8-byte pattern.

SetEmptyRgn empties a region.

SetRectRgn and RectRgn are almost the same, but they are given the data they need in different forms. Both set up the new contents for an already created region. They are given the coordinates of the region's new defining rectangle, with the rectangle defined by a Rect datatype record when given to RectRgn. The rectangle is defined for SetRectRgn by four separate integer values.

Gem

Standard Gem does not have an equivalent of regions.

Windows

MS Windows regions "appear" to be similar in nature to the Mac's. However, they differ in region building; the Windows GDI package isn't thrown into a graphics collection mode to build a region, as is done in Quickdraw. MS Windows region building routines aren't as flexible as the Mac's, but they represent an orthodox approach and should be adequate.

Here are the MS Windows region routines:

    FillRgn
    FrameRgn
    InvertRgn
    PaintRgn
    CombineRgn
    EqualRgn
    OffsetRgn
    CreateRectRgn
    CreateRectRgnIndirect
    CreateEllipticRgn
    CreateEllipticRgnIndirect
    CreatePolygonRgn

FillRgn fills the specified region associated with the specified display context with the specified brush. All the parameters are handles. PaintRgn does the same thing as FillRgn, except that the current brush for the display context is used.

FrameRgn, using the brush specified, draws a border around the indicated region. The width of the brush strokes is described by two more parameters (the assigned width of the horizontal border is independent of the set width of the vertical border).

InvertRgn inverts the colors within the specified region.

The CombineRgn function is provided to create a region by gluing together two other regions. The results are indicated by the returned value, which can be set to any of the following:

ERROR	Something is amiss.
NULLREGION	The result has no size.
SIMPLEREGION	The result is a single body.
COMPLEXREGION	The result is two or more bodies.

Additionally, a parameter of CombineRgn indicates how the two regions are to be merged. This style parameter may assume the following values:

RGN_AND	The new region is the intersection of the first two.
RGN_OR	The new region is the union of the first two.
RGN_XOR	The new region is the nonoverlapping portions of the first two regions.
RGN_DIFF	The new region is the area of the first region that is not in the second.
RGNCOPY	The new region is a copy of the first region.

The function EqualRgn returns TRUE if the two specified regions are identical and FALSE if they're not.

OffsetRgn is used to move a region on the display. Separate X and Y values are provided to move the region in both the X and Y directions independently with the same call.

CreateRectRgn creates a rectangular region; you provide it with two coordinate pairs representing a couple of points on the device, and it hands back a handle to the new region. CreateRectRgnIndirect does the same thing as CreateRectRgn, except instead of giving the routine four individual integer values, you give it a structure of type RECT. Using the same bounding box technique, CreateEllipticRgn and CreateElliptic-RgnIndirect both return handles to new elliptical regions.

CreatePolygonRgn returns a handle to a new region that is the shape of the polygon described by the array of POINT elements indicated by the pointer passed to the routine. The fill mode parameter for CreatePolygonRgn can be one of these two values: ALTERNATE or WINDING.

IIGS

All the Macintosh region handling routines are present in the IIGS.

Amiga

Amiga regions aren't quite the same as regions provided by the Mac or MS Windows. Instead, they are defined exclusively to be "the subset of a Raster bitmap in which drawing must take place . . . " In Macintosh/MS Windows vernacular, they are clipping regions. Also, Amiga regions are defined by a linked list of rectangular areas; arbitrary polygonal shapes are not supported.

To build an Amiga region, start by calling the routine NewRegion to allocate the space for the Region record. Then make one or more calls to the other region building routines (described shortly) to add ClipRect-type clipping rectangles to the list of clipping rectangles belonging to that region. These rectangles describe the domain of the region.

When actually used, the clipping rectangle list is "borrowed"; the region record is used to keep track of the clipping rectangles while the region is changed. When the region data are needed, only the clipping rectangle list (and not the region record) becomes involved. The clipping rectangle list temporarily becomes an Amiga **damage list**, a list of rectangles that encompass the area that has to be redrawn on a layer. A layer's DamageList pointer is changed to reference the clipping rectangle list when the information is needed (see Fig. 3–27).

The AndRectRegion routine is given pointers to a region and a rectangle record (as parameters). The intersection (the area contained within both the region and the rectangle) is calculated; this area becomes the new contents of the old region. OrRectRegion and XorRectRegion provide similar services; OrRectRegion replaces the old region with the union of the rectangle and the region's old contents, and XorRectRegion redefines the old region to contain the area that is contained either by the old region or by the rectangle, but not both (that is, everything but the rectangle-region intersection).

ClearRegion is used to reduce the region contents (and its size) to nothing.

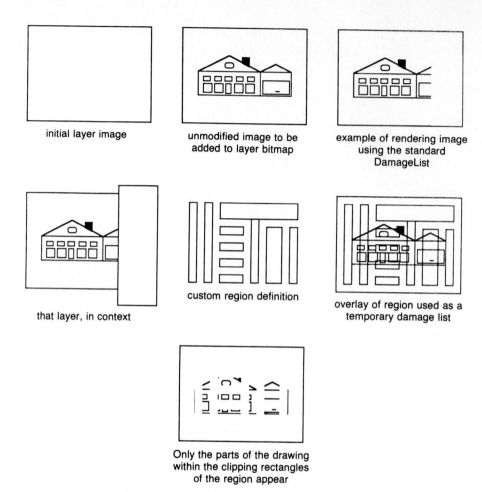

initial layer image

unmodified image to be added to layer bitmap

example of rendering image using the standard DamageList

that layer, in context

custom region definition

overlay of region used as a temporary damage list

Only the parts of the drawing within the clipping rectangles of the region appear

Figure 3–27 Building an Amiga clipping region and using it for layer redraws

DisposeRegion will move the dynamic storage allocated to a region back into the free memory pool.

PATTERN FILLS

Macintosh

The normal Quickdraw pattern size is 64 bits, organized as a square defined by 8 bytes. The pattern datatype is:

```
TYPE Pattern = PACKED ARRAY[0..7] of 0..255;
```

Because a pattern based on a mere 8 bytes is considered by some users to be insufficient, the developers of some Macintosh software have gone to great lengths to incorporate their own set of pattern fill support routines in their products. Challenger Software's Mac 3D drafting package allows the use of 8 x 8, 16 x 16, and 32 x 32 patterns.

There are three patterns supported by a Macintosh grafPort at one time. The **foreground** pattern, pnPat, is used by the Quickdraw pen to draw lines. The pnPat pattern is initially set to the solid black pattern. The **Paint** routines, such as PaintRgn and PaintPoly, use the pen pattern to fill a specified object. The **object fill** pattern, fillPat, is used by most of the Fill routines, like FillOval, but with a twist: The pattern to be used is given as a parameter, and the fillPat field is set by the function. The Fill routines make a number of calls to lower-level functions, where the fillPat pattern comes in handy. When designing Quickdraw, it was noted that each call to a Fill routine normally requires a different fill pattern, so the modal approach used with other grafPort fields doesn't hold water with fillPat.

Here are additional routines found in the Mac 128K ROMs and later models. They are discussed at greater length in the section on bitmaps.

CalcMask   Calculate destination bit image where paint can't leak.

SeedFill   Calculate destination bit image where paint can leak.

CopyMask   A version of CopyBits that copies bits only where there's a corresponding 1 in a bitmap built by CalcMask or SeedFill.

Here are new routines which are similar to CalcMask and SeedFill but operate on Mac II color PixMap data rather than just BitMap data:

CalcCMask   Same as CalcMask, only in color.

SeedCFill   Same as SeedFill, only in color. SeedCFill uses the source pixel map coordinate system, but SeedFill uses the source rectangle.

CopyCMask   Same as CopyMask, only for color transfers.

The Quickdraw routine BackPat is used to set the background pattern of the current Macintosh grafPort. The background pattern, kept in the bkPat field of a grafPort record, is used by routines like EraseRoundRect for "erasing." PenPat sets the foreground pen pattern. Calling the Pen-Normal routine will reset the foreground pen pattern to the default: black. PenNormal also returns a couple of other pen characteristics to their default settings: the pen nib size is set to 1-pixel by 1-pixel, and the pen drawing mode is set to patCopy.

Macintosh II

When you add color to the Macintosh pattern fills become more interesting. In the new color version the foreground pattern is called pnPixPat, the background pattern is called bkPixPat, and the fill pattern is called fillPixPat. The expanded pattern record is called pixPat (for pixel pattern), and is defined as follows:

```
PixPatHandle = ^PixPatPtr;          {A handle to a color pattern.}
PixPatPtr    = ^PixPat;             {A pointer to a color pattern.}
PixPat       = RECORD               {The color pixel pattern record.}
    patType:     INTEGER;           {The type of pattern.}
    patMap:      PixMapHandle;      {The pattern's pixMap (color bitmap).}
    patData:     Handle;            {The pixMap's data.}
    patXData:    Handle;            {The expanded pattern data.}
    patXValid:   INTEGER;           {Contains flags that indicate whether}
                                    { the expanded pattern is valid.}
    patXMap:     PatXMapHandle;     {A handle to the expanded pattern.}
    pat1Data:    Pattern;           {The old-style pattern/RGB color.}
END;
```

When the patType field is 0, the old Quickdraw pattern system is used, but with the new data structures. The old pattern size limits are still valid.

When the patType field is 1, everything about a pattern is defined using a pixel map defined with a patMap record. Only 72 pixels per inch are supported. The old pattern size limits are no longer valid, height and width can be any power of 2. Patterns can also be a single byte wide.

When the patType field is 2, dithering is supported. **Dithering** is what you do when you need more colors than you get with a video card—you use pixels of different colors mixed together over a screen area to fake the colors you can't directly generate. A routine called MakeRGBPat is available to build a pattern that approximates a color. Currently, Make-RGBPat constructs 125 different patterns in 4-bit mode, and 2197 patterns in 8-bit mode.

The expanded pattern record is used internally by Mac II Quickdraw. If something is changed, like the color table or the data for a pattern, the information in the expanded pattern is probably invalid, and should be recalculated; setting the patXValid field in pixPat to −1 forces the recalculation.

Here is the definition for the records that are related to expanded pixel patterns:

```
PatXMapHandle =      ^PatXMapPtr;   {A handle to an expanded pattern.}

PatXMapPtr =         ^PatXMap;      {A pointer to an expanded pattern.}

PatXMap = RECORD                    {The expanded pixel pattern record.}

     patXRow:        INTEGER;       {The number of rowbytes in pattern.}

     patXHMask:      INTEGER;       {The horizontal mask.}

     patXVMask:      INTEGER;       {The vertical mask.}

     lastCTable:     LONGINT;       {A seed value for last color table.}

     lastOfst:       INTEGER;       {The last global-local offset.}

     lastInvert:     LONGINT;       {The last invert value.}

     lastAlign:      LONGINT;       {The last horizontal alignment.}

     lastStretch:    INTEGER;       {The last stretch.}

  END;
```

Here is a list of the new routines that go with the pixPat record:

NewPixPat	Creates and partially initializes a pixPat record.
DisposPixPat	Used to release the storage belonging to a pixPat record.
CopyPixPat	For copying one pixPat record into another, including the handles.
MakeRGBPat	Creates a dithered color pattern that can be used to simulate a wide range of colors.
PenPixPat	Same as PenPat, but for color pixel patterns.
BackPixPat	Same as BackPat, but for color pixel patterns.

Gem

Gem fill patterns are uniquely identified with two integer numbers: a fill style number and a fill style index.

There are five predefined classes of fill styles:

hollow	Fill with current background color only

solid	Fill with current fill color
pattern	16-bit by 16-bit grid
hatch	16-bit by 16-bit grid
user-defined	16-bit by 16-bit grid

The other number, the index, is used to subdivide each of the major classes if necessary. The first two fill styles don't need to be indexed, and only one user-defined pattern can exist at a time.

Gem Fill patterns are formed by the contents of one or more planes, each consisting of sixteen 16-bit words. At the top left of each plane of the pattern is the most significant bit of the first word; at the bottom right is the least significant bit of the last (the 16th) word.

The routine vsf_interior is used to set the current fill style value, and vsf_style is used to set the current fill style index. vsf_color sets the fill color index. vsf_perimeter is used to turn the outlining of fill areas on and off; if outlining is on, then an outline of the fill area is drawn when an area is filled, using a solid line of the current fill color. vsf_udpat is used to enter a user-defined fill pattern.

A flood fill routine, vr_contourfill, is provided. This function flood fills a bordered area on the screen, using the current fill attributes. If there is a break in the border, the fill will ooze through the break and flood as much of the screen contents as Murphy's Law permits.

Another fill routine, vr_recfl, is designed just for rectangular areas. This routine uses the current fill attributes, but does not outline the fill area.

Windows

The stock fill patterns for MS Windows are simple. Anything having to do with a brush is actually a fill pattern.

There are a number of routines for manipulating brushes.

The function CreateSolidBrush returns a handle to a new brush; the one parameter for the routine is the RGB color of the brush, which otherwise has no pattern. If the brush can't be made, the routine returns a NULL value.

CreateHatchBrush is the function that creates a brush with a hatched pattern (indicated by the first parameter) and an RGB color (indicated by the second parameter). The first parameter, the index, can have the following values:

HS_HORIZONTAL	Defines a horizontal hatch

HS_VERTICAL	Defines a vertical hatch
HS_FDIAGONAL	Defines a 45-degree upward hatch from left to right
HS_BDIAGONAL	Defines a 45-degree downward from left to right hatch
HS_CROSS	Defines a horizontal and vertical cross-hatch
HS_DIACROSS	5-degree cross-hatch

CreatePatternBrush has a comfortable similarity to equivalent routines provided by the Macintosh and Gem environments. It is given a handle to a bitmap containing a pattern. A bitmap used as a brush pattern has a minor restriction; it can't be any smaller than 8-by-8-bits. The routine returns NULL if success wasn't met.

CreateBrushIndirect defines a brush given a pointer to a LOGBRUSH type record:

```
TYPE LOGBRUSH = RECORD              {The logical brush object record.}
     lbStyle: WORD;
     lbColor: INTEGER4;
     lbHatch: INTEGER2;
END;
PLOGBRUSH = ADR OF LOGBRUSH;       {A short pointer.}
LPLOGBRUSH = ADS OF LOGBRUSH;      {A long pointer.}
```

GetStockObject, mentioned in the section on the pen, creates a handle to a pen, brush, or font that has been given a predefined name and a variety of attributes. GetStockObject is a shortcut routine. Here are the predefined brushes; the index names are self-explanatory:

WHITE_BRUSH

LTGRAY_BRUSH

GRAY_BRUSH

DKGRAY_BRUSH

BLACK_BRUSH

HOLLOW_BRUSH

NULL_BRUSH

There is a current background mode that indicates how the background should be treated before something is brought on top of it in the foreground, such as text, brush, or pen drawing. There are two options: the TRANS-PARENT mode means that the background is not modified, and the OPAQUE mode means the background is filled with the current background color before the foreground drawing is started. The background mode is set by SetBkMode, which returns the previous mode. The current background mode is returned by GetBkMode.

When a polygon has overlapping sections (i.e., when some of the outline segments cross), filling the entire polygon indiscriminately sometimes loses some of the visual information. MS Windows supports two modes for filling polygons: ALTERNATE, which doesn't fill all the enclosed regions in the polygon, and WINDING, which does. The function SetPolyFillMode is used to set the current polygon fill mode, and GetPolyFillMode returns the current fill mode.

GetBrushOrg is used to return the current brush location on the output device. SetBrushOrg sets the current brush location and returns the previous brush location.

FloodFill is used to cover the display at the specified coordinates with the current brush pattern. The flood area bounding color is a parameter, so FloodFill knows where not to tread. The returned value is FALSE if the routine fails.

IIGS

There is a difference between the Macintosh and IIGS patterns. Both Macintosh and IIGS support an 8-by-8 pixel pattern. The IIGS pattern mask requires the same 8 bytes as the Mac pattern mask, but the IIGS pattern needs either 16 or 32 bytes, depending on whether the screen (or even the individual scan lines) is in 320- or 640-pixel mode. With 320-pixel mode each pixel requires 4 bits (to provide 16 colors); 640-pixel mode supports up to 4 colors, and therefore uses 2 bits per pixel. The IIGS mask doesn't carry color information, but the pattern does.

A single line of pixels is not a simple line of bits; there is depth (figuratively speaking), so a line of color pixels is called a **slice**.

BackPat, PenPat, and PenNormal are present in the IIGS. The fillPat field of the Mac GrafPort is not present in the IIGS version. The only use for fillPat is as a temporary current fill pattern for the lower-level Quick-draw routines. Macintosh application code doesn't set fillPat directly, and the fillPat value is valid during one high-level Quickdraw call anyway. The IIGS developers were not forced to include it, so they didn't.

Amiga

Flood is a common area-fill routine. It is given a pointer to the rastPort of interest. It also gets a floodmode value and a coordinate pair. The flood begins at the location indicated by the coordinate pair. If the floodmode value is 0, then the routine behaves consistently with other implementations of flood routines, filling pixels with the flood color if they don't match the current outline color (AOlPen). However, if the floodmode value is 1, then Flood does not behave so normally. The coordinate pair is also the location of a pixel; Flood will fill the other pixels with the outline color if their color matches the original color of that first pixel.

The BltPattern routine fills a rectangular area of the current raster bitmap, using the current drawing mode, fill pattern, and outline of a specified rastPort. Optionally influencing the result is another bitmap that is used as a mask. Simply put, it's a fill rectangle routine, but it uses the custom graphics hardware of the Amiga and is *fast*. BltPattern is also limited to working with bitmaps defined in the first 512K of RAM, the domain of the Amiga coprocessors.

The first BltPattern parameter is a rastPort pointer. The second is a pointer to the optional masking bitmap. The third, fourth, fifth, and sixth parameters form two coordinate pairs that define the target area, a rectangle in the rastPort raster coordinate space. The last parameter is the number of bytes per row, which is sometimes used in place of the second coordinate pair to designate the size of both the mask and the target rectangle. The mask bitmap must be as large as the target rectangle.

SetRast will set the entire raster bitmap of a rastPort to the indicated color. The routine needs a pointer to the rastPort and a color value that can range from 0 to 255 pixels.

SetAfPt is used to set a rastPort's current fill pattern, which is used by the AreaEnd and Flood routines. The macro requires a pointer to the rastPort, a pointer to the area fill pattern in RAM, and a value containing the length of the fill pattern in words.

SetDrPt is used to set a rastPort's current line fill pattern, which is used by the Draw, PolyDraw, and Move routines. The macro needs a pointer to the rastPort and the word containing the line fill pattern.

POLYGONS

The polygon is arguably the most useful graphic construct. Simple polygons can be used to build much larger pictures, such as those found in the computer-generated graphics by Digital Productions, Inc., for the movie *The Last Starfighter*. However, to use polygons in that way it helps to have a very fast processor, a large number of smaller processors, or a few processors that specialize in polygon-based graphics generation, none of which are presently available at mass-market prices.

The present forms of the Macintosh, Atari, and IBM PC machines support slow graphics with medium resolution, but the available processing power is nevertheless sufficient to execute code to produce polygon-based graphics.

Faster graphics engines make heavy use of the simplest polygons, like triangles and four-sided figures; depending on the application software, sometimes more complicated polygons are broken down into an associated group of simpler polygons. However, the commercially viable majority of applications using graphics on the Mac or PC work without high-velocity graphics; the polygon support by the Mac, PC, and Atari ST is rudimentary.

Macintosh

Quickdraw understands a polygon to be a sequence of connected lines which are represented in the Polygon record as lines drawn between connected Points. The Mac polygon data structure is of variable length, and the polyPoints array can be as long as necessary:

```
TYPE Polygon = RECORD
        polySize:           INTEGER;
        polyBox:            Rect;
        polyPoints:         ARRAY[0..0] of Point
END;
```

Because the size of a polygon record is dynamic, application code must use handles, not pointers. The Mac memory manager moves dynamic records without prior warning or permission, and handles to dynamic records are automatically kept up-to-date. Here are the definitions:

```
TYPE PolyPtr = ^Polygon;
     PolyHandle = ^PolyPtr;
```

To define a polygon, call the OpenPoly function to get a polygon handle (PolyHandle). To end a polygon definition, call ClosePoly. In much the same way as regions are defined, the OpenPoly and ClosePoly calls encompass the routine calls that can modify the polygon, like MoveTo and LineTo. Here is an example of polygon definition code on the Mac:

```
polygon := OpenPoly;            {Create polygon space and handle.}
  MoveTo(200,200);              {Move to one vertex of square.}
  LineTo(200,250);              {Trace out square in black and white.}
  LineTo(250,250);
  LineTo(250,200);
  LineTo(200,200);
ClosePoly;                      {Finish definition of 4-sided polygon.}
FillPoly(polygon,grey);         {Render polygon in a cheerful color,}
KillPoly(polygon);              { then return polygon space to system.}
```

The KillPoly routine wipes a polygon from the heap by returning the space to the free-memory pool. The handle to the polygon is surrendered as a parameter. You get to keep the handle, but another call to OpenPoly must be made to make the handle valid.

There are a number of polygon manipulation routines. OffsetPoly relocates the entire polygon in its coordinate plane; it is given separate horizontal and vertical change distances. FramePoly draws the polygon using the current draw modes described by the present grafPort record. FramePoly draws polygons bigger than the other polygon routines; the polyBBox field of the polygon record normally contains the entire polygon, but the polygon outline drawn by FramePoly will extend below and to the right of the actual polygon by the line width.

PaintPoly acts like any other QuickDraw paint routine, using the current pen pattern (the grafPort pnPat field) and drawing mode (pnMode) to render the specified polygon. ErasePoly draws the specified polygon using the background pattern (bkPat) and using the patCopy mode. InvertPoly swaps the white pixels with black ones and vice versa within the specified polygon. Finally, FillPoly renders the specified polygon with the given pattern.

Gem

For polygons that have to be filled, the Gem polygon draw routine is v_fillarea. v_fillarea can handle polygons with lines that cross, and draws the polygonal shape if the outlining is turned on. A v_fillarea polygon is intended to be a guaranteed-closed figure, according to the Gem standard.

For polygons that don't have to be filled, v_pline will probably do just as well, or for that matter v_pmarker. There is no routine provided to specifically draw a regular-sided polygon.

Windows

Polygon is the Windows polygon draw routine. A handle to the display context, a pointer to an array of type POINT, and an integer with the count of coordinate pairs in the POINT array are the parameters.

As mentioned previously, a polygon may have overlapping sections (which occurs when the polygon border crosses itself). When a polygon is complex, filling it entirely is sometimes too complete (see Fig. 3–28). There are two Windows polygon filling modes: ALTERNATE and WINDING. Filling a polygon using the ALTERNATE mode results in some of the enclosed regions not being filled. Filling with WINDING as the current mode results in the entire polygon being filled. The routine Polygon, after drawing a closed polygon, fills the interior with the current brush pattern.

The SetPolyFillMode routine is used to set the current polygon fill mode, and GetPolyFillMode returns the current polygon fill mode.

IIGS

The IIGS polygon is the same as the Macintosh polygon. The polygon routines OpenPoly and ClosePoly work the same, as do the rest: KillPoly, OffsetPoly, FramePoly, PaintPoly, ErasePoly, InvertPoly, and FillPoly.

Amiga

An Amiga polygon is built in the fashion of Macintosh and IIGS polygons. The Amiga software diverges from Apple machines after the completion of the polygon list: the polygon is immediately drawn, and then the list is lost. Presumably, a more permanent copy of the polygon coordinate list is

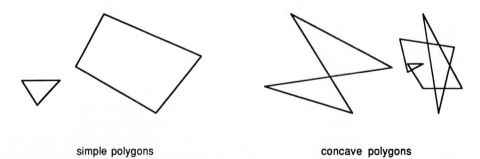

simple polygons   concave polygons

Figure 3–28 Simple and complex polygons

used to make the temporary low-level copy if the image is to be drawn repetitively, or the image is drawn onto a small bitmap once and then that image is copied onto other bitmaps.

The AreaDraw routine adds a coordinate pair to a list of coordinate pairs used to describe a polygon in a raster coordinate space. A rastPort pointer and a pair of raster coordinates are the parameters. This routine may return a −1 value, which means that the buffer containing the coordinate pairs has run out of space. AreaDraw doesn't draw anything by itself; that work is handled by AreaEnd. In the Amiga documentation the coordinate buffer is officially called a **vector list**.

A call to AreaMove means that the construction of a new polygon should be started. The pen is moved without drawing to the indicated raster coordinates (not screen coordinates). If there was an incomplete polygon under construction just before an AreaMove call, then an additional call to AreaDraw is automatically made to close the open polygon before the pen is moved to the beginning of the new polygon. A − 1 returned means that the coordinate pair list ran out of space.

When the AreaEnd routine is called, it means that the vector list that was built using AreaDraw and AreaMove is finally to be drawn. The involved rastPort is the only parameter. When the area fill using the current area-fill pattern and drawing mode is completed, the vector list is emptied and readied for the next AreaMove instruction. During drawing AreaEnd uses the TmpRas scratchpad area for temporary storage.

InitArea is the routine used to allocate and initialize a vector list. It is given a pointer to an AreaInfo record, a pointer to the beginning of the vector list buffer, and a value for the maximum number of coordinate pairs that can be held in the vector list—the buffer size. The vector list is thus prepared for a call to AreaMove.

CIRCLES, ELLIPSES, CURVES, AND ARCS

Macintosh

Most of the Macintosh circle, ellipse, and arc routines were mentioned in the section covering rectangles. A rectangle is used in Quickdraw to define the extent of a symmetric curved shape. Other parameters are provided to describe the start and end positions.

Gem

The Gem VDI Generalized Drawing Primitive (GDP) handles circles, ellipses, and arcs. The following binding routines are normally provided:

v_arc	Draws an arc.
v_pieslice	Draws an arc, filled.
v_circle	Draws a circle.
v_ellarc	Draws an elliptical arc.
v_ellpie	Draws an elliptical arc, filled.

These functions accept screen coordinates (either NDC or RC) and degrees, where appropriate, in units of tenths of a degree (90 degrees, for example, is passed as the integer value 900). The arc extent is specified as having a beginning angle and an ending angle.

Windows

The curved objects drawn by Windows and associated routines are:

Ellipse	Draws ellipse and circle.
Arc	Draws an elliptical arc.
Pie	Draws a pie-shaped wedge.

Each of the objects drawn is specified using a defining rectangle; the coordinates for the upper right and lower left corners of the rectangle are parameters to each routine as four separate integer values. The arc and pie routines require two additional coordinate pairs, one pair for each endpoint of the drawn elliptical arc. Fortunately, the endpoints do not have to exactly coincide with the arc line.

IIGS

The Macintosh routines and the IIGS routines are almost exactly the same. The major difference in their behavior is related to the availability of color on the IIGS and the shape of the pixels.

The Amiga doesn't currently provide basic curved-shape draw routines, though this is easy enough to remedy. Since Amiga, like the IBM, supports a number of screen pixel densities, this must be accounted for in any curved-shape draw library. The big difference between the IBM and

Amiga displays is that Amiga viewports with different resolutions can coexist on the screen, something IBM displays can't normally do.

CLIPPING

Clipping is used to handle picture rendering to the display or a subset of the display. Clipping is a way of life, preventing graphics that are too big for the area of the display from overwriting other sections (see Fig. 3–29).

Clipping is used to tell if part of a picture is going to be visible; if it isn't, then the programmer shouldn't bother calling routines to show it. Calling draw routines for objects that are off the page is a noticeable time-wasting effort on any kind of machine, especially micros. More intelligent drawing packages will make this decision for the application code. The windowing environments discussed here all have some built-in clipping.

The adept use of clipping will make drawing sequences go from needing an impossibly long time to finish to lickety-split completion. It is common for 99.999% of a large drawing to not fit on the display except with the most uncomfortable and extreme view settings (see Fig. 3–30).

Clipping affects only the image rendered. The entire coordinate range is still available, because clipping does not affect calculations made before a draw command. In Figure 3–31, some calculations are made, creating a shape; a clipping area is defined, a draw command is given, another clipping area is defined, and another draw command is given. Two visually different results will be obtained. The calculations involve coordinates that extend beyond one clipping area but not the other. Were the clipping to

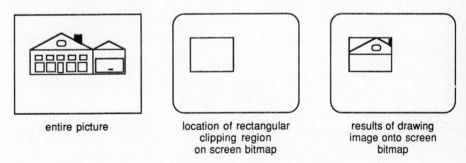

entire picture location of rectangular clipping region on screen bitmap results of drawing image onto screen bitmap

Figure 3–29 Picture, clipping region, and result of update

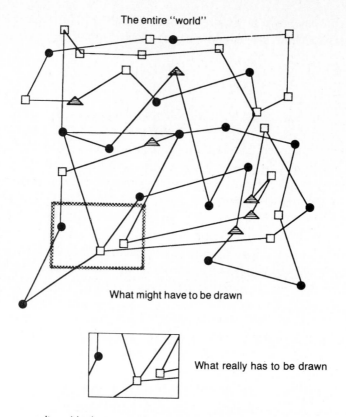

The entire "world"

What might have to be drawn

What really has to be drawn

It could take too much time for an application to draw the
off-screen parts of the picture.

Figure 3–30 Eliminating graphics that are obviously offscreen

have an effect on the calculations and not just the drawing, then the line
would be drawn the same way both times.

So, for this context, clipping does not change things in any stages
before drawing. (See Fig. 3–32 for an ineffective version of clipping.)

Macintosh

Much of the clipping work on the Macintosh is done not with rectangles
or polygons, but with regions.

The grafPort's clipRgn is the region that application code can use to limit
the area on the screen on which drawing will take place. Another grafPort
region, the visRgn, is controlled by the Macintosh Window Manager, and
describes the screen area that is viewable with respect to a window. If a

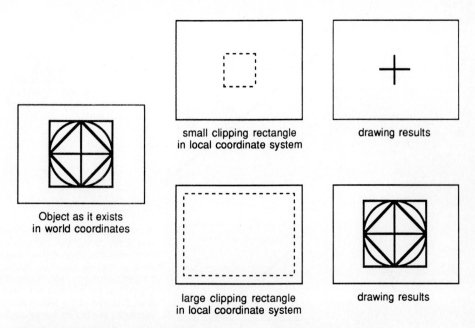

Figure 3–31 Effect of clipping rectangles on world coordinate objects

window is in the foreground, then the visRgn will coincide with the entire window. If the window is partially off-screen or behind another window, the visRgn will not contain the obscured parts of the window.

The clipRgn is initially huge; the visRgn is initially set to equal the grafPort's portRect.

The few clip region routines in Quickdraw are SetClip, GetClip and ClipRect. SetClip assigns the clipping region of the current grafPort to the region whose handle is provided in the parameter list of the call. A copy of the region is made and the clipRgn is assigned to it. GetClip does just the opposite: it makes a copy of the clipRgn and associates the copy with the region handle provided as the parameter to the call. Similar to SetClip but with a different graphic primitive, ClipRect forces the clipRgn of the current grafPort to be the equivalent size and shape of the rectangle described by ClipRect's only parameter.

The Macintosh clipping routines go a long way to limit the display contents to where they belong, but an application can still waste a considerable amount of CPU time on calculations that produce results that will not be visible. Do not expect that exclusive use of the basic clipping routines provided on the Mac will be satisfactory for applications employing a display list, for they may not exclude things soon enough. However, most Macintosh applications to date seem satisfactory.

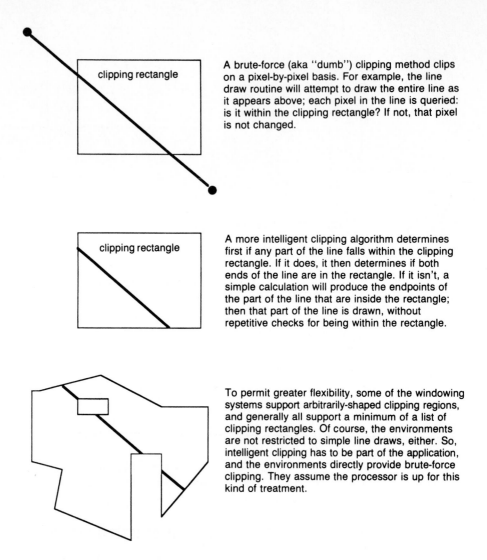

A brute-force (aka "dumb") clipping method clips on a pixel-by-pixel basis. For example, the line draw routine will attempt to draw the entire line as it appears above; each pixel in the line is queried: is it within the clipping rectangle? If not, that pixel is not changed.

A more intelligent clipping algorithm determines first if any part of the line falls within the clipping rectangle. If it does, it then determines if both ends of the line are in the rectangle. If it isn't, a simple calculation will produce the endpoints of the part of the line that are inside the rectangle; then that part of the line is drawn, without repetitive checks for being within the rectangle.

To permit greater flexibility, some of the windowing systems support arbitrarily-shaped clipping regions, and generally all support a minimum of a list of clipping rectangles. Of course, the environments are not restricted to simple line draws, either. So, intelligent clipping has to be part of the application, and the environments directly provide brute-force clipping. They assume the processor is up for this kind of treatment.

Figure 3–32 Clipping algorithms

The Macintosh II provides a transparent mode to be used with color images. The transparent mode replaces the destination pixel with the source pixel if the source pixel is not equal to the background color. Transparent mode is intended to be used with color bitmaps with large transparent holes. Using this for display clipping in many cases will provide much faster code than using the clipping region or CopyMask mask parameter equivalent.

When used with single-bit pixels, transparent mode reverts to OR.

Gem

There is but one clipping routine: vs_clip. vs_clip is used to turn clipping off or on. When clipping is turned on, vs_clip is also used to define the clipping rectangle, with its size and location specified either in Gem Normalized Device Coordinates or in raster coordinates, depending on how the output device was opened.

The clipping routine is automatically called by objc_draw before an object is rendered. The clipping rectangle is set to the size of the parent of the object being drawn.

Windows

As is true on the Macintosh, the Windows clipping area is a region, not simply a rectangle.

Most of the draw routines return a flag set to TRUE if the draw was successful, and FALSE if not. A FALSE is returned if the object to be drawn falls outside the display context clip region.

GetClipBox calculates a rectangle around the entire current clipping region. Since the clipping region is not necessarily rectangular, there may be some display space included within the rectangle that is not in the clipping region. The routine is given a display context handle and a pointer to a RECT data structure where the rectangle coordinates are to be inserted. The function returns with a flag that either tells of a problem (ERROR) or indicates the type of region (NULLREGION, SIMPLE-REGION, COMPLEXREGION).

IntersectClipRect creates a new current clipping region from the intersection of the old current clipping region and a rectangle specified by the four integer values (two coordinate pairs) that are passed to the routine. The return value is the same as that returned by GetClipBox.

OffsetClipRgn moves the display location of the current clipping region (for the specified display context). A delta-X and delta-Y coordinate pair is passed to the routine; the returned value is the same as that returned by GetClipBox.

ExcludeClipRect will take a rectangular-shaped chunk out of the current clipping region. The display context handle and the four coordinate values (two coordinate pairs) of the rectangle, are parameters; the returned value is the same as that of GetClipBox.

PtVisible returns TRUE if the requested device coordinates are within the clipping region of the specified display context, and FALSE if not.

IIGS

SetClip, GetClip, and ClipRect are present and are all the same as in Macintosh Quickdraw.

Amiga

A **clipping rectangle** is an area in which drawing can occur. A clipping rectangle list is zero or more clipping rectangles linked together into a list; drawing can occur within any of these rectangles. A ClipRect structure is used to contain one clipping rectangle; a number of ClipRect records can form a double-linked list. Its definition is as follows:

```
struct ClipRect {
    struct ClipRect    *Next;        /* Points to next ClipRect record. */
    struct ClipRect    *prev;        /* A pointer to the previous record. */
    struct Layer       *lobs;        /* A pointer to an associated Layer. */
    struct BitMap      *BitMap;      /* A pointer to an associated BitMap. */
    struct Rectangle   bounds;       /* The bounds rectangle for the clip. */
    struct Cliprect    *_p1, *_p2;   /* Used by the Amiga system. */
    LONG               reserved;     /* Reserved for Amiga system use. */
#ifdef NEWCLIPRECTS_1_1
    LONG               Flags;        /* Used only in layer allocation. */
#endif
}
```

The Amiga region is not merely the same as the clipping rectangle list, nor is it the equivalent of an Amiga ClipRect record. A Region record is used by the region routines to build and modify a ClipRect list. Sometimes the modifications involved are elaborate; the behind-the-scenes work is masked within the region. A ClipRect list alone can't be manipulated by the region routines.

A Layer record may also have a list of ClipRect records, with each ClipRect record containing a clipping rectangle.

When do ClipRect clipping rectangles meet Region clipping rectangles? If part of a layer has been modified in some way, then the clipping rectangle that contains the changed area of the layer's bitmap is used to modify a Region's clipping rectangle list. Eventually the Region's clipping rectangle list is used as a **damage list**, which is a list encompassing all the changed portions of the layer's bitmap to point out all areas "damaged" by the changes and needing redrawing. A region is a place for wholesale manipulation of an entire clipping rectangle list; a Layer record may point to a clipping rectangle list, but global manipulation of the list ought not to take place unless it is copied to a Region first. The region routines should be used to do the copying.

The Amiga part of the regions section describes Amiga's clipping regions and clipping region functions.

SwapBitsRastPortClipRect is used to display menus and other graphics quickly to avoid having the application program redraw them every time they're used. The routine is described in greater detail in the section on bitmaps.

LIST OF PRIMITIVES

Macintosh

line

rectangle (horizontal or vertical orientations only)

rectangle-based shapes: round-corner rectangle, arc, ellipse

region

polygon

pixel image (bitmap)

text

very limited color

picture (limited)

Mac II: chunky pixel image model

Mac II: upward-compatible extensions for elaborate color support

Gem

polyline

polymarker

polygon, text

rectangle

round-corner rectangle

arc

pie

circle

ellipse (elliptical arc and pie)

cell array

text

color

Windows

line

polyline

rectangle

round-corner rectangle

polygon

ellipse

arc

pie

color

IIGS

line

rectangle

region

polygon

pixel image (bitmap)

text

Some variations on the rectangle are provided, such as the ellipse, the circle, and round-cornered rectangle, with the limitation (as with Macintosh) that the objects cannot be drawn directly by Quickdraw II at an angle other than zero degrees with respect to the X- and Y-coordinate axes.

Amiga

line

polyline

rectangle

region (used for building clipping rectangle list only)

polygon

pixel image (bitmap)

layer (special bitmap)

hardware sprite

virtual sprite

blitter object (playfield)

animation object (group of blitter objects)

animation component (group of animation objects)

text

color

COLOR

Macintosh

The Mac 128K, 512K, and Mac+ systems are all equipped with black and white displays with square pixels. The color support is rudimentary, because only eight colors are supported by old Quickdraw: black, white, red, green, blue, cyan, magenta, and yellow. It was originally intended that all nonwhite colors appear as black on monochrome devices, but this has been sidestepped in use. Some applications have been developed that translate the monochrome fill and pen patterns, as shown on the Mac screen, into regions of color for hard copy on plotters and color printers (like Apple Imagewriters with color ribbons).

Quickdraw supports output devices that have 32 bits of color description per pixel, but the support is not extensive.

There are only three routines provided in ROM for color control purposes. ForeColor is used to set the foreground color of all the drawings in the current grafPort (the fgColor field). The default color is blackColor. BackColor does the same for the background color (the bkColor field); the default background color is whiteColor.

Finally, the ColorBit routine is used by color display or hard copy software to select the color plane into which Quickdraw should be drawing. Quickdraw can draw only on one plane at a time. ColorBit is given a number corresponding with a single bit plane, 0 through 31. It is *not* simply a 32-bit INTEGER value with all the planes selected via setting bits in corresponding positions of the word. The value 29 turns on only the 29th plane. The grafPort field involved is called colrBit, which is of type INTEGER.

Macintosh II

Macintosh II color is not the same as that supported by the Mac 128K, 512K, or Plus. Mac II Quickdraw has RGB color values that can range from (0,0,0) for black to (65535,65535,65535) for white. A Mac II color-graphics device can have up to 16 bits of resolution for each component (red, green, or blue), but it isn't mandatory.

A Macintosh II package called the **color picker** provides routines for converting RGB values to CMY, HLS, and HSV color model values. The acronyms stand for:

CMY	Cyan, magenta, yellow
HLS	Hue, lightness, saturation
HSV	Hue, saturation, value

The Mac II Quickdraw package supports chunky pixels, in which all the bits used to describe the color of a single pixel are consecutive in memory, perhaps all in the same byte or word. This is different from many color display systems which commonly consign each bit to a separate bit plane; the Amiga is one such system.

To "do it right," quite a bit of work was done to the original Quickdraw code. The result, Mac II Quickdraw, is upward-compatible with the original code so that Macintosh application code can't use Mac II Quick-draw as an excuse for not working on the Mac II. The original data structures such as grafPort and bitMap were left alone. New color versions of old data structures, such as CGrafPort for grafPort and PixMap for bitMap, have been created. New data structures are defined for handling RGBColor values, color tables, and mapping pixel values to RGBColor values. There are some descriptions of the new data structures in the sections on bitmaps and data structures.

A very important addition to Mac II Quickdraw is support for multiple screen devices that can be available at the same time. A new data structure, gDevice, is used by the Mac II to keep track of a single device. One screen device is active at a given moment, and can be selected with the routine SetDeviceAttribute. The default screen device is selected from the beginning automatically so that old code doesn't have to know about this new feature. Here is a list of the new gDevice support routines:

NewGDevice	Allocates a gDevice record and initializes the associated hardware device (by calling InitGDevice).
InitGDevice	Assigns the video device to the indicated mode; fills out the gDevice record to match the mode.
GetGDevice	Provides a handle to the current gDevice.
SetGDevice	Sets the current gDevice to the one indicated.
DisposeGDevice	Releases the space allocated to the specified gDevice record.
GetDeviceList	Fetches a handle to the entire list of all the gDevice records known to the Mac II environment at that time.
GetMainDevice	Returns a handle to the primary graphics device in the device list.
GetNextDevice	Returns a handle to the next graphics device in the device list.
TestDevice-Attribute	Used to test whether a given device is both an active device and a screen device.
GetMaxDevice	Provides a handle to the last device intersecting the indicated global rectangle.

To properly use color on the Mac II, you must use the routines RGB-ForeColor and RGBBackColor instead of ForeColor and BackColor. The old GetForeColor and GetBackColor routines work in either case.

There are new versions of the fill routines that should be used. They are:

FillCRect

FillCOval

FillCRoundRect

FillCArc

FillCRgn

FillCPoly

GetCPixel and SetCPixel can be used to respectively obtain and assign the RGB color value for the indicated pixel.

CopyBits has been rewritten to handle operations involving the new pixMap data structures as well as the old bitMap structures.

A Macintosh II color table is used to associate each currently displayable RGBColor value with a physically smaller index value. The smaller index values are used to represent pixel color in memory instead of the larger RGBColor values since an RGBColor record commonly uses 6 times more RAM than an index into a color table. Using the index implies that the number of colors simultaneously available is limited to the maximum number of addressable entries in the color table. With an 8-bit index, there are up to 256 different ColorSpec records in the color table, with each ColorSpec record containing one index and one RGBColor value. Here are some of the definitions:

```
TYPE RGBColor = RECORD          {The Mac II RGBColor record definition.}
          red:   INTEGER;       {The Red Component.}
          green: INTEGER;       {The Green Component.}
          blue:  INTEGER;       {The Blue Component.}
     END;
     ColorSpec = RECORD
          value: INTEGER;       {A pixel value.}
          rgb:   RGBColor;      {The associated RGB value.}
     END;
     CTabHandle = ^CTabPtr;
     CTabPtr = ^ColorTable;
     ColorTable = RECORD
          ctSeed:      LONGINT;       {A unique ID from the table.}
          transIndex:  INTEGER;       {The index of a transparent pixel.}
          ctSize:      INTEGER;       {The number of entries in the table.}
          ctTable:     ARRAY[0..0] OF ColorSpec;
     END;
```

Gem

A Gem color index value is a simple integer. Gem assumes that the color indices 0 and 1 are valid for every display device. More are available depending on the display hardware.

A Gem color intensity is an integer value from 0 to 1000. 0 means that there is no presence of a color, and 1000 means that the color intensity is cranked all the way up.

A color index can be mapped to a triad of color intensities. The Gem routine vs_color is used to assign a combination of red, green, and blue color intensities to an arbitrary color index value. IBM PC/AT display cards generally have preset color indices, as there aren't a large number of available colors to choose from.

The Atari ST provides monochrome graphics at 640 x 400 resolution, 4 colors in the 640 x 200 mode, and 16 color graphics at 320 x 200 resolution. There are 512 colors in the Atari ST palette, which means that the red, blue, and green guns each have only 8 real intensities.

Gem has a small number of object color set routines:

vsl_color	Sets the polyline color index.
vsm_color	Sets the polymarker color index.
vst_color	Sets the text color index.
vsf_color	Sets the fill color index.
vq_color	Returns the color mix for a given color index.

Windows

The display context (DC) is where some of the current color attributes are kept. There are three attributes in the DC that are most directly involved with color assignments and not drawing modes: the text color, the background color, and the color table.

Other color attributes are kept within the pen and brush structures, which are created as needed. The color attributes of a brush or pen are thus not set by fields that are contained in the display context. A DC *does* have fields for the current pen and the current brush; consequently (and indirectly) there are such things as current pen and brush colors.

Most of the details on how to set the color of pens and brushes are discussed elsewhere in this chapter. Look for explanations of the following routines: GetStockObject, CreatePen, CreatePenIndirect, CreateSolidBrush, CreateHatchBrush, CreatePatternBrush, CreateBrushIndirect, CreateBitmap (since a brush is really using a small bitmap), and CreateBitmapIndirect; there are others.

A Windows RGB color structure is a 32-bit value of which the lower significant three bytes contain valid color information. Each byte contains a color intensity value from 0 to 255. The lowest significant byte is the red intensity, the next higher significant byte is the green intensity, and the next byte is the blue intensity. Thus, Windows can directly support an RGB-Analog (RGBA) color display subsystem capable of displaying 2^{24} different colors. The RGB color structure is handled as a long integer in order that it may be returned as the value of a function without having to use a pointer, and to take advantage of the fact that good C compilers stick the function return value directly in a register so that its access is quick.

Each display context has a predefined RGB color table (the contents of which may vary based on the device type). The Windows manual unfortunately does not go into much detail, so it is presumed that this table is the method used to translate between the rich selectivity of the RGB color value and the limited color selection of most IBM-PC–family machines in use at the time of this writing. The table also seems to be intended to accommodate some of the color imaging differences between different output devices. For example, a picture displayed using a color tube using one palette of colors may not look as good when a hard copy is made using a color printer; the colors may have to be changed slightly to make up for differences in the color mix.

The routine SetPixel, mentioned earlier in this chapter, assigns a color to a specified device pixel, and GetPixel retrieves that RGB color value.

SetBkColor sets the current background RGB color to the indicated display context to what is specified by the second parameter. GetBkColor retrieves the color value.

SetTextColor sets the current text color of the mentioned display context to the indicated RGB color value. GetTextColor returns the current text color.

IIGS

Color on this machine does not follow the lead of the original Macintosh Quickdraw package (which supports 8 colors by name), but is capable of handling 32-bit pixels; a color picture would have a maximum of 32-bit planes. The "MacCaveat": you can set or reset the bits only one plane at a time. The IIGS, in what is (amusingly) called **Super High Resolution Mode**, embraces 2 or 4 bits per pixel, and the pixel codes are translated into RGB values for display with a Color Lookup Table. A 16-color scanline may have 320 pixels, and a 4-color scanline may have 640 pixels.

The IIGS grafPort has two color fields that are the same as the Macintosh grafPort, although the names are slightly different. FGColor is the foreground color for a grafPort, and BGColor is the grafPort background color. The IIGS grafPort does not have a colrBit field. The routines used to set and get the current foreground and background colors are SetForeColor, GetForeColor, SetBackColor, and GetBackColor. These names are different from the Macintosh equivalents, and they work a little differently. A IIGS ColorValue is 2 bytes (1 word) long, and contains 4 nybbles of information as shown in Figure 3–33.

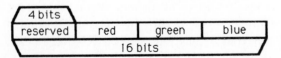

Figure 3–33 Apple 2GS ColorValue Composition

A IIGS ColorTable is a 16-word array of ColorValue entries. A Color-Table is used to convert a pixel's 2- or 4-bit code into an RGB ColorValue; the bit code is an index into the color table. This way it is possible to change the color of all the pixels on the screen with a value of 0, by just changing the value of the 0th entry of the appropriate ColorTable.

The IIGS supports the use of 16 different ColorTable arrays; each SCB contains 4 bits that identify which color table it is using. The 16 ColorTable arrays have hardwired addresses, and are the only ones that are used to actually map colors.

InitColorTable sets up a color table with the standard values. The values depend on the value of the color mode in the master SCB.

SetColorTable is used to assign all the entries in a color table; a pointer to an arbitrary array of ColorValue and a color table ID number are parameters. The ColorValue array is copied into the color table. GetColorTable can be used to copy the contents of one color table (addressed using the color table ID) to another (addressed by a pointer), which means that if you know the RAM addresses of the real color tables, you can use GetColorTable to copy into them (this will probably be a popular thing to do, but is not recommended).

SetColorEntry is used to change a single entry in a color table. GetColorEntry obtains a ColorValue entry in a color table.

A Scanline Control Byte (SCB) is used to describe the nature of an associated pixel image. For the screen an SCB describes the resolution and identifies the color table used with individual scan lines. Elsewhere SCBs identify the color table and the number of bits per pixel for entire pixel images. There is an SCB in every LocInfo record (the IIGS's version of the Macintosh BitMap), used to describe how to interpret the contents of the pixel image.

As you might expect, the IIGS's SCB requires a bumper crop of support routines: SetMasterSCB, GetMasterSCB, GetStandardSCB, SetSCB, GetSCB, and SetAllSCBs.

The Master SCB is used by Quickdraw II routines like InitPort and QD-Startup as a template whenever an SCB has to be initialized. The application passes what it wants the master SCB to QDStartup (nothing in Quickdraw II can be done without QDStartup being called first). The application can change its mind while running and change the master SCB by using SetMasterSCB; the value of the current master SCB can be obtained by calling GetMasterSCB.

The standard SCB is a particular predefined SCB value. QDII's GetStandardSCB returns a standard SCB value, as shown in Figure 3–34. The standard SCB is a convenience.

The routine SetSCB is used to set the SCB of the specified display scan line to the value indicated. SetSCB returns the previous value of the SCB. GetSCB retrieves the current value of the indicated scan line SCB. SetAllSCBs sets all the scan line control bytes to the preferred value.

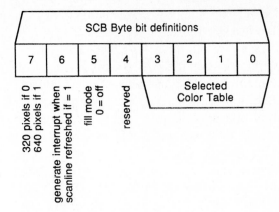

Figure 3–34 Apple 2GS Scanline Control Byte definition

Each LocInfo record, used to point to a IIGS pixel image that can be drawn in, has a Port SCB byte that sets the bit interpretation of the pixel image. For more information on the LocInfo record, see the section on data structures.

If active (= 1) the **fill mode** bit in an SCB means that entry 0 in that SCB's color table is ignored by the hardware, and that the pixel color index of 0 means "use the color last displayed."

Here are some mundane routines. GrafOn turns on the 640-by-200 pixel resolution mode. GrafOff turns off the 640-by-200 mode. These routines play with the IIGS New Video softswitch, affecting only what is displayed. Clear-Screen fills the screen memory with the specified word-sized value.

Amiga

Each Amiga RGB value in the color tables is a 16-bit value that has 4 fields of 4 bits each. Bits 0 to 3 contain the blue color value, bits 4 to 7 contain the green component, and bits 8 to 11 contain the red intensity. Bits 12 to 15 aren't used, but are reserved. A 4-bit value of 0 means minimum intensity, and 15 (decimal) means maximum intensity. This is the same composition as a IIGS Color table value.

GetRGB4 accepts a pointer to a ColorMap record and an entry number. GetRGB4 looks in the colormap table for the ColorMap record to see if the entry wanted is a legitimate RGB value. If it is the value of the RGB colortable entry is returned, and a − 1 is returned if it isn't.

LoadRGB4 is the routine used to copy wholesale a ViewPort's color palette from the colormap table that belongs to the indicated ColorMap record. Three parameters are passed to LoadRGB4: a pointer to the ViewPort record, a pointer to the ColorMap record, and a count of the number of ViewPort color entries to use in the color table. Color Table copies always start with the first color table entry. The hardware limit of 32 colors can be assigned at once.

SetRGB4 is used to change one RGB value entry for a ViewPort. There are five parameters: a pointer to the ViewPort; the color table entry number, which can range from 0 to 31; and three values, ranging from 0 to 15, individually describing the red, green, and blue intensities. SetRGB4 changes one entry faster than LoadRGB4 can change an entire palette of colors; the speed may be a factor in reducing system overhead, screen flicker, and noise.

To make a ColorMap record, GetColorMap is called with the required number of entries in the table as a parameter; the routine returns a pointer to the new record. FreeColorMap accepts a ColorMap record pointer and deallocates the space used by the record back to the system free queue.

The two things that wind up on the display, playfields and sprites, support a different number of colors. Hardware sprites can show 4 out of a choice of 16 colors, with two caveats: The first is that one of the four colors must be transparent. The second is that hardware sprites are paired when color is involved; two hardware sprites must share the same selection of colors.

Virtual sprites have the same constraints as hardware sprites.

To understand how Amiga bitmap colors work, it helps to understand the bigger picture: how ViewPorts relate to RastPorts, Layers, and BitMap records. The number of planes in a bitmap dictates the number of colors available; when are bitmaps created, and to whom do they belong? The complete answer is in the next section; for now, the partial answer is that a maximum of 32 colors are available because there are only 32 color registers in the Amiga model 1000. You can specify a bitmap to consist of from 1 to 6 bitplanes; it takes 5 to handle 32 colors at once. Anything using a bitmap, blitter objects, animation objects, layers, viewports, or animation components can have up to 32 colors.

Since the IIGS color table is only 16 entries long, it is suggested that software portable between the IIGS and the Amiga try to involve only 16, not 32, colors.

BITMAPS

A bitmap is a collection of data bytes that can be manipulated as a unit. The significance of each bit in a bitmap depends on the capabilities of the display circuitry, and whether the intended use of a given bitmap involves a complete set or a subset of those capabilities. Normally a bitmap is used to contain a bit image which is at some time visually presented on the display.

In its simplest form a bitmap is in the shape of a rectangle with each bit representing one screen pixel; a bit value of 0 means black, and a bit value of 1 means white. Bitmaps are not sparse arrays; they are solid, brute-force, contiguous storage representing *all* the bits between the top left and the bottom right corners of its rectangular shape. Bitmaps are globally intended to be fast display objects, appearing on the screen and vanishing all at once, and movable as single units without parts lagging behind. For the fastest display speed, they are not at all storage space-efficient.

Macintosh

A Mac bitmap is always in the shape of a rectangle. The Mac BitMap record describes where in the coordinate plane the bitmap is drawn, where the bitmap data are in memory, and how many bytes wide (horizontally) the bitmap is. Here is the Pascal datatype definition:

```
BitMap = RECORD
     baseAddr:    Ptr;
     rowBytes:    INTEGER;
     bounds:      Rect:
END;
```

The BitMap record does not contain the bitmap data, but it does have a pointer to them. This allows several BitMap records to point to the same bitmap data. The same image can be shown at several places on the display at once, for example.

On the Macintosh the bitmap data blob is called a bit image (Fig. 3–35). In the bit image rectangle the most-significant bit of the least-significant byte is at top left; the least-significant bit of the most-significant byte is at bottom right. Rows go across and columns go up and down. Two memory-adjacent bytes are normally in the same row, except when they are both boundary bytes of the rectangle; in other words, the rows are filled first, then the columns.

In the BitMap record the third field is a defining rectangle that establishes where in the coordinate plane the bitmap should be displayed. Normally the defining rectangle and the bit image are the same dimension. This means that any operations done to the bit image through a BitMap record will affect all the bit image contents. If the defining rectangle is smaller, then some of the bit image is excluded from any bitmap operations. The top left corner of the bit image is stapled to the top left of the defining rectangle of a BitMap record; when the defining rectangle is smaller than the bit image, the bits at the bottom or to the

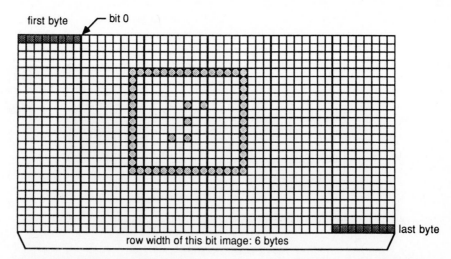

Figure 3–35 Macintosh bit image

right are left out of bitmap calculations. There are two powerful routines in Quickdraw that work with bitmaps: ScrollRect and CopyBits.

ScrollRect is handed a rectangular area on the display. It is also given two distance values, one for the horizontal change and the other for the vertical change. Finally, ScrollRect also uses several fields from the current grafPort: for the visible region, the clipping region, the grafPort rectangle, and the pointer to the current grafPort's bitmap. ScrollRect does a simple scroll operation on the contents of the bitmap at the intersection of all the regions and rectangles mentioned above. All the bits are moved to a new location on the display. The scroll can be horizontal (as shown in Fig. 3–36) or vertical. Bits that are pushed out of the intersection are clipped out of view. Bits that weren't visible before the scroll have to be eventually updated with other Quickdraw calls, but in the meantime ScrollRect places the background pattern in their stead. If a picture of a house were centered in a window and a ScrollRect were called, the house might be moved to the edge of the window, with part of the garage missing.

CopyBits, a regularly exercised routine, is used to copy (with one of the Quickdraw copy modes) a bit image from one bitmap to another. It is given a source bitmap, a destination bitmap, a transfer mode, source and destination rectangles (for scaling the copied bitmap image), and a handle to a region used for clipping the bit image at its destination (see Fig. 3–37).

The Macintosh Plus and all Macintosh systems that have upgraded to version 117 or later (known as the 128K-version) of the Mac ROM have the following three extra bitmap routines: SeedFill, CalcMask, and CopyMask.

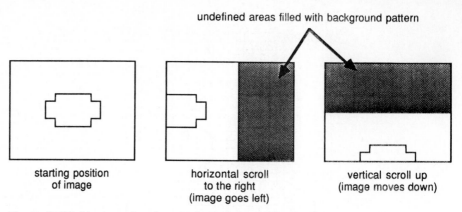

undefined areas filled with background pattern

| starting position of image | horizontal scroll to the right (image goes left) | vertical scroll up (image moves down) |

Figure 3–36 Horizontal and vertical scrolling of a bit image

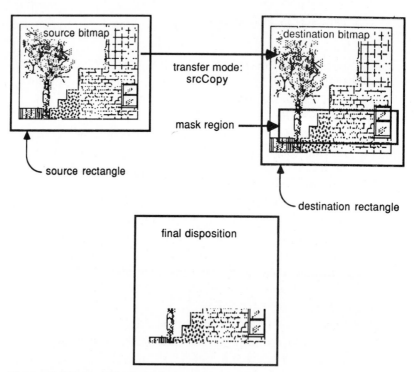

Figure 3–37 CopyBits in action

SeedFill is given a source bit image. It calculates a destination bit image, with 1's in the pixels where paint can leak from the starting seed point, à la MacPaint. SeedFill calls are not limited to the contents of the current port. SeedFill calls are also not stored in Quickdraw pictures. The source and destination rectangles can be anywhere within the source and destination bitmaps.

CalcMask is given a source bit image. It calculates a destination bit image, with 1's in the destination bits where paint can *not* leak from the outer edges, like the MacPaint lasso. Like SeedFill, CalcMask calls aren't limited to the current port contents and are not stored in Quickdraw pictures.

Finally, CopyMask is a version of CopyBits that copies a bit image from a source to a destination bitmap, but only where there is a 1 in a corresponding bit in a third bitmap. The third bitmap is used as a mask, but is not a region; it is a bitmap record with a rectangular local coordinate space.

Macintosh II

Color Quickdraw uses a pixel map instead of a bit map for drawing. In addition to all of a bit map's data, a pixel map carries with it a version number, packing format, two resolution values, physical pixel characteristics, a count of components per pixel, a count of bits per components, an offset value to the next plane, a handle to a color table, and room for expansion. Here are the type definitions:

```
PixMapHandle = ^PixMapPtr;          {Handle to a Mac II color pixel map.}
PixMapPtr    = ^PixMap;             {Pointer to a Mac II pixel map.}
PixMap = RECORD                     {The Mac II Color pixel map.}
    baseAddr:    Ptr;               {A pointer to pixel data.}
    rowBytes:    INTEGER;           {The offset to the next line.}
    bounds:      Rect;              {This rectangle encloses the bitmap.}
    pmVersion:   INTEGER;           {The pixMap version number.}
    packType:    INTEGER;           {This defines the data packing format.}
    packSize:    LONGINT;           {The length of the pixel data.}
    hRes:        Fixed;             {The horizontal resolution.}
    vRes:        Fixed;             {The vertical resolution.}
    pixelType:   INTEGER;           {This defines the pixel type.}
    pixelSize:   INTEGER;           {The number of bits in a pixel.}
    cmpCount:    INTEGER;           {The number of components in a pixel.}
    cmpSize:     INTEGER;           {The number of bits for each component.}
    planeBytes:  LONGINT;           {The offset to the next plane.}
    pmTable:     CTabHandle;        {The color map for this pixMap.}
    pmReserved:  LONGINT;           {This is for future use. MUST BE 0.}
```

To go with the new PixMap record are a small number of new routines. NewPixMap returns a handle to a pixMap data structure that is created and initialized for the occasion, but NewPixMap does not initialize other structures such as the color table for the pixMap. On the other hand, DisposPixMap is used to deallocate the storage for both a pixMap and the pixMap's color table. The

CopyPixMap routine is used to copy the contents of one pixMap to another, including the contents of the color table, not the color table handle. There is also SetCPortPix, which replaces the old SetPortBits routine when working with CGrafPort data structures; SetCPortPix sets the PortPixMap field of the current CGrafPort, but has no effect on a normal grafPort. The routines that exist in the previous versions of Quickdraw for the Macintosh and aren't replaced by new routines in Mac II Quickdraw for using color are still valid; even the routines that have been superceded on the Mac II can still be used, but without the exacting color control provided by the video card.

Gem

A record called an MFDB (Memory Form Definition Block) is used to describe the shape of the Raster area, the data format, and the Raster data starting location. In Pascal there is an MFDB record definition, along with type declarations for gptr and gempoint, two versions of pointers commonly used in Gem. Again, the integer datatype mentioned here is a 2-byte affair. The MFDB record, and odd bitmap formats, are required to handle the small variety of memory-mapped graphics displays available for the Gem target machines. The IBM PC CGA standard (the 640-by-200 one) has a memory map that is not arranged like 99 percent of other color graphics systems; dumping bitplane-oriented color bitmaps into CGA RAM untouched produces worthless visual effects.

```
TYPE
     gptr = ^LONGINT;              {A general 32 bit pointer.}
     gempoint = record            {Pointer is defined this way for easy access.}
            CASE BOOLEAN OF
                  TRUE:           (gp: gptr);
                  FALSE:          (hi: integer; lo: integer);
     END;
     MFDB = record                         {Memory Form Definition Block}
            mptr:          gempoint;       {A pointer to plane 1 of data.}
            formwidth:     integer;        {The width of data in bits.}
            formheight:    integer;        {The height of data in bits.}
            widthword:     integer;        {The width of data in words.}
            formatflag:    integer;        {0 = standard format; 1 = unstd format.}
            memplanes:     integer;        {The number of raster data planes.}
            res1:          integer;        {Reserved for future use.}
            res2:          integer;        {Reserved for future use.}
            res3:          integer;        {Reserved for future use.}
     END;
```

There are four VDI routines provided to handle rudimentary Raster operations. They are vro_cpyfm, vrt_cpyfm, vr_trnfm, and v_get_pixel.

vro_cpyfm (descriptively, Copy Raster Opaque) copies raster data from one MFDB raster data area to another. It is assumed that both source and destination MFDBs are in device-specific form; if they're not, they can be converted using the routine vr_trnfm, which is described below. vro_cpyfm is provided the two MFDB records and the coordinates for a source and a destination rectangle, allowing the transfer of a subset of MFDB raster data areas. If the source rectangle is larger than the destination rectangle, the destination rectangle gets bigger to accommodate the larger raster data requirements. If the source and destination rectangles overlap, the source area is not changed until the corresponding destination area is processed first; the copy will occur cleanly even though some overlap may be present. The kind of copy that takes place is indicated by the mode passed to vro_cpyfm, as shown in Figure 3–38.

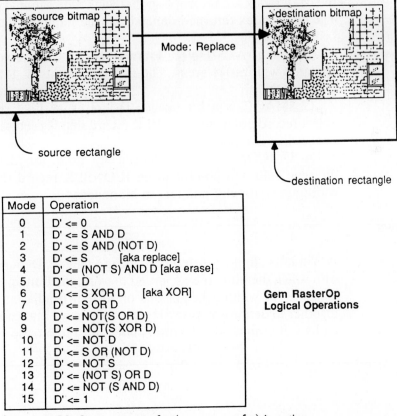

Mode	Operation
0	D' <= 0
1	D' <= S AND D
2	D' <= S AND (NOT D)
3	D' <= S [aka replace]
4	D' <= (NOT S) AND D [aka erase]
5	D' <= D
6	D' <= S XOR D [aka XOR]
7	D' <= S OR D
8	D' <= NOT(S OR D)
9	D' <= NOT(S XOR D)
10	D' <= NOT D
11	D' <= S OR (NOT D)
12	D' <= NOT S
13	D' <= (NOT S) OR D
14	D' <= NOT (S AND D)
15	D' <= 1

**Gem RasterOp
Logical Operations**

Figure 3–38 Gem vro_copyfm (or vrt_copyfm) in action

vrt_cpyfm (known as Copy Raster Transparent) also copies raster data from one MFDB raster data area to another. The difference is that the source raster area is monochrome only, and is copied to a color area. Separate color indices are specified for raster values of 0 and 1. Only four of the raster logical operations are meaningful: replace mode, transparent mode, XOR mode, and reverse transparent mode.

vr_trnfm provides a way to convert raster areas between the standard format and device-specific format. The standard format is a fairly common-sense arrangement, with each color plane occupying a contiguous section of memory and each plane being the same size and proportion as the other planes. The bit order is consistent, with the most-significant bit of the first word in a plane at the top left corner. The member planes are next to each other in numeric order in memory.

v_get_pixel is a quick way to find the color of a single pixel on the screen. Each corresponding bit on each available color plane is used to determine the pixel color. The returned color index values are preset for the standard form MFDB, but both the multiplane value for the pixel and the color index are returned so that your code can make up its own mind. The color index returned depends on the number of planes used by the system. (See Fig. 3–39.)

The Gem AES Object Library supports two object types that are affiliated with raster areas. The first type is the G_IMAGE; the second is G_ICON.

G_IMAGE is a bit image. The ob_spec field of the G_IMAGE object record points to a BITBLK record that is used to describe small bit images like cursors.

A G_ICON object is specifically used for defining icons. The ob_spec field is a pointer to an ICONBLK record that has fields with coordinate data and pointers to bit images.

Windows

A Windows bitmap is referenced using a handle. Depending on the device with which the bitmap is supposed to work, the bitmap is organized either in planes of width x height bits or so that n adjacent bits are grouped together to define one pixel. Here is the record that can be used to create a physical bitmap; this record is not itself the bitmap record:

```
TYPE BITMAP = RECORD
    bmType:             short;      {The bitmap type.}
```

```
bmWidth:            short;       {The pixel width of the bitmap.}
bmHeight:           short;       {The bitmap height in rasters.}
bmWidthBytes:       short;       {The byte width of the bitmap.}
bmPlanes:           BYTE;        {The number of color planes.}
bmBitsPixel:        BYTE;        {The number of adjacent bits per pixel.}
bmBits:        ADS OF INTEGER;   {The bit data in an integer array.}
bmWidthPlanes:      short;       {The byte number in each color plane.}
END;
```

The value for bmWidthBytes must indicate an equal or greater number of bits than bmWidth. The value for bmWidthPlanes is equal to bm-WidthBytes x bmHeight.

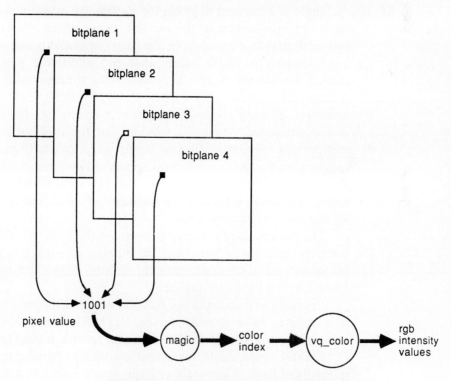

The process, "magic," that converts (in this case) a four bit pixel value into a color index, varies between Gem implementations; for the ST, the "magic" process appears to be nonexistant, for the default pixel values are the same as the color index values. The difference between pixel values and the color index values on IBM PCs depends on the display card.

Figure 3–39 The relationship between pixel, color index, and rgb intensity values

The routine PatBlt overlays some or all of the existing bitmap on the display with a brush pattern in a specified rectangular area. A display context handle as a parameter indicates the device. The rectangular area is described using the device coordinates of the top left corner, a value for the horizontal extent, and a value for the vertical extent. How the brush pattern is overlayed on the existing pattern is described by another parameter; there are 256 possible ternary raster operations, but PatBlt can be used with only a small subset of those, specifically the ones that do not involve a source bitmap. As an example, the raster operations with the common names PATCOPY, PATPAINT, PATINVRT, and DSTINVERT would work.

The function BitBlt goes a little farther than PatBlt; instead of using the current brush as the overlay pattern, BitBlt uses a bitmap from a display context. Not only is a target display context handle a parameter, but so is a separate source display context handle. The destination rectangle is described as being for PatBlt. An additional coordinate pair describes the location of the top left corner of the source bitmap on the source display context. All the 256 raster operations are available for use.

StretchBlt is BitBlt except that two additional parameters are included: the source X and Y extents. This routine uniformly resizes the bitmap rectangle from the source extents to match the extents of the target rectangle. The two rectangles are handled as though the source rectangle is a world coordinate space window and the destination rectangle is a viewport. If the destination rectangle were longer than the source rectangle, then the destination rectangle would contain a stretched version of the visuals of the source rectangle. It is like stealing a frame off of a color comic strip with a flattened blob of Silly Putty, and then stretching the blob so that the image elongates.

The parameters for CreateBitmap are the bitmap width and height (in bits), the number of bitplanes, the number of color bits per pixel, and a pointer to an array containing the bitmap data. The routine returns a handle to the bitmap it creates.

CreateBitmapIndirect is CreateBitmap, but the only parameter it gets is a pointer to a record of type BITMAP which contains the same information. CreateBitmapIndirect also returns a bitmap handle.

CreateCompatibleBitmap returns a bitmap handle; the new bitmap is guaranteed to work properly with the device associated with the indicated display context. That is, the number of color planes or the bits per pixel in the bitmap will match that of the device. The width and the height of the bitmap are also parameters.

Bitmap creation is different when a handle to a memory display context is passed to CreateCompatibleBitmap. When a memory display context is created, standard operating procedure is for Windows to assign a standard, stock, monochrome bitmap as the current bitmap. When a compatible bitmap is made to match that DC, the bitmap is actually made to mirror the format of the current bitmap.

It should be noted that a color memory DC can have as the current bitmap either a color or a black-and-white bitmap; the new compatible bitmap would still be built to match whatever is current for that DC.

SetBitmapBits stuffs the indicated bitmap with the bit data stored in an integer array. A byte count is also provided. Like most Windows routines, SetBitmapBits returns TRUE if successful, FALSE if not.

GetBitmapBits copies the contents of the indicated bitmap into an integer array. A byte count tells how many bytes to copy. GetBitmapBits returns the actual number of bytes copied.

When a bitmap is stretched or compressed, there are three different modes from which to choose that are used for reducing image distortion. The first mode, WHITE_ON_BLACK, favors white pixels over black ones. The second, BLACK_ON_WHITE, favors black pixels. The last, COLOR_ON_COLOR, is free of bias. SetStretchBltMode sets the current stretching mode for the indicated display context; GetStretchBlt-Mode returns the current stretching mode.

IIGS

Instead of the Macintosh BitMap, the IIGS Quickdraw II package supports a new record called LocInfo. The first released version of Macintosh Quickdraw allows pixel drawing to take place only in the RAM associated with the graphics display. Though it is possible to move the screen RAM around (there are two Mac screen RAM areas defined, but the alternate screen buffer is slowly evaporating from use), drawing still takes place in the screen RAM area. Quickdraw II permits pixel images to be anywhere in RAM and not just in the screen area, as long as there is a LocInfo record for each pixel image. The LocInfo record looks like a Mac BitMap record with some extra fields:

```
TYPE LocInfo = RECORD
      portSCB:                AnSCBByte;
      reserved:               BYTE;
      pointerToPixelImage:    QDPtr;
      Width:                  INTEGER;
      BoundsRect:             Rect;
END;
```

The Boundary Rectangle (BoundsRect) imposes a coordinate system on the pixel image; the BoundsRect surrounds the active portion of the pixel image. The Width field is the number of bytes in a slice of the pixel image, and must be a multiple of 8. It is apparent from the use of the pointer-ToPixelImage field (as a pointer and not a handle) that Apple construes the pixel image to be of static size and not subject to being moved by the memory manager, which is how Mac QD treats bit images.

The ScrollRect routine works on pixel images on the IIGS, and is used the same way as the ScrollRect routine on the Macintosh. The Macintosh CopyBits routine is replaced by Cortland's PaintPixels function, which uses the following parameters to copy a pixel image:

PtrToSourceLocInfo	In place of source bitmap record
PtrToDestLocInfo	In place of destination bitmap record
PtrToSourceRect	Source pixel image BoundRect coordinates
PtrToDestRect	Destination pixel image BoundRect coordinates
Mode	IIGS transfer modes: COPY, notCOPY, OR, notOR, XOR, notXOR, BIC, and notBIC
MaskHandle	The clipping region

Amiga

The Amiga bitmap is always rectangular, with multiple planes to represent more colors; a single bitplane bitmap can handle two colors (usually black and white); three bitplanes can be used to handle eight colors. The system provides up to 6 bitplanes per bitmap, but there are only 32 color registers, so normally a bitmap can handle 32 colors. There is an exception: the hold-and-modify mode of a viewport displays each pixel by stealing parts of the color of neighboring pixels. It requires an extra (sixth) bitplane and some mental gymnastics, but you can extort 4096 colors out of a viewport this way.

The BitMap record datatype is used by a number of other Amiga record types to provide basic information about the data in the bitmap. Here is the definition:

```
struct BitMap {
    UWORD BytesPerRow;          /* The length of rows. */
    UWORD Rows;                 /* The number of rows. */
```

```
UBYTE Flags;              /* Some attributes. */
UBYTE Depth;              /* The number of planes. */
UWORD pad;                /* An unused part of this structure. */
PLANEPTR Planes[8];       /* A pointer to each bitplane of the BitMap.*/
```

An Amiga viewport is not the same kind of entity as the one implied by the general computer science version. An Amiga viewport owns a bitmap that can be as large as 1024 by 1024 pixels; since the Amiga 1000 display isn't that large, the entire bitmap can't be visible at one time. An Amiga view is represented in software by a ViewPort record that describes what portion of the bitmap is visible and where. The ViewPort record also controls the resolution of the screen within its rectangular domain. More information on the ViewPort record is in the section on data structures, where the big picture is glued together.

The windowing environments use one bitmap for several different things at once; a simple example is Windows' directly supporting two tasks that access two tiled windows on a display. It is necessary to have one bitmap contain more than one, perhaps several, dissociated images that don't derail one another. On the Amiga more than one task may modify a single viewport bitmap (see Fig. 3–40).

The Amiga provides support for the multiple-related operations with Layers. Layers are used to control the scrolling and redrawing of a portion of a bitmap and can be used to overlay one bitmap (such as one belonging to a viewport) with all or part of another bitmap. This extends the size and availability of coordinate systems for application tasks.

The layer mechanism provides excellent decoupling between tasks competing for screen real estate. Though tasks can't access the screen at exactly the same time (there is only one main processor, after all), there is at least more opportunity for concurrent tasks to inadvertently run over one another's graphics than single-foreground task systems need to deal with. There is a lock mechanism for layers in case a number of tasks want to modify the same layer. Layers are assigned a display priority so that higher-priority layers are displayed over overlapping layers of lower priority.

The Amiga supports three kinds of layers, which differ in size, depth, and automation: simple-refresh, smart-refresh, and superbitmap. There is also a special kind of layer, a backdrop.

Simple-refresh layers aren't automated. The application software has to rebuild the graphic content of the layer every time something happens to it, such as something in front of the layer moving away. The reason is that there is no copy of the bit image off-screen. Normal Macintosh, Windows, and Gem software is written as though everything is done with

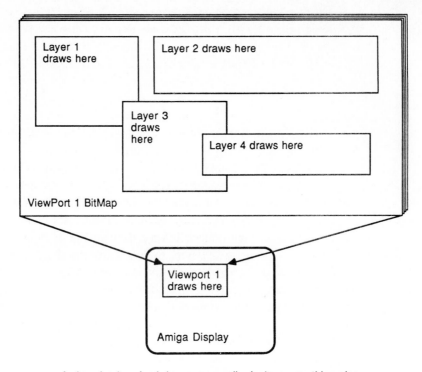

Amiga simple-refresh layers generally don't use anything else
other than part of a bitmap owned by a ViewPort. Smart-refresh
and superbitmap layers have additional resources; smart-refresh
layers store obscured pixels in automatic offscreen bitmaps, and
superbitmap layers have their own bitmap and have parts of it
copied into a designated area in the ViewPort bitmap.

Figure 3–40 Layers using a Viewport's bitmap as their own

simple-refresh layers, although Amiga simple-refresh layers cannot be
scrolled nondestructively; you have to redraw the entire visible portion of
a simple-refresh layer to simulate scrolling.

An important concept is that the bitmap for a simple-refresh layer is
normally a portion of the bitmap that really belongs to a viewport. The
bitmap could also be owned (and accessed only) by the layer; Amiga
bitmaps are designed to be flexible.

Smart-refresh layers have two places to put pixels. The first is the
visible part of the layer, which could be on the bitmap belonging to a
viewport; the second is in a variable list of tiny off-screen bitmaps which
contain all the pixels that are obscured from view.

When a smart-refresh layer is moved, or parts of the layer are revealed
or obscured, the Amiga system automatically determines how to react to
the changes and then implements them. For example, if a layer on top of

a smart-refresh layer is pushed aside, the no-longer-obscured pixels are automatically moved from the little off-screen bitmaps to the viewport bitmap — no redrawing by the application is needed.

The changes may involve changing the offscreen bitmap list for the layer, transferring pixels to an off-screen bitmap, or transferring pixels from an off-screen bitmap to the viewport bitmap. However, there is always only one copy of each pixel in a smart-refresh layer (Fig. 3–42); they are either in the part of the viewport bitmap assigned to the layer or in one of the off-screen bitmaps.

Smart-refresh bitmaps are most efficient when they're not very big. The contents of these bitmaps also cannot be scrolled nondestructively; smart-refresh bitmaps are *not* implemented on a screen as small "windows" looking onto larger bitmaps, like superbitmap layers. The entire layer bitmap is actually a mapped portion of the viewport's (or other) bitmap.

A **superbitmap layer** (Fig. 3–43) has one (possibly enormous: 1024 by 1024) off-screen bitmap that contains a copy of all the pixels belonging to the layer. The visible portion of the layer (on the viewport's bitmap) automatically receives copies of the visible pixels in the superbitmap. The layer acts like a normal window/viewport into a global coordinate space, but everything is pixel-oriented, so there is no scaling. A superbitmap layer can be scrolled by showing a different part of the superbitmap in the viewport's bitmap claimed by the layer.

A **backdrop layer** is a regular layer with a simple property. It can be a simple-refresh, smart-refresh, or superbitmap layer, but it must live behind any other layers created by the application. The "behindmost" layer attribute is present to simplify some bookkeeping that may arise in a multitasking system when selecting windows and bringing layers to the foreground; there are some layers that are not meant to be brought to the foreground.

A RastPort record is used to store the current status of a bitmap; whenever a Layer record is created, a RastPort record is created along with it to contain the current status of and control access into the layer's bitmap.

To summarize, a simple-refresh layer only works with one bitmap, usually a viewport's bitmap, and often just a rectangular part of it. The entire layer must be part of the bitmap. A superbitmap layer works with two bitmaps. An off-screen bitmap (that is, one not related at all to a viewport) contains the "backup copy" of the entire image belonging to the layer, and a "visible subset" of that image is copied into a part of another bitmap (belonging to a viewport). The visible subset can be smaller than the size of the entire superbitmap. A smart-refresh layer has its entire image mapped onto a bitmap (which is possibly owned by a viewport); the obscured portions of the image are kept in a dynamic list of smaller off-screen bitmaps.

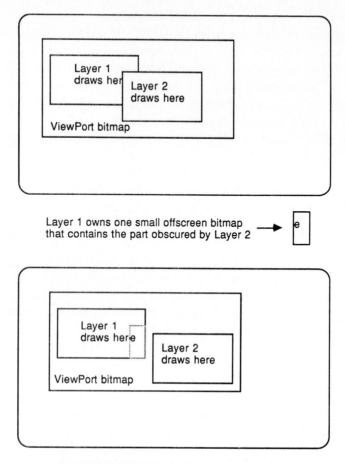

Layer 1 owns one small offscreen bitmap
that contains the part obscured by Layer 2

The offscreen bitmap that Layer 1 used to have
is moved back into the ViewPort bitmap when
Layer 2's area is moved to the side. Since Layer 1
is a smart-refresh layer, the transfer is done
automatically by the Amiga system, without
application code prompting.

Figure 3–41 Amiga smart-refresh layers

Amiga Layer Functions

BeginUpdate is used to start the visual reconstruction process of a
simple-refresh layer. The simple-refresh layer is the only kind of layer that
does not have a full image kept off-screen in a bitmap somewhere in
memory; it has to be redrawn. BeginUpdate swaps the current ClipRect
structure for the current DamageList structure. The DamageList identifies which parts of the layer (in rectangles) have to be rebuilt. For

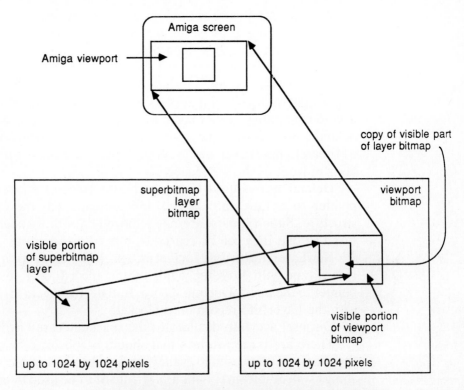

The Amiga superbitmap layer owns an offscreen bitmap. The
onscreen part of the layer is a copy of a part of the
superbitmap. If an obscured part of the superbitmap layer
becomes visible, copies of those pixels are sent to the viewport
bitmap automatically.

Figure 3–42 The Amiga superbitmap layer

parameters BeginUpdate only requires a pointer to the layer, and it locks
that layer from being modified elsewhere.

EndUpdate is used to unswap the current DamageList for the Clip-
Rect, and unlocks the layer. Every call to BeginUpdate must be followed
by an EndUpdate call.

BehindLayer requires a pointer to a LayerInfo record and another
pointer to a layer. Upon receiving these, the specified layer is moved behind
the other layers on the display. This operation, from the application-code
standpoint, is a simple one if the layers involved aren't simple-refresh types;
once-obscured parts of layers are automatically rebuilt from the off-screen
copies of the bitmap stored in RAM. If applications are using simple-refresh
layers, they will have to redraw the contents of the layers.

CreateBehindLayer returns a pointer to a new layer that has been created according to the seven (or eight) parameters. The eighth parameter is present only if a superbitmap layer is being made. The other parameters are a pointer to a LayerInfo record, a pointer to a bitmap record, the two coordinate pairs used to describe the locations of the upper right and lower left corners of the layer bitmap on the screen, and a word containing a set of layer attributes (flags). The new layer is placed behind other layers on the screen. CreateUpfrontLayer does the same job as CreateBehindLayer and uses the same parameters, but places the new layer in front of the other layers on the screen.

DeleteLayer is used to obliterate any trace of a layer; it requires a pointer to a LayerInfo record and a pointer to the victim, a Layer structure. Superbitmaps are not removed from the system by this command so that they can be reused by other Layer records.

NewLayerInfo is used to allocate space in storage for a new LayerInfo record, and initializes the fields of the record. The routine returns a pointer to the new LayerInfo record. Initially the layers that are associated with the LayerInfo record are unlocked.

DisposeLayerInfo deallocates the space allocated by NewLayerInfo.

There are three routines that should be obsolete by now. FattenLayerInfo is a routine used to evade incompatibilities between versions of the Amiga system software. FattenLayerInfo must be used by application code that uses the InitLayers routine on later releases of Amiga system software; Initlayers initializes (without space allocation) a LayerInfo record that is too small for later versions of Amiga software. ThinLayerInfo does the opposite of FattenLayerInfo, and deallocates the extra memory added to a LayerInfo record. The entire idea strikes me as foolish. Using NewLayerInfo is recommended for application code, but Commodore-Amiga should provide better allocation, initialization, and access routines than NewLayerInfo for environment-supported structures; it should not be necessary for application code to be modified when the low-level structures have been changed for any reason.

LockLayer reserves modification of a specified layer to the current task. The routine needs pointers to the LayerInfo record and the Layer record to be locked. The routine waits for tasks currently accessing the layer to finish before locking. UnlockLayer makes the layer (and its bitmap) available to other tasks after a call to LockLayer.

LockLayerInfo reserves modification of a specified LayerInfo record to the current task. UnlockLayerInfo unlocks the LayerInfo record.

LockLayers locks all the layers associated with the specified LayerInfo record. The current task will be the only one able to change its bitmaps. A call to UnlockLayers makes all the layers available again.

LockLayerRom is used to reserve a layer for the calling task; a pointer to the Layer record is given to the routine. No other task may modify the layer contents until the owner task calls UnlockLayerRom with a pointer to the same Layer record.

MoveLayer moves a layer (it can't be a backdrop) to a new position. Simple-refresh layers that have parts affected by this operation have the REFRESH bit set in the Flags field of the Layers record, and the affected areas are recorded in the DamageList. MoveLayer requires a LayerInfo record pointer, a Layer record pointer, a value for the change in the X axis (in pixels), and a similar value for the change in the Y axis.

MoveLayerInFrontOf is used to bring a specified layer in front of another specified layer in the display order. Affected simple-refresh layers have the REFRESH bit set; the areas are recorded in the DamageList.

ScrollLayer works with a superbitmap layer, copying bits from the superbitmap to the onscreen layer bitmap. Normally the superbitmap is much larger than the on-screen bitmap, so the scrolling that takes place is merely because the bits that are copied are displayed on the screen and shifted in position by one or more pixels in the X and/or Y directions. ScrollLayer needs a pointer to the LayerInfo record, a pointer to the Layer record, and values for delta-X and delta-Y. The delta values are the distances to scroll the layer bitmap, in pixels, from the last position set.

SizeLayer is used to adjust the size of the layer bitmap. The X and Y dimension changes are individually specified; the routine also needs pointers to the involved LayerInfo and Layer records. The top left corner of the layer bitmap is "nailed down." Any changes in the size of the bitmap are reflected by the new location of the lower right corner of the bitmap. The contents of a corresponding superbitmap are automatically copied when necessary to the layer bitmap.

SwapBitsRastPortClipRect is used to display menus and other graphics quickly to avoid having the application program redraw them every time they're used. At program startup the image of an object is built once in an off-screen bitmap using the standard selection of graphics and text functions. When it is necessary to display the image, a call to SwapBits-RastPortClipRect swaps the appropriate layer bitmap pixels for the off-screen bitmap pixels. *Voilà*, the image of a menu appears on the screen with the speed of the Amiga's DMA block move. The bits that had been in the layer bitmap have been temporarily sent to the off-screen bitmap! To make the image go away, call SwapBitsRastPortClipRect again to do the same operation, which this time will restore the pixels to their original habitats. It is usually more expensive to redraw the same image several times than it is to draw it once off screen and merely copy the image to the display each time it is needed.

SwapBitsRastPortClipRect requires two parameters, a pointer to the RastPort and a pointer to the ClipRect. The ClipRect bitmap contains the reusable graphics image, and the RastPort owns the real estate where the image temporarily takes residence.

UpfrontLayer brings a specified layer to the foreground in front of all the other layers. It requires a pointer to the LayerInfo record and a pointer to the Layer record.

WhichLayer provides the identity of the layer whose layer bitmap owns a specified pixel on the display. The pointer to the topmost layer at that location (if any) will be returned. NULL is returned if no candidates are found.

Amiga Bitmap Routines

There are some Amiga routines that are used to directly manipulate bitmaps. They are not concerned with Layer records. Scrolling a layer bitmap image directly using ScrollRaster probably won't make sense in many circumstances, and may cause the image to become discontinuous.

AllocRaster is the routine that creates a bitplane (the Mac's bit image) of indicated width and height in bits. If not successful AllocRaster returns a FALSE (an integer 0); if successful it returns a pointer to the bitplane. FreeRaster returns the bitplane RAM back to the system. The height and width of the bitplane must be provided with the pointer to the bitplane area, since FreeRaster doesn't otherwise know how big the bitplane is.

ScrollRaster is the scroll routine for the Amiga. The contents of a rectangular subsection of a raster can be slid on the display in two dimensions at once. ScrollRaster accepts separate parameters for the changes in X and in Y in raster coordinates, but their meanings are a little different from the delta values for the other machines. These delta values measure how much the image should be moved toward the origin of the raster coordinate system. Since the origin of a raster bitmap is usually at the top left corner, positive X and Y deltas indicate that scrolling should go to the left and upward.

The current background pen (BGPen) color is used to fill the area of the rectangle vacated by the moved bits.

The other parameters for moving raster bits are a RastPort pointer and the two coordinate pairs that define the affected subrectangle of the raster.

BltBitMap is the Amiga's workhorse bitmap copy routine. It can be used to copy a rectangular slice of a raster bitmap to anywhere on the same or another raster bitmap.

BltBitMap needs pointers to the source and destination BitMap records, the coordinate pairs of the top left corners of the source and destination rectangles, the extent of the rectangle to be copied (a pair of values, one for X and one for Y), a byte-wide parameter (Minterm) decreeing how the present occupants of the destination rectangle affect the transfer, a parameter identifying which bit planes are involved in the transfer (normally set to ALL), and a pointer to a temporary 1024 pixel buffer that is used only when the source and destination rectangles overlap on the same raster bitmap.

The source and destination rectangles must be the same size; no scaling is done.

The Minterm parameter contains a code identifying which logical operation to use for each bit involved in the transfer. These logical operations are similar in design to the 256 MS Windows raster operations.

The top left corner of either rectangle can be anywhere from (0,0) to (976,976).

The routine BltTemplate is the poor cousin of BltBitMap. It doesn't do anything interesting or fancy, just a simple copy operation from a specified bitmap to the raster coordinate space belonging to the RastPort mentioned in the parameter list. No logical operations, mask bitmaps, or bitplane masks are done.

The source rectangle is described using the following parameters: a pointer to the beginning of the data area; the copy rectangle's top left corner coordinate for the X axis (only), and the **source modulo**, or width, of the source data area. The destination rectangle is described with a pointer to the destination RastPort and the coordinates of the top left corner of the destination rectangle, using the destination raster coordinate space. The size of the copy rectangle is indicated with a pair of values, using the source raster coordinate space.

ClipBlit is similar in function to BltBitMap. ClipBlit has pointers to source and destination RastPort records, and no masking bitmap.

To initialize a bitmap, the InitBitMap routine is given a pointer to the owner, a BitMap record. The dimensions of the bitmap are also provided; they are the height and width of the bitmap and the number of bit planes. InitBitMap assumes that RAM has already been allocated for the bitmap. A bitmap can be as big as 1024-by-1024 pixels.

CopySBitMap is used to copy part of a layer's superbitmap to the layer's bitmap. SyncSBitMap goes the other way; it is used to copy a layer's bitmap into the layer's superbitmap. Both routines have only one parameter, a pointer to the layer.

ScrollVPort is used to scroll the contents of a ViewPort display rectangle. ScrollVPort is told which ViewPort, the X-axis scroll distance, and the Y-axis scroll distance (in pixels). The scroll distances are the changes to be made to move the ViewPort rectangle toward the origin of the coordinate space, the same as the X and Y parameters for Scroll-Raster. A positive X value moves the rectangle contents to the right, which is the same as moving the ViewPort rectangle to the left (over the larger raster coordinate space); a positive Y value moves the rectangle contents down (see Fig. 3–43).

SetWrMsk is used to set a RastPort's current bitplane write mask. The macro uses a pointer to the RastPort in question and the write mask in a 16-bit value. The least-significant 6 bits are the bitplane designators.

THE CURSOR

Macintosh

A Macintosh cursor is depicted on the display as a 16-bit by 16-bit (1 row = 2 bytes) pattern. Here is the record definition:

```
TYPE Cursor = RECORD
     data:    ARRAY[0..15] OF INTEGER;
     mask:    ARRAY[0..15] OF INTEGER;
     hotspot: Point;
END;
```

The first field in the Cursor record, data, is the cursor image. The second field, mask, is used to control how each of the bits of the cursor image is

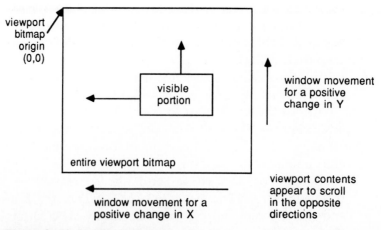

Figure 3–43 Scrolling viewports

displayed. If the mask bit is zero, then the color of a white cursor bit is displayed as the color of the screen pixel underneath it, and the color of a black cursor bit is the inverse of the screen pixel beneath it. This is the mask used when the text entry cursor is present while using MacWrite. When the mask bit is 1, the cursor bit color is whatever the cursor data array says it should be.

When the arrow cursor is used, such as when a menu pick is being made, the mask bits associated with the arrow shape bits are all 1, whereas the rest of the 16-by-16 box is zeroes; this makes some of the cursor block transparent and the arrow shape (including a white outline) opaque.

The hotSpot field is the reference point for the entire cursor for Quickdraw. When a mouse click is made, the location of the hotSpot coordinate over the screen coordinates is obtained by Quickdraw; those coordinates are translated into the local coordinates for the current grafPort and eventually made available to the application software in the form of a mouse down–event record.

The five routines provided in Quickdraw for manipulating the cursor are InitCursor, SetCursor, HideCursor, ShowCursor, and ObscureCursor. InitCursor sets the current cursor to the default image (the arrow pointing up and a little to the left), and makes the cursor visible. SetCursor is used to set what the cursor looks like. HideCursor makes the cursor invisible.

ShowCursor tries to make the cursor visible, but if the cursor level counter (decremented every time HideCursor is called) isn't zero, then the cursor won't appear. Each call to ShowCursor will increment the cursor level counter until it becomes zero; subsequent calls to ShowCursor will not cause the level counter to become greater than zero.

ObscureCursor causes the cursor to vanish from the display until someone nudges the mouse, whereupon the cursor will reappear. If you are very careful, you can press the mouse button and the cursor won't reappear. The Mac will notice very slight mouse movement—pushing the mouse button down will usually move the mouse enough to be noticed.

Macintosh II

The Mac II supports a color cursor, and does it with a data structure entirely alien to the old Cursor record.

```
END;

CCrsrHandle =^CCrsrPtr;        {Handle to a color cursor.}

CCrsrPtr =    ^CCrsr;          {A pointer to a color cursor.}
```

```
CCrsr =        RECORD              {The color cursor record definition.}
        crsrType:    INTEGER;      {The type of cursor.}
        crsrMap:     PixMapHandle; {The cursor pixMap.}
        crsrData:    Handle;       {The cursor data.}
        crsrXData:   Handle;       {The expanded cursor data.}
        crsrXValid:  INTEGER;      {The depth of expanded data (0=none).}
        crsrXHandle: Handle;       {Resrved for future use.}
        crsr1Data:   Bits16;       {A one-bit cursor.}
        crsrMask:    Bits16;       {The cursor's mask.}
        crsrHotSpot: Point;        {The cursor's hotspot location.}
        crsrXTable:  LONGINT;      {Used internally by Quickdraw.}
        crsrID:      LONGINT;      {Used internally by Quickdraw.}
END;
```

The new routines provided for handling color cursors are:

GetCCursor   Creates a new color cursor record, and uses the available color cursor resource (type 'ccsr') indicated by the provided resource ID parameter to initialize it.

SetCCursor   Used to select the current color cursor.

DisposCCursor   Deallocates the space alloted for a cursor record.

AllocCursor   Reallocates cursor memory to reflect changes that have occurred to the depth of a screen.

Gem

The Show Cursor (v_show_c) and Hide Cursor (v_hide_c) routines are the Gem equivalents of the Macintosh ShowCursor and HideCursor. If the cursor is visible, one call to v_hide_c will render it invisible. A call to v_show_c will return it to visibility. Four calls to v_hide_c normally require four calls to v_show_c to get the cursor back. An alternative method which will always succeed in getting the cursor back pronto is to call v_show_c with the reset flag parameter set to zero (0). If v_show_c is called with the reset flag set to a nonzero value, the number of calls to v_show_c and v_hide_c must match for the cursor to be visible.

An application may replace the standard cursor draw routine with vex_curv. This function is used to swap the address of the cursor draw routine with the address of a new cursor draw routine (vex_curv returns the old cursor routine address). The cursor swap routine does not remove the old routine from memory. Gem will use the new cursor routine until vex_curv is again called with a different address.

The cursor drawing routine is low-level; it must accept the XY location of the cursor in registers, and the calling/returning sequence is machine-dependent. On 8086-based systems register BX contains X, CX is Y, and the cursor draw routine is accessed using a CALL FAR instruction, returning with a RETURN FAR. On a 68000 system register d0.w contains X, d1.w contains Y, and to get to it and return from it one uses JSR (Jump To Subroutine) and RTS (Return From Subroutine).

If the application should suddenly find itself having to draw the cursor when it doesn't want to, the application should call the standard Gem cursor draw routine using the above rules.

Usually replacing the cursor draw routine isn't necessary; merely changing the cursor graphic (or the mouse form) will do. Gem VDI provides a routine to do just that: vsc_form. The parameters that vsc_form needs are called the **mouse form definition block**, and consist of the following: (1) the local XY coordinates of the cursor hotspot, which serves the same function as the Macintosh cursor hotspot; (2) the mask and the data color indices; (3) the 16-word bit-image of the cursor mask; and (4) the 16-word bit-image of the cursor data. The most-significant bit of the first word of each of the bit images is at the top left of the form.

Gem AES provides the routine graf_mouse for changing the mouse form. The binding routine for graf_mouse has two parameters; the first, gr_monumber, is the mouse form code, which has the following:

0	Arrow
1	Text cursor (vertical bar)
2	Hourglass
3	Hand with pointing finger
4	Flat hand, extended fingers
5	Thin cross hair
6	Thick cross hair
7	Outline cross hair
255	Mouse form stored in gr_mofaddr (see below)
256	Hide mouse form
257	Show mouse form

The second parameter, gr_mofaddr, is the address of a 35-word buffer containing a mouse form definition block (described above). The second parameter is valid only when gr_monumber is assigned the decimal value 255.

The application selects the mouse form appearing in the active window. Outside the active window area the mouse form must be an arrow or the kill-time symbol (the hourglass). Every time the mouse form crosses the active window boundary rectangle, an evnt_mouse event is passed to the application so that the application can make the appropriate mouse form change with graf_mouse. The event information is provided by an evnt_multi or an evnt_mouse call.

graf_mkstate provides the current mouse screen location, the state of the mouse buttons, and the keyboard state.

graf_watchbox is used to watch the mouse form closely as it enters and leaves a predefined box, but it is called only when a mouse button is pressed or held down. The routine returns a value when the mouse button is released. The box is contained in a Gem object tree. The state of the object changes as the mouse form enters and leaves the box (the box may change color or a pattern may disappear).

The Atari ST doesn't have hardware sprites, but the low-level support for the display for Gem treats the cursor as a software-generated sprite.

Windows

LoadCursor loads a unique cursor resource into RAM. If the resource is already in RAM, it is not reloaded. In either case a handle to the cursor resource is returned. The first parameter is a handle to a module instance (an executable file). The second parameter is a pointer to a C-style string containing the name of the cursor resource.

SetCursor sets the cursor image to the indicated bitmap. This bitmap is a cursor resource, and must have been loaded using LoadCursor.

SetCursorPos sets the screen position of the cursor. GetCursorPos returns the current cursor screen location; the X and Y values are placed into a record of type POINT.

ClipCursor limits the cursor movement to within a rectangular area of the display.

ShowCursor is used to control the visibility of the cursor image. If the one parameter to ShowCursor is TRUE the cursor display count is incremented; if the parameter is FALSE the value is decremented. The cursor is visible only if the cursor display count is a positive value.

IIGS

The size of the IIGS cursor is adjustable. The IIGS cursor record has two additional fields for the height and width of the cursor pixel image and mask:

```
TYPE Cursor = RECORD
        CursorHeight:  INTEGER;
        CursorWidth:   INTEGER;
        CursorImage:   ARRAY[1..CursorHeight,1..CursorWidth] of word;
        CursorMask:    ARRAY[1..CursorHeight,1..CursorWidth] of word;
        HotSpot:       Point;
     END;
```

Amiga

Intuition uses an Amiga sprite as its cursor. There are only two routines for cursor manipulation: SetPointer and ClearPointer.

SetPointer is used to assign a cursor symbol to an Intuition window. The routine needs six parameters: a pointer to the Window record, a pointer to a SpriteImage record, the height and width of the sprite image, and the X and Y offsets for the cursor's "hotspot."

ClearPointer accepts a pointer to a Window record; it is used to clear the window's current mouse pointer image. If the window is active, the default cursor image becomes visible immediately; otherwise the default image becomes visible when the window is activated.

DATA STRUCTURES

Macintosh

A grafPort record contains all the presently known facts about a region of the screen that is accessible to an application. Each of the fields is modifiable by the application; however, Apple recommends that grafPort fields be changed using the routines provided in Quickdraw and not by directly accessing the field—doing so permits Apple much more freedom to adjust the operation of the environment software (and correct glitches).

Here is the definition of the grafPort record and pointer:

```
TYPE GrafPtr  = ^GrafPort;

    GrafPort = RECORD
                device:      INTEGER;   {The logical output device number.}
                portBits:    BitMap;    {The drawing bitMap.}
                portRect:    Rect;      {The drawable subset of bitMap.}
                visRgn:      RgnHandle; {The visible region of portRect.}
                clipRgn:     RgnHandle; {The portRect drawable region.}
                bkPat:       Pattern;   {The current background pattern.}
                fillPat:     Pattern;   {The current fill pattern.}
                pnLoc:       Point;     {The current pen location.}
                pnSize:      Point;     {The current pen nib size.}
                pnMode:      INTEGER;   {The current pen draw mode.}
                pnPat:       Pattern;   {The current pen draw pattern.}
                pnVis:       INTEGER;   {The current pen draw status.}
                txFont:      INTEGER;   {The current text font.}
                txFace:      Style;     {The current text style attributes.}
                txMode:      INTEGER;   {The current text draw mode.}
                txSize:      INTEGER;   {The current text size.}
                spExtra:     LongInt;   {The current number of space pixels.}
                fgColor:     LongInt;   {The current foreground color.}
                bkColor:     LongInt;   {The current background color.}
                colrBit:     INTEGER;   {The current color plane.}
                patStretch:  INTEGER;   {The printer pattern expansion.}
                picSave:     Handle;    {The current picture info.}
                rgnSave:     Handle;    {The current region info.}
                polySave:    Handle;    {The current polygon info.}
                grafProcs:   QDProcsPtr; {The custom Quickdraw routines.}
    END;
```

A call to the standard Pascal new routine with an uninitialized pointer to a grafPort will create a valid data area for that pointer. A call to OpenPort afterward will initialize the new grafPort properly for use. An even later call to InitPort will reinitialize the grafPort record. ClosePort is used to deallocate the data areas of the grafPort pointed to by handles in the grafPort; a call to the standard Pascal dispose routine will get rid of the remains. Later use of remnants of a grafPort eliminated in this way will provide hours of entertainment (and debugging).

SetPort makes the specified grafPort the current one. GetPort returns a pointer to the current grafPort.

GrafDevice is the routine that assigns a grafPort to a logical output device (by updating the device field in the grafPort record).

SetPortBits is used to redefine the location in memory of the bitmap used for drawing output. Normally, this bitMap is part of the Mac display, but an off-display region of memory can be used; it just won't be seen immediately.

PortSize is used to adjust the normally drawable portion of the display assigned to the current grafPort; it changes the portRect field. No changes to the current screen contents are made.

MovePortTo moves the screen location of the drawable portion of the display assigned to the current grafPort; like PortSize, it changes the portRect field. No changes to the current screen contents are made.

Macintosh II

A CGrafPort is the color version of the grafPort record and is created with the Mac II window manager routines NewCWindow and GetNewCWindow. The changes made to the grafPort data structure to make the CGrafPort record were kept to a minimum; in fact, Mac II Quickdraw can tell the difference between a grafPort and a CGrafPort, so that many of the new color features are handled automatically and portably. Here is the CGrafPort definition:

```
CGrafPtr = ^CGrafPort;                    {Pointer to a color GrafPort.}
CGrafPort = RECORD
        device:       INTEGER;            {The device ID for font picking.}
        portPixMap:   PixMapHandle;       {The pixel map of the port.}
        portVersion:  INTEGER;            {The version of color Quickdraw;}
                                          {the high 2 bits are always set.}
        grafVars:     Handle;             {A handle to more fields.}
        chExtra :     INTEGER;            {The number of pixels that are}
                                          { used to widen all characters}
                                          { but the space character.}
        pnLocHFrac:   INTEGER;            {The horizontal pen fraction.}
        portRect:     Rect;               {The port rectangle.}
        visRgn:       RgnHandle;          {The visible region.}
        clipRgn:      RgnHandle;          {The clipping region.}
        bkPixPat:     PixPatHandle;       {The background pattern.}
        RGBFgColor:   RGBColor;           {The requested foreground color.}
        RGBBkColor:   RGBColor;           {The requested background color.}
        pnLoc:        Point;              {The pen location.}
```

```
        pnSize:       Point;              {The pin nib size}
        pnMode:       INTEGER;            {The pen transfer mode.}
        pnPixPat:     PixPatHandle;       {The pen pattern.}
        fillPixPat:   PixPatHandle;       {The fill pattern.}
        pnVis:        INTEGER;            {The pen visibility.}
        txFont:       INTEGER;            {The text font number.}
        txFace:       Style;              {The text character style.}
        txMode:       INTEGER;            {The text transfer mode.}
        txSize:       INTEGER;            {The text font size.}
        spExtra:      Fixed;              {pixel number used to widen}
                                          { the space character. }
        fgColor:      LONGINT;            {The actual foreground color.}
        bkColor:      LONGINT;            {The actual background color.}
        colrBit:      INTEGER;            {This is reserved.}
        patStretch:   INTEGER;            {Used internally by Quickdraw.}
        picSave:      QDHandle;           {The picture being saved.}
        rgnSave:      QDHandle;           {The region being saved.}
        polySave:     QDHandle;           {The polygon being built.}
        grafProcs:    QDProcsPtr;         {The low-level drawing routines.}
END;
```

Gem

As described above Gem objects are used by applications to build trees, which are used merely as Gem display instructions and not for higher-level, internal database needs. Also, objects are restricted to using normalized device or raster coordinates if Gem is to make any sense of them at all.

The tree arrangement of the object records is echoed in the display (see Fig. 3–44). A parent object will own a certain amount of display space; its children objects may have part or all of their parent's space, but no more than that.

To display a tree of objects, one only has to pass the top of the tree to the routine objc_draw, which will mastermind the rendering of the entire tree (no matter how complex or deep) on the display.

The main record declaration, in C, is:

```
typedef struct object {
    WORD    ob_next;     /* A pointer to the next sibling object. */
    WORD    ob_head;     /* A pointer to first child object. */
    WORD    ob_tail;     /* A pointer to last child object. */
    UWORD   ob_type;     /* Identifies what kind of object this is. */
```

```
    UWORD  ob_flags;      /* Various flags. */
    UWORD  ob_state;      /* The state of the present object. */
    LONG   ob_spec;       /* A pointer to type-dependent info. */
    UWORD  ob_x;          /* The relative screen coordinates of the */
    UWORD  ob_y;          /*     upper left corner of the object. */
    UWORD  ob_width;      /* The object width. */
    UWORD  ob_height;     /* The object height. */
} OBJECT;
```

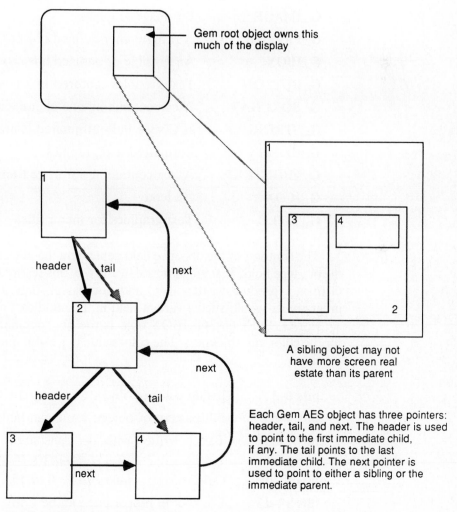

Gem root object owns this much of the display

A sibling object may not have more screen real estate than its parent

Each Gem AES object has three pointers: header, tail, and next. The header is used to point to the first immediate child, if any. The tail points to the last immediate child. The next pointer is used to point to either a sibling or the immediate parent.

Figure 3–44 Gem object trees

The interesting fields of the object type are ob_type, ob_flags, ob_state, and ob_spec; the rest are pointers to siblings or children objects, or screen coordinates which are relative to the parent object's area of the display. To decode the real screen coordinates of the object record in question, Gem AES provides objc_offset, the object relative to screen coordinate conversion routine.

Here are all the predefined ob_type values at present:

Type	What the object represents
G_BOX	A box containing graphics
G_TEXT	Text graphics
G_BOXTEXT	A box containing text graphics
G_IMAGE	Bit image graphics
G_PROGDEF	A programmer-defined object (go wild)
G_IBOX	An invisible or outlined box containing graphics
G_BUTTON	Text graphics centered in a box
G_BOXCHAR	A box containing one character
G_STRING	A C-style null-terminated character array
G_FTEXT	Formatted text graphics
G_FBOXTEXT	A box containing formatted text graphics
G_ICON	An icon
G_TITLE	Text graphics for menu titles

The contents of the ob_spec field depend on the object type contained in the ob_type field. You might notice by the way this record is constructed that Gem is a product written in C and not Pascal; only a *spiteful* ex-Pascal programmer would stick a variant field in the middle of a record like this.

For G_BOX and G_IBOX objects the ob_spec field contains values for the color and thickness. The color value is a 16-bit quantity divided into 5 fields:

bits 0–3	Inside color of object; value can be 0 to 15
bits 4–6	Fill pattern of object; value can be 0 to 7
bit 7	Text is written with: 0 = transparent mode, 1 = replace mode
bits 8–11	Color of text; value can be 0 to 15
bits 12–15	Color of border; value can be 0 to 15

The fill pattern values are defined:

0	Hollow fill
1–6	Dither patterns of increasing darkness
7	Solid fill

The G_BOXCHAR object keeps the single character it represents in the ob_spec field, along with the color descriptor and box outline thickness. A G_IBOX object differs from G_BOX in that the fields in the color descriptor for the G_IBOX fill pattern and internal color are ignored.

For G_TEXT, G_BOXTEXT, G_FTEXT, and G_FBOXTEXT objects the ob_spec field contains a pointer to a TEDINFO record which contains text-associated data. Part of the data includes a pointer to a character string that is somewhere in memory. The TEDINFO structure is described below.

The ob_spec field of G_TITLE, G_BUTTON, and G_STRING (no jokes!!) contains a pointer to a C-style null-terminated character string.

The G_IMAGE ob_spec field is used as pointer to a BITBLK record.

The all-purpose G_PROGDEF object uses the ob_spec field for a pointer to an APPLBLK record.

The ob_flags field is a bitfield. Each bit set indicates the existence of an attribute of the object. Here are the ob_flags values and their meanings:

SELECTABLE	Object can be selected by user
DEFAULT	Form library will examine object when user enters a carriage return.
EXIT	Form library will return control after exit condition is satisfied by user clicking on object
EDITABLE	Object is editable by user
RBUTTON	A radio button—push one down and the others pop up
LASTOB	Indicates object is the last object in the tree
TOUCHEXIT	Form library will return control after the exit condition is satisfied by user pressing the mouse button when the mouse form is over the object
HIDETREE	Makes a subtree invisible; objc_draw and objc_find will ignore the subtree

INDIRECT the value in the ob_spec field is actually a pointer to the actual value of the ob_spec field

The ob_state field is another bitfield. Each bit indicates the presence of a current condition. More than one of the object state conditions may be present at a time. The states are:

NORMAL Draw object in normal foreground-background colors

SELECTED Draw object highlighted by reversing the foreground-background colors

CROSSED An "X" is drawn in a box object

CHECKED Object is drawn with a check mark

DISABLED Object is drawn faintly

OUTLINED Outline appears around the box object

SHADOWED Object is drawn with a drop shadow

Here are a number of C code type-definitions for the structures pointed to and used by objects, as mentioned above:

```
typedef struct text_edinfo {
    LONG    te_ptext;       /* A pointer to character string: */
                            /* the string is not null terminated. */
    LONG    te_ptmplt;      /* A pointer to text string template; */
                            /* the string is not null terminated. */
    LONG    te_pvalid;      /* A pointer to the validation string. */
    WORD    te_font;        /* A font identification number. */
    WORD    te_junk1;       /* This is reserved for future use. */
    WORD    te_just;        /* This is the text justification type. */
    WORD    te_color;       /* The object color descriptor. */
    WORD    te_junk2;       /* Reserved for future use. */
    WORD    te_thickness;   /* The text box border width. */
    WORD    te_txtlen;      /* The length of text string data. */
    WORD    te_tmplen;      /* The length of template string data. */
} TEDINFO;
```

The innards of the TEDINFO record are explained in the section on low-level text editing support.

```
typedef struct icon_block {
     LONG  ib_pmask;     /* Apointer to mask bit image of icon. */
     LONG  ib_pdata;     /* A pointer to data bit image of icon. */
     LONG  ib_ptext;     /* A pointer to the icon's text string. */
     WORD  ib_char;      /* The letter to be drawn in the icon. */
     WORD  ib_xchar;     /* The X coordinate of ib_char char. */
     WORD  ib_ychar;     /* The Y coordinate of ib_char char. */
     WORD  ib_xicon;     /* The X coordinate of the icon. */
     WORD  ib_yicon;     /* The Y coordinate of the icon. */
     WORD  ib_wicon;     /* The width of the icon, in pixels. */
     WORD  ib_hicon;     /* The height of the icon, in pixels. */
     WORD  ib_xtext;     /* The X coord. of the icon text. */
     WORD  ib_ytext;     /* The Y coord. of the icon text. */
     WORD  ib_wtext;     /* The width of the icon's text rectangle. */
     WORD  ib_htext;     /* The height of icon's text, in pixels. */
} ICONBLK;

typedef struct bit_block {
     LONG  bi_pdata;     /* A pointer to the bit image.*/
     WORD  bi_wb;        /* The width of the bit image, in bytes. */
     WORD  bi_hl;        /* The height of the bit image, in pixels. */
     WORD  bi_x;         /* The X coord of bit image subset.*/
     WORD  bi_y;         /* The Y coord of bit image subset; */
                         /*  we may not want the entire image. */
     WORD  bi_color;     /* The object color descriptor; */
                         /*  this used to be called bi_blt. */
} BITBLK;

typedef struct appl_blk { /* This used to be called USERBLK. */
     LONG  ab_code;      /* A pointer to object driver routine. */
     LONG  ab_parm;      /* A generic parameter for driver. */
} APPLBLK;

typedef struct parm_blk {
     LONG  pb_tree;      /* A pointer to a tree of application defined */
                         /*  objects. */
     WORD  pb_obj;       /* An object index of an application defined */
                         /*  object.*/
                         /* If the following two fields are equal */
                         /*  then application is drawing and not changing */
                         /*  object. */
```

```
WORD    pb_prevstate; /* The old state of object to be changed. */
WORD    pb_currstate; /* The new state of the object. */
WORD    pb_x,          /* The X coord of object defining rect. */
        pb_y,          /* The Y coord of object defining rect. */
        pb_w,          /* The width in pixels of size rect. */
        pb_h;          /* The height in pixels of size rect.   */
WORD    pb_xc,         /* The X coord of clipping rectangle.*/
        pb_yc,         /* The Y coord of clipping rectangle.*/
        pb_wc,         /* The width in pixels of clip rectangle. */
        pb_hc;         /* The height in pixels of clip rect. */
LONG    pb_parm;       /* The value passed to appl for draw/chg. */
} PARMBLK;
```

Windows

The display context (DC) is used as a leash to control application program use of the output devices, primarily the main display, where several applications could be drawing at more or less the same time. In order to do any output to a device, a Windows application must ask Windows to create a DC, and the DC must be used thereafter to access that device. The actual DC is kept by Windows; an application only gets a Windows handle to it. The exact composition of a DC is not supposed to be known; any modification of the DC must be done via a Windows routine.

The DC clipping region is the last line of defense for a display device. The clip region restricts the results of draw commands to the agreed-upon area of the display; even if the application code should execute a number of draw commands with the intention of causing graphics to appear on the display outside the clip region, it won't work without cooperation by the DC.

In addition to the device associated display context, there is also the information context (IC) which is used to obtain information regarding a device without creating a display context.

When a window is created, normally a default display context is created with it. This default display context is maintained by Windows while the application is not using it (for example, right after a call to the ReleaseDC routine for that DC). When a default DC is returned to Windows, Windows restores the data in the DC to their original values, forcing the application to reassign the values to taste after the next call to the GetDC routine.

Applications can tell Windows to keep its hands off by defining the DC type when the window class is created. A CS_CLASSDC type DC is shared by all of the windows of a given class, and A CS_OWNDC type DC is privately owned by one window. Since Windows does not modify these kinds of DCs, it also does not automatically update these DCs when the associated window is changed; calls to ReleaseDC and GetDC must take place for the updates to happen.

When a display context is being shared between several windows, it is possible to hog a display context and prevent other windows from being changed. GetDC and ReleaseDC must be called just before and after the drawing is to take place.

Here is a table of the fields of interest in a display context, including what each field does, the default values, the routine normally used to modify the content of that field, and the routine used to query the value of the field:

Data	Default	Set	Query
Current Position	(0,0)	several, like MoveTo	GetCurrentPosition
Relabs Flag	ABSOLUTE	SetRelAbs	GetRelAbs
Text Color	Black	SetTextColor	GetTextColor
BackGround Color	White	SetBkColor	GetBkColor
Background Mode	OPAQUE	SetBkMode	GetBkMode
Drawing Mode	R2_COPYPEN	SetROP2	GetRop2
Mapping Mode	MM_TEXT	SetMapMode	GetMapMode
Polygon Fill Mode	ALTERNATE	SetPolyFillMode	GetPolyFillMode
Color Table	even distribution of full range of avail. colors		
Clipping Region	entire display	several: CreateRectRgn	GetClipBox (approximation)
Window Origin	(0,0)	SetWindowOrg	GetWindowOrg
Window Extents	(1,1)	SetWindowExt	GetWindowExt
Viewport Origin	(0,0)	SetViewportOrg	GetViewportOrg
Viewport Extents	(1,1)	SetViewportExt	GetViewportExt
Stretch Mode		SetStretchBltMode	GetStretchBltMode
Brush Origin		SetBrushOrg	GetBrushOrg
Extra Break Space		SetTextJustification	
Break Char Count		SetTextJustification	
Interchar Spacing	0	SetTextCharacterExtra	GetTextCharacterExtra
Pen		SelectObject	GetObject
Brush		SelectObject	GetObject
Font		SelectObject	GetObject
Bitmap		SelectObject	GetObject

While we are on the subject, there are a small number of routines that base query actions on a device display context: EnumFonts, EnumObjects, GetTextFace, GetTextMetrics, and GetDeviceCaps.

EnumFonts enumerates the available fonts for a device.

EnumObjects enumerates the pens and brushes available for a device.

GetTextFace returns the facename of the current font.

GetTextMetrics fills a buffer with a variety of useful measurements regarding the current font.

GetDeviceCaps returns a selected item regarding a display device from a wide selection. You tell it which item and which device you're interested in, and it returns the item.

The routine CreateDC makes a device-associated display context. There are four parameters to CreateDC; three are Windows long pointers to C-style (null-terminated) ASCII strings, and the fourth is a long pointer to a table of device-specific initialization information. The last pointer is NULL if the device needs no initialization information.

The first three character strings are the names of the device driver, the device, and the output medium. The output medium is the method used to talk to the device, like a serial or parallel port or a file.

If CreateDC is successful it returns a handle to the new DC; otherwise it returns a NULL value.

Using the function CreateCompatibleDC is an easy way to make a display context for a memory-associated DC that is compatible with a device DC or another memory DC. Once an image is built using a compatible memory DC (which might take a while), any fraction of the bit image can then be copied to the device in fast order. CreateCompatibleDC is supplied with an already-made display context and returns a new one.

The CreateIC routine is used to create an information context for the indicated device, which can be used to quickly obtain current information about a device without necessarily using a display context.

DeleteDC removes a specified display context from the system, deallocating any memory space that it used. If the DC were associated with a device and it were the last DC for the device, then the device would be told to close up shop, Windows would deallocate resources allotted to it, and the function would return TRUE. If the DC weren't the last for a device, the routine would return FALSE.

SaveDC stuffs the current state of a display context into a queue. The DC context can be arbitrarily changed and then restored to the saved state by using RestoreDC. SaveDC is given the DC handle and returns a level indicator; RestoreDC is given that level indicator and returns a result flag. When RestoreDC restores a display context that is not first in the queue, that DC is restored and the state information in the queue above the restored DC is blown away. All saved DCs share the same queue. RestoreDC returns TRUE if the prior state of a DC was successfully restored, and FALSE if not.

There may be a problem similar to the "chicken and egg" paradox when trying to glue the entire show together. How do the main display, DCs, and window descriptors relate?

In the context of the main display, a program normally communicates with its tiled window using a handle to the window descriptor. There is usually just a single tiled window per application.

Consider that the descriptor for a tiled window is at the top of the heap. From the window descriptor, the display context for either the client area of the window or the DC for the entire window (including caption bar, menus, and scroll bars) can be obtained. One way to get the client area DC is to use GetDC; to get the entire window DC, use GetWindowDC.

When a WM_PAINT message is sent to the application, it is time for the application to draw in the window. To be able to modify the contents of the window client area, MS Windows provides a preparation routine called BeginPaint. The application gives BeginPaint a window descriptor handle and a vacant PAINTSTRUCT type record. BeginPaint fills the PAINTSTRUCT record with information appropriate to the upcoming paint job (including a handle to the display context), and gives the record back to the application. BeginPaint also returns the DC handle separately, but this copy can be ignored.

This DC clipping region is restricted to the area of the display in need of painting, according to MS Windows. The application does its thing with the DC handle and a paint can. When done, the application calls End-Paint, passing the same window descriptor handle and the pointer to the PAINTSTRUCT record it handed to BeginPaint. The EndPaint call signifies the end of the paint job.

A routine of interest is ReleaseDC. Depending on how the window was created (see the discussion on window class and private display contexts), it may be necessary for a window procedure to release the display context. The world may change but the DC may not be updated automatically, and thus may get out of date. Not only that, but hanging on to a DC may keep it from being used by other components of a system, since a DC may be shared.

There are four other routines that may be appropriately mentioned in this section. GetObject is used to fill a specified RAM buffer (the third parameter) with the data defining an object pointed to by the first parameter, a handle to an object. The objects grabbed can be the types LOGPEN, LOGBRUSH, LOGFONT, or BITMAP. The buffer had better be big enough. The second parameter is the number of bytes that should be copied.

SelectObject is used to select an object for a display context and replace the previous object of the same type being used by the DC. The two parameters are an MS Windows handle to a display context and a handle to an object. The object can be a pen, brush, font, bitmap, or region.

SelectClipRgn selects the given region to be the clipping region for the display context indicated by the first parameter. A handle to the region is the second parameter.

DeleteObject kills a pen, brush, font, bitmap, or region. The storage allocated for defining the object is reclaimed by the system, and the handle to the object becomes invalid (unchanged but no longer pointing to anything significant).

IIGS

Here's the IIGS version of the grafPort, which is based on the Macintosh grafPort but is not exactly the same. The changes were made to support more freedom from the physical display when preparing graphic images, and to support the more complicated (color) pixel images of the IIGS.

```
TYPE GrafPort = RECORD
      portInfo:     LocInfo;       {* A Logical device (pixel image)}
      portRect:     Rect;          {The drawable subset of LocInfo.}
      clipRgn:      RgnHandle;     {The portRect drawable region.}
      visRgn:       RgnHandle;     {The visible region of portRect.}
      bkPat:        Pattern;       {The background pattern.}
      pnLoc:        Point;         {The current pen location.}
      pnSize:       Point;         {The current pen nib size.}
      pnMode:       INTEGER;       {The current pen draw mode.}
      pnPat:        Pattern;       {The current pen draw pattern.}
      pnMask:       Mask;          {* The current pen draw mask.}
      pnVis:        INTEGER;       {The current pen visibility status.}
      fontHandle:   Handle;        {* A handle to the current font.}
```

```
    fontFlags:    INTEGER;      {* }
    txface:       Style;        {The text style attributes.}
    txMode:       INTEGER;      {The current text draw mode.}
    SpExtra:      INTEGER;      {The current number of space pixels.}
    fgColor:      INTEGER;      {The current foreground color.}
    bgColor:      INTEGER;      {The current background color.}
    PicSave:      Handle;       {The current picture info.}
    RgnSave:      Handle;       {The current region info.}
    PolySave:     Handle;       {The current polygon info.}
    GrafProcs:    Pointer;      {The custom QDII std. routine pointer record.}
    UserField:    LongInt;      {*}
    SysField:     LongInt;      {*}
END;
```

The fields whose comments begin with an asterisk are unique to the IIGS for one reason or another.

OpenPort, InitPort, ClosePort, SetPort, GetPort, MovePortTo, SetOrigin, SetClip, GetClip, ClipRect, and BackPat work the same as on the Mac. GrafDevice and SetPortBits don't exist.

SetPortLoc and GetPortLoc are used to take care of the portInfo grafPort data. SetPortLoc is given a pointer to a LocInfo record and transfers the information to the current grafPort's LocInfo record. GetPortLoc copies the current grafPort's LocInfo data into the record pointed to by the parameter.

SetPortRect and GetPortRect are used to change and return, respectively, the portRect field of the current grafPort. Both routines use a pointer to a Rect(angle) record as a parameter.

SetPortSize is the IIGS version of Mac's PortSize, with a simple name change to conform to a standard with more clout and sense than precedence. The IIGS library is full of these name changes, so *beware*.

SetClipHandle and GetClipHandle are *not* SetClip and GetClip. Where SetClip and GetClip involve pointers to regions and the transfer of region contents, SetClipHandle changes the clipRgn field to be the handle of a different clip region, and GetClipHandle returns the current grafPort clipRgn handle.

SetForeColor, GetForeColor, SetBackColor, and GetBackColor are mentioned in the color section of this chapter. They are unique to Quickdraw II.

SetFont, GetFont, GetFontInfo, SetFontFlags, and GetFontFlags are mentioned in the section on low-level text in this chapter. They are also unique to Quickdraw II.

SetVisRgn copies the contents of the region (indicated by the region handle parameter) to the region belonging to the current grafPort visRgn handle. In the tradition of CopyRgn, SetVisRgn does not create a region, but it does change the region's content. GetVisRgn copies the current grafPort's visRgn region to the region that belongs to GetVisRgn's region handle parameter.

SetVisHandle changes the value of the current grafPort's visRgn handle, normally to make it point to another region that already exists. The contents of a region are not copied or moved. GetVisHandle returns a copy of the current visRgn handle.

There are six routines in QDII that manipulate the current grafPort handles to the polygon, region, and picture construction areas. The Set routines aren't meant to be used by mere application software; applications are supposed to use NewRgn, OpenPoly, ClosePoly, OpenRgn, CloseRgn, OpenPicture, and ClosePicture for building the dynamic records. The Get routines are fair game, though their use in application code is a sign of strange circumstances. SetPicSave, SetRgnSave, and SetPolySave assign values to the respective current grafPort save handles; GetPicSave, GetRgnSave, and GetPolySave return the respective grafPort save handles.

The routines SetGrafProcs, GetGrafProcs, and SetStdProcs all deal with the grafPort subrecord belonging to the grafProcs pointer field. As mentioned in the Macintosh section on the standard graphics rendering procedures, SetStdProcs is used to assign a QDProcs record to the current grafPort, with pointers initially pointing to the standard low-level drawing routines; the QDProcs record is then used to wrest away some of the drawing duties from the standard low-level Quickdraw routines by changing one or more of the pointers. If the grafProcs field is not NIL, then QD knows that the application program has a custom draw record and looks to it for the addresses of the draw routines to use. SetGrafProcs can be used to assign the grafProcs pointer in the current grafPort to point to an arbitrarily defined QDProcs record. GetGrafProcs obtains the graf-Procs pointer value of the current grafPort, so you'll know where the QDProcs record is if it exists.

The routines SetUserField and GetUserField are provided to permit read/write access to the userField field of the current grafPort. The userField is a pointer to an absolutely arbitrary address in memory, belonging to whatever the application code wants to be there. The userField is a way for application code to keep context-sensitive data that are based on grafPorts.

The SetSysField and GetSysField routines are used by the operating environment (and not application code) to attach and access data that are conveniently associated with a grafPort. These data items can be anything and anywhere. Keep your hands off!

Amiga

Manipulating the Amiga display involves working with a number of data structures. To have a good understanding of how the whole thing works is going to take much more than this book can give, although much of the wizardry can be revealed in a manner in keeping with the goals of this text.

An Amiga RastPort record is similar in purpose to a Macintosh GrafPort and a display context of MS Windows. In the Amiga one RastPort record contains current information about only one bitmap. A pointer to the RastPort record is needed by most of the Amiga's basic bitmap graphics routines (as a parameter) in order for them to know which bitmap to draw on and what all the current conditions are. Here is the definition of a RastPort record:

```
Struct RastPort {                      /* The current bitmap modes and attributes. */
    struct Layer *Layer;               /* A ptr. to a Layer record. */
    struct BitMap *BitMap;             /* A ptr. to a BitMap record. */
    USHORT       AreaPtrn;             /* A ptr. to an area-fill pattern. */
    struct TmpRas *TmpRas;             /* A ptr. to temp. buffer control record. */
    struct AreaInfo *AreaInfo;         /* A ptr. to an area vertex list. */
    struct GelsInfo *GelsInfo;         /* A ptr. to a graphics animation record. */
    UBYTE        Mask;                 /* The bitplane select draw mask. */
    BYTE         FgPen;                /* The foreground pen color. */
    BYTE         BgPen;                /* The background pen color. */
    BYTE         AOlPen;               /* The area outline pen color. */
    BYTE         DrawMode;             /* The pen drawing mode (see SetDrMd). */
    BYTE         AreaPtSz;             /* the size in words of AreaPtrn pattern. */
    BYTE         LinPatcnt;            /* A system var used for line patterns. */
    BYTE         dummy;                /* You wouldn't believe me if I told you. */
    USHORT       Flags;               /* Various and sundry bit flags. */
    USHORT       LinePtrn;             /* The line draw pattern. */
    SHORT        cp_x;                 /* The current pen X BITMAP coordinate. */
    SHORT        cp_y;                 /* The current pen Y BITMAP coordinate. */
    UBYTE        minterms[8];          /* The blitter control array. */
    SHORT        PenWidth;             /* The pixel width of pen lines. */
```

```
SHORT         PenHeight;     /* The pixel height of pen lines. */
struct TextFont *Font;       /* A ptr. to the current text info record. */
UBYTE         AlgoStyle;     /* The software adjustment font style */
                             /*  control byte. */
UBYTE         TxFlags;       /* The current text modes byte. */
UWORD         TxHeight;      /* The current font height. */
UWORD         TxWidth;       /* The current font char standard width. */
UWORD         TxBaseline;    /* The current baseline distance. */
WORD          TxSpacing;     /* The current char spacing distanc.e */
APTR          *RP_User;      /* A ptr to the Exec message port for task. */
UWORD         wordreserved[7];   /* The you never know department. */
ULONG         longreserved[2];   /* The you never know department. */
UBYTE         reserved[8];        /* The you never know department. */
```

A RastPort record can be initialized using the InitRastPort routine. Most of the fields of a RastPort are set to 0 or −1. The default drawing mode is JAM2, and the default font is called Topaz.

When a new layer is created (see the description in the sections on bitmaps and color), a RastPort comes with it. The layer record has a pointer to that controlling RastPort record. The RastPort record has up-to-date fields for the layer because of the way things were set up; by using either CreateUpfrontLayer or CreateBehindLayer, the RastPort and the Layer records know the layer type, where the bitmaps are, what parts of the bitmap are out-of-bounds and what parts aren't, where the neighbor Layer records are, and a small number of access control, scrolling, and message details.

The Layer record (and RastPort) is created with the help of a Layer_Info record, which is used to keep track of some of the needed context for the new Layer and RastPort records for cooperation with other Layer and RastPort records. LayerInfo records tie together related layers, permitting some Amiga layer functions to control all the related layers with a single effort (like locking all the layers under a specified Layer-_Info record). The Amiga layer functions involving Layer_Info records are covered in the section on bitmaps. Here is the Layer_Info record definition:

```
struct Layer_Info {          /* The control record for several layers. */
    struct Layer *top_layer; /* The first layer in this Info's list. */
    struct Layer *check_lp;  /* A mysterious system variable. */
```

```
    struct Layer *obs;              /* A mysterious system variable. */
    struct MsgPort RP_ReplyPort;/* Used for intertask communications. */
    struct MsgPort LockPort;        /* Used for intertask communications. */
    UBYTE Lock;                     /* The LayerInfo Lock status. */
    UBYTE broadcast;                /* */
    UBYTE LockNest;                 /* I don't have the vaguest idea. */
    UBYTE Flags;                    /* Padding. */
    struct Task *Locker;            /* A pointer to the present locking task. */
    UBYTE bytereserved[2];          /* Padding. */
    UWORD wordreserved[2];          /* Padding. */
    UnlockLayer byteres3[2];        /* Padding. */
}
```

Now we will discuss bitmap areas. Setting up a bitmap under a BitMap record is as easy as two calls; one to AllocRaster (actually, you need one AllocRaster call per bitplane in the bitmap), and one call to InitBitMap. The RastPort record, or a RasInfo record (in the case of an Amiga viewport record), will then have valid BitMap records to point to. Layer bitmaps are no different, for neither CreateUpfrontLayer nor CreateBehindLayer creates a bitmap when it creates a Layer record. Here is the BitMap definition:

```
struct BitMap {
    UWORD BytesPerRow;   /* The number of bytes required to store a row. */
    UWORD Rows;          /* The number of rows in the bitmap. */
    UBYTE Flags;         /* Some status and condition flags. */
    UBYTE Depth;         /* The number of bit planes in bit map. */
    UWORD pad;           /* A padding variable of size WORD. */
    PLANEPTR Planes[8];  /* Pointers to each bit plane in bitmap. */
}
```

Another RastPort field is a pointer to a private TmpRas record, which in turn has a field that points to a RAM area. The RAM is used as a scratchpad by some of the Amiga bitmap manipulation routines in the graphics library, like Flood, AreaEnd, AreaDraw, and AreaMove. The size of the RAM buffer is also kept by the TmpRas record.

Use the routine InitTmpRas to allocate and initialize the scratchpad area, initialize the TmpRas record, and assign the current RastPort's TmpRas pointer. Three parameters must be given: a pointer to the TmpRas record (the TmpRas record must exist already), a pointer to the beginning of the temporary scratchpad area, and the size of the temporary scratchpad. Subsequent calls to InitTmpRas, with different size values for the scratchpad, are handled intelligently; memory that is no longer required is deallocated, and more is allocated when necessary. There is one caveat: scratchpad buffers must reside in the first 512K of addressable RAM. This can be tough when multitasking.

It is now time for an illustration of the Amiga big picture (see Fig. 3–45). It is a fence with two groups of record types milling about on either side. This is seen more by the Amiga Intuition program than by applications; Intuition is paid to pay attention to details at this level.

The structures on the left side are used by application code to draw onto bitmaps. A RastPort contains the current state of modes and patterns for a bitmap. A bitmap can be associated with one or more Layer records; RastPort records are used to keep the current pen, pattern, and draw status for them. A LayerInfo record is used as a header to a linked list of Layer records that are related to one another. Layers are used for determining how bitmap images are to be drawn onto bitmaps in the event that the view has been changed.

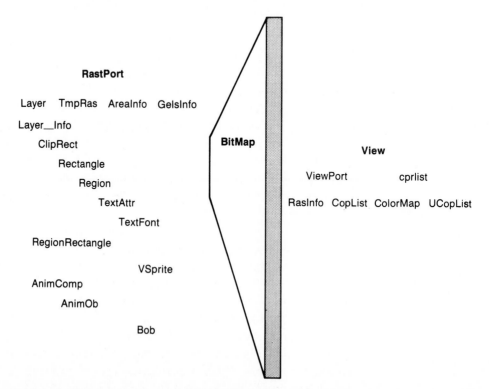

Figure 3–45 The Amiga graphics neighborhood

The fence is made of bitmaps and BitMap records. The BitMap record contains a little information about the size and shape of the bitmap it represents. BitMap records are used fluently by structures on either side of the fence.

The structures on the other side of the fence are involved with getting the contents of Amiga bitmaps that belong to viewports, blitter objects, and sprites onto the screen. These are the View, ViewPort, RasInfo, CopList, CprList, and UCopList records. The data tree composed of these records is called a **view**, since it represents a snapshot of the entire contents of the Amiga display.

The contents of the view have to be translated into a form that can be handled by the coprocessor in charge of the screen contents (the Copper). This other form is simply a Copper microprocessor instruction list (really a Copper program). The Copper is a microprocessor that executes a considerably different instruction set than the Motorola 68000 or Intel 8086 processors.

An entire Copper program is designed to run for about 1/60 of a second, which is coincidentally the time it takes the video beam to travel across the screen (in noninterlace mode). The program is brought to the attention of the Copper graphics coprocessor, and the screen comes to life. Normally a Copper program is run over and over.

A finished Copper program is *not* independent from what may be currently brewing in the view it has been derived from, since parts of the current bitmap data are used by the Copper (and blitter) to build the frame in real time. So there you have the germ of how the Amiga graphics system is intended to work: a Copper program is built using the layout of viewports and layer bitmaps, and then used repetitively while the bitmap contents are modified. Changes to the contents of a bitmap do not require a change in a Copper program, although changes to the layout of a view do. This is good, since creating a Copper program takes a noticeable amount of time.

The following is a description of the record types on the right side of the fence. Application programs intended to run under Intuition generally don't work directly with these structures. The view descriptions,, with their View, ViewPort, and RasInfo records, are part of the low-level guts of the Amiga display system, and are without any form of software protection. Intuition provides a layer of protection by performing all the view operations itself, at the request of any other task. It certainly is not a good idea for a number of concurrent application tasks to have to directly play with the low-level structures of the system. It is possible to bypass Intuition, but most of the time it is easier to just use it. Intuition gives you screens and windows, which are pretty flexible and consistent for most application needs.

A View record is the "majordomo" record of the Amiga graphics system. Its contents (including what it points to) represent the contents of the Amiga screen. The View record points to a list of ViewPort records. Here is the definition:

```
struct View {                       /* The majordomo display structure. */
    struct ViewPort *ViewPort;  /* Ptr. to first ViewPort record in a list.*/
    struct cprlist *LOFCprList; /* The Long Frame Copper List pointer; */
                                /*  both interlace and noninterlace. */
    struct cprlist *SHFCprList; /* The short Frame Copper instruction list;*/
                                /*  contains interlace only. */
    short DyOffset;             /* The View display screen XY offsets: */
    short DxOffset;             /*    NOTE: these are counter-ordered! */
    UWORD Modes;                /* Mode bit flags: */
                                /*  PFBA, DUALPF, HIRES, LACE, HAM, */
                                /*  SPRITES, VP_HIDÉ, GENLOCK_AUDIO */
                                /*  GENLOCK_VIDEO, EXTRA_HALFBRITE */

}
```

InitView is used to initialize a View record.

The View record for a given view (there may be more than one used in a system) points to a list of ViewPort records. The ViewPort describes/controls a particular part of the display described by the view. The ViewPort record has a pointer to a colormap table for determining what colors are available within the ViewPort's bitmap.

```
struct ViewPort {
    struct ViewPort *Next;      /* A ptr to the next ViewPort in View. */
    struct ColorMap *ColorMap;  /* A ptr to the header record for the color
                                /*  table. */
    struct CopList *DspIns;     /* Ptr to the display copper instruction */
                                /*  list. */
    struct CopList *SprIns;     /* A ptr. to the sprite copper instruction */
                                /*  list. */
    struct CopList *ClrIns;     /* A ptr to the color copper */
                                /*  instruction list. */
    struct UCopList *UCopIns;   /* A ptr. to the user-defined copper list. */
    SHORT DWidth;               /* Width of the visible displayed bitmap. */
    SHORT DHeight;              /* The height of vis. map, in pixels. */
    SHORT DxOffset;             /* The location of top left corner of map */
```

```
     SHORT DyOffset;              /*  on the Amiga display. */
     UWORD Modes;                 /* The same Modes bits as View. */
     UWORD reserved;              /* A new condo subdivision here soon. */
     struct RasInfo *RasInfo;     /* A ptr. to a BitMap (eventually). */
}
```

InitVPort is used to initialize a ViewPort record.

The ViewPort owns a bitmap that can be as large as 1024-by-1024 pixels, which means that the visible portion of the bitmap image may be smaller than the entire bitmap. The RasInfo record is used to point to the ViewPort's BitMap, and also to describe which part of that bitmap is showing through.

```
struct RasInfo {
     struct RasInfo *Next;  /* Points to another RasInfo record. */
     struct BitMap *BitMap; /* Points to the ViewPort's BitMap (and bitmap).*/
     SHORT RxOffset;        /* The X coord of top-left of visible corner. */
     SHORT RyOffset;        /* Y coord of ViewPort bitmap's visible part. */
}
```

Each ViewPort can have its own set of color settings for the color registers, so that its 32 available colors can be different from another View-Port's colors. Here is the record for keeping track of that information:

```
struct ColorMap {
     UBYTE Flags;
     UBYTE Type;
     UWORD Count;
     APTR ColorTable;
}
```

The CopList (premerged sublist), UCopList (user-defined Copper instruction stream), and cprlist (completely merged and sorted View Copper list) record types are used for grouping, sorting, and storing Copper instruction lists. The Copper programs are built using a small number of routines, like MakeVPort and DrawGList, sorted by SortGList. When the Copper instruction lists are being built there are four different sublists: display, sprite, color, and user-defined. These lists, when in sorted order, must be merged into one (or two) sorted Copper programs with

MrgCop, and then those Copper instruction lists are inserted into the display system by LoadView.

LoadView's single parameter is a pointer to the View record, which contains a pointer to the coprocessor instruction list. Clever use of the OFF_DISPLAY and ON_DISPLAY macros can help the presentation of the graphics generated with LoadView.

When MakeVPort builds a display Copper list for the ViewPort, a pointer to the new Copper list is placed in the DspIns field of the ViewPort. MakeVPort uses the default color table if the ViewPort doesn't have a ColorMap record.

INITIALIZATION AND TERMINATION

Macintosh

InitGraf is called once to initialize the Macintosh Quickdraw subsystem. The action initializes a few Quickdraw global variables. The address of the global variable record is passed to InitGraf as a parameter.

Gem

The routine freemem is used on the IBM PC family to return much of the memory initially allocated by MS-DOS to the Gem application so that other things may be used there, such as drivers and heap storage data.

appl_init is a Gem AES routine that has to be called if the application is to get very far. This routine returns a process ID number that uniquely identifies a task. If too many tasks have attempted to run at the same time, the return value is −1, a hint from Gem to the application that it should not proceed. This routine must be executed before opening any workstations.

appl_exit is called normally at the end of an application's runtime to tell Gem that the application is done. Gem cleans up where needed (deallocating buffers in heaps, etc.).

There are two sets of workstation open and close routines. The first set, v_opnwk and v_clswk, is used to set up and shut down, respectively, a physical device like a screen, printer, or plotter. The open workstation (v_opnwk) call loads a device driver, calls the driver's initialization function, and returns a go/nogo result. The close workstation (v_clswk) call is responsible for flushing device buffers and resetting the hardware to the state it was in before the open workstation call was executed. The Gem environment may be the only environment on a machine, in which case opening and closing the workstation is unnecessary. In fact, early versions of the Atari ST run Gem without these two routines working properly; not using them works fine.

The second pair of open and close routines is v_opnvwk, Open Virtual Screen Workstation, and v_clsvwk, Close Virtual Screen Workstation. When a virtual workstation is opened, a unique workstation environment record is initialized, and a Gem handle to that environment (aka the virtual workstation) is returned. This record is Gem's answer to the Macintosh grafPort, though it is not as extensive. Each open workstation has its own set of current attributes, including clipping rectangles. Like Apple's grafPort access routines, Gem's attribute and inquiry routines are provided to allow safe, controlled access to the fields in the workstation environment record, although Apple tells exactly how a grafPort is put together and Digital Research doesn't provide that information for its equivalent structure.

When a virtual workstation is closed, further attempts to gain access to it are unsuccessful. Both Gem AES and applications must use the handle for access; the open and close virtual workstation calls are Gem VDI routines.

v_clrwk, Clear Workstation, will erase the screen or, if the device is a printer, send a form feed to the device after erasing pending output in the device buffer.

The graf_handle routine provides the Gem VDI handle for the open screen workstation, in case it was misplaced after the open workstation call.

Windows

The CreateDC and CreateMemoryDC routines can be used to initialize a device driver. If used on the last DC of a device, DeleteDC will start some mop-up operations and release the resources allocated to the device. CreateWindow and DestroyWindow are the window manager initiate and terminate routines, but somewhere along the line they call the DC routines to get the real work done. CreateWindow can't make a move unless RegisterClass is called to set up a window class first.

IIGS

The Mac's InitGraf is replaced on the IIGS with QDBootInit, QDStartup, QDShutDown, QDVersion, and QDSTatus.

QDBootInit initializes Quickdraw II at boot time. Application code should not use this routine.

QDStartup takes the place of Mac's InitGraf for the IIGS. Quickdraw II is initialized, the current GrafPort is set to the standard port, the screen is cleared to specifications (a master SCB is passed to the routine), some pixel map buffers are allocated (QDStartup is told the maximum buffer size required by the application), and the program ID is registered.

QDShutdown deallocates whatever buffers were required by an application.

QDVersion returns the version number of the copy of Quickdraw II running on a machine.

QDStatus returns TRUE if Quickdraw II is active (if QDII has been successfully initialized).

Amiga

Amiga applications running underneath Intuition aren't responsible for initializing the runtime environment because Intuition is supposed to do that. The application normally uses one or more windows, and standard execution normally involves an Amiga screen, so the routines OpenWindow and OpenScreen are at least involved. The appropriate runtime library must be opened before an application attempts to execute some parts of the system code that is kept in libraries; this is done using OpenLibrary. Anything that has been opened should be closed prior to the end of an application's execution.

SetMenuStrip is used to assign entries in a window's menu bar, and ClearMenuStrip will remove the entries; problems may arise if ClearMenuStrip is not called before the window is deallocated.

EXTENDING AND INTERCHANGING CODE

Besides creating routines that aren't included in the normal libraries for a machine or windowing environment, you may need to try rearranging, adding, and replacing routines. There are sometimes hooks provided by the low-level software for this. Permitting developers to bypass the standard fare is vital.

Macintosh

There are a small number of Quickdraw graphic primitive routines that are used by other, higher-level Quickdraw routines (and consequently, application code) to draw something. Any grafPort record has a field (grafProcs) that, when its value is not the default NIL, points to a sub-record filled with procedure pointers. These are pointers to all the low-level graphic routines that are to be used by software using that grafPort. When the pointer to the QDProcs type record is NIL, then Quickdraw merely uses the standard primitives. When a QDProcs record is present, however, one or more of the pointers in the record may point to nonstandard low-level drawing routine that would be used.

An example of one of the default Quickdraw draw primitives is StdPoly. StdPoly is used by all the high-level polygon draw routines, like FillPoly and FramePoly, to do the actual drawing. StdPoly accepts a handle to a polygon descriptor and a drawing mode attribute called a GrafVerb, which is declared:

```
TYPE GrafVerb = (frame, paint, erase, invert, fill);
```

Although it is possible for an application to call the StdPoly routine directly rather than going through the higher-level routines like FillPoly or FramePoly, it would be bad form to do so. The QDProcs record is provided to allow independent swapping of the graphic primitive drivers; calling the Std routines directly bypasses the QDProcs record and prevents the routines from being changed.

One thing that comes to mind when the programmer is armed with this ability is the possibility of attaching a different display to the Macintosh, perhaps an external one that provides color, and using it without having to change most of the Quickdraw package and application code. I haven't the foggiest idea what this kind of effort involves beyond this mere speculation.

Here is the definition for the QDProcs type:

```
TYPE QDProcsPtr = ^QDProcs;

    QDProcs = RECORD
            textProc:   Ptr;
            lineProc:   Ptr;
            rectProc:   Ptr;
            rRectProc:  Ptr;
```

```
        ovalProc:    Ptr;

        arcProc:     Ptr;

        polyProc:    Ptr;

        rgnProc:     Ptr;

        bitsProc:    Ptr;

        commentProc: Ptr;

        txMeasProc:  Ptr;

        getPicProc:  Ptr;

        putPicProc:  Ptr;

END;
```

Standard Pascal does not go in for pointers to procedures or functions, but the C language has no such qualms. The Apple development Pascals, like any good Pascal compilers, have enough extensions to make computer-language purists turn funny colors.

The routine SetStdProcs is used to set up a QDProcs record to point to the standard primitives. The pointers can then be changed to indicate other primitive routines.

There are 13 default low-level routines:

StdText	The standard text draw routine.
StdLine	Draws lines.
StdRect	Draws rectangles.
StdRect	Draws round-corner rectangles.
StdOval	Draws ovals.
StdArc	Draws arcs.
StdPoly	Draws polygons.
StdRgn	Draws regions.
StdBits	Transfers bit images.
StdComment	Processes picture comments (that is, ignores them).
StdTxMeas	Measures Text width.
StdGetPic	Gets some bytes of a picture.
StdPutPic	Stores some bytes of a picture.

✳ **WARNING: Those who have ventured to deal directly with these routines have more often than not come back with many grey hairs. These routines were not originally implemented cleanly and can be the source of a number of application bugs that will require the user's setting breakpoints and traipsing through ROM to determine what on Earth is going on. Of particular interest is the StdTxMeas**

entry point, which appears to make font manager calls when handed strings of length 0.

Gem

Replacing the cursor draw routine is permitted; use vex_curv as discussed in the section on cursors. The primitive graphic routines are less involved than those in Mac's Quickdraw package; replacing them is a minor matter of providing a different draw routine and calling it. The Gem VDI does not do coordinate system translation beyond Normalized Device to Raster for the screen, so about the only thing that has to be done is to worry about the clipping rectangle. Gem AES routines do some coordinate translation when drawing child objects, but all that is needed is to call the objc_offset routine. The object support library includes a structure (the G_PROGDEF object) enabling a programmer to invent Gem screen objects and plug in the driver routines for them. The Gem AES object library will then automatically use the drivers when it encounters a programmer-defined object in an object tree.

Windows

LineDDA allows a programmer-specified routine to be used to draw a line.

The Escape routine allows direct access to a device driver. Since the GDI supports only so many functions, the application is permitted to call the device driver with an input data block, an output data block, and an escape number that identifies the low-level driver function wanted. Here are the predefined Escape functions:

NEWFRAME	Clear the display surface (and specify page name)
ABORTPIC	Erase everything written to the display
NEXTBAND	Used for "banding" applications
SETCOLORTABLE	Set an entry in the device color table
GETCOLORTABLE	Get an entry in the color table using an index
FLUSHOUTPUT	Zotz the device buffer contents

More functions can be defined by the device.

A program can pretty much have the run of the entirety of its tiled (or overlapping) window (both the frame and the client area), but going outside is destined to be a challenge.

IIGS

The IIGS QDII package has the same extensible properties as Macintosh Quickdraw. There is an additional entry in the grafProcs record for a routine that tells Quickdraw II whether it can use the scan line interrupts as timing for drawing the cursor without flicker. If an application wants to use the scan line interrupts, QDII can't use them.

Amiga

There is a significant distinction in Amiga software between raster bitmap manipulation and painting or drawing the contents of a bitmap. The Amiga excels in raster bitmap manipulation but has no advantage over the other machines for generating the contents of the raster bitmaps. The Amiga does not have a Quickdraw equivalent except for raster bitmap manipulation, and this component does not have interchangeable parts in the tradition of Quickdraw. Quickdraw allows you to select the "driver" routine for a display device or a graphic primitive, and Quickdraw will then attempt to use that software. The Amiga is designed so that if you want to approach the display rendering differently, you may bypass the existing software. For normal applications work, it isn't necessary to bypass the existing raster bitmap manipulation routines provided in ROM, but opportunities for customization abound when creating the graphic contents of bitmaps for later manipulation.

PICTURES

A picture is a group of graphic primitives and attributes that can be treated as a unit.

Each use of a graphic primitive (like the rectangle) is called an **instance** of a rectangle. Once a picture is defined, some graphics application packages permit the use of instances of a picture. Each instance could be slightly modified to conform to local requirements, just as instances of rectangles are rotated, sized, and filled.

Another useful property of pictures is that they can be **nested**: a picture may contain instances of other pictures. For example, the picture of a car might contain four instances of a picture of a tire, three instances of a picture of a windshield wiper (two in front and one in back), etc. The term **subpicture** is used when describing the instance of a picture that is used in another picture.

A picture is commonly implemented in memory as a linked list of graphic primitive records; the header of this particular list is another type of graphic primitive record called a picture.

Macintosh

Each Macintosh picture has a picture frame (which is nothing more than a defining rectangle) that is used to properly scale the instance to fit into its surroundings.

A Macintosh picture can include any number of any drawing commands, which makes it a dynamic structure that has to be referenced by the application code with a handle. Here are all the related definitions:

```
TYPE PicPtr = ^Picture;              {The direct pointer to a picture.}
     PicHandle = ^PicPtr;            {The handle to a picture record.}
     Picture = RECORD                {The Macintosh picture record. }
         picSize:      INTEGER;      {The size of the picture record.}
         picFrame:     Rect;         {The defining rectangle.}
         {The picture definition data starts here...}
     END;
```

The Macintosh method for handling picture definition is one that masks the construction details from most programming concerns. To begin creating a picture, call OpenPicture; OpenPicture returns a handle to the picture used to collect commands. To build the picture, call any number of any Quickdraw graphics routines after the OpenPicture call. To stop building the picture, call ClosePicture. To render the picture on the display, call DrawPicture; to deallocate the memory space assigned to a previously opened Picture record, call KillPicture.

The routine PicComment is used to insert variable-sized comments as entries within a Picture record.

Although it is possible for a picture instance to occur within a picture, do not try to build one picture while another picture is being built. A call to OpenPicture must be followed by a call to ClosePicture before the next OpenPicture call can be made.

Gem

Object records are used to build a tree that can be handled as a unit to describe a picture on the screen. Object trees can support a complicated hierarchy of images being used within images, but the extent of the picture depicted by an object tree is limited to the display raster, forcing a conversion from a virtual coordinate space supported by the application to the screen coordinate space before the tree can be built and displayed. In other words, transformations are handled outside of the object trees. Since no restrictions exist on how the coordinate space of an application may work, this is a flexible arrangement. It is expected that third-party libraries for the purpose of supporting world coordinate space manipulation will provide some development shortcuts.

Figure 3–46 is an illustration of how to build a Gem object tree and have it drawn on the display.

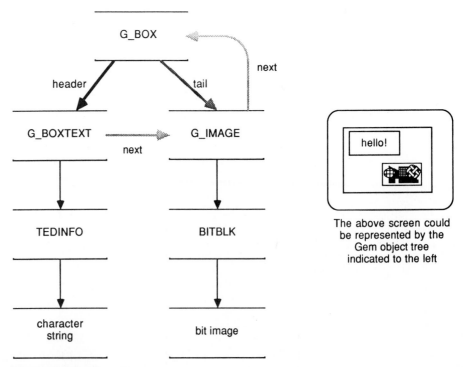

The above screen could be represented by the Gem object tree indicated to the left

Figure 3–46 Gem object tree

Windows

The things that come closest to already existing support for pictures are the metafile support routines. When some of the standard GDI commands are handed a metafile display context, the commands are stored in a pseudo-executable format in the metafile. When building of the metafile is done, the contents can be run through the PlayMetafile routine, which will call the standard GDI routines for each command in the metafile. The metafile routines are similar to the OpenPicture, ClosePicture, and Draw-Picture functions provided on the Macintosh.

CreateMetaFile is used to make a display context for a disk or memory-based metafile. CloseMetaFile closes the display context and replaces it with a handle to the metafile itself. GetMetaFile can be used to obtain a handle to a metafile that is on disk; all that is needed is the MS-DOS file name. CopyMetaFile is used to copy the contents of one metafile to another (disk or memory-based). DeleteMetaFile doesn't destroy a disk-based metafile, but it does remove the validity of the handle to it, as well as all resources it may have acquired. Finally, PlayMetaFile runs through all the stored commands in the metafile, executing them on the specified display context.

IIGS

The IIGS Picture handling routines are the same as those for the Macintosh.

Amiga

The Amiga does not provide routines for building or maintaining pictures. The Amiga initially did not come with an extensive graphic primitive support library (no circle draw routines for example), which is needed when supporting lists of graphic primitives as objects. There are many ways to handle pictures: the Macintosh capture-and-draw way is appropriate for some applications, but most others have to build their own sophisticated picture support. Gem's object-tree support is great for supporting object-oriented graphics manipulation, but it only provides for the visible half of picture data and offers little support for manipulating the data in an application's context.

LOW-LEVEL TEXT SUPPORT

One of the most useful capabilities of the windowing environments is their support for manipulating text. Providing a consistent set of rules for handling blocks of text data is a very simple way to make several independently developed application programs "accidentally" able to talk to each other, and much more fluently than "integrated" programs developed in the past few years.

The low-level text support consists of the routines involved with simple presentation graphics, and not any of the higher, record-oriented text manipulation routines. They get their own chapter.

Macintosh

Quickdraw does not handle carriage returns and line feeds by itself; it assumes that the application or utility code is intelligent enough to process formatting concerns by itself.

For selecting the current font for the present Mac grafPort, Quickdraw provides the TextFont routine.

For selecting one or more style attributes (bold, italic, underline, outline, shadow, condense, or extend), there is the TextFace routine.

TextMode is used to choose the current grafPort's text transfer mode. There are only three valid transfer modes: srcOr, srcXor, and srcBic; srcOr is the default.

TextSize is used to select the current font size.

SpaceExtra is available to set how many extra pixels go between each character in a line.

DrawChar draws the specified character to the right of the current pen position; the current pen position is advanced.

DrawString is given a Pascal standard string; the routine calls DrawChar once for each character in the string.

DrawText does almost the same thing that DrawString does; the difference is that DrawText is not given a Pascal standard string. DrawText is provided with a pointer into memory, an offset value (in bytes), and a byte count.

CharWidth provides the width (in coordinates) of a given character.

StringWidth provides the width (in coordinates) of a given string of characters.

TextWidth provides the width (in coordinates) of a given collection of characters stored in RAM.

GetFontInfo provides the status of the current grafPort's character font. The current size and style are taken into account. The returned record is defined:

```
TYPE FontInfo = RECORD
     ascent:  INTEGER;     {The height of character font above base line.}
     descent: INTEGER;     {The depth of character font below base line.}
     widMax:  INTEGER;     {The maximum width of any character in font}
     leading: INTEGER;     {The distance between Descent and next Ascent.}
                           { lines for text alignment (default).}
   END;
```

The 128K version of the Macintosh ROM has an extra routine for measuring characters: MeasureText. Starting from an arbitrary piece of text in RAM, MeasureText calculates the distance from the starting position to the right side of the character for each character encountered in a string. MeasureText is given the number of characters to measure, and a pointer to an array of integers longer by one than the number of characters. The array is returned with all the measured distances. MeasureText does not involve StdText.

Gem

The open workstation supports several current attributes that are used to display text. There are also five predefined objects that support low-level text drawing.

To set the writing mode for everything drawn to the display (including text), vswr_mode is used. The writing modes are replace, transparent, XOR, and reverse transparent.

vst_height is used to set the current character height in Normalized Device or raster coordinates. vst_point sets the character height using units of 1/72 of an inch (aka one standard **point**). vst_point returns a variety of size and width information.

vst_rotation is for setting a text drawing angle, so that text can be displayed vertically or at a 30-degree slant, for example.

To select the current type face, the vst_font routine is used to select between text faces that have already been loaded. To load fonts into memory, use the routine vst_load_fonts; to get rid of them, use vst_unload_fonts.

vst_color is provided to set the current color index for text.

vst_effects turns on and off special text effects. These effects are underline, thicken (bold), intensity (light or normal), outline, shadow, and skew (italics).

vst_alignment sets the horizontal and vertical alignment for text. The options are horizontally (text can be left, center, or right justified) and vertically (alignment can be baseline, half line, ascent line, bottom, descent, or top). The default alignments are left justified and baseline.

For asking what some of the various current text settings are, Gem provides vqt_attributes. The attributes available with this function are current textface number, text color index, text baseline rotation, horizontal and vertical alignments, writing mode, and character and cell proportions.

Another inquiry routine, vqt_extent, returns the coordinates for a box that contains a text string drawn with a rotated baseline (see Fig. 3–47). The coordinates are given such that the box touches the X and Y axes and the string is drawn in the first quadrant (the upper right quarter). This routine comes in handy for text-highlighting operations. All the special text effects attributes will affect the size of the box.

Yet another routine, vqt_width, is used to get the cell width for a particular character in the current type face. This value is not in points, it is in the current coordinate system.

vqt_name provides the current type face name in readable text, not in numbers. The routine returns a 32-character array; the first 16 characters contains the font name, and the next 16 characters describe the style and weight. For example, Caslon is the name of a type face; Bold Extended is the style and weight for this particular version of the Caslon font.

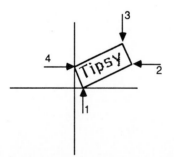

Figure 3–47 Rotated text rectangle

vqt_fontinfo provides sizing information for the current font. The current size and special effects are included in the equation because they change character cell proportions (see Fig. 3–40). The normal cell width and height are returned; the changes induced by the font special effects are returned in terms of changes to the normal cell proportions, like a width delta and left and right offsets.

The object information record type TEDINFO is used to keep track of each individual string that has been defined with current attributes. The attributes have to be stored in the TEDINFO record, along with a pointer to the string data, because the current attributes have a habit of changing after the string is defined. In the present form of TEDINFO not all the text attribute settings have entries. For example, the special effects options aren't represented.

Windows

TextOut writes a character string of a specified number of characters to the indicated display context. The coordinates of the beginning of the string are passed as two parameters, X and Y. The function returns TRUE if successful, FALSE if not.

CreateFont is an enormous can of worms. There are 14 parameters to this function; each of the parameters is a quality or attribute of the members of the font. CreateFont tries to find a font using all the qualities mentioned in the parameter list. If a perfect fit is not to be had, Create-Font uses a font that comes close, matching as many of the qualities as it can.

The qualities include font character height, font character width, text line draw angle (with reference to the bottom of the page), character draw angle, and font weight. The qualities also include a bumper crop of boolean flags: Italic, Underline, and StrikeOut. Also, there are a number of non-boolean, but simple attributes: CharSet can be ANSI_CHARSET or OEM_CHARSET; OutPrecision, ClipPrecision, and Quality all portray to what resolution their respective characteristics should be presented. PitchAndFamily is a hybrid value, with the lower 2 bits (of a byte) indicating the pitch type (default, fixed, or variable) and the high 4 bits

an example of normal, unmodified text
an example of text in bold face
an example of italicized text
an example of text in outline

Figure 3–48 Font sizing differences due to style

identifying the font family (for example, roman, swiss, typewriter, script, decorative or dontcare). Last but not least, lpFacename is a pointer to a string (C-style) containing the facename of the font. The function returns FALSE if it wasn't successful, and a handle to the font if it was.

The function CreateFontIndirect is the same as CreateFont, except that there is only one parameter: a pointer to a LOGFONT type record that describes what the font should look like. CreateFontIndirect also returns a handle to the font when successful and FALSE when unsuccessful. Here is what a LOGFONT record looks like:

```
TYPE LOGFONT = RECORD
        lfHeight:               INTEGER2;
        lfWidth:                INTEGER2;
        lfEscapement:           INTEGER2;
        lfOrientation:          INTEGER2;
        lfWeight:               INTEGER2;
        lfItalic:               BYTE;
        lfUnderline:            BYTE;
        lfStrikeOut:            BYTE;
        lfCharSet:              BYTE;
        lfOutPrecision:         BYTE;
        lfClipPrecision:        BYTE;
        lfQuality:              BYTE;
        lfPitchAndFamily:       BYTE;
        lfFaceName:             ARRAY[0..LF_FACESIZE] OF BYTE;
    END;
```

To set the current drawing color for text, pass the current display context and an RGB color structure to SetTextColor; it will return the old text color. To determine what the present text color is, use GetTextColor.

To prepare a text line for display using the TextOut routine, use SetTextJustification to tell the GDI how much extra space to use for justifying a line of text. This routine is also used to tell how many break characters (normally the space character) are on the line. In order to figure out how much padding to put in, the length of the text line without padding is calculated with the function GetTextExtent; just give the function the string and the number of characters and it will return the length and width in a single 32-bit integer. The height has the upper bunk in the integer.

These routines have a shortcoming: They don't properly handle more than one font per line. The application code has to break the line apart to separate the fonts and then individually feed each part to GetTextExtent, SetTextJustification, and TextOut.

To clear a running error counter, it is good form to call SetTextJustification with its space-to-add (TBreakExtra) field set to 0 after the entire line is displayed.

SetTextCharacterExtra is used to set the amount of space to surround each character (the **intercharacter spacing**). This routine returns the old value. GetTextCharacterExtra returns the current value.

EnumFonts is one of those routines that enumerates things and doesn't stop until all the present, appropriate things are enumerated. EnumFonts enumerates the present fonts for a device with the indicated facename (a C-style string).

The application gives EnumFonts a pointer to an application routine. It is up to EnumFonts to find each interesting font and hand the font data, one set at a time, to the application routine. EnumFonts provides four parameters: a LOGFONT type record, a TEXTMETRIC type record, an integer describing the font type, and an application-supplied data record. With this arrangement the application routine is solely concerned with the business of understanding the characteristics of one font, and nothing else that is out of context.

GetTextFace returns the currently selected font facename in a buffer. The routine is given a DC handle, a pointer to the buffer, and the size of the buffer in characters. The name is a C-style (null-terminated) character string; the function return value is the number of characters inserted into the buffer.

GetTextMetrics returns the currently selected font metrics. The routine is given a DC handle and a pointer to an empty TEXTMETRIC record. The function return value is TRUE if the call was successful and FALSE if it wasn't; the metrics should be in the TEXTMETRIC record.

IIGS

SetSysFont is used to set the system font. A font handle is the one parameter.

GetSysFont returns a copy of the current system font handle.

SetFont sets the indicated font (using a handle as the parameter) to the current font.

GetFont returns a copy of the handle to the current font.

GetFontInfo is given a pointer to a font information record so that it can put information on the current font into the record.

SetFontFlags and GetFontFlags respectively set and return the current font flags. The content of the font flags word is not currently defined.

SetTextFace sets the text face to the value passed to it, exactly as the Mac's TextFace routine does. GetTextFace returns the current text face. The two routines deal with the font attributes bold, italic, underline, outline, shadow, condense, and extend.

SetTextMode assigns the current text transfer mode, and GetTextMode returns what the current text transfer mode is. SetTextMode does the same work as the Mac's TextMode routine, but the modes aren't exactly the same. The modes here are COPY, notCOPY, OR, notOR, XOR, notXOR, BIC, notBIC, foreCOPY, notforeCOPY, foreOR, notforeOR, foreXOR, notforeXOR, foreBIC, and notforeBIC. The last eight modes are text mode specials used for drawing a font (monochrome) onto a color pixel map.

TextSize works the same on the IIGS as on the Macintosh.

SetSpaceExtra is the Mac's SpaceExtra routine, and GetSpaceExtra returns what the current spExtra value is.

DrawChar is the same as the Mac's DrawChar. DrawString, DrawText, CharWidth, StringWidth, and TextWidth are likewise the same. The new kids are DrawCString (the routine for people who insist on using NULL-terminated C-style strings), which draws a C language string the same way that DrawString works with Pascal compatible strings, CStringWidth (returns the width of the C-style string à la StringWidth), and the bounds routines, CharBounds, TextBounds, StringBounds, and CStringBounds (each of which accepts a pointer to a rectangle and a pointer to the respective namesake character-based data, and fills in the specified rectangle with bounds of the indicated data).

Amiga

The TextFont record type is used by application tasks to describe and point to an available font in RAM. There is one TextFont record for each font, per task. The composition of the TextFont type is the following:

```
struct TextFont {          /* A font may contain up to 255 chars */
    struct Node TextNode;      /* The record containing font name et al. */
    struct Message tf_Message; /* Reply message used when font removed. */
    UWORD tf_YSize;    /* The height of font in pixels. */
    UBYTE tf_Style;    /* The intrinsic font styles (with five available).*/
```

```
UBYTE  tf_Flags;     /* The global font preference settings. */
UWORD  tf_XSize;     /* The smallest character width, in pixels. */
UWORD  tf_Baseline;  /* The number of lines from char top to baseline.*/
UWORD  tf_BoldSmear; /* This is used to produce bold chars in font. */
UWORD  tf_Accessors; /* The number of tasks to open a given font. */
UBYTE  tf_LoChar;    /* The integer offset of first char in font. */
UBYTE  tf_HiChar;    /* The integer value of last character in font. */
APTR   tf_CharData;  /* The pointer to the font image data. */
UWORD  tf_Modulo;    /* The number of image data bytes per character. */
APTR   tf_CharLoc;   /* A ptr. to a bit offset/char width array. */
APTR   tf_CharSpace; /* A ptr. to a proportional spacing array. */
APTR   tf_CharKern;  /* A pointer to a kerning data array. */
}
```

When searching for a font on disk or in memory, an application task must provide the open font routine with a TextAttr type record filled with the information the system will need to track down the font. The record is defined as follows:

```
struct TextAttr {       /* This is used by AskFont, OpenFont, OpenDiskFont.*/
    strptr ta_Name;     /* The name of the font; C-style null terminated.*/
    UWORD ta_YSize;     /* The height of the font in pixels. */
    UBYTE ta_Style;     /* The intrinsic font style wanted. */
    UBYTE ta_Flags;     /* The preference settings for the font. */
}
```

The preference flags are for indicating things like ROMFONT (font in ROM), REVPATH (drawn from right to left), and PROPORTIONAL (the characters in this font have width and positioning independent from the other characters).

The AddFont routine is for adding a font to the RAM resident system font list (copy the font from disk to RAM for use by any task). The routine requires two parameters; the first is a pointer to the rastPort of interest and the second is a pointer to a record of type TextAttr.

The function AskSoftStyle returns a byte indicating which styles (Normal, Underlined, Bold, Italic, Extended) are software generateable for the current font, almost exactly like the other environments covered in this text. Those that are software- or algorithmically-generated, rather than intrinsic to the design of the font and unalterable, will have the corresponding bit in the byte set. AskSoftStyle requires a pointer to the RastPort in question, and returns the byte-sized bitset.

SetSoftStyle is used to modify the changeable (not intrinsic) software or algorithmic styles for a font. Three parameters are needed. The first is a pointer to the appropriate RastPort, the second is the byte containing the styles that should be active or inactive, and the third is the mask byte that tells SetSoftStyle which styles are changeable (this is the value returned by the AskSoftStyle routine).

AvailFonts is used to determine what fonts are available, on disk, in RAM, or both. The routine creates a single AvailFontsHeader record to contain the count of the number of different fonts encountered in the search. The routine also creates an AvailFonts record for each font it encounters; the font must fit the search criterion specified in the third parameter of the routine, which is either the value AFF_MEMORY (look for them in RAM), AFF_DISK (check the disk) or the union of both values for searching both locations. The first parameter for AvailFonts is a pointer to a RAM buffer hopefully large enough to store all the AvailFonts records and the one AvailFontsHeader record that will be created as a result of the call. The second parameter contains the buffer size in bytes. The AvailFontsHeader and AvailFonts records are defined as follows:

```
struct AvailFontsHeader {
    UWORD afh_NumEntries;       /* The count of the available fonts. */
}


struct AvailFonts {
    UWORD af_Type;              /* The font in AFF_MEMORY or AFF_DISK. */
    struct TextAttr af_attr;    /* A standard TextAttr record. */
}
```

ClearEOL will erase the rest of the line from the current pen position to the right end of the screen. The only parameter ClearEOL needs is a pointer to the appropriate RastPort. The height of the current font is used to determine the height of the rectangular area that will be cleared. The color of the rectangle is set to background pen color if the drawmode is JAM2; otherwise the color is 0.

ClearScreen will erase a rectangle from the current pen position to the bottom right corner of the current Raster bitmap. ClearScreen also needs as its only parameter a pointer to the appropriate RastPort record.

CloseFont is used to deallocate the RAM resources given to a font when it was brought into RAM with either OpenFont or OpenDiskFont.

Many fonts in RAM can take up an enormous amount of space, so using CloseFont is a good idea. CloseFont requires a pointer to the TextFont record for the font.

To scan the disk for a specific font, use OpenDiskFont; if the font is present, the font is brought into RAM and a TextFont record is created for it. If the font is not found, a NULL TextFont record pointer is returned by the routine. OpenDiskFont requires a pointer to a TextAttr record, with the record filled with information regarding the font to be used.

OpenFont is fancier than OpenDiskFont. OpenFont searches the system font list for a font that matches all the criteria mentioned in the TextAttr record parameter. If it doesn't find a perfect match, it tries to find a font with the same name but perhaps a different size or style. If it fails, it returns a NULL TextFont record pointer, but if it succeeds, the TextFont pointer returned is valid.

The routine RemFont is used to yank a font from the system font list. One task calling RemFont will not interfere with another task using the font, unless the second task tries to open the font again without calling AddFont or AvailFonts first. RemFont requires a pointer to a TextFont record of the font.

Text is the routine used to write an array of characters to the current raster bitmap using the currently selected font. The string is written to the raster bitmap starting at the current pen location. The first parameter is the pointer to the appropriate RastPort record, the second is a pointer to the beginning of the array of characters, and the third is the character count. The RastPort field DrawMode and the current algorithmic styles selected both affect the results.

The function TextLength returns the length in pixels of the graphically rendered image of a specified array of characters. TextLength uses the appropriate information in the indicated RastPort record (such as the font, style, and drawing modes) to determine the length of the bit image. The first parameter is the pointer to the RastPort, the second is a pointer to the array of characters to be measured, and the third is the array character count.

MISCELLANEOUS GRAPHICS SUPPORT ROUTINES

Macintosh

Random returns any number from -32768 to $+32767$ inclusive. The distribution is uniform, though a seed value is involved (the global randSeed) and Random does generate a reproducible pseudo-random sequence.

GetPixel is given the coordinates of a pixel on the display; it returns TRUE if the pixel color is black and FALSE if the color is white.

StuffHex translates the provided character string containing hexidecimal numbers into bit patterns and inserts them into RAM beginning at the specified address.

ScalePt is used to scale a width and height value, as provided in a Point record, from one defining rectangle to another. This scaling is based on the proportions of the rectangles with respect to each other. The initial width and height are with respect to the source rectangle; the returned values are with respect to the destination rectangle.

Gem

Inquire Input Mode, vqin_mode, provides the current input mode for the input device whose handle is provided. Four different input devices are supported: locator, valuator, choice, and string. Two different input modes are supported in the report: request and sample. **Request mode** is where the system waits for the data (such as a mouse click) to arrive, and **sample mode** is where the system uses the current state of an input device without waiting for a valid-data-present signal like the press of a mouse button.

Windows

GetDeviceCaps can be used to extract an encyclopedia of data on a single device and the capabilities of its driver.

IIGS

The Random routine (as on the Macintosh) has a buddy, SetRandSeed, that sets the value used to calculate the first value of a pseudo-random sequence of numbers returned by calling Random a number of times. Calling SetRandSeed with the same value will start the same sequence over again; providing a different value in the middle of one pseudo-random sequence will start a new sequence.

Amiga

BltClear places a 0 value in each byte of a block, starting at the indicated address and continuing for the specified number of bytes. The zeroed block must live in the first 512K of RAM.

MAPPING ROUTINES

A few routines are normally provided to convert coordinates from one coordinate system to another.

Macintosh

There are four routines, MapPt, MapRect, MapRgn, and MapPoly, that accept as parameters one graphic data structure (or a handle to one) and two rectangle descriptors. The graphic object fits within the coordinates of the first rectangle descriptor. These map routines are used to return the graphic object, but with the coordinates of the object changed to fit within the second rectangle descriptor (see Fig. 3–49). The two rectangles do not have to be related in any way; their proportions may be as different as their coordinates. The proportions of the graphic object are also changed to conform to the proportions of the destination rectangle.

MapPt returns the destination equivalent of the source coordinate, with the source coordinate being within a "source" rectangle and the destination coordinate being within a separate "destination" rectangle (probably of different proportions).

MapRect does the same job as MapPt, but for rectangles.

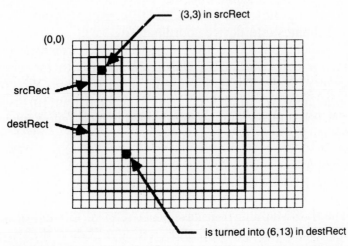

Figure 3–49 How objects are mapped from source rectangle to the destination rectangle

MapRgn does the same job as MapPt, but for regions.

MapPoly does the same job as MapPt, but for polygons.

As mentioned in the section on the point, Quickdraw has two routines, LocalToGlobal and GlobalToLocal, for mapping the point coordinates between the private coordinate system of a Macintosh GrafPort (discussed below) and a world coordinate space of an application.

Gem

objc_offset translates the parent or object-tree relative coordinates of a child object to Normalized Device or Raster Coordinates (depending on how the workstation was opened). This does not convert global or application coordinates to screen coordinates or vice versa; Gem doesn't provide coordinate system support beyond screen coordinates.

Windows

The function DPtoLP is used to convert device coordinates to logical coordinate points. One of the parameters is a pointer to a POINT array, and another is the number of POINT entries. Each element up to the number mentioned is converted. The current mapping mode, window, and viewport settings influence the conversion.

Going the other way, LPtoDP converts an array of logical POINT coordinates into device coordinates.

ClientToScreen converts the window coordinates of a specified point into screen coordinates which are relative to the origin of the entire display. ScreenToClient goes the other way, and WindowFromPoint determines which window contains a specified point (in display coordinates). These last three routines are defined to be Window functions, not Graphics Device Interface functions.

IIGS

The IIGS Mapping routines LocalToGlobal, GlobalToLocal, MapPt, MapRect, MapRgn, and MapPoly are identical to the Macintosh routines. With the map routines no grafPort data are involved, so the coordinate information could be entirely fictional.

Amiga

The Amiga doesn't have mapping routines. This situation probably won't last long.

SPECIALIZED PROCESSOR CONTROL

The present forms of the Macintosh, ST, and IBM machines do not rely on as general a class of processors to study as the central processor unit of the Motorola 68000 or Intel 8086, but instead use processors designed for dedicated applications such as graphics. The Amiga has the Copper, a generalized coprocessor responsible for handling graphics operations: sprite and playfield control, blitter control, and color palette control. The Copper also gets to play with the sound-generation hardware. What is important to the design of the Amiga is that the dedicated coprocessor is guaranteed to have enough horsepower and time to handle high-speed display list operations, something that the other machines cannot do. Although the Amiga, like the other machines, has some horsepower problems (and these problems can be embarrassingly obvious at times), the difficulties are usually centered on the load of the CPU and the state of the system support software. The Copper appears to perform its job in stellar form.

The Amiga also has a Blitter processor. The blitter processor is good for a small number of useful operations. It can:

- [ ] Copy bitplane image data
- [ ] Retrieve data from up to three sources as it prepares the result for a destination
- [ ] Provide 256 different logical operations for manipulating the 3 data sources into a result
- [ ] Deal with playfields of different sizes easily
- [ ] Scan source and destination areas forward or backward
- [ ] Do 15-bit shifts on up to 2 sources prior to the logic operation
- [ ] Mask the left and right data word from each horizontal line for logic operations on bit boundaries
- [ ] Detect nonzero logic operation results without storing the results back in memory
- [ ] Perform very, very, very fast area fills
- [ ] Perform line draws at arbitrary angles with patterns

Accessing the blitter is usually done via the routine library provided for high-level language support. Commodore/Amiga provides a manual with the exciting assembly-level details for high-performance applications like real-time games and tax preparation; these details are not available here because they take up an entire manual, and it is impossible to conduct a meaningful discussion while evading detail.

There are a few routines used to control the Copper coprocessor and some macros. Again, normal application programs that work with the Intuition user interface of the Amiga generally do not make direct use of these routines.

The routines in the graphics libraries that are associated with the Copper coprocessor are not as much direct Copper control routines as they are Copper instruction manipulation routines. The LoadView routine, mentioned in the data structures section, creates a new video frame by presenting to the Copper a coprocessor instruction list that has already been built. When the routine MakeVPort builds the Copper instruction list for the view, it doesn't interact at all with the Copper. The same is true for InitVPort, makeView, and MrgCop. The Copper accepts the lower-level orders in the Copper instruction list. It is possible for an application to create a Copper instruction list directly; such a thing is kept with a UCopList record, which is later used by MrgCop to bring the list into the combined instruction stream with the Copper instructions from the animation functions and the normal graphics Copper instructions. To support the construction of application (user)-defined Copper instruction lists, a small number of macros are provided: CEND, CINIT, CMOVE, and CWAIT.

The CEND macro is used to terminate a list of Copper instructions. The macro expects a pointer to a UCopList structure.

The macro CINIT initializes a UCopList structure; the UCopList can then accept Copper instructions until a CEND macro is run. The macro requires a pointer to the UCopList and a number for the maximum number of Copper instructions that can be added to the list.

CMOVE is the macro used to add a Copper move instruction to a list. The macro expects a pointer to a UCopList, the value of the instruction, and the register that is to receive the value. The "move" concept of the CMOVE macro means "move this value into this register at this time." The real Copper instruction is the value that will be shoved into the register. The values are moved into the hardware registers when the list is executed, not when the list is built.

A CWAIT macro is used to add a timing command to the end of a UCopList. When the list is executed, the timing command (CWait) holds up instruction execution until the video beam position is optimal. The instructions that will be added after the CWait in the UCopList list are sensitive to the location of the video beam on the display. CWAIT expects a pointer to the UCopList structure, the vertical position of the video beam, and the horizontal position of the beam. Execution continues when the beam reaches the indicated position on the display.

The single Blitter resource on an Amiga must be obtained with proper etiquette, since several tasks are usually clamoring for its services at the same time. There are three routines, one of which must be used to request the services of the Blitter: OwnBlitter (for long Blitter jobs) and QBlit and QBSBlit (for short ones).

OwnBlitter is used by an application to grab the Blitter resource. The application can keep the resource until it doesn't need it any longer, at which time it must run the DisownBlitter routine. DisownBlitter is used to released the Blitter resource so that another application task can use it. An OwnBlitter call inserts an entry into the Blitter Request Queue; when the blitter queue manager encounters that entry, the application will be reawakened and OwnBlitter will return from the call. OwnBlitter queue entries are low priority requests, and are pushed back in the queue by subsequent requests made using QBlit and QSBlit.

QBlit is used to make a request for the Blitter resource. The request is in the form of a BlitNode record which is added to the end of the Blitter queue. When a queued BlitNode record is selected, the blit queue manager uses a pointer in the BlitNode record to find the application routine that is to be run. This routine can do anything with the Blitter that it wants; when it returns, the next BlitNode record in the queue can be processed. The QBlit call is normally used for shorter Blitter jobs that don't involve the screen, since QBlit doesn't pay attention to the video scan timing. Using QBlit for screen updates is allowed, but the result might be hard on the eyes; screen flicker and hash occur when the display electronics access the same section of screen RAM that someone else is changing.

The QBSBlit routine does the same thing as QBlit, but permits access to the screen RAM only when the display hardware isn't using it. QBSBlit is preferred over QBlit for Blitter operations that involve the display, even though QBSBlit is slower.

For keeping the application in sync with the Blitter Request Queue, the WaitBlit routine can be used. This routine will return only when the request queue is empty; until then the application task is "rolled out" or "ready but waiting" to execute. WaitBlit is handy for two occasions: waiting for the queue to empty so that the application can call OwnBlitter or make a number of QSBlit and QBlit calls which will then be bunched together in the queue, and waiting for the queue to empty after the application has already queued some blitter operations with QSBlit and QBlit. In the second case WaitBlit returns because the Blitter has finished that application's requests, so WaitBlit can be used for wait-until-available and wait-until-finished sync problems.

Other Pertinent Amiga Control Functions

The VBeamPos function returns which scan line the video beam is on. The value becomes out of date for one of two reasons: the beam is moving too quickly, or the Amiga multitasks and the status of the task needing the information suddenly become ready-waiting (another task is executing) and thus unable to use the data when valid.

WaitBOVP is used to tell the Amiga scheduler to awaken the task when the video beam is on the scan line coinciding with the bottom of the indicated ViewPort record.

WaitTOF is used to tell the scheduler to awaken the task when the video beam is at the top of the next video frame and all the vertical-blanking routines have executed for the current vertical-blanking interval.

ANIMATION

This description of structures, macros, functions, and behavior is intended to provide a good idea, but not a complete description, of the Amiga animation facilities. It should be clear from this outline that the Amiga graphics subsystem is nothing like that of the other machines, and that the portable portion of the source of an application will not use Amiga animation routines or even similar algorithms. A product could not make an impact commercially if it relied on animation devised on an IBM PC, for instance, and then used the same techniques on the Amiga.

The Amiga provides coprocessors for making smooth-movement animation easier to achieve. Smooth animation is not easily done on the Macintosh, IIGS, IBM, or Atari machines, since it involves loading the central processor down with repetitive, high-speed changes to the graphics display; quite a number of software techniques have been developed to do a little bit of animation; these techniques are realized inevitably in assembler. Game program developers have been excited about the Amiga primarily because it allows them to use greater resolution displays and still do a great deal of smooth-motion animation.

The Amiga is a display/list–based machine, which means that for every spot of phosphor covered by the travels of the scanning video-beam, a dedicated processor decides what to place on the screen at that location. The Amiga's Copper coprocessor follows an entire stream of orders (aka a **view**) for each video frame in 1/60th of a second (noninterlaced). Assuming that an entire view is prebuilt, all that must be done to change the contents of the video frame completely is to present the Copper a different view (via the LoadView routine). It is possible to do this for a while, even for consecutive video frames. The Copper instruction stream is built from information derived from a data tree formed by a single View record, one or more ViewPort records, and the fleet of support structures, including bitmap data.

An Amiga view is composed of a number of viewports, each a rectangular area controlled with a ViewPort record.

All the viewports that are manipulated by a single task are glued together into a linked list and attached to a View record by a pointer. The code definitions for View, ViewPort, and other records are given in the data structures section earlier in this chapter.

Amiga viewports are strange and finicky things; you can't overlap them or place them horizontally next to each other. Viewports also cannot be placed next to each other vertically; a minimum of one scan line (and sometimes more) is necessary, depending on what has to be done to flush the viewport settings from the Amiga's display registers. The gist is that you can't use viewports with impunity. You can't get rid of them either; aside from describing the area of the display in its domain, a viewport has an attribute byte that controls the absence or presence of the following useful modes:

DUALPF	The viewport raster is two independent playfields
PFBA	If DUALPF is TRUE, then the second playfield has priority over the first
HIRES	The viewport raster would have 640 pixels horizontally if the raster covered the width of the screen.
LACE	Display the raster in interlace mode
HAM	Use hold and modify mode (lots and *lots* of colors, but little else)
SPRITES	Indicates that virtual sprites or hardware sprites are being used
VP_HIDE	Indicates that this viewport is obscured

by other viewports; the view will then not have display instructions for this viewport

EXTRA_HALFBRITE   "Reserved for future use," it says in the *Amiga ROM Kernel Manual, Volume I*

There is only one View used at a time on the Amiga display, which brings up a problem when several tasks are running in the system. Without Intuition, the user-interface package, there would undoubtedly be some problems with tasks interfering with each other's attempts to write to the display. The Intuition package sets up a layer between the graphic primitives that control the View and ViewPort structures and the application tasks that want to generate graphics. If a task wants to draw on the display, it should not make direct calls to routines like InitView, etc., but should instead rely on the bookkeeping abilities of Intuition by using Intuition screens and windows. There are times when using the graphic primitive routines are inescapable (such as when drawing polygons and polylines in a layer), but the OK routines don't directly subvert the working View records and viewport list. All the tasks generating graphics have to influence changes to View and ViewPort data structures; their voluntary use of Intuition routines awards Intuition the sole responsibility for direct modification of View and ViewPort records on behalf of the tasks. An uncooperative task sticks out like a grand piano in a marching band.

Cast of Characters: Amiga Animation Things

The Amiga implements a number of different objects for supporting animation. The lowest-level objects are the aforementioned hardware (simple) sprites, of which there are only eight to be shared among all the running tasks in a system.

Moving small graphic objects is a fundamental operation for most inter-active game software (if nowhere else), and is a considerable drag on main processor resources. It is common to identify frequently used operations and reimplement them in hardware so that the main processor does not have to do the work; Amiga sprites are the results of much earlier work in this direction. A **sprite** is an entity that is specifically supported by hardware, and whose sole purpose is to display on the screen a small graphic image. Sprites can be moved quickly and smoothly; a small bouncing ball can be imple-mented as a sprite. Sprite hardware is usually on guard for sprites that "collide" on the screen, a common test in game software.

Hardware sprites are controlled by hardware sprite DMA channels. Each hardware sprite can be a maximum of 16 pixels wide, but can be as high as the entire screen. Hardware sprites can have 4 of 16 colors, 1 of which is transparent; these sprites are also colored in pairs, which means that 2 hardware sprites use the same colors. Collisions on the screen that involve hardware sprites cannot be detected.

Here is the definition of the SimpleSprite record which is used by application software to control sprites through system function calls:

```
struct SimpleSprite {          /* A sprite descriptor record. */
    UWORD *posctldata;         /* A pointer to a SpriteImage record. */
    UWORD *height;             /* The height of the sprite in scan lines. */
    UWORD x,y;                 /* The current sprite viewport coordinates. */
    UWORD num;                 /* A unique sprite instance ID number. */
}
```

The SpriteImage record is used to contain the image of the sprite. The record is pointed to by the first field in a SimpleSprite record. Here is that definition:

```
struct SpriteImage {               /* A sprite image control record. */
    UWORD posctl[2];               /* The initial and final coordinates. */
    UWORD sprdata[2][height];      /* The sprite image definition. */
    UWORD reserved[2];             /* This is not used at this writing. */
}
```

Virtual sprites are next in line. Virtual sprites can be defined in RAM and kept there until they're needed. The system automatically copies or maps the virtual (software) sprite definition into a hardware sprite and displays the pattern. Virtual sprites have a strange limitation: only eight virtual sprites can be defined to be at one Y coordinate on the screen. Otherwise it is possible to have many, many virtual sprites on-screen, as is true with hardware sprites. You can define a million zillion virtual sprites, but their presence in the display sometimes involves clever thinking and the use of common software tools like a sledgehammer or crowbar. Virtual sprites have the same color limits as hardware sprites; 4 out of 16 colors can be used at 1 time per sprite, with 1 color being transparent. For the game developers collisions involving virtual sprites are detectable.

The following is the definition for a VSprite record, which (strangely enough) is used to define either virtual sprites or blitter objects (described shortly). A blitter object record uses a VSprite record to contain the current blitter object coordinates, for example. After a brief look the name of the VSprite structure seems inappropriate, so beware.

```
struct VSprite {   /* This is used by virtual sprites or blitter object recs.*/
     struct VSprite *NextVSprite;      /* The next VSprite record pointer. */
     struct VSprite *PrevVSprite;      /* The previous VSprite rec ptr. */
     struct VSprite *DrawPath;  /* The DrawPath data array ptr. */
     struct VSprite *ClearPath; /* The ClearPath data array ptr. */
     WORD    OldY,                     /* The previous sprite Y coordinate. */
             OldX;                     /* The previous sprite X coordinate. */
     WORD    Flags;                    /* The sprite attributes. */
     WORD    Y,                        /* The current Y coordinate. */
             X;                        /* The current X coordinate. */
     WORD    Height,                   /* The height of sprite in pixels: 0-200. */
             Width,                    /* The width of sprite in pixels. */
             Depth;                    /* The blitter object: up to 5 bitplanes. */
                                       /* vsprite: field not used. */
     WORD    MeMask,                   /* A collision handling routine mask. */
             HitMask;                  /* A collision handling routine mask. */
     WORD    ImageData;                /* This points to the image data if any. */
     WORD    *BorderLIne;              /* A collision detect border data pointer. */
     WORD    *CollMask;                /* A collision mask pointer. */
     WORD    *SprColors;               /* Sprite: a pointer to a colormap table. */
     struct Bob *VSpriteBob;           /* A pointer to a VSprite record. */
     BYTE    PlacePick,                /* Blitter object: an 8 bit color mask. */
             PlaneOnOff;               /*    An access event mask. */
     VUserStuff                        /* A programmer-extensible field. */
     VUserExt;                         /* A programmer-extensible field. */
};
```

The two "programmer-extensible" fields mentioned above are intended to be redefinable with C preprocessor include files containing #defines created by an application programmer. The idea is to make the above record larger to accommodate special-purpose fields that for some reason need to be included in each record of the above type. This author thinks programming tricks of this genre are best when left unused—ignore them.

It should be noted that Amiga sprites (both kinds) don't cooperate with Intuition very well. Intuition is comfortable with RastPort records, layers, raster bitmaps, and the soon-to-be-discussed blitter objects. Sprites are controlled below the Intuition layer, and Intuition does not force sprites to harmonize with the playfield graphics. Sprites are not clipped or limited by screen or window boundaries, nor can they be obscured by screens or windows.

Another instrument is the blitter object. Sprites are designed to be used as smallish, mobile, foreground objects on a background. Blitter objects are expected to cover more display real estate (i.e., the graphics are larger) than sprites, and move more ponderously since the blitter hardware is slower than the sprite DMA channels. Blitter objects can contain 32 different colors, many more than sprites get. Blitter objects are not limited to a width of 16 pixels; they are a rectangular section of a playfield bitmap that can be moved from bitmap to bitmap as well as around on a single bitmap, so a width limitation would be a considerable nuisance. The official short nickname for blitter object is "**bob,**" but since this book is filled with the terms of several machines, bob isn't used much here except in record, macro, and function names. The blitter object record definition is as follows:

```
struct Bob {                     /* A blitter object record definition */
    WORD flags;                  /* The blitter object attribute bits. */
    WORD *SaveBuffer;            /* The bitmap image temporary stor. */
    WORD *ImageShadow;          /* The blitter object shadow mask pointer. */
    Struct Bob    *Before,       /* The animation object member */
                  *After;        /*    priority fore & back pointers. */
    struct VSprite *BobVSprite;/* A VSprite record pointer. */
    struct AnimComp *BobComp;   /* An AnimComp record pointer. */
    struct DBufPacket *DBuffer;/* The Bob double buffer pointer. */
    BUserStuff                   /* A programmer-extensible field. */
    BUserExt;                    /* A programmer-extensible field. */
}
```

As mentioned above, it is the author's opinion that it is not smart to redefine the two redefinable entries in the end of the record type definition.

The Amiga system handles displayable blitter objects and virtual sprites as members of a **graphics element list**, a doubly linked list that is often sorted in increasing Y,X order using the function SortGList. When the function DrawGList is called to render the objects on the screen, the objects in the graphics element list provided for the function must be in increasing Y,X order.

One useful property of blitter objects that sprites lack is the ability to be hierarchically grouped. An **animation component** is a group of blitter objects that can be treated as a single object. One step above is the **animation object**, a group of animation components that can also be treated as a single object. Sequenced-drawing and motion-control animation can be performed using animation objects. A brief discussion of

Amiga animation follows shortly, after the AnimOb and AnimComp
record definitions and some descriptions of the associated linked lists.

```
struct AnimComp {
    WORD    Flags,               /* Animation component behavior attributes. */
            Timer,               /* The lifetime countdown variable. */
            TimeSet;             /* The lifetime of the animation component. */
    struct AnimComp *NextComp,   /* The next component in anim. obj. */
                    *PrevComp,   /* The previous component in anim. obj. */
                    *NextSeq,    /* The next component in sequence. */
                    *PrevSeq;    /* The previous component in sequence. */
    WORD (*AnimCRoutine)();      /* A pointer to a custom animation routine. */
    WORD    YTrans,              /* The initial Y translation of anim comp. */
            XTrans;              /* The initial X translation of anim comp. */
    struct AnimOb *HeadOb;       /* This points to an associated animation
                                 /*  object record. */
    struct Bob    *AnimBob;      /* A pointer to a blitter object list. */
}


struct AnimOb {              /* The animation object record definition, in C. */
    struct AnimOb *NextOb,   /* The next animation object in anim obj. list. */
                  *PrevOb;   /* The previous animation object in the list. */
    LONG    Clock;           /* The number of animate calls in object lifetime. */
    WORD    AnOldY,          /* The old animation object Y coordinate. */
            AnOldX;          /* The old animation object X coordinate. */
    WORD    AnY,             /* The current Y coordinate of object. */
            AnX;             /* The current X coordinate of object. */
    WORD    YVel,            /* The current Y component of velocity of obj. */
            XVel;            /* The current X component of velocity of obj. */
    WORD    YAccel,          /* The current Y component of acceleration. */
            XAccel;          /* The current X component of acceleration. */
    WORD    RingYTrans,      /* The reference position increment for Y. */
            RingXTrans;      /* The reference position increment for X. */
    WORD (*AnimORoutine)();  /* A custom animation routine pointer. */
    struct AnimComp *HeadComp; /* A pointer to the first AnimComp record. */
    AUserStuff               /* A programmer-definable entry. */
    AUserExt;                /* A programmer-definable entry. */
    }
}
```

A **blitter object list** itemizes all the blitter objects that comprise one animation object. Blitter objects are in the list in order of drawing priority; the highest-priority blitter object is the one on top of the others in the display. An **animation object list** is a list of active animation objects.

There are two types of **animation component lists**: The first is a list of animation component members, and the second describes the animation component drawing order.

There are two types of animation: sprite and playfield animation. **Playfield animation** involves blitter objects; **sprite animation** is done with hardware and virtual sprites.

Sprite animation is simple; move the sprites around in front of a playfield background, treating each sprite as an individual object.

Blitter object animation can be more complicated, thanks to the ability to group blitter objects (and to group groups of blitter objects). **Single blitter object animation** is merely nudging individual blitter objects around the display; each blitter object has a video priority to indicate which objects should be in front of other objects.

Multiple blitter object animation is more interesting. Groups of objects can have a velocity and an acceleration. Individual members of a group may also have individual velocities and accelerations relative to the group. For example, it is easy to have a group of two objects, a hand and a car window, moving from left to right on the screen, with the hand waving good-bye (by moving up and down); this is an example of motion control animation. The other kind of animation done with multiple blitter objects, sequenced drawing animation, is achieved by defining a number of discrete animation object positions that will, in turn and for a specified period of time, appear on the display. The animation object (AnimOb) record type is used to define the order and the positions.

The changes are not entirely automatic; the application task posting the animations must repetitively call the Animate routine to post the next contribution of graphics to the viewport list. The animation facilities are designed so that it is possible to program animation sequences ahead of time and have the Amiga animation system follow orders without undue intervention by the application program (unless a stimulus appears to force a different animation sequence before the completion of the posted material).

The GelsInfo (Graphics Element Information) record is defined as follows:

```
struct GelsInfo {         /* The Amiga graphic element information record. */
    BYTE          sprRsvd;   /* The availability of the hardware sprite. */
```

```
        UBYTE         Flags;            /* System flag bits. */
                                        /* The first and last records are empty, */
                                        /*  but there can be valid VSprite records */
                                        /*  between:*/
        struct VSprite *gelHead,        /* A pointer to a first VSprite rec (dummy).*/
                      *gelTail;         /* A ptr. to the last VSprite rec (dummy).*/
        WORD          *nextLine;        /* system use only: sprite line def */
        WORD          *lastColor;       /* system use only: sprite colr def */
        struct collTable *collHandler;  /* A ptr to a collision table. */
        SHORT         Leftmost,         /* The clipping rectangle boundary. */
                      rightmost,        /* The clipping rectangle boundary. */
                      topmost,          /* The clipping rectangle boundary. */
                      bottommost;       /* The clipping rectangle boundary. */
        APTR          firstBlissObject, /* An AnimOb record pointer. */
                      lastBlissObject;  /* An AnimOb record pointer. */
};
```

The DBufPacket record is used to keep track of double buffer RAM areas.

```
struct DBufPacket {             /* A double buffer pointer record. */
        WORD          BufX,     /* The last onscreen X coordinate. */
                      BufY;     /* The last onscreen Y coordinate. */
        struct VSprite *BufPath; /* A pointer to the drawing order control. */
        WORD          *BufBuffer; /* A pointer to a double RAM buffer area. */
}
```

Amiga Animation Graphics Routines

AddAnimOb is used to add an animation object to an animation object list. The routine requires a record of type AnimOb, a pointer to the last animation object (AnimOb) record in the list, and a pointer to the current RastPort.

The AddBob routine adds a specified blitter object to the current graphics element list. It needs a pointer to the blitter object record and a pointer to the current RastPort.

AddVSprite adds a virtual sprite (a VSprite record) to the current graphics element list. It needs a pointer to the virtual sprite record and a pointer to the current RastPort.

Animate updates the current position and velocity of each element in the current animation object list, and calls a custom animation routine if one is indicated by the animation object record. Animate doesn't draw the objects, it just nudges them around. When Animate is done chances are very good that the animation objects are out of increasing Y,X order, so a call to SortGList is in order before the list is drawn.

ChangeSprite is used to change the image of a hardware sprite. The routine requires a pointer to the current ViewPort that the hardware sprite is associated with, a pointer to a SimpleSprite record, and a pointer to a SpriteImage record. The SpriteImage record must be in the first 512K of RAM.

The **Collision Table** (CollTable) is a 16-entry table of pointers to routines. The collision routines are called when a collision is detected between movable animation objects like graphics elements and playfields. A collision occurs when the boundary of a graphics element overlaps that of a playfield or another graphics element.

The SetCollision routine is provided to assign collision routines to the individual entries of the CollTable. SetCollision needs an integer value ranging from 0 to 15 to indicate which entry in the CollTable is to be changed, a pointer to the routine to be added to the collision table, and a pointer to an appropriate graphic element information (GelsInfo) record.

The SetCollision routine has a partner, DoCollision, which is used to scan the entire current graphics element list for overlapping graphics elements or playfields. When a collision is detected, DoCollision doesn't return a TRUE or an integer value, but instead calls the appropriate collision-handling routine using the CollTable entries.

SortGList is used to sort the members of the current graphics element list into increasing Y,X order. This routine is required by the Amiga hardware, which can handle the graphics in an ordered list but not when they are out of order. It is difficult and expensive to have the electron beam scan the horizontal lines of a screen out of order. It is even more difficult to do part of a single horizontal line and then start another line, intending to come back and finish the first line later. The Amiga is designed around the premise that the video beam traverses the real estate of the screen in a simple, orderly, and involuntary fashion. If an entity is out of order in the list when DrawGList is called, the Amiga has to wait until the video beam returns to the right location before drawing that element. Drawing the rest of the data in the frame is delayed, and the effect is obvious and uncomfortable to watch. SortGList needs a pointer to the current RastPort as a parameter.

The InitAnimate macro is used to initialize the animation object list. This is a simple job, done by defining a pointer to the first animation object record in the animation object list. An initialization routine called InitGels is provided to initialize a graphics element list. InitGels needs pointers to two dummy virtual sprite records that are to be used as the head and tail of the list. InitGels also needs a pointer to the new graphics elements info (GelsInfo) record that will be set up.

DrawGList draws the contents of the current graphics element list. It needs a pointer to the appropriate RastPort and a pointer to the involved ViewPort. Blitter objects are included in the current raster bitmap, and virtual sprites are included in a Copper list.

GetGBuffers is used to allocate memory for buffers for an animation object. It requires three parameters: a pointer to an animation object (AnimOb) record, a pointer to the appropriate RastPort, and a boolean value where TRUE indicates that double buffering is to be used and FALSE that it isn't. The routine returns TRUE if the operation was successful. Calling FreeGBuffers with the same parameters will deallocate those buffers.

The routine GetSprite is called with two parameters, a pointer to a SimpleSprite record and an integer value that can range from 0 to 7. GetSprite tries to assign the indicated hardware sprite to an image, and if successful that sprite then belongs to the task executing the GetSprite routine. GetSprite returns a boolean value indicating the success of the attempt; since hardware sprites have limited access, success is certainly not guaranteed under every circumstance.

FreeSprite is the routine used to release a hardware sprite (all tasks have to share the limited number of hardware sprites), making it available to other tasks. The only parameter FreeSprite needs is the sprite number, an integer from 0 to 7.

To move a hardware sprite in a viewport display, the Amiga provides the MoveSprite routine. The parameters are a pointer to the ViewPort; a pointer to the SimpleSprite record; the new X coordinate (in pixels); and the new Y coordinate. The X and Y coordinates are relative to the top left of the viewport bitmap.

To eliminate a virtual sprite record from the current graphics element list, RemVSprite only needs a pointer to the VSprite record; it will remove the VSprite record and close the ranks in the list.

Each animation object component has two masks, the borderline mask and the collision mask, that have to be initialized before collisions can be detected properly. The routine InitMasks is used to initialize the masks for a virtual sprite, and the InitGMasks routine is used for an animation object. InitGMasks actually calls InitMasks once for each component in the indicated animation object. InitMasks needs a pointer to a virtual sprite (VSprite) record, and InitGMasks needs a pointer to an AnimOb record.

The RemBob macro is for yanking blitter object records from both the current graphics element list and the raster bitmap. The removal does not become visually effective until the next call to the DrawGList. It takes two calls to DrawGList to remove all the remains of a double-buffered blitter object. RemBob needs a pointer to the blitter object record and a pointer to the involved RastPort.

The RemIBob routine is harder than the RemBob macro: its effect, visually and internally, is *immediate*. RemIBob needs three parameters: (1) a pointer to the blitter object record to be removed from the list and raster bitmap, (2) a pointer to the appropriate RastPort record, (3) and a pointer to a ViewPort record.

3.5 Windows and their Managers

A **window manager** is used to create, remove, or adjust windows on the display. Using information that is provided by the window manager, an application can correctly draw on a display using the graphics library.

Digital Research's Gem, Microsoft Windows, Commodore's Amiga, and Apple's IIGS and Macintosh promote articulate window control by providing an option-filled smorgasbord of callable routines. The window manager services conducted by each package are similar enough to each other until you get close enough to see the programming details. Very few of each system's equivalent routines have the same name or use the same parameters, and the window data structures show slight similarities only because they are used for similar purposes.

DISTINCTIONS

The Macintosh permits building custom program features, such as unusual or new kinds of windows, and still allows use of the higher levels of support. Gem's window support doesn't let you add frame controls or define odd-shaped windows without rewriting a lot of code. Windows' tiled windows aren't something that can be fiddled with, but the child windows provide the extensibility that the Mac enjoys. The IIGS tries to emulate the Macintosh window manager while working with color, a lower vertical resolution, and a switchable horizontal resolution. The Amiga's fancy display hardware can handle demanding requirements; Intuition, the entire user-interface package, is an easy medium for defining custom controls (aka Amiga Gadgets) for juggling windows and data.

Gem is written to be moved around; it is the only package in the bunch to have been ported to a number of different machines, not just to the IBM PC and the Atari ST. Gem has the simplest window support of the packages discussed here, probably because of this original design objective.

VOCABULARY

Here is an introduction to many of the terms used to describe the components and features of the window managers. Some of the terms, like "screen," are used differently.

Macintosh

The Macintosh windows that are created by and belong to application programs are **application windows**. Windows that belong to desk accessories are called **system windows**. The bulwark Macintosh window type is a **document window**. The frame of a document window may have a close or "go-away" box, a title bar, scroll bars, and a size box. The scroll bar is an example of a control; controls are, incidentally, the domain of the Macintosh Control Manager.

Macintosh applications regularly have one active window on the Mac display. The active window has a highlighted title bar; the inactive windows don't.

Every Macintosh window has a **content region**, which is controlled by the application, and a **structure region**, which is the window frame and the content region put together. There are a number of optional regions, such as the go-away region, the drag region, and the grow region. These are used to help determine how the application should react if a mouse button event occurs when the cursor is over one of the regions.

The inherent difference between a primary Macintosh application and a desk accessory is supposed to be that an application gets the entire screen (allowing the application module to be huge), whereas a desk accessory normally requires one window, needs no menu bar, and is a resource that has to be added to the system file (see Fig. 3–50). A combination of circumstances has prompted the creation of some very elaborate desk accessory programs, but not many.

Microsoft

The Windows display has a work area for windows and an icon area for iconic windows. Iconic windows are those that can be closed, removed from the work area, and replaced by an icon in the icon area. Dragging the icon back into the work area swaps a displayed window with the window belonging to the icon. Double-clicking the icon will shove the window back into the work area (making room) and remove the icon from the icon area.

There are three main styles of windows: tiled, popup, and child (see Fig. 3–51). A window class has to be registered with Windows during runtime; a registered window class can then be used when creating one or more windows, each with the abilities and properties of that class.

The manipulative devices within the frame of a window are **controls**. The part of the window that can be pointed at with the mouse cursor and used to move the window around is the **caption bar**. There is a **size box** for adjusting the size of a window. The area inside a window that is controlled by the application is called the **client area**. Drawing in the client area is

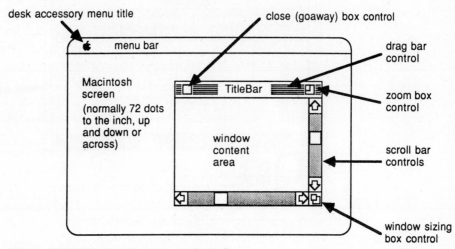

Figure 3–50 Macintosh screen and window

called **painting**, though text is drawn. **Destroying** a window means removing the window data structures from memory.

Gem

The part of Gem that most directly deals with the windows is the AES, or Application Environment Services. The binding routines that deal with windows have names that begin with the prefix wind_, although this may actually vary from language system to language system because the binding routines must be implemented by the language system authors and not necessarily by Digital Research.

A Gem window (shown in Fig. 3–52) is composed of a work area and a border area. The border area may contain a number of components, such as the title bar, a close box, a size box, an information line, and a full box. There may be vertical and horizontal scroll bars, with arrows and sliders. Gem has only one kind of window, and several windows may

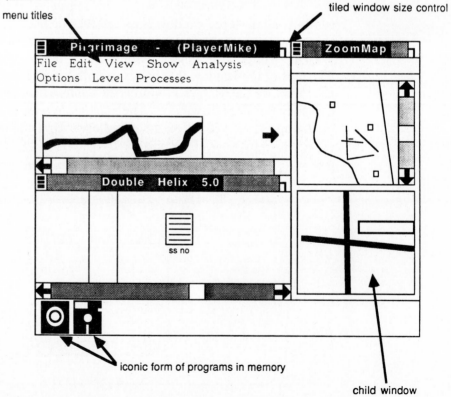

Figure 3–51 MS Windows display with three tiled windows present

overlap. Changing the work area of a window is called **updating**. Closing a window hides it, but deleting a window destroys it.

IIGS

The window terminology of the IIGS is essentially identical to that of the Macintosh. The big difference graphically is that IIGS windows look more like Gem windows than Macintosh windows. The IIGS supports color, and the scroll bar thumb is now a rectangle that changes size depending on the scrolling range and the domain of the screen axis with respect to the scrolling range (like Gem).

Amiga

The user-interface package for the Amiga is called Intuition. An Amiga Intuition screen is a backdrop for windows. Screens can vary in display modes, depth, and display position. It is important that a distinction be made between a physical display and an Intuition screen: several Intuition screens can coexist on the display.

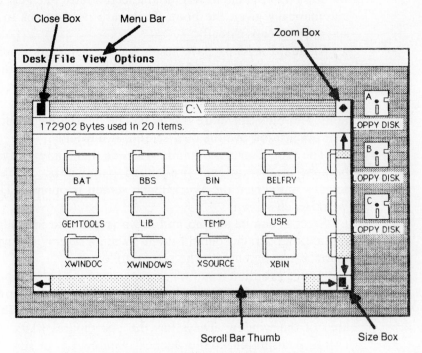

Figure 3–52 Example Gem window on a display

There are two horizontal display modes: low and high resolution. Low resolution is 320 pixels across, and high resolution is 640 pixels across. There are two vertical display modes: interlace and noninterlace. Interlace mode supports 400 lines vertically, and noninterlace supports 200 lines.

The sprite mode allows up to 8 movable physical sprites, each with 4 colors, 16 pixels horizontally, and any number of lines vertically. The Amiga supports any number of virtual sprites (with restrictions), using the eight physical ones. Intuition support for sprites of any kind is insubstantial.

Dual-playfield mode provides two independent display memories.

Hold-and-modify mode provides additional color capabilities.

Screen depth alludes to the number of bit planes that are used to describe the color of pixels within the screen area of the display. Normally a screen can be allocated up to 5 bit planes, and can show up to 32 different colors. Underneath the bit planes are color registers, which can be used to instantly adjust the actual displayed color across a screen.

There are standard screens and custom screens. A standard screen is automatically created in RAM and opened only when a window that uses one is opened with the OpenWindow routine. Likewise, when all the windows that belong to a standard screen have been closed, the screen is automatically given the boot. There are *no* routines to open and close standard screens directly.

Standard screens have predefined parameters, such as colors and display modes, that should not be modified by applications. The reason is that if an application doesn't have to define them, it doesn't have to assume that its screen is incompatible with the screens of other applications, and thus can share a screen. The alternative, to have each concurrent application own its own screen, is unwieldy.

The WorkBench is a standard screen that many utility applications use because of the rational predefined parameters. Also, when all other screens are closed the WorkBench screen is opened. There is only one WorkBench screen.

Screens can be slid up and down (much like Macintosh windows) to reveal other screens behind them. When a screen is moved, the windows that are associated with the screen follow it.

Amiga Intuition windows use a screen for a backdrop. There are a few different types of windows: **Borderless**, which is a window drawn without a border; **Gimmezerozero**, where the top left corner of the free-drawing area of the window always has the coordinates (0,0); **Backdrop**, which always is displayed as the deepest window on an Intuition screen; and **SuperBitMap**, which is used to show a part of a possibly very large bitmap.

The outer plane of a window contains the window title, **gadgets** (aka controls on other machines), and the window border. The inner plane or inner window is where graphics and text can be placed.

WINDOWS AND MULTITASKING

The presence of concurrently executing programs is a significant criterion, and an unforgiving one, for designing a windowing package. Much of the difference in the construction of event loops and other I/O code is attributable to multitasking, and the same is true for the design of the window managers.

The 68000-based Macintosh systems can normally run one single application task at a time, but several application programs can at least be coresident in memory, and a good number of desk accessories can be on-screen at one time. Some existing Macintosh software behaves as if the machine provides a form of multitasking. At this time a solution general enough to allow any two arbitrary main applications to run concurrently has not been released. The window manager can handle concurrently modified windows with help from additional code. The Macintosh can handle the same respectable number of windows that Windows and Amiga are designed to handle, though as in Windows and the Amiga, many aren't visible.

Gem supports a limited form of multitasking and is written to capitalize on the tasking prowess of the native operating system. Examples are Concurrent DOS by DRI and multitasking releases of MS-DOS (versions 5.0 and up). I expect Gem to work amicably with the multitasking operating system that Atari provides for the ST. Since Gem's window management currently drives windows only, and does not include virtual screens (like Switcher), Intuition screens, or Windows iconic and tiled windows, there is plenty of room for whatever graphical expansion is needed to properly handle concurrent tasks.

Windows supports multitasking among Windows-compatible applications. Each running application may own a window on the display. When convenient, the tiled window can be turned into a small icon at the bottom of the display, which can be reexpanded into a window at any time. This is an **iconic** window.

The IIGS is like the Macintosh in that it supports a single main task, but it does so with a slower CPU. I think it is unlikely that any kind of successful multitasking additions to the IIGS operating system will be made, though nongeneral solutions (like a Modula 2 system support for concurrency) should be expected.

The Amiga supports a multitasking environment, but addresses the partitioning of the display in a way much different from the way MS Windows does.

SCREENS VERSUS TILED WINDOWS

Using a windowing package alleviates the need for an application to know about many of the system-dependent details regarding the physical display. An application can generate all its output inside one or more windows, the exact sizes and placements of which can be system-dependent without requiring changes to any program code. Mac, Windows, and Gem are not the same when it comes to mapping windows to the display; portable code that uses two or three of these windowing systems will have to be written with respectful attention to this aspect.

Macintosh

It was initially decided that the 1984 Macintosh display, being only 512-by-342 dots on a 9-inch diagonal black-and-white tube, did not have enough screen real estate to support handling more than one principal application program at a time. Desk accessory programs were not intended to be very large or elaborate, and certainly would not clutter the display with many windows of any kind. For this and a number of other reasons, multitasking on the Mac was not immediately implemented.

The Mac screen is the property of one major application program at a time, with parts of the screen occasionally borrowed by desk accessories. With Andy Hertzfeld's Switcher, you can leap from one program to another in a matter of moments. To permit coresident but not concurrent applications, the Switcher program follows the guideline by showing the screen of one application program at a time. Andy's Servant program, intended to be a second-generation Finder/Switcher/resource editor facility, has not currently been officially released, but is available for testing purposes. Another program, Juggler, is an ambitious attempt to provide nonpreemptive multitasking.

Not only was using virtual Mac screens a relatively painless thing for Andy to do (since the menu bar on the Macintosh customarily appears at the top of the screen and outside any windows), it is also a sensible arrangement. Digital Research is among the companies that may have supplied the precedent for such a design, as DRI's Concurrent DOS supports a number of virtual screen-sized terminals per physical Concurrent DOS console; switching between the virtual screens is a matter of pressing some relatively unused key combinations.

Gem

Gem is designed to work with a wide range of physical display characteristics, such as from 320 by 200 pixels to 1024 by 800 pixels. Gem supports a varying number of colors per pixel, and can deal with strange nonlinear memory maps, such as the IBM CGA display card.

A Gem application owns the screen, and the application's menu bar appears at the top, with windows appearing below.

Unlike the current version of Windows, Gem VDI and AES do not contain software to drive concurrent tasks. Multitasking is left to the lower echelons of the operating system. Gem AES provides an event and message passing system that efficiently supports a concurrent environment. Application code will likely not have to be changed when moved to a multitasking version of an already existing single task operating system.

Microsoft

Windows directly supports the concurrent execution of applications. Windows also differs from Gem and Mac in that a Windows application does not automatically get the entire screen; when an application that uses Windows starts up, it can open one or more tiled windows.

The tiled windows of Windows act graphically as screens. Tiled windows are designed so that they cannot overlap each other; when one tiled window gets bigger, the other tiled windows shrink out of the way. Each tiled window has a title bar, and underneath it is normally a private menu bar.

Child windows are another kind of Windows window. These are completely contained within the client, or drawable, area of the application's tiled window. Child windows can overlap each other, but they are drawn as though they either fall behind the tiled window or are scaled by the relative size of the tiled window. The size of a screen cannot be changed, but changing the size of a tiled window (up to screen size) is no problem. A parent window is any kind of window that owns a child window.

While talking about different kinds of Windows windows, it is a good idea to mention that the third kind of window is the **popup**, which is designed to convey information of immediate importance and, when present on the screen, appear in front of the plane of the tiled windows. Popup windows are not subject to being contained by tiled windows, and in fact are preemptive, usually demanding user-interaction via a mouse click before permitting access to the tiled windows again. The MS popup window is similar to the Macintosh dialog and alert windows and the Gem dialog box. The IBM Presentation Manager, based on Windows, will not use tiled windows as a standard, but will use popup windows as Mac-like overlapping windows.

The MS tiling windows are unique in that an application's displayed main window can be swapped for its icon, allowing another application to have more of the display space. When the application has a tiled window, for example on the display, the tiled window can be removed and replaced by its corresponding icon at the bottom of the display in the icon area. Selecting the icon causes the icon to vanish and the tiled window to reappear in the window area.

A Mac application is normally invoked by double-clicking the mouse button when the cursor is over a program or data file icon. In Windows the only invokable form is an entry in an uppercase character-only directory listing.

Amiga

Amiga Intuition supports assigning overlapping windows to an Intuition screen. An Amiga screen is the functional equivalent of a Windows tiled window, although there are significant differences in how the problem was approached. Several display-size Intuition screens can be active at once; where tiled windows jockey for display space, Intuition screens overlap, and where tiled windows change size, Intuition screens don't change size at all. When an Intuition screen is slid downward, it is sliding off the visible part of the display.

IIGS

At this writing the IIGS does not have the equivalent of the Switcher or Servant programs for the Macintosh.

WINDOW MANAGEMENT INITIALIZATION

Initialization is done to reserve regions of memory, set up pointers, configure the display, and bring from disk into RAM the necessary system facilities. Two of the windowing packages (Mac and IIGS) need the application software to initiate all the environment-initialization work, and the others expect less.

Macintosh

The Macintosh initialization routines must be called first, and need be run only once. The Mac's window manager initialization routine is InitWindows. InitWindows draws a desktop and creates a window manager port. The window manager port is used as a reference for drawing window frames for new windows, since the window manager port describes the entire screen available to the application.

The Macintosh event manager relies on the window manager data structures being set up properly.

Microsoft

The first routine executed in a Windows application and written by the application developer must be called WinMain. WinMain governs the setup and the event handling loop of the application. The normal initialization duties involve calls to the routines RegisterClass, CreateWindow, and ShowWindow. There is no visible Windows equivalent to Mac's InitWindow routine, since the Windows environment is initialized not by an application, but by itself.

Gem

There are no initialization routines specifically for the Gem window manager, but the binding routine appl_init must be called before an application does anything else with Gem. The binding routine merely calls the application library initialization function within the Gem AES runtime package, as follows:

```
function appl_init: integer; { returns the application program ID }
```

The return value is the application program ID number used to tell Gem who is generating a request when the time comes; this is useful information when several tasks are running.

IIGS

WindBootInit is called at boot-time by the system; application code should not have to worry about it. WindStartup is called InitWindows on the Mac, but the parameter list was changed for the IIGS; the application should call WindStartup once to initialize the window manager. WindShutDown can be called to free RAM space allocated to the window manager. WNewRes is called after changing the screen resolution, forcing a redrawing of the screen contents in the new resolution. WindReset is used to reset the window manager.

Amiga

Intuition provides its own display initialization software, so applications don't have to set up the screen as on the Macintosh and the IIGS. It may be useful or necessary for an application to create its own screen with OpenScreen, over which it will eventually open one or more windows.

WINDOW TYPE REGISTRATION AND CREATION

Macintosh

The Macintosh has two window creation routines, NewWindow and GetNewWindow.

There are two ways to build a Macintosh window. The first method, a programming solution, is to specify the information with arguments to the window manager function, called NewWindow, and then show the window with ShowWindow. NewWindow expects a small flock of parameters that describe all of the properties of the new window.

The second method involves using a resource editor to create a window template resource. The window definition ID number indicates the resource ID of the associated window template. Calling GetNewWindow with the ID number makes the Mac track down the template resource and return a valid pointer to it (now in RAM); calling ShowWindow will make the window appear. Since placement and size are more easily

adjusted graphically and interactively than by tweaking numbers in parameter lists, interactive resource editors like ResEdit make the creation
of numerous window templates and other graphic objects viable. Once
created, the window template resource can be used to define more than
one window instance.

Microsoft

Microsoft's RegisterClass routine has no exact equivalent routine on the
Macintosh. The acts of defining window templates and formulating the
values for Apple's NewWindow are as close as Apple gets.

Microsoft's CreateWindow routine corresponds with Mac's GetNew-
Window function. Both assume that some effort has been made to
establish the identity of a window type, and both create a data record in
memory to describe the antics of a particular window (called an "instance"
of a window).

Gem

The Gem wind_create function is used to establish the kind of window
and provide the important graphic starting-point information: the X,Y
coordinate of one of the window corners and the absolute maximum width
and height of the window. The wind_open routine is used to display the
window; the X,Y coordinate and the initial dimensions of the window are
provided.

The Gem routine wind_get is used to get from Gem information
regarding a given window, such as the coordinates of the work area, the
relative positions of the scroll bar sliders, and the handle of the window
that is on top. This is commonly used, for example, to get the coordinates
for the Gem desktop window. The desktop is the backdrop area, the part
of the physical display available to an application; the coordinates of the
desktop should be a factor in determining where to put an application's
windows on the display

Amiga

To create a window, one only has to call OpenWindow with a pointer to
a filled-in NewWindow record. A description of the NewWindow record
appears in the section on window management data structures.

To create a custom screen, the OpenScreen routine is handed a pointer to a NewScreen record; see the data structure section for the record definitions.

Standard screens cannot be explicitly opened or created with a screen open routine. When a standard Intuition screen is needed, the NewWindow record that is used to create a window has a field, Type, that indicates the type of screen wanted. If the Type field shows that the WorkBench screen is wanted, then the window winds up on the WorkBench screen. If a custom screen is wanted, then the window is associated with the indicated (already created) custom screen. If a standard screen is not already in RAM, one will automatically be created.

IIGS

NewWindow is called to create a new window. A IIGS version of Mac's GetNewWindow does not currently exist, since the IIGS does not support resources. The parameters are different from those of the Macintosh version of NewWindow. Additional routines are supplied to adjust the color of the window's frame components.

PREDEFINED WINDOW TYPES

The predefined window definition types are those that are directly supported by an environment and require the least amount of effort to use. They are listed later in this section.

The whole idea behind a window manager is to permit applications to subdivide a physical display with dynamic partitions so that users can adjust things to their liking. Major partitions, like screens and tiled windows, are used to permit coexisting RAM-resident applications and concurrent tasks. Minor partitions, like document windows, are used to encapsulate similar objects and help identify the control and edit operations that can operate on them. Different document windows do not have to contain dissimilar objects, but they normally do. Special windows, like dialogs, are used to contain controls and editable text fields which are used for setting up commands and methods of operation. Alerts are for warnings of varied significance.

Macintosh and IIGS

The kinds of windows available on the Mac and the IIGS are disarmingly simply compared with those available on Windows, provided one is restricted to the predefined window types. The common way to pick the type of window is by mentioning the appropriate window definition ID when the window is created. Here are the predefined window definition IDs, and the kinds of windows they represent:

documentProc	A standard document window with optional size box, goaway box, title bar, drag bar, and zoom box
dBoxProc	An alert or modal dialog box
plainDBox	A plain box
altDBoxProc	A plain box with a shadow
noGrowDocProc	A document window without a size box
rDocProc	A window with rounded corners (the curvature of the round portions of the border is selectable)

The documentProc window has a size box so that it can be resized, and a goaway box option. The noGrowDocProc has no size box, but does have a goaway box option. The rDocProc has a goaway box option. The other windows are devoid of frame controls. Whether the goaway box is present for a particular window is defined by a flag in the WindowRecord of a window, a data structure that is defined later in this chapter.

The IIGS has about the same variety of windows as the Mac, for compatibility's sake. There is an information bar option that is extra, and a window can have a private menu bar within the window frame (used to handle more options with the lower-resolution display of the IIGS).

Window Frame Controls

Window frame controls on the Mac are handled in a way *much* different from the way they are handled in the IIGS. The IIGS solution makes more sense, and is discussed in detail in the section on window creation. The global effect of this difference is that the window creation code has a minor difference and the window record on the IIGS is different from that on Mac, which can be a major problem depending on how applications play with that record. There is an entire chapter on controls in Part 3 of this book.

Rolling Your Own Window Types

Beyond the predefined window definitions are the roll-your-owns. You must provide a custom window definition function to drive them. A window definition function is the code that does the hard work behind the presence of a Macintosh window; there is already code to handle each kind of window listed above. A window definition function (the name is misleading, as this function may actually be a number of routines) must be prepared to handle the following explicit operations on the Macintosh:

wDraw	Draw the window frame
wHit	Tell which region of the window the cursor was in when the mouse button was pressed
wCalcRgns	Calculate Mac's strucRgn and contRgn
wNew	An escape valve for accommodating extra initialization requirements
wDispose	An escape valve for accommodating extra disposal needs
wGrow	Draw the grow image
wDrawGIcon	Draw the size box in the content region

This list is expanded a bit on the IIGS and the names of the constants are probably a little different, but I currently don't have adequate documentation to itemize these differences. It is safe to say that the window definition function code can be considered to be system-dependent; I expect IIGS versions to be considerably different from Mac versions, and certainly machines of other makes have no close equivalent.

Gem

Here is a list of the window and window-like objects that Gem directly supports at this writing:

window	With all frame controls optional: close box, full box, title bar, up arrow, scroll bar, etc.
form	Controls and editable text fields within a Gem window
dialog box	Controls and editable text fields in a foreground box
alert box	Simple dialog box with contents defined by one

function call (form_alert); has text field, alert icon, and one to three button controls

error box   Used to report disk-operating system errors; the text string is generated by the form library

The attribute list for Gem windows is very short, since there is no provision for implementing custom windows and still being able to use Gem AES function calls to interact with them. Nor are there different major classes of windows, such as the Tiled and Child windows in Microsoft's product. The options are simply the window frame controls that are present. Here is the list; each option owns a bit in a 16-bit word:

NAME   The title bar is present.

CLOSE   The close box is present.

FULL   The full box is present.

MOVE   User can move the window.

INFO   The information line is present.

SIZE   The size box is present.

UPARROW   The up arrow is present.

DNARROW   The down arrow is present.

VSLIDE   The vertical slider is present.

LFARROW   The left arrow is present.

RTARROW   The right arrow is present.

HSLIDE   The horizontal slider is present.

Custom windowing has been done on the Atari ST with good success, so the fact that Gem doesn't support it should not eliminate the option, but it appears to be a more involved effort than that required for the Mac or Windows.

MS Windows

These are the major players in the Windows solution:

tiled   Used as the "screen" for an application; used like the Amiga Intuition screen to control or restrict an application's use of the physical display; tiled windows don't overlap each other

child   Used to subdivide the drawable area of tiled windows; child windows can overlap

popup   Foreground windows used as dialog and alert boxes, and to contain menu items

Tiled windows are similar in intent to Amiga Intuition screens, but are certainly not the same in how they are operated.

Child windows are nestable and overlappable; they provide a more generalized approach to window manipulation than Macintosh windows. The MS Windows examples that I have seen so far usually use child windows to subdivide the application's tiled window without giving the user the ability to move them around (so the child windows can't be made to overlap).

How Styles are Defined

There are a number of properties that can be assigned to a new Windows window class. The usual window frame controls are provided: the close window box, scroll boxes, bars, and arrows, and size box. Other attributes include generic window styles: tiled, popup, and child. An unusual frame option, the system menu, is available.

Here is a list of Microsoft Windows styles attributes:

WS_TILED   A tiled window: usually each task has one

WS_POPUP   This is a popup window used for pull-down menus and dialog boxes

WS_CHILD   Child windows subdivide tiled windows and other child windows

WS_ICONIC   Iconit tiled windows can be swapped off the display and replaced by an icon

WS_VISIBLE   An initially visible window

WS_DISABLED   An initially disabled window

WS_CLIPSIBLINGS   Exclude child and popup windows from this window's clipping region

WS_CLIPCHILDREN   Exclude child windows from this window's clipping region

WS_BORDER	This window has a border
WS_CAPTION	This window owns a caption bar
WS_DLGFRAME	This window has a double border (this attribute must not be used with caption)
WS_VSCROLL	This window has a vertical scroll bar
WS_HSCROLL	This window has a horizontal scroll bar
WS_SIZEBOX	A sizing control box on the top right of the window frame will be present
WS_SYSMENU	A system menu will be present

Class Styles

CS_VREDRAW	The window will be redrawn if the vertical size of the window has been changed
CS_HREDRAW	The window will be redrawn if the horizontal size of the window has been changed
CS_KEYCVTWINDOW	Makes space at the bottom for a window for key conversions
CS_DBLCLKS	Sends double-click messages to window
CS_OEMCHARS	OEM character translation
CS_OWNDC	Window gets private display context
CS_CLASSDC	Window class get display context; all windows of that class must share the DC
CS_MENUPOPUP	Custom menu popup window; usually associated with a menu bar
CS_NOKEYCVT	(Not documented)

Composite Style Definitions

WS_TILEDWINDOW	Standard tiled window with a caption, a system menu, and a size box

WS_POPUPWINDOW	Standard popup window with a border and a system menu
WS_CHILDWINDOW	The standard child window has no additional standard style attributes

Of the three generic window types (tiled, popup, and child), the tiled window is usually the boss. In Windows version 1.03 and earlier, the popup and child windows are associated with a task that owns a tiled window. The child windows may overlap each other, but tiled windows don't. Child windows are used to subdivide the client region (the drawing area) of a tiled window or other child windows into areas where different kinds of data may be presented. The three window types are not handled the same way, but fortunately most of the differences are processed by Windows and not by the application program. Later versions of Windows are rumored to drop tiled windows, replacing them with the more Mac-like overlapping popup/child windows.

Amiga

The major objects supported by the Intuition window manager are:

screen	Contains Intuition windows and graphics; used to describe the environment for those windows; controls the pixel resolution, the presence of interlace, the number of available colors, the presence of sprites, and the number of play-fields; screens can have gadgets
borderless	A window without default borders
Gimmezerozero	The top left of the drawable area of the window is always the local coordinates (0,0)
backdrop	The background window; this window is always positioned just before the screen in priority, and is not affected by its or any one else's screen priority system gadget
superbitmap	These have an off-screen bitmap; a subset is (usually) displayed with the superbitmap window

Amiga System Gadgets

Amiga Intuition window controls, or gadgets, are "sky's the limit" instruments. There are a small number of predefined system gadgets, which are listed below. It is possible to define one's own gadgets and associate them with a window. The system gadgets are:

sizing	For adjusting the window size and shape
depth arrangement	For easily adjusting the display order of windows and screens
drag	Occupies the window title bar if present, and enables you to move a window
close	Generates an event message indicating that the user wants to close the window

This list is provided here as a handy comparison of windows and screens. There is an entire chapter on controls and gadgets in Part 3.

VISIBLE DATA STRUCTURES

Here are the literal type declarations of the significant data structures used by each system. They aren't the same, but they secretly sing in four-part harmony when nobody is looking.

Microsoft

```
{ Microsoft Windows Window Class Descriptor }
type WNDCLASS = record
          style:          WORD;       {An attributes word.}
          lpfnWndProc:    FARPROC;    {The window procedure.}
          cbClsExtra:     int;        {The extra class bytes.}
          cbWndExtra:     int;        {The extra instance bytes.}
          hInstance:      HANDLE;     {The class module.}
          hIcon_:         HICON;      {The class icon.}
          hCursor_:       HCURSOR;    {The class cursor.}
          hbrBackground:  HBRUSH;     {The class background brush.}
```

```
            lpszMenuName:        LPSTR;        {The class menu.}
            lpszClassName:       LPSTR;        {The name of the window class.}
      END;
      PWNDCLASS =   ADR OF WNDCLASS;           {The short pointer definition.}
      LPWNDCLASS = ADS OF WNDCLASS;            {The long pointer definition.}
```

To create a window, the contents of a Windows WNDCLASS type record have to be defined by the application code. A WNDCLASS record contains a number of seemingly dissociated facts about a kind of window, such as whether the client area of a window is to be redrawn whenever the size or shape of the window is changed. Other specifiable tidbits include the identity of the icon associated with the window, the kind of background brush used, and the cursor shape.

To create and display a window in Windows, invoke the routine RegisterClass to register a new class of window described by a WND-CLASS record, call CreateWindow, and finally call ShowWindow to get the window visible on the screen.

Manipulating a window is only done by a variety of window support routines that change the contents of window records; changing window record fields directly by application code is forbidden. The window manipulation routines usually require one argument to be the handle to the window record. This handle is of type HWND, which is actually declared to be a word (16 bits). Though the Windows WNDCLASS data structure is known, it merely defines the selectable attributes of a window and is not the structure containing the window instance information.

Macintosh

A window record contains everything there is to know about an instance of a window type. Here is the datastructure:

```
{ Apple Macintosh window descriptor }

type WindowPtr = GrafPtr;                  {The Window indirect pointer.}
     WindowPeek = ^WindowRecord;           {The Window direct pointer.}
     WindowRecord = record                 {The WindowRecord definition.}
          port:              GrafPort;     {Points to grafPort record.}
          windowKind:        integer;      {The type of the window.}
```

```
    visible:            boolean;        {This is TRUE when visible.}

    hilited:            boolean;        {TRUE when highlighted.}

    goAwayFlag:         boolean;        {TRUE if goaway box present.}

    spareFlag:          boolean;        {A reserved field.}

    strucRgn:           RgnHandle;      {The structure region.}

    contRgn:            RgnHandle;      {The content region.}

    updateRgn:          RgnHandle;      {The update region.}

    windowDefProc:      Handle;         {The window definition function.}

    dataHandle:         Handle;         {Data used by windowDefProc.}

    titleHandle:        StringHandle;   {The window title string.}

    titleWidth:         integer;        {Title width is in pixels.}

    controlList:        ControlHandle;  {The window control list.}

    nextWindow:         WindowPeek;     {Pointer to next window in list.}

    windowPic:          PicHandle;      {The picture for drawing window.}

    refCon:             longint;        {The window reference value.}

end;
```

The predefined window types for the Macintosh are driven by a supplied window definition function that is kept in a system resource file or in ROM. Custom window definition code must be written for a custom window type, and it must be included in the application code that uses it. For example, there are presently no predefined window definition functions to handle heart-shaped windows or round windows with circular scroll bars.

Macintosh II

There are new routines in the window manager for supporting fancy color manipulation on the Mac II. Here is a list of the new routines, and a short description of what they do:

GetCWMgrPort Returns the address of a WMgrCPort record. The WMgrCPort is a color version of the old WMgrPort record.

SetDeskCPat Assigns the desktop pattern to the specified pixel pattern. If the PixPat record's patType field is zero, the old foreground/background colors are the pattern colors.

NewCWindow Creates a new color window. NewCWindow is a color version of NewWindow that uses a CGrafPort rather than a grafPort.

GetNewCWindow Creates a new color window from a window template resource and colors the window using a related window color table resource ('wctb') if present in the resource file.

SetWinColor Used to assign or change a color table for a window.

GetAuxWin Returns (if there is one) a handle to the auxiliary window record for a window.

Two routines, FindWindow, and PaintOne, have been modified; FindWindow now checks with a new menu bar definition procedure to ask if the point specified is somewhere in the menu bar, and PaintOne is rewritten to handle color faster and better.

Here are the pertinent new records that support coloration in windows on the Mac II.

```
{The color window manager for the Mac II includes the following records
 for choosing colors used to display the parts of a window.}


AuxWinHndl = ^AuxWinPtr;   {Handle to an auxiliary window record.}

AuxWinPtr = ^AuxWinRec;    {Pointer to an auxiliary window record.}

AuxWinRec = RECORD         {The auxiliary window record definition.}
               nextAuxWin:  AuxWinHndl;  {Handle to next AuxWinRec.}
               auxWinOwner: WindowPtr;   {Ptr to window.}
               winCTable:   CTabHandle;  {Color table for this window.}
               dialogCTable:Handle;      {Handle to dialog mgr records.}
               waResrv2:    Handle;      {Handle reserved.}
               waResrv:     LONGINT;     {For expansion.}
               waRefCon:    LONGINT;     {User constant.}
END;
WCTabHandle  = ^WCTabPtr;                {Handle to a window color table.}
WCTabPtr     = ^WinCTab;                 {Pointer to window color table.}
WinCTab      = RECORD                    {Window color table definition.}
               wCSeed:     LONGINT;   {Reserved.}
               wCReserved: INTEGER;   {Reserved.}
               ctSize:     INTEGER;   {Usually 4 for windows.}
               ctTable:    ARRAY [0..4] OF ColorSpec;
END;
```

Auxiliary records exist in a Mac II as part of a single linked list that the system controls; each auxiliary record has a handle to the control record for whom it managers color information. At the end of the linked list is the default auxiliary record, which points to the default color table. The defaults are used if no matching auxiliary records (and associated color table) is located first in the linked list.

Gem

Since Gem AES doesn't use C structures or Pascal records to communicate with the binding routines, and the standard binding routines are very simple, there aren't any compound types worth mentioning that have to be used when talking to Gem. Standard Gem windows are created with simple calls to the routines wind_create and wind_open.

IIGS

Apple is attempting to get programmers away from knowing what the internal structures look like. They eventually would like to be where Microsoft is now, with those structures out of sight completely. The IIGS window structure is not completely out of sight, since it emulates the Mac environment, but it is not exactly the same.

Amiga

Here is the data structure that is used to set up a new Intuition screen:

```
struct NewScreen {        /* Create a new screen with these parameters. */
    SHORT  LeftEdge,      /* Initial X coord position for screen (set to 0).*/
           TopEdge,       /* Initial Y coord position for screen. */
           Width,         /* 320 for low-res., 640 for hi-res. */
           Height,        /* Height of screen in pixel lines. */
           Depth;         /* Number of bits per pixel or bit planes in */
                          /*  screen.*/
    UBYTE  DetailPen,     /* Color register # for gadgets and title, etc. */
           BlockPen;      /* The Color register # for title bar, other */
                          /*  blockfills.*/
    USHORT ViewModes;     /* HIRES | INTERLACE | SPRITES | DUALPF | HAM */
    USHORT Type;                    /* Normally set: CUSTOMSCREEN. */
```

```
       struct TextAttr      *Font;               /* NULL if default font used. */
       UBYTE *DefaultTitle;                      /* NULL-terminated title str.*/
       struct Gadget        *Gadgets;            /* The gadget list pointer.*/
       struct BitMap        *CustomBitMap;       /* A pointer to the optional */
                                                 /*  private bitmap. */
}
```

Here is the NewWindow type record used to create a brand new window under Intuition (a pointer to this record is the argument to the OpenWindow routine):

```
struct NewWindow {
      SHORT  LeftEdge,       /* Initial X coord position of top-left of window. */
             TopEdge;        /* Initial Y coord position. */
      SHORT  Width,          /* Initial width in pixels. */
             Height;         /* Initial height in pixels (lines). */
      UBYTE  DetailPen,      /* Pen # for gadgets and title bar text draws. */
             BlockPen;       /* Pen # for block fills like window border. */
      USHORT IDCMPFlags;     /* Set these for setting up I/O ports to window. */
      ULONG  Flags;                     /* These values are listed below.*/
      struct Gadget       *FirstGadget; /* A pointer to the gadget list. */
      struct Image        *CheckMark;   /* Ptr to menu item checkmark image. */
      UBYTE  *Title;                    /* Null terminated window title str */
      struct Screen       *Screen;      /* Ptr to (custom only) screen */
                                        /*  structure. */
      struct BitMap       *BitMap;      /* A pointer to a SUPER_BITMAP */
                                        /*  refresh bitmap. */
      SHORT  MinWidth,                  /* Minimum window width in pixels. */
             MinHeight;                 /* Minimum window height in pixels. */
      SHORT  MaxWidth,                  /* Maximum window width in pixels. */
             MaxHeight;                 /* Maximum window height in pixels. */
      USHORT Type;                      /* The screen type. */
}
```

These are the flag bits:

WINDOWSIZING   Window size gadget present

SIZEBRIGHT	Size gadget at lower right of window, or
SIZEBOTTOM	Size gadget in the bottom border
WINDOWDEPTH	Window depth arrangement gadget present
WINDOWCLOSE	Window close gadget present
WINDOWDRAG	Window title bar is the drag gadget, too
GIMMEZEROZERO	Window is of Gimmezerozero type
SIMPLE_REFRESH	Window has no backup bitmap image
SMART_REFRESH	Window has auto off-screen backup bitmap
SUPER_BITMAP	Window has (possibly huge) off-screen backup bitmap, with refresh under application control
BACKDROP	Window is always behind other windows
REPORTMOUSE	Report mouse cursor movements (noisy!)
BORDERLESS	Window free of default border graphics
ACTIVATE	Window becomes active when opened
NOCAREREFRESH	Prevent refresh messages from appearing
ACTIVEWINDOW	Set if window active message to be sent
INACTIVEWINDOW	Set if window inactive message to be sent

Here is the current definition of the Intuition window structure:

```
struct Window {
    struct Window      *NextWindow; /* The pointer to the next window of the
                                    /*  screen. */
    SHORT  LeftEdge,                /* The left edge screen coordinates. */
           TopEdge;                 /* The top edge screen coordinates. */
    SHORT  Width,                   /* The window dimensions in pixels. */
           Height;                  /* The window dimensions in pixels. */
    SHORT  MouseY,                  /* The mouse coordinates relative to */
           MouseX;                  /*   The upper-left corner of window.*/
    SHORT  MinWidth,                /* The minimum window size. */
```

```
            MinHeight;
    SHORT   MaxWidth,                   /* The maximum window size. */
            MaxHeight;
    ULONG   Flags;                      /* The current flag settings. */
    struct Menu         *MenuStrip;     /* Points to the menu bar for window.*/
    UBYTE   *Title;                     /* NULL-terminated title string.*/
    struct Requester    *FirstRequest;  /* Ptr to active requester list.*/
    struct Requester    *DMRequest;     /* Ptr to the double-click requester.*/
    SHORT   ReqCount;                   /* The number of open requesters.*/
    struct Screen       *WScreen;       /* The pointer to this windows screen.*/
    struct RastPort     *RPort;         /* The RastPort ptr. for this window.*/
    BYTE    BorderLeft,                 /* The window border descriptors.*/
            BorderTop,
            BorderRight,
            BorderBottom;
    struct RastPort     *BorderRPort;
    struct Gadget       *FirstGadget;   /* Ptr to windows gadget list.*/
    USHORT *Pointer;                    /* Mouse pointer sprite image.*/
    BYTE    PtrHeight;                  /* The height of the pointer sprite.*/
    BYTE    PtrWidth;                   /* Width of sprite; must be <= 16.*/
    BYTE    XOffset,                    /* The pointer sprite offsets.*/
            YOffset;
    ULONG   IDCMPFlags;                 /* Flags for IDCMP ports for window.*/
    struct MsgPort      *UserPort,      /* User message port.*/
                        *WindowPort;    /* Window message port.*/

    struct IntuiMessage *MessageKey;
    UBYTE   DetailPen,                  /* text and gadget pen.*/
            BlockPen;                   /* block fill pen.*/
    struct Image        *CheckMark;     /* Custom checkmark for menu items.*/
    UBYTE   *ScreenTitle;               /* Screen title when window is active.*/
    SHORT   GZZMouseX;                  /* Mouse coordinates relative to the */
                                        /*  GimmeZeroZero inner window. */
    SHORT   GZZMouseY;
    SHORT   GZZWidth;                   /* Width of GZZ window inner window */
    SHORT   GZZHeight;                  /* Height of GZZ window inner window */
    UBYTE   *ExtData;                   /* Pointer to arbitrary block of data.*/
    BYTE    *UserData;                  /* Pointer to arbitrary block of data.*/
}
```

DISPLAYING A WINDOW

Macintosh, IIGS, and Gem

The Macintosh and IIGS have the routine ShowWindow for making a window visible. The equivalent Gem routine is wind_open. The Mac and IIGS routines for temporarily removing windows from the display are ShowHide and HideWindow. Gem provides wind_close. A wind_close may be followed by a wind_open without problems unless the window was deleted using Gem's wind_delete.

Microsoft

The Windows routine for making a window visible or invisible, or for making its Windows icon visible while making the tiled or popup window invisible, is ShowWindow. The parameter list accepts a Microsoft window handle and an integer value with five possible values: SHOW_FULL-SCREEN, HIDE_WINDOW, SHOW_OPENWINDOW, SHOW_O-PENNOACTIVATE and SHOW_ICONWINDOW. Because MS tiled windows may be represented by an icon on the display, the routine OpenIcon is provided to display the window on the screen and remove the icon. The routine CloseIcon does the opposite of OpenIcon and the same as ShowWindow with the SHOW_ICONWINDOW value as its second parameter. The only calls that work with MS popup and child windows is ShowWindow, with either HIDE_WINDOW or SHOW_OPENWIN-DOW as parameter values. SHOW_OPENNOACTIVATE is used for tiled or popup windows only.

Amiga

The OpenWindow and CloseWindow routines respectively create and destroy a window structure in RAM, so they don't have the same effect as other routines in this category. Intuition doesn't currently provide routines to directly control a window's visibility. You'll probably have to do weird things like yank the window record from the screen window list and then refresh the other windows, or redraw the window with pixel coordinates that are off-screen and bet that the owner doesn't have a large enough screen to show it.

Causing screens to vanish and appear at will doesn't appear to be consistent with the style of software being developed for the Amiga or other machines; when a running application needs a screen, that screen sticks around while the application executes or is RAM-resident. Screens have some of the same control operations as windows, but no provided routines can make the screens vanish and reappear at will without also removing the screen record from RAM.

WINDOW ADJUSTMENTS

Macintosh and IIGS

Some Macintosh routines are provided for adjusting the display priorities of windows. The window with the highest priority is the one that is shown without being eclipsed by any other window; it is on the front plane. A window with the lowest display priority is the one that is displayed "way in the back" or on the back plane. The Macintosh and IIGS have routines BringToFront and SendBehind for changing the priority order, and SelectWindow for bringing a window to the front and making it the active window.

Gem

A Gem application is not required to make function calls like these, because the Gem runtime package fields window display priority events itself. The Gem routines aren't available at the application level, and aren't mentioned anywhere in the Gem documentation. Gem does what is effectively a call to the application code by sending an update or redraw window event when it wants the application to redraw a part of a window. Gem sends the application the coordinates of the parts to be redrawn. The Gem function wind_set gives the application the option to set a specified window to be on the top.

Microsoft

Microsoft Windows' BringWindowToTop provides the obvious function, but only for popup and child windows, and not tiled windows. Only popup and child windows may overlap. SetActiveWindow is used to make a tiled or popup window the active window.

Amiga

Amiga windows and screens can have a system gadget move them to the foreground or to the background. If present, an Intuition backdrop window is always the last window before the screen, so having it own this kind of system gadget is inappropriate.

The two routines for controlling window display priority are Window-ToFront and WindowToBack. Each routine requires a pointer to the window record.

The four routines that control screen display priority are ScreenTo-Front, ScreenToBack, WBenchToFront, and WBenchToBack. The Work-Bench routines change only the single WorkBench screen that exists at one time; the other two routines work with any screen.

MISCELLANEOUS ROUTINES

Macintosh

The Macintosh's HiliteWindow is provided for highlighting an arbitrary window (whether it is active or not); FindWindow provides a pointer to the window where the cursor was when the mouse button was pressed; SetWTitle and GetWTitle assign and provide, respectively, the title string of a window.

Gem

Gem provides the single routine wind_set for changing some of the window frame information and settings (title, information line, scroll bar slider positions, and window position on the display) and bringing the specified window to the top. Also, wind_set can be used to tell Gem the coordinate addresses of a new default Gem desktop window, the "hindmost" or backdrop window from which other window addresses have to be determined.

Microsoft

Microsoft Windows has a FindWindow function, but this does not indicate which window is visible at a specified coordinate on the display. This version provides a Microsoft handle to a window; it is called with two parameters (two C language style (NULL character terminated) strings). One contains the Microsoft class name of the window and the other contains the name of the window.

The name of a Microsoft window is a parameter to CreateWindow.

Microsoft also provides EnumWindows, which causes the user-specified procedure mentioned in the parameter list to receive, one at a time, the handle of each existing tiled, iconic, and popup window. Child windows are enumerated by the routine EnumChildWindows. AnyPopup tells if a popup window is visible on the display. IsIconic tells if a tiled window exists, but is represented on the display by an icon rather than in the open window form. DrawIcon draws an icon on the given display.

IsWindowVisible returns a nonzero value if the specified window is being shown on the screen.

Amiga

The WindowLimits routine is provided to allow changes to the initial minimum and maximum dimensions of a window. The five parameters are a pointer to the window record, the new minimum width and height, and the new maximum width and height. If a value is not to be changed, the appropriate argument is set to 0.

ReportMouse is called to toggle the mouse movement messages. Sending TRUE and a pointer to a window record will cause mouse movement messages to be sent to the application. This can result in a voluminous stream of messages.

RethinkDisplay performs the Intuition global display reconstruction. Everything about the images displayed is reconstructed from the base upward.

WINDOW DYNAMICS

Macintosh

The Macintosh functions that are keyed to events, such as mouse-down, are executed by the application code from its event loop. No reaction to an event is handled automatically. Most commercially available products use entirely custom-authored event handlers, despite the availability of products like Apple's *MacApp* (which is supposed to provide some or all of this code already written for use).

When the Macintosh first came out, some programmers' primary complaint about Mac programming was (and still is) that it takes too long to write a reliable event-handling module. On the other hand, programmers working on products are in the habit of creating their own window classes and writing their own window and control animation; they don't use stock code!

My conclusion is that people who are making industrial-grade software hate the complexity involved, but "damn the torpedoes" and put up with it anyway. People who are writing school projects, minor utility programs, or hacking a program together can use the libraries and obtain adequate results and avoid much of the rigmarole.

Gem

Gem automates many window operations, such as the window frame control animation (dragging the window around, or sizing the window). The outcome of the control changes is reported to the application. The application has the responsibility of redrawing the window contents when appropriate.

Microsoft

Microsoft Windows likewise handles the processing of some of the window operations, stepping aside with a window message when an operation has been completed. For example, the Macintosh requires that an application program call the Mac routine DragWindow when a mouse-down event occurs (to draw a window outline that follows the cursor). Windows handles the window dragging itself, and tells the affected application afterward with a WM_MOVE message. Gem similarly provides the WM_MOVED message. The Microsoft and Gem messages provide a window handle and the new coordinates.

Incidentally, it is the popup-style window that is most like the windows used on the Mac.

IIGS

Event handling on the IIGS is almost the same as that on the Macintosh; in neither machine is it easy. To alleviate some of the difficulty in code writing, Apple is providing TaskMaster on the IIGS, a layer of system software used by the application to handle the mundane stuff. All users that have developed code for the Mac in the past have written nearly the same code for their applications; TaskMaster for the IIGS and MacApp for the Macintosh are attempts to alleviate the repetition and complexity.

CLOSING A WINDOW

Macintosh and IIGS

When a mouse-down event occurs in the goaway region of an Apple window, the routine TrackGoAway is usually called to watch for a mouse-up event within the same region. TrackGoAway reacts to moving the cursor out of the goaway box (region) (without releasing the button) by unhighlighting the close window box. TrackGoAway highlights the box when the cursor is within the region. If the button is released while the cursor is still in the box, then the routine returns TRUE.

Some Apple packages place a goaway box in a window frame and then ignore goaway box picks, or they interact properly but don't close the window afterward. This is obviously bending the guidelines, but it can be done (it is usually not done intentionally).

Gem

Gem handles the close window box interaction, and then reports to the owner of the window that a close window request has been made (using a WM_CLOSED message). The application, depending on the context of the operation, may at least call wind_close to make the window invisible, and then perhaps wind_delete.

Microsoft

Microsoft Windows provides the application with a WM_CLOSE message when the user requests that a window be removed.

Amiga

The Amiga standard screen is closed when the last window belonging to it is closed via CloseWindow. There is an exception: The CloseWorkBench routine is used to attempt to close the WorkBench window, but the attempt will fail if another task has open windows on it.

Amiga custom screens can be closed amicably with CloseScreen. A pointer to a screen record is the only argument.

DRAGGING A WINDOW

Macintosh and IIGS

The Macintosh DragWindow routine does the same sort of thing for a window's drag region that Mac's TrackGoAway routine does for the close window box. DragWindow draws the grey outline rectangle of the window around until the mouse button is released. The routine MoveWindow is usually called afterward to do the actual window relocation on the screen.

Gem

Gem handles the window dragging interaction, and then reports the finished act to the owner of the moved window. Included in this message is an update rectangle detailing the region of the display that is affected by the change (a coordinate pair plus the width and height of the window).

A change in a Gem window occurs in the following sequence: The application program calls wind_update to reserve the display list so that other tasks don't change the display in the middle of *its* change. Each Gem window is described by a list of rectangles each of which describes a part of a window that is either visible or obscured. Gem's wind_get routine is called, perhaps a number of times, to obtain (one at a time) each member of the window's rectangle list. Each rectangle is compared with the update rectangle to see if it intersects, or is entirely within the realm of, the update rectangle. If it overlaps, then that part of the window has to be redrawn. When the window updating is complete, another call to wind_update is made to unlock the display.

Microsoft

Again, the Windows application does not really know that a window has been moved until the WM_MOVE message arrives. The coordinate of the moved window (provided with the message) is unique, in that when a child window is moved, the coordinate is relative to the parent window; the coordinate is relative to the screen when a tiled window is moved.

Amiga

Intuition handles most of the window moving details. What your application code has to do depends on the types of windows that have been affected by the drag. Moving a screen doesn't affect window content.

Intuition always takes care of the contents of a window that is dragged. Windows that are eclipsed are also taken care of by Intuition. Windows that are exposed are a different story. If parts of a simple-refresh window are exposed by a drag operation involving a different window, then the application that owns the exposed window gets a REFRESHWINDOW message and should redraw the exposed contents. If parts of a smart-refresh window are exposed, Intuition handles the refresh and the application doesn't get a message. In this case a super-bitmap window is handled the same as a smart-refresh window, automatically.

ADJUSTING THE SIZE OF A WINDOW

Macintosh and IIGS

The Mac's GrowWindow is called (by the event loop) when the size box is picked; it draws a grey outline of the window, redrawing the size of the window outline to follow the cursor until the mouse button is released. When the button is released, the grey outline of the window is removed from the display. The application then calls SizeWindow to redraw the window frame, and uses other function calls to redraw the contents of the window.

Gem

Gem handles the window size adjustment interaction for the application. After the size adjusting is done and the mouse button is released, Gem sends a WM_SIZED message to the application. The application normally reacts with calls to wind_update, wind_get, and the appropriate draw routines (see the description of dragging a Gem window).

Microsoft

Windows also handles the window sizing. The application is told that the window size has been changed when a tiled window gets a WM_SIZE message. A WM_SIZE message is sent with a parameter describing the type of sizing that has taken place:

SIZEICONIC	The window icon has been made.
SIZEFULLSCREEN	The full screen size window has been made.
SIZENORMAL	A window other than full screen or icon has been made.

When the application is sent a WM_SIZE message for a window, it should normally react by calling ReleaseDC and GetDC, respectively releasing and getting the display context associated with that and perhaps other windows. Between the calls to ReleaseDC and GetDC are calls to routines that update the display context, unless Windows does that for the window (it depends on the display context type used to create the window class). Updating the display context must take place before painting the window.

When a window needs to be redrawn, for example after sizing or moving, Windows sends the window owner application a WM_PAINT message. The message has a PAINTSTRUCT type record describing the screen area to be drawn. For more information the application has to issue a call to BeginPaint, which returns the appropriate display context for the window, in addition to a flag that says "the window contents have been erased." The window updating is arranged by the application, which then calls EndPaint. EndPaint must be called eventually if BeginPaint has been called.

The messages WM_SIZE and WM_PAINT will be generated by a resizing of the window. They are different and require different reactions from the Microsoft application window procedure. The WM_SIZE message caused by a particular act will always appear before the WM_PAINT message, perhaps by several messages, due to the way the messages are queued. Processing caused by the appearance of a WM_SIZE message establishes where the window and window frame are, and processing caused by the appearance of WM_PAINT uses the existing context to draw within the correct boundaries.

The UpdateWindow routine can be called to make sure that a visible window is being displayed correctly. This includes child windows belonging to it.

Amiga

What an application needs to do when a window is resized depends on the type of window used. Applications receive a REFRESHWINDOW event and have to redraw the window when a smart-refresh or a simple-refresh window is made larger. A superbitmap window is handled automatically by Intuition.

When refreshing a window, make sure to surround the redraw code with calls to BeginRefresh and EndRefresh.

DRAWING THE CONTENTS OF A WINDOW

Macintosh

The contents of the window drawing area are handled with routines in other major components of the Macintosh environment. When a window is activated or changed in size, a couple of window manager routines must be called in conjunction with redrawing the contents of the modified window. The window manager's BeginUpdate routine is called to limit the (re)drawing of the modified window to the area that has changed recently. This is especially useful in situations in which a window that is partially obscured by an object is brought to the front (obscuring part of the object that used to be in front of it). It isn't necessary to redraw both entire windows, only the intersection part. BeginUpdate limits the visible region (visRgn) of the window to the changed area, so that draws will take place only where they are necessary. The Mac's EndUpdate routine is invoked to restore the draw region (the visRgn) to the entire visible part of the window drawing area. Between the calls to BeginUpdate and EndUpdate it may be necessary to call DrawGrowIcon to display the sizebox and scroll bar outlines, and then call the other appropriate Macintosh routines to draw the window controls and the window contents.

Gem

Redrawing the contents of a Gem window is handled by the application code, which first determines what part of a window should be redrawn. This is done using the information that was volunteered by Gem (such as the update rectangle data) when the window change message arrived and via subsequent calls to Gem's wind_get function. The actual window content changes are made using a variety of calls to Gem VDI functions.

Microsoft

As described in the previous section, Windows sends a WM_PAINT message to the application owning a window when it has to be drawn or redrawn. Calls to the BeginPaint and EndPaint routines flank the calls to routines for redrawing the client area of the window. The drawing messages can be prompted by calling UpdateWindow.

Amiga

When a REFRESHWINDOW event message appears, or when displaying the window contents for the first time, call BeginRefresh, do the drawing, and then call EndRefresh. This is not unlike what has to be done for all the other environments.

DRAWING/PAINTING SUPPORT ROUTINES

Macintosh

When the drawing area of a window is affected by changes to the window (by dragging of the size box or the appearance of another window on top of it), it is common to call SizeWindow to implement the changes. SizeWindow permits you to say that you'd rather have the application code modify (add or subtract parts of) the window's update region; otherwise SizeWindow will do it. The option is provided because you may not like the way SizeWindow does it. InvalRect can be called to add the affected rectangular areas to the region that has to be redrawn (the update region). InvalRgn does the same work, but with arbitrary Macintosh regions. Regions and rectangles can be removed from the update region by using ValidRect and ValidRgn; by calling those routines you are saying that the area in question does not need updating (see Fig. 3–53).

The region routines are slower than the rectangular version, but are proportionally easier to use.

Gem

The Gem AES is responsible for window change accounting; Gem tells what sections of a window are visible when the application calls the wind_get function a few times. Each call gets a descriptor for a visible space rectangle in the drawing area of the window. In other words, the application is told (after the fact) that a resizable window has been resized and that Gem would like the application to get around to filling in the visible contents of the application's windows. The application is told via the WM_ message events. The application still has to ask what needs to be drawn. Compared with the Macintosh Gem has fewer ways available for an application to control the window manipulation (unless you want to step by Gem altogether), since more of the window management responsibilities are held by the Gem AES.

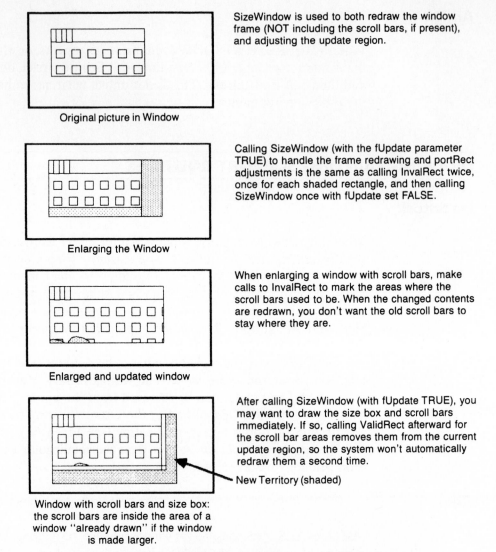

SizeWindow is used to both redraw the window frame (NOT including the scroll bars, if present), and adjusting the update region.

Original picture in Window

Calling SizeWindow (with the fUpdate parameter TRUE) to handle the frame redrawing and portRect adjustments is the same as calling InvalRect twice, once for each shaded rectangle, and then calling SizeWindow once with fUpdate set FALSE.

Enlarging the Window

When enlarging a window with scroll bars, make calls to InvalRect to mark the areas where the scroll bars used to be. When the changed contents are redrawn, you don't want the old scroll bars to stay where they are.

Enlarged and updated window

After calling SizeWindow (with fUpdate TRUE), you may want to draw the size box and scroll bars immediately. If so, calling ValidRect afterward for the scroll bar areas removes them from the current update region, so the system won't automatically redraw them a second time.

New Territory (shaded)

Window with scroll bars and size box: the scroll bars are inside the area of a window "already drawn" if the window is made larger.

Figure 3–53 Working with SizeWindow, InvalRect, InvalRegion, ValidRect, and ValidRegion routines

Microsoft

Update List Control Routines

Windows provides a way to react to event messages without writing more than a function call. The DefWindowProc routine, which means "default window procedure," will handle most messages in the standard Windows way. Note that this routine must be called by the application code, since Windows does not assume that you want DefWindowProc to be used for anything. Turning the meaning around, this allows an application to usurp some of the windowing responsibilities from Windows, and leaves it to the application to decide when to call DefWindowProc for handling window messages.

The Windows system requires that the routine with the name WndProc exist in the application code. WndProc must be callable by Windows because WndProc is going to receive *all* the messages that are intended for the application (and that window).

Display Contexts (DCs)

A display context record keeps the current status information for one or more windows, including foreground and background colors, patterns, fonts, draw modes, and the location and extent of a window. Windows gets the current window settings from the display context when it is told to update the contents of a window, as when drawing a line or filling in an area with a pattern. The application code can change the settings in the display context with Windows function calls like SelectObject.

There are three kinds of display context records: default, class and own. Each window usually gets its own default display context, but the class and own types are there for when their special properties are needed.

In order for class and own display contexts to be used without interference from Windows or another window, the application must make a call to GetDC. Default DCs are automatically maintained by Windows, which means that Windows modifies the DC during the time an application claims it. Class and own display contexts aren't maintained by Windows after the DC is claimed with GetDC. A call to ReleaseDC drops the claim, leaving Windows free to update the display context.

A class DC is shared by windows of the same class, so a call to ReleaseDC will unlock the display context previously reserved with a GetDC call. Not releasing the DC means that no other window of the same class can be updated.

An own DC is like a default display context (in that it is used by one window), but Windows does not automatically update the own DC like it does with default DCs; it must wait for the display context to be released. The application must then make another call to GetDC to get the updated display context. Drawing in windows that use own DCs must be done while the contents of the DC are current.

When a call to ReleaseDC is made with a default display context, the fields in the display context are reset to the original creation values! The application must then call GetDC to get the record back, and must replace the customized field values before using the display context again for updating the contents of a window.

Area and Region Marking

InvalidateRect marks for repainting a rectangular area within the display screen of the specified window. InvalidateRgn does the same for a region. The contents of the described area may be erased immediately when these routines are called if the value of the third parameter, bERASE, is TRUE.

ValidateRect removes a rectangle and ValidateRgn removes a region from the repaint list.

GetUpdateRect returns a rectangle that contains the region to be updated.

WINDOW SHUTDOWN

Macintosh and IIGS

The Macintosh provides CloseWindow and DisposeWindow for removing windows from use with a program; CloseWindow works with statically allocated window records, and DisposeWindow works with dynamically allocated window records. The Mac's HideWindow merely makes a window invisible; the window still exists and can be made visible with a call to ShowWindow. Strange things happen when doing operations with a closed or disposed window.

Gem

The Gem function wind_delete is used for deallocating the application's window and Gem's handle to the window. A call to wind_close before the call to wind_delete is mandatory.

Microsoft

Microsoft has CloseWindow, but this works only on tiled windows, and it removes the window from the display and replaces it with the window icon. DestroyWindow annihilates a window and its data structure, freeing the occupied memory for reuse.

Amiga

Custom screens can be removed with a call to CloseScreen; a pointer to the screen record for the screen to be destroyed is the only parameter. CloseScreen removes the screen from the display and reclaims the RAM space used for storing the screen. Standard screens can't be closed directly by function call, only by closing the last window in them (with CloseWindow). An exception is that the WorkBench screen can be closed with a call to CloseWorkBench if there aren't any open windows in the screen that belong to other tasks. If successful, the space allocated for the screen is reclaimed by the system.

Closing a window is done by calling CloseWindow. CloseWindow also causes the RAM used by the window to be reclaimed by the system.

ACCESSING THE FIELDS OF WINDOW DATA RECORDS

Macintosh

The Macintosh environment does not impede the direct access to any data structure. In general it is necessary to request the exact location of a given record before changing its contents, because the record can be moved during the course of program execution.

Gem

The fundamental Gem data structure, from the view of an application program, is what is supported by the Gem system itself (arrays of integers) or what is supported by the protective binding routines around Gem (however sophisticated the authors make them). Direct access to window records is not directly provided; it is necessary to use Gem function calls to change the Gem copy of a window record.

Microsoft

Windows provides a small number of record field access routines that are written in C style, rather than Pascal style; they put greater emphasis on the size of the datatype rather than on its identity or meaning. GetWindowWord, GetWindowLong, SetWindowLong, and SetWindowWord are provided a Microsoft handle to a window record controlled by the environment and an offset (of the datatype size) into the structure. Accessing a record using a pointer rather than a handle is not recommended.

IIGS

Like the Macintosh, the IIGS allows your application code to "get in there and rumba" with the data structures. However, some Apple software engineers are beginning to take a dim view of this, and are busily providing access routines, à la Windows, for the many fields in the various system-supported data structures. Apple would ideally like to reclaim the freedom of changing the fields around and adding new ones, but in the meantime will have to be satisfied by improving the reliability of application code. On the downside, the IIGS is a slower machine than the Macintosh; any additional function calls will add overhead that may be noticeable for repetitive calls to the same function. Repetitive calls are common.

Amiga

Amiga data structures are an open book to application software developers. At the time of writing the Amiga environment doesn't emulate the Macintosh by moving dynamic structures around in RAM without the knowledge of the application, so pointers rather than handles are used. Little effort has been made to provide structure field access routines.

EXTENSIBILITY

Additional window frame controls are common extensions to windows. Many new Macintosh products could not work without the added number of new window frame controls. These products were written assuming that a number of windows could be on the screen concurrently, whether on the small original Mac screen or the larger screens of later products.

Adding controls (aka gadgets) on the Amiga is simpler than on the Mac, since it doesn't require rewriting the equivalent of a Mac's (IIGS's) window definition function or control definition function. Windows child windows are good for freeform subdivision of any parent window, including the application's tiled window, and so can be used to identify areas where new controls exist; the code is not at all the same as that needed on the Amiga or the Macintosh. Custom controls in Gem have to be done by emulation (with object trees and software), since the variety of controls provided by Gem AES isn't great or extensible.

Other forms of customization involving windows are at least permitted by the Mac, IIGS, and Windows, but may be difficult to achieve on the Amiga or under Gem. Doing nonrectangular windows (à la Flash Gordon communicator display screens) is no simple matter with any windowing package. The resultant code is not going to be portable unless much of the lower level support code is also rewritten. SubLogic, Inc., had to provide a complete pseudo-Macintosh environment for the Microsoft Flight Simulator because of real-time requirements.

MULTITASKING AND TASK SWITCHING

Gem and Mac are presently single-task oriented, but additional utilities can be added to provide coresident programs and concurrency. Windows has multitasking. Application design considerations include whether the active window is the only one that may be updated, whether more than one task can occupy a single virtual screen, and whether a task which is updating the display prevents further display updates elsewhere until it is finished.

Gem

If Gem AES is waiting for an event to occur and detects the mouse button being pressed when the cursor is outside of the border of the active window, it will check to see if anything interesting is underneath the tip of the cursor. The AES sends no event messages if the cursor is over just the desktop, but if the cursor is over a window a window activation message is sent to the application that owns the window. If the previously active application is different from the new one, it will not receive the event record and will have to wait until it gets a window activation message.

Messages are sent only to the applications that should receive them. The application that owns the window that has been changed by the user will be the only one given the news that its window has been changed. If windows belonging to other applications are affected by the change, those applications will receive separate messages.

The present form of the Gem kernel supports a single application, three desk accessories, and the screen manager, either on an Atari ST or on an IBM PC. Each active task is allocated some CPU time, so that all the tasks appear to run concurrently. The Gem environment is not currently a proven multitasking package, though it is designed to be. The number of open windows that can be displayed, a maximum of eight, is a design constraint that will have to be dealt with in the application code.

Macintosh

The Macintosh Event Manager is less selective about who gets event records, for it allows the desk manager to check first to see if an event may be for a desk accessory. Since the existing Macintosh environment does not directly support multitasking, the running application gets the event record whether or not the event was intended for the application (the Mac routine GetNextEvent returns TRUE if it is, FALSE if it isn't).

The Macintosh Switcher program supports coresident applications, but they do not run concurrently, nor can their windows coexist on a single screen. An experimental program has been written (and nearly released) to support multitasking on the Macintosh; using this software, several applications were able to update coexisting, overlapping windows on a Macintosh screen without resorting to Switcher-like virtual screens. At the time of this writing it is not expected that the package will be released commercially. Apple is developing a package of its own, Juggler, but its current form supports a nonpreemptive scheduling method: applications voluntarily give up the CPU.

Microsoft

Since the Windows package supports multitasking for multiple applications (Windows desk accessories are merely other application programs), it is the most flexible of the three packages within the ideological confines of the operating system. Printer spoolers run in the background without special effort, and electronic mail software hums while the machine's display and user are preoccupied with other things. With respect to the tiled windowing, the concurrency is handled nicely on even slow machines because of the simplicity of the work required to contain the window updating for each task; the tiled windows require less overhead (since they are not overlapping) to determine which regions of the display are drawable—they are always rectangular in shape, free of clipped corners.

CONCLUSIONS

This chapter spends most of its time describing how impossibly different each of the window driving codes is going to look, yet the major operations provided by the window managers are both few and common.

Above the application's window management "drivers" lies the demarcation line for the system-independent routines. No direct references to the dependent data structures may exist above this line. Some effort to make some of the dependent code portable may be worthwhile, but the solution is likely to be application-dependent and therefore beyond the scope of this book to map with any accuracy.

The window manager code is rarely time-critical, and therefore can be implemented in a portable way without losing many points for slow responsiveness. Most of the window management code is executed once per window or screen during the lifetime of that object. An exception is the code used to set up the environment before and after a window update. Even so, when window locations and sizes are occasionally modified, the partial window redraw that is done usually needs significantly more CPU time than the window relocation.

The Manufacturers' Standard Issue Examples

The coding examples that have been provided by the manufacturers are not portable, nor are they *large* enough to be worth writing in a portable fashion, since converting them is about as time-consuming as rewriting them from scratch. Their purpose is to clearly demonstrate how the system works, and they use a direct coding style. Portable code will have additional conditional compilation, function calls, and type definitions, and will approach a solution in a more roundabout way. This code may be slower, but it usually doesn't lose much in readability (it often improves), and it certainly had better be more maintainable.

Trends

Some companies are now attempting to bring out very complicated products and are leaning toward efficient implementation on the individual environments; they appear to be less concerned about portability. The products on the different environments then become separately supported, and must stand alone. This path is not practical for everyone, and it makes it difficult for multimachine users to keep track of a particular product ("Whaddya mean, this isn't available on the IBM? It *has* to be! I *saw* it . . . didn't I?"). Underneath the marketing facades, some of the guts are invariably the same, unless projects are written entirely in assembly language.

Missing Features

I wouldn't hesitate to use customized windowing to make up for shortcomings in the standard features of one of the target machines for a product. That particular code isn't portable, but you already know that a great deal of the user-interface code isn't going to be portable either. I prefer to use the standard issue windowing if I can get away with it, since it's cheap, but many, many of the new packages find the basic window facilities, particularly the standard issue window frame controls, to be much too constraining. This makes software portability a stronger issue if it has to be considered at all.

3.6 Menus

Popup and pulldown menus are standard mechanisms used to interactively provide most (if not all) of a program's commands and make them unobtrusively apparent. Once the menu mechanism is understood, which is by most measurements a simple matter (learning what the mouse is for and how to use it is harder, since it requires some hand-to-eye coordination), people can use menus to learn what commands are available and to invoke them. Menus are nifty since they do not clutter expensive screen real estate except when they're wanted.

COMMAND INPUT METHODS

Menus can be used to demonstrate the other ways to invoke features. They can show what the text and the shortcut forms of the command invocation are.

The text form is the ancestral form of command entry: typing the command. It sometimes requires several (for instance, 20) keystrokes just for the command name, but normally takes anywhere from 1 to 8. An example of the command's text form is typing the word compress.

The shortcut form involves very few (one to three) keystrokes and uses special keyboard keys and key combinations, such as function keys, escape, and control key sequences. Random shortcut examples are pressing the F1 key and keying *Wordstar*'s ever-popular CONTROL-K D (actually, *Wordstar* doesn't provide a longer form). Another kind of shortcut is typing the shortened (but still unique) form of the complete command name: "c" or "comp"; this is standard under Digital Equipment's VMS operating system.

Four ways to invoke a hypothetical command are (1) selecting the menu item compress the file (see Fig. 3–54), (2) typing the word compress, (3) feeding the program a command file from disk with the word compress in it, and (4) pressing the control and P keys at the same time.

Many Macintosh programs provide shortcuts for some but not all menu items. Very few programs on the Macintosh accept commands in text form from the keyboard, although "keypunching" text or numeric data is the status quo. Indirect text command files are consequently also missing from most Macintosh packages; these are readable, editable text macro command files that could work across program boundaries. Macintosh software is evidently trying to emphasize interactive operations, and consequently ignoring (or at least not supporting) batch/macro/indirect command operation.

JOURNALING AND MACRO PACKAGES

There is another way to implement macro command files; the Macintosh was released with a journaling mechanism, which grabs and stores input

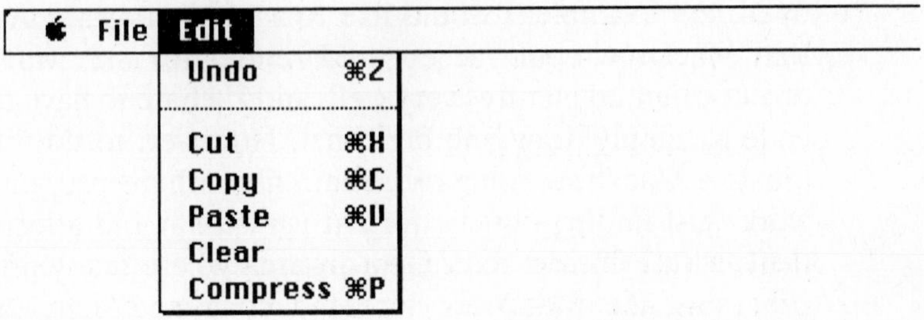

Figure 3–54 Menu with the word Compress and a Splat-C key equivalent

events as they come in and plays them back later to drive the same software in exactly the same way, only without having to press buttons again. It takes the mouse and keyboard input from the journal file. This software sits in the background and records mouse, mouse button, and key interactions, and then plays them back on command. The journaling mechanism was intended to be incorporated in an application for demos and in automating some of the testing process.

A small number of polished, commercially available journaling/macro packages, such as *Tempo*, make repetitive use of other programs bearable. If you are working with an application and you get to a point where a long stream of commands that have already been "canned" in a Tempo file is necessary, you can merely wake up that Tempo macro and it will do the interaction for you. The contents of a Tempo macro file are not pure, readable text, and can't be easily modified with program editors or word processors as though they were in a text file.

Tempo macros are not pure command streams. If a menu item is selected, the Tempo file contains a mouse-down event, a location, a mouse-up event, and a location; it does not contain the text form of the menu item. If that Tempo macro file were used with a version of the application that moved the positions of the menu items, the Tempo macro would not work properly.

DIGRESSION ON COMMAND INPUT DESIGN

Why is text command input important? It is my opinion that one program's output could be another program's input, regardless of the nature of the information. Witness how Unix utility programs work; one program feeding another commands or data is commonplace.

Although cut-and-paste operations are common on the Macintosh, other forms of program-to-program communication are not well developed. For example, I would like to write a program that creates graphics that MacDraw could accept and render for me; MacDraw draws large object-oriented pictures very well, and I'd hate to have to duplicate all that code to simply draw one big chart. However, to do this I would have to create a MacDraw-compatible data file with my program, which is tedious work (just finding out the format isn't easy) and a test of how MacDraw deals with incorrect data files, an area where many programs are soft. If programs like MacDraw accepted command files, there would be no problem! MacDraw could be the plotter for my simple 500-line program.

On the other hand, the Macintosh credo is to use the thing without *really* knowing how to type; such indirect command file "nonsense" flies against the path of the jet stream, because text forms of commands can be wordy or cryptic, and usually require typing skills.

It is possible for programs like Tempo to support readable, indirect command files by allowing macro nesting (translating text keywords into screen location/mouse button sequences when executing macros, and naming macros with text keywords when creating macros). Entire groups of macros would form a template for specific application programs, and all the commands could then have text forms. Even then, however, some context-sensitive information (e.g., graphics) would not be easily representable, so it is still not as satisfactory as having the application program having indirect command files built in (but it is better than nothing).

Menus are important; for elaborate programs it isn't necessary to memorize everything that's available, and the need to know how to type is relaxed; modal commands can be clearly identified for what they are intuitively by having the appearance of a dialog (request/form) box with a menu item selection.

DESIGN CONSTRAINTS

Menu bars and item lists have natural limitations that have forced some elaborate (and quirky) responses by system and application programmers. The first limit is the number of menu titles on a menu bar; one eyeful is normally limited to the number of characters than can comfortably fit across one screen. The second limit is the number of menu items in a single menu; one eyeful is limited to the height of the display. Most available applications have not bumped either limit, although I know some Macintosh owners who have run into problems because their systems have more than 30 desk accessories. Some applications have bumped the limits, bringing in a couple of changes by Apple (the menu item list now scrolls up and down for long lists). A number of programs require more than one menu bar, and at least one application scrolls the menu bar horizontally.

Another way to deal with too many related menu items is to use several columns, as is done for pen and fill patterns in MacPaint and Mac 3D. Yet another way is to use submenus to pop up when a menu item is pointed to with the mouse form. The submenu appears off to the left or right of the currently highlighted menu item.

Finally, chances are that many of the menu items will have to be put on a dialog box (Gem form or Amiga requester), as is done in early versions of Microsoft Word for the Macintosh. The thing to watch for here is that having to interact with dialog boxes for many simple commands is irritating.

The portability of long menus and numerous menus is questionable. It should be possible to port screens with 8 menus and up to 20 items per menu (without columnating individual menus), but this should be studied in context; long menu names will reduce the number, although long menu item names shouldn't be a problem. Also, not every environment supports popup submenus.

Macintosh support for menus is excellent, including about 35 routines. Gem provides 6 routines specializing in menus, MS Windows has 10, the IIGS has 50, and the Amiga has 5. The support quality can never be measured by a simple count of routines.

Here is a caveat: The exact meanings of some of the menu terms may differ between environments in confusing ways.

MENU COMPOSITION

Macintosh

A Macintosh menu list consists of zero or more menus. Normally each menu has a title and several menu items, which appear on the screen when the menu is selected with the mouse cursor (see Fig. 3–55).

A Mac shortcut (aka **keyboard equivalent**) for commands is defined to be any single key (except SHIFT) that is pressed at the same time that the Command key (aka "splat" or "the key with the flower symbol on it") is pressed. Shortcuts can be defined as part of the text of the menu item. The Macintosh shortcuts are case-insensitive ("x" = "X"), since the SHIFT key is ignored; any shifted symbol will be interpreted as the lowercase symbol on the same key. However, when specifying the key, always use the uppercase form of an alphabetic character for cosmetic reasons. The Command key is normally used to act as the control key for telecommunications use; the position of the 128K, 512K, and Mac Plus' Command key (to the left of the space bar) is much too creative.

A Macintosh menu item may have an icon to the left of the text, a check mark (or other symbol) all the way on the left of the item entry, and the shortcut keys, shown all the way on the right of the menu item entry. The

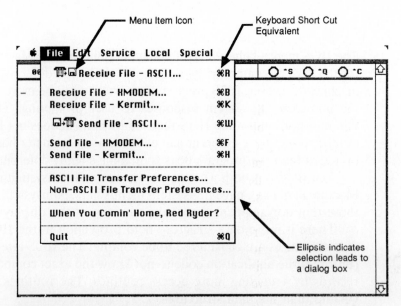

Figure 3—55 Macintosh menu (from Red Ryder by Scott Watson)

Macintosh provides different routines to finagle each of these components of menu items. The new Macs support submenus or popup menus containing submenu items, as does the Amiga; I have seen some minor software packages use them, even though they weren't supported at the time.

The text of the menu items is displayable with style attributes. Ghosted (disabled) menu items aren't selectable using the mouse.

Gem

Gem menu items can sport a check mark and a shortcut key displayed almost the same way as their Macintosh counterparts. Gem menu items do not normally have icons, although they can be bitmaps instead of text.

Gem's Menu items, like everyone else's, can be either disabled or enabled.

Windows

Microsoft calls the title of a Windows menu (found in a top-level menu or a horizontal menu bar) a top-level menu item; the things that appear when the menu is opened are popup menus.

IIGS

The IIGS menus behave in essentially the same way as Macintosh menus do for the sake of compatibility. Because of the speed differences between the machines, however, IIGS programmers are likely to be more concerned with the immediacy of system responses to user prompting. There are many different routines on the IIGS that the Macintosh does not have, and some of the routines have different names because a parameter has been changed or added (and the program does something slightly different).

The IIGS has both a system menu bar and nonsystem menu bars; the Macintosh doesn't have nonsystem menus bars. Nonsystem menu bars are those that don't appear across the very top of the display.

There is more data structure field protection in the IIGS. The menu data structures are considered to be volatile. The IIGS attempts to permit (or force) the application code to not know the exact composition of these records by providing more access routines. The routines are much less volatile than the data structures.

Amiga

The Amiga terminology is similar to that of Windows in that there are menus, menu items, and submenu items. The menu bar contains menu titles or categories, each menu contains menu items, and each menu item can have a popup menu that contains submenu items. Amiga menu items can have a check mark in front, a shortcut form to the right, and the command name in the center. Menu item text may also be graphic. Menus and menu items can be enabled or disabled.

COMMON ROOTS AND SUBTLE DIFFERENCES

There is a consensus between windowing packages on how menus are created, modified, displayed, and removed from service, although naturally few of the routines that do the work behave similarly; the data structures that are used demonstrate amazing divergence in design. Space for menus is allocated in heap storage to permit free-form changes at any time during runtime. If the windowing environment supports resources, menus are resources.

Selecting the title of a menu on the menu bar causes the contents of the menu to appear below it. Gem is odd in that the mouse button need not be pressed to cause the menu contents to appear; the mouse cursor has but to appear over the menu title. It takes a mouse button press elsewhere to get rid of the menu.

Both Gem and Macintosh show a single system menu bar across the top of the entire display, above the area where windows can live. Early Macintosh software didn't switch the contents of the system menu bar to match the active window, since only one major application could be running at once. Macintosh desk accessories usually add a menu to the menu bar when they are active and remove their menu when they are deactivated (and the Mac's main application's menus are selectively disabled when a desk accessory is active). The Apple IIGS menu bar's graphics are very similar to those of both Macintosh and Gem; in fact, the "look 'n feel" of IIGS windowing dynamics seems to be much more similar to Gem than to Macintosh. Quite a bit has to do with the resolution of the displays and the availability of color.

One divergence, perhaps temporary, between Macintosh and IIGS is the IIGS support for nonsystem menu bars (menu bars that appear somewhere other than across the top of the screen, such as across the top of a window). Apple indicates that one of the reasons for this is the number of problems with low screen resolution; my guess is that not enough menu titles will fit on the menu bar when using 320-by-200 pixel resolution. Apple doesn't recommend anything but light use of nonsystem menu bars.

With the Switcher program, each active application gets a virtual display, which is analogous to a Windows tiled window or an Amiga screen. With the Servant and Juggler programs, applications can share a screen, and the selection of the active window rolls in the application's current menu bar.

Windows menus appear across the top of tiled windows inside the tile frame. Each Windows tiled window functions like an entire Macintosh or Gem screen. Popup windows may also contain a menu bar.

Each Windows tiled window has a system menu that can be unique. Each Macintosh Switcher virtual screen acts like a complete regular screen, with one main application with its own desk accessory menu; that is, some of the contents are very likely to be unique. Gem does not directly support virtual screens or tiled windows, but it doesn't get in the way either, so multiple desk accessory menus are probably possible. The contents of an Amiga menu bar are entirely up to the owner application.

Each Amiga Intuition screen can have a menu bar across the top. Intuition screens are intended to perform much the same function as Windows tiled windows, with a completely different set of operational problems. Intuition screens stack and tend to obscure one another, but Windows tiled windows don't stack at all and tend to rob one another's display territory.

When establishing menus for an application, Macintosh, Windows, and Gem offer two methods, one that defines menu resources when the application is being built, and another that manipulates menus during the application's runtime. Macintosh and Windows provide resource construction software that builds resources using input in the form of a resource description language. No such resource building software currently exists for Gem, so menu resources have to be built using another custom-authored program (a much less programmer-friendly option). The Amiga doesn't support resources, so that much more has to be done at runtime.

The primary difference between the Macintosh and the IIGS is that the IIGS presently does not support resources.

Amiga directly supports popup submenus, as does Windows, but Gem and Macintosh do not.

The big addition for Macintosh II menu management are hierarchical submenus, popup menus that appear when a regular menu item is picked with the mouse button held down. The submenus are a cure for the otherwise unavoidable use of irritating modal dialog boxes to keep a list of choices that won't fit on a standard Macintosh screen under one menu bar. The other environments (except Gem) support hierarchical menus in one form or another.

DISPLAYING MENUS

Macintosh

DrawMenuBar is used to display the menu bar. It should be called by the application whenever a current menu or the menu bar has been modified; otherwise the changes may never be reflected by what is displayed.

MenuSelect is used to draw the selected menu while the mouse button is held down. More detail on this is provided in the section on controlling menu feedback.

Gem

Since interactions with the mouse and the display are not as tightly controlled by application programs under Gem as they are under Macintosh, Gem is in charge of drawing and redrawing menu bars and displaying menus when selected. All the application need do is give Gem the menu object tree, duly informing Gem that it is a *menu* object tree, via calls to menu_bar. Depending on the value of a flag parameter, menu_bar will either display or remove the visual representation of the menu object tree. The flag is set to 1 if the menu is to be displayed, and 0 if it is to be removed.

Other routines (like menu_tnormal) modify the way in which parts of the menu object tree are to be displayed, but nothing else does the actual drawing of the menu on the display. When the state of a menu item or title is changed, the change appears automatically (if that part of the menu is visible) without further interaction on the part of the application code.

Windows

Windows applications have to inform Windows when to redraw the menu bar, as on the Macintosh. This is usually when a menu change has been made. DrawMenuBar is the routine used. Windows takes care of menu interactions; this is different from the Macintosh. The first time a Windows application knows about a menu selection is through the message it gets from the Windows runtime environment.

IIGS

The IIGS has DrawMenuBar and MenuSelect. It also has MenuKey.

Amiga

Intuition support for menus is similar in this respect to Gem; there is no routine used just for drawing or redrawing the menu. It is sufficient to merely define or remove the menus using SetMenuStrip and ClearMenuStrip. The menu strip that is displayed at the top of the Amiga screen will be the one assigned to the current active window.

CREATING AND REDEFINING MENU ITEMS

Menu items are the individual, selectable choices within a menu that are normally hidden from view until a menu title is picked with the mouse, at which time the items for that menu become visible. The exact definition of "menu item" varies slightly between the windowing packages; the above definition is what it means when used in this book.

Macintosh

Menu items are defined during runtime using simple Pascal-compatible, readable ASCII strings embellished by a short list of flags or metacharacters. The rules for metacharacter are simple: it tells the system what special significance the next ASCII character in the string has.

A semicolon (";") or a return character (0d hexidecimal, 13 decimal) is used to separate menu items in a string (that is, the next character is the first character of a new menu item). This is for when more than one menu item is being defined with a single function call using AppendMenu.

AppendMenu is used to add one or more brand new menu items to the end of a menu. The routine requires a string defining the menu items and a handle to the receiving menu.

A circumflex ("^") indicates that the menu item being described owns an icon, and that the next character identifies the icon; this character can be one of the ASCII characters "1" through "9" (these have a value greater than 48 decimal). The system takes the ASCII value of this character, subtracts 48 decimal from it, then adds 256. The result determines the Macintosh resource ID of the icon. The arcane math is because menu icons can have resource ID numbers only from 257 to 511. Defining menu item icons this way only gets you the icons from 257 to 266; the alternate method is to use the SetItemIcon routine, which requires as parameters a handle to the menu in question, the menu item number (they are numbered from the top of the screen, starting with 1), and a byte with the icon number in it. SetItemIcon can be used to indicate any legitimate menu icon resource ID. GetItemIcon, incidentally, is used to get the resource ID of the icon associated with a menu item.

A bang ("!") means that the menu item is supposed to have a check or one of the other simple marks; the next character identifies which mark. Any ASCII character will do. Related to this metacharacter are the routines CheckItem, SetItemMark, and GetItemMark. All three operate on existing menu items. CheckItem will add a check mark to a menu item if the boolean handed it is TRUE, and remove one if FALSE. SetItemMark will set the mark character to anything; a 0 means no mark. GetItemMark returns the mark character presently assigned to the indicated menu item.

A less-than (" < ") means that the text should be displayed with a style attribute; the next character identifies the attribute. The characters and the attributes they represent are:

B   Bold

I   Italics

U   Underline

O   Outline

S   Shadow

Related to this are the routines SetItemStyle and GetItemStyle, which are used respectively to change and query the display styles of the existing indicated menu item.

A forward slash ("/") means that there is a shortcut for the item. The next ASCII character is the keyboard equivalent for the item. In the application this character is displayed in the menu item following the Command symbol. There is no routine to change the shortcut key assignment of an existing menu item.

A left paren ("(") implies that the item is disabled. No data character immediately follows. Disabling or enabling a menu item after its definition is done using the DisableItem or EnableItem routines; both routines require a handle to the menu and the menu item number.

Finally, a single dash ("–") means that a dividing line should appear across the menu; it takes the space of a menu item in the menu, and can't be selected.

Again, AppendMenu is used to append new menu items to the end of the indicated menu; the text defining the menu items can be embellished with the metacharacters just described. The GetItem routine is used to get the text string of an existing menu item without metacharacters.

SetItem is used to change the text of an existing menu item. For example, from "Turn Grid On" to "Turn Grid Off."

The routine InsMenuItem is used to stick menu items into a menu at the location specified by one of the parameters, the number of an item already in the list. Other parameters include the menu handle and a Pascal string of up to 255 characters. The string may contain a number of menu items; they are inserted in reverse order. This routine appears in the 128K version of the Macintosh ROM.

DelMenuItem removes specified individual menu items from a menu. Give it a menu handle and the item number, and it's in business. This routine appears in the 128K version of the Macintosh ROM.

Building Menus Before Runtime

The Macintosh is quite a bit ahead of the other environments when it comes to building and maintaining resources. It used to be that Macintosh resources were created primarily with RMaker (Resource Maker), which is a batch-oriented program that creates resources from a simple text file description. Apple Canada then wrote DialogCreator for interactively building dialog box resources. Apple has been providing REdit and ResEdit in one form or another (some of them working) for interactively editing much more than dialog boxes. Nowadays ResEdit is in a form where it can be used satisfactorily for several kinds of resource editing. RMaker or other resource compilers can be used as fail-safe utilities in cases where ResEdit falls short. It is much easier to build resources interactively, for the same reasons that people switch from manual typewriters to word processors.

The Macintosh Programmer's Workshop includes Rez for using text-form resource description files to build application-usable binary resource files, and DeRez for making readable text source from the binary resource files (going the other way). Here's an example of what might go into a Rez text file to describe some menus:

```
resource 'MENU' (128, "Apple", preload) {
    128, 0x7FFFFFFD, enabled, apple,
    {
        "About Sample…",
                noicon, nokey, nomark, plain;
        "-",
                noicon, nokey, nomark, plain
    }
};


resource 'MENU' (129, "File", preload) {
    129, 0x7FFFF6EF, enabled, "File",
    {
        "Quit",
                noicon, "Q", nomark, plain
    }
};


resource 'MENU' (130, "Edit", preload) {
    130, 0x3C, enabled, "Edit",
    {
        "Undo",
                noicon, "Z", nomark, plain;
```

```
        "-",
                noicon, nokey, nomark, plain;
        "Cut",
                noicon, "X", nomark, plain;
        "Copy",
                noicon, "C", nomark, plain;
        "Paste",
                noicon, "V", nomark, plain;
        "Clear",
                noicon, nokey, nomark, plain
    }
};
```

In this vernacular the first line of each statement starts with the keyword resource, followed by the resource-type keyword (in this case, menu). Within the parentheses in each first line are the resource ID number, the resource name, and the optional attributes.

Gem

Defining menu items is trickier in a Gem menu than in a Macintosh menu. Each menu item in a menu is represented as a Gem object record, which is part of an object record tree that represents the entire menu. This graphic data structure can either be constructed at runtime by the Gem application or be loaded in from a resource file on disk using the routine rsrc_load. The latter option requires that the menu's object tree be built beforehand using another Gem program (perhaps a resource editor or compiler), and stored permanently in the resource file.

A Gem menu item is represented in the object tree as an object record of type G_STRING that points to a null-terminated string in RAM. Each menu item is part of a linked list of records belonging to a G_BOX record. This parent stakes a claim on some screen territory for its children, who in this case form the contents of a single menu list. Because of its type, this G_BOX record is also responsible for drawing a box outline around the text of the menu items.

The title of a Gem menu is stored as a null-terminated string under an object record of type G_TITLE. The G_TITLE records of all the titles in the menu bar form their own linked list. This list belongs to another object record of type G_IBOX, since we don't want a box to be drawn around the menu bar titles.

The G_BOX records for each menu form their own linked list, which belongs to another record of type G_IBOX, which defines all the real estate that the menus collectively would take up if they were all open or visible. This G_IBOX record, along with a G_BOX record that owns the G_IBOX record owning the menu bar titles, are the kids of a single boss G_IBOX record. Figure 3–56 is an illustration of the hierarchy.

Like everything else graphical in Gem, a menu is defined as an object tree. This tree is created with another program and stored as a resource in a resource file. First, it is defined in C code as a number of initialized structures; the data are massaged and then written out to a file.

There are better ways to do this, and people are working on them.

The menu item object records each have a field called ob_state (object states) which contains bits that indicate the current state of the data of the object record. Some of these bits are used for menu items. The bits represent the following:

NORMAL	Object is drawn normally
SELECTED	Object is highlighted by reversing foreground and background
CROSSED	Not used for menu items; an X is drawn in the object
CHECKED	Object is drawn with a check mark
DISABLED	Object is drawn faintly
OUTLINED	Used for dialog boxes; an outline appears
SHADOWED	Used for boxes; a drop shadow appears

The text contents of an existing menu item record can be changed with the routine menu_text. The routine needs the menu item number, a pointer to the menu object tree, and a pointer to the update string. The update string cannot be any longer than the original string in the object tree, since the space for the entire object tree is allocated when it is created in memory (however it comes to be there) to the original length of the string.

The menu_icheck routine is used to turn on or off the checkmark that can appear next to the existing menu item text. It also requires a unique menu item ID number, a flag indicating whether to turn on or off the check mark, and a pointer to the object tree.

menu_ienable enables or disables a menu item, depending on the value of a boolean value parameter. The routine also needs a pointer to the menu object tree and the unique ID number for the menu item.

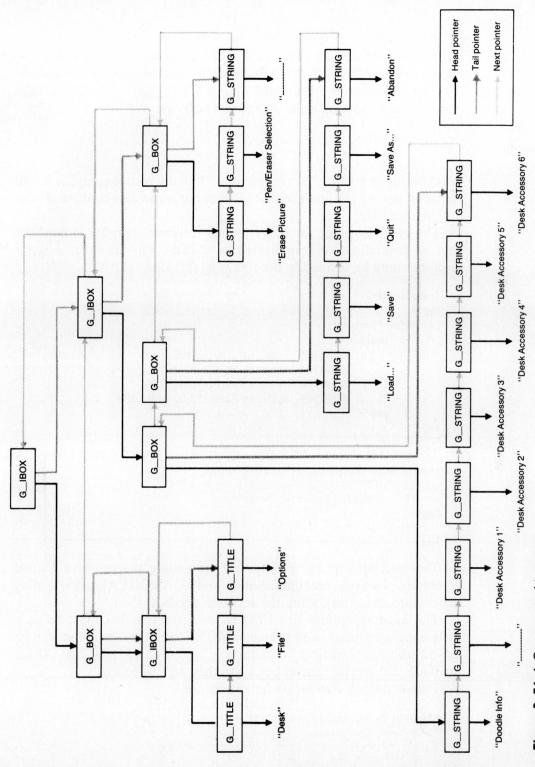

Figure 3–56 A Gem menu object tree

menu_register deals with the Gem desk accessory menu; it is used to add a menu item record to the desk accessory menu. There is only room for six desk accessories, which I find to be a rather strange and constraining limit. The routine returns the unique ID number of the menu item (0–5) unless something went wrong, in which case −1 is returned.

Windows

Windows menu creation is normally done with a resource compiler in the course of putting the application together, but it can also be done during program runtime.

The input language for the Windows resource compiler is nowhere near as generalized or complicated as C code. For example, a menu resource could be defined in the following fashion:

```
fiendish MENU
begin
    POPUP "Torture"
        begin
                MENUITEM "Tickling", DO_TICKLE
                MENUITEM "Lawrence Welk", DO_WELK
                MENUITEM "Being a Cub Fan", DO_CUBS
                MENUITEM "Basic vs Pascal", DO_ARGUEMENT
        end
end
```

The general syntax for the resource compiler used for menu resource and menu item definition is the following:

```
menuID      MENU, LoadOption MemOption
begin
    ItemDefinitions
end
```

The load options are PRELOAD for getting the resource loaded absolutely, positively, and immediately, and LOADONCALL, for loading the resource from disk when the software needs it.

The memory options are FIXED for resources that must be at a certain memory location all the time, MOVEABLE for those that can be moved arbitrarily (possibly for garbage collection), and DISCARDABLE for those that can be thrown out when they aren't needed.

Item definition statements for menus are:

```
MENUITEM text, result, OptionList
POPUP text, OptionList
```

The text field contains a double-quoted string. The backward slash ("\")
is a metacharacter that, when appearing in the string prior to one of the
following characters, flags a special character or function:

\a   Right justify the text in the string following

\t   Translates into a tab character in the string

The result field is the integer value returned when that menu item is
selected. The option list is one or more of the following:

MENUBREAK	Precede item with a new line.
MENUBARBREAK	Place item in a new column and separate the old and new columns with a bar; used for POPUP only.
CHECKED	Menu item has a checkmark in front.
INACTIVE	Item cannot be selected.
GRAYED	Item is displayed as grey and fuzzy rather than bold and sharp, and item is inactive.

As demonstrated in the example above, a POPUP statement may be
followed by a description of the popup menu's submenu items. This description may contain MENUITEM statements but not POPUP statements.

There is a special form of the MENUITEM command: MENUITEM
SEPARATOR, which is merely a dividing line. If it is a menu item, then
the separator is a vertical line; if it is a submenu item, then the separator
is a horizontal line.

Windows menu items can be bitmaps too. A bitmap resource can be
defined using the resource compiler's BITMAP one-line statement. The
BITMAP instruction points out a disk file with the bitmap in it, and the
contents of this file are added to the executable file being built.

MS Windows provides several routines for runtime menu item manipulation: CheckMenuItem, EnableMenuItem, HiliteMenuItem, and a
catchall routine called ChangeMenu. Whenever one of these routines is
called, it is usually a good idea to follow up with a call to DrawMenuBar
to force the screen image to immediately reflect the internal changes.

CheckMenuItem is given the Windows handle to a menu, the ID
number (an integer) of the menu item in the menu, and an integer value
that can either be MF_CHECKED or MF_UNCHECKED. All the
routine does is insert or remove a check mark from the menu item.

EnableMenuItem is given a menu handle, the menu item ID, and an integer value that can be MF_GRAYED, MF_ENABLED, or MF_DISABLED, and the routine will change the menu item to match the request.

HiliteMenuItem, aside from the menu handle and the item ID, also gets a window handle and a Flags parameter. The routine is used to control the highlighting for items on the menu bar only. The bit values for the Flags parameter are:

MF_BYCOMMAND	ID parameter is the menu item ID number
MF_BYPOSITION	ID parameter is an offset
MF_HILITE	Highlight the item (if zero remove highlighting)

The ChangeMenu routine can be used to add to and insert menu items in menus, or to modify menu items. The parameters are a handle to the menu to be changed, the integer ID number of the to-be-changed item or subitem, a catchall handle/pointer whose type and value depend on the selected operation, the integer ID number of the new menu item, and the ever-popular Flags parameter, an unsigned integer whose bits indicate the presence (or absence) of a change attribute or operation. The possibilities of the last are represented by the following C style constants:

MF_CHANGE	Change the specified item
MF_INSERT	Insert the new item prior to item specified
MF_APPEND	Add new item to end of menu
MF_DELETE	Remove item with extreme prejudice
MF_BYPOSITION	Item ID number to be changed actually is the position of the item
MF_BYCOMMAND	Item ID number to be changed actually is the ID number of the item to be changed
MF_GRAYED	Disable and dim the item
MF_ENABLED	Make the item selectable
MF_DISABLED	Item is not to be selectable
MF_CHECKED	Item is to have a check mark

MF_UNCHECKED	Item is not to have a check mark
MF_MENUBREAK	Item is to be placed in a new column
MF_MENUBARBREAK	Item is to be placed in a new column, and a bar placed between the new and old columns
MF_SEPARATOR	Item is a horizontal break line
MF_BITMAP	Item is a handle to a bitmap
MF_STRING	Item is a pointer to a C-style (terminated with an ASCII 00 or NULL) string
MF_POPUP	Item is a handle to a popup menu

In order to provide a menu item label, the function GetMenuString needs the handle to the menu, the ID number of the menu item, a pointer to a buffer long enough to contain the label, a value for how long the label can get before it has to be truncated (aka the maximum length), and a flag containing either of the constant values MF_BYPOSITION or MF_BY-COMMAND (both are mentioned above). A copy of the label string is placed in the buffer, and the function returns the length of the label.

A selected menu item is automatically highlighted.

IIGS

The IIGS support for menu item manipulation is not exactly the same as that provided by the Macintosh. The routines AppendMenu, SetItem, GetItem, DisableItem, EnableItem, CheckItem, SetItemMark, GetItem-Mark, SetItemStyle, and GetItemStyle are all present. Rather than Ins-MenuItem and DelMenuItem, the IIGS has InsertItem and DeleteItem.

The IIGS also has SetItemFlag, GetItemFlag, SetItemID, and Set-ItemBlink, but is missing SetItemIcon and GetItemIcon.

There is only one way to set up IIGS menus for an application. The Macintosh has two ways: before the application's runtime by building menu resources with resource manipulator programs, and during runtime with calls to menu manager routines. Doing it either way still requires routine menu manager calls to present the menus on the display, but when using resources most of the arrangement work is taken care of before runtime. Since the IIGS does not support resources, the only want to set up menus is with menu manager routine calls during the application's runtime.

The IIGS syntax for specifying menu items is not the same as that used on the Macintosh. Here is the format:

□ The first character of the menu list definition string is the menu title flag character.

□ Titles and items are terminated by the carriage return character.

□ The first character that is different from the title flag character to start a line becomes the menu item flag character.

□ A third character that begins a line in the same string is the string end character.

□ The metacharacters are:

"\" is the special character flag.

"*" is the shortcut flag character; the next character is the keyboard equivalent of the menu item.

"C" leads the marking character (i.e., check mark) for a menu item.

"B" emboldens the text in the menu item.

"I" italicizes the text in the menu item.

"U" underlines the text in the menu item.

"V" creates a dividing line underneath the current menu item.

"D" dims the current item or title.

"X" uses XOR highlighting for the menu item or title.

□ The sequence title-flag-character-@-carriage-return supplies the Apple logo as a menu title. No spaces should appear between the characters, and the XOR flag should not be used.

Some examples of menu title and item definitions are:

+FirstTitle	The " + " becomes the title flag character
−MenuItem1	The " − " becomes the menu item flag character
-MenuItem2\D*D	Keyboard equivalent is D and item is dimmed
−MenuItem3	Simple definition for the third menu item
+SecondTitle	Simple definition for the second title
−MenuItem1	Simple item definition for the second menu
−MenuItem2	Simple item definition for the second menu
−MenuItem3\BV	Shown in bold with a line drawn under it
−MenuItem4	Simple item definition (the fourth) for the second menu
	The end of the definitions

SetItemFlag and GetItemFlag are for setting and obtaining, respectively, two dissociated options: whether the item is underlined or not, and how the item is highlighted. There are two highlighting methods, XOR and redraw.

SetItemID accepts the current ID number of an item and a second number (which becomes the new ID number of that item).

SetItemBlink sets the number of times the item should blink when it is selected. Apparently this takes the place of the Macintosh routine SetMenuFlash.

Amiga

OnMenu is used to turn on a menu or menu item. The first parameter to the routine is a pointer to an Amiga window record, and the second parameter is an ID number of the menu or menu item (see Fig. 3–57).

OffMenu is used to turn off a menu, menu item, or menu subitem; the parameter list is the same as that of the routine OnMenu.

SetMenuStrip and ClearMenuStrip operate on a linked list of menu structures (the menu strip) to set up and take down the entire menu of an application. One of Amiga's unique characteristics in menu handling is that menus must be removed before an application's window is closed. Both routines need a pointer to the window record, and SetMenuStrip also needs a pointer to the first record in the menu strip.

**Macros Used to decode the MENUNUMBER value
provided by the MENULIST input event message**

MENUNUM	Provides the ordinal menu number (MENUNULL = no item selected)
ITEMNUM	Provides the ordinal item number (NOITEM = no item selected)
SUBNUM	Provides the ordinal sub-item number (NOSUB = no subitem picked)

For example (in C):
Mnumber = MENUNUM(value);
Inumber = ITEMNUM(value);
Snumber = SUBNUM(value);   Use these macros for upward compatibility

An Amiga Intuition Menu Selection Message Number

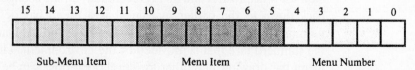

Figure 3–57 Amiga intuition menu, item, and sub-item selection decoding

ItemAddress translates the Amiga menu number into the address of the corresponding MenuItem record. The routine needs a pointer to the first record in the menu strip and a menu number.

THE MENU BAR

Macintosh

InsertMenu, DrawMenuBar, DeleteMenu, GetMenu, SetMenu, Clear-MenuBar, GetNewMBar, GetMenuBar, and SetMenuBar are Macintosh's menu bar operators.

InsertMenu is used to stick a menu into the list of menus. You provide the ID number of the menu already in the list in front of which to place the new menu. If you give it 0, it will add this menu to the end. The procedure also needs, of course, a handle to the new menu.

DrawMenuBar should be used whenever something concerning a menu or menu bar has been modified. It redraws the menu bar according to the data currently in the menu list.

DeleteMenu is given the ID number of a menu; it yanks that menu (and only that menu) from the menu list.

ClearMenuBar removes any trace of previously defined menus.

GetNewMBar is used to establish a list of menus. The routine is provided with the resource ID number of the menu bar. A RAM-based copy of the resource is used if it exists; otherwise it is obtained from disk.

GetMenuBar is called to make a clone of the current menu list. It returns a handle to the copy.

SetMenuBar copies the specified menu list (it is given a menu list handle) onto the current menu list, overwriting the old list.

GetMenu is used to get the handle to the menu of the specified window.

The SetMenu routine is for assigning a menu to an indicated window. If the handle to the menu is NULL, then the current menu for the window is removed.

Macintosh II

New for Macintosh II and family (eventually all the changes except color will drift back down to the earlier machines) is a menu bar definition function. This permits much easier development of custom menu bar handling routines beyond the standard fare that is provided by the environment. The routines that do the menu bar drawing, and other low-level operations can be temporarily replaced.

Gem

The menu_bar routine is actually a display routine, and doesn't add or subtract menus to the menu_bar. Runtime modifications to the Gem menu involve modification of the menu object tree, which requires the services of the Gem AES object routines (those prefixed with objc_).

Windows

The menus to be used are made known at runtime when the window class is registered (RegisterClass) or when the window is created (CreateWindow). The names of the popups that can be used are established before runtime with the resource compiler.

What Windows refers to as a "menu" is referred to as a "list of menus" on the Macintosh. The routines CreateMenu and DestroyMenu operate on the contents of the entire menu bar, not just one menu title and accompanying pull-down list. MS Windows calls a menu title a "top level (menu bar) menu item," thereby implying that menu titles can be treated as menu items.

To arbitrarily add or subtract menu titles at runtime, use the routine ChangeMenu (described elsewhere in this chapter).

CreateMenu merely returns a Windows handle to a new, empty menu.

DestroyMenu erases the contents of the specified menu and marks the space for demolition. The routine is given the handle to an existing menu. Again, this is for what is called a menu list on the Mac.

GetSubMenu provides the handle to a Windows popup menu. The popup menu is specified by the handle to the parent menu and an integer position indicator that starts with the value 0 for the first menu item. This routine avoids using the menu ID number.

IIGS

Some of the Macintosh menu bar routines are present: InsertMenu, DrawMenuBar, DeleteMenu, GetMenuBar, and SetMenuBar. The Mac's ClearMenuBar and GetNewMBar are missing.

The IIGS also has FixMenuBar, SetBarColors, GetBarColors, GetSysBar, and SetSysBar. If these are not enough, the routines SetTitleWidth, GetTitleWidth, SetMenuTitle, GetMenuTitle, SetMenuFlag, GetMenuFlag, and SetMenuID are also present.

FixMenuBar is provided to calculate the standard sizes for menu bars and menus to neaten the presentation of menu items and titles.

SetBarColors is used to assign the menu bar colors. Three parameters are required: NewBarColor (the normal bar color), NewInvertColor (the color the bar appears in when selected), and NewOutColor (the color of all the outlines and dividing lines of the menu bar). The formats are as follows:

parameter	bits	significance
NewBarColor	0–3	normal text color
	4–7	normal background color
NewInvertColor	0–3	selected text color
	4–7	selected background color
NewOutColor	4–7	outline and dividing line color

GetBarColors works a little differently. It returns a single LONG value: bits 0–7 contain the bar color, 8–15 contain the invert color, and 16–23 contain the outline color.

GetSysBar and SetSysBar manipulate the system menu bar, which on the IIGS is not the only kind of menu bar available. SetSysBar assigns a menu list to be the system menu bar, the menu bar across the very top of the display. GetSysBar returns a handle to the current system bar menu list, and SetSysBar expects a handle to a menu list. Consequently, SetMenuBar works a little differently. If you pass SetMenuBar a null handle, then the current menu is set to the system menu; otherwise it is set to whatever menu you give it.

SetTitleWidth is used to assign the width of a title, the selectable area. It requires the menu ID and the new width of the title as parameters.

GetTitleWidth returns the current title width; it requires the menu ID.

SetMenuTitle is provided the menu ID and a string containing the new menu title, and *voilà*, the menu has a new title.

GetMenuTitle returns a pointer to a string containing the title of the indicated menu.

GetMenuFlag is given the ID number of a menu; it returns the flag status bits for a menu record (specifically MenuNum.MenuFlag).

The SetMenuFlag routine is used for assigning new values to the status flags of a menu. The bits control the following options:

Menu Enabled or Disabled

Menu Title Displayed Normally or Inverted

Highlighting mode either XOR or Redraw

Menu Text, Color, or Application Defined

Finally, menus can have their ID numbers changed using the routine SetMenuID. Provide the routine with the old ID number of the menu and the new one, and the new ID shall replace the old.

Amiga

The two routines SetMenuStrip and ClearMenuStrip manipulate a list of menus with respect to a window. That's about it.

MANIPULATING THE DESK ACCESSORY MENUS

Macintosh

Here is an example of what generally is done to build an initial menu, including the desk accessories, "info on" entries, and other things that may be added to the desk accessory (Apple) menu (such as program help activation):

```
PROCEDURE SetUpTheMenus;                        {For a Macintosh application.}
BEGIN

    theMenuBar := GetNewMBar(Initdata.menubar[1]); {Get the first menu bar}
                                                   { from a resource file.}

    SetMenuBar(theMenuBar);                     {Must set up before drawing.}
    deskMenu := GetMHandle(appleMenu);          {Get MY apple menu and then}
    AddResMenu(deskMenu,'DRVR');                { add all the desk accessories.}
END;
```

Gem

Gem provides menu_register, which is used to add menu items to the desk accessory menu. It requires the desk accessory's process ID number (obtained as a consequence of using the Gem appl_init routine) and a pointer to the C-style string in RAM that contains the text of the menu entry.

Windows

In exchange for a handle to a tiled window and an action flag, the function GetSystemMenu returns a handle to either the original system menu or a copy of it. If the action flag is TRUE, the private copy of the system menu belonging to the indicated tiled window is annihilated; the handle returned is to the original system menu. If the action flag is FALSE, the handle returned is to a copy of the original system menu.

The Windows system menu is not the same as that of the Macintosh or the IIGS; to the Apple machines the system menu is always the entire menu bar across the top of the screen. The Windows system menu is the popup menu hiding underneath the box symbol at the top left of each tiled window frame.

IIGS

The desk accessory menu, by definition, is the first menu on the system menu bar. This is no different than on the Macintosh, except that the IIGS has menu bars that aren't across the top of the screen, and the placement of the desk accessory menu has to be mentioned in this context for it to be clear.

The IIGS menu manager doesn't have AddResMenu or InsertResMenu since the IIGS doesn't support resources. Initialization of the desk accessory menu has to be a little more elaborate, probably involving an initialized array of characters set up at compile time and then fed to NewMenu at runtime.

Amiga

Any program on disk or in memory is continually available for use even when one application is running, because of the multitasking kernel and the matching support provided by Intuition window and screen management. Under this circumstance no special structures or calls are provided for a desk accessory or system menu under the control of the application.

MENU INITIALIZATION, SETUP, AND TAKEDOWN

Macintosh

On the Macintosh there are InitMenus, NewMenu, GetMenu, Dispose-Menu, AppendMenu, AddResMenu, and InsertResMenu.

The Macintosh Menu subsystem is initialized with a single mandatory call to InitMenus. This routine requires no parameters.

NewMenu creates space for a single menu with an ID number specified in one of the parameters. The other parameter is a Pascal-compatible string containing the title of the menu; this is the text that appears on the menu bar. The menu title is what is called a "menu item" in Windows and Gem (and not a "submenu item").

GetMenu obtains a copy of a menu resource from a resource file, creating space for it in memory and returning a handle. The routine needs the resource ID of the menu. The handle to the menu definition procedure is stored in the menu record. The current menu list is not updated with this routine; use of routines that modify the current menu list (like Insert-Menu) is needed. This function must be used once only per menu; once a copy of a menu is RAM-resident, GetResource is used to reobtain the handle. ReleaseResource is used to deallocate the menu's heap storage.

DisposeMenu is used to release a menu's heap storage that had been allocated using NewMenu. It may be necessary to call DeleteMenu first to yank the menu out of a menu list; otherwise the menu list pointers will become corrupt.

Macintosh II

There are a few changes to the Menu manager for the Macintosh II, some of which will be transferred back to the older machines in time. The new menu manager routines are:

InitProcMenu	Creates a MenuList record, loads a 'mbdf' resource, and sets up a menu bar for an application by calling the menu bar definition function. This routine is used only for custom menu bars.
DelMCEntries	Deletes entries from the menu color information table. This can be used to remove one or all menu items of a menu.
GetMCInfo	Creates a new menu color information table record and copies the current color information table data to it.
SetMCInfo	Disposes of the current menu color information table, then creates a new current menu color information table and copies the provided menu color information table to it.
DispMCInfo	Disposes a menu color information table indicated by the provided handle.
GetMCEntry	Is used to track down the menu color information table entry belonging to the item identified by the provided menu ID number and menu Item number. A pointer to the entry is returned if successful, NIL if not.
SetMCEntries	This routine is used to assign or change any number of menu color information table entries at

MenuChoice one time. The routine is given an array of any length and the number of entries in the array. Returns a menu ID and menu item number of a disabled item that was under the mouse cursor at a mouse-up event. This information is not provided by MenuSelect, but may come in handy. If no menu item is involved, the item number is zero.

Many menu manager routines have been changed to properly handle the addition of a menu bar definition function, menu color information tables, scripts, and hierarchical menus. Also, odd quirks in the way that menu title highlighting worked in older Macintoshes have been repaired.

Gem, Windows, and Amiga

Initialization and takedown of their menu support facilities are handled as inconsequential subsets of other parts of their graphics supports. Amiga menus have to be dissociated from a window before the window is deleted.

IIGS

The IIGS provides MenuBootInit, MenuStartup, MenuShutDown, and MenuReset. For returning version information, MenuVersion is provided. None of these routines have the same names as their Macintosh counterpart, InitMenu.

The routines MenuBootInit and MenuReset are not described here beyond the fact that they exist.

MenuStartup is the routine used to initialize the system menu bar. No menus are assigned, and it becomes the current menu.

MenuShutDown dissolves any menus that have been allocated and closes the menu manager port.

MenuVersion simply returns a single word containing the menu manager's version number.

ADVANCED MENU-BUILDING ROUTINES

Macintosh

AddResMenu can be used to search all open resource files for resources of an indicated type. All the names of qualifying resources are appended to the provided menu except those with names beginning with the ASCII characters "." or "%". This is normally done in word processors to make a menu of all the available and unique font resources.

InsertResMenu does almost the same thing as AddResMenu; the appended names are inserted in the menu, but only after the indicated item (the item number is a parameter). If the item number is 0, then the names are inserted before the first existing item number.

Gem

Just for clarification, menus are made of Gem object records and are manipulated at runtime by operations such as adding and deleting menu items with Gem object routines like objc_add and objc_delete. Gem resources are also created this way, with another program that can be quickly cobbled together and used to build object trees and then stuff these resources into a file. Legitimate general resource compiler/editor facilities are very useful for this.

IIGS

The IIGS does not presently support resources, so the Mac's menu manager resource grabbing routines don't have counterparts on the IIGS.

MENU UTILITY ROUTINES

Macintosh

CalcMenuSize is provided to determine the dimensions of a menu. It is given the handle to the menu, and it sticks the dimensions in the menu record. These dimensions are not returned by the routine as either parameters or returned values.

CountMItems can be called to extract the number of items in a menu.

GetMHandle returns the handle of a menu in the current menu list that matches the menu ID number passed to the routine.

IIGS

The IIGS has CalcMenuSize and CountMItems, but doesn't have GetMHandle.

The added routines are MNewRes, InitPalette, SetTitleStart, and GetTitleStart.

MNewRes is a routine that is called when the resolution of the screen is changed; it signals that some adjustments are to be made by the manager. The system menu bar is redrawn when MNewRes is invoked.

InitPalette is called when the color palettes have been changed. The Apple logo that is displayed as the title for the desk accessory menu is a certain combination of colors that may be displayed incorrectly if the palettes are left the way they are.

SetTitleStart adjusts where the menu titles start (on the left side) in the menu bar. The parameter provided is the starting position, in pixels, from the left side of the bar; the value can vary from 0 to 127. GetTitle-Start provides the current value.

SPECIAL EFFECTS

Macintosh

FlashMenuBar is used to toggle the background and foreground colors of the current menu bar. If the provided menu ID number is 0, the entire bar flashes; otherwise the identified menu title flashes.

SetMenuFlash adjusts the number of times a menu item will blink when selected.

HiliteMenu is used to highlight (or turn off the highlighting of) the title of a menu in the menu bar.

Windows

FlashWindow can be used to momentarily draw the window frame in reverse.

Gem

The routine menu_tnormal controls whether a menu title is displayed normally or highlighted (reverse video). It requires a pointer to the Gem object tree that is the current menu, the unique ID number of the menu, and a flag set to 1 if the title is displayed normally and 0 if it is highlighted.

IIGS

HiliteMenu and FlashMenuBar are both present in the IIGS.

SetItemBlink, as mentioned in the section on menu items, sets the number of times the item should blink when it is selected. Apparently this takes the place of the Macintosh routine SetMenuFlash.

MENU DATA STRUCTURES

Below are the essential data structures that are directly involved with menus on each machine.

Macintosh

```
type noMark =            0;            {Mark symbols for MarkItem.}
     commandMark =       $11;
     checkMark =         $12;
     diamondMark =       $13;
     appleMark =         $14;
     TextMenuProc =      0;
     MenuPtr =           ^MenuInfo;
     MenuHandle =        ^MenuPtr;
     MenuInfo = RECORD
          menuId:        Integer;
          menuWidth:     Integer;
          menuHeight:    Integer;
          menuProc:      Handle;
          enableFlags:   LongInt;
          menuData:      Str255;
     END;
```

Macintosh II

The menu manager uses a color table that is different than those used by other Macintosh II managers. The menu color table is called a **menu color information table** (to distinguish it from the other color tables in use).

Gem

Gem menu lists, as stated above, are nothing more than Gem object trees. It is beyond the scope of this book to delve deeply into the mystical realm of Gem object data structure and object trees.

Windows

Windows hides the menu-related data structures, so that all you effectively can get at directly is the menu handle datatype that is used as a parameter on most of the menu routines. All modifications to menus are done via Windows menu support routines, and the manuals give little indication of how to work directly with the data structures (intentionally).

IIGS

No pertinent data are available at this time, but the IIGS routines should be very similar to Macintosh versions.

Amiga

```
struct MenuItem {
        struct          MenuItem *NextItem;   {Points to the next item in menu list.}
        SHORT           LeftEdge,             {The MenuItem select box area.}
                        TopEdge,
                        Width,
                        Height;
        USHORT          Flags;                {See the MenuItem flags description.}
        LONG            MutualExclude;        {The items on the same plane.}
        APTR            ItemFill;             {Pointer to ITEMTEXT controlled data.}
        BYTE            Command;              {Shortcut key for menu item.}
        struct          MenuItem *SubItem;    {Pointer to subitem list (popup).}
        USHORT          NextSelect;           {If MENUNULL, no other items selected.}
    };
```

CONTROLLING MENU FEEDBACK

Like almost everything else in the Macintosh, handling menu picks is not an automatic process as it is under Gem, Windows, or Intuition. When a mouse-down event occurs within the menu bar, the application is supposed to call MenuSelect to handle the graphic appearance of selected menus, and to return the identity of the selected menu item when the mouse button is released. Otherwise the screen picks are ignored and the menus won't pull down. MenuSelect expects the point coordinates of the mouse-press event. Two numbers, the menu ID and the menu item number, are returned as a single long integer.

MenuKey is used to map the character provided by a key-down event into the corresponding menu item pick. MenuKey accepts a one-character parameter and returns the menu ID and menu item number as a single long integer.

The IIGS also provides MenuKey and MenuSelect.

3.7 | Dialog, Form, Requester, and Alert

WHAT THEY ARE

The Macintosh, IIGS, Gem, and Windows have **dialogs** and **alerts**; Gem also has **forms**, and Amiga calls them **requesters**. Regardless of what they're called, their purpose is to get your attention, present information in the form of text, graphics, or controls, and sometimes allow you to edit text and change the status of the controls.

All the windowing packages support these predefined window types because (1) filling out forms is one of the most popular pastimes in commerce and government, and (2) people know how to control machines with switches, dials, and buttons. Their onscreen simulation is recognizable by most people. The packages discussed in this book provide the tools to do this: special predefined windows, some routines, and a number of graphic controls.

A control can be selected and adjusted with the mouse or keyboard. It is designed to look and act like a control device or paper icon that has been in use for years. For example, there are sliding-bar and rotating-knob volume controls on radios, "radio buttons" that get pushed out when a neighbor is pushed in, simpler buttons that light up when pushed, and check boxes. Controls generally flash or change color when selected, to present the idea that the parameter they represent is active, inactive, or started. Due to the volume of the material there is a separate section on controls/gadgets, leaving this one to discuss the routines and data structures that drive dialogs, and not the devices inside them.

In the Macintosh vernacular a dialog window contains a dialog box. While normal windows are used to show graphic and text data, dialog boxes show a collection of settings and/or present inquiries with predetermined fields. The text edit cursor might be blinking in one of the editable text fields.

Dialog boxes are flexible, and are able to contain a variety of controls. Alert boxes are not as flexible, but they are easier than dialog boxes to program. **Modal** dialogs "act like trolls" and won't allow you to step around; you must "pay" with an answer. **Nonmodal** dialogs (see Fig. 3–58) are not as single-minded, for you can interact with screen components other than nonmodal dialog. Alerts require user interaction for the alert to be satisfied, like modal dialogs; they seem to be more demanding than dialogs since they carry important messages or warnings (such as: ka-Boom!—resume or restart?) and provide no more than four buttons to choose from (i.e., OK, Cancel, and No).

MODAL VERSUS NONMODAL DIALOGS

A modal dialog does not allow menu picks or window activations to take place without a user first satisfying its requirements, even if mouse-picking

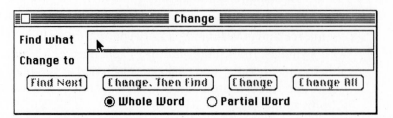

Figure 3–58 Macintosh nonmodal dialog box

a cancel button is all that is needed. Modal dialogs are imposing and demanding, but only for a short time; they appear after a command has been invoked, and vanish from the screen once they get all the absolutely necessary parameters for the command.

Nonmodal dialogs are not as ruthless or dominating, since other screen interactions are not turned off while they are present. They get out of the way for menu selections and window activations; they don't *need* interaction. Nonmodal dialogs also don't disappear from the screen when a command is invoked through them.

The output that is sent to inactive windows on a display that is showing a dialog box (or equivalent) is not blocked unless that code is handled in the application and done badly. For example, a dialog might crop up while using a telecommunications program. The remote machine may be sending a stream of characters which should be reflected by the contents of the visible part of the window that is supposed to show them. When the dialog is removed, the window will show characters that have come in since the dialog was summoned.

A common coding practice is that if a menu item command leads to a dialog of any type, the menu item entry is shown with an elliptical form (for example, "For Example . . . .").

Macintosh

There are modal and modeless dialog boxes, which are always enveloped by a dedicated window. The modeless boxes are contained by windows with a title bar and an optional goaway box, and the modal dialogs tend to have windows with no window frame controls. Modal dialogs, when they appear, are the foreground windows; they can be superceded temporarily by another modal dialog or alert box.

Macintosh alert boxes are less freeform (by design) than dialogs. They are in windows without frame controls, and the button that corresponds with pressing the return key has a heavier outline. Alerts can beep, too; in fact, depending on the number of consecutive occurrences of the alert condition, the alert graphics can be set to not appear the first couple of times, but just beep 0 to 3 times.

Gem

The dialog is one of four kinds of forms handled by the Gem form library. Two other kinds are alerts and error boxes (the latter is a special kind of alert box). A generic, or application-defined, form is also available. Application-defined forms technically are displayed in the same way as dialogs and alerts, with the Gem object library routine objc_draw. However, application-defined forms are shown within the drawing area of a Gem window; the other types appear in front of any windows, and are not affected by any clipping rectangles.

Gem forms are modal.

Windows

The control windows is the Windows generic term for windows that provide dialog and alert box functions. Windows dialog boxes are defined to be popup or child windows that contain window controls. Dialog boxes are either modal or modeless, depending on the needs of the code associated with the parent window.

There are message boxes (everyone else calls them alerts), which are implemented as popup or child windows and are created to show simple messages. They require a button pick with the mouse or keyboard to vanish.

There are also list boxes. Each is a special kind of window containing a list of any number of character strings; it can be equipped with a vertical scroll bar so that long lists don't have to be displayed with 4-point type. Selecting one of the strings evokes a message from the list box to the parent window. The parent window's code can highlight strings in the list box.

IIGS

The dialog manager documentation is not currently available. It is expected that the behavior of IIGS dialog and alert boxes will be exactly the same as the behavior of those in the Macintosh, with three exceptions: (1) the IIGS does not presently support resources, so any routines that are involved with dialog resources will not be present on the IIGS; (2) the IIGS presently supports color, whereas the Macintosh Plus, 512K, and 128K models don't (at least not very well), so some of the IIGS routines may be changed to accommodate some minor changes for color support; and (3) the IIGS developers (and Apple in general) are now more interested in protecting their ability to arbitrarily change data structures, so more dialog data structure access routines will be present and their use mandatory. A IIGS routine name is usually the same as the Mac counterpart if there have been no parameter changes, and different if the parameter list has been juggled.

Amiga

Amiga requesters (aka dialogs) are always modal, and come up in an existing window of an application. Though the requester is modal, input to *other* windows, even those belonging to the same application task, is permitted. Once responding to a requester is complete, the requester is removed and normal user interaction with that window is restored.

The simplest requester is called an **autorequest**. It presents a text statement and asks for a yes or no response in the form of selecting either the "yes" button or the "no" button with a mouse pick.

A normal requester doesn't behave differently from the regular dialog boxes of the other windowing packages.

A double menu requester is a special type that will appear in an application's window only after a double-click with the Amiga mouse menu button.

DATA STRUCTURES

Macintosh

```
{All the different types of dialog windows on the Macintosh:}


CONST dialogKind = 2;


{The following constants are for the dialog manager:}


    userItem  =    0;
    ctrlItem  =    4;
    btnCtrl   =    0;          {The low two bits specify the control type.}
    chkCtrl   =    1;
    radCtrl   =    2;
    resCtrl   =    3;
    statText  =    8;          {Static text.}
    editText  =   16;          {Editable text.}
    iconItem  =   32;          {Icon item.}
    picItem   =   64;          {Picture item.}
    itemDisable = 128;         {Disable item if set.}
    OK =           1;          {OK button is first by convention.}
```

```
      Cancel =      2;               {Cancel button is second by convention.}


   {The dialog manager datatype declarations.}


TYPE DialogPtr = WindowPtr;          {The dialog pointers are defined thus.}
     DialogPeek = ^DialogRecord;      {Yet another kind of dialog pointer.}
     DialogRecord = RECORD           {What a dialog contains:}
          window:       WindowRecord; { An entire Mac window record.}
          Items:        Handle;      { This points to 1st of list of items.}
          textH:        TEHandle;    { A handle to current editText item.}
          EditField:    INTEGER;     { An editText item number - 1.}
          EditOpen:     INTEGER;     { This is for internal use only.}
          ADefItem:     INTEGER;     { The default buttom item number.}
     END;
     DialogTHndl = ^DialogTPtr;       {A handle to a dialog template.}
     DialogTPtr =   ^DialogTemplate;  {A pointer to a dialog template.}
     DialogTemplate = RECORD          {The dialog template definition.}
          boundsRect:  Rect;          {This becomes the window portRect.}
          procID:       INTEGER;      {Window definition ID number.}
          visible:      Boolean;      {TRUE = visible.}
          filler1:      Boolean;      {Ubiquitous dummy variable.}
          goAwayFlag:   Boolean;      {TRUE = GoAway region present.}
          filler2:      Boolean;      {Ubiquitous dummy variable.}
          refCon:       LongInt;      {Reference value for window.}
          ItemsID:      INTEGER;      {Resource ID of item list.}
          title:        Str255;       {Pascal std title string.}
     END;


     AlertTHndl = ^AlertTPtr;         {Handle to alert record.}
     AlertTPtr =  ^AlertTemplate;     {The pointer to alert record.}
     AlertTemplate = RECORD           {The alert template record definition.}
          boundsRect:  Rect;          { The window boundary rectangle.}
          itemsID:      INTEGER;      { The resource ID number of item list.}
          stages:       StageList;    { The alert stage information.}
     END;


     StageList = PACKED ARRAY [1..4] OF RECORD { The alert staging record.}
          boldItem:  0..1;               {The default button number minus 1.}
```

```
        boxDrawn:  Boolean;        {TRUE = alert box to be drawn.}
        sound:    0..3;           {The sound number (or # of beeps).}
END;
```

Gem

The Gem form is represented as a Gem object tree (discussed at some length in the sections on graphics and menus). The handling differences between application-defined forms and the other types are provided by calling different Gem AES form library routines to set up the forms. The Gem object tree is built first, either during runtime or before, and stored in the executable file as a resource. When the time arrives, the object tree is used as a form by calling the appropriate form library routines. All object trees share the same object library routine, objc_draw, for rendering.

Windows

There are a small number of constants available for inspection. The structures for dialogs and dialog support are intended to be treated as black boxes. Dialogs and alerts are not complicated, but the controls that go in them are; they are discussed separately.

IIGS

Please refer to the comments made earlier regarding Macintosh/IIGS differences; the data structures are likely to be the same, but Apple is providing a greater number of data access routines to make intimate knowledge of those structures less (or not) necessary.

Amiga

Here is the definition of a requester record:

```
struct Requester {                          /* The requester definition, in C.*/
    struct Requester *OlderRequest;         /* A pointer maintained by Intuition.*/
    SHORT LeftEdge, TopEdge;                /* Used if to appear window relative.*/
    SHORT Width, Height;                    /* The size of the entire requester.*/
    SHORT RelLeft, RelTop;                  /* Used if to appear pointer relative.*/
    struct Gadget *ReqGadget;               /* The pointer to the gadget list.*/
    struct Border *ReqBorder;               /* Ptr to the optional border struct.*/
    struct IntuiText *ReqText;              /* Requester text in IntuiText struct.*/
    USHORT Flags;                           /* POINTREL: TRUE if pointer relative.*/
                                            /* PREDRAWN: TRUE if custom bitmap & */
                                            /*     ImageBMap points to it.*/
                                            /* There are others used by Intuition.*/
    UBYTE BackFill;                         /* Requester rectangle background pen.*/
    struct ClipRect ReqCRect;               /* Used to create the requester image.*/
    struct BitMap *ImageBMap;               /* Pointer to custom (only) bitmap. */
    struct BitMap ReqBMap;                  /* Used to create the requester image.*/
```

DIALOG MANAGEMENT INITIALIZATION AND TERMINATION

Macintosh

The routine InitDialogs sets up the dialog manager for the Macintosh. It has to be called only once and requires no parameters.

Gem

No form library routine calls are required for initialization.

Windows

No routines exist for initializing just the dialog management.

IIGS

The IIGS dialog manager initialization routines are:

DialogBootInit   This routine is called at initialization time; applications shouldn't have to know about it.

DialogStartUp   Initializes the dialog manager.

DialogShutDown   Stops the dialog manager and deallocates memory reserved for its operation.

DialogReset   Reinitializes to the default values some of the parameters that are used by the dialog manager.

Amiga

Initialization of Intuition's dialog management is handled from within, so there are no routines to call.

DIALOG AND ALERT CREATION AND DISPOSAL

Macintosh

NewDialog is one of those "high arity" routines, one that requires a large number of parameters (9) and returns a pointer to a new dialog record created by the call. NewDialog relies on NewWindow for most of the work; the first few parameters are required for that routine. The rest give dialog-specific information.

NewDialog accepts parameter information on:

The dialog's bounds rectangle

The dialog's title string

The location of the storage area for the dialog if it has already been allocated (the parameter is NIL if NewDialog is to provide storage)

Whether the dialog is visible or not

The ID number for the window

A pointer to the window that the new dialog window is to be drawn behind (− 1 if dialog goes out front)

Whether the goaway box is present in the dialog window frame

A long integer dummy that can contain anything to be associated with the new dialog

GetNewDialog does the same thing as NewDialog, only there are many fewer parameters. The secret is that GetNewDialog uses a dialog template resource for most of the data it needs. It needs the dialog resource ID number (an integer), a pointer to the storage area that follows the same rules as in NewDialog above, and a pointer to the window that the new dialog is to be drawn immediately behind (this also follows the same rules as used by NewDialog).

CloseDialog is used to eliminate the specified dialog from being displayed on the screen. It also removes the dialog record from the window list. The routine functions similarly to CloseWindow of the Mac's window manager; it reclaims the memory allocated to the control record, the control's region, the window's region and the text. DisposDialog goes a step farther and reclaims the space occupied by the dialog record and the dialog's item list, but leaves the icons and pictures alone.

CouldDialog is used to make certain that the specified dialog template record (with a resource ID number) is already in RAM from the disk file. It marks the record as unpurgeable. The dialog window definition function, the item list resource, and item resources are also checked and so marked. This routine is used to improve the speed of some operations involving the disk (if the stuff isn't in RAM, then the application has to go get them from the disk). The disk may not be in the system at the moment and may have to be swapped in, a real drag because it leads to a multitude of disk-to-drive inserts during operation. Using CouldDialog prevents that. FreeDialog unlocks all the elements again.

The Alert function is used to invoke the alert defined by the specified template. The value returned depends on what was actually done as a consequence of the call to Alert. This value can change depending on the number of consecutive calls to Alert for the same alert template resource.

The StopAlert function is nearly identical to the Alert function. The difference is that a stop icon is drawn in the top left corner of the box. The NoteAlert function similarly draws the note icon in the top left corner of the alert box, and the CautionAlert function provides a caution icon.

CouldAlert is used to guarantee that the alert resource specified (by its ID number) is in RAM, and locks it there until a subsequent call to FreeAlert is made for that alert resource.

Macintosh II

NewCDialog is the new routine added to the dialog manager to support color dialogs. It must be used instead of NewDialog so that a color grafPort is allocated rather than the old version.

Gem

Gem provides a number of object library routines for manipulating anything based on trees of Gem object records. Among them are the objc_add routine (which is used to add individual objects to a tree), objc_delete (used for deleting the indicated Gem object record from a specified tree), and objc_order (which is used to move object records around within an object tree).

The Gem form library routines are used with object trees that have been built by the application (during its runtime) with the above routines. Form library routines are also used with object tree resources, which are built by an application program cobbled together to simply build resources and placed in the executable file before runtime. During runtime, instead of the application calling the object library routines, the resources are accessible using the resource library routine rsrc_load. The form library routines of interest for creation and disposal operations are described below.

The form_error function is used to display a Gem error box. The routine requires but one parameter, an arbitrary integer error number. The routine returns the number identifying which exit button was used.

The form_alert function is used to show a Gem alert box. It requires two input parameters, an integer that identifies the default exit button and a pointer to the alert string. The function returns which exit button was used. The exit button values are:

0   no default

1   1st exit button

2   2nd exit button

3   3rd exit button

The form_center function is provided for centering a modal dialog box on the screen. This dialog is drawn on top of the previous screen object in the foreground, and not within any window. The function requires a pointer to the dialog object tree, the top left X and Y coordinates of the box, and the box's height and width. The routine modifies the coordinates of the top left of the box.

The form_dial function is used for four different operations. It is used to reserve or free screen real estate for a dialog box, and it is also used to animate a growing or shrinking rectangular outline. The Gem AES standard binding routine from Digital Research needs the integer flag parameter to identify which operation is wanted, the top left X and Y coordinates of the dialog box, and the width and height of the box. The Gem AES function itself requires a coordinate pair and a height and width for both the small and large versions of the dialog box to support the animation operations. The flag parameter can be as follows:

FMD_START	Reserve screen space for dialog box
FMD_GROW	Draw expanding box from small box to large
FMD_SHRINK	Draw shrinking box from large to small box
FMD_FINISH	Free space reserved for dialog box

Windows

After Windows dialog boxes are created, they accept input via their associated dialog input function. The declaration of the function takes the form:

```
BOOL FuncName( WindowHandle, Message, WordParam, LongParam ) /* in C */
```

The dialog input function is assigned when the routines CreateDialog or DialogBox are called by the application; Windows then knows where to send consequent event messages for a window.

The function CreateDialog makes a dialog box. The routine needs a handle to the instance of a module whose file contains the dialog template (a "resource"). CreateDialog also needs a pointer to a C-style string with the name of the dialog template in it, a handle to the window-owner of the new dialog box, and a pointer to the dialog function. Both of the pointers mentioned are long. The function returns a pointer to the dialog in RAM if successful, and a NULL value if not.

DialogBox also makes/renders a dialog box. The difference between this routine and CreateDialog appears to be solely in the return value of the function; DialogBox returns a 32-bit integer value. DialogBox does not return until it obtains an interactive response from the user in the form of a control window selection or "shortcut" key press.

IIGS

IIGS creation and removal routines are slightly different from their equivalent Macintosh routines. NewModalDialog creates a modal dialog and returns a pointer value to it. The NewModelessDialog routine does the same thing, but for a modeless dialog. GetNewModalDialog uses a dialog template (not a resource) to create a dialog box. CloseDialog erases the dialog from the screen and pulls the dialog record from the window list.

Amiga

The InitRequester routine initializes the provided requester record. The record could be initialized explicitly in application code, taking the place of the routine. This function does not allocate space, nor does it display the requester; it merely fills in some of the fields with nominal values for general use, particularly the system-oriented fields that the application could care less about, and afterward the application code can modify the fields it does care about.

DIALOG RESOURCE DEFINITION

Macintosh

There are a couple of resource compilers for the Macintosh, each providing a unique input grammer (see Fig. 3–59).

Gem

There is currently no resource compiler; dialog resources have to be constructed by small utility programs using Gem to create dialog object trees and then writing the object tree to a file.

Windows

An example of the Windows resource compiler for dialog construction follows:

```
ABOUTBOX DIALOG 22,17,144,75
STYLE WS_POPUP | WS_DLGFRAME
BEGIN
    CTEXT "Microsoft Windows"                -1, 37, 5, 68, 8
    ICON "shapes"                            -1, 9, 23, 0, 0
    CTEXT "Shapes application"               -1, 0, 14, 144, 8
    CTEXT "Version 1.01"                     -1, 38, 34, 64, 8
    CTEXT "Copyright (c) 1985, Microsoft Corp" -1, 5, 47, 132, 9
    DEFPUSHBUTTON "Ok"                       IDOK, 53, 59, 32, 14, WS_GROUP
END
```

```
/* This is from MacApp[TM], Copyright (C) Apple Computer 1985, 1986 */
/* First, include some necessary external definitions from resource files. */
include MacAppRFiles":Dialog.rsrc";   /* We need the dialog resource types.*/
include "ShowOffDialogs" 'CODE';      /* Need only the code segments here.*/
/* Second, create a DLOG and a DITL resource with the resource types. */
resource 'DLOG' (1501, purgeable) {   /* Defining DLOG type resource here.*/
    {60, 30, 200, 476},               /* These are box corner coordinates.*/
    dBoxProc,                         /* This is the dialog type. */
    invisible,                        /* This is the initial condition.*/
    noGoAway,                         /* No close box for this dialog. */
    0x0,
    1501,
    ""
};
resource 'DITL' (1501, purgeable) {   /* Matching DITL resource declaration.*/
    {                                 /* Array DITLarray with 11 elements. */
        {100, 30, 120, 110},          /* [1] Location of control.*/
        Button {                      /* We got a button. */
            enabled,                  /* It is selectable by default. */
            "OK"   };                 /* The button label is OK.*/
        {100, 350, 120, 432},         /* [2] At this location is */
        Button {                      /*  another button. */
            enabled,                  /* This is selectable as well. */
            "Cancel" };               /* It is the evil Cancel button. */
        {16, 20, 36, 190},            /* [3] At this location is some text */
        StaticText {                  /*  which is not intended to do much */
            disabled,                 /*  except sit there among the active */
            "Set margins to:"}; /*  controls as an external label. */
        {44, 30, 64, 90},             /* [4] Starting at this location are a*/
        RadioButton {                 /*  number of mutually exclusive */
            enabled,                  /*  controls called radio buttons. */
            "0\"" };                  /*  The label for one radio button. */
        {44, 90, 64, 150},            /* [5] Next radio button definition.*/
        RadioButton {                 /* Mac radio buttons are not automatic*/
            enabled,
            "1/2\"" };
        {44, 150, 64, 200},           /* [6] */
        RadioButton {                 /* Another radio button definition.*/
            enabled,                  /* It is selectable. */
            "1\"" };                  /* This is its label. */
        {44, 200, 64, 270},           /* [7] */
```

Figure 3–59 Examples of Rez dialog construction

```
RadioButton {              /* Another radio button definition.*/
      enabled,             /* It is selectable. */
      "1 1/2\"" };         /* This is the label.*/
{44, 270, 64, 330},        /* [8] */
RadioButton {              /* Another radio button definition.*/
      enabled,             /* It is selectable.*/
      "2\"" };                   /* This is its label.*/
{44, 330, 64, 400},        /* [9] */
RadioButton {              /* Another radio button definition.*/
      enabled,             /* It is selectable.*/
      "2 1/2\"" };         /* This is its label.*/
{70, 120, 100, 400},       /* [10] */
RadioButton {              /* Another radio button definition.*/
      enabled,             /* It can be selected with mouse.*?
      "Printable area of page" };
{0, 0, 0, 0},              /* [11] */
UserItem {
      disabled }


};
```

Figure 3–59 (Continued)

The general rule for the dialog statement of the resource compiler is as follows:

```
DialogName DIALOG LoadOption MemoryOption X, Y, Width, Height
OptionStatements
BEGIN
ControlStatements
END
```

ControlStatements are defined as follows:

```
ControlType Text, ID, X, Y, Width, Height[, Style]
```

DialogName is a unique number or alphanumeric string identifier. The LoadOptions are either PRELOAD or LOADONCALL, respectively meaning that the dialog is brought into memory at the beginning of runtime or brought in from disk only when the dialog is needed by the application. The MemoryOption field can be FIXED, MOVEABLE, and/or DISCARD-ABLE. The X, Y, width, and height parameters are the locations and dimensions of the dialog box. If the dialog box is a POPUP, then the coordinates are relative to the entire display; otherwise the coordinates are relative to a single child window.

Control statements are used to define any existing control windows (or areas) within the dialog. There are quite a few control widgets available; they are itemized and discussed in the section on controls and gadgets. Examples of types of controls are radio buttons, icons, and right-justified text.

IIGS

The IIGS does not currently support resources. However, the dialog manager does have dialog creation using a template that is not stored in a resource.

Amiga

The Amiga does not currently support anything like resources.

DIALOG DISPLAY

Macintosh

DrawDialog is used for no-response-required dialog boxes; these dialogs are present on the screen while something is going on in the application, and the dialog is provided to warn that the extended crunching is normal. The routine only needs a pointer to the dialog to be shown.

UpdtDialog (128K ROM) is a newer routine that improves on Draw-Dialog in that it is used to draw only items in the dialog box that are within the update region. This routine is used as a response when appropriate to an update event, between BeginUpdate and EndUpdate calls.

HideDItem squirrels away an item belonging to a specified dialog. That is, the item is removed from the screen (using EraseRect) and then given a display rectangle very far out of the pixel-addressing range of a Macintosh display. ShowDItem reverses this trick.

Macintosh II

The Mac II controls manager uses few new record definitions to support color in controls. There is a control color table, whose resource template is called 'cctb,' that is used when a control is constructed from a 'CNTL' resource if a matching 'cctb' resource is handy.

Auxiliary records exist in a Mac II as part of a single linked list that the system controls; each auxiliary record has a handle to the control record for which it manages color information. At the end of the linked list is the default auxiliary record, which points to the default color table. The defaults are used if no matching auxiliary records (and associated color table) are located first in the linked list.

There are but three new routines added to the Macintosh controls manager. They are:

SetCtlColor   Changes the values in the indicated control color table.

GetAuxCtl   Returns a handle to a control color table.

GetCVariant   Returns an integer variant code for the specified control.

Gem

The Gem AES object library routine objc_draw is used to render a Gem dialog. The whole ball of wax might involve Gem calls in the following order:

rsrc_gaddr	Track down the object tree in RAM
form_center	Center the dialog on the display
form_dial	Reserve the needed screen space for the dialog
form_dial	Draw the expanding box animation
objc_draw	Draw the dialog
form_do	Allow the user to interact with the dialog
form_dial	Draw the shrinking box animation
form_dial	Free the reserved screen space

The shrinking and expanding box animations are purely optional. Also, some binding routine packages may have turned the four-function form_dial routine into four different form library routines. The dialog displayed by the above becomes the foreground screen object.

To merely display a Gem form, just call objc_draw with the index to the form object tree. Then call form_do with the number of the active editable text field in the form and a pointer to the object tree as parameters. The form does not become the foreground object; it is displayed within a window.

To display an alert box, simply call form_alert. Similarly, just call form_error to display an error box.

Windows

The DialogBox function is used to display a dialog on the screen. The routine returns a 32-bit integer value. When it returns, the dialog box has been removed from the screen.

IIGS

Information is not currently available, but it is assumed that the draw routines for dialogs and alerts on the Macintosh will be very similar to those provided for the IIGS.

Amiga

DisplayAlert is used to show an alert box. It requires an alert number type, a pointer to a message string, and the total number of display lines required by the alert. The alert type is one of the following:

RECOVERY_ALERT	DisplayAlert returns TRUE on mouse selection button pressed, FALSE on mouse menu button pressed
DEADEND_ALERT	DisplayAlert always returns FALSE

AutoRequest is used to display an automatic requester and waits for user response. An auto requester is one that is predefined to request only yes/no or OK/cancel responses. AutoRequest requires a bunch of parameters: a pointer to the window owning the requester, a pointer to an IntuiText record that contains the description of the nature of the requester, a pointer to another IntuiText record that contains the string to be associated with a TRUE or positive response by the user, and another IntuiText record pointer pointing to the negative or FALSE IntuiText record (with the string to be associated with a FALSE user response). Either the positive or the negative string is displayed in the requester when the response is received; the AutoRequest routine returns TRUE or FALSE according to the response received.

Also required by the routine are the height and width of the requester rectangle and two flag parameters, PositiveFlags and NegativeFlags, which are for the Amiga IDCMP associated with the window involved in this AutoRequest.

BuildSysRequest is a significant requester routine for Intuition. It is used to construct and then display requesters. The function uses nearly the same parameter list as AutoRequest; the difference is that instead of a positive flags parameter and a negative flags parameter, BuildSysRequest has a single IDCMPFlags parameter.

The idea behind BuildSysRequest is to build a requester in a specified window (the first parameter for the routine is a pointer to a window record). If the requester is successfully built, then the Amiga IDCMP UserPort and WindowPort are set up to match the value in the IDCMPFlags parameter.

Intuition automatically calls DisplayAlert in case the construction of the requester is not successful; DisplayAlert tries its best to return a TRUE/FALSE answer to the code that called BuildSysRequest.

Providing a NULL value for the window pointer causes Intuition to automatically create a window for the requester.

The negativetext parameter to BuildSysRequest can not be NULL, though the positivetext parameter can be; there must always be an equivalent of a CANCEL option for a requester.

To get a user response, you are supposed to use the wait routine to watch the message port for the associated window.

FreeSysRequest frees up the memory allocated with a call to BuildSysRequest, and removes the requester currently in the specified window. It requires only the valid pointer to a window record.

SetDMRequest is used to attach to the specified window the special requester that is displayed (activated) with a double-click of the mouse-menu button. The routine requires a pointer to the window in question, as well as the pointer to the double-mouse-menu-button requester. This routine will not succeed if the DMRequester is already set and is being displayed. ClearDMRequest is used to clear the DMRequester from the specified window. This routine will not succeed (return TRUE) if the double-click requester is currently being displayed.

Finally, Request activates a requester. It needs a pointer to the requester and a pointer to the window that will contain the requester. The function returns TRUE if successful, and FALSE if not.

DIALOG MANIPULATION

Macintosh

IsDialogEvent determines if the specified event record describes an event to be handled as part of a modeless dialog. The routine returns true if it is an activation or update event for the dialog, or one that occurs within the active dialog.

The routine DialogSelect is called after IsDialogEvent reports that the event in question is associated with a modeless dialog. DialogSelect returns the item number of the dialog (and TRUE) if something was selected. DialogSelect updates or activates the modeless dialog when either of those two events are present. The routine also starts text editing interactions by displaying the text cursor or selecting text, returning TRUE if text was selected. Since DialogSelect doesn't handle keyboard equivalents of commands, that code must be provided if it is to be supported.

DlgCut is used to determine if there are any editText items in the specified dialog. If there are, the TECut routine from the TextEdit package is called to work on the currently selected text. The related routines DlgCopy, DlgPaste, and DlgDelete call different TextEdit routines to process text data.

Gem, IIGS, and Amiga

There are no additional routines.

Windows

DlgDirList is used to create a list that permits selection of files or directories. The DlgDirSelect routine obtains the currently selected entry in the directory/file list built by DlgDirList, and copies it into a string indicated by the provided long pointer.

MapDialogRect is used to convert dialog box coordinates to client coordinates.

DIALOG ITEM MANIPULATION

Dialog items are any things that go inside dialog/requester boxes, and can range from text to radio buttons.

Macintosh

ParamText is used to swap strings in static text items. These fields are used for "fill-in-the-blanks" purposes. The substrings that ParamText is looking for (in the static text items of a dialog or alert box) are "^0" through "^3". When it finds one, it replaces that substring with the appropriate one provided as an argument to ParamText. ParamText is given four parameters, param0 through param3, all of which are of the type Str255 (standard-unstandard Pascal strings).

GetDItem needs a pointer to a dialog and the number of the item. It returns the type identifier (an integer) to that item, a handle to the item, and a display rectangle for that item. With this information it is possible to arbitrarily change that item's type and content.

SetDItem is the partner of GetDItem. It is used to assign new values to the item that is specified uniquely by a pointer to the parent dialog box and the integer ID number of the item. The values that can be changed are the item type, the display rectangle for the item, and a handle to the data appropriate for an item of that type. The item is not redrawn by this routine.

FindDItem (128K ROM) is used to track down an item empirically. You give the routine a pointer to the dialog and the coordinates of a point within the dialog box, and FindDItem returns the item number whose display rectangle includes that location. If the point doesn't fall within the rectangle of any item in the dialog, the value -1 is returned.

The GetIText procedure hands over a copy of the text string belonging to an item. The routine is given a Macintosh handle to the item.

SetIText assigns a new text string to an item; that item is then drawn by this routine. The routine needs a handle to the item and a Pascal format string.

SellText is used to select a range of characters in the string of an item. The text selected is highlighted unless the range is length 0, in which case a simple edit caret (the vertical blinking bar) is placed in the desired position in the string. This is normally used right after a bogus user text entry that the application wants to note as unacceptable by highlighting the incorrect text. The routine needs a pointer to the dialog box, the item number, and the start and end positions in the text of the item (as integer values).

GetAlrtStage returns a value from 0 to 3. The alert stage is the number of times an alert has consecutively been prodded through something occurring in the application; this allows different reactions by the application to the user trying to do something illegal. For example, the alert box may not show up the first time that a user tries to select something outside the addressable region of the screen, but the second time it just might, and the third time that alert might be downright insulting. ResetAlrtStage is used to reset the current alert stage value to 0, the first alert stage.

Gem

objc_change is used to modify the location and dimensions of the clip rectangle of an object, and the state of the object. The version of the Gem binding routine provided by Digital Research requires the following nine arguments:

A pointer to the object tree (it doesn't have to be a dialog or form object; the object library works on object trees, which are used by every complicated entity supported by Gem)

The number of the object in the tree to be modified

A zero value; this parameter is reserved but not used yet

The X and Y coordinates of the top left of the clip rectangle

The width and height in pixels of the clip rectangle

The new state value for the object

A draw code for the object; 1 = redraw object, 0 = don't redraw.

The function returns a 0 if an error occurred and a positive value if no error was encountered.

The state of the object can be one or more of the following:

NORMAL

SELECTED

CROSSED

CHECKED

DISABLED

OUTLINED

SHADOWED

The routine objc_edit needs a few parameters: the address of the dialog/form's object tree in RAM, an integer number identifying the object in the tree to be edited, a single input character (from the user), the present character position index, and an integer identifying the function to be performed. The routine returns the new character position index.

The character position index points to the location in the object's data at which the edit will occur.

This object routine works only with objects of type G_BOXTEXT or G_TEXT.

Windows

GetDlgItem is provided to track down the handle of a dialog item. You provide the routine with a handle to the dialog and the integer ID number of the dialog item; GetDlgItem returns the handle to the dialog item.

The GetDlgItemInt function is mostly mundane; it converts a dialog item string into an integer value. It requires the handle to the dialog and the (unique ID) number of the dialog item. The routine returns TRUE in the address pointed to by a third argument if there were no errors. A fourth argument, if TRUE, instructs SetDlgItemInt to check for a leading minus sign; if this argument is FALSE then the routine doesn't check. The function returns the converted integer value.

SetDlgItemInt goes the opposite way of GetDlgItemInt; it is given an integer value, a dialog handle, and a dialog item number and stuffs a string version of the integer value in the dialog item string. SetDlgItemInt also has a flag that tells the routine whether the value can be signed or not.

SetDlgItemText takes the string handed to it and assigns it to a dialog item. The routine gets a handle to a dialog and the ID number of the dialog item to be modified.

GetDlgItemText obtains the string contained by a dialog item. It gets a Windows handle to a dialog and the ID number of the dialog item from which the string is copied.

CheckDlgButton sticks or removes a check mark from the specified dialog item, depending on the value of a boolean. It requires a handle to the dialog and the ID number of the dialog item. If the boolean argument is TRUE the check mark is placed in the dialog item; it is removed if FALSE.

IsDlgButtonChecked is given the handle to the dialog and the dialog item ID number; it returns TRUE if the dialog item has a check, and FALSE if not.

CheckRadioButton is given the handle to a dialog and three dialog item ID numbers. The first is the first of a sequence of radio button dialog items; the second is the last of that sequence. All those radio buttons are unchecked (they better have consecutive ID numbers!). Then the dialog item with the third ID number is checked.

SendDlgItemMessage is used to send a message to the specified dialog item, which is addressed in the same way as the other routines mentioned in this section. The message is in the form of an unsigned integer, and there is a word-sized argument and a long-sized argument to contain additional information for the dialog item's window procedure. The function returns a 32-bit integer sent by the window procedure.

For modeless dialogs IsDialogMessage can be used to determine if a dialog box message has been processed yet. The routine is given a handle to the dialog box window and a long pointer to a MSG record. The function returns TRUE if the message was used, and FALSE otherwise.

IIGS

No information regarding the IIGS is available at this time; however, it is expected that the IIGS will support the same foundation of routines (with perhaps some minor changes) that is currently available on the Macintosh. Since the dialog item routines do not involve resource manipulation but may involve color, some changes may be expected.

Amiga

There are six routines that have to do with dialog items, which on the Amiga are called **gadgets**. These routines are AddGadget, OnGadget, OffGadget, RefreshGadgets, RemoveGadget, and ModifyProp.

AddGadget adds a gadget to a list of gadgets assigned to a requester. The composition of gadgets is covered in a different section, so here we only describe how to add a gadget that is already built. The routine needs a pointer to the window or screen record, a pointer to the gadget, and the position number for the gadget in the gadget list.

OnGadget needs a pointer to the gadget, a pointer to the screen or window, and a pointer to the requester (if there is one, null if not). The routine activates the gadget. OffGadget, which requires the same parameters, turns the indicated gadget off.

The RefreshGadgets routine is used to tell Intuition to redraw a list or part of a list of gadgets. The first argument is a pointer to the first gadget in the list to be redrawn, and the other two parameters are pointers to the window or screen and to the requester (if one exists). All the gadgets in the gadget list after the gadget indicated will be redrawn.

ModifyProp gives you the ability to modify the parameters of a proportional gadget. It has eight arguments: a pointer to the gadget, a pointer to the screen or window record, a pointer to the requester (if any), a Flags parameter, horizontal and vertical pot (percentage) parameters, and horizontal and vertical body parameters. The pot values are the degrees to which a gadget is set, ranging from 0 to 100 percent. The body values are the smallest increments that the gadget can be changed by.

DIALOG SOUND SUPPORT

Macintosh

The routine ErrorSound is used to set the sound procedure for dialogs and alerts. The sole argument to ErrorSound is a pointer to the custom sound procedure. Sending this routine a 0 will turn off sound altogether for dialogs and alerts, and also stop the menu bar from blinking; what power!

DIALOG INTERACTION

This section describes how each windowing package uses dialog controls to get user responses.

Macintosh

Once a modal dialog is displayed on the screen, ModalDialog is called to handle the user interactions. ModalDialog is in charge until the user makes a selection that ends the dialog session. ModalDialog changes the appearance of selected buttons in the open dialog, handles text editing, and beeps if mouse cursor selections outside the dialog box are made.

Macintosh nonmodal dialogs are processed differently, requiring routines like IsDialogEvent and DialogSelect.

IsDialogEvent determines if an event is an interaction with a dialog. This function accepts an EventRecord record that just came from the most recent call to GetNextEvent. TRUE is returned when:

A dialog window is active

It is an activate event for a dialog

It is an update event for a dialog

It is a mouse-down event in the content region of an active dialog

IsDialogEvent is present to handle modeless dialog windows. The routine only needs the one argument.

If TRUE is returned, the usual thing to do is first check for shortcut (keyboard equivalent) events, and then hand off the record to the function DialogSelect. DialogSelect processes events for modeless dialogs. DialogSelect returns TRUE if the event involves a dialog item that is enabled; also returned (as arguments) are the item number and a pointer to the dialog.

When the event involves an editText item, DialogSelect will select the text or show a flashing grey caret at the insertion point.

DialogSelect doesn't handle keyboard equivalents of commands, but it does handle key-down events associated with editText items, allowing text entry and editing. After processing such an event the routine returns TRUE if the editText item is enabled, and FALSE otherwise.

A mouse-down event in a control prompts DialogSelect to call TrackControl and then return TRUE or FALSE depending on the result of the interaction.

DlgCut, DlgCopy, and DlgPaste are provided to allow the basic scrap buffer (cut-buffer) editing operations with editText items in a dialog window. DlgDelete is provided to permit editText item deletions.

Gem

After a dialog or form has been drawn (with objc_draw), the Gem AES routine form_do processes any interactions. For alerts use the Gem routine form_alert; for error boxes call the form_error routine. Both form_alert and form_error internally call form_do.

Windows

The Windows routine DialogBox displays a dialog and handles the interactions between the user and the dialog box.

Amiga

Request is used to display an Intuition requester. Once this happens any other kind of I/O to the window that owns the requester, other than gadget selection, is blocked. Transactions then come across an Amiga IDCMP (Intuition Direct Communication Message Port). The application is then supposed to wait for an IntuiMessage record to come across the IDCMP.

AutoRequest is the alternative to full-fledged requesters; an auto requester is one that has a single yes/no option. Calling AutoRequest draws the requester and handles the user interaction with the requester.

DisplayAlert renders an alert box and handles the user interaction with the box, returning the results when done.

MISCELLANEOUS ROUTINES

Windows

DlgDirList builds a list of files or directories. Once the list is made it can be displayed, and a user can select from the list or merely know what files are present.

The routine is normally called from a routine driving a dialog box. The five arguments are a handle to the dialog, a path specification pointer (a pointer to a string), an ID number of an MS Windows list box (where the list is inserted), an ID number of a static text control, and an integer that describes what kinds of files should be included in the list. These are the possible attributes:

Read-only file

Hidden file

System file

Subdirectory

Archive

Drive bit

Exclusive bit

They can be combined to be more specific.

DlgDirSelect copies the current file/directory selection from the directory list (which was built by DlgDirList) and sticks it into the buffer pointed to by one of the arguments.

MapDialogRect converts device-independent dialog coordinates into window coordinates. It needs a handle to the dialog box and a rectangle record for arguments.

DIALOG EXTENSIONS

In each of the windowing packages support is provided for a certain variety of controls (or gadgets). The degree of ease with which you may define unique controls, bring them into an application, and have the window environment support them, varies quite a bit. Gem is not as forgiving about expanding its base set of dialog controls as are Mac, IIGS, or Windows. Mac, IIGS, and Windows permit the application to define custom routines for processing item and dialog events/messages, making it is easier to add code to support odd dialog controls. All things considered, odd dialog controls are probably harder to code than are any of the controls that are already provided; it is much easier to use the existing controls. When you get down to it, a dialog control or gadget is merely a microcosm of interactive graphics; as such it is always possible to create more dialog controls, but possibly not within the existing frame of dialog control support.

Macintosh

The Mac's ModalDialog routine is called after a modal dialog routine is created and displayed in the foreground. The routine handles interactions within the dialog box until something happens that allows it to return. When it does return, it returns with the value of the dialog item selected by the user in one of the arguments.

There is a standard routine used to filter events when they are being generated while ModalDialog is running. When ModalDialog gets an event, it queries this standard event filter routine, which tells the caller if the event is one of those that should be dealt with.

It is possible to write a nonstandard filter routine and have Modal-Dialog use it. If ModalDialog is to use the standard event filter software, the filterProc parameter is set to 0 (NIL). If a nonstandard filter routine is defined, the filterProc parameter is a pointer to that routine. The filter procedure is to be defined with the following header:

```
FUNCTION CustomEventFilter(        theDialog:    DialogPtr;
                           VAR     theEvent:     EventRecord;
                           VAR     itemHit:      INTEGER): BOOLEAN;
```

The name of the function is up to you.

As discussed in the section on controls and gadgets (dialog items), the Macintosh easily supports user-defined and supported items. One of the item types is indicated by the constant userItem; this tells the application that the item won't be handled by any system-supported code.

The routine supporting the application-defined item that you write should have a declaration like the following:

```
PROCEDURE AnyOleItemFuncName(     the Window:    WindowPtr;
                                  itemNo:        INTEGER );
```

Gem

The form_do routine handles normal interactions with a dialog or alert. This includes only the predefined text and controls. To add controls requires writing a different routine that does the job of form_do to handle them. The form_do routine not only checks for events that take place within the screen area allocated to the dialog box, it also traverses the dialog box object tree to find the lowest-order component where the mouse cursor was at the time of the (mouse-down) event. Depending on the type of object it finds, form_do acts as Gem's agent and provides feedback, such as changing the color of a button, to the user.

While Apple and Microsoft still handle event captures and message generation when you write custom dialog control drivers, Gem requires that you also handle the events for a dialog.

Gem's standard set of dialog controls is not rich or fancy compared with the other environments, so it may be more necessary to "go out on a limb" when developing programs using Gem. The Gem form library and object library do support text operations of reasonable complexity for local, fixed format editing.

Windows

This windowing package provides a rich set of controls for dialogs. Among the set is a "user-definable" (actually an application-definable) button, where the graphics processing is up to the application. A Windows application has more global control over the processing of the messages that come in from the Windows runtime system. Also, when a dialog is created, it is possible to specify a custom function for processing the messages that are generated during dialog box interaction; it is at least a simple matter to patch into the existing dialog box support framework with custom dialog controls drivers. The architecture of the Windows package makes custom dialog controls at least conceptually fathomable.

Amiga

The gadget support for the Amiga assumes that you want to develop custom gadgets (controls) for dialog boxes, and for that matter other kinds of windows. It is possible, in fact, to devise custom gadgets for the window frames.

Intuition is designed to allow assigning custom graphics to gadgets, either bitmap or line-draw based. There is a distinction supported by Intuition between a gadget that is not selected and one that is selected, so all an application has to do is provide two forms of gadget graphics; it does not have to be too concerned with rendering gadget graphics.

Gadgets may also have no imagery at all.

An in-depth discussion of the flexibility of Amiga gadgets appears in the next section.

3.8   Controls, Gadgets, and Icons

All the controls in use around the frames of windows, and within dialog and alert boxes, are very simple uses of graphic icons. This section compares the standard window, dialog, and alert controls (and gadgets) of each environment covered in this book, and then winds up with an extrapolation of iconic interfaces as they might exist.

OVERVIEW

Gem, Windows, Macintosh, and IIGS have controls. On the Amiga they're called gadgets. A control is a device that is used to adjust the way a program works. A control is not a data item, nor is it part of a data base, but it is part of a program. The presence and operation of a control may depend on the presence of data.

Controls are the firmament of an iconic user interface. Here is what they provide graphically, sometimes without burdening the display with text description:

- ☐ The presence of a decision
- ☐ The opportunity to make a decision
- ☐ A current status
- ☐ The kind of decision that can be made
- ☐ With clever and consistent positioning, the significance of the status
- ☐ The impact of a decision
- ☐ A missing control, or a control shown to be unselectable, also carries meaning

Using Controls

Making a decision with a control normally involves moving the mouse cursor over a part of the control and one of the following: pressing the mouse button; pressing and then releasing the mouse button; pressing the button twice; and pressing the button, dragging the mouse, and then releasing the button. There are other methods; some controls might need text entry. Alternative methods of controlling the movement of the select cursor are by using a bit pad, digitizer puck, light pen, or cursor keys. Some mice have more than one button; pressing a particular button may influence a control differently.

Learning Safely

Controls have to make visual and cognitive sense. To help the learning process and to prevent accidents, controls that lead to destructive actions do not usually have the last say as to whether the act occurs; they are backed up by the appearance of an alert box, complete with text description and another control. In good software people can play with controls without getting burned. In the event that a mistake is made, good software can also back up a change, though considerable clock time might pass.

General Types

In the current windowing environments there are only a few types of standard, supported controls. None of the environments restrict you from designing your own controls (the reason for the success of big windowing environments is that they provide a mechanism for you to employ graphic icons in software systems), but some are better at it than others.

Most of the predefined controls have two possible states, represented by two different patterns that are visible at different times. Some controls have parts that move around, or have changing alphanumeric text fields. Some have all three kinds; the MacWrite scroll bar has arrows whose two states are selected and dormant, the scroll bar thumb which moves from side to side or top to bottom, and the file page number which appears inside the thumb.

WINDOW CONTROLS

Macintosh and the IIGS

Though all IIGS Macintosh controls are associated with a window, the GoAway, Drag, Zoom, and Grow Controls for a window are unique. They are drawn by the machine's window definition code when the window frame is drawn. Also, tracking these controls is done by routines in the window manager, not the controls manager. The presence of the window controls depends on the type of window created; there are a few predefined window types that are covered by the stock Mac window definition code and involve various configurations in which some or all of the window controls are present. Custom windows require custom window definition code.

The GoAway control is a little square in the top left portion of a window, within the rectangle that contains the window title (if there is one) and the Drag control. Picking the GoAway control is supposed to lead to the program closing and removing the window from the display.

The Drag control is the rectangle across the top of the window frame that contains the window title and the GoAway control. To use it, press the mouse button with the cursor over the drag control; you should then be able to move the window around on the screen until you release the mouse button.

The Grow control is stationed at the bottom right corner of the window. Pressing the mouse button with the cursor over the Grow control will enable you to drag the control around on the screen and consequently resize the window to taste.

The Zoom control is located at the top right corner of the window. Selecting the zoom box symbol will cause the window to be redrawn, taking over a good portion of the screen in the process. Reselecting the zoom box causes the window to be redrawn in its previous size.

When a mouse-down event comes in for a window, the Macintosh window definition code is given the location of the mouse cursor and the window descriptor record, and is asked to return one of the following constant values:

wNoHit	Pick does not involve any window controls
wInContent	Mouse pick is within the window content region and not in the grow region (if the window is active)
wInDrag	Mouse pick occurred in the drag region
wInGrow	Mouse pick happened in the grow region; will only happen if it was the active window
wInGoAway	Mouse pick occurred in the goaway region; will happen only if it was the active window
wInZoomIn	Mouse pick is in zoom region for zooming in
wInZoomOut	Mouse pick is in zoom region for zooming out

The window definition code is considered to be the low-level interpreter of mouse-down actions for a window, and is called by the window manager routine FindWindow. FindWindow is used to track down in which window (if any) the mouse-down event took place. If a window is involved, FindWindow uses the appropriate window definition code to track down which part of the window; both the part and a pointer to the window record are returned. The constants that identify the part returned by FindWindow are:

inDesk	None of the following
inMenuBar	Pick took place in the menu bar

inSysWindow	Pick took place in the system window
inContent	Pick took place in the content region of a window, excluding the grow region if it is the active window
inDrag	Pick took place in the drag region
inGrow	Pick took place in the grow region
inGoAway	Pick took place in the goaway region
inZoomIn	Pick took place in the zoom in region
inZoomOut	Pick took place in the zoom out region (same as zoom in)

The grow and goaway controls of a window are not visible and not selectable when the window is not active.

When one of the above values is returned (except for inDesk), the application is expected to react by calling one of the routines that drives the rest of the sequence of events to conclude the control section. These routines are executing. They must watch the mouse cursor being moved while the mouse button is down, and then return appropriate status and data when the button is released.

When inGoAway is returned, the application should call the window manager function TrackGoAway, which will watch the mouse activity until the mouse button is released. If the mouse button was released while the cursor was still in the goaway region, then TrackGoAway returns TRUE; otherwise it returns FALSE. While the cursor is in the GoAway region, TrackGoAway is supposed to display the alternate form of the GoAway control, an asterisk. How the control is highlighted is again up to the window definition code for that window. It is important to note that, while TrackGoAway is executing, the main event loop is not doing anything else.

Similar behavior is expected of the application when values inDrag or inGrow are returned; the routine DragWindow is called for inDrag, and GrowWindow is called for inGrow. The routines MoveWindow and Size-Window change the window record after DragWindow and GrowWindow, respectively, do the move and grow animation and then return the changes.

Zooming depends on the state of the window (whether it has already zoomed out or in), but the consequence of a zoom box selection is to call TrackBox, which works like TrackGoAway but for the zoom box. Depending on the returned result of TrackBox, you may have to call ZoomWindow to effect the change in the window size.

The interface for the window definition code is shown below. Window definition code, which could be any number of procedures and functions, has to handle seven operations:

wDraw	Draw the window frame
wHit	Tell where the mouse cursor was when the mouse-down event occurred
wCalcRgns	Determine strucRgn and contRgn
wNew	Do "extra" window initialization
wDispose	Do "extra" window cleanup
wGrow	Render this window's grow image
wDrawGIcon	Draw the size box

The declaration of an example window definition function (the one at the top of all the window definition code) is:

```
function WinDefFunc(    variation:    integer;   (* Window type variation.*)
                        theWindow:    WindowPtr;(* Window record pointer. *)
                        operation:    integer;   (* wDraw, etc *)
                        param:        LongInt    (* Operation dependent. *)
                        ):            LongInt;   (* Return value when approp.*)
```

IIGS—Macintosh Differences

There are some differences between Macintosh window frame controls and those available on the IIGS. The IIGS windows and those on Macintoshes with 128K (or larger) ROM can have a zoom box. On the IIGS the size of the scroll thumbs (or indicators) is proportional to the ratio between the range of the world coordinate system addressed by the scroll bar and the extent of the displayable portion of the coordinate system in the window. Gem's thumbs are exactly like those on the IIGS.

The returned results from FindWindow (see the description in the Mac section above) have different constant names, and there are more of them:

wNoHit	A near miss
wInDesk	Pick on the desktop
wInMenuBar	Pick on the system menu bar
wInSysMenu	Pick in a system window

wInContent	Pick in a window content region
wInDrag	Pick in drag region
wInGrow	Pick in grow region
wInGoAway	Pick in goaway region
wInZoom	Pick in zoom region
wInInfo	Pick in information bar
wInHScroll	Pick in vertical scroll bar
wInVScroll	Pick in horizontal scroll bar
wInFrame	Pick in window, excluding the areas mentioned above

Other differences of interest may include the IIGS frame color control routines SetFrameColor and GetFrameColor, which are used to adjust the colors of each of the visible fields in a window frame; the frame, title, title bar, content background, close box, zoom box, grow box, and information bar colors are individually adjustable.

Improvements

The Macintosh code required to watch controls has prompted the development of "canned" application code that does most of the work already, so that all that needs to be done is to use the routines. The Apple IIGs solution for this is called TaskMaster, and unless you are defining unusual window classes, it is probably unnecessary for your code to directly interact with the window and control animation routines.

Gem

When a Gem window is created, all the window frame controls that are going to be present have to be mentioned in a bit field argument to the wind_create routine. These controls are:

CLOSE	Close box
FULL	Full box (select it to toggle window between full screen and the preset size)
MOVE	Move bar (coincides with the window title bar)
SIZE	Size box
UPARROW	Up arrow

DNARROW	Down arrow
VSLIDE	Vertical slider (aka "thumb" or indicator)
LFARROW	Left arrow
RTARROW	Right arrow
HSLIDE	Horizontal slider

When a window is on the screen, any interaction with the window frame controls is processed by Gem first. The application doesn't find out about the interaction until Gem sends the application an event message detailing the significant results. The application is responsible for the consequences of control interaction and not for the real-time parts (like watching the mouse being dragged around, as is done by Mac application code).

There doesn't appear to be an easy way using the Gem AES Window Library to define custom windows, much less create custom window frame controls. To do this seems to require extensive work with object trees and custom event messages. I don't know for certain how to do this satisfactorily without entirely bypassing Gem.

Windows

The window frame controls for a window are specified as window style attributes in the a Style bitfield argument for the CreateWindow routine. Here are the attributes that have to do with controls:

WS_ICONIC	Create a TILED window that is initially iconic (window is displayed as an icon in the icon area)
WS_SYSMENU	Window is given a system menu box in caption bar
WS_CAPTION	Window has a caption bar
WS_SIZEBOX	Window has a sizing box
WS_VSCROLL	Window has a vertical scroll bar control
WS_HSCROLL	Window has a horizontal scroll bar control

Like Gem, Windows applications do not have to take part in driving the real-time parts of interacting with controls; the Windows runtime does all that. The results of control interactions are sent as messages to an application's window message queue, where they are extracted by Get-Message, forwarded by DispatchMessage, and fielded (again) by the application's ShapesWndProc routine. Some additional details on these routines are available in the section on events.

Custom window frame controls are possible, depending on the type of Windows window involved. Tiled windows aren't very flexible, but child windows are; it's possible to nest them so that one child window acts as the frame for another. Custom control manipulation takes place with the application doing all of the work (including animation) unless normal Windows controls are employed.

Amiga

Amiga controls, called gadgets, reside in the frames of both windows and screens. These are called **system gadgets**, and are predefined by Intuition (for consistency). The other kind of gadgets, custom application gadgets, are discussed in the next section.

Here is a list of the predefined system gadgets:

Sizing	For changing the size of a window
Dragging	For dragging screens and windows
Depth Arrangement	For changing the display priority of a window/screen
Close	For requesting window close

When you select a Close gadget, a close window request message is broadcast to the program that owns the window. The program is then expected to do whatever it wants, but ideally it should call the CloseWindow routine. It is an option because it may be nice to be able to display a requester (just to be sure) before the call to CloseWindow is made.

The depth arrangement gadget is handy; you not only use it to bring a window to the foreground, you can also use it to send a window to the background to reveal windows that may have been entirely obscured.

The sizing and dragging gadgets work just like those of Gem and Windows, with the exception that resizing can be blocked for a while by making arrangements beforehand. If a program is using an IDCMP port for messages, the SIZEVERIFY flag of the IDCMP may be set and a message will be generated when the sizing gadget is selected.

Here are the names of the bits that have to be set in the Flags field of an Intuition NewWindow record for the window to have the system gadgets:

WINDOWCLOSE

WINDOWDEPTH

WINDOWDRAG

WINDOWSIZING

Custom Window Frame Gadgets

The Gadget record has position fields that can be set so that the gadget winds up in the border of a window (only). The flag bits to study are kept in the Activation field:

RIGHTBORDER

LEFTBORDER

TOPBORDER

These custom window gadgets can be added to a window's repertoire through the AddGadget routine, and yanked with the RemoveGadget routine.

DIALOG AND ALERT CONTROLS

Macintosh

The Mac control manager routines are used to make, display, change, and remove controls, monitor user-interaction with a control, and report the control settings.

The following are standard Macintosh control types:

buttons	Round-corner rectangles with text inside; when selected they lead to immediate action; when held they can lead to continuous action.
check boxes	Squares that reflect a current setting that is to be used in the future; a check box either has a check in it or is empty; when selected the state of the check box is changed, but nothing immediate should occur.

radio button Two or more round "check boxes" in which only one is "set" at a time in a group; the set radio button contains a round black circle, the rest are empty; like check boxes, changing the states of radio buttons should not invoke immediate action. Mac supports the graphics but does not change the states of other radio buttons in a group when one button is changed.

dials The scroll bar (the only predefined dial on the Mac); sports a moving part called an indicator (the "thumb" on the Mac scroll bar) that can be dragged with the mouse.

Any dialog control can be inactive; this is indicated by the control label text being drawn as a fuzzy halftone, rather than in black, and by the control being displayed without grey tone or black color.

Highlighted or selected buttons are drawn inverted (black). Selected state controls like check boxes and radio buttons are drawn with a thicker outline, since selection only leads to a semipermanent change of state that is indicated by the symbol displayed within.

Elaborate controls can have several parts, each identified with an integer number from 1 to 253 (excluding, for some reason, the value 128). Parts of controls are manipulated by identifying the part with the control and the part number.

Custom controls can be defined by creating new **control definition code**, which is the low-level module that drives control operations, and is the code that everything else uses. The control definition function can handle the following operations:

drawCntrl	Draw the control
testCntl	Test where the mouse button was pressed
calcCRgns	Calculate control's region or indicators
initCntl	Execute any further control initialization
dispCntl	Execute any further control cleanup
posCntl	Reposition and update control indicator
thumbCntl	Determine dragging indicator parameters
autoTrack	Execute control action procedure

Gem

There aren't too many predefined Gem controls for Gem Forms and Dialog, Alert, and Error boxes. A control is implemented in Gem in the same way as everything else that is graphic (as a Gem object). Using the defined object primitives and several of the Graf Library routines, a small number of controls become available with little effort. It is possible (by building object trees) to define anything that can act as a mouse-controllable graphic object, and reflect state changes in the controls by changing the object tree on the fly.

The Gem AES Form and Dialog box, driven by the Gem form_do routine, understand that objects in an object tree that are of type G_BOXTEXT can be selectable buttons. The OBJECT structure flags for G_BOXTEXT objects that are intended to be used in this way should have the SELECTABLE and EXIT bits set. One of the buttons must also have bits set for DEFAULT and LASTOB.

Technically, Gem can use graphic object records and trees to handle more than the simple controls that are most directly provided, but obviously to do so is more challenging than simply saying "OK, put a circular scroll bar right there in the dialog."

Graf Library Routines

For animation prompted by selecting controls, or just for everyday graphics window editing, there are six graphics animation routines from the Gem AES Graf Library:

graf_rubberbox draws an animated box outline that changes size from a fixed screen location as the mouse cursor is moved.

graf_draqbox is used to animate moving a box. The mouse cursor is kept to the same point within the box outline.

graf_growbox and graf_shrinkbox are used to animate a growing or shrinking box respectively. The initial and final coordinates (and proportions) are provided as arguments.

graf_movebox draws a moving box without distorting the size of the box.

graf_slidebox draws a box that is allowed to move within a parent box.

For a little more information on Gem object trees, check out the graphics section in this book.

The Gem Alert box is, incidentally, defined not by using an object tree, but by a call to form_alert with a text string containing all the needed text and button information. form_alert builds a temporary object tree from the text string and displays it.

Windows

The Microsoft approach to controls is quite different from that of Gem or the Macintosh. A control is defined to be a child window used by any program for I/O. Controls are a "big deal" in Windows.

There are defined control classes, styles, messages, notification codes, and notification messages.

Controls can be created, either by using CreateWindow or by defining Dialog box controls with a resource script.

Control Classes

Here are the predefined Windows control window types:

BUTTON	Rectangular child window that can have two states
EDIT	Rectangular child window for containing editable text
STATIC	Used to prettyprint other controls; noninteractive
ListBox	The strings in a string list box are controls
ScrollBar	Typical scroll bar control

The available predefined control styles are shown below. A control type may have one or more of these styles.

These are button control styles:

BS_PUSHBUTTON	Mouse-selectable box containing a string; parent notified
BS_CHECKBOX	Two-state square; if set a small box appears; the parent window is not notified when selected
BS_RADIOBUTTON	A two-state square grouped with others so that only one in the group can be set at a time; the application must drive this function

BS_AUTOCHECKBOX	Like checkbox, only this automatically toggles its state when selected
BS_3STATE	Like the checkbox, only capable of showing a greyed third state, which is used to show that the control is disabled
BS_AUTO3STATE	A three-state checkbox that automatically toggles when selected
BS_GROUPBOX	A rectangle used to group several other controls together
BS_USERBUTTON	A button that tells the parent window when it is selected

These are edit control styles:

ES_LEFT	Unframed left-justified text field
ES_RIGHT	Unframed right-justified text field; text is justified on user input
ES_CENTER	Unframed center-justified text field
ES_FRAMED	Draw frame around edit field
ES_NOTEFOCUS	Notify parent when Windows input focus is gained or lost
ES_NOCHANGE	Create an uneditable edit control, but the characters in the control are selectable
ES_NOTECLICK	Control should notify parent when control is selected
ES_MULTILINE	Make a multiple line edit control
ES_AUTOVSCROLL	Make a multiple line edit control with auto vertical push scrolling (window contents move to accommodate window space needs)
ES_AUTOHSCROLL	Make a multiple line edit control with auto horizontal push scrolling

These are static control styles:

SS_LEFT	Make left-justified text field

SS_RIGHT	Make right-justified text field
SS_CENTER	Make center-justified text field
SS_ICON	Draw an icon
SS_BLACKRECT	Draw a filled rectangle (black)
SS_GRAYRECT	Draw a filled rectangle (grey)
SS_WHITERECT	Draw a filled rectangle (white)
SS_BLACKFRAME	Draw a box with colored frame (black)
SS_GRAYFRAME	Draw a box with colored frame (grey)
SS_WHITEFRAME	Draw a box with colored frame (white)
SS_USERITEM	Make a user-defined item
SS_ENTERPRISE	Blatant attempt to insert joke into finished copy

Here are the list box control styles:

LBS_NOTIFY	Notify parent window when string clicked or double-clicked
LBS_MULTIPLESEL	Toggle string selection on click/double-click; allows multiple string selection
LBS_SORT	Sort strings in listbox alphabetically
LBS_NOREDRAW	Do not update listbox display if changes made

Finally, here are the predefined scroll bar styles:

SBS_VERT	Make vertical scroll bar
SBS_LEFTALIGN	Make vertical scroll bar along left edge of window
SBS_RIGHTALIGN	Make vertical scroll bar along right edge of window
SBS_HORZ	Make a horizontal scroll bar
SBS_TOPALIGN	Make horizontal scroll bar along top edge of window
SBS_BOTTOMALIGN	Make horizontal scroll bar along bottom edge of window

IIGS

The IIGS controls manager is similar to its counterpart on the Macintosh. The control definition function operations are expanded; it handles, for example, the redrawing of controls that have been moved on the display.

Amiga

There are four types of application gadgets:

Boolean	Extricate TRUE/FALSE type answers
Proportional	Freeform slider/knob-based analog device emulation
String	Text edit fields
Integer	Text edit fields interpreted to be integers only

There are two ways to render gadgets:

Hand-Drawn	Uses free-form bitmap images (via Image record)
Line-Drawn	Uses an Intuition Border structure instance

There is a third kind of gadget rendering:

No Displayed Image	It is sufficient that the gadget be located somewhere on the display, but without visible representation

Gadget Selection
A program can be notified immediately by a GADGETDOWN message that a gadget has been selected. With the RELVERIFY flag set the GADGETDOWN message isn't generated, but a GADGETUP message is sent when the mouse button is released over the gadget.

Gadget Selection Region
A gadget selection area is described in terms of offset coordinates (in pixels) from the border of the containing screen, window, or requester. The height and width are also described in pixels, in terms of distances from the border or as a static height and width.

Follow The Mouse Option

There is a flag available for gadget definition that, if set, causes mouse movement messages to be broadcast while the gadget is selected.

Highlighting

Selected gadget highlighting is done with one of the following methods:

None	The GADGHNONE bit in the Flags field of a Gadget record must be set
Color Complement	The color of the select area of a gadget is bitwise inverted. The GADGHCOMP bit should be set in the Flags field of a Gadget record.
Draw Box Outline	The GADGHBOX bit is set in the Flags field.
Image	Set SelectRender field of Gadget record to custom Image record
Alternate Border	Set SelectRender field of Gadget record to custom Border record

Disable/Enable Control

Setting the GADGDISABLE bit in the Flags field of the Gadget record will render a gadget unselectable.

CONTROL ROUTINES AND DATA STRUCTURES

Macintosh

Here is the Macintosh version of the ControlRecord; the IIGS version is likely to be similar, but no necessarily the same:

```
Type ControlRecord = RECORD
    nextControl:      ControlHandle;     { Points to next control record.}
    contrlOwner:      WindowPtr;         { Point to control's window.}
    contrlRect:       Rect;              { Enclosing rectangle.}
    contrlVis:        BOOLEAN;           { TRUE if visible, FALSE if not.}
    contrlHilite:     BOOLEAN;           { TRUE if highlighted.}
    contrlValue:      INTEGER;           { Current control setting.}
    contrlMin:        INTEGER;           { Minimum selectable setting.}
```

```
contrlMax:          INTEGER;            { Maximum selectable setting.}
contrlDefProc:      Handle;             { Control's definition function.}
contrlData:         Handle;             { Data used by contrlDefProc.}
contrlAction:       ProcPtr;            { Default action procedure.}
contrlRfCon:        LongInt;            { control's reference value.}
contrlTitle:        Str255;             { Control's title string.}
ControlPtr =        ^ControlRecord;     { Pointer to a control record.}
ControlHandle =     ^ControlPtr;        { Handle to a control record.}
```

Control Manipulation Routines

NewControl and GetNewControl are both used to establish new controls. The created control is added to the top of the control list for the specified window. NewControl has nine arguments, since everything about the control is specified in the parameters. GetNewControl has only two arguments, since most of the design information is supplied in the control template in the resource file from which GetNewControl builds the control. Both routines return a handle to the new control.

NewControl accepts the following parameters: a pointer to the window that gets the control; the bounds rectangle for the new control; the title string for the control; a boolean indicating the visibility of the control; the initial, minimum and maximum values; the control definition ID; and a private reference value that will make sense only to the application.

GetNewControl requires a pointer to the owner window and the control template resource ID number.

DisposeControl accepts one parameter, a handle to the control, and removes any trace of it from the system.

KillControls removes all trace of every control owned by the window specified in the routine's only argument.

SetCTitle is used to redefine the title string for a control. The control is redrawn. The GetCTitle routine is used to return the title string of the specified control as an argument, changing nothing else.

The routine HideControl is used to hide a control from view. Anything obscured by the control will become visible. The ShowControl routine will make an invisible control visible; if the window that contains the control is not obscured by other windows, then the control will appear on the display.

DrawControls is used to render all the controls that belong to the indicated window. The oldest controls will overlap the youngest if there are conflicts.

HiliteControl is used to highlight part of a control. A Mac IIGS control can have 253 different parts, so the routine is given a handle to the control and an integer number identifying the part to highlight. Pass HiliteControl a 254 or a 255 and the entire control is rendered as an inactive control. The value 254 is used for controls that can still be identified as the selected control, even when inactive.

TestControl is used to determine which part of the control contains the location specified by a Point type record, normally the location of the cursor during a mouse-down event. The function returns the part number; if the control is inactive (and visible), the value returned is 254. Invisible controls, or controls inactive with the value 255 (see HiliteControl above) cause a value of 0 to be returned.

The routine FindControl accepts a global coordinate and a pointer to a window record. It returns a handle to the control that contains the coordinate. It also returns the integer value identifying the part of the control within which the coordinate falls, using the same rules that TestControl follows.

TrackControl is the "animation" routine for controls. When a user selects a part of an active control, TrackControl should be called to watch what the user does with the control until the mouse button is released again. The routine is given a handle to the control being animated, the initial coordinate selected with the mouse, and a pointer to the control definition function. When the mouse button is released, the integer value identifying the part of the control in which the cursor is returned.

MoveControl can be used to move the indicated control around within the window (a pointer to which is also an argument of the procedure). Two other parameters indicate the new local horizontal and vertical coordinates.

DragControl is used to animate dragging a control around on the screen; it draws a grey outline on the screen following the movements of the mouse cursor. When the mouse button is released, the control is redrawn at the new location.

SetCtlValue and GetCtlValue are used to assign and obtain, respectively, the current setting of the indicated control. Upon assignment the control is redrawn to reflect the change.

SetCtlMin and GetCtlMin are used to access the indicated control's minimum possible setting. SetCtlMax and GetCtlMax are likewise used to access the indicated control's maximum possible setting.

SetCRefCon and GetCRefCon are for accessing the specified control's reference value. This reference value can be anything that fits in a long integer, as needed by the application code. Go wild!

SetCtlAction and GetCtlAction are used to assign and return, respectively, a pointer to the action procedure for the indicated control. These routines access the action procedure pointer field in the control record.

Gem

Object trees are used for almost everything under Gem, and controls are no exception. A description of Gem object trees can be found in the section on graphics.

The Gem AES functions that are provided, form_do and form_alert, are given an object tree which they interpret as being an entire form or dialog. Gem AES controls appear as members of the dialog object tree; they do not appear as isolated objects. In contrast, a Gem AES window frame control isn't part of an object tree, and is not controlled using the form routine library; Gem keeps track of windows and window frame controls internally, and window frame controls are created when the window is created.

Custom application routines will have to be written to interpret different object trees to your taste, as Gem provides your application only with the few members of the form library, and leaves you to your own devices when it comes to emulating the fancier controls of the other environments. You must start with Gem mouse-down event messages to find out if a mouse-pick has occurred within a particular area of the display; you must also supply the code that drives the graphic interactions.

Windows

An application talks to predefined controls by way of the routines Send-Message and PostMessage. There are no routines that can be called to directly manipulate the appearance of a predefined Windows control. Windows informs an application of activity (possibly involving a predefined control) with a message sent to the application's appropriate parent window. The application may react by changing the status displayed by the control. This is done by sending the control a control message (via SendMessage). Windows is the actual recipient of the control messages, and will change the image of the control accordingly.

Here is a play-by-play account of what happens. Windows leaves it to the application to interpret certain events within the domain of its windows. A mouse-down message in a parent window may be further interpreted by the application as a selection within a child window; further interpretation may reveal that the child window is a control. The application makes the required internal changes, and then tells Windows to change the appearance of the control to match. The original event message is simple and generalized; it is one of the "reply" messages that the application sends back to Windows that changes the control.

Controls that have no precedents in Windows will have to be treated as original creations by the application; code will have to be provided by the application to drive the control's image. In this case a reply message to Windows to change the state of the control is not sent.

Amiga

Here is the definition for a Gadget data structure.

```
struct Gadget {
      struct Gadget *NextGadget; /* The next gadget in the linked list.*/
      SHORT        LeftEdge,     /* Location & dimensions of the gadget */
                                 /*  select box.*/

                   TopEdge,
                   Width,
                   Height;
      USHORT       Flags;        /* The flag bits for the gadget.*/
      USHORT       Activation;   /* More flags used to describe attributes.*/
      USHORT       GadgetType;   /* Even MORE flags to state gadget type.*/
      APTR         GadgetRender; /* Ptr. to current gadget image record.*/
      APTR         SelectRender; /* Ptr to the alternate (or highlighted) */
                                 /* version of the gadget image.*/
      struct IntuiText *GadgetText; /* A text string associated with gadget.*/
      LONG         MutualExclude;   /* Bits used to exclude other gadgets.*/
      APTR         SpecialInfo; /* Ptr to addl data needed for proportional,*/
                                /*  string, and integer gadgets.*/
      USHORT       GadgetID;    /* The programmer customizable entry.*/
      APTR         UserData;    /* The programmer custom entry: sky's limit.*/
```

The following record is used to store the additional information required by proportional gadgets:

```
struct PropInfo {             /* Proportional gadget (addl.) information.*/
    USHORT Flags;             /* Additional feature flag bits.*/
    USHORT HorizPot;          /* Percent of horizontal.*/
    USHORT VertPot;           /* Percent of vertical.*/
    USHORT HorizBody;         /* Range of horizontal selectivity.*/
    USHORT VertBody;          /* Range of vertical selectivity.*/
    USHORT CWidth;            /* Real width of container.*/
```

```
USHORT CHeight;            /* Real height of container.*/
USHORT HpotRes,            /* Horizontal increment size.*/
       VPotRes;            /* Vertical increment size.*/
USHORT LeftBorder;         /* Real left border of container.*/
USHORT TopBorder;          /* Real top border of container.*/
```

A similar record exists for string gadgets:

```
struct StringInfo {        /* For string gadgets.*/
    UBYTE *Buffer;         /* Pointer to a null-terminated string buffer.*/
    UBYTE *UndoBuffer;     /* Ptr. to an edit buffer to reverse dumb changes.*/
    SHORT BufferPos;       /* Initial cursor character position in buffer.*/
    SHORT MaxChars;        /* Number of characters in buffer, including NULL.*/
    SHORT DispPos;         /* Position of first displayed char in buffer.*/
    SHORT UndoPos;         /* Position of first character kept in undo buffer.*/
    SHORT NumChars;        /* Currently buffered character count.*/
    SHORT DispCount;       /* Number of chars visible in container.*/
    SHORT  CLeft,          /* Left location of container.*/
           CTop;           /* Location of the top of the container.*/
    struct Layer *LayerPtr; /* The layer that this gadget is in.*/
    LONG LongInt;          /* Contains the integer value of data string.*/
    struct KeyMap *AltKeyMap; /* Points to an alternate key map.*/
```

AddGadget is used to add a gadget to the list of the indicated screen or window. RemoveGadget is used to do the reverse.

OnGadget will turn the indicated gadget on, making it selectable; the routine needs a pointer to the gadget record, a pointer to the screen or window structure, and an optional pointer to the requester that may own the gadget. OffGadget is used to disable a gadget; it uses the same argument list as OnGadget.

RefreshGadgets is used to redraw all the gadgets that belong to the indicated screen, requester, or window.

ModifyProp is provided to allow changing the operational parameters of a proportional gadget. When the contents of the proportional gadget record are modified, the gadget is redrawn with the new values in mind.

SYNOPSIS

There are two major classes of controls: window frame controls and controls that wind up in dialog and alerts. Window frame controls are a separate issue under Gem, Macintosh, IIGS, and Amiga. On the Amiga controls are called gadgets, and the predefined window (and screen) controls are called system gadgets. Under Windows window frame controls are handled the same as other controls; controls are client windows, which are controlled through Windows using standard messages. Screen interactions with controls result in the generation of standard messages.

Figure 3–60 is a table of the essential operations of controls:

```
* Example Resource File for Filigree

FiligreeRes

Type DLOG
,111 (4)
Info Dialog
94 70 232 442
Visible GoAway
1
0
111

Type DITL
,111
4
*    1
BtnItem Enabled
104 142 129 227
Heavy

*    2
StatText Disabled
22 61 39 302
Phil Foglio Filigree Generator v0.1

*    3
StatText Disabled
56 8 91 367
Demo for TVT by Michael Brian Bentley.\0DCopyright notice goes here.

*    4
IconItem Enabled
14 21 46 53
111
```

Figure 3–60A Old resource compiler source for example modal dialog

Operation on Control

System or Environment	Define and Create at Runtime	Define in Resource Create from Resource Template	Remove
Macintosh	NewControl	GetNewControl	DisposeControl KillControls
2GS	NewControl	No Equivalent	DisposeControl KillControls
MS Windows (Excludes Edit Controls)	CreateWindow (for edit controls. Other controls can be defined only in dialog resources)	CreateDialog DialogBox (EndDialog)	DestroyWindow EndDialog
Amiga	AddGadget	No Equivalent	RemoveGadget
Gem (Excludes Form Text-field Editing)	objc_add	rsrc_load, rsrc_gaddr, but not as easy as other window systems	objc_delete

Figure 3–60B How each window system implements common control operations

Operation on Control

Move	Select/Highlight	Drag	Activate
MoveControl (Control Definition Function: drawCntl)	HiliteControl (given a value of 1 through 253) (Control Definition Function: drawCntl)	DragControl (Control Definition Function: dragCntl)	HiliteControl (given a value from 0 to 253)
MoveControl (Control Definition Function: drawCntl)	HiliteControl (given a value of 1 through 253) (Control Definition Function: drawCntl)	DragControl (Control Definition Function: dragCntl)	HiliteControl (given a value from 0 to 253)
MoveWindow	Send message BM_SETSTATE to the control with the SendMessage routine	Handled by MS Windows	EnableWindow ShowWindow: SHOW_OPENWINDOW
Change fields in Gadget record: LeftEdge, TopEdge	Set the SELECTED bit in the Gadget record Flags field is toggled	Handled by Intuition	OnGadget (affects GADGDISABLED bit in field Flags of Gadget record
objc_order (may affect location on display); Change ob_x, ob_y fields in OBJECT record	objc_change	graf_dragbox	objc_change

Figure 3–60B (continued)

Operation on Control

System or Environment	Deactivate	Control Visibility	Animate
Macintosh	HiliteControl (given values 254 or 255)	HideControl ShowControl	TrackControl DragControl (Control Definition Function: autoTrack)
2GS	HiliteControl (given values 254 or 255)	HideControl ShowControl	TrackControl DragControl (Control Definition Function: autoTrack)
MS Windows (Excludes Edit Controls)	EnableWindow ShowWindow: HIDE_WINDOW (also see Control Styles BS_3STATE and BS_AUTO3STATE)	ShowWindow: HIDE_WINDOW ShowWindow: SHOW_OPENWINDOW (IsWindowVisible)	Handled by MS Windows
Amiga	OffGadget	Zero the GADGIMAGE flag, and set GadgetRender pointer to NULL, to render invisible (but still Active). Return the pointer value and set the Flag to restore visibility.	Set the FOLLOWMOUSE flag to turn on mouse movement reports. Used with GADGIMMEDIATE flag bit to report on mouse button down when gadget is selected. You are told which gadget is picked.
Gem (Excludes Form Text-field Editing)	objc_change	Adjust HIDETREE bit in ob_flags field of OBJECT record	Use members of the GRAF library: graf_rubberbox, graf_dragbox, graf_movebox, graf_growbox, graf_shrinkbox

Figure 3–60B (continued)

Operation on Control

Test (Which part of control is cursor in)	Find	Draw	Initialization
TestControl	FindControl	(Control Definition Function: drawCntl)	(Control Definition Function: initCntl)
TestControl	FindControl	(Control Definition Function: drawCntl)	(Control Definition Function: initCntl)
Handled by MS Windows	Handled by MS Windows	Handled by MS Windows	Done in code with calls to SetDlgItemInt
Handled by Intuition (see Animate)	Handled by Intuition (see Animate)	RefreshGadgets (redraws ALL gadgets)	Application code sets up Gadget record, etc. to taste
Normally handled by Gem; wind_find	Normally handled by Gem; wind_find	wind_calc, objc_draw	OBJECT record set from resource file or by application code; Add OBJECT to tree via object-add

Figure 3–60B (continued)

Operation on Control

System or Environment	Termination	Manipulate Position Indicator	Manipulate Position Range	Change Selection Area
Macintosh	(Control Definition Function: dispCntl)	(Control Definition Function: thumbCntl) SetCtlValue (Control Definition Function: posCntl)	GetCtlMin SetCtlMin GetCtlMax SetCtlMax	SizeControl (Control Definition Function: calcCRgns)
2GS	(Control Definition Function: dispCntl)	(Control Definition Function: thumbCntl) SetCtlValue (Control Definition Function: posCntl)	GetCtlMin SetCtlMin GetCtlMax SetCtlMax	SizeControl (Control Definition Function: calcCRgns)
MS Windows (Excludes Edit Controls)	Handled by MS Windows	SetScrollPos (Scroll Bar Thumb) GetScrollPos	SetScrolllRange	Handled by MS Windows
Amiga	Handled by Intuition (via RemoveGadget)	ModifyProp	ModifyProp	See Animate, Drag; change fields in Gadget record: Width, Height
Gem (Excludes Form Text-field Editing)	objc_delete	For frame controls: wind_set, wind_get	For frame controls: wind_set, wind_get	Modify object records accordingly in application code

Figure 3–60B (continued)

Operation on Control

Manipulate Control Value	Manipulate Control Caption (Title)	Is User Selecting THIS Control Right Now?	Is Message for THIS Dialog?
SetCtlValue GetCtlValue	GetCTitle SetCTitle	TestControl	Must be determined by application
SetCtlValue GetCtlValue	GetCTitle SetCTitle	TestControl	Must be determined by application
CheckDlgButton CheckRadioButton SendMessage: BM_SETCHECK IsDlgButtonChecked SendMessage: BM_GETCHECK	GettDlgItmInt GetDlgItemText SetDlgItmInt SetDlgItemText	SendMessage: BM_GETSTATE	IsDialogMessage
Change PropInfo record contents; Use ModifyProp	Change the GadgetText char array contents (pointed to by Gadget record)	No Equivalent; see Animate	Intuition includes this data with message
Modify object record in application code; use objc_change for simple controls	Modify object record in application code	graf_watchbox	Gem includes this with message

Figure 3–60B (continued)

3.9 | Advanced Text Editing Support

The Macintosh has an additional layer of support for text editing operations beyond that mentioned in Section 3.7. The design and implementation of these routines may or may not be adequate for all applications; many developers foresake the use of the TextEdit routines in favor of their own versions that at least follow the TextEdit/Mac user-interface standard.

Since the standard libraries for Windows, Gem for the PC or ST, and Amiga do not provide equivalents, it may be necessary to write your own set of higher-level text routines for those machines. The advanced text support library for the Apple IIGS currently has not been described; it is not expected to be the same as the present form of the Macintosh TextEdit routine library. Third-party libraries may also be available to provide equivalent services, so it will be a point of interest to look for them and find out what machines they are for.

The Macintosh TextEdit routines provide basic editing functions (including text scrolling, insertion, and deletion), cut buffer operations, and translating mouse activity into text operations. A majority of Macintosh products use the text operation standards that are supported by TextEdit. This has had a remarkable impact on the ease of learning Mac software.

The TextEdit routines commonly use a Macintosh handle to an edit record containing a ridiculous amount of useful information about a handy array of characters. The record type is defined as follows:

```
TYPE CharsHandle =       ^CharsPtr;    {Character block handle.}

     CharsPtr =          ^Chars;       {Character block pointer.}

     Chars =             PACKED ARRAY[0..32000] OF CHAR;   {Char. block.}

     TEPtr =             ^TERec;       {Macintosh TERec handle definition.}

     TEHandle =          TEPtr;        {Macintosh TERec pointer definition.}

     TERec = RECORD                    {TML Pascal version of TextEdit record.}

          destRect:      Rect;         {Destination rectangle: entirety.}

          viewRect:      Rect;         {View rectangle: visible portion.}

          selRect:       Rect;         {Select rectangle.}

          lineHeight:    Integer;      {Line height, ascent to ascent.}

          fontAscent:    Integer;      {Current font ascent: caret drawn here.}
```

```
selPoint:      Point;        {Selection point(mouseLoc).}

selStart:      Integer;      {Start of selected highlighted text.}

selEnd:        Integer;      {End of highlighted text.}

active:        Integer;      {This field <> 0 if active.}

wordBreak:     ProcPtr;      {Word break routine.}

clikLoop:      ProcPtr;      {Click loop routine.}

clickTime:     LongInt;      {Time of first click.}

clickLoc:      Integer;      {Character location of click.}

caretTime:     LongInt;      {Time for next caret blink.}

caretState:    Integer;      {On/active Booleans.}

just:          Integer;      {The fill style.}

TELength:      Integer;      {The length of text below.}

hText:         Handle;       {Ahandle to actual text}

recalBack:     Integer;      {<>0 if recal in background.}

recalLines:    Integer;      {The line being recalled.}

clikStuff:     Integer;      {This field is used internally.}

crOnly:        Integer;      {Set to -1 if CR line breaks only.}

txFont:        Integer;      {The text Font.}

txFace:        Style;        {The text Face.}

txMode:        Integer;      {The text Mode.}

txSize:        Integer;      {The text Size.}

inPort:        GrafPtr;      {Pointer to the GrafPort.}

highHook:      ProcPtr;      {The highlighting routine.}

caretHook:     ProcPtr;      {The caret draw routine.}

nLines:        Integer;      {The number of lines.}

lineStarts:                  {Actual line starts themselves.}
               ARRAY [0..16000] OF Integer;

END;
```

The TERec destRect field is the extent of where text would be on the screen if you could see it. Anything that is visible on the Macintosh screen has to be within the extent of TERec's viewRect rectangle. The destination rectangle could be much larger than the view rectangle, and the character locations would be calculated to form lines within the destination rectangle, but the characters wouldn't be visible unless they fell inside the view rectangle (see Fig. 3–61).

lineHeight is the distance between ascent lines in lines of text. font-Ascent is the distance between the text baseline and ascent line.

The selStart field contains the character position value (a simple integer) where characters are presently selected (highlighted). The selEnd field is the value of the character position of the last character that is selected.

The just field is 0 for left-justification of text, 1 for center-justification, and −1 for right-justification.

The teLength field contains the number of characters controlled by the text edit record.

The hText field is a Macintosh handle to the text data area.

The crOnly field, when positive, wraps text at the destination rectangle's right edge. When negative, the ends of lines are always marked by a carriage return (0d hexidecimal).

The txFont field specifies the font. The txFace field specifies the character style. The txMode field indicates the pen draw mode. The txSize field shows the font size. All these fields control the entire contents of the data area handled by the one edit record.

The inPort field points to the GrafPort associated with the edit record.

The highHook field points to an assembly routine that handles the text

Figure 3–61 The destination and viewing rectangles of a Macintosh text edit record

highlighting. The caretHook field points to a caret drawing routine, also (usually) written in assembler.

The nLines field has the number of lines in the text block controlled by this edit record.

The lineStarts array, a dynamic data structure with as many elements as are required (one of the reasons you have to point to the record with a Macintosh handle and not just a pointer), contains the character position of the first character in each line.

The wordBreak field points to an assembly routine used to figure out the extent of a word when a user double-clicks the mouse button with the mouse positioned over it. This is for highlighting the entire word. The same routine is used for figuring out where the wrap occurs in a line longer than the width of the view rectangle.

The clikLoop field points to an assembly routine that is called repeatedly when the mouse button is held down and the cursor is within the text block. The routine handles automatic text scrolling.

THE MACINTOSH TEXTEDIT ROUTINES

TEInit is the TextEdit initialization routine. This routine must be executed once only, even though the application doesn't directly use TextEdit routines. Other parts of the Mac system use them and rely on the application's initializing TextEdit for them. TEInit allocates a handle to an empty TextEdit scrap.

TENew accepts set rectangle records for the view and destination rectangles, and returns a handle to an allocated and initialized edit record. The view and destination records use the current GrafPort for a coordinate system. TENew can be used a multitude of times for getting a number of edit records.

TEDispose accepts the handle to an edit record and absorbs the resources allocated to it.

The TESetText routine is handed a pointer to an array of characters, the number of characters in the array, and a handle to an edit record. The characters are added to the edit record text data block. The destination location is specified by the selection range of the edit record.

TEGetText accepts a handle to an edit record and provides a handle to the character block that belongs to the edit record.

TEIdle is called repeatedly to blink the caret (the text insertion point bar symbol). Apple suggests that TEIdle be called once per event loop round.

TEClick is used to move, extend, shrink, or place the text selection zone. TEClick modifies the selection fields in the provided (by handle parameter) edit record, and moves the text highlighting around. The routine is given the coordinate point of the location of the mouse cursor when the mouse button was pressed (in local coordinates; use GlobalTo-Local to convert the event record cursor location from global to local), and a boolean value that is TRUE if the shift key was down when the mouse button was pressed, and FALSE if not. This last indicates that the user means to extend the selection range that exists already. Single words are highlighted by double-clicks.

TESetSelect moves the highlighted text zone on the display to the selection range mentioned in the parameter list. The handle to the involved edit record is also provided as a parameter. The selStart and selEnd fields in the edit record are assigned the new values.

TEActivate merely highlights the text in the selection range in the view window belonging to the indicated edit record, and makes the text insertion caret visible if appropriate. This routine needs to be executed every time a Macintosh window with an edit record becomes active. TEDeactivate un-highlights the text in the selection range and turns the caret off. This routine is called when a window with an edit record becomes inactive. Both routines require one parameter, the handle to the involved edit record.

TEKey replaces the selection range in the text specified by the provided edit record with the specified character. The insertion point is placed immediately after the inserted character in the view rectangle. The backspace character tells TEKey to just replace the selection range text with the insertion point.

TECut inserts the selection range text into the TextEdit scrap buffer (aka a "cut" buffer) and removes any trace of the text from the view window. The previous contents of the TextEdit scrap buffer are overwritten. This only requires a handle to the edit record.

TECopy does almost the same thing as TECut, but neither removes the text from the view window nor fiddles with the selection range. This only requires a handle to the edit record.

TEPaste copies the contents of the TextEdit scrap buffer into the edit record in place of the selection range text, or at the insertion point. This only needs a handle to an edit record.

TEDelete removes all trace of the selection range text from the view window. The view window is redrawn if necessary.

TEInsert is used to insert text into an edit record text block. The location and length of the character array and a handle to the edit record are the parameters. The current insertion point of the edit record is used.

The TESetJust routine is used to assign the current justification of text in the view window of an edit record. The routine needs a handle to the edit record and an integer value with one of the following meanings:

−1	Right-justification
0	Center-justification
1	Left-justification

TEUpdate draws the text specified by the indicated edit record within the rectangle also specified in the parameter list.

TextBox is given a pointer to an array of characters, the count of characters in the array, a rectangle, and a justification value ($-1, 0,$ or 1). The routine draws the specified text within the rectangle using the required justification.

TEScroll scrolls the text in the view rectangle of the specified edit record. The amount scrolled is given by two other parameters, an X-coordinate delta and a Y-coordinate delta, in pixels.

TEFromScrap and TEToScrap could be executed after a scrap buffer operation to return a result code of type OSErr. If no error occurred from the scrap operation, the value returned is 0. If something other than 0 was returned, well, you'll have to look in Apple's *Inside Macintosh*, or *Inside the Apple IIGS* in the chapter on Operating System Utilities for the codes.

Here are some minor routines: TEScrapHandle is used to return a handle for the TextEdit scrap buffer. TEGetScrapLen returns the size of the TextEdit scrap buffer in bytes. TESetScrapLen is used to assign the size of the TextEdit scrap buffer. The parameter is the size in bytes.

Last but not least is TECalText; this is used to redetermine where the beginning of each line of text controlled by the specified edit record is, and consequently changes all the entries in the lineStarts array. The routine is used if anything significant and related has been adjusted, such as the destination rectangle or anything else that might force a shuffle of words on a line.

Macintosh II

The new TextEdit package for the Mac II accommodates the new Script Manager, through which simple use of international text is possible. The modifications are backward compatible, but using many of the new features requires use of some new routines.

The Style data structure is a new record that is used to keep track of all the styles that are used in the text of an edit record. Another new data structure is used for keeping a table of individual style entries for a style record. Another new record keeps the height of the text contained in an edit record. Older Macs will get these improvements.

These are the new routines:

TEStylNew	Creates a new style edit record with style information, and does some initialization. The new style edit record hasn't changed, but some of the fields are interpreted differently by the new Mac system software.
SetStylHandle	Sets the style handle of the specified edit record to the indicated value. This routine is provided to avoid having applications directly modify edit records.
GetStylHandle	Retrieves a handle to the style record of an edit record.
GetStylScrap	Creates a style scrap record (StScrpRec) and copies the current edit record style information into it. This routine is similar to TECopy.
TEStylInsert	Used to insert some text just before the indicated selection range. The text is redrawn where needed.
TEGetOffset	Returns the character offset in an edit record's text data that corresponds with the specified point.
TEGetPoint	The opposite of TEGetOffSet, it returns the coordinates that correspond to the indicated text offset in the text data of an edit record.
TEGetHeight	Returns the accumulated height of the lines of text that are associated with a specified edit record.
TEGetStyle	Returns the style information for a specified character in the text of the indicated edit record.
TEStylPaste	Pastes text from the desk scrap into the text of the indicated edit record. Exactly how the paste is done depends on where the insertion point is and what text is currently selected.
TESetStyle	Assigns the style of currently selected text data and (on request) redraws the changed text.
TEReplaceStyle	Used to change one specified style to another in the indicated text edit record. On request, the changed text is redrawn.

3.10 | Resources

As mentioned briefly in Part 1 and at length in Part 2, a **resource** is a collection of bytes that is given a name and a type. Resources are kept in binary files. They can be borrowed and modified by operating system or application code. Resources can be preloaded from disk and kept in RAM, or loaded as required. The exact details depend on the window system.

Resources can be used for everything if the window system is up to it. Macintosh resources contain almost everything definable; the Macintosh version of an executable file is called a **resource file**, and executable code is kept in **code resources**.

The contents of a resource can be a mystery to everything except the software that directly uses and modifies them. Most routines that use a resource accept a pointer or handle to it as an argument. If the routine is given a resource of the wrong type, the routine probably won't realize (because it doesn't look) that it has been given the wrong thing. The results are unpredictable.

The exact composition of predefined resources may not be public knowledge, since some developers of window systems like to be able to change them. This forces you to use system functions for editing operations, something the window system developers also control. If application developers commonly edited the contents of predefined resources directly, modifications would break too much code.

RESOURCE COMPILERS AND EDITORS

There are resources that can be created with utility programs like resource compilers and editors. The resource compiler accepts a text description of one or more resources, from which it produces a resource file. A resource editor is used to interactively create and edit predefined types of resources graphically. Since the resource compiler uses numbers (rather than the hand and eye) to size and position display objects, it is generally easier to adjust resources with the editor. Currently, resource editors don't handle as many different resources as do resource compilers. Programmers that use them go by "anything that works," since resource construction software is not currently a science.

DECOMPILERS

Because resource contents tend to be well-defined (even if they are hidden), there are also resource **decompilers**. These create a text file containing the description of resources in a resource file. The description can be turned right around and fed to the resource compiler to recreate the resource! A decompiler handles the predefined types of resources that it is designed for.

PREDEFINED RESOURCE TYPES

Macintosh

Apple Computer has predefined a number of resource types. Custom resource types are everywhere. The purpose of each of these resources is not always obvious.

A resource type identifier is defined to be a 4-character literal, so there is some mnemonic value to the ID, but not much. The chart of Macintosh Reserved Resource Words on pages 336–337 lists some of these identifiers.

MS Windows

There are nowhere near as many predefined resource types as found on the Macintosh. Figure 3–62 is a list of Windows resources.

Gem

Predefined Gem resources are very few in number. Graphic objects are described as Gem AES object trees, without distinction between one kind of object tree and another. Object trees can be kept in a file as a resource. Figure 3–63 is a list of Gem resources.

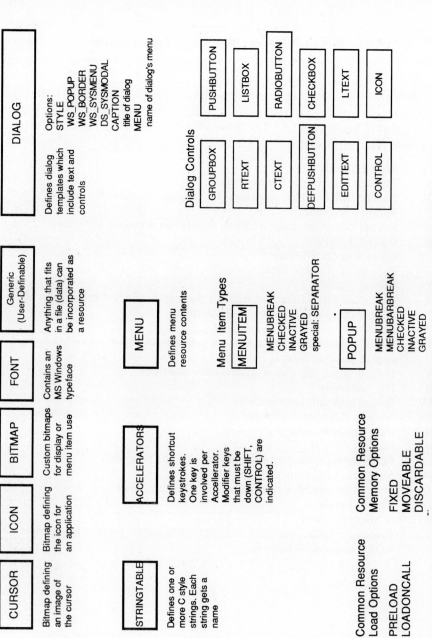

CURSOR

Bitmap defining an image of the cursor

ICON

Bitmap defining the icon for an application

BITMAP

Custom bitmaps for display or menu item use

FONT

Contains an MS Windows typeface

Generic (User-Definable)

Anything that fits in a file (data) can be incorporated as a resource

DIALOG

Defines dialog templates which include text and controls

Options:
STYLE
WS_POPUP
WS_BORDER
WS_SYSMENU
DS_SYSMODAL
CAPTION
    title of dialog
MENU
    name of dialog's menu

Dialog Controls

GROUPBOX	PUSHBUTTON
RTEXT	LISTBOX
CTEXT	RADIOBUTTON
DEFPUSHBUTTON	CHECKBOX
EDITTEXT	LTEXT
CONTROL	ICON

MENU

Defines menu resource contents

Menu Item Types

MENUITEM

MENUBREAK
CHECKED
INACTIVE
GRAYED
special: SEPARATOR

POPUP

MENUBREAK
MENUBARBREAK
CHECKED
INACTIVE
GRAYED

ACCELERATORS

Defines shortcut keystrokes. One key is involved per Accellerator. Modifier keys that must be down (SHIFT, CONTROL) are indicated.

STRINGTABLE

Defines one or more C style strings. Each string gets a name

Common Resource Load Options

PRELOAD
LOADONCALL

Common Resource Memory Options

FIXED
MOVEABLE
DISCARDABLE

Figure 3–62 Microsoft Windows predefined resource types, options, and components

---

Macintosh Reserved Resource Type Names

Apple reserves all the resource type names that can be made entirely of lowercase ASCII characters and ASCII characters with the high bit set (ASCII values greater than 7f hexidecimal or 127 decimal). The following list contains the predefined, reserved resource type names.

ALRT	Alert Template
bmap	Bit maps used by the Control Panel
BNDL	Bundle; defines all the resources of a program related to the Finder
CACH	RAM cache (code)
CDEF	Control definition function (code); defines how a control will behave
CNTL	Control Template
CODE	Executable Code Segment
ctab	Used by the Control Panel
CURS	Cursor
DITL	Dialog (or Alert) Item List; contains the graphic and text descriptions of things displayed in a Dialog or an Alert box
DLOG	Dialog
DRVR	Driver; contains executable code for a desk accessory or for an I/O device such as the disk drive
DSAT	Default system alert table (system error manager)
FCMT	File comments
FKEY	Special keyboard key sequences
FMTR	3½-inch disk format software
FOND	Font Family Record
FONT	Font
FREF	File Reference; used to define the icon for the program
FRSV	Numbers of the fonts that are reserved
FWID	Font width; describes the dimensions of an entire font
ICN#	Icon and mask
ICON	A Macintosh Icon
INIT	Executable Code; contains a keyboard configuration routine, for example, written in assembly language

Macintosh Reserved Resource Type Names — cont'd

insc	Installer script
ITL	International resource
LDEF	List definition (for the list manager)
MACS	String that is part of the system bundle (BNDL)
MBAR	Menu Bar
MDEF	Menu definition
MENU	Menu
MINI	Minifinder
NBPC	Name binding protocol (Appletalk)
NFNT	128K ROM font
PACK	Package; contains normally disk-resident selections of executable routines
PAPA	Printer access protocol (Appletalk)
PAT	QuickDraw Pattern
PAT#	QuickDraw Patterns (generally more than one)
PDEF	Printer definition
PICT	QuickDraw Picture
PREC	Printer Record
PRER	Device type for Chooser desk accessory
PRES	Device type for Chooser desk accessory
PTCH	ROM patch code
RDEV	Device type for Chooser desk accessory
ROvr	Code for overriding ROM resources
ROv#	List of ROM resources to override
SERD	Serial driver
STR	String; a single Pascal string of up to 255 characters
STR#	Strings; a number (generally more than 1) of Pascal strings, each up to 255 characters in length
*TEXT	Text; any number of characters
WDEF	Window definitions
WIND	Window template

Generally, Gem resources contain:

Icons
Objects
Object Trees
Pictures (bitmaps)
Strings

More Specifically, the Gem resource routine library knows of these structures (as per the descriptions for rsrc_gaddr and rsrc_saddr):

Object Tree	An array of Gem objects, interconnected by index pointers to form a tree hierarchy
OBJECT	Header record for a single object; contains coordinates, fore and aft index pointers, width and height values, attribute fields, and type specific data. The objects that are supported are listed below
TEDINFO	Text editing control record
ICONBLK	Icon description record
BITBLK	Bitmap (bitblock) physical description record
APPLBLK	A record used to indicate the code that should be used to render the graphics for the associated object
PARMBLK	Parameter data that relates to an object; contains size, location, current and old state information
string	Null-terminated (C-style) character array
imagedata	Data for BITBLK, ICONBLK records

Object Types

G_BOX
G_TEXT
G_BOXTEXT
G_IMAGE
G_PROGDEF
G_IBOX
G_BUTTON
G_BOXCHAR
G_STRING
G_FTEXT
G_FBOXTEXT
G_ICON
G_TITLE

Figure 3–63 Table of Gem Resources

WINDOW SYSTEM RESOURCE SUPPORT

Macintosh

Initialization

InitResources is used by the system, and should not be called by applications. It is used to pull into RAM the Macintosh resource map for the system resource file. InitResources returns a reference number for the map, which is stored in the global INTEGER variable SysMap. Global variable SysMapHndl contains a handle to the system resource map.

The system resource file can be referenced either by the actual reference number kept in SysMap or by the reference number 0.

RsrcZoneInit is called by the system to clean up resources after a previous application is finished with them. Resource files are closed and references to RAM-resident system resources in the current system resource map are zeroed. This routine needs no parameters.

Resource File Operations

CreateResFile makes a new, empty resource file. The routine expects one argument, a string with the file name in it.

OpenResFile is given the name of a resource file to open. If the file exists, it is opened and the resource map is copied from the file into RAM. Resources that are marked to be loaded when the file is open are read into memory. The reference number for the file is returned.

The most recently opened resource file becomes the current resource file, the first file to be searched for resources. Files opened earlier (and still open) will be searched in the reverse of the order in which they were opened; the system resource file, opened first, is searched last.

CloseResFile will close the specified open resource file; it expects the reference number provided by OpenResFile. CloseResFile housecleans in both memory and the closing file by calling the appropriate routines. Occupied RAM is released, and updates to the resource file are made. The RAM for the resource map is reclaimed.

CurResFile is used to get the reference number of the current resource file. More than one resource file can be open, but only one is the current file. Calling CurResFile right after an application starts to run will return its reference number.

HomeResFile accepts a handle to an open resource file and returns the file's reference number.

UseResFile is employed to turn the resource file specified by the provided reference number into the current resource file. Other files that have been searched for resources before this file was checked are entirely ignored. This may change when another resource file is opened, or perhaps when UseResFile is called again.

ResError can be called at any time after a resource manager routine is executed, and will find out if an error has occurred. A zero value returned means no error was detected.

Resource Manipulation Routines

LoadResource is given a handle to a resource; it loads the resource into RAM unless the resource is already there.

ReleaseResource reclaims the memory used by a RAM-based resource. The resource map handle for the resource is set to NIL.

DetachResource leaves the RAM-based resource in memory, but still sets the resource map handle to NIL. This is used if your code wants to keep the copy of the resource to itself.

SetResLoad is a resource manager control routine; it is given a boolean parameter indicating whether resources should be loaded into RAM with other resource manager routines or not. TRUE means load them; FALSE means don't. If this parameter is set to FALSE for too long, it could mean disaster.

GetResource returns a handle to a resource indicated by a resource ID number and a resource type value. The resource is copied into RAM. The routine will return NIL if it doesn't find it or if it can't fit it into RAM when it does find it.

The function GetNamedResource does the same job as GetResource, but uses a name string instead of an ID number. The name string is Pascal-compatible.

Get1Resource (128K ROM) returns a handle to a resource indicated by a resource ID number and a resource type value. The resource is copied into RAM. The routine will return NIL if it doesn't find it or if it can't fit it into RAM when it does find it. Get1Resource only searches the current resource file; otherwise it is the same as the function GetResource.

The function Get1NamedResource (128K ROM) does the same job as Get1Resource, but uses a name string instead of an ID number. The name string is Pascal-compatible. Get1NamedResource is a cousin of Get-NamedResource.

CountResources counts the resources of a given type in the open resource files, and returns the number.

GetIndResource provides the handles to all the resources of a given type, one at a time per call. You have to give it an index that can range from 1 to the value returned by the CountResources routine.

Count1Resources (128K ROM) is given a resource type, and it returns the number of that kind of resource in the current file.

Get1IndResource (128K ROM) is used to return a handle to each resource of a given type. The routine is called once for each resource, and it needs an integer index value that ranges from 1 to the value returned by Count1Resources. Get1IndResource also needs the type of the resource.

The CountTypes routine counts the number of types of resources in all the open resource files.

GetIndType is used to scan for available resource types in the open resource files. It is given an index number from 1 to the value returned by CountTypes, and it returns the matching resource type in a parameter of type ResType.

Count1Types (128K ROM) returns the INTEGER number of resource types in the current resource file.

Get1IndType (128K ROM) is used to scan the current resource file for unique resource types, one at a time. The routine accepts an index that ranges from 1 to the value returned by Count1Types. Each call with a different index returns another unique resource type.

Resource File Editing Routines

AddResource adds a new resource to a resource file. Required are a handle (that is not a handle to a resource) to the RAM-based data to be written, a resource type value, an ID number for the resource, and the name of the resource in an extended-Pascal style string.

RmveResource is given a handle to a resource, which is yanked out by the roots from the current resource file. First the resource reference is removed, then the resource data are removed (the latter when the resource file is updated).

UpdateResFile needs the reference number of a resource file. When it is called, the resource file indicated is updated and compacted.

WriteResource writes the data to the file for the resource indicated (by a handle, the routine's only parameter) if that resource's resChanged attribute bit is set.

Resource Information Utilities

UniqueID is given a resource type value and returns an ID number not currently used by any resources. If UniqueID returns a value from 0 to 127, don't use the number (it is reserved for system resources); call UniqueID again.

Unique1ID (128K ROM) returns a new unique ID number. The number is unique with respect to the current resource file only.

GetResInfo accepts a handle to a resource and in return provides the ID number, type, and name of the resource.

GetResAttrs provides an INTEGER value that contains the attributes for a resource. The routine requires a handle to the resource. The attributes describe the following properties, with each property assigned a bit:

Low-order byte bit	Function
7	usually 0, 1 = system reference (never used)
6	1 = load into system heap, 0 = application heap
5	1 = purgeable, 0 = not purgeable
4	1 = locked, 0 = unlocked
3	1 = protected, 0 = not protected
2	1 = preloaded, 0 = do not load when file opened
1	1 = written to resource file, 0 = not written
0	reserved

SizeResource provides the size of a resource. The value is the number of bytes. A handle to the resource is required, and a LONGINT is returned.

MaxSizeRsrc (128K ROM) returns the size of a resource (a LONG-INT) by looking at the RAM-based resource map, not by looking on the disk. Going to the disk was the bane of early Macintosh software, when many Macs had but one disk drive.

Resource Editing Routines

SetResInfo is used to change the name and ID number of a resource, given a handle to the resource.

SetResAttrs sets the resource attribute value to the provided value. The routine also needs a handle to the resource.

ChangedResource tells the resource manager that it should write the contents of the resource back to the resource file when the file is updated. The entire resource map for the file is also to be written. The routine needs a handle to the modified resource in RAM.

Calling the SetResPurge routine will cause the system to check before a purge to see if a RAM-based resource has data that have been modified.

If the resource is in the application heap and the resChanged bit is set, the data will be written to the resource file. SetResPurge accepts a boolean parameter which should be TRUE to write changed data to the resource file, and FALSE if it shouldn't be done.

The routines GetResFileAttrs and SetResFileAttrs are used to manipulate resource file attributes. You can make a resource file read-only, and have the file compacted and the map written on updates.

Miscellaneous Resource Routines

RsrcMapEntry (128K ROM) provides the offset of the resource reference from the beginning of the resource map, enabling your software to access a resource directly and not with a handle. RsrcMapEntry returns a LONGINT with the offset; it requires a handle to the resource. I venture a guess that someone with a need for high access speed, and little need for the other ROM routines, asked for this.

The OpenRFPerm (128K ROM) routine is OpenResFile with two extra parameters to set the read/write permissions and specify the directory/volume the file is in.

Windows

AddFontResource copies a font from the indicated file into the Windows RAM-based font table. Any font in the table can be used by any application. The single parameter to the routine is a long pointer to the null-terminated string containing the font resource file name. The parameter can *alternatively* be a handle to a loaded module, with the handle in the low word and a zero in the high word.

RemoveFontResource requires the same parameter as AddFontResource. It is used to remove a font resource from the font table in RAM. The function returns TRUE if the action was successful. The font is not actually removed from the RAM font table until all the references made to the font by applications (and system software) are released.

LoadBitmap is used to load a device-independent bitmap into RAM. The routine needs a handle to the module containing the bitmap and a pointer to a null-terminated string containing the name of the bitmap. The routine returns a handle to the usable RAM-based resource.

LoadCursor works the same way as LoadBitmap, only it works on cursors. LoadCursor can also be used to yank predefined cursors, by setting the handle to NULL and the Name pointer to a constant corresponding to the predefined cursor pattern. Here is a list of the predefined cursors:

IDC_ARROW	Arrow
IDC_UPARROW	Vertical arrow
IDC_CROSS	Crosshairs
IDC_IBEAM	I-BEAM (text edit) cursor
IDC_WAIT	Hourglass cursor

LoadIcon works the same way as LoadCursor, only for icons. The predefined icons are:

IDI_APPLICATION	Default application symbol
IDI_NOTE	Alert symbol
IDI_ERROR	Error symbol

LoadMenu works the same way as LoadIcon, LoadCursor, and Load-BitMap, but for menus. There are no predefined menus.

LoadString loads a string from a module into RAM. It needs a handle to the module, the ID of the string, the location of the string buffer in RAM in which to put the string, and the maximum size of the buffer. The function appends a NULL terminator onto the string after copying it into the buffer. LoadString returns the length of the actual data in the string, including the NULL terminator.

LoadAccelerators is used to get a table of shortcut keypresses (Windows accelerators) from a module indicated by the first parameter, a handle. The second parameter to the routine is a long pointer to a buffer where the accelerator table is to be placed in RAM.

FindResource can be used to track down a resource in a resource file. The routine requires a handle to the module containing the resource, a long pointer to the name string of the resource (NULL-terminated), and a long pointer to a string containing the type of the resource. The routine returns a handle to the resource. The name and type string pointers can also be integer IDs of the name or type, respectively, of the resource.

The resource types are:

RT_CURSOR	Cursor
RT_BITMAP	Bitmap
RT_ICON	Icon
RT_MENU	Menu

RT_DIALOG	Dialog
RT_STRING	String
RT_FONTDIR	Font
RT_FONT	Font
RT_ACCELERATOR	Keyboard shortcut keys table

LoadResource is used to haul a RAM copy of the resource (indicated by the resource handle parameter) from the file (indicated by the file handle parameter). The function returns a handle to the resource in RAM.

AllocResource has to be used to parcel out RAM for each memory-resident copy of resources. Some of the other resource manager routines, such as LoadResource, call AllocResource. This function requires three parameters: a handle to the module containing the resource, a handle to the resource, and an integer value describing the amount of RAM to allocate if the value is not zero (otherwise the allocation will be based on the size of the resource). This last parameter may come in handy if a hefty number of resources are to come and go and you want to dispense with the garbage collection that will be involved if all the resources are a different size.

FreeResource is used to release a chunk of RAM that has been claimed by a resource. It needs a handle to the memory, and it returns TRUE if the RAM has been released. FreeResource doesn't release the memory until the number of FreeResource calls involving that resource matches the number of LoadResource calls for the same resource.

AccessResource is used to open the resource file and return a handle to the file. The file is ready to be read from the beginning of the resource indicated by the resource handle parameter. The application can then read the resource and place it anywhere it wants in memory. The function also requires a handle to the module containing the resource.

SizeofResource requires a handle to the module containing the resource and a handle to the resource. It returns the size of the resource in bytes.

SetResourceHandler requires a handle to the module containing the resource, a long pointer to the name string of the resource, and a long pointer to a function. The function is used to set up the employ of a custom resource loading procedure when the indicated resource is needed.

The custom loading routine should accept three parameters: the first is a handle to the memory block for the resource, the second is a handle to the module that contains the resource to be loaded, and the third is a handle to the resource.

Gem

The Gem AES routine rsrc_load is for loading a resource file into RAM. The standard binding routine needs one parameter, the address of the string that contains the name of the file.

The routine rsrc_free reclaims the memory allocated during the rsrc_load call.

The rsrc_gaddr routine tracks down the address of a data structure in memory. The record is identified by two values, an integer constant that indicates the type of the record and an integer index value for the record.

The routine rsrc_saddr is used to store an address value inside an arbitrary data structure. It requires three parameters: the type of the data structure as described by an integer constant, the index or offset into the data structure, and the base address of the data structure.

rsrc_obfix calculates a screen location of an object in pixels from its Gem character coordinates. The binding routine needs the index of the object and the address of the tree that contains the object. Since the location of an object tree object depends on the location of the objects above it in the tree, the base address of the tree must be provided.

PART 4 Program Orchestration

4.1 | Methods and Automation

This book is written assuming that software written with well-understood methods gets better results than software written informally with incomplete and ad hoc methods. This is especially true when a number of people are involved and when the product has to be portable. Portable designs always require much more forethought than nonportable designs.

Covered in this section are a small number of existing design and diagraming methods, as well as the idea of automating some of the design work. I think that computer-aided software design is a necessity, so some existing packages are mentioned with capsule comments describing both their intended function and what they're good for.

WHAT IS A GOOD IDEA

It is normal to have only a "good idea" of how a system will go together before any of the code is written. A good idea is not the same as exact knowledge, but it usually provides at least one starting point for development. This foothold on the unknown has been enough for many projects, regardless of budget size, to be wheeled directly from prototype code development to product just after a dollop of market polish is hastily smeared on it.

From Light Bulb to Paper Napkin to *POWIE!*(code)

The foothold of a "good idea" project is a precarious place from which to implement a fast, clean product. Hold back and let the ideas merge into a plan that can be committed to disk and paper.

Contrasting products born from orchestrated software projects and disorganized forethought are a buyer's dilemma not unlike the one faced by a used car buyer. Some people take care of new cars, but others never change the oil. The car that suffered early will certainly cost more to run than the car that has had its oil changed every 2,000 miles. It is likely that the negligent owner knew that he was going to sell the car in a year; discreet mistreatment of the car may not change its 1-year-old value. What does the owner care about the car after it is sold? On the other hand, the person who takes good care of a car is probably less certain about selling it after a year, so a sharp used-car buyer spends time searching for clues.

Software buyers have it a little easier than car buyers, since the object isn't a one-of-a-kind. The questions are easier to get answers for. Is the program version 1.0 or brand new? Have there been a successful number of releases in a timely fashion? Does the program work? Is the program, currently the best choice, going to be competitive against later releases of other software?

Down deep people hate to change packages or machines. Though they rarely say it, they want the package to last *forever* once it is in their library.

Here are some other questions: Will this package survive Father Time? If the program is copy-protected, will someone else (users, if nobody else) pick up and support the package if the company that made it vanishes?

PROTOTYPING

Good use of formal development methods prevents developing most sections of code as if they were prototypes. Prototyping code is for removing bad assumptions and spotlighting forgotten and unknown dark alleys (you don't know if parts of a design will work, or you know that a design won't work but aren't certain why).

There are two ways to prototype. The first way is to merely barricade oneself in a room and use the time on the computer to create routines and design concurrently. There is not much predefinition of the routines on paper or how they interface with each other. The second way adds committing a fuzzy design to paper and working out a small prototype implementation from that. In either case prototype development is useful and fun but horrendously expensive, because the code gets tossed when it doesn't work.

Programs can be described without writing a line of corresponding code. Once designed, the writeups can be handled all at once to people adept at weaving implementations. All the books that describe analysis and design methods (see the section entitled "For Further Reading") tirelessly talk about making descriptions to evaporate overhead while keeping the creative parts of design and coding. They say it also removes the tight temporal handcuffs between design and coding, permitting people to spend more time on what they want to do and are good at doing.

The window systems help break different ground in the user interfaces. Each new program using them currently does something unique to stretch the realm. For example, Challenger Software's Mac 3D package uses circular scroll bars, something I've never seen before. Odesta's Helix products have been praised for their imaginative use of graphics for database design. Clearly some of the user interface details are going to be open for discussion, so prototyping some of that code is a good idea.

Another area that has enough novelty to warrant some prototyping is that of the overall organization of a program under a windowing environment. Things like event loops (normal fare in process control and real time systems) rarely made it into accounting packages until machines like the Macintosh became popular. There are examples provided by the books dedicated to the individual machines, and Windows and Gem Toolkits come with a number of examples of disk. Assuming that these examples are fathomable, nobody should be in the dark regarding how things are done, given one system. The ultimate trick is how to make the application code reasonably portable!

COMMUNICATION AND MEMORY

The two good reasons for building a document are memory, because few people are capable of accurately remembering details of a large project, and communication, because the document reflects the state of the project at any given moment. People can reliably refer to it instead of a person, which reduces the need for everyone to know details about parts of the project with which they aren't involved. That knowledge may give you a warm feeling, but it may also slow you down.

OK, How? By Capturing Connectivity

The trick is in knowing how to make such a document. Most descriptions of software development tell what *not* to put into a good document. Tomes such as system documents are tough to build, with the pressure aimed at programmers to write software and little else. Making the proper design documents by hand is very difficult, time-consuming, and perhaps not worthwhile.

Since the big picture is tedious to have and hold, software should be used to capture project design information and keep it in a database. Such systems have enough intelligence to complain about ambiguities and other design faults. Drawing a large number of diagrams and not knowing how correct they are is like writing several thousand lines of C language code without using a compiler once; it is likely that you will discover that reality has parted company from the implementation.

CASD (Computer-Aided Software Development) systems that help automate diagraming and data dictionary maintenance have been commercially available for some time. These programs are going to quickly get better and much cheaper; currently the usable ones cost over $800. Their unique feature and battle cry is that they *maintain the connectivity of the components of the design database*. This means that, if two elements are related somehow, moving one of the elements doesn't detach the bond between them, and the other connected elements aren't forced to move unless you want them to.

The design document contents have to be mechanically consistent for problem areas to visibly grate against the natural order of the work. When well-defined terminology and graphics are used, problems can be detected by simple inspections or walk-throughs. Few questions asking what the finished system will do and how the system will do it will need more than looking at the right diagram and following the train of thought. If that can't be done, there's a problem. A document's authority becomes iron if it is accurate, and the concept of "correct" will be unconsciously felt and repeatedly verifiable. With a document like that, nobody in his or her right mind would drift from its recipe. The availability of a CASD system provides a way of automating some of the mundane work so that global consistency can be more easily attainable.

WORDS AND PICTURES

The idea that "one picture is worth a thousand words" is especially apropos in design documentation because most of the useful methodologies involve working with building a suite of pictures of various (but well defined!) kinds.

Dataflow Diagrams

Dataflow diagrams show "what" a system has to do and not how to do it. The fine line drawn between the "what to do" and the "how to do it" is not obvious the first time around. Using the limited variety of components allowed in a dataflow diagram, not enough information can be expressed to pin down physical details such as order of execution, module size, data structure size, or number of lines of code (in short, anything concrete or physical that relates to the implementation of a system). Despite this apparent shortcoming, dataflow diagrams are not designed to irritate people.

If one accepts the idea that writing bug-free, easily-maintainable code is more expensive in time and cost than talking about a program in general terms, then it requires no tremendous leap of logic to understand that one would like to have a concise way to talk about programs in general (the guidelines) without having to write something that must work. One of the assumptions made with dataflow diagrams is that any early description involving the order in which parts of a system run is likely to be completely inaccurate. This acts like loud static during a shortwave radio broadcast, clouding the useful information. If it is going to be wrong, then not enough of the system has been defined. Don't describe those ideas in the dataflow diagrams.

There are four graphic components to dataflow diagrams. **Processes** are things that generate output from input, and are represented by a circle with an identification number and a name (see Fig. 4–1).

A **dataflow** is a named path that is used by a single kind of data item or structure. The data travel from one end of the flow path to the other, in single file. There is no way to show the frequency of data elements traversing the path or the timing by which elements may arrive; it is assumed that a data element may show up at any time. Such extra information is considered to be a physical (design or implementation)

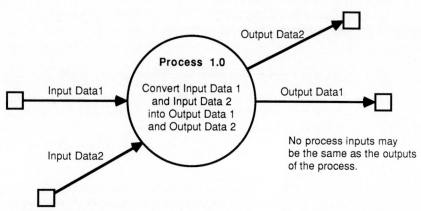

Figure 4–1 Example of a DFD process

concern. Not only is there no way to describe how many records may be stacked up in the conduit waiting for processing by the process(es) at the receiving end, there is no way to indicate signals (flags).

The dataflow path (Fig. 4–2) is represented by an arrow, normally drawn with an arc. The names for the dataflow arrows are as descriptive as the process names. Naturally the exact contents of any given abstract record traversing the conduit is not in full view in a dataflow diagram; this is left to other parts of the project document, such as the data dictionary.

A **store** (Fig. 4–3) is a place to keep data. In reality a store could represent a disk-based file, a linked-list in RAM, an array, a single variable, or anything used to keep data around for a while. In any case, the dataflow representation is the same, a pair of parallel horizontal lines.

Finally, a **terminator** is used to define an arbitrary source or sink of data that belongs outside the domain of the problem being defined. It could eventually represent a terminal display or keyboard, a (yech) card punch, magtape (for very long term data stores), but the distinction is not significant to a dataflow of a system. Terminators are the small boxes in Figure 4–4.

Dataflow diagrams are used to describe what entire systems have to do in a detached or logical way. Since the construction rules for dataflow diagrams are so simple, it is easy to learn how to look over these diagrams and find defects. First-time users, because of their lack of experience with dataflow diagrams, often do not know what they are looking for when scanning for errors. Prior to learning all the properties of dataflow diagrams, they often want to add more features to them. There are some situations that aren't properly handled by dataflow diagrams, but changing the composition of the dataflow diagram is probably going to be less satisfactory than using an entirely different type of diagram. Like so many other sets of diagraming rules, the success of dataflow diagrams relies on what is not depicted.

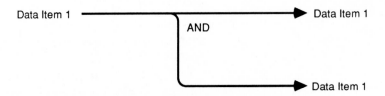

Data Item 1 is given to two receivers. Dataflow diagrams do not distinguish between whether two physical copies of items, or two pointers to one single record, are used.

Figure 4–2 Example of a dataflow path

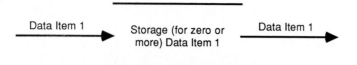

Figure 4–3 Example of a dataflow diagram store

A suite of dataflow pictures shows processes that talk to each other with data. The processes are highly cohesive, meaning that they can have high-precision names. For example, the names SquareRoot, MergeRippleWith-Peppermint, and UnlockBackDoor imply single well-defined operations, but a process called ManageKeypressEvents implies an indefinite variety of operations (depending on the key that was pressed), and would have to be refined (see Fig. 4–1).

Note that one of the cohesive processes seems to imply a continuous operation: a continuous stream of ripple mixed with a stream of peppermint ice cream. Processes in dataflow diagrams start work when data appears in their in baskets, and will continue to generate output until the input data stop coming.

Processes that are highly cohesive normally have tamer I/O requirements. For example, the variety of data that SquareRoot has to accept and generate is implicitly better understood than the I/O required by ManageKeypressEvents.

One of the limitations of dataflow diagrams is that a process is assumed to always be present and active: it will accept data elements when they appear, and will subsequently generate data elements. This assumption drives people nuts because such a diagram "cannot possibly" describe how most programs are implemented. This is why some folks desperately add bells and whistles to dataflow diagrams to force them to work "properly."

The distinction between what is to be done and how it is done is demonstrated by the following story.

Twenty-five students are told to develop a fancy communications program for a software engineering course assignment. They know the operating system to use, the language in which it is supposed to be written, the protocols to implement, and the modems that will be used with it; all the physical questions are listed with answers on the assignment description.

Two months later 25 entirely different communications programs are handed in to be graded. For the sake of argument, let us assume the incredible and say that all of them work.

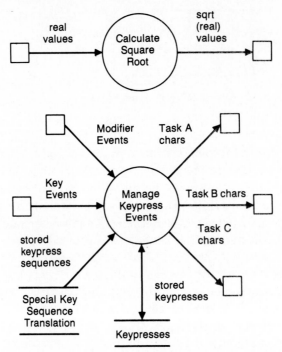

Figure 4–4 Example dataflow processes: an easy one and a hard one

These programs differ in every way, except (we assume) that they all fulfill the outlined base requirements. One version creates several little programs that run simultaneously, each task handling part of the required work. Another program emulates multitasking with a polling loop at the top of the program, continuously sampling sources of data and commands. A third program is written without either a master I/O-event loop or multitasking, and instead relies on modes to either accept user commands or transfer files, but not both at once.

Dataflow diagrams avoid limiting the options for implementing a program by not demonstrating the order that the processes of the system will execute. This is poles apart from a flowchart, which spends most of its soul vigorously and unambiguously telling all who will listen that line 34 will *always* execute immediately after line 33, ifs, ands, and buts excluded! Fancier flowcharts show the order of execution of entire routines, but nevertheless do the job in the same way as a programming language does. Flowcharts tend to be more readable than assembly code source (so they're used often in assembly-based projects), but flowcharts do nothing that Pascal or C source can't do better (so they're not at all popular with Pascal or C programmers).

It isn't correct that order of execution is ignored while a program is being described with dataflow diagrams. Other types of diagrams are developed, usually in parallel with dataflow diagrams, that do have that information. Revising a design iteratively brings the description of the design and implementation of the system closer to logical description in a stepwise manner, during which some of the timing details may be worked out in the other diagrams.

In the sample dataflow diagram in Figure 4–5, note that process CarefullySelectManuscriptForReading feeds process SkimManuscript with the data items called CarefullySelectedManuscript; the details that are left out of this graphic connection fill the rest of the design document. Logically the process cannot provide CarefullySelectedManuscript items if there are no Submissions in either the Slush Pile or the High Priority Pile, and SkimManuscript can't skim more than one manuscript at a time. This dataflow diagram only describes the average, or steady-state, condition of a machine, and does not describe the handling details of the kind of data being pushed around. It is important to understand the processes in a DFD are assumed to have enough smarts to know when to hand out and accept its data items.

There is therefore little reason to describe how many data items can be "queued up" in a data flow path like the one labelled CarefullySelectedManuscript. In Figure 4–5 I include file symbols where things exist that act like files (or like directories), such as the HighPriorityPile and the SlushPile. They're mentioned in the DFD because there really are things called "slush piles" where uninspected manuscripts are kept, but technically this DFD doesn't need them although they indicate that the steady-state condition of the dataflow path between FilterKnownAuthors and CareFullySelectManuscriptForReading is expected to have a number of manuscripts in the queue.

What a process does can be described by a short verb-object phrase (Lift Hood, Clear Buffer Contents, or Transfer All Swag To Bigger Bag), and the data elements it accepts are what it uses to generate new data elements. A program or subprogram can be described using one or more (usually many) processes. Chances are good that a complete set of dataflow diagrams used to describe the class assignment would correspond with a number of the finished programs, despite the differences in the implementations.

A **signal** is a boolean value (yup/nope, or TRUE/FALSE, or OK/ERROR) that is considered to impart not processable data, but only timing or activation information. For this reason dataflow diagrams may not be

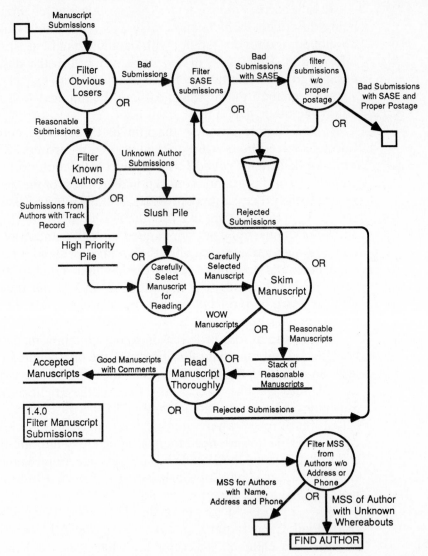

Figure 4–5 Simple example of a dataflow diagram: a book/magazine submissions editor

appropriate for fully describing signal-based systems, like many process control applications with devices. Dataflow diagrams are one of the tools in the arsenal. They do not do everything. Once the simple nuances of dataflow diagrams are understood, they can be drawn fast and can be quickly read with understanding.

Nested Dataflow Diagrams

Dataflow diagrams are hierarchical. For example, in the following diagram the highlighted process has a "lower" dataflow diagram that describes its function more accurately in the second diagram. The index numbers indicate this relationship. Dataflow diagrams are hierarchical because any given single dataflow diagram is supposed to be understandable, but should exclude greater detail when it can be avoided.

Each dataflow diagram, for example, should have around seven processes and the appropriate associated dataflow arrows.

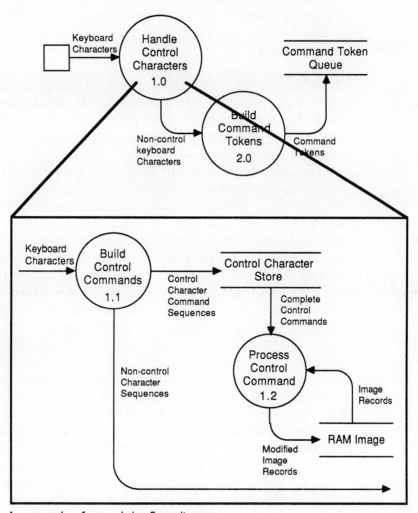

An example of nested dataflow diagrams

Creating a Dataflow Diagram

To give some idea how a dataflow of a system is constructed, here is a short list of things that are done. First, the outputs and inputs to a system are defined to help provide the context in which the system has to work. The outputs and inputs are generally the well-understood parts of a system to be analyzed. Second, a series of processes is created using the already-defined parts of the dataflow diagram, usually by starting from the outputs and working backward into the guts of the system until the inputs are encountered on the other side.

Sometimes several iterations will have to be made to get the diagram into the most appropriate form. For this reason it is suggested that the first few renditions of a particular diagram be done first with paper and pencil.

Nassi-Shneiderman Charts

Nassi-Shneiderman charts (see Fig. 4–6) are rigorous flowcharts. If a segment of code can be described using Nassi-Shneiderman charts, then the code is well organized. The code may be harder to read for other reasons, such as meaningless variable names (like a1 or z) or improperly indented text.

Flowcharts can be used to design code that does not conform to rules used to describe good structures. Nassi-Shneiderman charts can't. Flowcharts are collections of statements loosely connected by lines, which makes for easy free-form construction. Nassi-Shneiderman charts are built like Aztec and Mayan mosaics, with each component of a chart carefully fitted among the others. Flowcharts were popular in the dawn of software development because of the lack of building constraints. Few people had any idea what good development rules were, outside of the ones picked up with experience and the intuitive few. Also, most work was done without high-level languages, not even FORTRAN or Cobol. Nassi-Shneiderman charts could not be used to describe some of the necessary and common coding practices of that time. Since high-level languages became popular, Nassi-Shneiderman charts can now be used, including assembler projects based on machines with rich instruction sets. Nassi-Shneiderman charts are now used in part to confirm that a number of important rules are followed during code implementation.

It isn't possible to tack a sequence of instructions on to a Nassi-Shneiderman chart without a proper beginning and a correct (and predictable) termination. The chart will be visibly incomplete.

If the implementation of a system is correct, Nassi-Shneiderman charts can easily be generated from the source code to confirm adherence to the

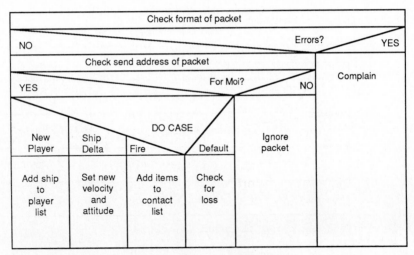

Figure 4–6 Example Nassi-Shneiderman chart

original design document, part of which could be Nassi-Shneiderman charts completed before coding began. Flowcharts are also generatable from source code (even badly organized source code), but an automatically-generated flowchart may not exactly match a hand-drawn one, whereas two Nassi-Shneiderman charts of the same routine are going to be pretty close.

It is also possible to automatically create structure charts from the source code. If a system was implemented without an eye toward clean design, the structure chart generated for it (if one can be generated at all) will be amazing. One routine, for example, may reference 30 different routines, making it difficult to understand what the big routine does. Utility routines near the bottom of the chart may commonly reference top control routines, for normal processing as well as exception processing. Single files may be used to define a number of unrelated data structures for a large program.

The same fate can befall flowcharts; the flowchart of an incomprehensible routine is likely to be incomprehensible. Nassi-Shneiderman charts give up at the first sign of an unstructured construct, such as a goto into the midst of a block of code with otherwise one entrance and one exit.

Components of Nassi-Shneiderman Diagrams

Figure 4–7 shows a list of the components of a Nassi-Shneiderman diagram.

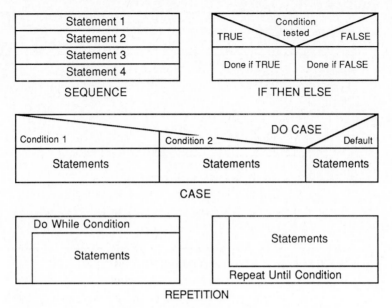

Figure 4–7 List of Nassi-Shneiderman components

Structure Charts

Structure charts demonstrate in a single eyeful all the real-world interface requirements for a design. It shows the names of all the functions and procedures in a system, and describes who calls what. Structure charts aren't used to display the order of execution of routines; they would be intolerably hard to read and maintain.

Where a suite of dataflow diagrams show what needs to be done, a structure chart tells how to do it. The structure chart's composition does this by incorporating symbols showing the relationships of things that have names, like FORTRAN subroutines, Pascal Procedures, and C functions. This includes data in memory. Files do not have a particular symbol because of the variety of ways that data in files are accessed.

Structure charts are not tolerant of the generalizations used in dataflow diagrams. They don't go beyond describing what routines do (by making mention of each line of code as do flowcharts, pseudocode, or Nassi-Shneiderman diagrams). But then, if an entire system were described solely using flowcharts or Nassi-Shneiderman diagrams, the description would be so voluminous (for even small projects) that a single glance at them would reveal information regarding only single routines. A single glance at a structure chart reveals how several routines relate to one another. They are used to get the bugs out of the interfacing between routines and data.

A structure chart is flat. All the routines in the structure chart are displayed by name (and their function described if the names are short, à la old FORTRAN). Dataflow diagrams can be nested, where a process can be broken down into a number of processes, stores, and dataflows on a different dataflow diagram (the relationship is shown as a DFD with a similar but longer index number). Structure chart elements cannot be broken down further—a function or data item is the smallest component that can be given a name.

The Unwieldy Size of Structure Charts

Although theoretically there ought to be just one structure chart for a single system, this structure chart could require a sheet of paper the size of one side of one of the World Trade Center buildings in New York City. The common practice is to make structure charts human-scale in size by chopping the diagram apart at the low traffic points (aka lowest coupling and cohesion).

Any set of structure charts can get bulky, contributing to the amount of time dedicated to maintaining diagrams of this type. It has historically been difficult to maintain an accurate, complete set of charts with data and control flows by hand. For this reason it is recommended that no structure charts or similar diagram systems should be attempted without help from a computer.

Iterative Refinement

The structure charts are developed from the suite of dataflow diagrams. A better suite of dataflow diagrams is developed from the realization of a more concrete design while the structure charts are developed. Refinements in a system progress iteratively until someone yells *"enough,"* time runs out, or no worthwhile or noticeable improvement has taken place for the amount of time spent on them.

Living Documents

Any system changes until it is branded "mature," which is usually when nobody can be coerced into working on it any longer. The document that describes that system also has to change, always before the code is changed. The initial development of a successful system is usually a brief segment of the system's timeline. An accurate, in-depth working document is a magnificent tool to have (see Figs. 4–8, 4–9, and 4–10).

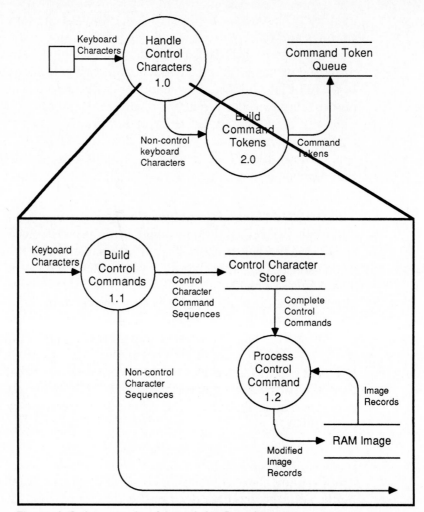

Figure 4–8 An example of nested dataflow diagrams

Extra information that may be added to structure charts without making them more difficult to read is organizational, such as source file names and directory locations. Other concrete information should be added whenever it impacts on the organization of the system or the structure of the interfaces of a group of routines. For example, in a multi-CPU environment a group of routines may make sense to only one type of available CPU, so the design constraint might be mentioned.

What does a structure chart provide as a service? It is a form of advanced warning that shows the extent of a design and the influence of changes on a design. Additions to a system (when described as changes to

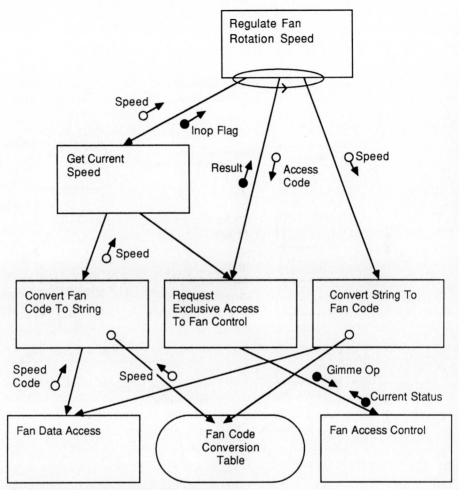

Figure 4–9 An example of a structure chart

parameters and new functions) and changes to old functions or deletions can be clearly mapped ahead of time.

When implementation jobs are assigned while using structure charts, they can be defined with an eye toward debugging the interfaces between major parts of a system. A great deal of time is spent getting the parameter lists between caller and callee to match. When they don't match, the discrepancy may be detected at a number of stages—compile time, link time, unit testing, system testing, or field use. When the parameters don't match exactly, it can mean that one of the routines was built with incorrect information, which could mean problems other than the parameter lists not matching. One routine is wrong.

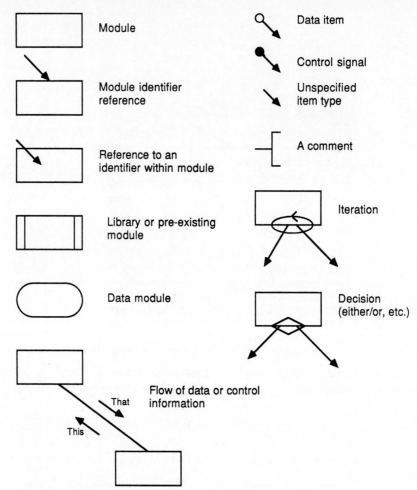

Figure 4–10 Some structure chart symbols

Very Briefly, Warnier-Orr

Warnier-Orr is a charting system that seems very appropriate for business application code design rather than scientific, real-time, or engineering development. This is only my opinion, and perhaps not that of Ken Orr, et al.

The diagrams used in the Warnier-Orr methodology are very similar in looks to those used by Yourdon. Warnier-Orr entity diagrams look like dataflow diagrams, but the rules are poles apart. While Yourdon processes are designed for high cohesion, a Warnier-Orr entity is not constrained by its cohesive property. It is an object that incorporates all that is required to maintain data; in Yourdon terms an entity is a manager. Every possible type of transaction that can be posted between entities is placed in the diagram with connecting arrows.

The Warnier-Orr equivalent for structure charts involves many long curly brackets (see Fig. 4–11). It is tempting to say that a Warnier-Orr chart is a structure chart that is rotated to the left with the boxes and arrows replaced by curly brackets, but this is not at all true. Warnier-Orr charts demonstrate order of execution and clearly identify initialization and termination. Pure structure charts don't show order of execution, and they exclude initialization and termination details. Warnier-Orr charts do not show interface details, but do demonstrate at a glance hierarchical relationships of large sections of code. Structure charts focus on demonstrating the interfaces between modules and procedures.

EXAMPLES OF AUTOMATED DEVELOPMENT STEPS

As mentioned before, tedious operations that are repeated ad nauseum deserve automation as much as possible. The act of automating some of the processing should not hamper any of the creative processes, and ought to speed up the entire development cycle.

What does a text editor program do that a simple manual or electric typewriter can't? It places the subject matter in a more accessible form. A document in the form of a file is accessible and changeable:

- ☐ Changes can be made without having to make hard copy
- ☐ Any number of copies can be produced
- ☐ Revision information can be kept in as accessible a form as the working copy
- ☐ Text can be formatted freely
- ☐ Several output devices can be used, ranging in quality from a quick dot-matrix output to an offset typesetter

Noting the successful graphics editing programs, automating some of the chart building tasks is a worthwhile job (especially the error detection duties). Since there are spelling checker programs, and there can also be data dictionary consistency programs. Since programs that support connectivity aren't currently in as high a demand as word processors (*everybody* uses those), they cost more, are fewer in number, and aren't as good.

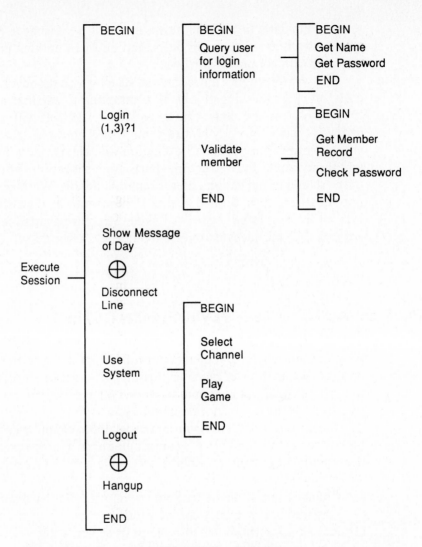

Figure 4–11 An example Warnier-Orr diagram

Making Do With What You Have

Word processors like the venerable WordStar editor can be used for producing several kinds of documents: Pascal source files, theses, magazine articles, record catalogs, and pictures using ASCII characters. If you have something to do with your personal computer and you don't have the exactly appropriate software tools for the work (you might be unable to afford the program, or the program doesn't exist and you don't want to write it), you might be able to make do with what software you do have.

There aren't many low-cost programs specifically made for editing correct design diagrams. It is possible to use readily available programs (like MacDraw, MacPaint, Filevision, Mac3D, or their equivalents for the IBM, ST, and Amiga) for building the charts, though the automatic detection of design faults will suffer. At least you'll be able to make copies of the document and make revisions (like making changes in text files). Some programs can be easily used in a role of design-aide for large graphics needs (vast structure charts). Others aren't so hot.

Please remember that the following comments regarding the software packages in question are likely to be out of date; they are examples of usage only, and present these packages only in a positive sense.

MacPaint is a program that provides a free-form, bit-oriented graphics scratchpad. With it you can create single-page sized illustrations. There are a flock of programs similar to MacPaint for the other machines with bit-mapped graphics displays (making the wheel rounder is a favorite pastime). MacPaint provides control of individual pixels, but the size of the canvas is limited. Since changes to the image affect the bitmap directly, and not a separate display list (used in MacDraw) to rebuild the image at will, Mac-Paint behaves radically different from the way MacDraw behaves. MacDraw, for example, allows you to grab a circle after it is drawn and move it about the canvas without affecting the rest of the canvas; in MacPaint this maneuver would cause parts of the canvas image to be overwritten with the circle image. There are equivalents on every graphics machine.

MacDraw, with its display/list-based graphics database, is more suited for developing design documents in most cases. It is, in fact, possible to extract meaningful information from a MacDraw data file with other programs.

Mac3D has additional features (over MacDraw) that make it possible to more easily develop large structure charts and other hierarchical diagrams that contain a great deal of graphic data. For example, the glue attribute allows the end of a line to be bound to a box; when the box is moved, the line adjusts to follow, but the movement of the entire line does not mimic the movement of the box. The endpoint of the line that isn't directly glued to the box stays stationary to the canvas, with the line becoming longer or shorter as the other endpoint follows the box. This means that if a function has many references and you have to move where it lies on the structure chart, you don't have to go through the tedium of moving the reference lines one at a time to the new location. However, Mac3D is not designed to maintain connectivity, and so is hardly an ideal solution for this need.

COMPUTER-AIDED SOFTWARE DESIGN PACKAGES

Cheap Ones

Dezign for the IBM PC is a program that supports the Jackson design methods. The program uses a standard 80-character by 24-line ASCII display without bit-mapped graphics. A single display's worth of information can contain 3 rows of 5 functions, plus a single function at the top of the display. Any number of displays can be in a suite, although in the version that I own (perhaps an old version) the data files are statically allocated and require a constant n blocks of space. To go beyond the number of displays that can fit in a set of files, the user must build a new set of larger files and copy the data to these files.

Associations are demonstrated with horizontal and vertical lines between the function descriptions. The functions are represented as rectangles.

Once a suite of data structure charts and functional charts have been described, the frames of the procedures can be generated from the suite. Dezign also supports some error and consistency checking.

Design by Meta Software is a Macintosh tool based on Petri Nets, applicable to developing a suite of hierarchical dataflow pictures. Design is not intended to be wedded to one methodology, but to be applicable to many. It is currently the least expensive Macintosh graphics package I've encountered that properly supports connectivity. Meta Software charges a goodly sum for the privilege of directly accessing its database and adding your own code.

Structure Chart from Excel Software is another inexpensive program with an inexpensive name, but at least with this one you don't have to guess what it does. It runs on the Macintosh.

Expensive Ones

At the 1985 National Computer Conference Arthur Young, James Martin, and Database Design, Inc., demonstrated a program for building a variety of diagram types for system analysis and design. The program was implemented using an early version of Gem, and appeared to have respectable performance characteristics on an IBM PC. In that version of the program (which didn't appear to have a name yet), the dataflow diagrams were built using the constraints of horizontal and vertical lines only, and the processes were represented by boxes.

In this program the different chart types are arranged hierarchically; a lower-level breakdown of a function in a Jackson style diagram is a dataflow diagram. To get to the DFD one picks the function box, and the corresponding dataflow window appears in the foreground.

Yourdon, Inc., provides an excellent-looking package called *The Analyst Toolkit* for the IBM PC, a series of programs that assist in creating dataflow diagrams, entity relationship diagrams, state transition diagrams, and free-form graphics. The picture-building actions are similar to those used in MacDraw, where a palette of graphic symbols provides a selection of draw modes. Selecting a circle in the palette means Create New Process, and choosing one of the arrowheaded lines or arcs starts one of the Create New Data Path modes. Another palette for commands occupies the screen across the bottom, and file name information is displayed on the top line. The graphics are displayed in the center without windows.

The Analyst Toolkit has error and consistent checking (the international symbol for NO is displayed on top of bad components) and a data dictionary.

Tektronix also has a package available for developing dataflow diagrams. It works by way of typing in descriptive text; you watch the program building the diagram from it. For example, "a to b" would cause the Tektronix system to draw a circle with "a" in it, a circle with "b" in it, and a dataflow path from process a to process b. This system is currently available on select Unix-based systems.

Abvent of Beverly Hills, California, provides the Anatool package for the Macintosh. It supports Yourdon-style dataflow diagrams, a data dictionary, and standards specifications. A process has to be described either by another dataflow diagram (hierarchically) or by a text specification, lest it fail the consistency checks. Like the other Mac packages mentioned here, it follows the Macintosh user guidelines pretty well.

McDonnell Douglas Professional Services Company provides ProKit*ANALYST and DFDdraw, two programs for the IBM PC family. DFDdraw is a dataflow diagram engine, and ProKit*ANALYST provides the features of DFDdraw in addition to extensive report-generation facilities aimed at describing the status of a system under development.

Nastec Corporation's Design Aid for IBM PC and DEC VaxStations is a system that supports a multitude of chart systems: Yourdon, Gane and Sarson, and Warnier-Orr.

Excelerator, Excelerator/RTS, and Customizer by Index Technology Corporation are products that work on an IBM PC. They support, respectively, normal Yourdon diagrams, real-time and control-critical systems design, and customization of the first two packages for specific requirements.

StructSoft, Inc., provides PCSA for the IBM PC, which supplies the usual dataflow diagraming and data dictionary functions with its own unique advantages.

I have also seen large companies rely on extensive in-house developed design programs that are based on the Warnier-Orr methodology. This software is used for the development of large business applications. Big outfits sometimes use packages like this as part of their "secret weapons" arsenal and never allow them to be sold.

HYBRID SYSTEMS

Mainstay, Inc.'s Visual Interactive Programming System (V.I.P.) is a graphic design medium of sorts. Each possible primitive command is represented on the screen as a box with a name, and the system helps you create individual boxes by indicating value ranges and fields to fill in before the primitive becomes useful. When a connected set of boxes is defined such that a program or program fragment has interactively been built, you can run it.

From the graphic representation of programs can come textual descriptions. One kind of description is the language in which V.I.P. programs are represented in files. V.I.P. is also designed to generate any kind of text description, including C and Pascal, from the representation in graphics. The V.I.P. system is also intended to insulate application software from the differences between window systems, though V.I.P.'s success in this venture has not yet been demonstrated (see Fig. 4–12).

The V.I.P. system is presented here because it is an attempt to merge program design graphics with the act of programming. Other systems, such as Dezign, can create program, function, procedural frames, and even code, from the information stored in its dictionary. The framing is language-independent. The V.I.P. system has a low floor but a fairly high ceiling, since it supports a limited form of object-oriented programming.

SUMMARY

With single-person projects formal methods provide keener insight. With multi-person projects formal methods inspire communication. Use well-defined design methods for a one-person project or one involving a number of teams, and find the software and machines that will help you use these methods. Do not settle for software that is too constraining, and be very aware of possible new objectives that may interfere with present

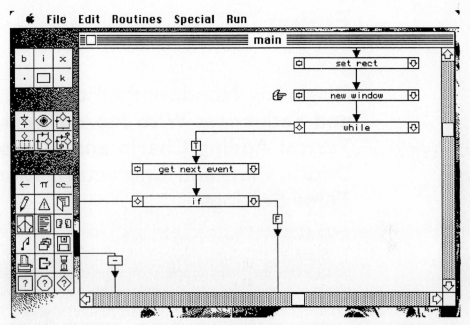

Figure 4–12 The Visual Interactive Programming screen with program fragment

development efforts. There is great notation for every kind of application that gets to the point without the plodding tedium of implemented code; find it and use it.

Epilog

Disguising Nondescript Positions, States, and Sequences With More Familiar Terms; Adding Charm and Memorabilia, Depth, Plot, and Characterization To Terse Settings

What do you use display objects for?

Some of the display objects that are supplied by the windowing packages are the computer science versions of squeezing oil from rock. The popup and pulldown menus, windows, dialogs, pushing-hand icons, and scroll bars are all (in part) low-horsepower workaround for small displays.

These same objects are insurance *against* display improvements; when the IBM PC came out, the 640-by-200 pixel graphics were a big deal, but that was several years ago. Relatively inexpensive displays now support 640-by-480 pixel color graphics, and monochrome displays go over 1024-by-960 pixels. A correctly written windowing application has no problem working with any of these displays without modification, since it is the responsibility of the window system to maintain the device drivers. If an entirely new display appears after the software is sold, the display manufacturer can present you with a driver that you can load into your window system. No upgrades to buy, and no fuss.

However, that isn't all.

There used to be a clearly defined boundary between how things are done in the world and how they are done with the computer. Computers (especially personal ones) have made doing many things easier and faster, but the methods that are used have always had to be learned since they weren't already part of everyday experience.

Software is being written to emulate the outside. People have found that if an operation supported by a computer looks, smells, sounds, and behaves like something in the physical world, a user can draw from his or her vast experience in the world to understand:

☐ What the operation is doing
☐ How the computer is doing it

☐   What the operation can do

The last point is significant. It means that a user who is relatively naive in using a computer does not have to experiment with the software to find out what its capabilities and limits are. His or her physical world experience has probably crossed its path several times. If the computer version is faithful, then how it works is mostly understood.

AN ELABORATE EXAMPLE

For example, the screen might show a door with a sign on it that says "Library." You touch the door, and hear and see the door unlatch and swing open. You see your camera (as yourself) enter, and hear the door close behind you. You see shelves with books, a card catalog, and someone behind the information desk. You ask, "Do you have a phone book?" and the librarian asks in reply, "For any place in particular, or perhaps Chicago?" You reply, "Chicago Yellow Pages." The librarian asks, "Business or Commercial Yellow Pages?" You reply, "Business." The librarian says, "Hang on, I'll be back in a moment," and gets up and walks to the far side of the room and through a door (which closes). You see another librarian try to enter the room, but the door wouldn't open. After a while, the librarian comes back, and a copy of a Yellow Pages book icon appears on the information desk. The librarian asks, "Do you want to check out this book?" and you reply, "Sure." The librarian then says, "You may carry this book for two days. If you let the due date expire, the book will *automatically return to the library*." You say, "I'd like to change the policy to return to the library if not used in a day." The librarian says, "OK." The book appears in your personal, local directory system.

This example may seem overly wordy, but what actually happened was that you asked your machine to dial out to a database somewhere, you talked with the database through your computer, and you returned with a set of rules for accessing part of that remote database. Your computer is going to flush the information when you stop using it, but you know you can go back to the "library" and get it again! Open the "book" and your computer will establish a connection with that part of the remote database. Which one? It usually doesn't matter. The average person may not know databases from aircraft rudders, but does know how to go to the library and ask the librarian for a phone book. There are many problems with the way this example may work (it might rely on heavy use of the keyboard, something we're trying to get away from), but you should have the idea.

CONTROLS ARE OBJECTS

A simple example of the physical world in current software are **controls**, which are software emulations of things like on/off buttons, rotating knobs, and sliding bar potentiometers. New entertainment software that is written in the tradition of Original Adventure relies on custom controls, icons, and animation, but doesn't stop there. Controls are a subset of display objects, obviously, but less obvious is that display objects are a subset of objects.

An **object** is a definable something that interacts with other objects using a set of rules. In this context an object is a software entity (like a program or part of one), so these rules are implemented in code. A display object is one particular type of object that owns an image that appears on a display. How can objects interact with each other? Well, ideally, any way you can think of. For example, objects of type A run around a system eating objects of type B.

Programs can be implemented in terms of objects. In the Library program above the librarian object moved from the book room object to the search room object to use the telecommunications object. Your you object went to the library object to track down a copy of the Chicago Yellow Pages, which is represented as a reference object that has an icon. That librarian does the job of a librarian, but doesn't perform as a lion tamer. The telecommunications object lives in the search room because it can be used by only one person at one time, and the search room only has space for one person.

The short-term future of user interfaces, as I see it, will continue the current trend of developing and using icons (objects), some of which will be superbly animated, carry sound, and be free of subtitles. There are some simple icons: the little icons for floppy disk, hard disk, and editor file; all the controls in a dialog and alert box; Mac 3D's circular scroll bar; and the more mundane type that all the user-interface packages have for scrolling windows. These simple ones are going to have some complicated company. A few people have been making a living writing programs and routine libraries that animate icons, but the number of such jobs will increase. Of course most software will not strive to emulate the physical world to the extent of my example, but it could if desired.

We appear to be designing and building places in software where spoken and written languages like English are less necessary.

PORTABILITY

Portability will always cost you something: performance, maintainability, sanity. As far as graphics are concerned, portability is a matter of how many times the product is going to be upgraded, how many machines are going to be targeted, the size of the product, how different the target environments are, and how nasty the graphic operations are going to be. The current window systems are not terribly different, especially between the Apple Macintosh and Microsoft Windows, but if you are spending most of your time writing animation software you will be ultrasensitive to their differences. Portability will gain you something; don't ignore a large portion of your market by following a bad development path to a finished product.

IMMEDIATE CONCERNS

Other developers and I have continuously crossed swords with the Moriarty of small computers: storage limitations. If it wasn't a shortage of RAM, it most certainly was a problem with not having enough disk storage. Hundreds of programs have died on the vine because they would have needed much too much storage. The problem is still very bad, because now we have figured out exactly what to do with *billions* of bytes of storage in single programs but have no way to store it all cheaply.

Storage is something that both graphics and digitized sound use by the barrelful. A single 30-second digitized passage of Beethoven can hog most of a 400K disk; 30 seconds of music is OK for the startup page of a game, but it couldn't be conveniently used for a music survey program. Pictures and accurately digitized sound are commodities that have been used *sparingly* in microcomputer software. Algorithmic approaches have been emphasized, characterized by simple stick graphics without shading or depth, and repetitive, homogenous drawings.

Both raw sound and picture data can be stored on disk in a compressed format, but I can see uses for orders of magnitude of more graphics and sound than we currently get. The solution is to use compression and get bigger disks. Where are those CD-ROMS?

Controls have been mostly graphic, but sound has been used to reinforce their operation. Controls have been limited to very simple graphics and animation. The use of more elaborate controls will require more storage, because the code to drive the controls has to share the same space as the large bitmaps and digitized passages used by the same software, assuming that elaborate controls are going to take up more space. I believe that controls are dependent on more processing power and imagination.

An alternative to handy on-site mass storage is a fast connection to sources of information that you don't own and are located somewhere else. The connections to these dialup services has been by telephone with a modem. Mass market modems have recently made it to 9600 bps, but this is hardly fast enough. To me local area networks aren't as interesting as a redesign in the current telephone system to abolish modems and permit reasonably high data transfers on a dialup.

Displays seem to be getting better, but at a slow pace. If we should see a breakthrough in display technology (Please? I mean, we're still using *vacuum tubes*? Get real), we will suddenly see a brand new demand for much better processing power. Again.

FINALLY

We have been dealt a very good hand; let's do something with it. Now.

Appendixes

A For Further Reading

Here is a list of good books to include in a library. It is not exhaustive. It includes the books used as reference for *The Viewport Technician*.

Apple Computer. *Inside Macintosh.* 5 vols. Menlo Park, Calif.: Addison Wesley, Inc., 1986.

> If you try to work on the Macintosh without having these books handy, you will fail. It is very simple; there are no other Macintosh references that come close to these for accuracy, competence, clarity, and completeness. They are not flawless, but they are indispensable and a tough act to follow.

Chernicoff, Stephen. *Macintosh Revealed.* 2 vols. Berkeley: Hayden Book Company, 1985.

> *Inside Macintosh* is too densely packed and random a reference from which to learn Macintosh programming from scratch, yet many developers did it since nothing else was available. Now there is *Macintosh Revealed*, which presents the capabilities of the Macintosh system in a well-written and step-by-step way. The size of the two-volume set shouldn't daunt anyone since much of the contents are in the form of graphics, tables, and listings.

Clark, Randy and Koehler, Stephen. *The UCSD Pascal Handbook.* Englewood Cliffs, N.J.: Prentice-Hall, Inc., 1982.

> This is a dandy reference for a very popular dialect of Pascal that influenced the design and operation of many other Pascal compiler and interpreter systems.

DeMarco, Tom. *Concise Notes on Software Engineering.* New York: Yourdon Press, 1979.

> The essence of structured analysis and design, tools, walkthroughs, encapsulation, data driven design, and an introduction to software engineering metrics. Books on software engineering tend to run long-winded, but this one is a spectacularly brief 93 pages, and the significant points are presented.

DeMarco, Tom. *Controlling Software Projects.* New York: Yourdon Press, 1982.

> This book discusses the costs of system development, what goes wrong, and how to improve matters considerably. Most software projects, when they die, die a little too late to save the participants grief and money. Significant projects are unwieldy things that require good methods to finish; this book introduces many of the needed ideas.

Duntemann, Jeff. *Complete Turbo Pascal.* Glenview, Ill.: Scott, Foresman and Company, 1986.

Duntemann, Jeff. *Turbo Pascal Solutions.* Glenview, Ill.: Scott, Foresman and Company, 1987.

> These two enjoyable books will guide you into Turbo Pascal expertise. They keep the Borland manuals honest with the clearest voice imaginable in technical writing.

Durant, David; Carlson, Geta; and Yao, Paul. *Programmer's Guide to Windows*. San Francisco: Sybex, Inc., 1987.

This 646-page effort is one of the best (of the few) books on the market that addresses the act of programming applications using Microsoft Windows. Learning Windows is not an easy experience; learning Windows with Microsoft's toolkit manuals alone is not (at all) recommended. Arm yourself with *Programmer's Guide to Windows*, however, and things will start to work in your favor. This book is to *Microsoft Windows Toolkit* what *Macintosh Revealed* is to *Inside Macintosh*.

Gerits, K.; Englisch, L.; and Bruckmann, R. *Atart ST Internals*. Grand Rapids, Mich.: Abacus Software, Inc., 1985 (originally published in Dusseldorf, West Germany by Data Becker GmbH in 1985).

Here we have a technical description of the major ICs in the Atari ST: the 68000, the custom ICs (Glue, MMU, DMA, and Shifter), the Western Digital 1772 floppy controller, and other ICs. The I/O interfaces are discussed: Video, Centronics, RS-232, MIDI, Cartridge slot, the floppy interface, and the DMA interface. 150 pages are used to cover the low-level operating environment software, including GEMDOS, XBIOS, BIOS, and Graphics A-line trap routines, and how interrupts work on the ST. Also included is a 200-page listing of the early Atari ST BIOS. This book is a useful reference if you know your way around a microcomputer system enough to know that you might need some of this useful (but arcane) information, and may come in handy for those who want a good look at what arcane information looks like. The writing is "wetter" than most technical reference books.

Harbison, Samuel P. and Steele, Guy L., Jr. *A C Reference Manual*. Englewood Cliffs, N.J.: Prentice-Hall, Inc., 1984.

If you haven't got the hang of Kernighan and Ritchie's *The C Programming Language*, then this may be more your cup of tea, though both are technical treatments and can't be considered easy reads by novice C programmers. *A C Reference Manual* covers the C language issue by issue. Examples run rampant, and the C language is described unambiguously with a variation of Backus-Naur Form (BNF) notation. The book is also good for coding practice hints.

Leemon, Sheldon. *Inside Amiga Graphics*. Greensboro, N.C.: Compute! Publications, Inc., 1986.

This is a good programmer's handbook dedicated to the Amiga's graphics. It has 300 pages, is spiral-bound and clearly written, contains both an index and a function summary, and has many code examples. One thing it doesn't have (for some reason) is many illustrations, but it otherwise stands by itself in its class.

Martin, James and McClure, Carma. *Diagramming Techniques for Analysts and Programmers*. Englewood Cliffs, N.J.: Prentice-Hall, Inc., 1985.

This is an excellent survey of the popular diagramming methods in use today. It does the important job of comparing and contrasting each of the diagram systems. The text relies heavily on illustrations.

Mical, Robert J. and Deyl, Susan. *Intuition, The Amiga User Interface*. West Chester, Pa.: Commodore-Amiga, Inc., 1985.

Commodore-Amiga. *Amiga ROM Kernel Manual.* 2 vols. West Chester, Pa.: Commodore-Amiga, Inc., 1985.

Commodore-Amiga. *Amiga Hardware Manual.* West Chester, Pa.: Commodore-Amiga, Inc., 1985.

Commodore-Amiga. *AmigaDOS Technical Reference Manual.* West Chester, Pa.: Commodore-Amiga, Inc., 1985.

Commodore-Amiga. *AmigaDOS Developer's Manual.* West Chester, Pa.: Commodore-Amiga, Inc., 1985.

These are the standard documents issued by the manufacturer of the Amiga. As long as they are kept up to date, the ROM Kernel Manuals are a good, quick place to find obscure details. In the editions used for this book, the print in Volume 2 was small and far from offset quality. The entire set is a good source of information, aided by a small number of technical books written by independent authors. Commercial versions are printed by Addison-Wesley, Inc.

Microsoft, Inc. *Microsoft Windows, Windows Write, etc.* Seattle, Wash.: Microsoft, Inc., 1986.

This contains the Windows runtime environment that you don't get when you buy the *Microsoft Windows Software Developer's Kit.* If you have version 1.03 of the Developer's Kit, you'll need the matching version 1.03 of the runtime environment. For the straight dope on later versions, check with Microsoft.

Microsoft. *The Microsoft Windows Software Development Kit.* 3 vols., many disks. Seattle, Wash.: Microsoft, Inc., 1987.

You can't do any Windows work without this package, since the interface to the Windows runtime has to be linked into your application's executable file. Owning a copy of the Toolkit is the legal recourse. Version 1.03 of the Toolkit comes with Pascal and C examples (for Microsoft compilers), a Windows-compatible debugger that takes some getting used to, and three binders of robust documentation. The three binders contain:

Volume 1: *Update and Programmer's Utility Guide*

Volume 2: *Quick Reference, Programming Guide, and Application Style Guide*

Volume 3: *Programmer's Reference*

Microsoft pays some attention to their forums on the Genie and CompuServe dial-in computer services, but they provide better developer support to those who pay and access the Microsoft Windows support BBS.

Mortimore, Eugene P. *Amiga Programmer's Handbook.* Berkeley: Sybex, Inc., 1986.

The earliest version of this work was not the easiest or most accurate reference on the Amiga, but it did contain insights that seemed to exist nowhere else, and above all it did exist. It still exists, in an excellent form.

Norton, Peter. *Inside the IBM PC.* Bowie, Md.: Brady Communications Co., 1984.

If you work with IBM PCs, you know this guy. Mr. Norton has been a one-man show in producing good software utilities and writing excellent books. *Inside the IBM PC* hands you the essential machine details of the PC: hardware, disk formats, the contents of ROM, some display details, how the speaker and the I/O ports work, and how MS-DOS is put together. While the IBM Technical Reference Manuals are brief, dry, withdrawn, and boring, this book is useful, outgoing, and entertaining. It propels those nitty-gritty details into your mind.

Stroustrup, Bjarne. *The C++ Programming Language.* Menlo Park, Calif.: Addison Wesley, 1986.

Both Modula 2 and C++ are free of many of the problems infecting C and Pascal. Stroustrup's book is an excellent technical journey into C++, but knowledge of C is mandatory and a general understanding of computer languages comes in handy. The significance of the C++ language will balloon when more C++ compilers (not just C++ preprocessors for regular C compilers) become available.

Szczepanowski, Norbert and Gunther, Bernd. *The Atari ST GEM Programmer's Reference.* Grand Rapids, Mich.: Abacus Software, Inc., 1986 (originally published in Dusseldorf, West Germany by Data Becker GmbH in 1985).

The essentials of GEM AES and VDI are presented here much in the form that they are given by the *IBM PC Gem Developer's Toolkit* by Digital Research, Inc. Each Gem routine is given a page, with the entries in the Gem parameter arrays itemized, and the C language binding routine declaration listed at the end of each entry. This book lacks programming examples, but the title does clearly mention that it is a reference book (implying that it isn't a tutorial).

Vinge, Vernor. *True Names.* New York, NY: Blue Jay Books, 1984.

A science fiction story that extrapolates the progress in user interface design, with an afterword by Marvin Minsky. There aren't many books in this one's class, nor are there many that treat the subject of advanced computing with such authority.

B Routines

EVENT MESSAGES AND ROUTINES

Macintosh

Modifiers
activeFlag
btnState
cmdKey
shiftKey
alphaLock
optionKey

Events
nullEvent
mouseDown
mouseUp
keyDown
keyUp
autoKey
updateEvt
diskEvt
activateEvt
networkEvt
driverEvt
app1Evt

app2Evt
app3Evt
app4Evt

Toolbox Functions
GetNextEvent
EventAvail
GetMouse
Button
StillDown
WaitMouseUp
GetKeys
TickCount
GetDblTime
GetCaretTime

Operating System Functions
PostEvent
FlushEvents
GetOSEvent

OSEventAvail
SetEventMask
GetEvQHdr

Masks
mDownMask
mUpMask
keyDownMask
keyUpMask
autoKeyMask
updateMask
diskMask
activMask
networkMask
driverMask
app1Mask
app2Mask
app3Mask
app4Mask
everyEvent

Gem

Functions
evnt_keybd
evnt_button
evnt_mouse
evnt_mesag
evnt_timer
evnt_multi
evnt_dclick

Events
MD_SELECTED
WM_REDRAW
WM_TOPPED
WM_CLOSED
WM_FULLED
WM_ARROWED
WM_HSLID

WM_VSLID
WM_SIZED
WM_MOVED
AC_OPEN
AC_CLOSE

Windows

Functions
WinMain
PostQuitMessage
GetMessage
PeekMessage
TranslateMessage
TranslateAccelerator
SetWindowsHook
DispatchMessage
GetMessagePos
GetMessageTime
SendMessage
PostMessage
ReplyMessage
WaitMessage
PostAppMessage
SendAppMessage
WndProc
DefWindowProc

Application Messages
WM_CREATE
WM_DESTROY
WM_SETVISIBLE

WM_ENABLE
WM_SETFOCUS
WM_KILLFOCUS
WM_SIZE
WM_ACTIVATE
WM_MOVE
WM_ERASEBKGND
WM_SYSCOLORCHANGE
WM_CLOSE
WM_QUERYOPEN
WM_QUERYENDSESSION
WM_ENDSESSION
WM_INITMENU
WM_MOUSEMOVE
WM_LBUTTONDOWN
WM_LBUTTONUP
WM_RBUTTONDOWN
WM_RBUTTONUP
WM_LBUTTONBLCLK
WM_RBUTTONBLCLK
WM_KEYDOWN
WM_KEYUP
WM_CHAR
WM_DEADCHAR

WM_TIMER
WM_COMMAND
WM_VSCROLL
WM_HSCROLL
WM_PAINT
WM_QUIT
WM_INITDIALOG
WM_SETDRAW
WM_GETTEXT
WM_GETTEXTLENGTH

System Messages
WM_SYSKEYDOWN
WM_SYSKEYUP
WM_SYSCHAR
WM_SYSDEADCHAR
WM_SYSCOMMAND

Clipboard Messages
WM_RENDERFORMAT
WM_RENDERALLFORMATS
WM_DESTROYCLIPBOARD
WM_DRAWCLIPBOARD

Amiga

IDCMP Flags
  (Event Message Types)
MOUSEBUTTONS
MOUSEMOVE
DELTAMOVE
GADGETDOWN
GADGETUP
CLOSEWINDOW
MENUPICK
MENUVERIFY
REQSET

REQCLEAR
REQVERIFY
NEWSIZE
REFRESHWINDOW
SIZEVERIFY
RAWKEY
NEWPREFS
DISKINSERTED/DISKRE-
  MOVED

IDCMP Functions
ModifyIDCMP
ReplyMsg
Wait

Console Functions
Open
Write
Read
OpenDevice
SendIO
DoIO

Macintosh QuickDraw Routines

Operations Involving
  GrafPorts
InitGraf

OpenPort
InitPort
SetPort

GetPort
GrafDevice
SetPortBits

PortSize
MovePortTo
SetOrigin
SetClip
GetClip
ClipRect
BackPat

Calculations that Use Rectangles

SetRect
OffsetRect
InsetRect
SectRect
UnionRect
PtInRect
Pt2Rect
PtToAngle
EqualRect
EmptyRect

Graphics with Rectangles

FrameRect
PaintRect
EraseRect
InvertRect
FillRect

Low Level, Customizable Quickdraw Primitives

SetStdProcs
StdText
StdLine
StdRect
StdRRect
StdOval
StdArc
StdPoly
StdRgn
StdBits
StdComment
StdTxMeas
StdGetPic
StdPutPic

Cursor Manipulation

InitCursor
SetCursor

HideCursor
ShowCursor
ObscureCursor

Graphics with Ellipses

FrameOval
PaintOval
EraseOval
InvertOval
FillOval

Graphics with Color

ForeColor
BackColor
ColorBit

Text Manipulation

TextFont
TextFAce
TExtMode
TextSize
SpaceExtra
DrawChar
DrawString
DrawText
CharWidth
TextWidth
GetFontInfo
MeasureText (128K)

Graphics with Round-corner Rectangles

FrameRoundRect
PaintRoundRect
EraseRoundRect
InvertRoundRect
FillRoundRect

Current Pen Control Routines

HidePen
ShowPen
GetPen
GetPenState
SetPenState
PenSize
PenMode
PenNormal

MoveTo
Move
LineTo
Line

Polygon Initialization and Disposal

OpenPoly
ClosePoly
KillPoly
OffsetPoly

Graphics with Polygons

FramePoly
PaintPoly
ErasePoly
InvertPoly
FillPoly

Picture Initialization, Drawing, and Disposal

OpenPicture
ClosePicture
PicComment
DrawPicture
KillPicture

Calculations with Regions

NewRgn
DisposeRgn
CopyRgn
SetEmptyRgn
SetRectRgn
RectRgn
OpenRgn
CloseRgn
OffsetRgn
InsetRgn
SectRgn
UnionRgn
DiffRgn
XorRgn
PtInRgn
RectInRgn
EqualRgn
EmptyRgn

Graphics with Regions
FrameRgn
PaintRgn
EraseRgn
InvertRgn
FillRgn

Misc Routines
Random
GetPixel
StuffHex

Bitmap Operations
ScrollRect
CopyBits

SeedFill (128K)
CalcMask (128K)
CopyMask (128K)

Point Calculations
AddPt
SubPt
SetPt
EqualPt

Mapping Routines
MapPt
MapRect
MapRgn
MapPoly

ScalePt
LocalToGlobal
GlobalToLocal

Graphics with Arcs
FrameArc
PaintArc
EraseArc
FillArc

Macintosh II Color Quickdraw Routines

cGrafport Manipulation
OpenCPort
InitCPort
CloseCPort

PixMap Manipulation
NewPixMap
DisposPixMap
CopyPixMap
SetCportPix

PixPat Manipulation
NewPixPat
DisposPixPat
CopyPixPat
PenPixPat
BackPixPat
GetPixPat
MakeRGBPat

Fill QD Primitive Routines
PillCRect
FillCOval
FillCRoundRect
FillCArc
FillCRgn
FillCPoly

Color Utility Routines
RGBForeColor
RGBBackColor
SetCPixel
GetCPixel
GetCTable
GetForeColor
GetBackColor

Icon Resources
GetCIcon
PlotCIcon

PixMap Operations
CopyPix
CopyCMask
SeedCFill
CalcCMask

Picture Manipulation
OpenCPicture

Other Miscellaneous Routines
GetSubTable
UpdatePixMap
MakeItable

AddSearch
AddComp
SetClient
QDError

Graphics Device Descriptor Operations
InitGDevice
NewGDevice
DisposGDevice
SetGDevice
GetGDevice

Entry Operations
ProtectEntry
ReserveEntry
SetEntry
SaveEntries
RestoreEntries

Misc Color Operations
Color2Index
Index2Color
InvertColor
RealColor

Cursor Handling Routines
GetCCursor
SetCCursor
AllocCursor

IIGS QuickDraw II Routines

QuickDraw II Global Routines
QDBootInit
QDStartup
QDShutDown
QDVersion
QDStatus
SetSysFont
GetSysFont

Operations Involving GrafPorts
InitGraf
OpenPort
InitPort
ClosePort
SetPortLoc
GetPortLoc
SetPortRect
GetPortRect
SetPortSize
MovePortTo
SetPort
GetPort
SetOrigin
SetClip
GetClip
SetClipHandle
GetClipHandle
ClipRect
BackPat

Calculations that Use Rectangles
SetRect
OffsetRect
InsetRect
SectRect
UnionRect
PtInRect
Pt2Rect
PtToAngle
EqualRect
EmptyRect

Graphics with Rectangles
FrameRect
PaintRect
EraseRect
InvertRect
FillRect

Low Level Primitives
SetStdProcs
StdText
StdLine
StdRect
StdRRect
StdOval
StdArc
StdPoly
StdRgn
StdPixels
StdComment
StdTxMeas
StdGetPic
StdPutPic
SetIntUse
GetAddress

Cursor Manipulation
InitCursor
SetCursor
HideCursor
ShowCursor
ObscureCursor

Graphics with Color
SetForeColor
GetForeColor
SetBackColor
GetBackColor
SetColorEntry
GetColorEntry

Graphics with Ellipses
FrameOval
PaintOval
EraseOval
InvertOval
FillOval

Text Manipulation
SetFont
GetFont
GetFontInfo
SetFontFlags
GetFontFlags
SetUserField
GetUserField
SetSysField
GetSysField
SetTextFace
SetTextMode
GetTextMode
TextSize
SetSpaceExtra
GetSpaceExtra
DrawChar
DrawString
DrawCString
DrawText
CharWidth
TextWidth
StringWidth
CStringWidth
CharBounds
TextBounds
StringBounds
CStringBounds
GetFontInfo

Graphics with Round-corner Rectangles
FrameRoundRect
PaintRoundRect
EraseRoundRect
InvertRoundRect
FillRoundRect

Picture Initialization, Drawing, and Disposal
OpenPicture
ClosePicture
PicComment
DrawPicture
KillPicture

Bitmap Operations
ScrollRect
PaintPixels

Misc Routines
Random
SetRandSeed
GetPixel
StuffHex
ClearScreen

Polygon Initialization and Disposal
OpenPoly
ClosePoly
KillPoly
OffsetPoly

Graphics with Polygons
FramePoly
PaintPoly
ErasePoly
InvertPoly
FillPoly

Current Pen Control Routines
PenNormal
MoveTo
Move
LineTo
Line
HidePen
ShowPen
GetPen
GetPenState
SetPenState
SetPenSize
GetPenSize
SetPenMode
GetPenMode

Mapping Routines
MapPt
MapRect
MapRgn
MapPoly
LocalToGlobal
GlobalToLocal

Point Calculations
AddPt
SubPt
SetPt
EqualPt
ScalePt

Calculations with Regions
NewRgn
DisposeRgn
CopyRgn
SetEmptyRgn
SetRectRgn
RectRgn
OpenRgn
CloseRgn
OffsetRgn
InsetRgn
SectRgn
UnionRgn
DiffRgn
XorRgn
PtInRgn
RectInRgn
EqualRgn
EmptyRgn

Graphics with Regions
FrameRgn
PaintRgn
EraseRgn
InvertRgn
FillRgn

Graphics with Arcs
FrameArc
PaintArc
EraseArc
FillArc

Color and Resolution
GetStandardSCB
SetMasterSCB
GetMasterSCB
SetSCB
GetSCB
SetAllSCBs
InitColorTable
SetColorTable
GetColorTable
GrafOn
GrafOff

More GrafPort Access Routines
SetPenPat
GetPenPat
SetSolidPenPat
SetPenMask
GetPenMask
SetBackPat
GetBackPat
SetSolidBackPat
SolidPattern
SetVisRgn
GetVisRgn
SetVisHandle
GetVisHandle
GetPicSave
GetRgnSave
GetPolySave
SetGrafProcs
GetGrafProcs

Untouchables
SetPicSave
SetRgnSave
SetPolySave

Amiga Graphics Library

Blitter Control Routines
OwnBlitter
DisownBlitter
QBlit
QBSBlit
WaitBlit

Blitter Graphics Routines
BltBitMap
BltClear
BltPattern
BltTemplate
Clipblit

Nondestructive Bitmap Scrolling
ScrollVPort
ScrollLayer

RGB Color Values
LoadRGB4
GetRGB4
SetRGB4

Point Operations
ReadPixel
WritePixel

View and Viewport Record Manipulation
InitView
InitVPort

Video Beam Timing
VBeamPos
WaitBOVP
WaitTOF

Raster Allocation and Deallocation
AllocRaster
FreeRaster

Dumb Bitmap Scroll Routines
ScrollRaster

Copper Macros
CEND
CINIT
CMOVE
CWAIT

Graphics Element List Processing
Animate
DrawGList
SortGList

Copper List Deallocation
FreeCopList
FreeCprList
FreeVPortCopLists

Color Map Routines
GetColorMap
FreeColorMap

Copper Instruction List Manipulation
MakeVPort
LoadView
MrgCop

Region Routines
NewRegion
OrRectRegion
XorRectRegion
AndRectRegion
ClearRegion
DisposeRegion

Text Display Routines
ClearEOL
ClearScreen
Text

Text Measurement
TextLength

Font Style Manipulation
AskSoftStyle
SetSoftStyle

LayerInfo Record Manipulation
DisposeLayerInfo
FattenLayerInfo
ThinLayerInfo
NewLayerInfo
LockLayerInfo
UnlockLayerInfo

Simple Refresh Layer Operations
BeginUpdate
EndUpdate

Superbitmap Operations
CopySBitMap
SyncSBitMap

Sprite Manipulation
InitMasks
ChangeSprite
FreeSprite
GetSprite
MoveSprite
AddVSprite
RemVSprite

Layer Access Control
LockLayer
UnlockLayer
LockLayers
UnlockLayers

ROM-based Layer Access Control
LockLayerRom
UnlockLayerRom

Layer Manipulation
MoveLayer
MoveLayerInFrontOf
SizeLayer
WhichLayer
BehindLayer
UpfrontLayer
InitLayers

Layer Control
CreateBehindLayer
CreateUpfrontLayer
DeleteLayer

Bitmap Flood
Flood

Graphics Element Initialization
InitAnimate

Gel Collision Control
SetCollision
DoCollision

Init Graphics Element List, Masks
InitGels
InitGMasks

Font Control
AvailFonts
AskFont
CloseFont
OpenDiskFont
OpenFont
RemFont
SetFont
AddFont

Line Draw Routines
Draw
PolyDraw

Blitter Object Control
AddBob
RemBob
RemIBob

Fast Bitmap Swapper
SwapBitsRastPortClipRect

Animation Object Control
AddAnimOb
FreeGBuffers
GetGBuffers

Display Record Initialization
InitBitMap
InitRastPort
InitTmpRas

Polygon Routines
InitArea
AreaDraw
AreaEnd
AreaMove

Rectangle Graphics
RectFill

Pen and Pattern Control
SetAfPt
SetAPen
SetBPen
SetDrMd
SetDrPt
SetOPen
SetRast
SetWrMsk

Pen Movement
Move

Gem VDI and AES Graphics Routines

Object Record Manipulation
objc_add
objc_delete
objc_draw
objc_find
objc_offset
objc_order
objc_edit
objc_change

Bitmap Form Conversion
vr_trnfm

Draw Mode Control
vswr_mode
Bitmap Copy
vro_cpyfm
vrt_cpyfm

Text Query Routines
vqt_attributes
vqt_extent
vqt_width
vqt_name
vqt_fontinfo

Text Control
vst_height

vst_point
vst_rotation
vst_font
vst_color
vst_effects
vst_alignment

Graphics Routines
v_bar
v_arc
v_pieslice
v_circle
v_ellarc
v_ellpie
v_ellipse

v_rbox
v_rfbox
v_justified
v_pline
v_pmarker
v_gtext
v_fillarea
v_cellarray
v_contourfill
v_recfl

Polyline Control
vsl_type
vsl_udsty
vsl_width
vsl_color
vsl_ends

Line Query Routines
vql_attributes

Polymarker Query
vqm_attributes

Polymarker Controls
vsm_type
vsm_height
vsm_color
vsm_string

Fill Area Query
vqf_attributes

Cursor Control
vsc_form
v_show_c
v_hide_c
vq_mouse

Area Fill Controls
vsf_interior
vsf_style

vsf_color
vsf_perimeter
vsf_updat

Input Handling Routines
vsm_locator
vsm_valuator
vsm_choice

Input Query Routines
vrq_locator
vrq_valuator
vrq_choice
vrq_string

Color index RGB Color Value
vq_color
vs_color

Point Operations
v_get_pixel

MS Windows Graphics Device Interface Routines

Display Context Manipulation
CreateDC
CreateCompatibleDC
CReateMemoryDC
DeleteDC
SaveDC
RestoreDC

Text Control
SetTextJustification
GetTextExtent
SetTextCharacterExtra
GetTextCharacterExtra

Graphics Routines
GetCurrentPosition
LineTo
Polyline
Rectangle
RoundREct
Ellipse
Arc

Pie
PatBlt
BitBlt
TextOut
SetPixel
GetPixel
FloodFill
LineDDA

Pen Movement
MoveTo

Clipping Region Manipulation
IntersectClipRect
OffsetClipRgn
ExcludeClipRect

Clipping Region Query
GetClipBox

Background Mode Control
SetBkMode
GetBkMode

Global Query
EnumFonts
EnumObjects
GetDeviceCaps

Device Environment
SetEnvironment
GetEnvironment

Object (Tool) Manipulation
GetStockObject
CreatePen
CreatePenIndirect
CreateHatchBrush
CreatePatternBrush
CreateBrushIndirect
DeleteObject
GetBrushOrg

SetBrushOrg
UnrealizeObject

Current DC Status Query and Control
SelectObject
SelectClipRgn
GetObject
SetRelAbs
GetRelAbs

Polygon Routines
SetPolyFillMode
GetPolyFillMode
Polygon

Mapping Routines
SetMapMode
GetMapMode
DPtoLP
LPtoDP
ClientToScreen
ScreenToClient
WindowFromPoint

Bitmap Manipulation
CreateBitmap
CreateBitmapIndirect
CreateCompatibleBitmap
SetBitmapBits
GetBitmapBits

Metafile Manipulation
CreateMetaFile
CloseMetaFile
GetMetaFile
CopyMetaFile
DeleteMetaFile

Color
SetBkColor
GetBkColor
SetTextColor
GetTextColor
GetSysColor
SetSysColor

Cursor Routines
SetCursor
SetCursorPos
ClipCursor
GetCursorPos
ShowCursor

Caret Routines
CreateCaret
DestroyCaret
HIdeCaret
ShowCaret
SetCaretPos
SetCaretBlink
GetCaretBlinkTime

StretchBlt Routines
SetStretchBltMode
GetStretchBltMode
StretchBlt

Direct Device Manipulation
Escape

Point Query Routines
PtVisible
PtInRect

Drawing Mode
SetROP2
GetRop2

Window Control
SetWindowOrg
GetWindowOrg
SetWindowExt
GetWindowExt

Viewport Control
SetViewportOrg
GetViewportOrg
SetViewportExt
GetViewportExt

Region Graphics
FillRgn
FrameRgn
InvertRgn
PaintRgn

Font Query
GetTextFace
GetTextMetrics

Font Manipulation
CreateFontIndirect
CreateFont

Window Graphics
DrawText
DrawIcon

Window Painting Red Tape Routines
BeginPaint
EndPaint

Region Manipulation
CombineRgn
EqualRgn
OffsetRgn
CreateRectRgn
CreateEllipticRgn
CreateEllipticRgnIndirect
CreatePolygonRgn

Rectangle Routines
SetRect
SetRectEmpty
CopyRect
InflateRect
IntersectRect
UnionRect
OffsetRect
IsRectEmpty
PtInRect
RectVisible
FillRect
FrameRect
InvertRect

WINDOWING ROUTINES

Macintosh

Initialization
InitWindows
GetWMgrPort

Allocation
NewWindow
GetNewWindow
CloseWindow
DisposeWindow

Generic Window Operations
SelectWindow
HideWindow
ShowHide
ShowWindow
HIliteWindow
FrontWindow
TrackGoAway
DrawGrowIcon

Window Display Order
BringToFront
SendBehind

Window Region Update Operations
InvalRect
InvalRgn
ValidRect
ValidRgn
BeginUpdate
EndUpdate

Movement and Sizing
FindWindow
MoveWindow
DragWindow
GrowWindow
SizeWindow

Title Operations
SetWTitle
GetWTitle

Low Level Utilities
CheckUpdate
ClipAbove
SaveOld
DrawNew
PaintOne
PaintBehind
CalcVis
CalcVisBehind

High Level Utilities
SetWRefCon
GetWRefCon
SetWindowPic
GetWindowPic
PinRect
DragGrayRgn

Gem

wind_create
wind_open
wind_close

wind_delete
wind_get
wind_set

wind_find
wind_update
wind_calc

Amiga

Workbench Operations
OpenWorkBench
WBenchToBack
WbenchToFront
CloseWorkBench

Screen Operations
CloseScreen
MakeScreen
MoveScreen
OpenScreen
ScreenToBack
ScreenToFront

ShowTitle
RethinkDisplay

Window Operations
WindowLimits
WindowToBack
WindowToFront
CloseWindow
MoveWindow
OpenWindow
SizeWindow
ViewPortAddress
SetWindowTitles

SetPointer
ModifyIDCMP

Gadget Operations
AddGadget
RefreshGadgets
RemakeDisplay
RemoveGadget
OffGadget
OnGadget
ModifyProp

Window Refresh
BeginRefresh
EndRefresh

Microsoft Windows

Window Msg Procedures
WndProc
DefWindowProc
CallWindowProc

Window Class Registration
RegisterClass
GetClass

Window Manipulation
CreateWindow
DestroyWindow
ShowWindow
CloseWindow
MoveWindow

EnumWindows
EnumChildWindows
BringWindowToTop

Window Queries
IsWindow
IsWindowVisible

Popup Query
AnyPopup

Window Icon Operations
OpenIcon
IsIconic
DrawIcon

Text Draw Operations
DrawText

Record Field Access
GetClassWord
GetClassLong
SetClassWord
SetClassLong
GetWindowWord
GetWindowLong
SetWindowWord
SetWindowLong

MENU SUPPORT ROUTINES

Mac Drawing
DrawMenuBar
HiliteMenu
FlashMenuBar

Mac Menu Manipulation
InsertMenu
DeleteMenu

Mac Menu Bar Manipulation
ClearMenuBar
GetNewMBar
GetMenuBar
SetMenuBar

Mac 128K ROM Menu Item Routines
InsMenuItem (128)
DelMenuItem (128)

Mac Menu Item Access
AppendMenu
AddResMenu
InsertResMenu
SetItem

GetItem
DisableItem
EnableItem
CheckItem
SetItemMark
GetItemMark
SetItemStyle
GetItemStyle
SetItemIcon
GetItemIcon

Mac Menu Manager
InitMenus
GetMenu
NewMenu
DisposeMenu

Mac User Interaction
CalcMenuSize
GetMHandle
MenuSelect
MenuKey
SetMenuFlash
CountMItems

Gem Menu Routines
menu_bar
menu_icheck
menu_ienable
menu_tnormal
menu_text
menu_register

Windows Menu Routines
CreateMenu
DestroyMenu
ChangeMenu
DrawMenuBar
CheckMenuItem
EnableMenuItem
HiliteMenuItem
GetSubMenu
GetSystemMenu
GetMenuString

Amiga Menu Routines
ClearMenuStrip
ItemAddress
OnMenu
OffMenu
SetMenuStrip

IIGS Drawing
DrawMenuBar
HiliteMenu
FlashMenuBar

IIGS Menu Manipulation
InsertMenu
DeleteMenu

IIGS Menu Bar Manipulation
SetSysBar
GetSysBar
SetMenuBar
GetMenuBar
SetTitleStart
GetTitleStart

IIGS MenuItem
InsertItem
DeleteItem

IIGS Menu Record Access
SetTitleWidth

GetTitleWidth
SetMenuTitle
GetMenuTitle
SetMenuFlag
GetMenuFlag
SetMenuID

IIGS Menu Manager
MenuBootInit
MenuStartup
MenuShutDown
MenuVersion
MenuReset
NewMenu
DisposeMenu

IIGS Menu Item Access
SetItem
GetItem
EnableItem
DisableItem
CheckItem
SetItemMark
GetItemMark

SetItemStyle
GetItemStyle
SetItemFlag
GetItemFlag
SetItemID

IIGS Menubar Color
SetBarColors
GetBarColors

IIGS Screen and Color Utilities
MNewRes
InitPalette

IIGS User Interaction
FixMenuBar
CalcMenuSize
MenuSelect
MenuKey
MenuRefresh
SetItemBlink
CountMItems

DIALOG BOX SUPPORT ROUTINES

Macintosh

Initialization
InitDialogs
ErrorSound
SetDAFont

Dialog Manipulation
NewDialog
GetNewDialog
CloseDialog
DisposDialog
CouldDialog
FreeDialog

Dialog Event Handling
ModalDialog
IsDialogEvent
DialogSelect

DlgCut
DlgCopy
DlgPaste
DlgDelete
DrawDialog
UpdtDialog (128)

FilterProc function
MyFilter

Dialog Item Manipulation
ParamText
GetDItem
SetDItem
FindDItem (128)
ShowDItem (128)
HideDItem(128)

GetIText
SetIText
SelIText
GetAlrtStage
ResetAlrtStage

Alert Manipulation
Alert
StopAlert
NoteAlert
CautionAlert
CouldAlert
FreeAlert

Custom Item Draw
MyItem (*)

Custom Sound Control
MySound (*)

Gem

Form Routines
form_do

form_dial
form_alert

form_error
form_center

Windows

Dialog Routines
CreateDialog
DialogBox
DlgDirList
DlgDirSelect
MapDialogRect

GetDlgItem
SetDlgItemInt
GetDlgItemInt
SetDlgItemText
GetDlgItemText
CheckDlgButton

IsDlgButtonChecked
CheckRadioButton
SendDlgItemMessage
IsDialogMessage

CONTROLS, DIALOG ITEMS, GADGETS

Macintosh

Initialization and Allocation
NewControl
GetNewControl
DisposeControl
KillControls

Control Display
SetCTitle
GetCTitle
HideControl
ShowControl
DrawControls
UpdtControl (128)
HiliteControl
Draw1Control (128)

Mouse Whereabouts
TestControl
FindControl
TrackControl

Control Movement and Sizing
MoveControl
DragControl
SizeControl

Control Setting and Range
SetCtlValue
GetCtlValue
SetCtlMin
GetCtlMin
SetCtlMax
GetCtlMax

CRefCon
SetCRefCon
GetCRefCon

Control Action
SetCtlAction
GetCtlAction

Roll Your Own
MyControl

Gem

Controls
Gem controls are predefined;
their manipulation is buried
within the function of the various
AES divisions. Most useful are
the object library routines.

Windows

Controls

MS Windows controls are also predefined; their creation and manipulation is provided for by the system, and are part of the function support for dialogs and windows.

SetScrollPos
GetScrollPos
SetScrollRange
GetScrollRange

Amiga

Intuition Gadgets
AddGadget
OnGadget

OffGadget
RefreshGadgets
RemoveGadget

ModifyProp

MAC TEXT EDIT ROUTINES

TextEdit Initialization
TEInit

Edit Record Manipulation
TENew
TEDispose

Edit Record Text Manipulation
TESetText
TEGetText

Insertion Point and Selection Control
TEIdle
TEClick
TESetSelect
TEActivate
TEDeactivate

Char Editing
TEKey

Scrap Buffer Operations
TECut
TECopy
TEPaste
TEDelete
TEInsert

Text Display Operations
TESetJust
TEUpdate
TextBox
TEScroll

Scrap Manipulation
TEFromScrap
TEToScrap
TEScrapHandle

TEGetScrapLen
TESetScrapLen

Start-of-line Calculations
TECalText

AutoScroll Operations
TESelView (128K)
TEPinScroll (128K)
TEAutoScroll (128K)

Mac II Additions
TEStylPaste
TESetStyle
TEReplaceStyle
TEGetStyle
GetStylHandle
SetStylHandle
GetStyleScrap
TEStyleInsert
TEGetPoint
TEGetHeight

RESOURCE MANAGER ROUTINES

Macintosh

Initialization
InitResources
RsrcZoneInit

Resource File Manipulation
CreateResFile
OpenResFile
CloseResFile

Error Reporting
ResError

Active Resource File
CurResFile
HomeResFile
UseResFile

Resource Manipulation
CountTypes
Count1Types (128)
GetIndType

Get1IndType (128)
SetResLoad
CountResources
Count1Resources (128)
GetIndResource
Get1IndResource (128)
GetResource
Get1Resource (128)
GetNamedResource
Get1NamedResource (128)
LoadResource
ReleaseResource
DetachResource

Resource Information
UniqueID
Unique1ID (128)
GetResInfo
GetResAttrs
SizeResource
MaxSizeRsrc

ResFile Attributes
GetResFileAttrs
SetResFileAttrs

Resource Modification
SetResInfo
SetResAttrs
ChangedResource
AddResource
RmveResource
UpdateResFile
WriteResource
SetResPurge

Resource System Reference
AddReference
RmveReference

New Misc
RsrcMapEntry (128)
OpenRFPerm (128)

Gem

Resource Manipulation
rsrc_load

rsrc_free
rsrc_gaddr

rsrc_saddr
rsrc_obfix

Windows

Resource Manipulation
AddFontResource
RemoveFontResource
LoadBitmap
LoadCursor

LoadIcon
LoadMenu
LoadString
LoadAccelerators
FindResource

LoadResource
AllocResource
FreeResource
AccessResource
SizeofResource
SetResourceHandler

C Declarations

These function "declarations" are taken from the *Amiga ROM Kernel Manual* Volume 2, and do not include routines added to the list in 1987. They are presented here using C language conventions.

/* AMIGA EXEC ROUTINES */

```
AddDevice( device )
AddHead( list, node )
AddIntServer( intNum,  interrupt )
AddLibrary( library )
AddPort( port )
AddResource( resource )
AddTail( list, node )
AddTask( task, initialPC, finalPC )
memoryBlock =    allocate( freeList, byteSize )
memList =        AllocEntry( memList )
memoryBlock =    AllocMem( byteSize, requirements )
signalNum =      AllocSignal( signalNum )
trapNum =        AllocTrap( trapNum )
size =           AvailMem( requirements )
Cause( interrupt )
result =         CheckIO( iORequest )
CloseDevice( iORequest )
CloseLibrary( library )
ColdReset(  )
Deallocate( freeList, memoryBlock, byteSize )
error =          DoIO( iORequest )
Enqueue( list, node )
node =           FindName( start, name )
port = FindPort( name )
task = FindTask( name )
FreeEntry( memList )
FreeMem( memoryBlock, byteSize )
Freesignal( signalNum )
FreeTrap( trapNum )
conditions =     GetCC(  )
message =        GetMsg( port )
InitStruct( initTable, memory, size )
```

```
Insert( list, node, listNode )
library =          MakeLibrary( vectors, structure, init, dataSize, segList )
error =            OpenDevice( devName, unitNumber, iORequest, flags )
library =          OpenLibrary( libName, version )
resource =         OpenResource( resName )
PutMsg( port, message )
error =            RemDevice( device )
node =             RemHead( list )
RemIntServer( intNum, interrupt )
error =            RemLibrary( library )
Remove( node )
RemPort( port )
RemResource( resource )
node =             RemTail( list )
RemTask( task )
ReplyMsg( message )
SendIO( iORequest )
oldSignals =       SetExcept( newSignals, signalMask )
oldFunc =          SetFunction( library, funcOffset, funcEntry )
oldInterrupt =     SetIntVector( intNumber,  interrupt )
oldSignals =       SetSignal( newSignals, signalMask )
oldSR =            SetSR( newSR, mask )
oldPriority =      SetTaskPri( task,  priority )
Signal( task, signals )
SumLibrary( library )
oldSysStack =      SuperState(  )
UserState( sysStack )
signals =          Wait( signalSet )
error =            WaitIO( iORequest )
message =          WaitPort( port )
```

/* AMIGA GRAPHICS ROUTINES */

```
AddAnimOb( anOb, anKey, RPort )
AddBob( Bob, Rport )
AddFont( textFont )
AddVSprite( VS, Rport )
AllocRaster( width, height )
AndRectRegion( region, rectangle )
Animate( key, RPort )
error =            ( int ) AreaDraw( rp, x, y )
AreaEnd( rp )
error =            AreaMove( rp, x, y )
AskFont( rastPort, textAttr )
enable =           AskSoftStyle( rastPort )
```

```
planes =            BltBitMap( SrcBitMap, SrcX, SrcY, DestBitMap, DestX, DestY,
                         SizeX, SizeY, Minterm, Mask, TempA )
BltClear( memBlock, bytecount, flags )
BltPattern( RastPort *, char *, x1, y1, maxx, maxy, bytecnt )
BltTemplate( source, srcX, srcMod, destRastPort, destX, destY, sizeX,
             sizeY )
CEND( c )
ChangeSprite( vp, s, newdata )
struct CopperList *CINIT( c, n )
ClearEOL( rastPort, graphicsLib )
ClearRegion( region )
ClearScreen( rastPort )
CloseFont( font )
CMOVE( c, a, v )
CopySBitMap( layer * )
CWAIT( c, v, h )
DisownBlitter( )
DisposeRegion( region )
DoCollision( RPort )
Draw( rp, x, y )
DrawGList( RPort, VPort )
Flood( rp, mode, x, y )
FreeColorMap( colormap )
FreeCopList( coplist )
FreeCprList( cprlist )
FreeGBuffers( anOb, RPort, db )
FreeRaster( p, width, height )
FreeSprite( pick )
FreeVPortCopLists( viewport )
GetColorMap( entries )
GetGBuffers( anOb, RPort, db )
GetRGB4( colormap, entry )
Sprite_Number =   GetSprite( sprite, pick )
InitArea( AreaInfo *, buffer *, maxvectors )
InitBitMap( bm, depth, width, height )
InitGels( head, tail, GInfo )
InitGMasks( anOb )
InitMasks( VS )
InitRastPort( rp )
InitTmpRas( rmpras *, buffer *, size )
InitView( view )
InitVPort( vp )
LoadRGB4( vp, colormap, count )
LoadView( View )
LockLayerRom( layer )
MakeVPort( view, viewport )
Move( rp, x, y )
MoveSprite( vp, sprite, x, y )
```

```
MrgCop( View )
rgn =              ( struct Region * ) NewRegion(  )
font =              OpenFont( textAttr )
OrRectRegion( region, rectangle )
OwnBlitter(  )
PolyDraw( rp, count, array )
QBlit( bp )
QBSBlit( bsp )
penno =            ( int ) ReadPixel( rp, x, y )
RectFill( rp, xmin, ymin, xmax, ymax )
error =            RemFont( textFont )
RemIBob( Bob, Rport, VPort )
RemVSprite( VS )
ScrollRaster( rp, dx, dy, xmin, ymin, xmax, ymax )
ScrollVPort( vp )
SetAPen( rp, pen )
SetBPen( rp, pen )
SetCollision( num, routine, GInfo )
SetDrMd( rp, mode )
error =            SetFont( rastPort, font )
SetRast( RastPort, pen )
SetRGB4( vp, n, r, g, b )
newStyle =         SetSoftStyle( rastPort, style, enable )
SortGlist( RPort )
SyncSBitMap( layer * )
error =            Text( RastPort, string, count )
length =           TextLength( rastPort, string, count )
UnlockLayerRom( layer )
pos =              VBeamPos(  )
WaitBlit(  )
WaitBOVP( ViewPort )
WaitTOF(  )
WritePixel( rp, x, y )
XorRectRegion( region, rectangle )
```

/* AMIGA INTUITION ROUTINES */

```
SHORT AddGadget( Pointer, Gadget, Position )
AllocRemember( RememberKey, Size, Flags )
AutoRequest( Window, BodyText, PositiveText, NegativeText, PositiveFlags,
             NegativeFlags, Width, Height )
BeginRefresh( Window )
BuildSysRequest( Window, BodyText, PositiveText, NegativeText, IDCMPFlags,
                 Width, Height )
```

```
ClearDMRequest( Window )
ClearMenuStrip( Window )
ClearPointer( Window )
CloseScreen( Screen )
CloseWindow( Window )
BOOL CloseWorkBench(  )
CurrentTime( &Seconds, &Micros )   ULONG Seconds,  Micros;
DisplayAlert( AlertNumber, String, Height )
DisplayBeep( Screen )
DoubleClick( StartSeconds, StartMicros, CurrentSeconds, CurrentMicros )
DrawBorder( RastPort, Border, LeftOffset, TopOffset )
DrawImage( RastPort, Image, LeftOffset, TopOffset )
EndRefresh( Window, Complete )
EndRequest( Requester, Window )

FreeRemember( RememberKey, ReallyForget )
FreeSysRequest( Window )
GetDefPrefs( PrefBuffer, Size )
GetPrefs( PrefBuffer, Size )
InitReuqester( Requester )
IntuiTextLength( IText )
ItemAddress( MenuStrip, MenuNumber )
MakeScreen( Screen )
ModifyIDCMP( WindowIDCMPFlags )
ModifyProp( Gadget, POinter, Requester, Flags, HorizPot, VertPot, HorizBody,
            VertBody )
MoveScreen( Screen, DeltaX, DeltaY )
MoveWindow( Window, DeltaX, DeltaY )
OffGadget( Gadget, Pointer, Requester )
OffMenu( Window, MenuNumber )
OnGadget( Gadget, POinter, Requester )
OnMenu( Window, MenuNumber )
OpenScreen( NewScreen )
OpenWindow( NewWindow )
BOOL OpenWorkBench(  )
PrintIText( RastPort, Itext, LeftEdge, TopEdge )
RefreshGadgets( Gadgets, Pointer,  Requester )
RemakeDisplay(  )
USHORT RemoveGadget( PoInter, Gadget )
ReportMouse( Window, Boolean )
Request( Requester, Window )
RethinkDisplay(  )
ScreenToBack( Screen )
ScreenToFront( Screen )
SetDMRequester( Window, DMRequester )
SetMenuStrip( Window, Menu )
SetPointer( Window, Pointer,  Height,  Width,  XOffset,  YOffset )
SetWindowTitles( Window, WindowTitle,  ScreenTitle )
ShowTitle( Screen,  ShowIt )
```

```
SizeWindow( Window, DeltaX, DeltaY )
ViewAddress( )
ViewPortAddress( Window )
WBenchToBack( )
WBenchToFront( )
WindowLimits( Window, MinWidth, MinHeight, MaxWidth, MaxHeight )
WindowToBack( Window )
WindowToFront( Window )
```

/* AMIGA LAYERS ROUTINES */

```
BeginUpdate( l )
BehindLayer( li, l )
CreateBehindLayer( ll, bm, x0, y0, x1, y1, flags[, bm2] )
CreateUpFrontLayer( ll, bm, x0, y0, x1, y1, flags[, bm2] )
DeleteLayer( li, l )
DisposeLayerInfo( li )
EndUpdate( l, flag )
FattenLayerInfo( li )
InitLayers( li )
LockLayer( li, l )
LockLayerInfo( li )
LockLayers( li )
MoveLayer( li, l, dx, dy )
BOOLEAN MoveLayerInFrontOf( layertomove, target )
NewLayerInfo( )
ScrollLayer( li, l, dx, dy )
SizeLayer( li, l, dx, dy )
SwapBitsRastPortClipRect( rp, cr )
ThinkLayerInfo( li ) _
UnlockLayer( l )
UnlockLayerInfo( li )
UnlockLayers( li )
BOOLEAN UpfrontLayer( li, l )
layer =             ( struct Layer * ) WhichLayer( li, x, y )
```

/* GEM VDI ROUTINES */

```
WORD v_clrwk( handle ) WORD handle;
WORD v_clswk( handle ) WORD handle;
WORD v_opnwk( work_in, handle, work_out ) WORD work_in[], *handle, work_out[];
WORD v_updwk( handle ) WORD handle;
```

```
WORD vq_chcells( handle, rows, columns ) WORD handle, *rows, *columns;
WORD v_exit_cur( handle ) WORD handle;
WORD v_enter_cur( handle ) WORD handle;
WORD v_curup( handle ) WORD handle;
WORD v_curdown( handle ) WORD handle;
WORD v_curright( handle ) WORD handle;
WORD v_curleft( handle ) WORD handle;
WORD v_curhome( handle ) WORD handle;
WORD v_eeos( handle ) WORD handle;
WORD v_eeol( handle ) WORD handle;
WORD vs_curaddress( handle, row, column ) WORD handle, row, column;
WORD v_curtext( handle, string ) WORD handle; BYTE *string;
WORD v_rvon( handle ) WORD handle;
WORD v_rvoff( handle ) WORD handle;
WORD vq_curaddress( handle, row, column ) WORD handle, *row, *column;
WORD vq_tabstatus( handle ) WORD handle;
WORD v_hardcopy( handle ) WORD handle;
WORD v_dspcur( handle, x, y ) WORD handle, x, y;
WORD v_rmcur( handle ) WORD handle;
WORD v_form_adv( handle ) WORD handle;
WORD v_output_window( handle, xy ) WORD handle, xy[];
WORD v_clear_disp_list( handle ) WORD handle;
WORD v_bit_image( handle, filename, aspect, x_scale, y_scale, h_align,
v_align, xy )
     WORD handle, aspect, x_scale, y_scale, h_align, v_align;
     WORD xy[];
     BYTE *filename;
WORD vq_scan( handle, g_height, g_slice, a_height, a_slice, factor ) WORD
handle, *g_height, *g_slice, *a_height, *a_slice, *factor;
WORD v_alpha_text( handle, string ) WORD handle; BYTE *string;
WORD vs_palette( handle, palette ) WORD handle, palette;
WORD v_sound( handle, frequency, duration ) WORD handle; WORD frequency; WORD
duration;
WORD vs_mute( handle, action ) WORD handle; WORD action;
WORD vqp_films( handle, names ) WORD handle; BYTE names[];
WORD vqp_state( handle, port, filmnum, lightness, interlace, planes, indexes )
     WORD handle, *port, *filmnum, *lightness, *interlace, *planes, *indexes;
WORD vsp_state( handle, port, filmnum, lightness, interlace, planes, indexes )
     WORD handle, port, filmnum, lightness, interlace, planes, *indexes;
WORD vsp_save( handle ) WORD handle;
WORD vsp_message( handle ) WORD handle;
WORD vqp_error( handle ) WORD handle;
WORD v_meta_extents( handle, min_x, min_y, max_x, max_y )
     WORD handle, min_x, min_y, max_x, max_y;
WORD v_write_meta( handle, num_ints, ints, num_pts, pts )
     WORD handle, num_ints, ints[], num_pts, pts[];
WORD vm_filename( handle, filename ) WORD handle; BYTE *filename;
WORD v_pline( handle, count, xy ) WORD handle, count, xy[];
WORD v_pmarker( handle, count, xy ) WORD handle, count, xy[];
```

```
WORD v_gtext( handle, x, y, string) WORD handle, x, y; BYTE *string;
WORD v_fillarea( handle, count, xy) WORD handle, count, xy[];
WORD v_cellarray( handle, xy, row_length, el_per_row, num_rows, wr_mode,
colors )
     WORD handle, xy[4], row_length, el_per_row, num_rows, wr_mode, *colors;
WORD v_bar( handle, xy ) WORD handle, xy[];
WORD v_arc( handle, xc, yc, rad, sang, eang )
     WORD handle, xc, yc, rad, sang, eang;
WORD v_pieslice( handle, xc, yc, rad, sang, eang )
     WORD handle, xc, yc, rad, sang, eang;
WORD v_circle( handle, xc, yc, rad ) WORD handle, xc, yc, rad;
WORD v_ellipse( handle, xc, yc, xrad, yrad ) WORD handle, xc, yc, xrad, yrad;
WORD v_ellarc( handle, xc, yc, xrad, yrad, sang, eang )
     WORD handle, xc, yc, xrad, yrad, sang, eang;
WORD v_ellpie( handle, xc, yc, xrad, yrad, sang, eang)
     WORD handle, xc, yc, xrad, yrad, sang, eang;
WORD v_rbox( handle, xy ) WORD handle, xy[];
WORD v_rfbox( handle, xy ) WORD handle, xy[];
WORD v_justified( handle, x, y, string, length, word_space, char_space)
     WORD handle, x, y, length, word_space, char_space; BYTE string[];
WORD vst_height( handle, height, char_width, char_height, cell_width,
cell_height )
     WORD handle, height, *char_width, *char_height, *cell_width,
*cell_height;
WORD vst_rotation( handle, angle ) WORD handle, angle;
WORD vs_color( handle, index, rgb ) WORD handle, index, *rgb;
WORD vsl_type( handle, style ) WORD handle, style;
WORD vsl_width( handle, width ) WORD handle, width;
WORD vsl_color( handle, index ) WORD handle, index;
WORD vsm_type( handle, symbol ) WORD handle, symbol;
WORD vsm_height( handle, height ) WORD handle, height;
WORD vsm_color( handle, index ) WORD handle, index;
WORD vst_font( handle, font ) WORD handle, font;
WORD vst_color( handle, index ) WORD handle, index;
WORD vsf_interior( handle, style ) WORD handle, style;
WORD vsf_style( handle, index ) WORD handle, index;
WORD vsf_color( handle, index ) WORD handle, index;
WORD vq_color( handle, index, set_flag, rgb )
     WORD handle, index, set_flag, rgb[];
WORD vq_cellarray( handle, xy, row_len, num_rows, el_used, rows_used, stat,
colors )
     WORD handle, xy[], row_len, num_rows, *el_used, *rows_used, *stat,
colors[];
WORD vrq_locator( handle, initx, inity, xout, yout, term )
     WORD handle, initx, inity, *xout, *yout, *term;
WORD vsm_locator( handle, initx, inity, xout, yout, term )
     WORD handle, initx, inity, *xout, *yout, *term;
WORD vrq_valuator( handle, val_in, val_out, term )
     WORD handle, val_in, *val_out, *term;
```

```
WORD vsm_valuator( handle, val_in, val_out, term, status )
     WORD handle, val_in, *val_out, *term, *status;
WORD vrq_choice( handle, in_choice, out_choice )
     WORD handle, in_choice, *out_choice;
WORD vsm_choice( handle, choice ) WORD handle, *choice;
WORD vrq_string( handle, length, echo_mode, echo_xy, string)
     WORD handle, length, echo_mode, echo_xy[]; BYTE *string;
WORD vsm_string( handle, length, echo_mode, echo_xy, string )
     WORD handle, length, echo_mode, echo_xy[]; BYTE *string;
WORD vswr_mode( handle, mode ) WORD handle, mode;
WORD vsin_mode( handle, dev_type, mode ) WORD handle, dev_type, mode;
WORD vql_attributes( handle, attributes ) WORD handle, attributes[];

WORD vqm_attributes( handle, attributes ) WORD handle, attributes[];
WORD vqf_attributes( handle, attributes ) WORD handle, attributes[];
WORD vqt_attributes( handle, attributes ) WORD handle, attributes[];
WORD vst_alignment( handle, hor_in, vert_in, hor_out, vert_out )
     WORD handle, hor_in, vert_in, *hor_out, *vert_out;
WORD v_opnvwk( work_in, handle, work_out ) WORD work_in[], *handle,
work_out[];
WORD v_clsvwk( handle ) WORD handle;
WORD vq_extnd( handle, owflag, work_out ) WORD handle, owflag, work_out[];
WORD v_contourfill( handle, x, y, index ) WORD handle, x, y, index;
WORD vsf_perimeter( handle, per_vis ) WORD handle, per_vis;
WORD v_get_pixel( handle, x, y, pel, index ) WORD handle, x, y, *pel, *index;
WORD vst_effects( handle, effect ) WORD handle, effect;
WORD vst_point( handle, point, char_width, char_height, cell_width,
cell_height )
     WORD handle, point, *char_width, *char_height, *cell_width, *cell_height;
WORD vsl_ends( handle, beg_style, end_style) WORD handle, beg_style,
end_style;
WORD vro_cpyfm( handle, wr_mode, xy, srcMFDB, desMFDB )
     WORD handle, wr_mode, xy[], *srcMFDB, *desMFDB;
WORD vr_trnfm( handle, srcMFDB, desMFDB ) WORD handle, *srcMFDB, *desMFDB;
WORD vsc_form( handle, cur_form ) WORD handle, *cur_form;
WORD vsf_udpat( handle, fill_pat, planes ) WORD handle, fill_pat[], planes;
WORD vsl_udsty( handle, pattern ) WORD handle, pattern;
WORD vr_recfl( handle, xy ) WORD handle, *xy;
WORD vqin_mode( handle, dev_type, mode ) WORD handle, dev_type, *mode;
WORD vqt_extent( handle, string, extent ) WORD handle, extent[]; BYTE
string[];
WORD vqt_width( handle, character, cell_width, left_delta, right_delta )
     WORD handle, *cell_width, *left_delta, *right_delta; BYTE character;
WORD vex_timv( handle, tim_addr, old_addr, scale )
     WORD handle, *scale; LONG tim_addr, *old_addr;
WORD vst_load_fonts( handle, select ) WORD handle, select;
WORD vst_unload_fonts( handle, select ) WORD handle, select;
WORD vrt_cpyfm( handle, wr_mode, xy, srcMFDB, desMFDB, index )
     WORD handle, wr_mode, *srcMFDB, *desMFDB, xy[], *index;
WORD v_show_c( handle, reset ) WORD handle, reset;
```

```
WORD v_hide_c( handle ) WORD handle;
WORD vq_mouse( handle, status, px, py ) WORD handle, *status, *px, *py;
WORD vex_butv( handle, usercode, savecode ) WORD handle; LONG usercode,
*savecode;
WORD vex_motv( handle, usercode, savecode ) WORD handle; LONG usercode,
*savecode;
WORD vex_curv( handle, usercode, savecode ) WORD handle; LONG usercode,
*savecode;
WORD vq_key_s( handle, status ) WORD handle, *status;
WORD vs_clip( handle, clip_flag, xy ) WORD handle, clip_flag, xy[];
WORD vqt_name( handle, element_num, name ) WORD handle, element_num; BYTE
name[];
WORD vqt_font_info( handle, minADE, maxADE, distances, maxwidth, effects )
     WORD handle, *minADE, *maxADE, distances[], *maxwidth, effects[];
```

/* GEM AES BINDING ROUTINES */

```
WORD appl_init( )
WORD appl_exit( )
WORD appl_write( rwid, length, pbuff )  WORD rwid; WORD length; LONG pbuff;
WORD appl_read( rwid, length, pbuff )  WORD rwid; WORD length; LONG pbuff;
WORD appl_find( pname )  LONG pname;
WORD appl_tplay( tbuffer, tlength, tscale )
     LONG tbuffer; WORD tlength; WORD tscale;
WORD appl_trecord( tbuffer, tlength )  LONG tbuffer; WORD tlength;
WORD appl_bvset( bvdisk, bvhard )  UWORD bvdisk; UWORD bvhard;
UWORD evnt_keybd( )
WORD evnt_button( clicks, mask, state, pmx, pmy, pmb, pks )
     WORD clicks; UWORD mask; UWORD state; WORD *pmx, *pmy, *pmb, *pks;
WORD evnt_mouse( flags, x, y, width, height, pmx, pmy, pmb, pks )
     WORD flags, x, y, width, height; WORD *pmx, *pmy, *pmb, *pks;
WORD evnt_mesag( pbuff )  LONG pbuff;
WORD evnt_timer( locnt, hicnt )  UWORD locnt, hicnt;
WORD evnt_multi( flags, bclk, bmsk, bst, m1flags, m1x, m1y, m1w, m1h,
            m2flags, m2x, m2y, m2w, m2h, mepbuff, tlc, thc, pmx, pmy,
            pmb, pks, pkr, pbr  )
     UWORD flags, bclk, bmsk, bst;
     UWORD m1flags, m1x, m1y, m1w, m1h;
     UWORD m2flags, m2x, m2y, m2w, m2h;
     LONG mepbuff; UWORD tlc, thc;
     UWORD *pmx, *pmy, *pmb, *pks, *pkr, *pbr;
WORD evnt_dclick( rate, setit )  WORD rate, setit;
WORD menu_bar( tree, showit )  LONG tree; WORD showit;
WORD menu_icheck( tree, itemnum, checkit )  LONG tree; WORD itemnum, checkit;
WORD menu_ienable( tree, itemnum, enableit )  LONG tree; WORD itemnum,
enableit;
```

```
WORD menu_tnormal( tree, titlenum, normalit )  LONG tree; WORD titlenum,
normalit;
WORD menu_text( tree, inum, ptext )  LONG tree; WORD inum; LONG ptext;
WORD menu_register( pid, pstr )  WORD pid; LONG pstr;
WORD menu_unregister( mid )  WORD mid;
WORD objc_add( tree, parent, child )  LONG tree; WORD parent, child;
WORD objc_delete( tree, delob )  LONG tree; WORD delob;
WORD objc_draw( tree, drawob, depth, xc, yc, wc, hc )
     LONG tree; WORD drawob, depth; WORD xc, yc, wc, hc;
WORD objc_find( tree, startob, depth, mx, my )
     LONG tree; WORD startob, depth, mx, my;
WORD objc_order( tree, mov_obj, newpos )  LONG tree; WORD mov_obj, newpos;
WORD objc_offset( tree, obj, poffx, poffy )
     LONG tree; WORD obj; WORD *poffx, *poffy;
WORD objc_edit( tree, obj, inchar, idx, kind )
     LONG tree; WORD obj; WORD inchar, *idx, kind;
WORD objc_change( tree, drawob, depth, xc, yc, wc, hc, newstate, redraw )
     LONG tree; WORD drawob, depth; WORD xc, yc, wc, hc;
     WORD newstate, redraw;
WORD form_do( form, start )  LONG form; WORD start;
WORD form_dial( dtype, ix, iy, iw, ih, x, y, w, h )
     WORD dtype; WORD ix, iy, iw, ih; WORD x, y, w, h;
WORD form_alert( defbut, astring )  WORD defbut; LONG astring;
WORD form_error( errnum )  WORD errnum;
WORD form_center( tree, pcx, pcy, pcw, pch )  LONG tree;
     WORD *pcx, *pcy, *pcw, *pch;
WORD form_keybd( form, obj, nxt_obj, thechar, pnxt_obj, pchar )
LONG form; WORD obj; WORD nxt_obj; WORD thechar; WORD *pnxt_obj; WORD *pchar;
WORD form_button( form, obj, clks, pnxt_obj )
     LONG form; WORD obj; WORD clks; WORD *pnxt_obj;
VOID graf_rubbox( xorigin, yorigin, wmin, hmin, pwend, phend )
     WORD xorigin, yorigin; WORD wmin, hmin; WORD *pwend, *phend;
VOID graf_dragbox( w, h, sx, sy, xc, yc, wc, hc, pdx, pdy )
     WORD w, h; WORD sx, sy; WORD xc, yc, wc, hc; WORD *pdx, *pdy;
VOID graf_mbox( w, h, srcx, srcy, dstx, dsty )
     WORD w, h; WORD srcx, srcy, dstx, dsty;
VOID graf_growbox( orgx, orgy, orgw, orgh, x, y, w, h )
     WORD orgx, orgy, orgw, orgh; WORD x, y, w, h;
VOID graf_shrinkbox( orgx, orgy, orgw, orgh, x, y, w, h )
     WORD orgx, orgy, orgw, orgh; WORD x, y, w, h;
VOID graf_watchbox( tree, obj, instate, outstate )
     LONG tree; WORD obj; UWORD instate, outstate;
VOID graf_slidebox( tree, parent, obj, isvert )
     LONG tree; WORD parent; WORD obj; WORD isvert;
WORD graf_handle( pwchar, phchar, pwbox, phbox )
     WORD *pwchar, *phchar; WORD *pwbox, *phbox;
WORD graf_mouse( m_number, m_addr )  WORD m_number; LONG m_addr;
WORD graf_mkstate( pmx, pmy, pmstate, pkstate )
     WORD *pmx, *pmy, *pmstate, *pkstate;
```

```
WORD scrp_read( pscrap )  LONG pscrap;
WORD scrp_write( pscrap )  LONG pscrap;
WORD fsel_input( pipath, pisel, pbutton )  LONG pipath, pisel; WORD *pbutton;
WORD wind_create( kind, wx, wy, ww, wh )  UWORD kind; WORD wx, wy, ww, wh;
WORD wind_open( handle, wx, wy, ww, wh )
    WORD handle; WORD wx, wy, ww, wh;
WORD wind_close( handle )  WORD handle;
WORD wind_delete( handle )  WORD handle;
WORD wind_get( w_handle, w_field, pw1, pw2, pw3, pw4 )
    WORD w_handle; WORD w_field; WORD *pw1, *pw2, *pw3, *pw4;
WORD wind_set( w_handle, w_field, w2, w3, w4, w5 )
    WORD w_handle; WORD w_field; WORD w2, w3, w4, w5;
WORD wind_find( mx, my )  WORD mx, my;
WORD wind_update( beg_update )  WORD beg_update;
WORD wind_calc( wctype, kind, x, y, w, h, px, py, pw, ph )
    WORD wctype; UWORD kind; WORD x, y, w, h; WORD *px, *py, *pw, *ph;
WORD rsrc_load( rsname )  LONG rsname;
WORD rsrc_free(  )
WORD rsrc_gaddr( rstype, rsid, paddr )  WORD rstype; WORD rsid; LONG *paddr;
WORD rsrc_saddr( rstype, rsid, lngval )  WORD rstype; WORD rsid; LONG lngval;
WORD rsrc_obfix( tree, obj )  LONG tree; WORD obj;
WORD shel_read( pcmd, ptail )  LONG pcmd, ptail;
WORD shel_write( doex, isgr, iscr, pcmd, ptail )
    WORD doex, isgr, iscr; LONG pcmd, ptail;
WORD shel_get( pbuffer, len )  LONG pbuffer; WORD len;
WORD shel_put( pdata, len )  LONG pdata; WORD len;
WORD shel_find( ppath )  LONG ppath;
WORD shel_envrn( ppath, psrch )  LONG ppath; LONG psrch;
```

{MAC QUICKDRAW ROUTINES}

```
        {
            These declarations were taken from the file
            Quickdraw.p Version: 2.0a3.1
            Copyright Apple Computer, Inc. 1984–1987
            All Rights Reserved
        }

PROCEDURE InitGraf(globalPtr: Ptr); INLINE $A86E;
PROCEDURE OpenPort(port: GrafPtr); INLINE $A86F;
PROCEDURE InitPort(port: GrafPtr); INLINE $A86D;
PROCEDURE ClosePort(port: GrafPtr); INLINE $A87D;
PROCEDURE SetPort(port: GrafPtr); INLINE $A873;
PROCEDURE GetPort(VAR port: GrafPtr); INLINE $A874;
PROCEDURE GrafDevice(device: INTEGER); INLINE $A872;
PROCEDURE SetPortBits(bm: BitMap); INLINE $A875;
PROCEDURE PortSize(width, height: INTEGER); INLINE $A876;
PROCEDURE MovePortTo(leftGlobal, topGlobal: INTEGER); INLINE $A877;
PROCEDURE SetOrigin(h, v: INTEGER); INLINE $A878;
```

```
PROCEDURE SetClip(rgn: RgnHandle); INLINE $A879;
PROCEDURE GetClip(rgn: RgnHandle); INLINE $A87A;
PROCEDURE ClipRect(r: Rect); INLINE $A87B;
PROCEDURE BackPat(pat: Pattern); INLINE $A87C;
```

{ Cursor Routines }

```
PROCEDURE InitCursor; INLINE $A850;
PROCEDURE SetCursor(crsr: Cursor); INLINE $A851;
PROCEDURE HideCursor; INLINE $A852;
PROCEDURE ShowCursor; INLINE $A853;
PROCEDURE ObscureCursor; INLINE $A856;
```

{ Line Routines }

```
PROCEDURE HidePen; INLINE $A896;
PROCEDURE ShowPen; INLINE $A897;
PROCEDURE GetPen(VAR pt: Point); INLINE $A89A;
PROCEDURE GetPenState(VAR pnState: PenState); INLINE $A898;
PROCEDURE SetPenState(pnState: PenState); INLINE $A899;
PROCEDURE PenSize(width, height: INTEGER); INLINE $A89B;
PROCEDURE PenMode(mode: INTEGER); INLINE $A89C;
PROCEDURE PenPat(pat: Pattern); INLINE $A89D;
PROCEDURE PenNormal; INLINE $A89E;
PROCEDURE MoveTo(h, v: INTEGER); INLINE $A893;
PROCEDURE Move(dh, dv: INTEGER); INLINE $A894;
PROCEDURE LineTo(h, v: INTEGER); INLINE $A891;
PROCEDURE Line(dh, dv: INTEGER); INLINE $A892;
```

{ Text Routines }

```
PROCEDURE TextFont(font: INTEGER); INLINE $A887;
PROCEDURE TextFace(face: Style); INLINE $A888;
PROCEDURE TextMode(mode: INTEGER); INLINE $A889;
PROCEDURE TextSize(size: INTEGER); INLINE $A88A;
PROCEDURE SpaceExtra(extra: Fixed); INLINE $A88E;
PROCEDURE DrawChar(ch: char); INLINE $A883;
PROCEDURE DrawString(s: Str255); INLINE $A884;
PROCEDURE DrawText(textBuf: Ptr; firstByte, byteCount: INTEGER); INLINE $A885;
FUNCTION CharWidth(ch: char): INTEGER; INLINE $A88D;
FUNCTION StringWidth(s: Str255): INTEGER; INLINE $A88C;
FUNCTION TextWidth(textBuf: Ptr; firstByte, byteCount: INTEGER): INTEGER;
     INLINE $A886;
PROCEDURE GetFontInfo(VAR info: FontInfo); INLINE $A88B;
PROCEDURE MeasureText(count: INTEGER; textAddr, charLocs: Ptr); INLINE $A837;
```

{ Point Calculations }

```
PROCEDURE AddPt(src: Point; VAR dst: Point); INLINE $A87E;
PROCEDURE SubPt(src: Point; VAR dst: Point); INLINE $A87F;
PROCEDURE SetPt(VAR pt: Point; h, v: INTEGER); INLINE $A880;
FUNCTION EqualPt(pt1, pt2: Point): BOOLEAN; INLINE $A881;
PROCEDURE ScalePt(VAR pt: Point; fromRect, toRect: Rect); INLINE $A8F8;
PROCEDURE MapPt(VAR pt: Point; fromRect, toRect: Rect); INLINE $A8F9;
PROCEDURE LocalToGlobal(VAR pt: Point); INLINE $A870;
PROCEDURE GlobalToLocal(VAR pt: Point); INLINE $A871;
```

{ Rectangle Calculations }

```
PROCEDURE SetRect(VAR r: Rect; left, top, right, bottom: INTEGER);
    INLINE $A8A7;
FUNCTION EqualRect(rect1, rect2: Rect): BOOLEAN; INLINE $A8A6
FUNCTION EmptyRect(r: Rect): BOOLEAN; INLINE $A8AE;
PROCEDURE OffsetRect(VAR r: Rect; dh, dv: INTEGER); INLINE $A8A8;
PROCEDURE MapRect(VAR r: Rect; fromRect, toRect: Rect); INLINE $A8FA;
PROCEDURE InsetRect(VAR r: Rect; dh, dv: INTEGER); INLINE $A8A9;
FUNCTION SectRect(src1, src2: Rect; VAR dstRect: Rect): BOOLEAN; INLINE $A8AA;
PROCEDURE UnionRect(src1, src2: Rect; VAR dstRect: Rect); INLINE $A8AB;
FUNCTION PtInRect(pt: Point; r: Rect): BOOLEAN; INLINE $A8AD;
PROCEDURE Pt2Rect(pt1, pt2: Point; VAR dstRect: Rect); INLINE $A8AC;
```

{ Graphical Operations on Rectangles }

```
PROCEDURE FrameRect(r: Rect); INLINE $A8A1;
PROCEDURE PaintRect(r: Rect); INLINE $A8A2;
PROCEDURE EraseRect(r: Rect); INLINE $A8A3;
PROCEDURE InvertRect(r: Rect); INLINE $A8A4;
PROCEDURE FillRect(r: Rect; pat: Pattern); INLINE $A8A5;
```

{ RoundRect Routines }

```
PROCEDURE FrameRoundRect(r: Rect; ovWd, ovHt: INTEGER); INLINE $A8B0;
PROCEDURE PaintRoundRect(r: Rect; ovWd, ovHt: INTEGER); INLINE $A8B1;
PROCEDURE EraseRoundRect(r: Rect; ovWd, ovHt: INTEGER); INLINE $A8B2;
PROCEDURE InvertRoundRect(r: Rect; ovWd, ovHt: INTEGER); INLINE $A8B3;
PROCEDURE FillRoundRect(r: Rect; ovWd, ovHt: INTEGER; pat: Pattern);
    INLINE $A8B4;
```

{ **Oval Routines** }

```
PROCEDURE FrameOval(r: Rect); INLINE $A8B7;
PROCEDURE PaintOval(r: Rect); INLINE $A8B8;
PROCEDURE EraseOval(r: Rect); INLINE $A8B9;
PROCEDURE InvertOval(r: Rect); INLINE $A8BA;
PROCEDURE FillOval(r: Rect; pat: Pattern); INLINE $A8BB;
```

{ **Arc Routines** }

```
PROCEDURE FrameArc(r: Rect; startAngle, arcAngle: INTEGER); INLINE $A8BE;
PROCEDURE PaintArc(r: Rect; startAngle, arcAngle: INTEGER); INLINE $A8BF;
PROCEDURE EraseArc(r: Rect; startAngle, arcAngle: INTEGER); INLINE $A8C0;
PROCEDURE InvertArc(r: Rect; startAngle, arcAngle: INTEGER); INLINE $A8C1;
PROCEDURE FillArc(r: Rect; startAngle, arcAngle: INTEGER; pat: Pattern);
    INLINE $A8C2;
PROCEDURE PtToAngle(r: Rect; pt: Point; VAR angle: INTEGER); INLINE $A8C3;
```

{ **Polygon Routines** }

```
FUNCTION OpenPoly: PolyHandle; INLINE $A8CB;

PROCEDURE ClosePoly; INLINE $A8CC;
PROCEDURE KillPoly(poly: PolyHandle); INLINE $A8CD;
PROCEDURE OffsetPoly(poly: PolyHandle; dh, dv: INTEGER); INLINE $A8CE;
PROCEDURE MapPoly(poly: PolyHandle; fromRect, toRect: Rect); INLINE $A8FC;
PROCEDURE FramePoly(poly: PolyHandle); INLINE $A8C6;

PROCEDURE PaintPoly(poly: PolyHandle); INLINE $A8C7;
PROCEDURE ErasePoly(poly: PolyHandle); INLINE $A8C8;
PROCEDURE InvertPoly(poly: PolyHandle); INLINE $A8C9;
PROCEDURE FillPoly(poly: PolyHandle; pat: Pattern); INLINE $A8CA;
```

{ **Region Calculations** }

```
FUNCTION NewRgn: RgnHandle; INLINE $A8D8;
PROCEDURE DisposeRgn(rgn: RgnHandle); INLINE $A8D9;
PROCEDURE CopyRgn(srcRgn, dstRgn: RgnHandle); INLINE $A8DC;
PROCEDURE SetEmptyRgn(rgn: RgnHandle); INLINE $A8DD;
PROCEDURE SetRectRgn(rgn: RgnHandle; left, top, right, bottom: INTEGER);
    INLINE $A8DE;
PROCEDURE RectRgn(rgn: RgnHandle; r: Rect); INLINE $A8DF;
PROCEDURE OpenRgn; INLINE $A8DA;
PROCEDURE CloseRgn(dstRgn: RgnHandle); INLINE $A8DB;
PROCEDURE OffsetRgn(rgn: RgnHandle; dh, dv: INTEGER); INLINE $A8E0;
PROCEDURE MapRgn(rgn: RgnHandle; fromRect, toRect: Rect); INLINE $A8FB;
PROCEDURE InsetRgn(rgn: RgnHandle; dh, dv: INTEGER); INLINE $A8E1;
PROCEDURE SectRgn(srcRgnA, srcRgnB, dstRgn: RgnHandle); INLINE $A8E4;
PROCEDURE UnionRgn(srcRgnA, srcRgnB, dstRgn: RgnHandle); INLINE $A8E5;
```

```
PROCEDURE DiffRgn(srcRgnA, srcRgnB, dstRgn: RgnHandle); INLINE $A8E6;
PROCEDURE XorRgn(srcRgnA, srcRgnB, dstRgn: RgnHandle); INLINE $A8E7;
FUNCTION EqualRgn(rgnA, rgnB: RgnHandle): BOOLEAN; INLINE $A8E3;
FUNCTION EmptyRgn(rgn: RgnHandle): BOOLEAN; INLINE $A8E2;
FUNCTION PtInRgn(pt: Point; rgn: RgnHandle): BOOLEAN; INLINE $A8E8;
FUNCTION RectInRgn(r: Rect; rgn: RgnHandle): BOOLEAN; INLINE $A8E9;
```

{ Graphical Operations on Regions }

```
PROCEDURE FrameRgn(rgn: RgnHandle); INLINE $A8D2;
PROCEDURE PaintRgn(rgn: RgnHandle); INLINE $A8D3;
PROCEDURE EraseRgn(rgn: RgnHandle); INLINE $A8D4;
PROCEDURE InvertRgn(rgn: RgnHandle); INLINE $A8D5;
PROCEDURE FillRgn(rgn: RgnHandle; pat: Pattern); INLINE $A8D6;
```

{ Graphical Operations on BitMaps }

```
PROCEDURE ScrollRect(dstRect: Rect; dh, dv: INTEGER; updateRgn: RgnHandle);
    INLINE $A8EF;
PROCEDURE CopyBits(srcBits, dstBits: BitMap; srcRect, dstRect: Rect;
                              mode: INTEGER; maskRgn: RgnHandle);
    INLINE $A8EC;
PROCEDURE SeedFill(srcPtr, dstPtr: Ptr; srcRow, dstRow, height,
                              words: INTEGER; seedH, seedV: INTEGER);
    INLINE $A839;
PROCEDURE CalcMask(srcPtr, dstPtr: Ptr; srcRow, dstRow, height,
                              words: INTEGER); INLINE $A838;
PROCEDURE CopyMask(srcBits, naskBits, dstBits: BitMap; srcRect, maskRect,
                              dstRect: Rect); INLINE $A817;
FUNCTION GetMaskTable: Ptr;
```

{ Picture Routines }

```
FUNCTION OpenPicture(picFrame: Rect): PicHandle; INLINE $A8F3;
PROCEDURE ClosePicture; INLINE $A8F4;
PROCEDURE DrawPicture(myPicture: PicHandle; dstRect: Rect); INLINE $A8F6;
PROCEDURE PicComment(kind, dataSize: INTEGER; dataHandle: Handle);
    INLINE $A8F2;
PROCEDURE KillPicture(myPicture: PicHandle); INLINE $A8F5;
```

{ The Bottleneck Interface }

```
PROCEDURE SetStdProcs(VAR procs: QDProcs); INLINE $A8EA;
PROCEDURE StdText(count: INTEGER; textAddr: Ptr; numer, denom: Point);
    INLINE $A882;
```

```
PROCEDURE StdLine(newPt: Point); INLINE $A890;
PROCEDURE StdRect(verb: GrafVerb; r: Rect); INLINE $A8A0;
PROCEDURE StdRRect(verb: GrafVerb; r: Rect; ovWd, ovHt: INTEGER);
    INLINE $A8AF;
PROCEDURE StdOval(verb: GrafVerb; r: Rect); INLINE $A8B6;
PROCEDURE StdArc(verb: GrafVerb; r: Rect; startAngle, arcAngle: INTEGER);
    INLINE $A8BD;
PROCEDURE StdPoly(verb: GrafVerb; poly: PolyHandle); INLINE $A8C5;
PROCEDURE StdRgn(verb: GrafVerb; rgn: RgnHandle); INLINE $A8D1;
PROCEDURE StdBits(VAR srcBits: BitMap; VAR srcRect, dstRect: Rect;
                                 mode: INTEGER; maskRgn: RgnHandle);
    INLINE $A8EB;
PROCEDURE StdComment(kind, dataSize: INTEGER; dataHandle: Handle);
    INLINE $A8F1;
FUNCTION StdTxMeas(count: INTEGER; textAddr: Ptr; VAR numer, denom: Point;
                             VAR info: FontInfo): INTEGER; INLINE $A8ED;
PROCEDURE StdGetPic(dataPtr: Ptr; byteCount: INTEGER); INLINE $A8EE;
PROCEDURE StdPutPic(dataPtr: Ptr; byteCount: INTEGER); INLINE $A8F0;
```

{ Misc Utility Routines }

```
FUNCTION GetPixel(h, v: INTEGER): BOOLEAN; INLINE $A865;
FUNCTION Random: INTEGER; INLINE $A861;
PROCEDURE StuffHex(thingptr: Ptr; s: Str255); INLINE $A866;

PROCEDURE ForeColor(color: LongInt); INLINE $A862;
PROCEDURE BackColor(color: LongInt); INLINE $A863;
PROCEDURE ColorBit(whichBit: INTEGER); INLINE $A864;
```

MAC II COLOR QUICKDRAW ROUTINES

{ Routines for Manipulating the CGrafPort }

```
PROCEDURE  OpenCPort(port: CGrafPtr); INLINE $AA00;
PROCEDURE InitCPort(port: CGrafPtr); INLINE $AA01;
PROCEDURE CloseCPort(port: CGrafPtr); INLINE $AA02;
```

{ Routines for Manipulating PixMaps }

```
FUNCTION  NewPixMap:PixMapHandle; INLINE $AA03;
PROCEDURE DisposPixMap(pm: PixMapHandle); INLINE $AA04;
PROCEDURE CopyPixMap(srcPM,dstPM: PixMapHandle); INLINE $AA05;
PROCEDURE SetCPortPix(pm: PixMapHandle); INLINE $AA06;
```

{ Routines for Manipulating PixPats }

```
FUNCTION  NewPixPat:PixPatHandle; INLINE $AA07;
PROCEDURE DisposPixPat(pp: PixPatHandle); INLINE $AA08;
PROCEDURE CopyPixPat(srcPP,dstPP: PixPatHandle); INLINE $AA09;
PROCEDURE PenPixPat(pp: PixPatHandle); INLINE $AA0A;
PROCEDURE BackPixPat(pp: PixPatHandle); INLINE $AA0B;
FUNCTION  GetPixPat(patID: INTEGER): PixPatHandle; INLINE $AA0C;
PROCEDURE MakeRGBPat(pp: PixPatHandle; myColor: RGBColor); INLINE $AA0D;


PROCEDURE FillCRect(r: Rect; pp: PixPatHandle); INLINE $AA0E;
PROCEDURE FillCOval(r: Rect; pp: PixPatHandle); INLINE $AA0F;
PROCEDURE FillCRoundRect(r: Rect; ovWd,ovHt: INTEGER; pp: PixPatHandle);
     INLINE $AA10;
PROCEDURE FillCArc(r: Rect; startAngle,arcAngle: INTEGER; pp: PixPatHandle);
     INLINE $AA11;
PROCEDURE FillCRgn(rgn: RgnHandle; pp: PixPatHandle); INLINE $AA12;
PROCEDURE FillCPoly(poly: PolyHandle; pp: PixPatHandle); INLINE $AA13;


PROCEDURE RGBForeColor(color: RGBColor); INLINE $AA14;
PROCEDURE RGBBackColor(color: RGBColor); INLINE $AA15;
PROCEDURE SetCPixel(h,v: INTEGER; cPix: ColorSpec); INLINE $AA16;
FUNCTION  GetCPixel(h,v: INTEGER): ColorSpec; INLINE $AA17;
PROCEDURE GetForeColor(VAR color: RGBColor); INLINE $AA19;
PROCEDURE GetBackColor(VAR color: RGBColor); INLINE $AA1A;
```

{ Transfer Mode Utilities }

```
PROCEDURE OpColor(color: RGBColor); INLINE $AA21;
PROCEDURE HiliteColor(color: RGBColor); INLINE $AA22;
```

{ Color Table Handling Routines }

```
PROCEDURE DisposCTable(cTable: CTabHandle); INLINE $AA24;
FUNCTION GetCTable(ctID: INTEGER): CTabHandle; INLINE $AA18;
```

{ Color Cursor Handling Routines }

```
FUNCTION GetCCursor(crsrID: INTEGER): CCrsrHandle; INLINE $AA1B;
PROCEDURE SetCCursor(cCrsr: CCrsrHandle); INLINE $AA1C;
PROCEDURE AllocCursor; INLINE $AA1D;
PROCEDURE DisposCCursor(cCrsr: CCrsrHandle); INLINE $AA26;
```

{ **Icon Handling Routines** }

```
FUNCTION GetCIcon(iconID: INTEGER): cIconHandle; INLINE $AA1E;
PROCEDURE PlotCIcon(theRect: Rect; theIcon: cIconHandle); INLINE $AA1F;
PROCEDURE DisposCIcon(theIcon: cIconHandle); INLINE $AA25;
```

{ **PixMap Handling Routines** }

```
PROCEDURE CopyPix(srcPix,dstPix: PixMap; srcRect,dstRect: Rect;
                                mode: INTEGER; maskRgn: RgnHandle);
    INLINE $A8EC;
PROCEDURE CopyCMask(srcPix: PixMap; maskBits: BitMap; dstPix: PixMap;
                                srcRect,maskRect,dstRect: Rect);
    INLINE $A817;
```

{ **Picture Routines** }

```
FUNCTION OpenCPicture(picFrame: Rect): PicHandle; INLINE $AA20;
```

{ **Text Routines** }

```
PROCEDURE CharExtra(extra: Fixed); INLINE $AA23;
```

{ **GDevice Routines** }

```
FUNCTION   GetMaxDevice(globalRect: Rect) : GDHandle; INLINE $AA27;
FUNCTION   GetCTSeed : LONGINT; INLINE $AA28;
FUNCTION   GetDeviceList : GDHandle; INLINE $AA29;
FUNCTION   GetMainDevice : GDHandle; INLINE $AA2A;
FUNCTION   GetNextDevice(curDevice: GDHandle) : GDHandle; INLINE $AA2B;
FUNCTION   TestDeviceAttribute(gdh: GDHandle; attribute: INTEGER) : BOOLEAN;
    INLINE $AA2C;
PROCEDURE SetDeviceAttribute(gdh: GDHandle; attribute: INTEGER; value:
                                BOOLEAN); INLINE $AA2D;
PROCEDURE InitGDevice(unitNum: INTEGER; mode: LONGINT; GDH: GDHandle);
    INLINE $AA2E;
FUNCTION   NewGDevice(unitNum: INTEGER; mode: LONGINT) : GDHandle;
    INLINE $AA2F;
PROCEDURE DisposGDevice(gdh: GDHandle); INLINE $AA30;
PROCEDURE SetGDevice(gd: GDHandle); INLINE $AA31;
FUNCTION   GetGDevice:GDHandle; INLINE $AA32;
```

{ **Color Manager Interface** }

```
FUNCTION Color2Index(VAR myColor: RGBColor): LONGINT;   INLINE $AA33;
```

```
PROCEDURE Index2Color(index: LONGINT; VAR aColor: RGBColor);   INLINE $AA34;
PROCEDURE InvertColor(VAR myColor : RGBColor );   INLINE $AA35;
FUNCTION  RealColor(color: RGBColor): BOOLEAN;   INLINE $AA36;
PROCEDURE GetSubTable(VAR myColors:CTabHandle; iTabRes:integer;
                       targetTbl:CTabHandle);   INLINE $AA37;
PROCEDURE MakeITable(cTabH: CTabHandle; iTabH: ITabHandle; res: INTEGER);
     INLINE $AA39;
PROCEDURE AddSearch(searchProc: ProcPtr);   INLINE $AA3A;
PROCEDURE AddComp(compProc: ProcPtr);   INLINE $AA3B;
PROCEDURE DelSearch(searchProc: ProcPtr);   INLINE $AA4C;
PROCEDURE DelComp(compProc: ProcPtr);   INLINE $AA4D;
PROCEDURE SetClientID(id: INTEGER);   INLINE $AA3C;
PROCEDURE ProtectEntry(index: INTEGER; protect: BOOLEAN);   INLINE $AA3D;
PROCEDURE ReserveEntry(index: INTEGER; reserve: BOOLEAN);   INLINE $AA3E;
PROCEDURE SetEntries(start, count: INTEGER; aTable: CSpecArray);
     INLINE $AA3F;
PROCEDURE SaveEntries(srcTable, resultTable: CTabHandle; VAR selection:
                       ReqListRec);   INLINE $AA49;
PROCEDURE RestoreEntries(srcTable, dstTable: CTabHandle; VAR selection:
                       ReqListRec);   INLINE $AA4A;
FUNCTION QDError: INTEGER;   INLINE $AA40;
```

MAC TOOLBOX ROUTINES

```
{
       These declarations are taken from the file ToolIntf.p
       Version 2.0a3.1
       Copyright Apple Computer, Inc. 1984–1987
       All Rights Reserved
}
```

{ General Utilities }

```
FUNCTION BitAnd(long1, long2: LongInt): LongInt; INLINE $A858;
FUNCTION BitOr(long1, long2: LongInt): LongInt; INLINE $A85B;
FUNCTION BitXor(long1, long2: LongInt): LongInt; INLINE $A859;
FUNCTION BitNot(long: LongInt): LongInt; INLINE $A85A;
FUNCTION BitShift(long: LongInt; count: INTEGER): LongInt; INLINE $A85C;
FUNCTION BitTst(bytePtr: Ptr; bitNum: LongInt): BOOLEAN; INLINE $A85D;
PROCEDURE BitSet(bytePtr: Ptr; bitNum: LongInt); INLINE $A85E;
PROCEDURE BitClr(bytePtr: Ptr; bitNum: LongInt); INLINE $A85F;
PROCEDURE LongMul(a, b: LongInt; VAR dst: Int64Bit); INLINE $A867;
FUNCTION FixMul(a, b: Fixed): Fixed; INLINE $A868;
FUNCTION FixRatio(numer, denom: INTEGER): Fixed; INLINE $A869;
FUNCTION HiWord(x: LongInt): INTEGER; INLINE $A86A;
FUNCTION LoWord(x: LongInt): INTEGER; INLINE $A86B;
FUNCTION FixRound(x: Fixed): INTEGER; INLINE $A86C;
PROCEDURE PackBits(VAR srcPtr, dstPtr: Ptr; srcBytes: INTEGER); INLINE $A8CF;
PROCEDURE UnPackBits(VAR srcPtr, dstPtr: Ptr; dstBytes: INTEGER);
```

```
      INLINE $A8D0;
FUNCTION SlopeFromAngle(angle: INTEGER): Fixed; INLINE $A8BC;
FUNCTION AngleFromSlope(slope: Fixed): INTEGER; INLINE $A8C4;
FUNCTION DeltaPoint(ptA, ptB: Point): LongInt; INLINE $A94F;
FUNCTION NewString(theString: STR255): StringHandle; INLINE $A906;
PROCEDURE SetString(theString: StringHandle; strNew: STR255); INLINE $A907;
FUNCTION GetString(stringID: INTEGER): StringHandle; INLINE $A9BA;
PROCEDURE GetIndString(VAR theString: STR255; strListID: INTEGER;
            index: INTEGER);
FUNCTION Munger(h: Handle; offset: LongInt; ptr1: Ptr; len1: LongInt;
            ptr2: Ptr; len2: LongInt): LongInt; INLINE $A9E0;
FUNCTION GetIcon(iconID: INTEGER): Handle; INLINE $A9BB;
PROCEDURE PlotIcon(theRect: Rect; theIcon: Handle); INLINE $A94B;
FUNCTION GetCursor(cursorID: INTEGER): CursHandle; INLINE $A9B9;
FUNCTION GetPattern(patID: INTEGER): PatHandle; INLINE $A9B8;
FUNCTION GetPicture(picID: INTEGER): PicHandle; INLINE $A9BC;
PROCEDURE GetIndPattern(VAR thePat: Pattern; patListID: INTEGER;
                index: INTEGER);
PROCEDURE ShieldCursor(shieldRect: Rect; offsetPt: Point); INLINE $A855;
PROCEDURE ScreenRes(VAR scrnHRes, scrnVRes: INTEGER);
```

{ for Font Manager }

```
PROCEDURE InitFonts; INLINE $A8FE;
PROCEDURE GetFontName(familyID: INTEGER; VAR theName: STR255); INLINE $A8FF;
PROCEDURE GetFNum(theName: STR255; VAR familyID: INTEGER); INLINE $A900;
PROCEDURE SetFontLock(lockFlag: BOOLEAN); INLINE $A903;
FUNCTION FMSwapFont(inRec: FMInput): FMOutPtr; INLINE $A901;
FUNCTION RealFont(famID: INTEGER; size: INTEGER): BOOLEAN; INLINE $A902;
```

{ new 128K ROM }

```
PROCEDURE SetFScaleDisable(scaleDisable: BOOLEAN); INLINE $A834;
PROCEDURE FontMetrics(VAR theMetrics: FMetricRec); INLINE $A835;
```

{ for Event Manager }

```
FUNCTION EventAvail(mask: INTEGER; VAR theEvent: EventRecord): BOOLEAN;
    INLINE $A971;
FUNCTION GetNextEvent(mask: INTEGER; VAR theEvent: EventRecord): BOOLEAN;
INLINE $A970;
FUNCTION StillDown: BOOLEAN; INLINE $A973;
FUNCTION WaitMouseUp: BOOLEAN; INLINE $A977;
PROCEDURE GetMouse(VAR pt: Point); INLINE $A972;
FUNCTION TickCount: LongInt; INLINE $A975;
FUNCTION Button: BOOLEAN; INLINE $A974;
PROCEDURE GetKeys(VAR k: KeyMap); INLINE $A976;
```

```
FUNCTION GetDblTime: LongInt; INLINE $2EB8, $02F0;
FUNCTION GetCaretTime: LongInt; INLINE $2EB8, $02F4;
```

{ for Window Manager }

```
PROCEDURE ClipAbove(window: WindowPeek); INLINE $A90B;
PROCEDURE PaintOne(window: WindowPeek; clobbered: RgnHandle); INLINE $A90C;
PROCEDURE PaintBehind(startWindow: WindowPeek; clobbered: RgnHandle);
     INLINE $A90D;
PROCEDURE SaveOld(window: WindowPeek); INLINE $A90E;
PROCEDURE DrawNew(window: WindowPeek; fUpdate: BOOLEAN); INLINE $A90F;
PROCEDURE CalcVis(window: WindowPeek); INLINE $A909;
PROCEDURE CalcVisBehind(startWindow: WindowPeek; clobbered: RgnHandle);
     INLINE $A90A;
PROCEDURE ShowHide(window: WindowPtr; showFlag: BOOLEAN); INLINE $A908;
FUNCTION CheckUpdate(VAR theEvent: EventRecord): BOOLEAN; INLINE $A911;
PROCEDURE GetWMgrPort(VAR wPort: GrafPtr); INLINE $A910;
PROCEDURE InitWindows; INLINE $A912;
FUNCTION NewWindow(wStorage: Ptr; boundsRect: Rect; title: STR255;
                   visible: BOOLEAN; theProc: INTEGER; behind: WindowPtr;
                   goAwayFlag: BOOLEAN; refCon: LongInt): WindowPtr;
     INLINE $A913;
PROCEDURE DisposeWindow(theWindow: WindowPtr); INLINE $A914;
PROCEDURE CloseWindow(theWindow: WindowPtr); INLINE $A92D;
PROCEDURE MoveWindow(theWindow: WindowPtr; h, v: INTEGER;
                   BringToFront: BOOLEAN); INLINE $A91B;
PROCEDURE SizeWindow(theWindow: WindowPtr; width, height: INTEGER;
                   fUpdate: BOOLEAN); INLINE $A91D;
FUNCTION GrowWindow(theWindow: WindowPtr; startPt: Point;
                   bBox: Rect): LongInt; INLINE $A92B;
PROCEDURE DragWindow(theWindow: WindowPtr; startPt: Point; boundsRect: Rect);
     INLINE $A925;
PROCEDURE ShowWindow(theWindow: WindowPtr); INLINE $A915;
PROCEDURE HideWindow(theWindow: WindowPtr); INLINE $A916;
PROCEDURE SetWTitle(theWindow: WindowPtr; title: STR255); INLINE $A91A;
PROCEDURE GetWTitle(theWindow: WindowPtr; VAR title: STR255); INLINE $A919;
PROCEDURE HiliteWindow(theWindow: WindowPtr; fHiLite: BOOLEAN); INLINE $A91C;
PROCEDURE BeginUpdate(theWindow: WindowPtr); INLINE $A922;
PROCEDURE EndUpdate(theWindow: WindowPtr); INLINE $A923;
PROCEDURE SetWRefCon(theWindow: WindowPtr; data: LongInt); INLINE $A918;
FUNCTION GetWRefCon(theWindow: WindowPtr): LongInt; INLINE $A917;
PROCEDURE SetWindowPic(theWindow: WindowPtr; thePic: PicHandle); INLINE $A92E;
FUNCTION GetWindowPic(theWindow: WindowPtr): PicHandle; INLINE $A92F;
PROCEDURE BringToFront(theWindow: WindowPtr); INLINE $A920;
PROCEDURE SendBehind(theWindow, behindWindow: WindowPtr); INLINE $A921;
FUNCTION FrontWindow: WindowPtr; INLINE $A924;
PROCEDURE SelectWindow(theWindow: WindowPtr); INLINE $A91F;
FUNCTION TrackGoAway(theWindow: WindowPtr; thePt: Point): BOOLEAN;
     INLINE $A91E;
```

```
PROCEDURE DrawGrowIcon(theWindow: WindowPtr); INLINE $A904;
PROCEDURE ValidRect(goodRect: Rect); INLINE $A92A;
PROCEDURE ValidRgn(goodRgn: RgnHandle); INLINE $A929;
PROCEDURE InvalRect(badRect: Rect); INLINE $A928;
PROCEDURE InvalRgn(badRgn: RgnHandle); INLINE $A927;
FUNCTION FindWindow(thePoint: Point; VAR theWindow: WindowPtr): INTEGER;
     INLINE $A92C;
FUNCTION GetNewWindow(windowID: INTEGER; wStorage: Ptr;
                behind: WindowPtr): WindowPtr; INLINE $A9BD;
FUNCTION PinRect(theRect: Rect; thePt: Point): LongInt; INLINE $A94E;
FUNCTION DragGrayRgn(theRgn: RgnHandle; startPt: Point; boundsRect,
               slopRect: Rect; axis: INTEGER;
               actionProc: ProcPtr): LongInt; INLINE $A905;
```

{ new 128K ROM }

```
FUNCTION TrackBox(theWindow: WindowPtr; thePt: Point;
                partCode: INTEGER): BOOLEAN; INLINE $A83B;
PROCEDURE ZoomWindow(theWindow: WindowPtr; partCode: INTEGER; front: BOOLEAN);
     INLINE $A83A;
```

{ for TextEdit }

```
PROCEDURE TEActivate(h: TEHandle); INLINE $A9D8;
PROCEDURE TECalText(h: TEHandle); INLINE $A9D0;
PROCEDURE TEClick(pt: Point; extend: BOOLEAN; h: TEHandle); INLINE $A9D4;
PROCEDURE TECopy(h: TEHandle); INLINE $A9D5;
PROCEDURE TECut(h: TEHandle); INLINE $A9D6;
PROCEDURE TEDeActivate(h: TEHandle); INLINE $A9D9;
PROCEDURE TEDelete(h: TEHandle); INLINE $A9D7;
PROCEDURE TEDispose(h: TEHandle); INLINE $A9CD;
PROCEDURE TEIdle(h: TEHandle); INLINE $A9DA;
PROCEDURE TEInit; INLINE $A9CC;
PROCEDURE TEKey(key: CHAR; h: TEHandle); INLINE $A9DC;
FUNCTION TENew(dest, view: Rect): TEHandle; INLINE $A9D2;
PROCEDURE TEPaste(h: TEHandle); INLINE $A9DB;
PROCEDURE TEScroll(dh, dv: INTEGER; h: TEHandle); INLINE $A9DD;
PROCEDURE TESetSelect(selStart, selEnd: LongInt; h: TEHandle); INLINE $A9D1;
PROCEDURE TESetText(inText: Ptr; textLength: LongInt; h: TEHandle);
     INLINE $A9CF;
PROCEDURE TEInsert(inText: Ptr; textLength: LongInt; h: TEHandle);
     INLINE $A9DE;
PROCEDURE TEUpdate(rUpdate: Rect; h: TEHandle); INLINE $A9D3;
PROCEDURE TESetJust(just: INTEGER; h: TEHandle); INLINE $A9DF;
FUNCTION TEGetText(h: TEHandle): CharsHandle; INLINE $A9CB;
FUNCTION TEScrapHandle: Handle; INLINE $2EB8, $0AB4;
FUNCTION TEGetScrapLen: LongInt;
PROCEDURE TESetScrapLen(length: LongInt);
```

```
FUNCTION TEFromScrap: OsErr;
FUNCTION TEToScrap: OsErr;
PROCEDURE SetWordBreak(wBrkProc: ProcPtr; hTE: TEHandle);
PROCEDURE SetClikLoop(clikProc: ProcPtr; hTE: TEHandle);
```

{ new 128K ROM }

```
PROCEDURE TESelView(hTE: TEHandle); INLINE $A811;
PROCEDURE TEPinScroll(dh, dv: INTEGER; hTE: TEHandle); INLINE $A812;
PROCEDURE TEAutoView(auto: BOOLEAN; hTE: TEHandle); INLINE $A813;
```

{ Box drawing utility }

```
PROCEDURE TextBox(inText: Ptr; textLength: LongInt; r: Rect; Style: INTEGER);
    INLINE $A9CE;
```

{ for Resource Manager }

```
FUNCTION InitResources: INTEGER; INLINE $A995;
PROCEDURE RsrcZoneInit; INLINE $A996;
PROCEDURE CreateResFile(fileName: STR255); INLINE $A9B1;
FUNCTION OpenResFile(fileName: STR255): INTEGER; INLINE $A997;
PROCEDURE UseResFile(refNum: INTEGER); INLINE $A998;
FUNCTION GetResFileAttrs(refNum: INTEGER): INTEGER; INLINE $A9F6;
PROCEDURE SetResFileAttrs(refNum: INTEGER; attrs: INTEGER); INLINE $A9F7;
PROCEDURE UpdateResFile(refNum: INTEGER); INLINE $A999;
PROCEDURE CloseResFile(refNum: INTEGER); INLINE $A99A;
PROCEDURE SetResPurge(install: BOOLEAN); INLINE $A993;
PROCEDURE SetResLoad(AutoLoad: BOOLEAN); INLINE $A99B;
FUNCTION CountResources(theType: ResType): INTEGER; INLINE $A99C;
FUNCTION GetIndResource(theType: ResType; index: INTEGER): Handle;
    INLINE $A99D;
FUNCTION CountTypes: INTEGER; INLINE $A99E;
PROCEDURE GetIndType(VAR theType: ResType; index: INTEGER); INLINE $A99F;
FUNCTION UniqueID(theType: ResType): INTEGER; INLINE $A9C1;
FUNCTION GetResource(theType: ResType; ID: INTEGER): Handle; INLINE $A9A0;
FUNCTION GetNamedResource(theType: ResType; name: STR255): Handle;
    INLINE $A9A1;
PROCEDURE LoadResource(theResource: Handle); INLINE $A9A2;
PROCEDURE ReleaseResource(theResource: Handle); INLINE $A9A3;
PROCEDURE DetachResource(theResource: Handle); INLINE $A992;
PROCEDURE ChangedResource(theResource: Handle); INLINE $A9AA;
PROCEDURE WriteResource(theResource: Handle); INLINE $A9B0;
FUNCTION HomeResFile(theResource: Handle): INTEGER; INLINE $A9A4;
FUNCTION CurResFile: INTEGER; INLINE $A994;
FUNCTION GetResAttrs(theResource: Handle): INTEGER; INLINE $A9A6;
PROCEDURE SetResAttrs(theResource: Handle; attrs: INTEGER); INLINE $A9A7;
```

```
PROCEDURE GetResInfo(theResource: Handle; VAR theID: INTEGER;
                VAR theType: ResType; VAR name: STR255); INLINE $A9A8;
PROCEDURE SetResInfo(theResource: Handle; theID: INTEGER; name: STR255);
    INLINE $A9A9;
PROCEDURE AddResource(theResource: Handle; theType: ResType; theID: INTEGER;
                name: STR255); INLINE $A9AB;
PROCEDURE RmveResource(theResource: Handle); INLINE $A9AD;
FUNCTION SizeResource(theResource: Handle): LongInt; INLINE $A9A5;
FUNCTION ResError: INTEGER; INLINE $A9AF;
```

{ new 128K ROM }

```
FUNCTION Get1IndResource(theType: ResType; index: INTEGER): Handle;
    INLINE $A80E;
FUNCTION Count1Types: INTEGER; INLINE $A81C;
FUNCTION Get1Resource(theType: ResType; theID: INTEGER): Handle; INLINE $A81F;
FUNCTION Get1NamedResource(theType: ResType; name: STR255): Handle;
    INLINE $A820;
PROCEDURE Get1IndType(VAR theType: ResType; index: INTEGER); INLINE $A80F;
FUNCTION Unique1ID(theType: ResType): INTEGER; INLINE $A810;
FUNCTION Count1Resources(theType: ResType): INTEGER; INLINE $A80D;
FUNCTION MaxSizeRsrc(theResource: Handle): LongInt; INLINE $A821;
FUNCTION RsrcMapEntry(theResource: Handle): LongInt; INLINE $A9C5;
FUNCTION OpenRFPerm(fileName: STR255; VRefNum: INTEGER;
                permission: SignedByte): INTEGER; INLINE $A9C4;
```

{ for Control Manager }

```
FUNCTION NewControl(curWindow: WindowPtr; boundsRect: Rect; title: STR255;
                visible: BOOLEAN; value: INTEGER; min: INTEGER;
                max: INTEGER; contrlProc: INTEGER;
                refCon: LongInt): ControlHandle; INLINE $A954;
PROCEDURE DisposeControl(theControl: ControlHandle); INLINE $A955;
PROCEDURE KillControls(theWindow: WindowPtr); INLINE $A956;
PROCEDURE MoveControl(theControl: ControlHandle; h, v: INTEGER); INLINE $A959;
PROCEDURE SizeControl(theControl: ControlHandle; w, h: INTEGER); INLINE $A95C;
PROCEDURE DragControl(theControl: ControlHandle; startPt: Point; bounds: Rect;
                slopRect: Rect; axis: INTEGER); INLINE $A967;
PROCEDURE ShowControl(theControl: ControlHandle); INLINE $A957;
PROCEDURE HideControl(theControl: ControlHandle); INLINE $A958;
PROCEDURE SetCTitle(theControl: ControlHandle; title: STR255); INLINE $A95F;
PROCEDURE GetCTitle(theControl: ControlHandle; VAR title: STR255);
    INLINE $A95E;
PROCEDURE HiliteControl(theControl: ControlHandle; hiliteState: INTEGER);
INLINE $A95D;
PROCEDURE SetCRefCon(theControl: ControlHandle; data: LongInt); INLINE $A95B;
FUNCTION GetCRefCon(theControl: ControlHandle): LongInt; INLINE $A95A;
```

```
PROCEDURE SetCtlValue(theControl: ControlHandle; theValue: INTEGER);
     INLINE $A963;
FUNCTION GetCtlValue(theControl: ControlHandle): INTEGER; INLINE $A960;
FUNCTION GetCtlMin(theControl: ControlHandle): INTEGER; INLINE $A961;
FUNCTION GetCtlMax(theControl: ControlHandle): INTEGER; INLINE $A962;
PROCEDURE SetCtlMin(theControl: ControlHandle; theValue: INTEGER);
     INLINE $A964;
PROCEDURE SetCtlMax(theControl: ControlHandle; theValue: INTEGER);
     INLINE $A965;
FUNCTION GetCtlAction(theControl: ControlHandle): ProcPtr; INLINE $A96A;
PROCEDURE SetCtlAction(theControl: ControlHandle; newProc: ProcPtr);
     INLINE $A96B;
FUNCTION TestControl(theControl: ControlHandle; thePt: Point): INTEGER;
     INLINE $A966;
FUNCTION TrackControl(theControl: ControlHandle; thePt: Point;
               actionProc: ProcPtr): INTEGER; INLINE $A968;
FUNCTION FindControl(thePoint: Point; theWindow: WindowPtr;
               VAR theControl: ControlHandle): INTEGER; INLINE $A96C;
PROCEDURE DrawControls(theWindow: WindowPtr); INLINE $A969;
FUNCTION GetNewControl(controlID: INTEGER; owner: WindowPtr): ControlHandle;
     INLINE $A9BE;
```

{ new 128K ROM}

```
PROCEDURE UpdtControl(theWindow: WindowPtr; updateRgn: RgnHandle);
     INLINE $A953;
PROCEDURE Draw1Control(theControl: ControlHandle); INLINE $A96D;
```

{ for Dialog Manager }

```
PROCEDURE InitDialogs(resumeProc: ProcPtr); INLINE $A97B;
FUNCTION GetNewDialog(dialogID: INTEGER; wStorage: Ptr;
               behind: WindowPtr): DialogPtr; INLINE $A97C;
FUNCTION NewDialog(wStorage: Ptr; boundsRect: Rect; title: STR255;
               visible: BOOLEAN; theProc: INTEGER; behind: WindowPtr;
               goAwayFlag: BOOLEAN; refCon: LongInt;
               itmLstHndl: Handle): DialogPtr; INLINE $A97D;
FUNCTION IsDialogEvent(event: EventRecord): BOOLEAN; INLINE $A97F;
FUNCTION DialogSelect(event: EventRecord; VAR theDialog: DialogPtr;
               VAR itemHit: INTEGER): BOOLEAN; INLINE $A980;
PROCEDURE ModalDialog(filterProc: ProcPtr; VAR itemHit: INTEGER);
     INLINE $A991;
PROCEDURE DrawDialog(theDialog: DialogPtr); INLINE $A981;
PROCEDURE CloseDialog(theDialog: DialogPtr); INLINE $A982;
PROCEDURE DisposDialog(theDialog: DialogPtr); INLINE $A983;
FUNCTION Alert(alertID: INTEGER; filterProc: ProcPtr): INTEGER; INLINE $A985;
FUNCTION StopAlert(alertID: INTEGER; filterProc: ProcPtr): INTEGER;
```

```
      INLINE $A986;
FUNCTION NoteAlert(alertID: INTEGER; filterProc: ProcPtr): INTEGER;
      INLINE $A987;
FUNCTION CautionAlert(alertID: INTEGER; filterProc: ProcPtr): INTEGER;
      INLINE $A988;
PROCEDURE CouldAlert(alertID: INTEGER); INLINE $A989;
PROCEDURE FreeAlert(alertID: INTEGER); INLINE $A98A;
PROCEDURE CouldDialog(DlgID: INTEGER); INLINE $A979;
PROCEDURE FreeDialog(DlgID: INTEGER); INLINE $A97A;
PROCEDURE ParamText(cite0, cite1, cite2, cite3: STR255); INLINE $A98B;
PROCEDURE ErrorSound(sound: ProcPtr); INLINE $A98C;
PROCEDURE GetDItem(theDialog: DialogPtr; itemNo: INTEGER; VAR kind: INTEGER;
                   VAR item: Handle; VAR box: Rect); INLINE $A98D;
PROCEDURE SetDItem(dialog: DialogPtr; itemNo: INTEGER; kind: INTEGER;
                   item: Handle; box: Rect); INLINE $A98E;
PROCEDURE SetIText(item: Handle; text: STR255); INLINE $A98F;
PROCEDURE GetIText(item: Handle; VAR text: STR255); INLINE $A990;
PROCEDURE SelIText(theDialog: DialogPtr; itemNo: INTEGER; startSel,
                   endSel: INTEGER); INLINE $A97E;
```

{ routines designed only for use in Pascal }

```
FUNCTION GetAlrtStage: INTEGER; INLINE $3EB8, $0A9A;
PROCEDURE ResetAlrtStage; INLINE $4278, $0A9A;
PROCEDURE DlgCut(theDialog: DialogPtr);
PROCEDURE DlgPaste(theDialog: DialogPtr);
PROCEDURE DlgCopy(theDialog: DialogPtr);
PROCEDURE DlgDelete(theDialog: DialogPtr);
PROCEDURE SetDAFont(fontNum: INTEGER); INLINE $31DF, $0AFA;
```

{ new 128K ROM }

```
PROCEDURE HideDItem(theDialog: DialogPtr; itemNo: INTEGER); INLINE $A827;
PROCEDURE ShowDItem(theDialog: DialogPtr; itemNo: INTEGER); INLINE $A828;
PROCEDURE UpdtDialog(theDialog: DialogPtr; updateRgn: RgnHandle);
      INLINE $A978;
FUNCTION FindDItem(theDialog: DialogPtr; thePt: Point): INTEGER; INLINE $A984;
```

{ for Desk Manager }

```
FUNCTION SystemEvent(myEvent: EventRecord): BOOLEAN; INLINE $A9B2;
PROCEDURE SystemClick(theEvent: EventRecord; theWindow: WindowPtr);
      INLINE $A9B3;
PROCEDURE SystemTask; INLINE $A9B4;
PROCEDURE SystemMenu(menuResult: LongInt); INLINE $A9B5;
FUNCTION SystemEdit(editCode: INTEGER): BOOLEAN; INLINE $A9C2;
```

```
FUNCTION OpenDeskAcc(theAcc: STR255): INTEGER; INLINE $A9B6;
PROCEDURE CloseDeskAcc(refNum: INTEGER); INLINE $A9B7;
```

{ for Menu Manager }

```
PROCEDURE InitMenus; INLINE $A930;
FUNCTION NewMenu(menuId: INTEGER; menuTitle: STR255): MenuHandle;
      INLINE $A931;
FUNCTION GetMenu(rsrcID: INTEGER): MenuHandle; INLINE $A9BF;
PROCEDURE DisposeMenu(menu: MenuHandle); INLINE $A932;
PROCEDURE AppendMenu(menu: MenuHandle; data: STR255); INLINE $A933;
PROCEDURE InsertMenu(menu: MenuHandle; beforeId: INTEGER); INLINE $A935;
PROCEDURE DeleteMenu(menuId: INTEGER); INLINE $A936;
PROCEDURE DrawMenuBar; INLINE $A937;
PROCEDURE ClearMenuBar; INLINE $A934;
FUNCTION GetMenuBar: Handle; INLINE $A93B;
FUNCTION GetNewMBar(menuBarID: INTEGER): Handle; INLINE $A9C0;
PROCEDURE SetMenuBar(menuBar: Handle); INLINE $A93C;
FUNCTION MenuSelect(startPt: Point): LongInt; INLINE $A93D;
FUNCTION MenuKey(ch: CHAR): LongInt; INLINE $A93E;
PROCEDURE HiLiteMenu(menuId: INTEGER); INLINE $A938;
PROCEDURE SetItem(menu: MenuHandle; item: INTEGER; itemString: STR255);
      INLINE $A947;
PROCEDURE GetItem(menu: MenuHandle; item: INTEGER; VAR itemString: STR255);
      INLINE $A946;
PROCEDURE EnableItem(menu: MenuHandle; item: INTEGER); INLINE $A939;
PROCEDURE DisableItem(menu: MenuHandle; item: INTEGER); INLINE $A93A;
PROCEDURE CheckItem(menu: MenuHandle; item: INTEGER; checked: BOOLEAN);
      INLINE $A945;
PROCEDURE SetItemIcon(menu: MenuHandle; item: INTEGER; iconNum: Byte);
      INLINE $A940;
PROCEDURE GetItemIcon(menu: MenuHandle; item: INTEGER; VAR iconNum: Byte);
      INLINE $A93F;
PROCEDURE SetItemStyle(menu: MenuHandle; item: INTEGER; styleVal: Style);
      INLINE $A942;
PROCEDURE GetItemStyle(menu: MenuHandle; item: INTEGER; VAR styleVal: Style);
      INLINE $A941;
PROCEDURE SetItemMark(menu: MenuHandle; item: INTEGER; markChar: CHAR);
      INLINE $A944;
PROCEDURE GetItemMark(menu: MenuHandle; item: INTEGER; VAR markChar: CHAR);
      INLINE $A943;
PROCEDURE SetMenuFlash(flashCount: INTEGER); INLINE $A94A;
PROCEDURE FlashMenuBar(menuId: INTEGER); INLINE $A94C;
FUNCTION GetMHandle(menuId: INTEGER): MenuHandle; INLINE $A949;
FUNCTION CountMItems(menu: MenuHandle): INTEGER; INLINE $A950;
PROCEDURE AddResMenu(menu: MenuHandle; theType: ResType); INLINE $A94D;
PROCEDURE InsertResMenu(menu: MenuHandle; theType: ResType;
                  afterItem: INTEGER); INLINE $A951;
PROCEDURE CalcMenuSize(menu: MenuHandle); INLINE $A948;
```

{ new 128K ROM }

```
PROCEDURE InsMenuItem(theMenu: MenuHandle; itemString: STR255;
                afterItem: INTEGER);  INLINE $A826;
PROCEDURE DelMenuItem(theMenu: MenuHandle; item: INTEGER);  INLINE $A952;
```

{ for Scrap Manager }

```
FUNCTION GetScrap(hDest: Handle; what: ResType; VAR offset: LongInt): LongInt;
    INLINE $A9FD;
FUNCTION InfoScrap: pScrapStuff; INLINE $A9F9;
FUNCTION LoadScrap: LongInt; INLINE $A9FB;
FUNCTION PutScrap(length: LongInt; what: ResType; source: Ptr): LongInt;
    INLINE $A9FE;
FUNCTION UnloadScrap: LongInt; INLINE $A9FA;
FUNCTION ZeroScrap: LongInt; INLINE $A9FC;
```

{ package manager }

```
PROCEDURE InitAllPacks; INLINE $A9E6;

PROCEDURE InitPack(packID: INTEGER); INLINE $A9E5;
```

MAC II TOOLBOX ROUTINES

{ Text Edit }

```
FUNCTION   TEStylNew(destRect,viewRect: Rect): TEHandle;   INLINE $A83E;
PROCEDURE  SetStylHandle(theHandle: TEStyleHandle; hTE: TEHandle);
FUNCTION   GetStylHandle(hTE: TEHandle): TEStyleHandle;
FUNCTION   TEGetOffset(pt: Point; hTE: TEHandle): INTEGER; INLINE $A83C;
PROCEDURE  TEGetStyle(offset: INTEGER; VAR theStyle: TextStyle;
                        VAR lineHeight,fontAscent: INTEGER; hTE: TEHandle);
PROCEDURE  TEStylPaste(hTE: TEHandle);
PROCEDURE  TESetStyle(mode: INTEGER; newStyle: TextStyle; redraw: BOOLEAN;
                hTE: TEHandle);
PROCEDURE  TEReplaceStyle(mode: INTEGER; oldStyle,newStyle: TextStyle;
                        redraw: BOOLEAN; hTE: TEHandle);
FUNCTION   GetStylScrap(hTE: TEHandle): StScrpHandle;
PROCEDURE  TEStylInsert(text: Ptr; length: LONGINT; hST: StScrpHandle;
                hTE: TEHandle);
FUNCTION   TEGetPoint(offset: INTEGER; hTE: TEHandle): Point;
FUNCTION   TEGetHeight(startLine, endLine: LONGINT; hTE: TEHandle):
                LONGINT;
```

{ Color Control Manager }

```
Procedure SetCtlColor(theControl:ControlHandle;newColorTable: CCTabHandle);
     INLINE $AA43;
Function GetAuxCtl (theControl:ControlHandle; VAR ACHndl:AuxCtlHndl) :
     BOOLEAN; INLINE $AA44;
Function GetCVariant (theControl:ControlHandle) : INTEGER; INLINE $A809;
```

{ Color Window Manager }

```
Procedure GetCWMgrPort(VAR wport: CGrafport); INLINE $AA48;
Procedure SetWinColor(theWindow: WindowPtr; newColorTable: WCTabHandle);
     INLINE $AA41;
Function GetAuxWin (theWindow: WindowPtr; VAR awHndl: AuxWinHndl) : BOOLEAN;
     INLINE $AA42;
Procedure SetDeskCPat(deskPixPat: PixPatHandle); INLINE $AA47;
Function NewCWindow(wStorage: Ptr; boundsRect: Rect; title: Str255;
                 visible: BOOLEAN; procID: INTEGER; behind: WindowPtr;
                 goAwayFlag: BOOLEAN; refCon: LONGINT): WindowPtr;
     INLINE $AA45;
Function GetNewCWindow(windowID: INTEGER; wStorage: Ptr;
                 behind: WindowPtr): WindowPtr; INLINE $AA46;
Function GetWVariant (theWindow: WindowPtr) : INTEGER; INLINE $A80A;
```

{ Menu Manager }

```
Procedure InitProcMenu(resID: INTEGER; aVariant: INTEGER); INLINE $A808;
```

{ Color Menu Manager }

```
PROCEDURE DelMCEntries (menuID, menuItem : INTEGER); INLINE $AA60;
FUNCTION GetMCInfo : MCInfoHandle; INLINE $AA61;
PROCEDURE SetMCInfo (menuCTbl : MCInfoHandle); INLINE $AA62;
PROCEDURE DispMCInfo (menuCTbl : MCInfoHandle); INLINE $AA63;
FUNCTION GetMCEntry (menuID, menuItem : INTEGER) : MCInfoPtr; INLINE $AA64;
PROCEDURE SetMCEntries (numEntries : INTEGER; menuCEntries : MCInfoPtr);
     INLINE $AA65;
FUNCTION MenuChoice : LONGINT; INLINE $AA66;
```

{ Dialog Manager }

```
FUNCTION NewCDialog(dStorage: Ptr; boundsRect: Rect; title: STR255;
                 visible: BOOLEAN; procID: INTEGER; behind: WindowPtr;
                 goAwayFlag: BOOLEAN; refCon: LONGINT; items: Handle):
DialogPtr; INLINE $AA4B;
```

{ **Font Manager** }

```
PROCEDURE SetFractEnable(fractEnable: Boolean);
```

{ **Resource Manager** }

```
FUNCTION RGetResource(theType: ResType; theID: INTEGER): Handle; INLINE $A08C;
```

MICROSOFT WINDOWS

```
                    { Microsoft Windows routines, from Windows version 1.03
                    Copyright © 1986 Microsoft Corporaton. All Rights Reserved. }

FUNCTION    MAKELONG ( w1_,w2_: WORD ): LONG;
FUNCTION    LOWORD ( l: LONG ): WORD;
FUNCTION    HIWORD ( l: LONG ): WORD;
FUNCTION    LOBYTE ( w: WORD ): BYTE;
FUNCTION    HIBYTE ( w: WORD ): BYTE;
FUNCTION    MAKEPOINT ( l: LONG ): POINT;


FUNCTION    RegisterWindowMessage ( l: LPSTR ): WORD;
FUNCTION    RGB ( r,g,b: BYTE ): DWORD;
FUNCTION    GetRValue ( d: DWORD ): BYTE;
FUNCTION    GetGValue ( d: DWORD ): BYTE;
FUNCTION    GetBValue ( d: DWORD ): BYTE;
FUNCTION    GetMessage ( l: LPMSG; h: HWND; w,x: WORD ): BOOL;
FUNCTION    PeekMessage ( l: LPMSG; h: HWND; w,x: WORD; b: BOOL ): BOOL;
FUNCTION    TranslateMessage ( l: LPMSG ): BOOL;
FUNCTION    DispatchMessage ( l: LPMSG ): LONG;
FUNCTION    SwapMouseButton ( b: BOOL ): BOOL;
FUNCTION    GetMessagePos: DWORD;
FUNCTION    GetMessageTime: long;
FUNCTION    GetSysModalWindow: HWND;
FUNCTION    SetSysModalWindow ( h: HWND ): HWND;
FUNCTION    SendMessage ( h: HWND; w,x: WORD; l: LONG ): long;
FUNCTION    PostMessage ( h: HWND; w,x: WORD; l: LONG ): BOOL;
FUNCTION    PostAppMessage ( h: HANDLE; w,x: WORD; l: LONG ): BOOL;
PROCEDURE   ReplyMessage ( l: long );
PROCEDURE   WaitMessage;


FUNCTION    DefWindowProc ( h: HWND; w,x: WORD; l: LONG ): long;
PROCEDURE   PostQuitMessage ( i: int );
FUNCTION    CallWindowProc ( f: FARPROC; h: HWND; w,x: WORD; l: LONG ): long;
FUNCTION    InSendMessage: BOOL;
FUNCTION    GetDoubleClickTime: WORD;
FUNCTION    RegisterClass ( l: LPWNDCLASS ): BOOL;
FUNCTION    CreateWindow ( l,m: LPSTR; d: DWORD; i,j,k,n: int; h: HWND; o:
                        HMENU; p: HANDLE; q: LPSTR ): HWND;
```

```
FUNCTION   IsWindow ( h: HWND ): BOOL;
FUNCTION   DestroyWindow ( h: HWND ): BOOL;
FUNCTION   ShowWindow ( h: HWND; i: int ): BOOL;
FUNCTION   FlashWindow ( h: HWND; b: BOOL ): BOOL;
FUNCTION   OpenIcon ( h: HWND ): BOOL;
FUNCTION   CloseWindow ( h: HWND ): int;
PROCEDURE  MoveWindow ( h: HWND; i,j,k,l: int; b: BOOL );
FUNCTION   IsWindowVisible ( h: HWND ): BOOL;
FUNCTION   IsIconic ( h: HWND ): BOOL;
FUNCTION   AnyPopup: BOOL;
PROCEDURE  BringWindowToTop ( h: HWND );
PROCEDURE  DrawText ( h: HDC; l: LPSTR; i: int; m: LPRECT; w: WORD );
FUNCTION   DrawIcon ( h: HDC; i,j: int; k: HICON ): BOOL;

FUNCTION   CreateDialog ( h: HANDLE; l: LPSTR; i: HWND; f: FARPROC ): HWND;
FUNCTION   DialogBox ( h: HANDLE; l: LPSTR; i: HWND; f: FARPROC ): int;
PROCEDURE  EndDialog ( h: HWND; i: int );
FUNCTION   GetDlgItem ( h: HWND; i: int ): HWND;
PROCEDURE  SetDlgItemInt ( h: HWND; i: int; w: WORD; b: BOOL );
FUNCTION   GetDlgItemInt ( h: HWND; i: int; b: LPBOOL; c: BOOL ): WORD;
PROCEDURE  SetDlgItemText ( h: HWND; i: int; l: LPSTR );
FUNCTION   GetDlgItemText ( h: HWND; i: int; l: LPSTR; j: int ): int;
PROCEDURE  CheckDlgButton ( h: HWND; i: int; w: WORD );
PROCEDURE  CheckRadioButton ( h: HWND; i,j,k: int );
FUNCTION   IsDlgButtonChecked ( h: HWND; i: int ): WORD;
FUNCTION   SendDlgItemMessage ( h: HWND; i: int; w,x: WORD; l: LONG ): long;
FUNCTION   CallMsgFilter ( l: LPMSG; i: int ): BOOL;

FUNCTION   OpenClipboard ( h: HWND ): BOOL;
FUNCTION   CloseClipboard: BOOL;
FUNCTION   GetClipboardOwner: HWND;
FUNCTION   SetClipboardViewer ( h: HWND ): HWND;
FUNCTION   GetClipboardViewer: HWND;
FUNCTION   ChangeClipboardChain ( h,i: HWND ): BOOL;
FUNCTION   SetClipboardData ( w: WORD; h: HANDLE ): HANDLE;
FUNCTION   GetClipboardData ( w: WORD ): HANDLE;
FUNCTION   RegisterClipboardFormat ( l: LPSTR ): WORD;
FUNCTION   CountClipboardFormats: int;
FUNCTION   EnumClipboardFormats ( w: WORD ): WORD;
FUNCTION   GetClipboardFormatName ( w: WORD; l: LPSTR; i: int ): int;
FUNCTION   EmptyClipboard: BOOL;
FUNCTION   IsClipboardFormatAvailable ( w: WORD ): BOOL;

FUNCTION   SetFocus ( h: HWND ): HWND;
FUNCTION   GetFocus: HWND;
FUNCTION   GetActiveWindow: HWND;
FUNCTION   GetKeyState ( i: int ): int;
FUNCTION   SetCapture ( h: HWND ): HWND;
PROCEDURE  ReleaseCapture;
```

```
FUNCTION   SetTimer ( h: HWND; s: short; w: WORD; f: FARPROC ): short;
FUNCTION   KillTimer ( h: HWND; s: short ): BOOL;
FUNCTION   EnableWindow ( h: HWND; b: BOOL ): BOOL;
FUNCTION   IsWindowEnabled ( h: HWND ): BOOL;
FUNCTION   LoadAccelerators ( h: HANDLE; l: LPSTR ): HANDLE;
FUNCTION   TranslateAccelerator ( h: HWND; i: HANDLE; l: LPMSG ): int;
FUNCTION   GetSystemMetrics ( i: int ): int;


FUNCTION   HiliteMenuItem ( h: HWND; i: HMENU; w,x: WORD ): BOOL;
FUNCTION   GetMenuString ( h: HMENU; w: WORD; l: LPSTR; i: int; x: WORD ): int;
PROCEDURE  DrawMenuBar ( h: HWND );
FUNCTION   GetSystemMenu ( h: HWND; b: BOOL ): HMENU;
FUNCTION   CreateMenu: HMENU;
FUNCTION   DestroyMenu ( h: HMENU ): BOOL;
FUNCTION   ChangeMenu ( h: HMENU; w: WORD; l: LPSTR; x,y: WORD ): BOOL;
FUNCTION   CheckMenuItem ( h: HMENU; w,x: WORD ): BOOL;
FUNCTION   EnableMenuItem ( h: HMENU; w,x: WORD ): BOOL;
FUNCTION   GetSubMenu ( h: HMENU; i: int ): HMENU;
PROCEDURE  EndMenu;


FUNCTION   GrayString ( h: HDC; i: HBRUSH; f: FARPROC;
                        d: DWORD; j,k,l,m,n: int ): BOOL;
PROCEDURE  UpdateWindow ( h: HWND );
FUNCTION   SetActiveWindow ( h: HWND ): HWND;
FUNCTION   GetWindowDC ( h: HWND ): HDC;
FUNCTION   GetDC ( h: HWND ): HDC;
FUNCTION   ReleaseDC ( h: HWND; i: HDC ): int;
FUNCTION   BeginPaint ( h: HWND; l: LPPAINTSTRUCT ): HDC;
PROCEDURE  EndPaint ( h: HWND; l: LPPAINTSTRUCT );


FUNCTION   GetUpdateRect ( h: HWND; l: LPRECT; b: BOOL ): BOOL;
PROCEDURE  InvalidateRect ( h: HWND; l: LPRECT; b: BOOL );
PROCEDURE  ValidateRect ( h: HWND; l: LPRECT );
PROCEDURE  InvalidateRgn ( h: HWND; i: HRGN; b: BOOL );
PROCEDURE  ValidateRgn ( h: HWND; i: HRGN );


PROCEDURE  ScrollWindow ( h: HWND; i,j: int; l,m: LPRECT );
FUNCTION   SetScrollPos ( h: HWND; i,j: int; b: BOOL ): int;
FUNCTION   GetScrollPos ( h: HWND; i: int ): int;
PROCEDURE  SetScrollRange ( h: HWND; i,j,k: int; b: BOOL );
PROCEDURE  GetScrollRange ( h: HWND; i: int; l,m: LPINT );
FUNCTION   SetProp ( h: HWND; l: LPSTR; i: HANDLE ): BOOL;
FUNCTION   GetProp ( h: HWND; l: LPSTR ): HANDLE;
FUNCTION   RemoveProp ( h: HWND; l: LPSTR ): HANDLE;
FUNCTION   EnumProps ( h: HWND; f: FARPROC ): int;


PROCEDURE  SetWindowText ( h: HWND; l: LPSTR );
FUNCTION   GetWindowText ( h: HWND; l: LPSTR; i: int ): int;
FUNCTION   GetWindowTextLength ( h: HWND ): int;
```

```
FUNCTION    SetMenu ( h: HWND; i: HMENU ): BOOL;
FUNCTION    GetMenu ( h: HWND ): HMENU;
PROCEDURE   GetClientRect ( h: HWND; l: LPRECT );
PROCEDURE   GetWindowRect ( h: HWND; l: LPRECT );
PROCEDURE   AdjustWindowRect ( l: LPRECT; l2: long; b: BOOL );
FUNCTION    MessageBox ( h: HWND; l,m: LPSTR; w: WORD ): int;
FUNCTION    MessageBeep ( w: WORD ): BOOL;

FUNCTION    ShowCursor ( b: BOOL ): int;
FUNCTION    SetCursor ( h: HCURSOR ): HCURSOR;
PROCEDURE   SetCursorPos ( i,j: int );
PROCEDURE   GetCursorPos ( l: LPPOINT );
PROCEDURE   ClipCursor ( l: LPRECT );

PROCEDURE   CreateCaret ( h: HWND; i: HBITMAP; j,k: int );
FUNCTION    GetCaretBlinkTime: WORD;
PROCEDURE   SetCaretBlinkTime ( w: WORD );
PROCEDURE   DestroyCaret;
PROCEDURE   HideCaret ( h: HWND );
PROCEDURE   ShowCaret ( h: HWND );
PROCEDURE   SetCaretPos ( i,j: int );

PROCEDURE   ClientToScreen ( h: HWND; l: LPPOINT );
PROCEDURE   ScreenToClient ( h: HWND; l: LPPOINT );
FUNCTION    WindowFromPoint ( p: POINT ): HWND;
FUNCTION    ChildWindowFromPoint ( h: HWND; p: POINT ): HWND;

FUNCTION    GetSysColor ( i: int ): DWORD;
PROCEDURE   SetSysColors ( i: int; l: LPINT; m: LPlong );
FUNCTION    CreateDC ( l,m,n,o: LPSTR ): HDC;
FUNCTION    CreateIC ( l,m,n,o: LPSTR ): HDC;
FUNCTION    CreateCompatibleDC ( h: HDC ): HDC;
FUNCTION    DeleteDC ( h: HDC ): BOOL;
FUNCTION    SaveDC ( h: HDC ): short;
FUNCTION    RestoreDC ( h: HDC; s: short ): BOOL;

FUNCTION    MoveTo ( h: HDC; s,t: short ): DWORD;
FUNCTION    GetCurrentPosition ( h: HDC ): DWORD;
FUNCTION    LineTo ( h: HDC; s,t: short ): BOOL;
FUNCTION    Polyline ( h: HDC; l: LPPOINT; s: short ): BOOL;
FUNCTION    Polygon ( h: HDC; l: LPPOINT; s: short ): BOOL;
FUNCTION    Rectangle ( h: HDC; s,t,u,v: short ): BOOL;
FUNCTION    RoundRect ( h: HDC; s,t,u,v,w,x: short ): BOOL;
FUNCTION    Ellipse ( h: HDC; s,t,u,v: short ): BOOL;
FUNCTION    Arc ( h: HDC; s,t,u,v,w,x,y,z: short ): BOOL;
FUNCTION    Pie ( h: HDC; s,t,u,v,w,x,y,z: short ): BOOL;
FUNCTION    PatBlt ( h: HDC; s,t,u,v: short; d: DWORD ): BOOL;
FUNCTION    BitBlt ( h: HDC; s,t,u,v: short; i: HDC;
                     w,x: short; d: DWORD ): BOOL;
```

```
FUNCTION    StretchBlt ( h: HDC; s,t,u,v: short; i: HDC;
                              w,x,y,z: short; d: DWORD ): BOOL;
FUNCTION    TextOut ( h: HDC; s,t: short; l: LPSTR; u: short ): BOOL;
FUNCTION    SetPixel ( h: HDC; s,t: short; d: DWORD ): DWORD;
FUNCTION    GetPixel ( h: HDC; s,t: short ): DWORD;
FUNCTION    FloodFill ( h: HDC; s,t: short; d: DWORD ): BOOL;
PROCEDURE   LineDDA ( s,t,u,v: short; f: FARPROC; l: LPSTR );
FUNCTION    FillRect ( h: HDC; l: LPRECT; i: HBRUSH ): int;
FUNCTION    FrameRect ( h: HDC; l: LPRECT; i: HBRUSH ): int;
FUNCTION    InvertRect ( h: HDC; l: LPRECT ): int;

FUNCTION    FillRgn ( h: HDC; i: HRGN; j: HBRUSH ): BOOL;
FUNCTION    FrameRgn ( h: HDC; i: HRGN; j: HBRUSH; s,t: short ): BOOL;
FUNCTION    InvertRgn ( h: HDC; i: HRGN ): BOOL;
FUNCTION    PaintRgn ( h: HDC; i: HRGN ): BOOL;
FUNCTION    PtInRegion ( h: HRGN; s,t: short ): BOOL;

FUNCTION    GetStockObject ( s: short ): HANDLE;
FUNCTION    CreatePen ( s,t: short; d: DWORD ): HPEN;
FUNCTION    CreatePenIndirect ( l: LPLOGPEN ): HPEN;
FUNCTION    CreateSolidBrush ( d: DWORD ): HBRUSH;
FUNCTION    CreateHatchBrush ( s: short; d: DWORD ): HBRUSH;
FUNCTION    SetBrushOrg ( h: HDC; i,j: int ): DWORD;
FUNCTION    GetBrushOrg ( h: HDC ): DWORD;
FUNCTION    UnrealizeObject ( h: HBRUSH ): BOOL;
FUNCTION    CreatePatternBrush ( h: HBITMAP ): HBRUSH;
FUNCTION    CreateBrushIndirect ( l: LPLOGBRUSH ): HBRUSH;

FUNCTION    CreateBitmap ( s,t: short; b,c: BYTE; l: LPSTR ): HBITMAP;
FUNCTION    CreateBitmapIndirect ( b: LPBITMAP ): HBITMAP;
FUNCTION    CreateCompatibleBitmap ( h: HDC; s,t: short ): HBITMAP;
FUNCTION    CreateDiscardableBitmap ( h: HDC; s,t: short ): HBITMAP;
FUNCTION    SetBitmapBits ( h: HBITMAP; d: DWORD; l: LPSTR ): BOOL;
FUNCTION    GetBitmapBits ( h: HBITMAP; l: long; m: LPSTR ): long;
FUNCTION    SetBitmapDimension ( h: HBITMAP; s,t: short ): DWORD;
FUNCTION    GetBitmapDimension ( h: HBITMAP ): DWORD;
FUNCTION    CreateFont ( s,t,u,v,w: short;
                        b,c,d,e,f,g,h,i: BYTE; l: LPSTR ): HFONT;
FUNCTION    CreateFontIndirect ( l: LPLOGFONT ): HFONT;
FUNCTION    CreateRectRgn ( s,t,u,v: short ): HRGN;
FUNCTION    CreateRectRgnIndirect ( l: LPRECT ): HRGN;
FUNCTION    CreateEllipticRgnIndirect ( l: LPRECT ): HRGN;
FUNCTION    CreateEllipticRgn ( s,t,u,v: short ): HRGN;
FUNCTION    CreatePolygonRgn ( l: LPPOINT; s,t: short ): HRGN;
FUNCTION    DeleteObject ( h: HANDLE ): BOOL;
FUNCTION    SelectObject ( h: HDC; i: HANDLE ): HANDLE;
FUNCTION    SelectClipRgn ( h: HDC; i: HRGN ): short;
FUNCTION    GetObject ( h: HANDLE; s: short; l: LPSTR ): short;
```

```
FUNCTION    SetRelAbs ( h: HDC; s: short ): short;
FUNCTION    GetRelAbs ( h: HDC ): short;
FUNCTION    SetBkColor ( h: HDC; d: DWORD ): DWORD;
FUNCTION    GetBkColor ( h: HDC ): DWORD;
FUNCTION    SetBkMode ( h: HDC; s: short ): short;
FUNCTION    GetBkMode ( h: HDC ): short;
FUNCTION    SetTextColor ( h: HDC; d: DWORD ): DWORD;
FUNCTION    GetTextColor ( h: HDC ): DWORD;
FUNCTION    GetNearestColor ( h: HDC; d: DWORD ): DWORD;
FUNCTION    SetROP2 ( h: HDC; s: short ): short;
FUNCTION    GetROP2 ( h: HDC ): short;
FUNCTION    SetStretchBltMode ( h: HDC; s: short ): short;
FUNCTION    GetStretchBltMode ( h: HDC ): short;
FUNCTION    SetPolyFillMode ( h: HDC; s: short ): short;
FUNCTION    GetPolyFillMode ( h: HDC ): short;
FUNCTION    SetMapMode ( h: HDC; s: short ): short;
FUNCTION    GetMapMode ( h: HDC ): short;

FUNCTION    SetWindowOrg ( h: HDC; s,t: short ): DWORD;
FUNCTION    GetWindowOrg ( h: HDC ): DWORD;
FUNCTION    SetWindowExt ( h: HDC; s,t: short ): DWORD;
FUNCTION    GetWindowExt ( h: HDC ): DWORD;
FUNCTION    SetViewportOrg ( h: HDC; s,t: short ): DWORD;
FUNCTION    GetViewportOrg ( h: HDC ): DWORD;
FUNCTION    SetViewportExt ( h: HDC; s,t: short ): DWORD;
FUNCTION    GetViewportExt ( h: HDC ): DWORD;
FUNCTION    GetClipBox ( h: HDC; l: LPRECT ): short;
FUNCTION    IntersectClipRect ( h: HDC; s,t,u,v: short ): short;
FUNCTION    OffsetClipRgn ( h: HDC; s,t: short ): short;
FUNCTION    ExcludeClipRect ( h: HDC; s,t,u,v: short ): short;
FUNCTION    PtVisible ( h: HDC; s,t: short ): BOOL;
FUNCTION    SetRect ( l: LPRECT; i,j,k,m: int ): int;
FUNCTION    SetRectEmpty ( l: LPRECT ): int;
FUNCTION    CopyRect ( l,m: LPRECT ): int;
FUNCTION    InflateRect ( l: LPRECT; i,j: int ): int;
FUNCTION    IntersectRect ( l,m,n: LPRECT ): int;
FUNCTION    UnionRect ( l,m,n: LPRECT ): int;
FUNCTION    OffsetRect ( l: LPRECT; i,j: int ): int;
FUNCTION    IsRectEmpty ( l: LPRECT ): BOOL;
FUNCTION    PtInRect ( l: LPRECT; p: POINT ): BOOL;
FUNCTION    RectVisible ( h: HDC; l: LPRECT ): BOOL;
FUNCTION    CombineRgn ( h,i,j: HRGN; s: short ): short;
FUNCTION    EqualRgn ( h,i: HRGN ): BOOL;
FUNCTION    OffsetRgn ( h: HRGN; s,t: short ): short;

FUNCTION    SetTextJustification ( h: HDC; s,t: short ): short;
FUNCTION    GetTextExtent ( h: HDC; l: LPSTR; s: short ): DWORD;
FUNCTION    SetTextCharacterExtra ( h: HDC; s: short ): short;
FUNCTION    GetTextCharacterExtra ( h: HDC ): short;
```

```
FUNCTION    GetMetaFile ( l: LPSTR ): HANDLE;
FUNCTION    DeleteMetaFile ( h: HANDLE ): BOOL;
FUNCTION    CopyMetaFile ( h: HANDLE; l: LPSTR ): HANDLE;
FUNCTION    PlayMetaFile ( h: HDC; i: HANDLE ): BOOL;
FUNCTION    Escape ( h: HDC; s,t: short; l,m: LPSTR ): short;
FUNCTION    EnumFonts ( h: HDC; l: LPSTR; f: FARPROC; m: LPSTR ): short;
FUNCTION    EnumObjects ( h: HDC; s: short; f: FARPROC; l: LPSTR ): short;
FUNCTION    GetTextFace ( h: HDC; s: short; l: LPSTR ): short;
FUNCTION    GetTextMetrics ( h: HDC; l: LPTEXTMETRIC ): BOOL;
FUNCTION    GetDeviceCaps ( h: HDC; s: short ): short;
FUNCTION    DeviceModes ( h: HWND; i: HANDLE; l,m: LPSTR ): LPSTR;
FUNCTION    SetEnvironment ( l,m: LPSTR; w: WORD ): short;
FUNCTION    GetEnvironment ( l,m: LPSTR; w: WORD ): short;

FUNCTION    DPtoLP ( h: HDC; l: LPPOINT; s: short ): BOOL;
FUNCTION    LPtoDP ( h: HDC; l: LPPOINT; s: short ): BOOL;

FUNCTION    GetVersion: WORD;
FUNCTION    GetCodeHandle ( f: FARPROC ): HANDLE;
FUNCTION    GetModuleHandle ( l: LPSTR ): HANDLE;
FUNCTION    GetModuleUsage ( h: HANDLE ): int;
FUNCTION    GetModuleFileName ( h: HANDLE; l: LPSTR; i: int ): int;
FUNCTION    GetInstanceData ( h: HANDLE; n: NPSTR; i: int ): int;
FUNCTION    GetProcAddress ( h: HANDLE; l: LPSTR ): FARPROC;
FUNCTION    MakeProcInstance ( f: FARPROC; h: HANDLE ): FARPROC;
PROCEDURE   FreeProcInstance ( f: FARPROC );

FUNCTION    LoadLibrary ( l: LPSTR ): HANDLE;
FUNCTION    FreeLibrary ( h: HANDLE ): HANDLE;

FUNCTION    AnsiToOem ( l,m: LPSTR ): BOOL;
FUNCTION    OemToAnsi ( l,m: LPSTR ): BOOL;
FUNCTION    AnsiUpper ( l: LPSTR ): BYTE;
FUNCTION    AnsiLower ( l: LPSTR ): BYTE;
FUNCTION    AnsiNext ( l: LPSTR ): LPSTR;
FUNCTION    AnsiPrev ( l,m: LPSTR ): LPSTR;

FUNCTION    GetTempDrive ( b: BYTE ): BYTE;
FUNCTION    GetTempFileName ( b: BYTE; l: LPSTR; w: WORD; m: LPSTR ): int;
FUNCTION    OpenFile ( l: LPSTR; m: LPOFSTRUCT; w: WORD ): int;

FUNCTION    GlobalAlloc ( w: WORD; d: DWORD ): HANDLE;
FUNCTION    GlobalCompact ( d: DWORD ): DWORD;
FUNCTION    GlobalDiscard ( h: HANDLE; ): HANDLE;
FUNCTION    GlobalFree ( h: HANDLE ): HANDLE;
FUNCTION    GlobalHandle ( w: WORD ): DWORD;
FUNCTION    GlobalLock ( h: HANDLE ): LPSTR;
FUNCTION    GlobalReAlloc ( h: HANDLE; d: DWORD; w: WORD ): HANDLE;
FUNCTION    GlobalSize ( h: HANDLE ): DWORD;
```

```
FUNCTION   GlobalUnlock ( h: HANDLE ): BOOL;
FUNCTION   GlobalFlags ( h: HANDLE ): WORD;
FUNCTION   LockData ( i: int ): HANDLE;
FUNCTION   UnlockData ( i: int ): HANDLE;
FUNCTION   LockSegment ( w: WORD ): HANDLE;
FUNCTION   UnlockSegment ( w: WORD ): HANDLE;

FUNCTION   LocalAlloc ( w,x: WORD ): HANDLE;
FUNCTION   LocalCompact ( w: WORD ): WORD;
FUNCTION   LocalDiscard ( h: HANDLE ): HANDLE;
FUNCTION   LocalFree ( h: HANDLE ): HANDLE;
FUNCTION   LocalHandle ( w: WORD ): HANDLE;
PROCEDURE  LocalFreeze ( i: int );
FUNCTION   LocalHandleDelta ( i: int ): int;
FUNCTION   LocalInit ( w: WORD; p,q: PSTR ): BOOL;
FUNCTION   LocalLock ( h: HANDLE ): PSTR;
PROCEDURE  LocalMelt ( i: int );
FUNCTION   LocalNotify ( f: FARPROC ): FARPROC;
FUNCTION   LocalReAlloc ( h: HANDLE; w,x: WORD ): HANDLE;
FUNCTION   LocalSize ( h: HANDLE ): WORD;
FUNCTION   LocalUnlock ( h: HANDLE ): BOOL;
FUNCTION   LocalFlags ( h: HANDLE ): WORD;
FUNCTION   FindResource ( h: HANDLE; l,m: LPSTR ): HANDLE;
FUNCTION   LoadResource ( h,i: HANDLE ): HANDLE;
FUNCTION   FreeResource ( h: HANDLE ): BOOL;
FUNCTION   LockResource ( h: HANDLE ): LPSTR;
FUNCTION   SetResourceHandler ( h: HANDLE; l: LPSTR; f: FARPROC ): FARPROC;
FUNCTION   AllocResource ( h,i: HANDLE; d: DWORD ): HANDLE;
FUNCTION   SizeofResource ( h,i: HANDLE ): WORD;
FUNCTION   AccessResource ( h,i: HANDLE ): int;
FUNCTION   MAKEINTRESOURCE ( i: int ): LPSTR;
FUNCTION   Yield: BOOL;
FUNCTION   GetCurrentTask: HANDLE;
FUNCTION   SetPriority ( h: HANDLE; i: int ): int;

FUNCTION   InitAtomTable ( i: int ): BOOL;
FUNCTION   AddAtom ( l: LPSTR ): ATOM;
FUNCTION   DeleteAtom ( a: ATOM ): ATOM;
FUNCTION   FindAtom ( l: LPSTR ): ATOM;
FUNCTION   GetAtomName ( a: ATOM; l: LPSTR; i: int ): WORD;
FUNCTION   GetAtomHandle ( a: ATOM ): HANDLE;
FUNCTION   MAKEINTATOM ( i: int ): LPSTR;

FUNCTION   GetProfileInt ( l,m: LPSTR; i: int ): int;
FUNCTION   GetProfileString ( l,m,n,o: LPSTR; i: int ): int;
FUNCTION   WriteProfileString ( l,m,n: LPSTR ): BOOL;
PROCEDURE  FatalExit ( i: int );
FUNCTION   Catch ( l: LPCATCHBUF ): int;
PROCEDURE  Throw ( l: LPCATCHBUF; i: int );
```

```
FUNCTION    CreateMetaFile ( l: LPSTR ): HANDLE;
FUNCTION    CloseMetaFile ( h: HANDLE ): HANDLE;
FUNCTION    GetMetaFileBits ( h: HANDLE ): HANDLE;
FUNCTION    SetMetaFileBits ( h: HANDLE ): HANDLE;
FUNCTION    GetCurrentTime: long;
FUNCTION    IsChild ( h,i: HWND ): BOOL;


FUNCTION    GetWindowWord ( h: HWND; i: int ): WORD;
FUNCTION    SetWindowWord ( h: HWND; i: int; w: WORD ): WORD;
FUNCTION    GetWindowLong ( h: HWND; i: int ): LONG;
FUNCTION    SetWindowLong ( h: HWND; i: int; l: LONG ): LONG;
FUNCTION    GetClassWord ( h: HWND; i: int ): WORD;
FUNCTION    SetClassWord ( h: HWND; i: int; w: WORD ): WORD;
FUNCTION    GetClassLong ( h: HWND; i: int ): LONG;
FUNCTION    SetClassLong ( h: HWND; i: int; l: LONG ): LONG;


FUNCTION    GetParent ( h: HWND ): HWND;
FUNCTION    EnumChildWindows ( h: HWND; f: FARPROC; l: LONG ): BOOL;
FUNCTION    FindWindow ( l,m: LPSTR ): HWND;
FUNCTION    EnumWindows ( f: FARPROC; l: LONG ): BOOL;
FUNCTION    GetClassName ( h: HWND; l: LPSTR; i: int ): int;
FUNCTION    SetWindowsHook ( i: int; f: FARPROC ): FARPROC;


FUNCTION    CreateConvertWindow ( l: LPSTR; h: HANDLE; m: LPSTR ): HWND;
PROCEDURE   ShowConvertWindow ( h: HWND; b: BOOL );
PROCEDURE   SetConvertWindowHeight ( i: int );
FUNCTION    IsTwoByteCharPrefix ( i: INTEGER1 ): BOOL;


FUNCTION    LoadBitmap ( h: HANDLE; l: LPSTR ): HBITMAP;
FUNCTION    LoadCursor ( h: HANDLE; l: LPSTR ): HCURSOR;
FUNCTION    LoadIcon ( h: HANDLE; l: LPSTR ): HICON;
FUNCTION    LoadMenu ( h: HANDLE; l: LPSTR ): HMENU;
FUNCTION    LoadString ( h: HANDLE; w: WORD; l: LPSTR; i: int ): int;
FUNCTION    AddFontResource ( l: LPSTR ): short;
FUNCTION    RemoveFontResource ( l: LPSTR ): BOOL;
PROCEDURE   MoveConvertWindow ( s,t: short );
PROCEDURE   ConvertRequest ( h: HWND; l: LPKANJISTRUCT );
FUNCTION    SetConvertParams ( s,t: short ): BOOL;
PROCEDURE   SetConvertHook ( b: BOOL );
FUNCTION    IsDialogMessage ( h: HWND; l: LPMSG ): BOOL;
PROCEDURE   MapDialogRect ( h: HWND; l: LPRECT );
FUNCTION    DlgDirList ( h: HWND; l: LPSTR; i,j: int; w: WORD ): int;
FUNCTION    DlgDirSelect ( h: HWND; l: LPSTR; i: int ): BOOL;


FUNCTION    OpenComm ( l: LPSTR; w,x: WORD ): short;
FUNCTION    SetCommState ( d: LPDCB ): short;
FUNCTION    GetCommState ( s: short; d: LPDCB ): short;
FUNCTION    ReadComm ( s: short; l: LPSTR; i: int ): short;
FUNCTION    UngetCommChar ( s: short; i: INTEGER1 ): short;
```

```
FUNCTION   WriteComm ( s: short; l: LPSTR; i: int ): short;
FUNCTION   CloseComm ( s: short ): short;
FUNCTION   GetCommError ( s: short; c: LPCOMSTAT ): short;
FUNCTION   BuildCommDCB ( l: LPSTR; d: LPDCB ): short;
FUNCTION   TransmitCommChar ( s: short; i: INTEGER1 ): short;
FUNCTION   SetCommEventMask ( s: short; w: WORD ): LPWORD;
FUNCTION   GetCommEventMask ( s: short; i: int ): WORD;
FUNCTION   SetCommBreak ( s: short ): short;
FUNCTION   ClearCommBreak ( s: short ): short;
FUNCTION   FlushComm ( s: short; i: int ): short;
FUNCTION   EscapeCommFunction ( s: short; i: int ): short;
```

Index